AMERICAN
HORTICULTURAL
SOCIETY

AMERICAN HORTICULTURAL SOCIETY

Northwest

Smart Garden™ REGIONAL GUIDE

Rita Pelczar

PETER PUNZI

DK Publishing, Inc.

DK

LONDON, NEW YORK, MUNICH,
MELBOURNE, AND DELHI

Senior Editor Jill Hamilton
Designers Megan Clayton, Susan St. Louis
Project Director Sharon Lucas
Creative Director Tina Vaughan
Production Manager Chris Avgherinos
DTP Designer Milos Orlovic
Picture Research Jo Walton
Image Coordinator Chrissy McIntyre
Publisher Chuck Lang

Horticultural editor Ray Rogers

Contributing writers Madeline Farbman, S. Jane von Trapp
Design assistance Sylvia Figueroa, Miesha Tate,
Mark Johnson-Davies, Jaye Tang, Stephanie Sumulong
Editorial assistance Christine Heilman
DK Photo Access Library: Mark Dennis,
Neale Chamberlain, Rosemary Firth,
Additional photo research: Louise Thomas

First American Edition, 2003
04 05 10 9 8 7 6 5 4 3 2

Published in the United States by
DK Publishing, Inc.
375 Hudson Street
New York, New York 10014

DK Publishing, Inc. offers special discounts for bulk purchases for sales
promotions or premiums. Specific, large-quantity needs can be met with
special editions, including personalized covers, excerpts of existing guides,
and corporate imprints. For more information, contact Special Markets
Department, DK Publishing, Inc., 375 Hudson Street, New York, NY 10014
Fax: 800-600-9098.

Library of Congress Cataloging-in-Publication Data

Punzi, Peter.
Northwest / by Peter Punzi.
p. cm. -- (SmartGarden regional guide)
ISBN 0-7894-9366-7 (PBF)
1. Gardening--Northwest, Pacific. I. Title. II. Series.
SB453.2.N83P86 2003
635.9'09795--dc21
2003010174

Reproduced by Colourscan, Singapore
Printed and bound in the USA by RR Donnelly

See our complete product line at
www.dk.com

CONTENTS

Foreword 6

PART I

THE TEN
SMARTGARDEN™ TENETS

Know yourself 10

Assess your site 16

Adapt when necessary 26

Pick the best plants 32

Take good care of the earth 40

Work with nature 52

Manage pests for a healthy garden 60

Keep a garden journal 70

Consult the pros 74

Have fun! 78

PART II

PLANT CATALOG

Catalog Contents 82

Trees 84

Shrubs 128

Conifers 218

Climbers 242

Herbaceous Plants 252

PART III

GARDENING TECHNIQUES

Selecting Plants 384

Planting 388

Pruning 396

Propagation 402

APPENDICES

Governmental resources 408

Horticultural web sites 409

Regional gardens 410

Index 412

Acknowledgments 419

Photo credits 420

FOREWORD

The Pacific West Coast has been a frequent destination for this North Carolina native. The lush way many of the plants grow, the seasonal changes and mixes of plants, and the unique native plants I saw in this region made me realize that the factors ruling a Carolina gardener do not operate here. Pacific Northwest winters and summers are milder than where I grew up. The plants look more like they were growing in southern England than North America.

Now, as it was then, successful gardening is based on coordinating factors such as light, temperature, water, and nutrients, and coping with the elements, critters, and the gardener's age. Advances in technology are making plant selection easier; recently the USDA Plant Hardiness Zone Map was updated using current information from weather stations around the country. The development of the AHS Plant Heat Zone Map in 1997 completed the circle of information available to determine the total range of temperature tolerance for each cultivated plant. In time, all of the coded plants listed in this book and others will be available online, accessible by zip code.

The passage of time has brought many wonderful innovations to gardening in the Northwest, yet over the course of my career, I have increasingly become aware of the mistakes that people live with in their gardens day after day that reduce the pleasures of gardening. Too many gardeners put up with plants that have outgrown their space, or are barely surviving.

This leaves the gardener with crucial questions to answer. How can I replace and replant with the most desired effects and create a SMARTGARDEN™? What tasks can I attempt and what should I have a professional do? And how do I accomplish this while being a good steward of the earth? The SMARTGARDEN™ program described in this book answers all these questions and many more. Using these ideas and techniques, you can create a garden that is successful, environmentally responsible, easy to maintain, and – most important – fun!

I know you will enjoy the process of re-evaluating your garden and your gardening practices from this new perspective!

H. Marc Cathey, PhD
President Emeritus,
American Horticultural Society

AMERICAN HORTICULTURAL SOCIETY

Northwest

SMARTGARDEN™ REGIONAL GUIDE

PART I

THE TEN SMARTGARDEN™ TENETS

These tenets offer the key to a scientifically sound, environmentally responsible approach to gardening. An assessment of your site and lifestyle directs your gardening choices with maximum efficiency. Integration of new technologies with proven practices and the effective use of available resources provide guidance for selection and maintenance of your garden plants. Most importantly, each practice is considered with respect to its environmental impact, to help you make the most responsible gardening choices.

KNOW YOURSELF

A lot of thought should go into gardening before you even pick up a trowel. Since you are going to determine the garden's dimensions, style, and makeup – and you will be primarily responsible for its maintenance – the best place to begin is to take a reading of your personal likes and dislikes and your abilities and limitations. In subsequent tenets we will consider the characteristics of the site, appropriate criteria for selecting plants, and ways to ensure that your gardening efforts reap successful results by using an environmentally responsible approach. But before you can begin to put that important information to good use, it is critical to examine your preferences, priorities, and point of view.

Be realistic

As much as you would enjoy spending many hours in your garden, you have other commitments that limit your availability, and you may be sharing your outdoor space with others who prefer nongardening activities. Physical constraints might also inhibit your gardening pursuits, and your budget may not accommodate your elaborate gardening visions. However, with some thoughtful planning and a bit of compromise, your SMARTGARDEN™ can oblige your varied outdoor requirements, limitations in time and physical ability, and, yes, even a budget that lacks a certain desired heft.

What you want
The owners of this property made careful decisions about how they wanted to use their space. Another owner might well have decided to plant the area entirely in grass and shrubs, and a third could have created a playground.

In a nutshell: think about your time, your physical condition, and your budget, and take on a garden only of the size and complexity you can handle.

The space-time continuum

Once you know where a garden best fits within the overall landscape, the next step is to determine its size and shape. While the shape is largely a design consideration, the size depends a great deal on the kinds of plants you want to grow and the time you have to tend them.

Some gardens will require little of your time once they are established. A bed of flowering shrubs underplanted with a groundcover needs only occasional attention. An extensive flower bed or large vegetable patch, on the other hand, needs regular tending throughout the growing season. Of course, the bigger the garden, the more time it requires to plant, weed, harvest, deadhead, edge, and prune. The best plan is to start small, then expand if you find you have the space, time, resources, and energy.

Planning the site

When deciding where to place your garden and what size to make it, you need to consider not only the conditions that make it suitable for growing plants, but also how the garden will be integrated into the landscape as a whole. If you have children who need space for a swingset or to play games, siting your garden at the other end of the yard might be wise – at least until they outgrow these activities. Obviously, you need a plan.

Fully integrated
A carefully considered mixture of plants and hardscaping – the nonplant elements – results in a garden that beautifully blends with and complements the house. Container-grown plants generally require more care than those that are grown in the open ground.

Garden Plans

Whether your garden aspirations are complex and ornate or you are planning on a somewhat more modest scale, you should map out your garden on paper before you pick up your trowel or buy your first plant. Although these garden plans may vary in complexity from a rough sketch to an exquisitely executed artwork, there are just a couple of basic types of sketches that you need to use at this stage. The first one is used to map out existing features and microclimates, information that you need to determine which plants will thrive and where. A more detailed garden sketch, which should be done on graph paper to scale, shows your entire property – both physical features and garden areas.

Unless you are starting with an empty lot, you will need to sketch the existing features of your landscape, such as the house, walkways, and driveway. The more accurate your sketch, the more useful it will be for planning. Don't forget to note sunny and shady areas, hedges and fences that block the wind, unusually wet or dry spots, neighboring buildings, attractive or unattractive views, and other positive and negative features.

You may find that you want to make adjustments: remove a tree, repair or improve a walkway, relocate the doghouse. Some of these changes will be easy; those that are more complex can be completed over time. Make corresponding notes on your plan to track the direction in which you are heading.

Next make a list of the activities that you enjoy doing in the yard. Of course, you also need to consider anyone who may spend a significant amount of time in the yard, whether it be your spouse or partner, children, or anyone else. The landscape use checklist (opposite) will help you identify the various uses and activities that fit your space and budget.

Once you have a prioritized list of gardening and nongardening activities for your yard, you can begin designating areas for each. Some areas will overlap, so make sure that the activities are compatible for use of the same space – playing football in the herb garden just won't work. On the other hand, patios and decks are perfect locations for container gardens and adjacent raised beds. Keep in mind that different kinds of plants (for example, perennials, vegetables, and shrubs) can often be combined in the same garden area as long as they have similar cultural requirements.

Making a plan

This exercise is useful for those who have just acquired a new property as well as for those who are considering a major (or even minor) relandscaping project. Documenting existing conditions will point you in the right direction when the time comes to choose specific elements.

FEATURES TO CONSIDER FOR THE SKETCH

When drawing a sketch of your property, include all features that are permanent or at least long-term. Once your sketch is completed, you may want to make several copies. That way you can try out different designs for arranging beds and hardscaping features on paper before you actually get to work.

Don't forget to include any of the following features that are applicable. There may well be more features in your yard that you will need to include.

- Perimeter of the yard
- House
- Driveway
- Walkways and paths
- Garage, shed, or other service outbuildings
- Gazebo, patio, deck
- Hammock
- Swingset/sandbox
- Pool
- Doghouse, kennel, run
- Existing trees
- Existing beds or gardens
- Hedges, fences, walls
- Water faucets
- Areas of sun and shade
- Wet or dry areas
- Views to highlight
- Views to hide

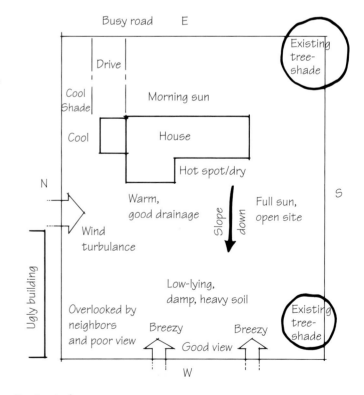

Putting it down on paper
All of the important cultural and design elements of the property have been included in this sketch. Note that there are no specific plant features indicated except for the trees, which are being considered more as producers of shade than as living plants. Consideration of individual plants comes later.

KEEP YOUR PLANS FLEXIBLE

Don't fret if there isn't room in your landscape to accommodate all of the activities you have in mind. Long-range planning can extend your choices, and spreading the implementation of your plan over the course of several years also reduces the shock to your bank account.

As you and the others who use your yard mature, priorities for landscape use will change. The area designated for a sandbox for youngsters might be transformed into a patio after a few years. Once the old swing set in the back yard has lost its appeal, it can be replaced with a mixed border or small vegetable garden.

Like children, plants grow up, and their increasing size alters the landscape. Perennials that once filled in between young evergreen shrubs may need to be moved as the shrubs reach their mature size. Aggressive perennials may be overrunning your borders. Choices must be made; something will need to go. As your trees expand in height and spread over the years, the area beneath them becomes shadier. If the grass growing in the trees' shadow becomes thin and weak, it may be time to replace it with a shade-loving groundcover or a simple mulch, or perhaps you will choose to thin or raise the crown of the tree (*see* p. 29) to allow more light to reach the grass.

Remember: plants don't live forever. The demise of a plant often opens up opportunities for including new and perhaps more interesting plants in its place.

Adapting to physical challenges

If you or members of your household have physical limitations, consider these in your planning. Raised beds and containers can be built and placed to increase accessibility. Paved walkways can put outlying beds within easy reach of those who might otherwise be able to enjoy them only from a distance, and stepping-stones or paths within planting areas afford easier and safer movement through the garden for maintenance.

Easier access
If gardening is difficult for you, growing plants in a raised bed such as this one will bring them up to your level. Even if you are not an active gardener, the plants will be closer to your eyes and nose.

LANDSCAPE USE CHECKLIST

Planning space to accommodate your outdoor pastimes will help you determine the best placement and size of your plantings, and prioritizing these areas will help you develop a working plan.

Nongarden areas/activities:

- Relaxing (including deck and/or patio)
- Outdoor cooking/eating
- Swimming
- Sports and active play
- Sandbox, tree house, playhouse, swing set
- Utility areas: trash cans, air conditioning/heating units, compost pile

- Work and storage spaces: garden shed, cold frame, firewood storage
- Pet areas
- Paths and walkways
- Driveway/parking
- Lawn
- Other, including walls and fences and overhead structures

Garden areas:

- Vegetable/fruit
- Herbs
- Flower beds
- Woodland garden
- Shade trees
- Wildflower meadow or naturalized area

- Foundation plantings
- Pond
- Containers
- Raised beds
- Cut flowers
- Hedges
- Specimen trees and shrubs

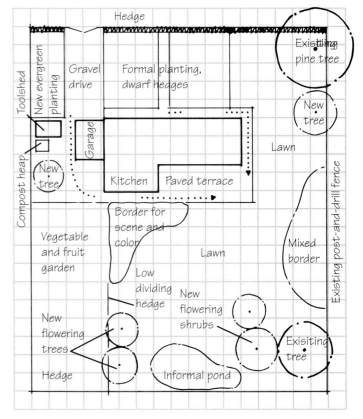

One step closer
The first sketch shown to the left is now fleshed out with desired planted areas (beds, borders, hedges, and the like) and hardscape features (driveway, terrace, and pond). The template is now ready to be made into a reality.

Careful selection and placement of plants within the landscape is important for physically challenged gardeners. Once established, many trees, shrubs, and groundcovers will require a minimum of care. These can be placed at the periphery of the yard. More labor-intensive gardens should be placed where they are most easily accessed and where tools and water are located nearby. Also remember the potential danger posed by thorny trees and shrubs, low branches, and surface roots. Of course, these points apply to any sensibly designed garden, but they are of more obvious and immediate importance to the physically challenged.

A number of ergonomically designed gardening tools make gardening easier if physical ability is limited. Despite our best efforts to remain fit, chances are that eventually we will all lose some mobility or strength. Your SMARTGARDEN™ should become easier to maintain as plants mature, but no garden is maintenance-free. Fortunately, physical limitations needn't eliminate gardening activities, particularly if they are carefully considered in your garden plan.

Lawns and turf alternatives

One repetitive chore that consumes a great deal of gardening time is mowing the lawn, and maintaining a healthy lawn can be a genuine challenge in many parts of the country. Irrigation systems may be necessary in areas that experience extended periods of dry weather during the growing season. Weeds, insect pests, and diseases may necessitate the use of pesticides or biological controls that can be costly and time-consuming to apply. This doesn't mean that you should exclude all turf from your landscape, but be aware that it is an area that requires a significant investment in time and money if you want it to look good. To reduce the expense in hours and dollars, reduce the size of the lawn. A small area of grass is much easier to maintain than a large expanse.

If you decide to reduce the lawn area of your yard, you have a number of options. Consider alternative plantings such as a wildflower meadow or a large bed of groundcovers, which will require some seasonal care – perhaps two or three times a year – but not nearly the time and effort involved in trying to maintain a perfect lawn.

LAWNS AND ALTERNATIVES

A healthy lawn ties the garden together and creates space.

Lawns can provide some of the most versatile outdoor living spaces. When properly maintained, they provide a rugged surface that can stand up to the traffic of daily outdoor activities. The tradeoff is that lawns can demand more time and resources than any other space in your landscape. Just think of the time-consuming tasks of mowing, fertilizing, aerating and thatching, and spraying. When rainfall is irregular, a lawn requires supplemental watering. Lawns also require more fertilizer per square foot than any other gardening area. If you choose to have a lawn, you can reduce many of these efforts if you choose the proper varieties of grass for your lawn. Cool-weather

grasses are the best choices in the Northwest, except at the extreme south of the range (southern Nevada, Utah, and Colorado). Along the West Coast to the Cascade Mountains is considered the cool and wet region. Rainfall is plentiful through most of the year with the exception of midsummer. The best lawn-type grasses in this area are: colonial bentgrass, Kentucky bluegrass, fine fescue, and perennial ryegrass. The rest of the Northwest region is cool and dry. Most cool-weather grasses will require much more supplemental watering over the course of the year in the cool and dry areas. When supplemental water is available, the cool-weather grasses listed for the cool wet coastal areas can be used. In addition rough bluegrass, creeping bentgrass and turf-type tall fescue can also be grown. In areas without supplemental water, grow drought-resistant native grasses such as buffalograss, fairway wheatgrass, and gramagrass (a warm-weather grass). In southern Nevada, Utah, Colorado, and Kansas, use varieties of turf-type fescues, regionally adapted bluegrass varieties, and cold-tolerant varieties of bermudagrass (which is a warm-season grass), gramagrass, and buffalograss. It is always best to use blends of these grasses rather than a single variety. Your local extension service

(see the Appendix, p.410) will have lists of the latest and best-adapted varieties for your local area. A recent trend is the formulation of ecology (also called ecolawn) mixes. Ecology mixes, which are mixtures of drought-resistant grasses and ground-hugging flowering perennials suitable for specific regions, are designed to be watered about once a month in the summertime and mowed every 3–4 weeks. They also require very little fertilizing or treatments for pest and diseases.

Both a conventional lawn and a graveled area fill the roles of unifier and provider of spaciousness.

Another alternative to lawns are the various soil coverings, such as paving, gravel, or mulch. These can serve as walkways or seating areas. Individual planting beds and trees can be extended by removing the turf between them and connecting the areas with mulch. Use broad curves for the outline of the mulched area to facilitate mowing, because mowing around a large area that contains several trees takes much less time than mowing around individual trees. Although the initial cost and labor output of creating these areas may be greater, the reduction in maintenance time and expense over the long run may be significant.

Low-maintenance plantings

Every garden – even the simplest container garden – requires some maintenance, but there are definitely some plants that require less attention than others. Consult your nursery, extension service, and other local experts (*see* Appendices, *pp. 408–411*) to identify such plants for your immediate area. Also, there are certain strategies that minimize the effort you must put into a planting for it to look good.

Many of these strategies are simply a matter of working with nature rather than against it: select plants that are adapted to the specific conditions present in your yard; water plants deeply rather than frequently so that roots grow downward and are capable of retrieving water over a greater area; remove weeds before they set seed and spread; and use mulch to conserve water and suppress weeds. Building raised beds and containers and filling them with soil may seem like a lot of work initially, but once constructed, they can provide a planting area that is within easy reach for maintenance.

A SMARTGARDEN™, when carefully analyzed, designed, implemented, and maintained, can reward any gardener for years.

Stay off the grass
Not a single blade of grass figures into this part of the property. Designed for low maintenance, it provides a pleasant sitting and socializing area while incorporating easy-care plants in both gravel and a raised bed. The solitary but exuberant container provides some color and serves as a focal point.

ASSESS YOUR SITE

The best place to begin your journey toward a SMARTGARDEN™, as with any project that involves change, is first to determine where you stand. Take a look around your property. Observe the existing vegetation, the lay of the land, the soil, the degree of light and shade, and know your average temperature ranges and your first and last expected frost dates.

Evaluating strengths & limitations

If your yard is shady, plants that thrive in low light levels will be the most successful. If part of your yard is shaded and another area receives full sun, your options increase; however, siting a plant in the area that satisfies its particular light requirement is essential. If your region receives limited precipitation during the growing season, consider xeriphytic plants (those with low water requirements); if you have wet areas, a bog garden might be your best choice. Although these factors limit gardening options, each can be viewed as a strength if the appropriate plants and garden style are chosen.

Examine the existing plants carefully. Are there trees or shrubs that are struggling to survive or that require excessive maintenance? Plants that outgrow their space or suffer from chronic disease or pest problems may be the wrong ones for your site, and it may be best to remove them entirely.

Evaluating the existing nonplant features in your landscape is an important part of your site analysis. Are there problem areas – a steep slope or an awkward swale? Are your walkways functional? Have you set aside areas for relaxation? Does everyone have space to pursue outdoor interests?

Your observations will point you toward those improvements that need to be made to maximize your gardening success and satisfaction with the least amount of strain on you, your resources, and the environment. Your site analysis will also provide clues for selecting plants (or other nonplant features) that will fit in with your conditions.

It helps to know something about basic plant requirements with respect to the environment, including aspects of soil; how temperature, shade, and exposure define your selection of garden plants; and how microclimates present options for savvy gardeners. After you examine your existing growing conditions, you may decide to make some changes or improvements. In Tenet 3, methods for modifying your site will be outlined. But first let's take a look at what you have to work with.

Get to know your soil

Becoming familiar with the character of your soil is key to your gardening success. Important aspects include texture, structure, drainage and water-holding capacity, pH (acidity or alkalinity), and fertility.

One way to get to know your soil is to have it professionally analyzed. A soil test reveals details about your soil's chemistry that cannot be observed with the naked eye. Soil test kits for home use are available in a wide range of prices and sophistication. You can also send a soil sample to a local soil-testing lab. Public soil-testing labs are relatively inexpensive, but they may be slow during peak seasons. Private soil-testing labs may be a bit more costly, but they are often faster and some offer more extensive tests than those available through the extension labs.

Metamorphosis
Combining careful planning with smart horticultural practices will transform this neglected yard into a beautifully integrated area (opposite) that will easily accommodate a wide variety of gardening and leisure activities.

SOIL TEST REPORT

A soil test report provides basic information about the fertility of your soil. It is very useful when you are determining the amounts of fertilizer to add (or to hold off on adding) to your soil.

Potassium moves through soil slowly and is rarely present in low levels

Magnesium is essential for plant activites, most notably for photosynthesis, and its chemistry is closely linked to pH and calcium levels

High levels of calcium are usually linked to a high pH reading and interfere with the availabilty of other minerals

Phosphorus moves through soil fairly quickly but is easily replaced

NOTE *Optimum levels are based on general garden conditions for a wide range of plants. Some vegetable crops and ornamentals require different levels.*

Macronutrients (pounds/acre)

Phosphorus: 67 *(Below Optimum)*
Potassium: 360 *(Above Optimum)*
Magnesium: 202 *(Optimum)*
Calcium: 1917 *(Above Optimum)*

by Mehlich 3 extraction

P
Mg
Ca

Below Optimum — Optimum — Above Opt.

Very Low | Low | Medium | High | Very High

50% pore spaces (air and water)

45% weathered rock and mineral particles

About 5% organic matter

The space between Healthy, productive soil contains the same amount of space (taken up by air and water) as it does actual particles. Smart gardening practices strive to preserve this balance.

Soil texture

All soils are made up of solid material and spaces between the solids – in roughly equal proportions by volume. About 90 percent of the solid portion of most soil is weathered rocks and minerals. These particles are classified according to size, and are, from smallest to largest, clay, silt, and sand. Most soils are a combination of particle sizes, often with one or another predominating. The relative amounts of each type of particle determines the soil texture. Loam is a soil that contains roughly equal amounts of all three soil particle types and is usually well suited for growing a very wide range of garden plants.

A soil's texture has a major influence on such soil characteristics as water retention and nutrient movement. For example, a sandy soil drains faster than a clay soil, and a clay soil retains nutrients better than a sandy one; therefore, watering and fertilizing schedules should be adjusted accordingly.

Soil texture will also influence your selection of plants. Some plants – those that generally have low water requirements – thrive in a sharply drained, sandy soil. Others benefit from a more constant supply of moisture and nutrients; these usually grow better in a loam or clay loam, which hold on to water longer and release it more slowly than sandy soil. You can get an idea of the texture by rubbing some dry soil between your fingers. Sandy soil has a gritty feel to it; silt is much smoother; and clay, when dry, forms dense, hard clumps that are not easily broken apart. When wet, clay can be formed into balls or ropes.

Soil structure

The structure of a soil is determined by how the various solid portions of the soil are arranged – particles can be separate, as in the case of pure sand, or bind together to form clusters, or aggregates (tiny clusters of particles). The arrangement has significant impact on the movement and retention of water, nutrients, and air in the soil.

The remaining solid part of the soil is organic matter, which makes soil more conducive to plant growth by enabling the formation of soil aggregates. Aggregates form when soil organisms break down organic matter into humus, an amorphous, gummy material that binds particles together (*see* The nature of humus, *p. 31*). Pore spaces between the aggregates are relatively large, and yet smaller spaces between soil particles occur within the aggregates. This combination provides a balance between the movement of water and air and the retention of moisture and nutrients, and makes it easier for plant roots to grow down through the soil.

To improve soil structure, spread organic matter on the soil surface and incorporate it into the upper six to eight inches (15–20cm) of soil every year in areas that are cultivated on an annual basis. For more permanent areas, work organic matter into the soil at planting time. After that, organic mulches can be applied around plants each year; the activities of soil organisms and other natural processes will incorporate much of the organic matter into the soil.

Drainage/water-holding capacity

Plant roots require both air and water for healthy growth. The pore spaces in soil accommodate both, but during rain or irrigation, water forces air out of the pores. Drainage refers to the movement of water through the soil; water-holding capacity is the ability of a soil to retain water after rainfall or irrigation. During dry periods, air-filled pores predominate. Coarse-textured (sandy) soils tend to drain quickly, retaining little water. They also warm up faster in the spring and are generally easy to work. Fine-textured (clay) soils retain both water and nutrients longer than a sandy soil and may become waterlogged. The same material – organic matter – that improves the drainage of a heavy clay soil can increase the capacity of a light sandy soil to retain water.

Different areas of your property may drain very differently. After a heavy rain, one area may stay wet much longer than others. If you plan to garden in a wet spot, you should choose plants that are well adapted to such conditions.

SOIL DRAINAGE TEST

To assess your soil's drainage, perform the following test. Wait at least a few days after the last rain until your soil has dried a bit, then dig a hole 4 inches (10cm) deep, large enough to accommodate a 46-ounce (1.4kg) can. Remove the top and bottom of the can and place it in the hole, firming the soil around the outside. Fill the can to the top with water, then observe how long it takes to drain. Ideally, the water level will drop about two inches (5cm) in an hour. This indicates that your soil drains well but also will retain the moisture necessary for the healthy growth of a wide variety of garden plants.

If the water level drops less than an inch (2.5cm) after an hour, your soil does not display sufficient drainage to accommodate many plants. Either limit your choice of plants to those that like constant moisture, or take measures to improve the drainage. If the water level drops four inches (10cm) in an hour, your soil drains too fast, and unless you plan to grow only plants that tolerate very dry soils, you will need to add organic matter to help retain soil moisture (and will also need to water as necessary).

Remember that different areas of your landscape may display marked differences in drainage and this test should be done in each one.

Soil pH

The acidity or alkalinity of your soil is critical to plant health. The measurement of the degree of acidity or alkalinity, the pH scale, rates solutions from most acidic (0) to most alkaline (14), with 7 being neutral.

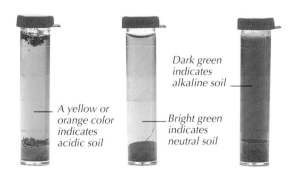

Determining pH
Kits are available for testing the acidity, neutrality, or alkalinity of your soil at home. They give a good general indication of pH.

A yellow or orange color indicates acidic soil

Dark green indicates alkaline soil

Bright green indicates neutral soil

The pH of your soil is determined by many factors, such as the type of rock from which the soil originated, the amount of preciption, and the type of vegetation growing in it.

The optimal soil pH for most plants is between 6.0 and 7.0. Deficiencies of essential nutrients often occur outside of this range, damaging plants and sometimes making them more susceptible to diseases and pests. Furthermore, acidic soils inhibit the survival of certain beneficial organisms, including earthworms, mycorrhizal fungi, and many bacteria. These organisms are responsible for the decay of organic matter and thereby help plants obtain nutrients.

Soil pH can be modified (to change soil pH, see p.30), but to determine which materials and how much you will need to add to your soil, you will first need to perform a soil test (see the opposite page).

Soil fertility

There are 16 essential nutrients necessary for plant growth. Carbon, hydrogen, and oxygen are derived from air and water, and the remaining nutrients are supplied from the soil. These are classified as macronutrients, secondary nutrients, and trace elements. Macronutrients – nitrogen (N), phosphorus (P), and potassium (K) – are needed by plants in large quantities; secondary nutrients – calcium (Ca), magnesium (Mg), and sulfur (S) – are needed in moderate quantities; and trace elements – boron (B), chlorine (Cl), copper (Cu), iron (Fe), manganese (Mn), molybdenum (Mo), and zinc (Zn) – are essential but needed only in very minute quantities. Determining the existing nutrient levels in your soil can help identify the kind and amount of fertilizers needed.

The acid test
Some plants, including azaleas (left) and rhododendrons and their relatives, thrive only in acidic soils. They will fail if not provided the conditions that maintain acidity.

pH				
4	5	6	7	8	9
Acidic			Neutral		Basic

nitrogen

calcium and magnesium

phosphorus

potassium

sulfur

iron, magnesium, zinc, copper, cobalt

molybdenum

boron

Not All are Alike
The availability of nutrients in the soil depends on the pH level. Note how many of them are less available in acidic soils.

Something's Missing
The yellowing leaves of this raspberry could be a result of an iron or magnesium deficiency in the soil.

Types of fertilizer

There are many different kinds of fertilizers available that can supply essential nutrients to your plants. Derived from a variety of sources, both natural and synthetic, they are available in a range of formulations that have been developed for different uses, from fast-acting foliar sprays to timed-release pellets. Some contain a single nutrient, and others multiple nutrients.

The three mineral nutrients used in the greatest quantity by plants are nitrogen (N), phosphorus (P), and potassium (K). A fertilizer that contains all three macronutrients is called a complete fertilizer. The three numbers on a bag of a complete fertilizer – the analysis – refer to the percentages by weight of nitrogen (N), phosphorus (phosphate, expressed as P_2O_5), and potassium (potash, expressed as K_2O), in that order.

Many complete fertilizers contain other nutrients that are also essential for healthy plants but are used in smaller quantities (secondary and micronutrients). These are usually listed on the label.

Organic fertilizer is derived from an organic – or once-living – source. Cow, horse, poultry, and sheep manures, fish emulsion, alfalfa and soybean meals, wood ashes, and compost are examples of organic fertilizers. Since most are somewhat lower and more

Apply it correctly
Spread the appropriate amount of fertilizer in a ring around a plant at and beyond its dripline – the outermost reach of its branches – then work it into the soil or cover it with mulch.

variable in nutrient content than chemical fertilizers, you will need to use more of the material to obtain the nutrition your plants require. Because organic fertilizers are typically slow to break down in the soil, they have several advantages over chemical fertilizers: they remain available to plants over a longer period of time, they don't leach out of the soil as quickly, and they don't usually "burn" (dehydrate) roots. One of the most significant qualities of organic fertilizers is that they improve the structure and ecological balance of soil, which promotes healthy plant growth.

FERTILIZER FORMULATIONS

Fertilizer comes in many forms. Many synthetic fertilizers are available in a dry, granulated form, which is easy to spread, and the nutrients are usually readily available. Some granulated fertilizers are coated with sulfur or plastic so that their nutrients are slowly released over time.

Some synthetic fertilizers are sold as concentrated liquids or powders that require diluting. These are applied as liquids to the soil around plants or as a foliar spray. Foliar fertilizing using a water soluble solution can provide quick relief for plants that are suffering from a nutrient deficiency.

Fertilizer spikes are compressed, dry fertilizer that has been formed into a stakelike solid. Commonly used for trees and shrubs, they are inserted into holes drilled into the soil around the root zone.

Manure can be fresh or dried, resulting in a considerable difference in weight and nutrient content, not to mention smell.

NUTRIENT CONTENT OF FERTILIZERS
(ALL VALUES ARE APPROXIMATE)

	% Nitrogen (N)	% Phosphorus (P_2O_5)	% Potassium (K_2O)
Organic			
Animal manure	0.6	0.1	0.5
Compost	0.5	0.3	0.8
Bone meal	2	14	-
Sewage	7	10	-
Seaweed meal	2.8	0.2	2.5
Blood meal	12	-	-
Mushroom compost	0.7	0.3	0.3
Rock phosphate	-	26	12
Wood ash	0.1	0.3	1
Cocoa shells	3	1	3.2
Inorganic			
Balanced fertilizers	available in various proportions		
Ammonium nitrate	35	-	-
Superphosphate	-	20	-
Muriate of potash	-	-	60
Potassium sulfate	-	-	49

Urban soils

Soils in urban environments often suffer from detrimental effects of construction and high-density populations. Compaction, contamination, poor drainage, nutrient imbalances, and excess temperatures are common. When the force of foot and vehicular traffic is exerted on the soil, it compresses and compacts the soil and breaks up soil aggregates. Compacted soil is a major cause of tree decline in urban environments.

Soil contamination often occurs when building materials are spilled or dumped. Some contaminants are toxic to plants, while others cause more indirect damage, such as altering the soil pH. On badly contaminated sites, gardening may be limited to raised beds and containers filled with imported soil.

In addition to suffering nutrient imbalances, many urban soils are infertile simply because topsoil and organic matter are often removed during construction, leaving an infertile subsoil that drains poorly and has very poor aeration. Taking the time to improve your soil is usually the best solution (*see* Building soil with organic matter, *p. 30*).

Heat absorbed by buildings, roads, sidewalks, and vehicles adds considerably to the air temperature of the urban environment, which in turn raises the soil temperature. This "heat-island effect" can significantly alter the chemical and biological characteristics of soil. One of the easiest and safest ways to counteract this effect is to apply an organic mulch to the soil surface (*see* The mulch advantage, *p. 46*).

Temperature ranges

All plants have an optimal temperature range for growth. They also have temperature limits (both high and low), beyond which injury or death is likely to occur. These temperatures vary from one plant to another – some plants have a wide temperature range, others are far more limited – a major reason that locations with widely different climates support distinct plant species. Gardeners deal with this preference for temperatures on a daily basis.

Bring on the cold
Bunchberry (*Cornus canadensis*) tolerates severe cold (to USDA Zone 2).

Sheltered beauties
Pacific coast irises (*Iris innominata* and others) thrive in a protected spot.

Keep me warm
Most gardeners in the Northwest need to provide a protected spot for loquats (*Eriobotrya japonica*).

USDA Hardiness Zones

Winter hardiness is the ability of a plant to survive the winter conditions in a given location. Other factors in addition to cold influence hardiness, including soil moisture, humidity, and buffeting winds. While a dianthus may tolerate frigid temperatures in a garden, it often fails to survive winters where soils stay wet, and although a number of broad-leaf evergreens thrive in cold temperatures, these evergreens may suffer severe desiccation if exposed to winter winds.

°F	Zones	°C
below -50°	1	below -46°
-50° to -40°	2	-46° to -40°
-40° to -30°	3	-40° to -34°
-30° to -20°	4	-34° to -29°
-20° to -10°	5	-29° to -23°
-10° to 0°	6	-23° to -18°
0° to 10°	7	-18° to -12°
10° to 20°	8	-12° to -7°
20° to 30°	9	-7° to -1°
30° to 40°	10	-1° to 4°
above 40°	11	above 4°

To help American gardeners identify plants that survive winter temperatures in their region, the USDA created the Plant Hardiness Zone Map. The 1990 edition includes 11 hardiness zones based on average annual minimum temperature. An updated edition of the map, under development, will include 15 hardiness zones – the four new zones will help gardeners in subtropical regions select appropriate plants. Plants in this book have been assigned hardiness codes that match the 15 zones on this map.

Thousands of plants have been coded to the USDA Plant Hardiness Zone Map according to the lowest temperatures they will survive. Also considered in the rating is the plant's cold requirement: many plants require a certain amount of cold in order for their buds to break dormancy in the spring. Therefore, the hardiness rating is actually a range from the coldest zone in which the plant will survive to the warmest zone that satisfies its cold requirements.

The influence of cold temperatures on plant survival is more complicated than simply the lowest temperature experienced by the plant. Other factors such as the rate of temperature drop, the duration of the cold, the amount of temperature fluctuation, and the snow or mulch cover on the soil around the plant.

AHS Heat Zones

On the opposite end of the thermometer, the amount of heat that plants are exposed to in summer is equally critical. For this reason the American Horticultural Society Plant Heat Zone Map was developed in 1997. AHS President Emeritus Dr. H. Marc Cathey supervised the development of the map, using data collected from the National Climatic Data Center and the National Weather Service. The map divides the US into 12 heat zones according to their average annual number of "heat days." A heat day is defined as a day in which temperatures reach or exceed 86° F (30° C).

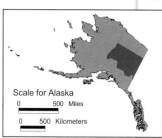

Scale for Alaska
0   500 Miles
0   500 Kilometers

Average Number of Days per Year Above 86°F (30°C)	Zone
<1	1
1 to 7	2
>7 to 14	3
>14 to 30	4
>30 to 45	5
>45 to 60	6
>60 to 90	7
>90 to 120	8
>120 to 150	9
>150 to 180	10
>180 to 210	11
>210	12

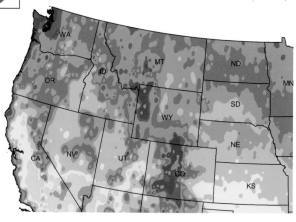

AHS Heat Zone 1 averages less than one heat day per year, while Zone 12 averages more than 210.

Like hardiness zones, the heat zones for a particular plant are given as a range. The first number indicates the hottest zone in which it will grow successfully; the second represents the zone with the minimum amount of summer heat necessary for it to complete its annual growth cycle.

As for cold hardiness, heat tolerance in plants involves more than just temperature. Summer rainfall – and the lack of it – limits the successful cultivation of many plants. High humidity rings the death knell for many plants that thrive in drier conditions with similar heat. Some plants are able to thrive in warmer zones if nights are cool. Qualities of the soil – its fertility, acidity or alkalinity, and drainage – also influence the summer survival equation. These factors should also be taken into account when selecting plants.

Although temperature is not the only determinant involved in a plant's ability to thrive in summer conditions, it is an important factor, and one that has been extensively assessed for the use of gardeners. For specific zones for many plants that grow in the Northwest, see the Plant Catalog.

Identify light and shade levels

As you stroll around your yard, observe which areas receive full sun and which areas are shaded by trees or surrounding structures. Because light levels change with the time of day, the season, and from one year to the next, this is an ongoing project. As the sun travels across the sky, a shady morning garden may be basking in full sun by early afternoon. In summer, when deciduous trees are in full leaf, a bed that received spring sun may be densely shaded. The angle of the sun as seasons change also alters the level of light in a garden. Furthermore, as trees mature, they cast increasingly broader shadows – beds that were planted in full sun several years ago may become cloaked in the shade of trees that grow nearby.

As your garden matures, stay abreast of changing light levels and the impact on your plants.

To assess your garden's current level of light, examine the shade patterns several times during the course of a sunny day. Note areas that receive shade in the morning, midday, and early and late afternoon. By noting the position of surrounding trees (taking into consideration whether they are deciduous or evergreen) and estimating the changing angle of the sun, you should be able to approximate the light levels in your garden for the entire year with reasonable accuracy.

Identifying your garden areas according to the light categories on this page will help you select plants with corresponding light requirements.

Full sun

Areas that receive at least six hours of direct sun during the day are considered in full sun and are desirable for vegetables, fruit, roses, and a wide range of flowering plants. Some plants that thrive in full sun in cooler areas, however, may require some afternoon shade in warmer areas of the Northwest.

Full shade

Areas beneath trees with a dense canopy where no direct sunlight penetrates and reflected light is reduced, or that stand in the all-day shadow of tall buildings or evergreens, are considered to be in full shade. Careful selection of plants for such minimal light levels (and the reduced moisture levels that often occur in areas with low light) is necessary.

Partial shade

Some gardens receive dappled shade throughout the day. If you stand in dappled shade, you should be able to glimpse portions of the sky through the leaves above. Other gardens are more densely shaded for a part of the day but receive bright sunlight for two to six hours. Both are considered partially shaded. A wide variety of plants are suited to this level of light.

Identify your microclimates

Areas within the same yard can present quite a variety of growing conditions, and it is important to recognize the garden limitations and possibilities of each. A microclimate – a portion of your yard where growing conditions differ from surrounding areas – can be a dry, shady spot or one that is constantly wet. It may be a narrow strip that is protected by a hedge, or an area warmed by its proximity to a building or stone wall.

To identify microclimates in your yard, note areas that seem slightly out of sync with the rest of the yard or other yards in the neighborhood – spots where spring flowers open earlier or later than others of the same kind, locations where blooms last longer, or areas that require more or less frequent watering than surrounding areas. These observations will suggest the need for plants that accommodate the nuances of your microclimate. They may also offer the opportunity to grow plants beyond the prevailing cultural limitations (particularly the overall hardiness and heat zone ratings) of your landscape.

EXISTING VEGETATION

Trees provide shade, and shady areas are typically several degrees cooler than adjacent areas in the sun. Shady spots also tend to stay wetter longer. Some plants that thrive in the sun where summers are cool can be grown in warmer climates if they are provided some shade. Dense vegetation can also block or reduce winds that cause a rapid loss of moisture by plants and soil. Planting a windbreak to provide protection from prevailing winds is one way you can help create a microclimate in your yard.

Microclimates are not static, however, especially those influenced by vegetation. As plants grow or are pruned or removed, conditions can be dramatically altered: a sunny garden may become shaded as the tree canopy expands; a wet area may become drier as groundcover plants grow and absorb more water; and a shade garden may be exposed to full sun if an old tree becomes damaged and needs to be removed. The gardener, as always, must be adaptable.

STRUCTURES AND HARDSCAPING

A house, garage, fence, or wall can also serve as a windbreak. These structures cast shade as well – the north side of a wall running east to west tends to be cooler and damper; the sunny south side will be notably warmer and drier. Such a wall creates two distinct microclimates that are separated by mere inches. Each side will support a culturally distinct set of plants. Although the difference in climate on either side of a wall that runs north to south is more subtle, the west side will tend to be warmer than the east side.

In temperate zones, a south-facing wall, particularly if it receives full sun, is a great place to grow sun-loving tropical or subtropical vines – such as *Bougainvillea* and black-eyed Susan vine (*Thunbergia alata*) – as annuals. The soil warms earlier in the spring, boosting early growth, and because the wall collects and holds heat,

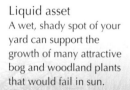

Liquid asset
A wet, shady spot of your yard can support the growth of many attractive bog and woodland plants that would fail in sun.

Dry oasis
A shady dry spot has been transformed into a refuge with the masterful use of gravel, water, and adaptable plants.

moderating cooler night temperatures, growth will continue later into the autumn.

Because the area is cooler, plants growing on the north side of a building emerge from dormancy later than those on the south side. Air temperatures are influenced by the material and color of nearby structures: white or light colors reflect daytime light and heat back onto the plants; dark colors absorb heat.

SOIL SURFACES
The color of paved surfaces and mulch has a similar effect on nearby plants. Dark mulches absorb heat and can be used to warm the soil. Light-colored paving reflects light and heat back to surrounding areas. Heat-tolerant plants that thrive in sunny locations are usually the best choices near unshaded driveways and sidewalks.

WATER
Large bodies of water have a moderating effect on temperature, but even a backyard pond or pool can contribute a similar influence. Plants located at the edge of a pond not only have more water available in the soil, but they also benefit from a more humid environment created by evaporation from the pond.

COASTAL GARDENS
Gardens located near the seashore have special requirements. Plants must be able to tolerate salt spray, strong winds, and sandy soil. However, the moderate temperatures and higher humidity allow

for growing a broader palette of plants, including marginally hardy ones. Soil can be improved with organic matter, and windbreaks can provide protection. Solid walls do not afford as much protection as salt-tolerant trees and shrubs. These plants act as filters to the salt spray as well as a buffer to the wind. Once a living barrier is established, less tolerant plants can be grown and benefit from the nurturing aspect of the ocean.

TOPOGRAPHY
Unless your yard is flat, its topography will influence your growing conditions. Marginally hardy plants and those that produce cold-sensitive, early spring flowers are more likely to be damaged by frosts if they are located in a frost pocket. Slopes also affect runoff: water can collect in a low area, making an ideal location for a bog garden. Steep slopes can be tamed and runoff reduced by using retaining walls to create level planting areas.

A nod to Monet
Open water provides limitless opportunities to create artistic compositions of plants, structures, and the reflected sky.

A little protection
Even a thinly constructed fence can provide enough wind protection to give shelter to delicate ferns and marginally hardy plants.

ADAPT WHEN NECESSARY

So you've assessed yourself and your lifestyle and have critically analyzed your site. Now it's time to make some decisions about your gardening conditions. Reconciling your personal interests, style, and budget with the physical limitations of your yard may require some compromises. But if any reasonable improvements to your site will enhance the long-term success of your garden, they should be considered. Drastic changes are not recommended for a SMARTGARDEN™, particularly those that will be difficult or time-consuming to maintain.

Fixed and variable factors

Certain aspects of a gardening site – temperature extremes, rainfall, elevation, proximity to city or the ocean – cannot be altered, and the plants you grow should be inherently compatible with those existing conditions. Radical attempts to change your microclimate are generally unfruitful and a frustrating waste of your time.

On the other hand, some modifications can alter the growing conditions significantly to the advantage of your gardens. Adding soil amendments such as organic matter (*see p. 30*) or limestone or iron sulfate to decrease or increase the acidity (*see* Adjusting soil pH, *p. 30*) is often necessary, particularly in areas where builders have removed topsoil. Regrading a backyard to improve drainage, or removing trees to allow more light into an area, may dramatically expand your gardening opportunities. The cost of such major modifications should be evaluated against the potential results. Sometimes compromises in garden size, placement, plant selection, and hardscaping options (nonplant features, such as patios) offer satisfying and less costly solutions.

Conditions vary, depending on the location of your garden within the landscape. Parts of your yard may be in full sun while others are shaded; some areas may be exposed to persistent winds from which other areas are protected; drainage patterns may result in a wet zone in one part of the yard and dry conditions in another. Identifying the distinct characteristics of each area provides the gardener with an opportunity to grow plants with varied requirements within a single landscape. Matching the requirements of the plants you want to grow as closely as possible to the conditions of a particular site will minimize adaptations that are necessary for healthy growth.

Staying dry
Make the best of an extremely fast-draining area by creating a dry garden, using drought-tolerant plants set among stones, gravel, and sand. The stepping stones and plants used here cleverly suggest a stream running through a woodland.

Smart redirection
Instead of trying to grow grass in a wet spot, the owners of this property converted part of their land into a lush planting of woodland plants shaded by small trees.

Raise it up
Raised beds and supplemental irrigation enable this gardener to grow vegetables in an area that would otherwise produce smaller, poorer-quality crops. Carefully amended soil, using copious amounts of organic matter, helps work the magic.

The benefits of time

Keep in mind that time is an important dimension in gardening. An instant SMARTGARDEN™ is an oxymoron. Good things take time. Building a healthy soil doesn't happen overnight; it is an ongoing process. Likewise plants, particularly trees and shrubs, increase in size over the years, and they should be spaced with an eye toward their mature size. Purchasing large plants to give your garden an established feeling from the start has its drawbacks: larger plants are more expensive, and they often have more difficulty becoming established than smaller

Worth the wait
Starting from scratch may at first seem daunting, but the satisfaction of watching a landscape grow over time is one of the major pleasures of gardening. Heavy work at first gives way to installing the structural "bones" of a garden area, followed by planting and then enjoying the rewards of all of your planning and hard work.

stock. By the time a large plant has settled in and has begun to produce significant growth, a specimen that was smaller at planting time might even have caught up with the larger one.

Time can be viewed as a wonderful dynamic – you can witness your garden's change from season to season and from year to year as the design you envisioned becomes a reality. As plants and beds mature, they often require less maintenance because after their roots become well established, appropriately selected trees and shrubs will not require much attention, and, as groundcovers fill in, the need for weeding is reduced.

Raised beds for variety

Sometimes the plants you want to grow are at odds with your soil. Plants that require excellent drainage are poor choices for heavy, clay soils. On the other hand, a light, sandy soil will not sustain plants that require abundant moisture without reliable, abundant irrigation. If you want to include plants in your landscape with requirements that vary significantly from your native soil, consider growing them in raised beds or containers. Given the finite quantity of soil involved, its characteristics can be easily manipulated to suit the needs of desired plants.

Although limited in space, these gardens can be constructed or placed in sun or shade, protected or exposed locations, and watered frequently or minimally. They can also be built to accommodate easy access for gardeners who have difficulty bending or working in ground beds. The flexibility of raised beds gives the gardener an enormous selection of plants that might otherwise be ill suited for the conditions of the site (*see also p. 13*).

Culling the existing landscape

Before you begin adding plants to your landscape, it is important to review those that are already there. Some may have suffered damage or neglect and are now simply eyesores. Others may require a bit (or more) of maintenance. Certain plants in your yard may require significant time and energy to keep them healthy and attractive. This is particularly common with plants that were sited in inappropriate conditions in the first place. Transplanting to a different spot in the landscape or removing them altogether may be necessary.

Small trees and shrubs are often planted too close together. Although the short-term effect may be pleasing, after a number of years plants eventually become too crowded for their space. If such plants exist in your yard, determine if their value is worth the effort of constant pruning. Is transplanting them to another location a possibility, or should you simply remove them entirely?

Most suburban lots can accommodate very few large trees. If the trees that were planted decades ago have overtaken the lot, you may want to consider removing one or two, or at least thinning their branches to allow more light to penetrate. Limbing up the tree – that is, removing the lower branches – can increase light penetration as well, and it opens the area beneath the tree for use.

Severe damage from disease, insects, winds, lightning, or other environmental stresses may have affected some trees and shrubs in your yard, and you should ask yourself if they are worth saving – it may be time to consider a replacement. Pruning or removing large trees may require a professional arborist.

WHEN TO CALL THE ARBORIST

Most home gardeners can learn from classes or books how to do most of their own home pruning, but there are cases where the scale of the pruning or the condition of the plants in question can make doing the operation yourself very risky. It takes considerable skill to drop large branches or entire trees where they will do no harm, especially if the tree is close to a house or plants that you don't want injured. Clean and informed pruning cuts need to be made so that the tree heals rapidly. This is especially true when you are dealing with removal of large limbs that interfere with power lines or building structures, dead, diseased, or dying limbs that pose a hazard, or limbs that have been compromised by storms or other acts of nature, such as lightning.

Arborists, popularly known as tree surgeons, are professionals trained in tree care. They can diagnose problems, recommend treatments, and fertilize, prune, spray, and cut down and remove trees safely. If there is any doubt in your mind whether or not you can handle a pruning situation, always consider employing a professional or at least consulting one.

Certified arborists are trained to make decisions on the safety of a tree and if and where it should be pruned or perhaps removed. Always use arborists that are members of National Arborist Association (NAA) or the American Society of Consulting Arborists (ASCA) or are members and have been certified by the International Society of Arboriculture (ISA).

A job for the professional
Removing large limbs and felling trees are both best left to trained professional arborists.

Thinning and Limbing Up

When large trees limit the opportunities for growing other plants in a yard, either because they take up a great deal of space, or they cast dense shade, removal is not your only option.

Thinning a tree involves removing a percentage of its branches so that more air and light can penetrate through the remaining canopy without stimulating a great deal of vigorous, new growth. This is accomplished by cutting specific branches back to where they connect to a larger limb. This type of pruning is often beneficial to the tree: weak, unhealthy, and crowded branches can be removed, and air circulates better through the canopy. Plants that are growing beneath the tree will receive more light. If you want grass to grow under a tree with a dense canopy, thinning is critical.

Limbing up the tree is the technique of removing low limbs back to the main trunk in order to allow access to the area beneath the canopy; it effectively raises the crown. Ideally this process should begin early in the tree's training, but it can be done to large trees as well. When removing lower limbs from a young tree, do it gradually – this will cause less shock and promote a stronger trunk. As the tree gains height and girth, continue to remove the lowest branches. Generally, the best time to prune trees is when they are dormant, during the fall and winter.

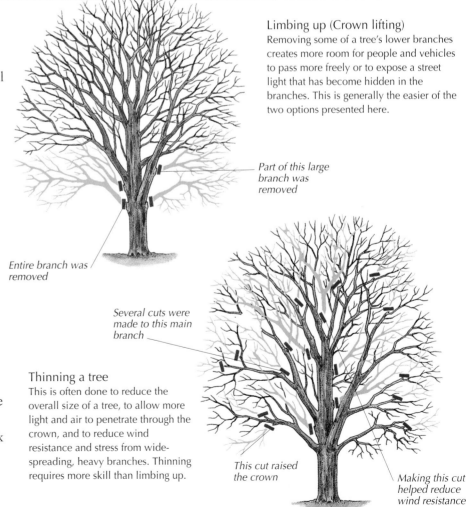

Limbing up (Crown lifting)
Removing some of a tree's lower branches creates more room for people and vehicles to pass more freely or to expose a street light that has become hidden in the branches. This is generally the easier of the two options presented here.

Part of this large branch was removed

Entire branch was removed

Several cuts were made to this main branch

Thinning a tree
This is often done to reduce the overall size of a tree, to allow more light and air to penetrate through the crown, and to reduce wind resistance and stress from wide-spreading, heavy branches. Thinning requires more skill than limbing up.

This cut raised the crown

Making this cut helped reduce wind resistance

Adapting soil conditions

Whether refining an existing garden or working an area that is new to cultivation, a number of conditions can be fairly easily modified, such as adjusting pH and modifying drainage and structure.

Many of these changes – particularly those involving the soil – are most easily addressed prior to planting. Once a garden has been planted, your ability to incorporate soil amendments is restricted. Whenever you dig soil, take the opportunity to incorporate amendments. It takes much longer for fertilizer and limestone to reach plant roots when placed on the surface of the soil than it does when those materials are mixed throughout the root zone.

ADJUSTING SOIL PH

As mentioned in Tenet 2, a soil test provides important information about your soil. If your existing soil pH restricts your selection of plants, you can adjust it by mixing certain minerals into the soil. Limestone – usually ground or dolomitic – is applied to raise the pH (decrease the acidity). Wood ashes also tend to raise the pH of soil. Elemental sulfur or iron sulfate are the most commonly recommended supplements for lowering pH. Aluminum sulfate can also be used to decrease acidity, but it may cause aluminum toxicity in some plants. Many sources of organic matter, including pine needles, oak leaves, unlimed compost, and green manure (cover crops that are plowed into the soil), will increase the soil acidity as they are broken down by microorganisms. Peat moss is also an acidifier, but its use should be avoided because it takes so long – centuries – for it to regenerate in its native bogs. The amounts of various materials needed to produce the desired pH level will vary depending on your soil texture and the amount of change needed. Modifying the soil pH takes time; it may require repeated applications.

An extreme case
You may not have ducks taking up permanent residence in your yard, but many properties have spots that are poorly drained. Either take measures to drain the area, or consider creating a bog garden or even a pond.

DEALING WITH DRAINAGE

If your soil drains too slowly, you have several options. You can limit your selection to plants that like wet soils, add material to the soil to improve drainage, or build raised beds and fill them with good, loamy soil before planting. To improve drainage of a compacted soil, add organic matter. If the subsoil is compacted, you may need to break up the hardpan or add subsurface drainage tiles or pipes that will carry excess water away from planting areas.

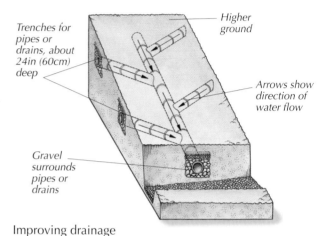

Trenches for pipes or drains, about 24in (60cm) deep

Higher ground

Arrows show direction of water flow

Gravel surrounds pipes or drains

Improving drainage
Connect pipes or tiles in a gravel-filled trench. On sloping ground, lay the pipes or tile drains to run parallel to the ground. On level ground, slope the pipes away from ground level.

For vegetable gardens with poor drainage, a hill-and-furrow planting method can be practiced: broad rows can be built up several inches above the soil surface, with furrows running between the rows to divert excess water. Conversely, if your soil drains too quickly, use the furrows for planting. Rain or irrigation water will be channeled into the furrows where plants are growing.

For gardens where the soil drains too quickly, the addition of organic matter will improve the water-holding capacity, and mulching will reduce evaporation loss. But supplemental irrigation may be necessary unless you choose plants that thrive in dry soils.

Building soil with organic matter

Organic matter – compost, leaf mold, grass clippings, rotted manure, or any material that was once alive – has a nearly miraculous power to improve almost any soil. Added to a clay soil, it facilitates drainage by creating soil aggregates with pore spaces between them; in a sandy soil, it bolsters water retention. The best way to provide continuous, well-balanced nutrition for plants is to build up the soil with organic matter.

As soil organisms digest organic matter, they release nutrients in a usable form for plants to absorb through their roots. Unlike quick-release chemical fertilizers that offer a glut of nutrients that may wash away with the next rain, decomposition of organic matter is a continuous process; nutrients are released slowly over a long period of time.

There are many good sources of organic matter, and many are free and readily available. Kitchen and yard wastes can be composted and within a few months yield a rich soil supplement (*see* Composting wastes, *p. 56*). Leaves raked during the fall become

Manure

Mushroom compost

Peat

Brown gold
Here are just three of the many kinds of organic matter that can be added to improve the structure and water retention of soil.

crumbly leaf mold, especially if they are chopped and mixed with a bit of soil to encourage their decomposition. Manure is often free for the hauling from a nearby farm or stable, or it can be purchased in bags from a home-supply or hardware store. Green manure is a cover crop that is sown, grown, and then turned back into the soil. A winter cover crop is an efficient method of adding both nutrients and organic matter to a vegetable garden. A distinction is often made between leguminous and nonleguminous cover crops. Both add organic matter to the soil, but legumes, such as clover and vetch, contribute additional nitrogen as a result of their symbiotic relationship with nitrogen-fixing *Rhizobium* bacteria in the roots. As the legume roots decompose, nitrogen is released into the soil. Of course, the amount of specific nutrients depends on the source and condition of the organic matter. For example, most compost contains 1.5 to 3.5 percent nitrogen, 0.5 to 1 percent phosphorus, and 1 to 2 percent potassium. Wood ashes – which tend to raise pH – contain little nitrogen, 1 to 2 percent phosphorus, and 3 to 7 percent potassium.

A soil well furnished with organic matter will sustain a healthy population of organisms, resulting in both improved soil structure and nourishment for your garden plants. This is recycling at its best.

HOW MUCH ORGANIC MATTER?

The amount of organic matter that you need to add to a given soil depends to a large degree on the soil temperature, which directly affects the rate at which microorganisms digest the organic matter in soil. Remember that if the rate of decomposition is greater than the rate at which you add organic matter to the soil, the organic matter content will drop. Of course, the converse is true as well.

The average amount of organic matter recommended to add annually to garden soils is 3 inches (8cm). The Northwest covers AHS Heat Zones from 1 to 10. Therefore, if you are in the colder AHS Heat Zones (1–2) you may be able to add less, say one to two inches, and if you are in the warmer end of the range (8–9), you should use up to 4 or 5 inches (10–13cm).

The optimal organic matter level is 5 to 7 percent in the top 12 to 24 inches (30–61cm) of the soil, where the bulk of most plants' root systems are located. Unless your soil is tested for organic matter in a laboratory, you need to guesstimate the content by observing the soil.

Observe your soil each year throughout the growing season, and make notes on how it looks and feels. If it seems to be getting lighter in color and less structured (fewer aggregates), then increase the amount of organic matter you add each year. You may need to add much more organic matter during the first few years to bring your levels up to par. In any case, using organic matter appropriately will build your soil and will enable your plants to grow more healthily.

The nature of humus

After organic matter is thoroughly decomposed by soil microorganisms, it produces a material called humus, which exists as a very thin layer around soil particles. There is some misunderstanding about this term. The material commonly sold in bags that bear the label "humus" – usually compost or peat – would be more accurately labeled "humus-producing material," because microorganisms use it to make true humus, which is the end product of organic matter decomposition.

Humus contributes significantly to the soil environment by facilitating the aggregation of soil particles (which improves soil structure), holding nutrients against the force of leaching, increasing aeration, retaining water, and acting as a buffer to moderate a soil's acidity or alkalinity.

The carbon:nitrogen ratio

Not all organic matter is equal (*see* Nutrient Content of Fertilizers, *p. 20*). One of the most critical characteristics of organic matter in terms of plant nutrition is the ratio of carbon to nitrogen (C:N ratio). Fresh organic matter has a high carbon content compared to its nitrogen content. As the organic matter is broken down, the ratio changes – the relative amount of nitrogen increases. In most fully matured compost, the C:N ratio is between 30:1 and 10:1.

Now it's time to choose the plants and other features for your SMARTGARDEN™!

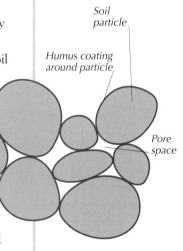

Soil particle

Humus coating around particle

Pore space

Up close
This diagram shows a much enlarged view of a few particles of soil. Each particle is coated with humus, the end product of microbial breakdown of organic matter. Humus aids in the retention of moisture and nutrients and promotes the formation of aggregates, which in turn leads to increased pore space: all very good things for soil.

PICK THE BEST PLANTS

One of the most important steps in establishing and maintaining a SMARTGARDEN™ is selecting the right plants. Matching the cultural requirements of plants with your specific garden environment significantly increases the likelihood of successful cultivation and minimizes the maintenance effort. Preferences for water, light, soil type and acidity, tolerance of wind, humidity, salt spray, and air pollution, and resistance to diseases and pests are important factors in plant selection. Some conditions, such as soil pH, can be adjusted to accommodate the needs of desired plants. Others, such as salt spray near coastal regions or air pollution near industrial areas, are essentially fixed and limiting factors in the selection process.

Practical considerations

Identifying the USDA Plant Hardiness and AHS Heat Zones of your site is a logical first step in choosing plants you would like to grow. If a plant does not have the hardiness or heat tolerance for the zone in which you garden, you should choose another plant, unless you are willing to take extra measures to protect it. For example, tropical and subtropical plants can be grown in a container outdoors in temperate zones and brought indoors for winter (*see* Tender Tropicals, *p. 38*). Consult the Zone maps on p. 22 to determine your USDA Hardiness Zone and your AHS Heat Zone. Use those numbers as a starting point to select plants that will thrive in your garden's temperatures.

There may be areas of your yard that are unsuitable or impractical for growing plants of any kind. Consider a nonplant alternative such as a fence (in place of a hedge), a walkway, patio, or deck (in place of a lawn, bed, or similar planting), or a gazebo (in place of a large shade tree). These spaces are important elements of a landscape because they provide you with a minimum-maintenance area for moving through your gardens comfortably, or room for relaxing and enjoying your planted areas.

So you have an area in your yard and you want it to do something, but you need to consider the options: Provide shade? Simply look nice? Attract birds? Smell good? Block a view? Separate one area from another? Cover the ground? Provide a space for active play?

What are the site's physical factors, including sun, water, soil, wind, and microclimate? Will it support plants? If no, use the site for some other purpose, or think hard about what you would need to do to modify it. If yes, then consider the specific plant features you'd like and require: leaves, flowers, fruit, form, bark, fragrance, size, shape, longevity, adaptabilty, productivity, hardiness, specific needs such as pruning, support, or deadheading to look its best, and its susceptibility to pests and diseases.

Choose plants that meet the desired criteria and will grow well in the available microclimate, and determine how many will be needed.

The next consideration is your budget. If you can wait for a small plant to grow to its mature size, or let groundcovers and other similar plants multiply, you will not need to spend as much. You should also determine when you will buy the plant, and when it will go into the ground.

Two solutions
Using plants is not always the solution to a given landscape problem: the conditions and the planning process may logically lead you to choose a hardscaping option over a garden.

Compromise
Instead of draining this area, the gardener chose to create a pond feature with hardscaping leading right up to it. Plants adapted to the conditions thrive, and the entire area is a place of delight instead of one of constant maintenance.

Plant categories

Plants are grouped according to their lifespan. The major categories are annuals, biennials, perennials, and woody plants.

ANNUAL

An annual completes its life cycle in a single season. It grows from seed, develops vegetatively, bears flowers, produces seed for the next generation, and then dies, all in less than a year.

BIENNIAL

A biennial requires two growing seasons to complete its life cycle. Most biennials produce vegetative growth their first season; they flower, produce seed, and die their second season.

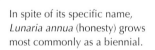

In spite of its specific name, *Lunaria annua* (honesty) grows most commonly as a biennial.

Calendula, or pot marigold (*Calendula officinalis*), is a commonly grown annual.

PERENNIAL

A perennial is a plant that lives for more than two years, and a herbaceous perennial is a nonwoody perennial that survives from one growing season to the next because its roots or underground storage organs (such as a bulb, corm, or tuber) persist.

Turtleheads (*Chelone* species) are native perennials adapted to moist borders and bog gardens.

Sun-loving perennial
Achillea species (yarrows) are mostly tough, adaptable perennials that grow well in dry, sunny spots.

WOODY PLANT

A woody plant is also a type of perennial, but it possesses a more permanent structure that persists above ground from season to season. Woody plants may be deciduous (shedding their leaves each year) or evergreen. Examples include shrubs, trees, and some climbers and groundcovers.

Hydrangea species and cultivars are all woody plants that are widely used in shrub borders and as specimens.

Beautyberries (*Callicarpa* species) often die back extensively – sometimes right back to soil level after a hard winter – but they are nonetheless woody plants and will produce a woody framework over time.

Perennials grown as annuals

Some plants are referred to as annuals in spite of being perennial in their native habitat or another Hardiness Zone. This has led to confusion among gardeners. True annuals – plants that grow, flower, produce seed, and die in a single growing season – have a Hardiness Zone of zero because they cannot tolerate cold winter temperatures, and hardiness is not an issue.

Many plants that are grown as annuals in temperate climates, such as sweet basil, snapdragon, coleus, and moonflower, are perennial in warm climates; such plants are sometimes called horticultural annuals, meaning that they can be grown as annuals in regions where they will not survive as perennials. They may also be referred to as tender perennials.

Four o'clocks (*Mirabilis jalapa*) produce rootstocks that will overwinter in milder areas if given protection, such as a deep mulch.

Snapdragons (*Antirrhinum* species and cultivars) often overwinter and produce many flowers their second year.

Although many are perennials or even shrubs in their native lands, *Impatiens* of many kinds are widely grown as tender annuals.

Plant adaptations

Why do some plants flourish in full sun while others languish unless they are provided shade? Why do some plants thrive in bogs and others in deserts? Although most garden plants have roughly the same structure – roots, stems, leaves, flowers – nuances in their morphology equip them for a wide variety of conditions. This is fortunate, because there are plants whose requirements and preferences match your conditions. Understanding the characteristics that make a plant suited to particular conditions will help you recognize those that are likely to do well in your garden environment.

Desert grasses
A great many grasses are adapted to growing in very dry and often hot areas and thrive in well-drained soils and even gravel.

SHADE

Plants that grow best in the shade tend to have large, flat leaves with a fairly thin outer layer of cells, called the epidermal layer. This allows maximum space and minimum resistance for absorbing light needed for photosynthesis and growth. In general, plants that grow in shady conditions tend to produce fewer flowers and seeds than those grown in sun – this limited reproductive activity conserves a great deal of energy that can be directed toward vegetative growth. Thus, the ornamental display of many shade gardens relies more heavily on foliage color and texture than on flowers.

Shady situation
Savvy gardeners prize shade for the opportunities it provides to create garden pictures using foliage color and texture as well as overall plant habit.

HEAT AND DROUGHT

Xeriphytic plants have developed several strategies for reducing water loss and dealing with high temperatures. Many have smaller leaves with a thick, waxy layer, called the cuticle, on the leaf surface that protects it from drying out as well as providing some protection against insects. Both the reduction in surface area and protective coating minimize moisture loss. Alpine plants that survive in areas where soil water is frozen for much of the year, and unavailable for absorption by plants, often exhibit similar traits.

Another adaptation that enables many plants to tolerate dry climates is pubescence – the presence of fine hairs – on leaves. These hairs help shade the leaf surface from the hot sun and trap moisture lost by the leaf through transpiration, thus maintaining a higher humidity level immediately around the leaf surface. The higher humidity reduces the transpiration pressure in the leaf, slowing the rate of moisture loss.

Leaf arrangement and color also affect the absorption of heat. Leaves that point upward, arranged vertically toward the sun – such as *Yucca* and *Phormium* – absorb less heat than those with leaves oriented at right angles to the stem. Light-colored plants (typical of many heat-tolerant plants, including several species of *Euphorbia, Sedum,* and *Verbascum*) absorb less heat than dark plants.

COLD AND WIND

Some plants that grow well in cold, windy sites have a prostrate growth habit, minimizing their exposure to drying winds. Trees and shrubs that survive in regions with cold winters are sensitive to environmental signals such as decreasing day length, initiating changes that prepare them for winter. As temperatures decrease, certain solutes – dissolved substances – accumulate in cells, reducing the likelihood of their freezing and rupturing. This is essentially making use of plant "antifreeze."

Resistant roses
Rosa rugosa var *alba* and its many relatives thrive in hot, dry, cold, and windy sites.

Site-specific challenges

Identifying the varied growing conditions of your site will help you select plants that will thrive with the least amount of assistance on your part. For example, an area of your yard that drains poorly and remains wet for long periods of the season is a likely site for a bog garden. The sunny strip alongside the street or driveway, subject to reflected heat and baking sun and far from the water faucet, lends itself to a xeriphytic planting of drought-tolerant plants. The shady north side of your house is a likely spot for shade-loving shrubs and groundcovers.

The conditions of some gardening sites are more challenging than others, and they may significantly restrict plant selection. If you live by the seashore, you should select plants that tolerate salt spray and wind. If your soil is rich in limestone, plants that thrive in alkaline soil are a logical choice. Trees that have proven to adapt to the stresses of air pollution and compacted soil are the best options for planting alongside busy streets and in high-traffic urban areas. The lists in the Plant Catalog offer you a guide to regionally adapted plants for a wide variety of specific conditions and uses.

Some areas may represent exceptions to the general conditions that are present in your yard and may offer possibilities for growing plants beyond those typically suited for your region or location (*see* Identify your microclimates, *p. 24*).

Four combinations
You can create spectacular gardens in almost any given condition: sunny and dry (upper left), sunny and wet (upper right), shady and dry (lower left), and shady and wet (lower right).
Only the most extreme conditions – such as the darkest, driest woodland or a sunny lake – will preclude you from achieving the garden you want.

Plants for local conditions

Plant breeders have developed varieties of plants with qualities that make them particularly well adapted to certain conditions, often extending the area in which that plant has traditionally been grown.

Many, if not most, of the cultivated plants that we grow have been selected because someone thought they were (for example) showier, bigger, smaller, healthier, or more fruitful than other plants like it. It may have been a planned cross that was part of a breeding program at a major seed company, or it may have been a serendipitous event – a gardener noticing a plant that was somehow different in some significant way than others. Sometimes seed of the selection observed and saved by a gardener is passed around to friends and handed down to children.

New varieties are continually being developed, grown, and compared at commercial seed companies and public institutions. Many regional plant breeding programs are associated with land grant colleges (*see* Appendix *p. 408*) or botanic gardens and arboreta (*see p. 410–411*).

Research has led to the breeding and selection of plants that better withstand environmental adversity. This means that certain varieties may extend the growing range or conditions where the plant can be successfully grown.

Discriminating variety selection can also reduce the impact of pests and diseases that frequently infest gardens in your locale. There may be varieties of the plants you want to grow that display an inherited resistance or tolerance to the problem. This preventive approach to pest and disease control is a simple way to reduce the need for applying pesticides. Local garden centers and Extension Services are often able to provide the names of disease- and pest-resistant varieties of fruits, vegetables, and ornamental plants for your area.

Mature size and growth habit

Trying to achieve a mature appearance in your new garden is tempting, but it can lead to problems. If you space your plants too closely together, the result is almost always unsatisfactory. Plants soon become crowded, they may become more susceptible to disease, and they compete for water and light. Flower and fruit production may be reduced. Often, their growth habit is altered – instead of full, wide-spreading branches, plants may appear sparse and gangly as they stretch in search of light.

When deciding which plants to include in your yard and where you want to place them, be sure you have room to accommodate the mature size of each selection, no matter what its eventual size will be. Repeated pruning of a shrub during the growing season will be made unnecessary if your initial selection is based on the desired mature size. Many nurseries supply the mature dimensions on the plant tag or label. Consult the Plant Catalog to avoid making a major mistake.

TIPS FOR TRANSITIONING TENDER TROPICALS

You can expand your Northwest plant palette by including tender tropical perennials in your garden or in containers on your patio. Tender tropical perennials are perennials that can be grown outdoors in temperate regions (as found in the Northwest) during the summer but must be protected in the winter. Many tender perennials can be grown in containers on patios or even sunk into the ground to add interest in your garden beds. Some of the easiest tender tropical perennials to grow in containers are the same plants sold as tropical houseplants. *Abutilon* (Flowering Maples), *Ficus*, and *Dracaena* are just some examples. In addition, there are even more exotic tropical perennials you can consider including Bananas (*Musa* and *Ensete*), *Citrus*, *Bougainvillea*, *Canna*, *Lantana*, Gingers of many kinds, *Heliconia*, *Hibiscus*, *Plumeria*, Palms, *Clerodendrum*, tropical *Jasminum* (jasmines), *Gardenia*, *Pelargonium* (especially the fragrant geraniums) and even the beloved Poinsettia (*Euphorbia pulcherrima*). The key is determining the best way to overwinter your

Cannas (*Canna* species and cultivars) produce lush, bold foliage and brilliantly colored flowers.

tender tropicals. Many tender tropicals never go dormant and will need to be kept in a greenhouse, sunroom, or large sunny window. Others, such as cannas whose rhizomes can be stored for the winter, or pelargoniums (geraniums) which can be overwintered bare-root, can be stored in a shaded, cool, frost-free location such as a garage or basement.

But be mindful of the transitions from outdoors to indoors and vice versa. Remember, plants grown indoors are not exposed to wind or direct sunlight, and glass reflects a great deal of UV radiation, so they will be less able to withstand the rigors of growing outdoors. Also, indoor greenhouse conditions can be warmer and much more humid than outdoor conditions. Keep in mind that plant leaves adapt to their environment relatively slowly, so accustom your plants outdoors in spring gradually, a few hours a day, slowly building up the time to prevent sunscald or drying out from wind and low humidity.

The transition to growing indoors after summering outside should include a thorough inspection and appropriate control for pests and diseases that may have infected the plants while they were outdoors. The pest problem will be more pronounced in enclosed areas. It will also be easier to treat and spray plants while they can still be brought outdoors. Furthermore, indoor winter conditions are less than ideal for many tropicals, lowering their resistance to pests and diseases.

Variations on the theme
Plants are very adaptable and respond to pruning and training to produce an amazing variety of shapes, including the espalier and standard shown here.

Training your plants from an early age to enhance their natural habit or to direct growth in a certain manner can be an effective way of managing plant size. Particularly in a small garden, carefully pruned specimen plants can serve as focal points and accents. Some plants can be trained to grow against a wall, a technique known as espalier; this requires a minimum of garden space and can be a very effective use of a blank wall.

Another choice you will be confronted with when selecting your plants is which size to purchase. Although a larger plant may give you a fuller look than a smaller version of the same plant, you will need to weigh the additional expense against the immediate effect. In a few seasons, small plants often catch up to plants that were larger at the time of purchase (*see* The benefits of time, *p. 28*).

If the growth habit of a plant is something worth featuring, be sure to provide adequate room. For example, a Harry Lauder's walking stick (*Corylus avellana* 'Contorta') is best placed in an open area where its unusual form can be appreciated. A low, spreading plant such as creeping juniper needs plenty of lateral room to develop; otherwise, it may overtake nearby plants or walkways.

If you do start with young plants, it is still possible to achieve a mature look while waiting for them to grow. Maintain temporary herbaceous plantings in the space between young woody plants. Annuals survive for only a single season, and as your trees and shrubs spread in the coming years, perennials can be dug and transplanted to other areas.

Tree forms

Trees may be the biggest of all the voices in your garden choir, but they do show a remarkable range of differences. Use these differences to create a varied backdrop for the rest of your garden plants and structures.

Multistemmed

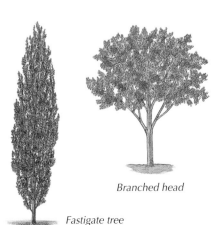

Fastigate tree

Branched head

Weeping standard

Growth habits

There are many shapes a plant can take, whether naturally or by manipulation though horticultural practices. It is often best to consider a plant's shape before thinking about its flowers – the shape will remain long after the flowers are gone.

Clump-forming

Cushion or mound-forming

Climbing and scandent

TAKE GOOD CARE OF THE EARTH

Every garden activity we undertake has a ripple effect on our plants, soil, water, and wildlife. We apply fertilizer to our lawns and, depending on the type and quantity, it can either bolster a healthy soil environment or leach through the soil and pollute local streams. By encouraging certain plants to grow and removing others, we influence whether and what wildlife inhabits our gardens. The material that we select to surface our paths and driveways also has an impact – positive or negative – on water runoff and soil erosion.

Choices and compromises

In our efforts to develop and maintain satisfying landscapes, we must try to achieve our goals without putting a strain on our environment. Simply by adjusting watering schedules, selecting the most effective mulch material, or timing the application of a pest control measure with precision, we can increase the efficiency of our gardening efforts and minimize the effect on the environment.

Some of the modifications we make in our gardens may require a balanced counteraction. For example, removing debris from a bed to keep it neat deprives soil of organic matter. Replacing the leaves with an organic mulch such as compost or shredded bark, however, supplies the organic matter while achieving the desired tidy appearance. Recognizing the impact of our activities, using resources efficiently and avoiding waste, must become second nature in the SMARTGARDEN™.

Whether planning a new bed, maintaining a lawn, or pruning a tree, gardening activities require choices. Consideration of environmental consequences should be an important part of the criteria you use for selecting one activity or technique over another.

Basic decisions such as whether an area should be maintained as lawn or developed into a bed, whether or not to encourage wildlife (and if so, which kind), and whether a tree that casts dense shade should be removed all need to be weighed against their impact on the overall landscape. Sometimes a compromise in expectations, material, technique, or timing can be effective in achieving the desired change without causing significant environmental consequences.

Another example of compromise is reducing the amount of nitrogen fertilizer applied to plants that are subject to water stress – vegetative growth may be reduced, but so will the water needs of the plant. You can reduce serious disease or pest problems by adjusting your planting schedule for several vegetable crops. Thinning the canopy of a tree that casts dense shade, rather than removing it entirely, can accomplish the desired outcome of increasing light penetration to your lawn without destroying a habitat and food source that supports a variety of wildlife.

Using every corner
Growing a wide range of plants makes efficient use of limited space and also attracts a diverse mix of wild creatures (many beneficial) into your garden.

Beneficial for all
Gardening in an age of shrinking habitats and resources should make every enlightened gardener consider both the plants and the wildlife that depend on them when making gardening decisions. The beauty many creatures bring is an added benefit.

white hairs that shade the leaf surface and prevent moisture loss. Many ornamental grasses and prairie natives have deep roots that range far to seek water. Some plants orient their leaves so that the minimum amount of sunlight falls on their surfaces, reducing leaf temperature. These and other characteristics of drought-tolerant plants minimize the need for supplemental watering (*see* Plant adaptations, *p. 36*).

You do not need to limit your plant selection to drought-tolerant species. Plants that require more frequent watering, however, should be grouped together, ideally close to a water source. By designing your garden according to the plants' water requirements, it is easier to develop efficient watering systems tailored to the needs of different sections of the garden.

REDUCING RUNOFF

A great deal of potentially beneficial garden moisture is lost to runoff. Careful grading of your beds can help direct the flow of water to where it will be most useful. Studies suggest that significantly more water penetrates into the soil through a diverse planting of groundcovers than through turf, and reducing your lawn area will also increase water absorption.

A rain barrel that collects water from the roof saves water that would otherwise be lost as runoff. Several manufacturers produce plastic rain barrels with hardware to connect the downspout with the barrel, and a faucet so you can access the water. Rain barrels can be attached to drip irrigation systems or simply

Someone's dinner table
Don't forget that, although lawns may be falling out of favor with some gardeners, they are still very popular with robins and other creatures that depend on them for food. Sensible watering practices help maintain a food source while not draining a valuable natural resource.

Conserving water

Given the droughts and higher average temperatures many parts of the country have been experiencing in recent years, not to mention the increase in population density, water consumption for gardening purposes is a growing concern. By combining strategies of conservation and efficiency, both water quantities consumed and the effort in delivering it can be reduced.

While all plants need water to thrive, some need less than others, and some plants are better equipped than others to obtain and retain water. For instance, succulent plants store water in their fleshy leaves or their stems and underground structures for use when needed. Leaves of lamb's-ears (*Stachys* spp.) and wormwood (*Artemisia* spp.) are covered with fine

Not thirsty
Drought-tolerant plants, such as junipers, lavender cotton, and sedums, grow well even when their natural water supply is short, and they adapt easily when irrigation water is scarce or when the gardener chooses not to provide supplemental water.

used to fill your watering can. An added benefit of collecting rainwater in areas with wells that supply hard water – water that contains a high level of soluble salts – is that since rainwater is soft, it will not cause mineral deposits that can clog up drip irrigation nozzles, and you can use the water on plants that need acidic soil conditions. Don't forget to cover barrels and other containers to control mosquitoes.

Solid-surface walkways and driveways prevent water from penetrating into the soil, and the water that runs off of these surfaces often leads to erosion or drainage problems. When installing a driveway or walkway, consider using a permeable surface through which rainwater can be absorbed. Driveways can be constructed of gravel, and beautiful walks and patios can be fashioned from unmortared stone set in sand.

Dry quarters
Even some tiny plants can get by without much water: saxifrages and *Aubrieta* are completely at home in a spot that provides little water; in fact, many grow best in such a setting.

NATURAL RECYCLING AND REDUCING RUNOFF

The Northwest region is rife with waterways and watersheds. Smaller tributaries lead to larger bodies of water, usually rivers, and eventually into lakes or reservoirs. These above-ground water systems are a major source of our water supply. Using this water wisely and keeping it as clean as possible is a major objective for those who need to use this water, and that means everyone.

Aquifers, underground deposits of fresh water, are connected to above-ground water systems. Personal well water, in addition to many local and regional water supplies, is drawn from these aquifers. Many aquifers are in danger today from excessive pumping of water from them and from slow but consistent contamination by chemicals and other byproducts of human activities.

Nitrogen, a principal nutrient required for plant growth and first number in the chemical analysis on fertilizer labels, is just one of many chemicals that affect the quality and health of our waterways and aquifers. While a great deal of the dissolved nitrogen occuring in our waterways comes from agricultural practices, a sizeable amount is derived from our personal gardening activities: the nitrogen we apply to our gardens and lawns may end up being carried away after a rainstorm, for example.

Nitrogen is a good indicator for the general health and impact of runoff and is measured constantly.

Gardeners can make a positive impact on our waterways and watersheds by following the gardening conservation practices outlined in this book, but we could make the opposite negative impact if we fail to be diligent in our efforts to make

sure our water remains clean. Remember, it is not just our water supply but also estuaries, lakes, and wildlife habitat that are affected. No matter where you live in the Northwest, your yard and gardens have only a few degrees of separation from some important source of water for humans or wildlife. Keep it clean.

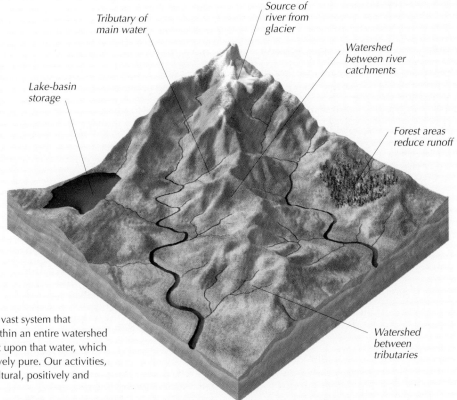

Tributary of main water

Source of river from glacier

Watershed between river catchments

Lake-basin storage

Forest areas reduce runoff

Watershed between tributaries

It's all connected
A river and its network of tributaries forms a vast system that collects and recycles the water that flows within an entire watershed area. Humans and all other life is dependent upon that water, which needs to be in constant supply and be relatively pure. Our activities, agricultural and industrial as well as horticultural, positively and negatively affect our water.

Supplementing nature

Water requirements are affected not only by the type of plant and the density of the planting, but also by a number of environmental variables such as temperature, wind, sunlight, and season. Soils also vary in their capacity to retain water. Thus there is no fixed rule for how often you will need to water: observing your plants and checking your soil offer the best clues.

Plants provide several clues when they are suffering from a lack of water. The observant gardener looks for these signs and waters thoroughly before the plant suffers long term or irreversable damage. The following are common symptoms or clues to water stress. The symptoms you first notice will vary somewhat from one kind of plant to another:

• dullness or a subtle change in foliage color
• reduced growth
• reduction in flowers or fruit
• wilting or curling of leaves
• a lawn turns dull, then bluish, and eventually straw-colored or brown

Where to water
Knowing where to water is as important as knowing when. Direct it to the base of the plant and to the soil, so that the water goes directly to the root zone. Unless they are quite dirty, don't bother to water the leaves and stems.

WHEN TO WATER

Although there are no fixed rules on when and how much to water, understanding the concept of evapotranspiration is crucial to knowing when to water your garden. Air and soil temperature, wind frequency, intensity and amount of sunlight, and season are all factors involved in evapotranspiration, the rate at which water is lost to the atmosphere by the earth (evaporation) and by the plants (transpiration). The majority of the Northwest states are on the low end of the evapo-transpiration rate, experiencing less than 15 inches (38cm) of water loss per year. The exceptions are North and South Dakota, Nebraska, and Kansas. These states see a loss 15 to 20 inches (38–51cm) of water per year.

When we water our garden plants and lawns, we are concerned with maintaining the level of the overall soil moisture, which is the difference between the evapo-transpiration rate and the rainfall, as well as the water-holding capacity of the soil.

Nevada, Western Utah, central east Washington (in the rainshadow of the Cascades), eastern Oregon (also in the rain-shadow of the Cascades), and the Big Horn and Rocky Mountain areas of Wyoming and Colorado all have low levels of soil moisture, so gardeners in those areas need to check soil-moisture levels frequently and provide water accordingly. The southern Puget Sound region of Washington, extending down into the Portland area of Oregon, as well as the eastern edges of North Dakota, South Dakota, Nebraska, and Kansas require less frequent levels of monitoring and irrigation.

All plants should be watered when they are first set out, and regular watering should continue until their roots are well established. It is important to water thoroughly (and at the base of the plants; you don't need to give plants a shower when you water them) to encourage deep root development. Plants with an extensive and deep root system can obtain more water from the soil and are less subject to injury from temperature fluctuations.

Early morning or evening (in other words, before or after the heat of the day), are the best times to water – less will be lost to evaporation. Avoid wetting plant foliage because wet leaves are more prone to disease.

HAND WATERING

Using a watering can or hose with a water breaker to deliver a drink to your gardens allows you to get "up close and personal" with your plants on a regular basis. You are likely to detect disease and insect problems soon after they appear. This system requires a great deal of time and may be impractical for large gardens. It is, however, perfectly suited for special, individual plants, small beds, and for those plants growing in containers.

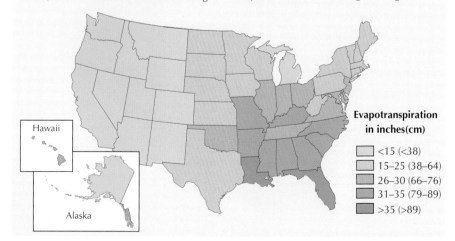

Hawaii

Alaska

Evapotranspiration in inches(cm)

	<15 (<38)
	15–25 (38–64)
	26–30 (66–76)
	31–35 (79–89)
	>35 (>89)

TRICKLE IRRIGATION

One of the most efficient watering systems is drip or trickle irrigation. It takes some effort to set up initially, but in the long run it saves time. Trickle systems can be designed to accommodate any garden size or style. Water is delivered directly to the root zone of desired plants or areas through emitters at the end of water tubes. Little water is lost to evaporation or wasted on areas between plants. The spacing of emitters and rate of flow can be adjusted as necessary. This system can also be used for container plants. If your water is hard, however, you may find that the narrow tubes become clogged with minerals. If a tube is clogged or becomes displaced, plants can suffer before the problem is noticed and rectified.

SOAKER HOSES

Also called a seep hose, a soaker hose allows water to drip out slowly into the soil along the length of the hose. Soakers are similar to drip systems but are easier to move from place to place. They are particularly useful in vegetable gardens, where they can be stretched along the rows, and in densely planted flower beds, where they can be wound through the entire planting area.

SPRINKLERS

For permanent plantings, an automated sprinkler system can be installed underground, preferably before the garden is planted. The hardware of these systems must be checked and maintained for efficiency, and plants near nozzles must be monitored; if they grow over the nozzles, they may block or divert the spray. These systems can be programmed to run on a timer.

Portable sprinkler systems are relatively inexpensive and versatile, but they rarely deliver a uniform spray. Hoses connect the water source with a variety of sprinkler attachments – fans, oscillators, and pulsating heads. A significant amount of water from sprinklers is lost to evaporation, and use of overhead sprinklers may lead to an increase in foliar disease problems.

Soaking a raised bed
Because soil dries out faster in a raised bed that in the open ground, growing vegetables or other plants this way often requires supplemental irrigation. A soaker hose provides water directly to the soil with very little loss by evaporation.

Wasting water
Sprinkler systems are a valuable method of applying water to lawns and gardens, but be sure to maintain the piping and hardware for maximum efficiency, and do your best to avoid waste by making sure the system is on only when water is needed

Mulching for moisture

Mulching around plants conserves moisture in a number of ways. By physically covering the soil, less moisture is lost to surface evaporation, and the temperature in the root zone in mulched soil is less than for bare soil, especially in hot sun. Mulches inhibit the growth of weeds that compete with your plants for water, and mulches help prevent soil crusting, the dry surface layer that impedes water penetration into the soil, leading to runoff and erosion.

Summer mulches are particularly important for soil moisture retention as well as weed control. But wait until the soil has had a chance to warm up in the spring before applying it, or new growth may be delayed. The best time to mulch depends on the plants you grow. In the vegetable garden, cool-season vegetables such as peas and spinach can be mulched much earlier than heat-loving tomatoes and melons. Give perennials enough time to emerge from the soil before mulching your flower beds.

In a climate with cold winters and warm summers, mulching to provide winter protection is most effective when applied after the ground has become cold and plants have entered dormancy. Mulching too early can delay normal maturation of growth for winter. Many perennials will benefit from a winter mulch after their tops have died back. This helps moderate winter moisture and temperature levels in the soil, which are especially critical with new plants and those with limited root systems.

There are some disadvantages to mulching, but paying attention to when and how much mulch you apply can minimize these. For example, some animals such as mice and rabbits may find an organic mulch to be a suitable spot to build their nests. These garden inhabitants can cause damage to shrubs and young trees in winter if they gnaw at the base of trunks or stems. Do not allow mulch to build up around the base of plants. This problem can be further minimized by waiting until after you have experienced several hard frosts before you apply the winter mulch. Mice and rabbits will likely have already found another location for their winter home by then. In spring, mulch needs to be pulled back from perennials to allow new growth to emerge and to prevent a buildup of excessive moisture around stems, which can lead to disease.

The mulch advantage

Mulching with the right material, applied at a proper depth and at the appropriate time, provides numerous advantages to garden plants in addition

Mulchberries
They're called strawberries for a good reason: gardeners long ago realized the value of mulching these plants, so much so that straw became part of their standard culture and of *Fragaria*'s common name.

Recycling into mulch
All of the mulching materials above (from the top, they are bark, compost, and leaves) could come from the garden to which they are returned. Recycling all heathy plant debris makes good sense.

to retaining moisture and suppressing weeds. Mulch protects plant roots from extremes of heat and cold and creates a physical barrier between foliage and soil-splashing rain, which helps prevent the spread of disease. In vegetable gardens, mulch keeps the fruit – such as tomatoes, squash, cucumbers, and melons – clean, preventing their direct contact with the soil, where fruit-rotting organisms often lurk. Also, mulching may reduce the need for fungicides.

Mulching does not in itself warm or cool a soil; rather, it moderates the temperature changes that would result from sun or wind on the soil. This influence is accomplished by shading the soil from the hot sun during the day and by the retention of moisture. Since water changes temperature more slowly than air, the more moisture contained in soil, the slower the rate of temperature change around a plant's roots. Often winter damage occurs to the roots of plants, not because of the low temperature to which they are subjected, but because of rapid changes in temperature of a dry soil. These rapid

changes can cause perennials to heave out of the soil, exposing their roots to cold, dry air, killing the plant. Mulching helps minimize such losses.

HOW MUCH MULCH?

How much mulch should you apply? Too much can impair plant growth by suffocating roots and preventing moisture from reaching the soil. Too thin a layer will not sufficiently suppress weed growth or retain moisture. A two- to three-inch (5–8cm) layer of organic mulch is usually appropriate. Replace the mulch as it breaks down instead of mulching too thickly at the beginning of the season. Always keep mulch away from the crown or stems to avoid the buildup of excessive moisture, which increases the likelihood of disease. In vegetable gardens and annual beds, organic mulch can be incorporated into the soil at the end of the season to improve soil structure and fertility. Around permanent plantings, mulch breaks down gradually, releasing nutrients that are carried to the roots by rain. In both cases, using an organic mulch promotes a healthy soil environment.

MULCHING MATERIALS

The mulch you select depends on availability, personal taste, and the type of garden. Both organic and inorganic mulches are available, and every one is suited to different types of garden applications.

Straw works well in the vegetable garden, but can look messy and contribute unwanted weed seeds to a perennial border. More attractive organic mulches, such as shredded bark, pine straw, or cocoa hulls, are a better choice for flower beds, trees, and shrubs.

Mulching defense
For woody plants, apply a mulch to cover the entire root zone. Leave a 4-6in (10-15cm) gap around the stem base; mounding mulch onto woody stems may cause rot.

The color of the mulching material will affect its absorption or reflection of solar heat. Dark-colored mulches absorb more heat, warm the soil earlier in the spring, and maintain the heat later into autumn. Light-colored mulches absorb less heat, but they reflect heat and light upward toward the plants, promoting faster growth and fruit maturation.

Plants themselves can serve as a mulch as they spread to cover the soil surface, crowding out weeds and shading the soil from the heat of the sun. Clematis benefit from such a mulch; many of them require a cool, shaded location for the roots along with plenty of sun for the above-ground portions of the plant. These requirements are met when the clematis is planted at the base of a shrub – the shrub provides a living mulch for the roots as well as support for the clematis vine to grow upon.

Of course, plants require water, so although a mulch of living plants is an effective method of weed control and soil temperature moderation, it may actually increase the water requirement for the area.

In a woodland garden, trees and shrubs annually provide their own mulch of leaves and needles. Be sure that leaves and needles are raked off of desired groundcovers and herbaceous perennials growing beneath trees.

Mutual benefit
Plants can be their own mulch or provide one for others: here, a clematis and *Tropaeolum polyphyllum* cover the soil for each other and produce a very attractive combination in the process.

Weed barrier fabrics (landscape fabric, or geotextiles, material made out of polypropylene fibers) allow water and air to penetrate but prevent weed growth. They can enhance the efficiency of an organic mulch, and are usually placed directly on the soil surface, with slits cut through them for planting. Mulch, such as shredded bark or cocoa shells, is usually applied on top to hold the fabric in place and provide a more attractive appearance.

Inorganic mulches include plastic, pebbles, and marble and stone chips. Black plastic is often used to mulch tomatoes, melons, cucumbers, and other hot-season vegetables, which benefit from the heat captured by the plastic and transferred to the soil, in addition to its virtual total suppression of weeds. Rock gardens and beds of cacti and succulents generally require drier conditions, and they may resent the moisture retained under a layer of shredded bark. Mulching with gravel or stones is probably the best solution for such gardens.

Don't wait
Try not to let weeds progress this far before tackling them. Many methods are available for controlling weeds, including hand-weeding, but using most methods will not make you feel like you're reenacting one of the labors of Hercules.

Managing without chemicals

Keeping your garden neat and preventing weeds from taking over doesn't require chemical warfare. Weeds can be pulled, cut, burned (where legal), smothered, and suppressed – the most effective method of control depends upon the types of weeds you are dealing with and the specific garden situation.

In a new garden, weeding can require a good bit of effort. As garden plants become established and spread to cover the open ground, your weeding efforts will lessen, particularly if you practice some routine weed-management tasks. Eliminate your weeds before they become established and reseed themselves. It is more productive to spend a little time weeding on a routine basis than to let the weeds get an upper hand, eventually requiring a major cleanup effort. Mulching after you weed will prevent many weeds from returning (*see* The mulch advantage, *p. 46*).

Solarization provides excellent initial weed control for a new planting. The area to be solarized should be mowed very low and watered well. Cover it with black plastic, secured at the edges, and leave it for at least six weeks – longer if possible. The temperature in the top several inches of soil rises significantly, baking the surface vegetation as well as most weed seeds, roots, and soil pathogens.

To suppress the germination of weed seeds, corn gluten can be applied to a soil surface. This material, which is a natural byproduct of milling corn, is a good source of nitrogen, and it inhibits seed germination. Applied to established lawns, it prevents the germination of crabgrass and other annual weeds. It can be applied in a vegetable garden after vegetable plants have emerged. It is also useful in establishing a groundcover bed: groundcover plants are set, corn gluten is applied and watered in, the bed is mulched, and weeds are suppressed.

Edging a bed with a solid barrier – brick, stone, or wood, for example – helps prevent creeping weeds from gaining entry.

A flame thrower is an effective tool for weeding nonflammable surfaces such as gravel paths, paved patios, and driveways, as well as for spot treating persistent weeds. Never use a flame thrower close to desirable plants that may be scorched, or near a flammable mulch or other flammable surface.

Both useful and beautiful

A simple edging of wood or stone or similar material keeps creeping weeds such as Canada thistle and quackgrass at bay and will provide a very attractive addition to an otherwise very utilitarian part of your garden.

Encouraging desirable wildlife

Every year, more and more land is being cleared for homes and businesses, and wildlife habitats are being reduced or destroyed. Your SMARTGARDEN™ can be a haven for wildlife with a little planning. The three basic needs of wildlife – food, water, and shelter – can easily be met in a garden if you consider the type of wildlife you want to encourage and provide for them by including plants that produce nectar, flowers, seeds, and fruit, a source of water, and suitable habitats for nesting.

Adding feeders to your garden to supplement the plants will carry the banquet through the garden's lean times. Birdbaths or a small pond can provide sufficient water for your visitors, but remember to change the water frequently so that it stays clean. If possible, leave some areas of the yard undisturbed for shelter. Dead trees and hollow logs provide homes for many wild creatures, as do unraked leaves (also see the Plant Catalog for plants to attract wildlife).

Maintaining a wildlife-friendly garden contributes to a well-balanced environment. Birds and bats feed on insects; butterflies, bees, and many other insects (and some bats) pollinate flowers; moles feed on grubs of root-eating beetles. Avoid using pesticides that will harm pollinating insects or birds, and be sure to read all pesticide labels carefully for warnings about potential dangers to wildlife.

Of course, not all forms of wildlife contribute to the health of your plants. Some wildlife may not be as welcome to your garden as others. There are some animals you would rather discourage from grazing in your azaleas, nibbling away at your bulbs, or feasting

Useful "Plain Jane"
Even something as common and familiar as Queen Anne's lace (*Daucus carota*, from which carrots were bred) will attract butterflies and other beautiful and beneficial organisms.

on your sweet corn. As with insect pests, take the approach of determining just how much damage the particular critter is likely to inflict on your plantings, and if the level is unsatisfactory, take precautions to prevent the destruction.

There are a number of techniques available to discourage deer, raccoons, voles, squirrels, and other potentially destructive forms of wildlife from damaging your plantings. Selecting plants that are unappetizing to the specific animal is a start – almost nothing eats daffodils! But that approach may be too limiting for your gardening aspirations. Other methods for discouraging foragers include constructing sturdy and deep fences or barriers, using repellents, strategically placing a scarecrow or an owl or snake lookalike, and keeping a big dog.

Water magnet
Water attracts birds and others animals to your garden just as much as flowers and bird seed. They need to drink and bathe just like gardeners do, and some creatures, such as frogs and dragonfly larvae, will take up residence in a suitable water feature.

NORTHWESTERN WILDLIFE

Ladybird beetle
This ladybug is looking for aphids and other pests to eat, as will its offspring.

The Northwest boasts a plethora of wildlife communities, from the tundra to sagebrush deserts. We as gardeners share our yards with these wildlife communities. Here is an overview of some of the different forms of wildlife you may encounter in your Northwest garden. As more and more land is taken over for human habitation, the areas left for wildlife shrink. More and more wild species are becoming accustomed to existing close to man and, by creating a wildlife-friendly garden, you can do much to encourage and protect them. Many birds, butterflies and small mammals can survive alongside man, and by adding a pool you can attract frogs and dragonflies. Depending on the size of your property and the diversity of planting, you can provide suitable habitats for a wide range of birds, animals and insects. Many of these will be beneficial and will aid you in keeping pests under control. Snakes, spiders, and toads may not be your favorite garden guests but they play an important role in reducing plant problems. The following list contains some of the more common wildlife you may find in your garden.

Bullock's Oriole
Admittedly beautiful, many birds are also our greatest natural allies against pests.

Over-wintering birds feed on weed seeds and the egg masses of garden pests if you encourage them to stay by putting out feeders. Those commonly found include: • Mallard • American Kestrel • Northern Flicker • Downy Woodpecker • American Crow • Common Raven • Barn Swallow • Black-capped Chickadee • Red-breasted Nuthatch • Dark-eyed Junco • Oregon Junco. Spring brings an influx of birds either passing through or that will stay all summer. They all help by feeding on seeds and emerging insect pests. Some that you are likely to see are: • Killdeer* • Common Nighthawk • Rufous Hummingbird (west of the mountain ranges) • American Robin • Hermit Thrush • Cedar Waxwing* • Warbling Vireo* • Yellow Warbler • Bullock's Oriole* • Evening Grosbeak* • Black Headed Grosbeak* • Purple Finch* • House Finch • American Goldfinch* • SpottedTowhee* • Sparrows

Mammals
Many small mammals will make their home in your garden and feed on seeds and insects, sometimes causing damage in the process. Some larger ones, like skunks and raccoons will also find their way in, but others, like groundhogs and deer are best excluded if possible. You may catch glimpses of some of these, others are more obvious:
Bats • Raccoon • Muskrat • Beaver • Deer Mouse • Northern Flying Squirrel • Squirrels • Dusky Shrew • Red Fox • Skunks • Deer • Least Chipmunk • Red-backed Vole • Meadow Vole • White Tailed Jackrabbit • Nuttall's Cottontail.

Red Admiral
Butterflies can eat garden plants as larvae, but few cause major damage.

Reptiles and amphibians
These are the gardener's friends, eating many of the pests that attack plants. The following species should be encouraged:
Common Garter Snake (found in all but the hotter southern regions) • Rubber Boa (western half of Northwest) • Painted Turtle (all but Southwest states) • Short Horned Lizard • Sagebrush Lizard • Pacific Treefrog (Pacific Northwest only) • Tiger Salamander (all but westernmost states) • Plains Spadefoot (Plains states) • Western Toad (west of the mountains) • American Toad (easternmost states) • Northern Leopard Frog

(*species not found in Alaska).

Flying Squirrel
They plant trees, just like their cousins do.

Butterflies and moths
These insects add movement and color to a summer garden. Encourage them by growing plants rich in nectar and by providing a patch of wet mud or very shallow pool area. Some of the more common and striking are: • Monarch and Queen

Garden Spider
They're not creepy or scary: spiders are another vital part of natural systems at work in your garden.

Butterflies* • Crescent Butterflies • Great Spangled Fritillary • Tortoiseshells • Mourning Cloak • Lady and Red Admiral Butterflies • Gray Hairstreak* • Black Swallowtail* • Hawk Moths* • Tiger Moth*. Other insects and invertebrates include: • Honeybees • Orchard Mason Bees • Yellow Mud Dauber* • Dragonflies • Black and Yellow Garden Spider* • Giant Water Bug • Millipedes • Fungus-feeding nematode roundworms.

Red Fox
Mammals also benefit from the conditions provided by gardens.

WORK WITH NATURE

Every aspect of gardening, from selecting your site and your plants to accommodating their spread and cleaning up debris, will be easier and more successful if you work with nature to achieve your goals. Although a garden alters a landscape to some extent, it should exist in harmony with its environment. The key is to follow nature's leads and to harness its forces to work on your behalf.

Learning from natural habitats

Plants with similar growth requirements should be grouped together in your garden, growing as they would in their natural habitat. Shrubs and perennials that thrive in low light can be planted beneath trees that furnish the necessary shade; those that require constant moisture can be grouped in a bog garden or at the edge of a pond; and those that thrive in full sun and dry soil can be combined in a sunny rock garden or xeriphytic planting.

In addition to grouping plants that share similar natural habitats, keep in mind any additional cultural requirements or special care that the plants might need when you are planning your garden. For example, vegetables and annual flowers generally require more fertilization and water than established perennials and woody plants. If the vegetable or annual flower beds are positioned within easy reach of a water faucet or rain barrel, their additional needs can be easily accommodated. Natural cycles of growth, reproduction, and decomposition can be put to work to your garden's advantage, and many problems can be avoided if you mimic natural patterns and solutions for reducing plant stress.

Just as the environment affects the growth of plants in your garden, everything you do in your garden has an impact on the environment. As environmentally responsible gardeners and stewards of the Earth, working in cooperation with nature rather than attempting to control it just makes good sense.

Natives and non-natives

One way to increase the odds that your plants are well adapted to your conditions is to select plants native to your region. By incorporating indigenous species, your garden not only reflects its geography, but it will also help sustain native wildlife.

Be sure that the natural habitats of your plant choices are reflected in the conditions within your yard. If your yard is open and sunny, it may be ideal for meadow wildflowers or rock garden plants. If it is heavily shaded, woodland natives are more appropriate. Regional wildflower and native plant societies can assist you with identifying native species and finding responsible retail sources.

Never collect plants from the wild without permission. Rare plants – those that may be difficult to obtain, but are not necessarily endangered – are put at risk when collectors dig them and remove them from their natural habitat. Many plants can be obtained without exploiting natural populations. Many nurseries, native plant societies, and private growers propagate their own rare plants and offer plants or seed for sale or exchange. Also, permission is sometimes given to individual plant collectors or native plant societies to dig and remove native plants from construction sites before the area is graded or built upon. In this way, many stands of both rare and common natives have been saved from the bulldozer.

Seize the shade
Although it may be considered a drawback by some, a shady spot – or entire property – presents a vast number of exciting opportunities for creating beautiful garden compositions and restful havens.

Worth copying
Many natural habitats are worth recreating in your garden, and some of the most popular are the wetlands: lakes, ponds, streams, bogs, wet prairies, and marshes. As with all habitats, it is important to know what constitutes a wetland and how it can be best and most easily maintained.

REGIONAL HABITATS WORTH RECREATING

High-alpine tundra vegetation paints a colorful picture in Alaska's Denali National Park.

The Northwest embraces a wide variety of wildlife communities, from tundra and riparine (river) habitats to sagebrush deserts and coastal rainforests. At one time all the various ecosystems spread across the country. Now in many areas, our cities and roads, as well as our homes and gardens, are dividing these communities into progressively smaller areas with less diversity. With a little thought and effort we can approximate the qualities of some of these communities. Although a home garden will never have the scale necessary to realize a larger ecosystem, components can be borrowed to make an ecosystem vignette. Here are some Northwest communities you can emulate at home, with commercially available native plants from those communities.

Alpine and Mountain Meadow

These mountain habitats have very short seasons, and the flowering plants are usually low growing and very hardy, usually covered and protected by a blanket of winter snow. Gardeners may consider these "rock garden" plants.

• American Globeflower (*Trollius laxus*) • Columbines (*Aquilegia caerulea, A. flavescens*) • Western Anemone (*Anemone occidentalis*) • Bitterroot (*Lewisia rediviva*) • Mountain Phlox (*Phlox diffusa*) • Elephant Heads (*Pedicularis groenlandica*) • Quamash (*Camassia quamash*) • Western Azalea (*Rhododendron occidentale*) • Rosy Indian-paintbrush (*Castilleja rhexiifolia*) • Red penstemon (*Penstemon barbatus*).

Examples: Denali National Park, AK; Rocky Mountain National Park, CO; Glacier National Park, MT; High Uintas

Wilderness Area, UT; Mount Rainier National Park, WA; and Grand Teton National Park, WY.

Great Plains Grassland

This habitat covers a large area across the Northwest region. The areas closest to mountains (such as the Rocky Mountains) get the least amount (sometimes as little as 10in/30cm) of rainfall due to the mountain's rain shadow. Other areas get more rain (20in/50cm), but there are no large trees. In their place is a variety of grasses and forbs (herbaceous plants that are not grasses). Suggested plants include:

Fringed Sage (*Artemisia frigida*) • Buffalo Grass (*Buchloe dactyloides*) • Blue Grama Grass (*Bouteloua gracilis*) • Great Plains Yucca (*Yucca glauca*) • Prairie larkspur (*Delphinium carolinianum*) • Purple Poppy Mallow (*Callirhoe involucrata*) • Scarlet Globe Mallow (*Sphaeralcea coccinea*) • Fragrant Leadplant (*Amorpha nana*) • Wyoming Indian-paintbrush (*Castilleja linariifolia*) • Pink Plains Beardtongue (*Penstemon ambiguus*) • Plains Tickseed (*Coreopsis tinctoria*) • Sego Lily (*Calochortus nuttallii*) • Four winged Saltbush (*Atriplex canescens*) • Rocky Mountain Juniper (*Juniperus scopulorum*).

Examples: Comanche National Grasslands, CO; Cimmaron National Grassland, KS; Benton Lake National Wildlife Refuge, MT; and Oglala National Grassland, NE.

The Humboldt National Forest in Nevada includes several communities, among them grassland as well as forested areas.

Pacific Coast / Lowland Douglas Fir Forests

Forests of the Pacific Coast as well as interior lowland forests all share Douglas Fir as an integral species. Near the Pacific coast it is a pioneer tree that grows very large, some approaching 300ft (100m). Farther east toward the Rockies they can be climax trees at higher elevations that only reach 100ft (30m). These rich woodland areas are quite multilayered, having low-growing perennials and small and large shrubs, as well as towering trees. Gardeners using these sample plants may start a woodland garden and may already have many of the larger trees on their property. Suggested plants include:

Douglas Fir (*Pseudotsuga menziesii*) • Grand Fir (*Abies grandis*) • Western Hemlock (*Tsuga heterophylla*) • Western Redcedar (*Thuja plicata*) •

Forests, such as this one in Olympic National Park in Washington, can be recreated in spirit and on a smaller scale in some home gardens.

Western White Pine (*Pinus monticola*) • Creambush Oceanspray (*Holodiscus discolor*) • Vine Maple (*Acer circinatum*) • Bigleaf Maple (*Acer macrophyllum*) • Pacific Rhododendron (*Rhododendron macrophyllum*) • Salal (*Gaultheria shallon*) • Sitka Spruce (*Picea sitchensis*) • Redwood (*Sequoia sempervirens*) • Vanilla leaf (*Achlys triphylla*) • Redwood Sorrel (*Oxalis oregona*) • Western Sword Fern (*Polystichum munitum*) • Deer Fern (*Blechnum spicant*).

Examples: Boise National Forest, ID; Beaverhead National Forest, MT; Umpqua National Forest, OR; and Olympic National Forest, WA.

Endangered and threatened plant species are those that the federal government has recognized as being in danger of extinction and are protected by law. The most common cause for this status is reduction or loss of the natural habitat of the species, but commercial collection of rare plants has also threatened their survival. Responsible propagation by native plant growers of species that are rare or at risk has increased considerably in recent years; this helps increase the population and the availability of these vanishing plants to consumers. You should always investigate commercial sources of rare plants to be sure they were nursery propagated and were not collected from the wild.

The term "native plant" is the source of some confusion. Plants have been introduced from one area to another throughout the history of mankind, and some plants have adapted so well to their new environments over such a long period of time that it is often hard to distinguish the natives from the introduced species.

Coastal native
Iris innominata and other Pacific Coast irises thrive in milder parts of the Northwest.

Spring surprise
Prized mostly for its large, umbrella-like leaves, *Darmera peltata* also sends up cheerful flowerheads that gradually appear as the foliage expands.

Some plant traffic between geographic areas predates human history, seeds having been conveyed by glacial movements, floods, prehistoric animals, or other means. The field of botanical archaeology has made interesting discoveries about prehistoric plant movement that continues to shed more light on the natural distribution of plants.

For the purpose of this book, however, a native species is one that, as far as can be determined historically, is indigenous – native – to the *state or region*. (More broadly, the issue is defining what is meant by the "region": is it a given continent, country, or state, or is it the area within 25 miles/ 40km of your property?) An exotic species is one that has been introduced from outside the region. An invasive exotic is one that has adapted so well to its new environment that it has escaped cultivation and is capable of overtaking the habitats of native plants.

The nativity of species within a genus is often widespread. For example, the genus *Quercus* – the oaks – includes species that are indigenous to regions within North America as well as Europe, the Middle East, Asia, and Northern Africa. Species of *Iris* hail from countries as widespread as China, Japan, Ukraine, Afghanistan, Turkey, Algeria, and the United States – from Alaska to the Mississippi Valley. Obviously, even though they are closely related, plants with such diverse native habitats have an equally wide range of cultural requirements. Thus, although you can probably grow more than one species of oak or iris in your garden, others of the same genus will need a different habitat.

Non-native plants from regions with similar climates and soils can add diversity to your landscape. To get ideas for plants that will grow well in your garden, observe plants that thrive in other nearby gardens, and ask your neighbors and staff at local public gardens as well. But take care to avoid those that are too well adapted. When these plants encroach upon your garden, diligent efforts are often necessary to limit their spread or eliminate them from your yard.

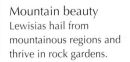

Mountain beauty
Lewisias hail from mountainous regions and thrive in rock gardens.

INVASIVE AND NOXIOUS WEEDS

A weed is any plant that is growing in a place where it is not desired. Invasive weeds are those that have risen above this definition to become more serious problems. Federal and/or state law designates plants as noxious if they are "overly aggressive, difficult to manage, parasitic, poisonous, or carriers or hosts of serious insects or diseases."

There are three basic ways that weeds can be controlled, involving physical, chemical, and biological techniques.

Physical techniques include cultivating, tilling, mulching, solarizing (heating soil using clear plastic), and burning (using a weed torch).

Chemical techniques include the use of selective and nonselective herbicides that can either be manmade (so-called "chemical" pesticides) or are derived from natural sources (such as concentrated vinegar, fatty acids, and citrus oils).

Biological techniques include the strategic use of cover or smother crops (which requires at least one season to work), as well as the use of insect pests that are host-weed specific. The Western Society for Weed Science published *Biological Control of Weeds in the West*, which contains information on approved biological controls for specific weeds as well as their availability. The book is available from the Western Society of Weed Science at P.O. Box 10342, Helena, MT 59604 or http://www.wsweedscience.org.

Plants that are recognized as serious pests have been put on federal and state lists of noxious weeds (see the box above). Legislation and regulation efforts to eradicate and control the spread of these pests is ongoing at federal, state, and local levels.

Multiplication and division

Many garden plants reseed themselves. This natural process can work to your benefit – providing new plants for next year's garden – or it can create unnecessary weeding. Before selecting a plant and placing it in a bed, determine whether and how prolifically it self-sows.

Many biennials – plants that complete their life cycle over the course of two growing seasons – can become permanent features in your garden through the process of self-sowing. The flowers of woodland forget-me-not (*Myosotis sylvatica*), honesty (*Lunaria annua*), and several foxgloves (*Digitalis* spp.) produce seeds that germinate and grow vegetatively the first season and develop flowers the next. With such plants, it is important to recognize the nonflowering plant so that it can be left to grow – and not inadvertently weeded – to bloom the following year.

Many annuals and perennials also self-sow. Some are such prolific seed producers that weeding the seedlings becomes a chore. If this is the case, deadheading the spent blooms before they have a chance to disperse their seed will reduce or eliminate the problem.

Many of the garden flowers that are sold in nurseries or by seed companies are hybrids – varieties produced by controlled crosses of specific parent lines – so their seedlings often do not resemble the parent plant in some important aspects. Be aware that your seedlings may be shorter, taller, less disease resistant, or a different color than their parent. Open-pollinated varieties, on the other hand, generally produce seed that is "true to type." Seed of such flowers or vegetables can be collected from these plants for growing the following year with some confidence about their inherited characteristics.

Herbaceous perennials that thrive in your garden may require dividing every few years. Take advantage of this natural increase to acquire more plants. For most perennials that bloom in spring, summer or fall division is recommended. Summer or fall bloomers are usually divided in spring.

Although the procedure varies somewhat with specific plants, division generally involves digging the entire clump, cutting it into smaller sections, discarding old, worn-out portions, replanting the vigorous divisions, and watering them thoroughly.

Composting wastes

One way you can work with nature to improve your soil is to build a compost pile. Here, kitchen and garden wastes are converted into a nutrient-rich soil amendment. It takes several weeks to months for raw organic matter to become thoroughly decomposed and garden-ready in an active compost pile. There are a variety of factors that influence the rate of decomposition; the most important are the size of

Composting bin
A simple cage constructed from lumber and chicken wire holds garden refuse and other materials as it breaks down into compost.

the organic matter, moisture and temperature, air circulation, and the carbon/nitrogen ratio. Organic matter that has been shredded decomposes faster than if it has been left whole, because there is more surface area exposed. Decomposition rates are higher when conditions are warm and damp than when they are cold and dry. Air circulation increases the rate of composting because the organisms responsible for decomposition need sufficient air to do their job.

However, other than occasional turning, and a bit of added moisture when it's very dry, nature – in the form of industrious micro- and macroorganisms – does most of the work for you.

COMPOST BINS AND TOOLS

A number of useful products are available to help you produce your own compost. Compost bins can be constructed out of wood, heavy-gauge wire fencing, cinder blocks, or other common materials. They can also be purchased ready-made. Designs range from simple bins to more elaborate constructions that feature cone-shaped tubs, interlocking layered shelves, and twist-top ventilation systems. Some designs feature tumblers or drums that rotate to facilitate mixing. Mixing or stirring an open compost pile can be done with a garden fork or a compost aerator, a tool specifically designed for the purpose, composed of a shaft with handles or a bar at one end for holding, and short paddles on the other end that are inserted into the pile, then turned and lifted.

Vermicomposting is a system using redworms, night crawlers, or earthworms in an enclosed container to break down organic matter such as grass clippings and kitchen wastes. The worm castings that are shed are a rich source of nutrients as well as a good source of organic material.

In an undisturbed woodland environment, the seasonal accumulation of leaves on the forest floor is part of a natural recycling process. As the leaves are decomposed by the soil organisms that digest it, a steady supply of nutrients is released for use by woodland plants. In an effort to keep a garden neat, this cycle is often interrupted; leaves are raked and removed to a sanitary landfill (or worse, burned). The nutrients can be restored, however, and the neatness maintained, if the raked leaves are composted and the finished compost returned to the garden. Once the compost is ready, it can be incorporated into the soil or applied as a topdressing or mulch. It is also a useful addition to a soil mixture for raised beds and containers. In an active compost pile, most weed seeds are killed by the heat that is generated during the decomposition process, but a few may survive. These are easily removed soon after they germinate in your garden.

By composting your kitchen and garden wastes, you are working with nature to improve the growing conditions for your plants while simultaneously reducing your contribution of solid waste to your local landfill.

Prettier and stronger
A more sturdily constructed compost bin (it's easy to build) is more attractive and holds up longer than a simple cage (left).

The view inside
Removing the front panel of the bin reveals the correct method of layering different materials in a compost pile.

General household waste
Plant remains are OK, but avoid including meat scraps and bones, which attract vermin.

Old straw
Make sure your compost pile heats up to destroy seeds contained in straw.

Weeds
As with straw above, a properly constructed and managed hot pile kills most weed seeds.

Hedge clippings
The smaller, thinner, and softer the clippings, the faster they will break down.

Bring it on
Good compost is best made from a wide variety of materials. Included on this page are just a few possibilities, including the spent bedding plants above.

Aiding natural selection

Cleaning up a garden at the end of a growing season will improve its appearance through winter and, more importantly, contribute to its health the next season. This often involves a bit of "editing" – removing plants, plant parts, or pests.

• Branches of trees and shrubs that are damaged beyond repair should be removed with clean cuts. Stems displaying disease symptoms such as cankers or sunken lesions are usually best removed to prevent the further spread of disease.

• Minimize next year's insect pests by removing and disposing obvious signs of infestation such as the "bags" of bagworms and the nests of fall webworms.

• Remove weeds before they go to seed.

• Rake leaves to avoid matting that may suffocate lawn or groundcovers; compost both weeds and leaves (but remember: no pest- or disease-infested material onto the pile; this material is best discarded along with your household trash)

• After they have died naturally or succumbed to frost, cut annuals at ground level, leaving the roots to break down in the soil; this is a particularly good practice where erosion is a problem. Or remove the plants, roots and all, then compost everything.

• Clean structures and stakes you plan to reuse. Those that cannot withstand winter weather should be removed, cleaned, and stored until conditions are suitable again in spring.

• Perennial plants that die back in autumn can be cut to the ground unless they contribute to your winter landscape or provide food or cover for desirable wildlife.

Eliminating flowered stalks
Removing flowered stalks of herbaceous plants not only improves their appearance but may also stimulate further flowering. A small scattering of fertilizer at this time will also help.

Reducing stress

Just like humans, garden plants look and perform better if their level of stress is reduced.

Transplanting can be traumatic for plants and may lead to a condition commonly known as "transplant shock." To avoid this, allow seedlings grown indoors or in a greenhouse the opportunity to acclimate to their new environment gradually (called "hardening off"). Place them in a protected spot outdoors for a few days before transplanting them. Stress will be further minimized if you transplant on a still, overcast day. It also helps to drench soil balls with a high-phosphorus liquid fertilizer to stimulate root growth.

During dry weather, wind can cause serious damage by increasing a plant's transpiration (moisture loss) rate. When moisture lost through leaves exceeds the rate at which it is replaced by roots, leaves appear scorched or may drop off. This can happen during cold weather as well, when soil water is frozen and little is available to plants. Siting a garden where plants are sheltered from prevailing winds can prevent such damage, or wind-tolerant plants can be grown as wind breaks to protect nearby plants.

Underground chills and summer sweats are another source of plant stress. Rapid fluctuations in soil temperature in winter can damage roots. This problem can be avoided by watering thoroughly in autumn and mulching to help retain the moisture. Temperature fluctuates less rapidly in moist soil than in dry soil. In warm climates, mulching and watering provide similar protection particularly during hot, dry periods when soil absorbs lots of radiant heat during the day. Watering during dry periods and shading the soil with mulch help reduce heat and moisture stress that can lead to injury.

Safe haven
Hardening off under some sort of cover enables plants to make a safe transition from their early life indoors to growing in the open ground and in the face of the elements.

MANAGE PESTS FOR A HEALTHY GARDEN

Integrated pest management (IPM) is a sustainable and environmentally sensitive approach to garden disease and pest problems. IPM was initially developed for commercial growers as a means of merging all available information regarding a crop and its documented or potentially troublesome pests and diseases into a comprehensive plan of action to maximize production and quality and to minimize environmental risks. IPM has been adapted as a useful tool for home gardeners and is a perfect fit with the SMARTGARDEN™ philosophy: to follow nature's leads and to harness her forces to work on your behalf.

Keeping the proper perspective

IPM is a multistep process. It includes taking steps to prevent problems or to reduce their severity, identifying and monitoring problems that do arise (using physical and natural control measures first), and, if necessary, applying the least toxic pesticide at the proper rate and at the proper time. When dealing with garden diseases and pests, it is important to keep in mind that a certain amount of damage is tolerable. Trying to maintain every leaf and flower in perfect condition is impossible. Accepting a level of tolerable imperfection does not mean ignoring damage when it occurs. The SMARTGARDEN™ approach is to assess the damage, identify the cause, estimate the potential for further damage, and, depending on that assessment, continue to monitor the problem and adjust cultural practices to reduce its spread, or proceed with a specific control measure. The key is to strive for balance rather than perfection.

An ounce of prevention

One of the best methods for dealing with plant problems is to prevent them from occurring. Healthy, well-adapted plants are less likely to be seriously damaged by the diseases or pests that invade the garden. They can withstand an infection (from diseases) or infestation (from insects or other animals) better than a plant that is struggling from the stress of neglect or placement in an inappropriate site.

Allies
Ladybird beetles (also widely called ladybugs) and a host of other insects and creatures can be recruited in the battle against plant pests.

How many should be tolerated
This colorful caterpillar is the larva of the beautiful black swallowtail butterfly. A few will not cause much damage, but large numbers would pose a threat. It's up to you whether to reduce or eliminate them or leave them alone.

How much is too much?
Gardeners who practice IPM know when the level of damage from a pest's activities has reached an unacceptable level.

Resistance or something else?
The hosta shown above is free of slug damage, while the one to the right has obviously been severely attacked. The difference between the two could be the result of thicker, tougher leaves than are common to many hostas, or it could be due to the the gardener's efforts.

RESISTANT VARIETIES

Most plant diseases and many pests are quite specific for the host plants that they will infect or infest. A disease that infects your lawn most likely will do no damage to your trees or shrubs. An insect that bores into pine trees will probably leave your other trees and shrubs, as well as your herbaceous plants, alone.

Susceptibility to diseases and pests varies from one variety of plant to another. Plant breeders have used this phenomenon to impart disease- and pest-tolerance and resistance to an ever-increasing number of new varieties of the plants we grow in our gardens.

Selecting varieties that are resistant to pests and diseases that are common in your area is an easy way to give your garden plants an advantage. For example, some tomato varieties are resistant to several fungal wilts, viral diseases, and certain nematodes that can devastate a susceptible variety. By selecting varieties of hosta with thicker, more substantial leaves, damage by slugs is often avoided or at least lessened.

SANITATION

Removal and disposal of disease-infected or pest-infested plants and plant remains from the garden is an important cultural tool that should be incorporated into your gardening efforts throughout the growing season. It should also be a designated part of your annual clean-up activities. Remember: although the heat generated by a well-managed compost pile is sufficient to kill pests and most disease-causing organisms, seriously diseased plants are best kept out of the compost pile, just as a precaution.

Many pests and disease-causing organisms overwinter in or on the remains of their former host, and if left in the garden will be ready and waiting to cause problems come spring. When practical, remove the source before the pest or disease has a chance to spread. Also, before you introduce any new plant into your garden, inspect it for pests and the symptoms of disease.

OTHER PREVENTION TECHNIQUES

Other cultural methods for preventing pest and disease problems include mulching to create a physical barrier between soil-borne spores and potential hosts, using physical barriers such as netting or row covers to exclude egg-laying female insects, planting to ensure adequate air circulation between plants, planting early or late to avoid a pest or disease at a predictable time each year, and removal of garden plants or weeds that may serve as alternative hosts to disease organisms or pests.

RESISTANT PLANTS

Here are a few plants that have shown resistance to some of the most common pests and diseases in the Northwest. Remember: resistance (the ability of a plant to withstand a pest) is not the same as immunity (not experiencing the problem at all).

Anthracnose: *Cornus kousa* and its hybrids with *C. florida*, such as 'Appalachian Spring'; *Plantanus* x *acerifolia* 'Yarwood', 'Liberty', 'Columbia', and 'Bloodgood' (Sycamores); 'Sweet Charlie' Strawberry

Aphids: *Lonicera* 'Freedom' (Honeysuckle), 'Canby' thornless Red Raspberry, 'New Generation' Lupines.
Black vine weevils: P.J.M. Rhododendrons, as well as other rhododendrons that have rolled-under leaf edges.
Borers: River Birch, especially 'Heritage'
Botrytis Blight: *Petunia* 'Lavender Wave' and 'Tidal Wave Silver'.
Slugs & Snails: Thick, waxy-leaved host as, including 'Krossa Regal', 'Blue Moon', 'Halcyon', 'Gold Edger', 'Shade Fanfare', and *H. sieboldiana* 'Elegans'; some *Pulmonaria* (Lungwort).

CROP ROTATION

Rearranging (rotating) the placement of plants from one season to the next is a valuable means of outwitting pests and diseases in vegetable gardens and annual beds. Most diseases and many insects are rather specific in their selection of host plants, and many survive the winter as eggs or spores in the soil around the plant that was the pest's host during the previous growing season. Replanting the same crop in the same space increases the probability of reinfection. Make it more difficult for the pest or disease: move your beans to the other side of the garden, and plant marigolds where you had China asters last year. This simple avoidance technique can significantly reduce recurring problems.

Year 1

LEGUMES AND POD CROPS

Okra
Hyacinth beans
Scarlet runner beans
Lima beans
Snap beans
Peas
Broad beans

Year 2

ALLIUMS (ONIONS)

Bulb onions
Pickling onions
Scallions
Shallots
Welsh onions
Oriental bunching
Onions
Leeks
Garlic

Year 4

BRASSICAS

Kales
Cauliflowers
Cabbages
Brussels sprouts
Sprouting broccoli
Broccoli
Oriental mustards
Chinese broccoli
Bok choi
Mizuna greens
Chinese cabbages
Komatsuna
Kohlrabi
Rutabagas
Turnips
Radishes

Year 3

SOLANACEOUS, ROOT, AND TUBEROUS CROPS

Sweet peppers
Tomatoes
Wonderberries
Eggplants
Celery
Beets
Taro
Carrots
Sweet potatoes
Parsnips
Scorzonera
Salsify
Potatoes

Rotation of vegetable crops
Vegetables are divided into four groups: legumes and pod crops; alliums; brassicas; and solanaceous, root, and tuberous crops. Sweet corn and summer and winter squash do not fit into the major groups, but they still should be rotated. If you are growing only a small amount of these, it may be possible to include them in one of the groups (such as alliums). Otherwise, treat them as a separate group and rotate everything on a five-year basis.

Diagnosing and assessing damage

If you are unfamiliar with the plant problem confronting you, take a Sherlock Holmes approach: use all available clues and resources to pin down the culprit. Numerous books and publications are available to assist your diagnosis. Furthermore, local Cooperative Extension offices, botanical gardens, nurseries, and plant societies maintain diagnostic clinics and horticultural hotlines. Many of these can be conveniently contacted on the Internet (*see* Appendix, *p. 408* for regional resources).

You may have an expert horticulturist to whom you can turn with any plant problems. But no matter whom you ask, the prognosis will be based on the information that you provide. The more detailed observations you make, the more accurate the advice you will receive. Whenever possible, you should provide one or more specimens of the plant that demonstrate progressive symptoms for the expert to examine. Each specimen should be more than just a single leaf; it is helpful and sometimes necessary to see more than one leaf attached to a bit of stem to identify the plant as well as the problem.

Once you identify the specific cause of your problem, the next step is to learn more about the disease or pest and determine how much damage is likely to occur and whether and what type of control measures are warranted.

NOTING DAMAGE

• When did you first notice the damage?
• What are the symptoms? Examine all parts of the plant and be as precise as possible.
• Are the symptoms on more than one plant or kind of plant?
• How rapidly do the symptoms progress?
• How long has the plant been growing in its current location?
• Which kinds of treatment (for example, fertilizer, insecticide, herbicide, mulching) have been applied to the plant or to surrounding areas recently?
• Have you ever noticed this problem before? If so, is it different this time?
• Has there been any change in soil grade in the area surrounding the plants?
• Has there been any other change in the area surrounding the plant?

Know your enemy

Familiarizing yourself with the most common pests and diseases of the plants you grow is a major step to outwitting them. By knowing their appearance, life cycle, feeding and overwintering habits, potential hosts, and natural predators, you can work with nature to tilt the balance in favor of your garden plants.

For example, fireblight is a bacterial disease that infests apples, pears, pyracantha, hawthorn, quince, and several other ornamental plants, typically causing sudden twig dieback. Serious damage can often be avoided by limiting the use of nitrogen fertilizer on susceptible plants, since succulent new growth, which is stimulated by nitrogen, is most prone to infection. If the disease does cause dieback, pruning out and destroying infected stems will generally stop (or at least slow down) the spread of the disease before it causes serious damage. Left untreated, the infection may move into older wood, where it forms cankers in which the bacteria overwinter. More extensive removal of branches displaying such cankers may be required at this point.

Knowledge of the life cycle of a pest or disease-causing organism enables the gardener to apply countermeasures at the time when they will be most effective. For instance, parasitic nematodes effectively control several lawn pests,

COMMON PESTS AND DISEASES

INSECTS AND OTHER INVERTEBRATES
Aphids suck sap from plants and excrete honeydew, on which sooty molds grow.
Beetle grubs are the larvae of various species of beetles. They feed on the roots of lawns, shrubs, and other plants.
Black vine weevils are small, flightless beetles with narrow heads and snouts. Adults feed at night and notch the edges of leaves, and larvae feed on roots.
Borers include wood-boring larvae of clearwing moths and beetles. The larvae eat bark and sapwood as well as the interior heartwood. Holes and oozing, hardening sap are the main symptoms.
Slugs and snails are slow-moving, soft-bodied mollusks ranging in size from one inch to over 8 inches. They eat leaves.

DISEASES
Anthracnose includes several species of fungi that attack leaves, stems flowers, and fruits.

Botrytis blight (also called gray mold) usually infects old blossoms but can spread quickly to herbaceous plants.
Mildews attack leaves. Downy mildew appears as a grayish mold on the underside of leaves, and powdery mildew appears on the top. Symptoms include dark water-soaked lesions that expand.
Wilts are soil fungi that block vascular tissue, resulting in wilting, yellowing, and browning of leaves and often death of the plant.

Many snails have voracious appetites

Catch it in time
Diseases such as rusts (above), if caught early in their development, may be controlled by nonchemical means. Severe cases, however, may need chemicals for total control.

including Japanese beetle grubs. But they must be applied when the target pest is active; the nematodes persist for only about two weeks. By knowing that the grubs become active as the soil warms in spring, the nematodes can be applied when the grubs begin to feed.

PHYSICAL CONTROLS
Many pests and diseases can be controlled by physical means. For example, handpicking the pest or pruning diseased stems or branches is sufficient in many cases to prevent further spread. Brute force is sometimes effective: a hard spray of water can knock down a population of aphids or mites to a tolerable level. Colorado potato beetles and tomato hornworms can often be eliminated by hand – the pests are simply picked off the host plant and destroyed. This method is effective, however, only when the gardener is vigilant (and prepared for gore!).

Barriers can also prevent pest damage: a cardboard collar around young vegetable seedlings checks their destruction by cutworms. Tree wraps – sticky bands of material that are placed around the trunk of a tree – prevent the larvae of gypsy moths and similar leaf-eating caterpillars from reaching the tree's susceptible foliage. Tubular plastic cages and wraps placed around young trees protect their bark from the gnawing of mice or rabbits. Floating row covers made of a thin, light, and water-permeable fabric can block many flying pests from infesting vegetable plants. Birds can be thwarted from eating your cherries or blueberries by covering the trees or shrubs with a protective net before the fruit ripens.

When pesticides are necessary
The goal when using a pesticide is to achieve control with the minimum impact on the rest of the environment. Applying the right material at the wrong time, to the wrong plant, or at the wrong dilution can negate its effect or, even worse, cause more damage than the pest itself. Whenever you decide to use a pesticide, it is critical to follow all label instructions for safety.

DIRECTIONS FOR HANDLING
• Eliminate or minimize human, pet, and nontarget plant exposure to the pesticide. This is particularly important when dealing with concentrated formulations.
• Wear protective clothing, and wash it after use, separately from other laundry.
• Wash equipment used for measuring, mixing, and applying the pesticide, and store in a secure, designated location.
• Wash down or flush any hardscaped or soil areas that were exposed to pesticides or where pesticides may have been inadvertently spilled.
• Store pesticides in a safe, secure (preferably locked) location – out of the reach of children and pets – in their original containers and according to the label instructions.
• Thoroughly wash your hands and face – or better, shower – after applying pesticides.
• Dispose of unused pesticides and empty pesticide containers according to the label instructions.
• Keep a record of the application; include date, material applied, and plants treated.

Population explosion
Whiteflies are a widespread insect pest of both indoor and outdoor plants. Their populations can build up to large numbers quickly, and their sugary secretions support the growth of black sooty molds. As with most plant problems, early detection and diligent inspection will help keep them at bay.

Many synthetic chemical pesticides formerly available have been banned for environmental and safety reasons. A variety of environmentally friendly, nonchemical pest control alternatives have been developed, many derived from plants or minerals. These pesticides generally break down quickly into safe byproducts and thus are good choices for the pests they control. Like any pesticide, they may be toxic to humans or other nontarget animals and should be applied with care according to the manufacturer's instructions.

Types of pesticides

Pesticides work by direct contact, ingestion, or making the plant distasteful to pests. Some pests and diseases are susceptible just during one phase of their life cycle. Therefore, timing may be critical to achieving an acceptable level of control.

Contact pesticides require direct contact with an external part of the pest for effective control. They must be applied where the pest is or will be present. If a pest feeds on the underside of leaves, the pesticide should be applied to the leaf undersides. If only the upper surface of the leaf is sprayed, the pesticide may have little or no effect.

Other pesticides work only after ingestion – they must be consumed by the pest. Leaf-eating caterpillars and beetles are often controlled by an ingested pesticide that is applied to the foliage of the host plant. Many biological controls such as Bt (bacteria that control specific leaf and root eating pests) must also be ingested by the pest to be effective (*see* Beneficial microbes, *p. 69*).

Systemic pesticides are absorbed and carried within a plant. Sprayed on the foliage or applied to the soil, they are taken in by the plant and kill the pest when it feeds on plant tissues.

Repellents do not kill the pest but instead prevent it from harming the host plant by making it less appealing. Hot pepper sprays and predator urine are examples of repellents designed to keep animals from devouring garden plants. These generally require frequent application.

Chemical pesticide formulations

Some pesticides can be applied directly, while others require diluting prior to application. Be sure always to dilute concentrated pesticides to the correct strength for the pest you are trying to control, and the host to which it is applied. Most pesticides are available in one or more of the formulations detailed below:

• Aerosols are ready-to-use sprays – usually contact poisons – that are under pressure. The pesticide is emitted as a fine mist.
• Dusts are finely ground pesticides combined with a fine inert powder that acts as a carrier. These are generally ready to apply from the bag.
• Granular formulations are similar to dusts, but the carrier is a larger particle, usually an inert clay. This formulation is most commonly used for pesticides that are applied to the soil.
• Liquid concentrates are similar to wettable powders except that the concentrated pesticide is in liquid form.
• Wettable powders are water-soluble pesticides that are usually combined with a wetting agent to make mixing easier. They are mixed with water prior to application. They are usually applied as a spray but may be watered into soil when appropriate.

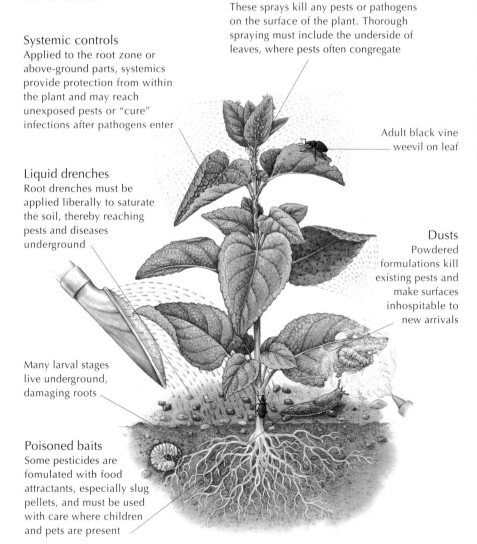

The way chemicals work
Different problems require chemicals to be applied in different ways. A combination of application methods may be needed to achieve a satisfactory level of control.

Systemic controls
Applied to the root zone or above-ground parts, systemics provide protection from within the plant and may reach unexposed pests or "cure" infections after pathogens enter

Liquid drenches
Root drenches must be applied liberally to saturate the soil, thereby reaching pests and diseases underground

Many larval stages live underground, damaging roots

Poisoned baits
Some pesticides are fomulated with food attractants, especially slug pellets, and must be used with care where children and pets are present

Contact sprays
These sprays kill any pests or pathogens on the surface of the plant. Thorough spraying must include the underside of leaves, where pests often congregate

Adult black vine weevil on leaf

Dusts
Powdered formulations kill existing pests and make surfaces inhospitable to new arrivals

Chemical pesticide alternatives

There are many alternatives to chemical pesticides that are available for combating garden pests and diseases, and many are just as effective as stronger chemical pesticides if they are used correctly.

BOTANICAL INSECTICIDES

Certain compounds extracted from plants are effective in controlling a variety of pests. Some of the more commonly available are:

• neem: repels some pests and interrupts the life cycle of many plant-eating caterpillars and beetles after ingestion.
• pyrethrum: an effective, broad-spectrum contact poison
• rotenone: commonly applied as a dust for short-term control of many leaf-eating caterpillars and beetles
• sabadilla: both a contact and stomach poison, effective against many true bugs, leaf-eating caterpillars, and thrips
Keep in mind that just because a pesticide is classed as a botanical, it may still be very toxic; rotenone in particular is very toxic to fish. Like any other pesticide, these must be used with extreme care, and always read the label.

INSECTICIDAL SOAPS

Derived from fatty acids and potassium salts, insecticidal soaps are applied as a dilute spray. They damage cell membranes of soft-bodied pests such as aphids, leafhoppers, whiteflies, and spider mites, and make them slip off the plant. In order to be effective, insecticidal soaps must come into direct contact with the pest. Some particularly sensitive plants can be damaged by insecticidal soaps; check the manufacturer's instructions and, if you are unsure, test the product on a small part of the plant first.

HORTICULTURAL OILS

These are refined petroleum products that are commonly used on dormant plants to smother overwintering insects and mites. Formulations called summer-weight oils can be applied to many plants during the growing season for controlling scales, whiteflies, and certain diseases. However, some plants are susceptible to damage by oils so, as with all pesticides, you should read all of the instructions carefully.

Vegetable oils, which are derived from agricultural crops, may also be used to control pests such as aphids, spider mites, whiteflies, thrips, and scales. However, these oils should not be used on begonias, fuchsias, or seedlings of any plant because they can damage the leaves.

Double protection
Rotenone (also called derris) has been applied to this plant to protect the leaves, and the square collar at the base protects the stem.

MINED MATERIALS

Another component of the arsenal of pest control weapons is material that is mined from the earth. Sprinkling diatomaceous earth – fossilized single-celled aquatic organisms – around plants provides a physical barrier against soft-bodied slugs and snails. Copper strips can be used as barriers to prevent damage by slugs and snails. Copper- and sulfur-based sprays and dusts can control fungal diseases such as powdery mildew and botrytis. These products can be detrimental to predatory mites, however, and should not be sprayed on young apples. Furthermore, the buildup of copper in the soil may be harmful to worms and, as it runs off into neighboring waterways, will affect fish.

Nature's pest control

Another method of thwarting garden pests is to enlist their natural enemies to work for you. Insects, nematodes, mites, microbes, and other organisms that feed upon or infect a plant pest are known as biological controls, and they are among the most effective ways of dealing with troublemakers in your garden. Beneficial organisms are fairly specific with respect to creatures they infect or consume, and they pose minimal danger to humans and other nontarget animals.

Some of the organisms that gardeners often lump together under the term "insects" are more correctly known simply as arthropods. Technically, true insects – such as ants, grasshoppers, butterflies, and beetles – are distinguished from other groups of common garden arthropods such as arachnids (spiders and mites) and crustaceans (pillbugs and sowbugs). Most of these creatures are neutral when it comes to their effect on garden plants; that is, they neither harm nor benefit them. They may, however, be a food source for birds, bats, or other wildlife, or they may help decompose organic matter. So in a sense, even though they do not directly help or harm plants, arthropods help maintain a well-balanced environment. Many arthropods benefit garden plants by hunting and eating other insects and mites that feed on plants. Others parasitize pests, often by laying their eggs inside the body of the pest, where they eventually hatch and consume their host; then the emerging female adults complete the cycle by laying eggs in new hosts. Predatory mites often consume plant-feeding spider mites. Many spiders build webs and feed on whatever prey wanders in and gets stuck. Others, such as wolf, jumping, and crab spiders, actively seek their prey on plants or on the ground. Among the pests they help control are leafhoppers, aphids, and numerous beetles and caterpillars. Learn to recognize these garden-friendly creatures, and avoid spraying pesticides when they are present.

Sowbugs may occasionally be a problem, however, because they are sometimes attracted in large numbers to seedlings, feeding on them at ground level. If necessary, a colony of sowbugs can be destroyed by pouring boiling water on them.

COMMON PARASITES AND PREDATORS

Damsel bugs eat aphids, insect eggs, and larvae.
Ground beetles are general feeders, eating nearly any garden pest that spends time on or in the top few inches of soil.
Hunting wasps (there are several species) capture a wide range of plant pests to feed to their young.
Lacewings feed on aphids, too, as well as many scale insects, small caterpillars, mites, and thrips.

On patrol
A ground beetle actively searches for many kinds of garden pests to eat. .

Lady beetles (ladybugs), in both their larval and adult stage, control pests. They prefer aphids but will also consume other small, soft-bodied plant feeders.
Parasitic wasps: several types, including braconids and *Trichogramma*, lay their eggs inside the bodies of a host. The eggs hatch, feed on the host, and eventually kill it. Occasionally, small white projections that resemble grains of rice are visible on the larvae of infected hosts. These are the cocoons of the wasp, and, if observed, the caterpillar should be left alone so the wasps can emerge to continue their beneficial activities.
Predatory stink bugs eats fairly large insects, including potato beetle larvae and a variety of caterpillars.
Spined soldier bugs consume the larvae of a variety of notorious plant pests including gypsy moth, Colorado potato beetle, and Mexican bean beetle.
Syrphid fly: the larval stage can consume dozens of soft-bodied plant-feeding insects in a single day.
Tachinid flies parasitize a variety of pests including caterpillars, true bugs, and beetles. Adults lay their eggs on the host insect. Soon after, the eggs hatch and the maggots tunnel into the host, eventually killing it.

Lone hunter
A solitary wasp has captured an insect to take back to its nest for its young.

Attracting beneficial organisms

You can encourage predators and parasites of plant pests to inhabit your garden. Beneficial organisms can be purchased from distributors of natural pest controls. Make sure that when you release beneficial insects, there are pests for them to feed on; otherwise, they will seek another garden with a more tempting menu. Another problem that you may encounter is that some predaceous insects, such as the praying mantis, will feed on beneficial insects as well as your pests.

Either attracting or releasing beneficial insects into your garden will not give you instant results – your pests may be around for several days – but once the predators or parasites arrive, they will work to control the pest until the pest population is depleted. Do not apply any insecticides to your garden while your beneficials are doing their job or you may eliminate them.

On target
Place containers of beneficial organisms on or near the plants you want to protect.

Beneficial nematodes

Some nematodes – microscopic, eel-like roundworms – are plant pests, but others are beneficial, residing in soils and infecting and reproducing in garden pests that spend part of their life cycle in the soil. Beneficial nematodes are effective for managing black vine weevil larvae, white grubs, and Japanese beetle grubs, among others. The nematodes penetrate a host insect through natural body openings, multiply within the host's body, and release bacteria that multiply and kill the pest.

Native populations of beneficial nematodes are generally too low to provide effective pest control. However, beneficial nematodes can be purchased and applied to your lawns and gardens. Timing of the application is critical, and as with all pest-control products, it is important that you follow all of the label directions carefully. When correctly applied, beneficial nematodes not only provide excellent control of the target pest but are extremely safe to humans and other nontarget animals because they can only inhabit particular hosts, for example, the vine weevil.

Beneficial microbes

Some microbial organisms can be recruited to control pests. *Bacillus thuringiensis* (Bt) is a bacterium available in several different varieties, each of which is effective against specific pests. The bacterium produces a protein that is toxic to a variety of insects, causing paralysis of their mouthparts or gut. Bt var. *kurstaki* (Btk) controls several destructive caterpillars, such as cabbage caterpillars, cabbage loopers, gypsy moth, tomato hornworm, and codling moths, as well as corn borers. Other strains, Btt and Bt var. san diego, provide control of leaf-eating beetles such as the Colorado potato beetle. It is important to select the appropriate variety of the bacterium for the pest at hand. Bt degrades in sunlight and, consequently, it must be reapplied in order to remain effective.

A related species, *B. popilliae*, controls Japanese beetles by infecting the grubs – the soil-borne larval stage – with a disease known as milky spore. The bacteria reproduce in the host and remain in the soil when the host dies, providing a long-term source for infection of other grubs.

Attracting predators
Even a small bit of wildflower meadow will attract large numbers of beneficial predatory and parasitic organisms into your garden.

KEEP A GARDEN JOURNAL

The more you know about your site, your plants, and potential problems you may encounter, the more success you will experience in gardening. Although numerous resources are available to guide your gardening endeavors, the most important is your own experience. Keeping records is among the most valuable gardening activities you can perform. Both your successes and failures provide lessons that will make you a better gardener.

A garden diary

Interrupting your planting or weeding efforts to jot down notes in a diary might seem like a nuisance at the time, but it will help you plan your garden efforts this season and for years to come. Record the names of those plants that have performed famously as well as those you'd rather forget – and be sure to indicate which is which! The moments you take to note your observations will save you time in the long run. When you repeat a mistake because you forgot a previous failure, not only is it a waste of time and effort, but it may result in the loss of an entire growing season or even longer.

A gardening diary is a simple way to keep track of what is happening in your yard. Some allow for multiple years' entries on the same page. Typically, one page is allotted to every week of the year, and it is divided to accommodate four or five years' worth of

records. This allows you to look back to see what was going on in the garden at the same time in previous seasons. However, less elaborate systems can work just as well. A simple notebook or a calendar with enough room for your entries can accommodate any important details. The critical aspect of a garden diary is not what it looks like, but that you write in it. Regularly.

While garden notes needn't be lengthy, a few items are very important to include. Be sure to record the full name, including cultivar or variety, of any plant you acquire. Note the planting date and the plant's location in the yard. Then, when it's time to replant your strawberries and you want the same (or a different) variety than you planted half a dozen years ago (was it 'Surecrop' or 'Tristar'?), it is just a matter of checking your records. When you order vegetable and annual flower seeds, you can sit down with your notes, ordering those varieties you considered tops in the past and avoiding those that were disappointing. Having a record of where you purchased a given plant is sometimes helpful, especially for those hard-to-find varieties.

Diagrams of planting plans are also helpful. A sketch of your vegetable garden will assist planning future crop rotation schedules. A bed layout will remind you of the location of bulbs, ephemeral perennials (plants that complete their annual growth cycle in a very short time), or perennials that emerge late in the season, avoiding accidental damage when you are working in your garden before or after these plants are visible.

Making notes
Recording garden observations as you make them will produce a valuable record for the future. It can be as simple or as literary as you wish.

The four seasons
Many experienced gardeners strive to have something of interest in their gardens throughout the year. Noting when plants bloom or show other interesting features will be useful as you plan color combinations or theme gardens for a particular season. Clockwise from top left: Columbine (*Aquilegia formosa*), Beebalm (*Monarda didyma*),, Christmas Rose (*Helleborus niger*), and Vine Maple (*Acer circinnatum*). Growing these four plants would provide all-season interest.

The march of time
Photographs, especially if taken at regular intervals, document the progression of a garden (or even a single plant) from the time of its establishment to mature beauty.

Information to include

Your records should include as much of the following information as possible about your plants and their basic and specialized care:

• Source: where you obtained the plant (nursery, friend, local plant sale)
• Provenance: the plant's place of origin (where it was previously grown)
• Date acquired
• Size and condition
• Special characteristics that set the plant apart
• Exact planting location
• Dates of application of fertilizer and pesticides
• Notes on propagation where applicable
• Pruning schedule
• Additional care required

• Flowering and fruiting times. Observations about plant growth are helpful as you plan additions. Perhaps you want a shrub that blooms at the same time as those in an existing planting, or a raspberry that ripens after your blackberries. Keeping track of planting and harvesting dates in the vegetable garden helps you plan for an extended harvest.
• Diseases, pests, cultural problems. Many pests can be avoided by planting earlier or later than the pest's arrival to the garden (doing this is especially useful in vegetable gardening). This necessitates, however, knowing when to expect the unwanted visitor. Because these dates vary even within a region, the best source of this information is your own garden records. The onset of a disease or pest infestation is equally important to note on ornamental plants so that you can be prepared to minimize damage.

On screen
Suitable computer software can be an invaluable aid in keeping track of the comings and goings (and successes and failures) of your garden plants over the years.

Planting Record.XLS

	A	B	C	D	E
1	PLANT NAME	SOURCE	DATE PLANTED	PLANTING LOCATION(S)	NOTES
2	Acer griseum x 3	Atlock	10/23/96	far corner	first things planted
3	Viburnum plicatum tomentosum 'Shasta'	Veronica Nursery	5/17/97	lamp post	growing slowly as of '99 - too dry?
4	Thuja occidentalis 'Smaragd' x7	B&B Nursery	5/30/97	far corner	3 dead spring '98 - take down the red maple!
5	Liquidambar syraciflua	Bowman's Nursery	5/31/97	near rear spruce	excellent fall color
6	Emmenopterys henryi	DCH Auction	6/5/97	near rear spruce	dead summer '97 - too hot and dry
7	Buxus sempervirens upright selection x 10	Atlock	7/2/97	along front fence	hedge to block view
8	Betula nigra 'Little King'	Scott Hort lecture '95	7/2/97	near front spruce	4" tall when received
9	Heptacodium mikanoides	Atlock ex Haskell's	7/3/97	near Betula 'LK'	prune to reveal bark

Sheet1 / Sheet2 / Sheet3

Many gardeners have developed a personal computerized plant record system. Data can be added to files quickly, and multiple years of records can be conveniently stored. You can develop a long-range plan and keep track of your progress. Be sure to keep a backup of all your gardening files just in case something happens to the computer!

Some of the most fascinating garden records are photographs. A spectacular garden is all the more dramatic when you can compare the "before" and "after" shots. Growth of trees, combinations of perennials, and successful container plantings can be documented for future referral. Also, a photograph can be very helpful to someone trying to diagnose a plant problem or identify a plant.

Other items for the record

Always record modifications you make to your soil. Keep your soil tests from year to year, and make note of any amendments you incorporate. Records of your soil fertility and pH are most useful when changes can be observed over time. Be sure to identify areas that receive different treatments.

Routine maintenance such as mulching, watering, fertilizing, and pruning should be recorded. Knowing the quantities of mulch and fertilizer you use in a season helps estimate future purchases.

By studying the phenology of the plants in your landscape – their cycles of growth and development over the course of the year – you can time gardening activities to your specific conditions. The optimum time to plant particular seeds, to apply insecticides, to release beneficial insects, and other gardening activities can be determined by observing the growth cycle of your plants and relating their various stages to the environment as a whole. Because plants respond to environmental stimuli, such as day length and temperature, their growth cycles can be used to indicate other similarly stimulated events such as the arrival of an insect pest or the emergence of a weed. Applying preemergent crabgrass control to the lawn as the forsythia flowers fade is an example of a phenologically based practice. Similarly, when an insect infestation is first observed in your yard, look around and take note of what is blooming. If the insect reappears in following years when the same plant is in bloom, you can reasonably schedule your pest control methods to coincide with that particular plant's blooming time.

Timing is everything
One way to control crabgrass is to apply a preemergent weedkiller to the soil as local forsythia flowers begin to fade. This is well before you would notice even seedling crabgrass, so make a note in your diary.

CONSULT THE PROS

In today's media-rich environment, the challenge is not so much to find information about whatever topic you seek as it is to filter the available resources to make sure you locate those that are most reliable and valuable to you and your gardening efforts. The books, periodicals, websites, television and radio shows, and gardens that are most useful to you are largely determined by two factors: your gardening interests and your location.

Gathering information

If you are investigating the possibility of developing a rock garden, for example, you can find books, magazines, and websites devoted to the subject. To apply the information you gather to your backyard, you can look to more regional resources, such as a nearby botanical garden, a local chapter of a rock garden society, your state's cooperative extension service, and periodicals with a regional focus. Obtain the best resources available to you, then integrate the information into your garden plan.

The printed word

Certain resources become like trusted friends – you return to them time after time for advice. A stroll down the gardening aisle of a well-stocked bookstore will reveal that there are titles for nearly every conceivable aspect of gardening. But all gardening references are not equal and can, themselves, add significantly to your expenditures before you even start planting. Although some books, like this one, have a regional perspective, many are written from a more general point of view, and some will reflect conditions quite unlike those that you confront. Take this into consideration when looking for advice from a nonregional reference.

Magazines and journals can inspire you with examples of what other gardeners are doing as well as keep you up to date on recent advances. There are many periodicals to choose from, for every level of gardening and for just about any specialty. Some of these are national with a broad scope, but you can also find ones for your particular geographic region. Many plant societies, botanic gardens, and nurseries publish a newsletter, packed with useful information.

Local and regional newspapers are another source of timely gardening information. Weekly gardening columns offer growing tips on a local level and many include reviews of new gardening books. Newspapers may cover gardens worth visiting in your area, as well as local gardening programs and events.

Landscape painters

Employing a professional landscape designer or architect and contractor will not be inexpensive, but the results gained from your investment should be very rewarding: you'll have an attractive and useful landscape feature, and it will be done the right way.

The printed word
Many reference books are available to buy from bookstores or to research at libraries. It's a good idea to consult more than one volume to get multiple (and often different!) insights on a given plant's characteristics and garden potential.

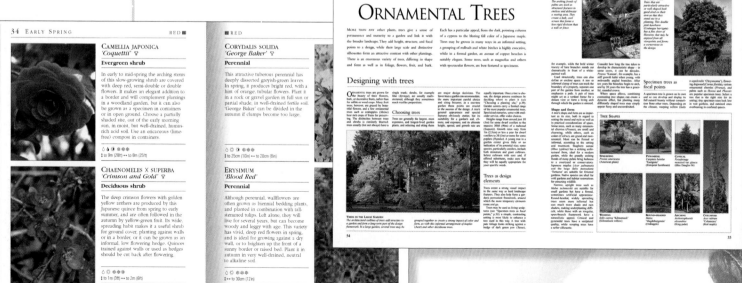

The electronic approach

Websites on every gardening specialty have cropped up over the last few years. A quick search on the Internet can reveal hundreds of articles about any gardening topic. You can spend hours surfing the Internet for specific information or just enjoy exploring the breadth of subjects covered. Nearly every plant society and botanical garden, and many state cooperative extension services and university horticulture departments, have websites that you are welcome to peruse without subscription. Expert advice on almost any gardening subject is often only an e-mail away.

Many organizations may have regional chapters with individual websites. These can be a helpful source of local expert advice and can inform you of meetings, classes, and other events in your area. If you are looking for information on a specific plant, for example daffodils or roses, or a particular gardening topic, such as rock gardens or bonsai, start with the appropriate national organization and go from there. Many organizations are listed on more general gardening websites, and the national organizations usually provide links to regional sites. *(For gardening websites see the appendix).*

A gardening list serve – an electronic conversation among a group of gardeners – provides you with opportunities to ask, receive, and offer advice, and to share gardening experiences. Many organizations

sponsor list serves. The accuracy of such advice, of course, depends upon the participants, but conversations are often lively and stimulating. If you are a member of the American Horticultural Society (AHS), you can learn about various list serves by visiting the Society's website (www.ahs.org), then join one of many ongoing conversation about potentially any gardening subject.

Many local radio and cable television stations are getting into the gardening act with shows that highlight local gardens, gardeners, and timely and regionally appropriate gardening information. Tune in and see what's new.

Being there

Although written and electronic references are invaluable aids to gardening, nothing is quite the same as a visit to a real garden for learning what you need to know and for inspiring you with ideas. Regional botanical gardens and arboreta afford visitors a chance to see plants they have read or heard about in a real growing situation, and experts are often available to answer your questions.

Some public gardens offer classes and workshops on a variety of subjects, and some provide training for Master Gardeners. Most offer volunteer opportunities, which is a great way to work with trained gardening staff, learning garden techniques first hand from the experts.

Red Butte Gardens and Arboretum, Salt Lake City, Utah
The largest botanical and ecological center in the Intermountain West features floral gardens, a Children's Garden, and a variety of educational programs.

Denver Botanic Gardens
The Tropical Conservatory houses an extensive display of tropical plants that can be viewed from a simulated banyan tree. Many other gardens, facilities, and programs make the DBG one of the premier horticultural institutions in the United States.

MASTER GARDENERS

The Master Gardeners program began in the early 1970s in Washington State as a means of training volunteers to help gardeners find reliable solutions to their gardening problems. Today there are master gardener programs in every state, coordinated by the Cooperative Extension Service in each state.

Programs vary somewhat from one state to another, but in general, volunteers are selected and trained in basic horticultural practices. Training often includes plant identification, diagnosis of plant problems with appropriate recommendations for treatment, soil and fertilizer recommendations, lawn care, pesticide use and safety, organic gardening, ornamental gardening, and a variety of other topics.

In return for their training, Master Gardeners volunteer a certain number of hours in service. These opportunities may include participation in plant clinics, assisting with soil test reports, answering horticultural hotlines, conducting garden tours, or performing other activities that are aimed at disseminating reliable gardening information to the American public.

Two hundred universities, public gardens, and nurseries throughout the United States and Canada are home to All America Selection (AAS) display gardens. These gardens provide visitors with the opportunity to see how recent award-winning introductions (vegetables, flowers, and herbs) perform in a garden setting.

Close to home

Don't overlook a garden simply because it doesn't have a name: within your neighborhood there may be landscapes that deserve a closer look. Most gardeners love to show off the fruits of their labor, and some of the best advice available to you may be from the man or woman next door who shares both your growing conditions and your enthusiasm for gardening.

Taking note of the plants that your neighbors grow, how they grow them, and how they tackle problems that arise can provide insight and ideas for your own yard. A gardening acquaintance may alert you to the arrival of a pest or show you a new plant that is just the ticket for your perennial border. Putting your heads together to find a solution for a common problem multiplies your available resources.

As your garden comes of age and neighbors observe your success, they are likely to ask you for advice. Be generous. Share your enthusiasm for gardening and your respect for the environment. You too have become a valuable resource by following the SMARTGARDEN™ tenets!

THE COOPERATIVE EXTENSION SERVICE

The Land-grant College System is a part of the US Department of Agriculture's Cooperative State Research, Education, and Extension Service (CSREES). The CSREES's mission is "to advance knowledge for agriculture, the environment, human health and well being, and communities." The Hatch Act of 1887 established the cooperative bond between the USDA and the nation's Land-grant colleges, maintained through the allocation of annual federal funds to the Land-grant colleges for research. Although the majority of past research focused on farms and agriculture, it later expanded to research on ornamental horticulture and home gardening. There is one Land-grant college in each of the 50 states. Each Land-grant college hosts the Cooperative Extension Service, which is a great resource for home gardeners. Many counties have local offices that provide information produced by the state Service and also distribute more localized materials.

The Northwest Land-grant colleges are:
University of Alaska, Fairbanks, AK
Colorado State University, Fort Collins, CO
University of Idaho, Lewiston, ID
Kansas State University, Manhattan, KS
Montana State University, Bozeman, MT
University of Nebraska, Lincoln, NE
University of Nevada, Reno, NV
North Dakota State University, Fargo, ND
Oregon State University, Corvallis, OR
South Dakota State University, Brookings, SD
Utah State University, Farmington, UT
Washington State University, Puyallup, WA
University of Wyoming, Laramie, WY

(Specific information is available in the Appendix.)

Cutting edge
Faculty members at local and regional agricultural colleges often spend part of their time researching new techniques and breeding new plants. Their printed and electronic publications are a valuable resource.

HAVE FUN!

Lots of people have yards; some have gardens. A yard is the area that surrounds your house. A garden, on the other hand, is a creation that enhances that space with sights, fragrances, and sounds that inspire and fulfill. The yard around your house is what you begin with; a garden is what it can become. Whether your garden is a woodland teeming with towering trees and flowering shrubs, a deep border of colorful perennials, a vegetable patch that stocks your table, or a simple windowbox overflowing with annuals, it should be fun for you and for those who visit.

The vision

Visualizing your dream garden can occupy many delightful of hours looking through books and magazines for ideas, visiting botanical gardens, and imagining a bed here, a pond there, and over there, perhaps a trellis . . . it's a pleasant thing to daydream about your green activities. Planning for it to become a reality, and taking the measured steps necessary to assure success, is even more exciting. Witnessing the transformation of your yard into a SMARTGARDEN™ through choosing great plants, maximizing efficient practices, and nurturing a friendly, healthy environment, is a thrill that grows over time.

The challenge

Achieving a SMARTGARDEN™ is a challenge beyond simply planting a few perennials and trees around a patch of grass. It requires you to consider the question: how do you develop a garden, making the most of your landscape, while at the same time merging seamlessly into the rhythms and flow of nature? Your answer is both the task and the reward of its creation. Compromises will be necessary, and you may not see instant dividends on your investment, but over time you will enjoy the compounded benefits of a lovely garden and a healthy, balanced environment. Because you planned for it, your investment will continue to grow over time.

The gardening practices described in this book are designed to make the most of your gardening activities, using all available resources to streamline efforts so that you can concentrate on the gardening activities that you find particularly rewarding and have plenty of time to enjoy the fruits of your labor. Of course there will be some surprises. You will make changes as you go along, learning from and adapting to what works best for you. It is dynamic, challenging, and exciting, and, as every gardener comes to know, there is no such thing as a "finished" garden. The ongoing processes of planning, planting, maintaining, experiencing, refining, and sharing is part of the thrill.

The reward

Although many gardens are pleasant to look at, a SMARTGARDEN™ is a delight to experience on many levels. It harmonizes with its surroundings, enhancing its environment without dominating it. The soil is alive and teeming with beneficial organisms. The plants fit their site and space – and they flourish! Birds and butterflies are welcome, encouraged by the diversity of vegetation and friendly habitat. It's exciting to know your plants intimately while taking pride in their performances and anticipating their changes through the seasons and the years.

People garden for many reasons: to enjoy nature, spend time outdoors, cultivate particular plants, grow their own food, attract wildlife, and create a pleasing, comfortable environment. For most gardeners, it is a combination of such goals. Some people garden because they enjoy the solitude, while others consider it an opportunity to spend time productively in the company of friends or family. It is a perfect activity for intergenerational bonding: senior gardeners have a wealth of experience they can share with young garden enthusiasts. Whether alone or with company, most of us garden because it's fun.

Some gardeners find satisfaction in neat rows of plump tomatoes, while others take pleasure in a casual meadow of wildflowers or an elaborate pond for night-blooming waterlilies. No matter which type of garden you choose, it can be grown following these ten tenets. This kind of garden affords you the opportunity to express your taste and style and then to watch it grow, knowing that it is a healthy and safe environment for all who visit. That knowledge will amplify the joy you derive from your garden.

Whether you are starting from scratch or you are improving an existing garden, smart gardening will help you embrace the vision, meet the challenge, and enjoy the rewards of bringing plants, animals, and structures together into a green and living whole.

Savoring the results
A well-planned and maintained garden that follows SMARTGARDEN™ principles will bring endless pleasure to its owners, no matter the style or level of horticultural interest. The choices are up to you!

PART II

PLANT CATALOG

including Trees, Shrubs, Conifers, Climbers, *and* Herbaceous Plants

One of the three most critical factors for the success of any SMARTGARDEN™ is choosing the right plant for the right spot. In this section, more than 4,000 plants that grow well in the Northwest are grouped by physical characteristics or horticultural requirements, with information on light and moisture needs, cold and heat tolerance, and maximum height and width. Below is a key of symbols:

PLANT CATALOG CONTENTS

TREES

Moist or wet soils	86
Dry soils and sunny sites	88
Acidic soils	90
Alkaline soils	92
Clay soils	94
Coastal exposure	96
Exposed windy sites	98
Air-polluted sites	100
Large stature	102
Medium stature	104
Small stature	106
Spreading or weeping	108
Ornamental spring flowers	110
Ornamental summer flowers	112
Colorful fall foliage	114
Decorative berries or fruit	116
The fruit garden	118
Ornamental bark	120
Specimens	122
Screening and windbreaks	124
Resistant to deer browsing	126

SHRUBS

Dry soils and sunny sites	130
Shady sites	134
Moist or wet soils	138
Drought-tolerant	140
Acidic soils	142
Alkaline soils	144
Clay soils	146
Coastal exposure	150
Exposed windy sites	152
Air-polluted sites	154
Large stature	158
Medium stature	160
Small stature	162
Yellow or orange flowers	164
Blue, purple, or lilac flowers	166
Red or pink flowers	168
White or creamy flowers	170
Winter flowers	172
Early spring flowers	174
Late spring flowers	176
Early summer flowers	178
Mid- to late summer flowers	180
Fragrant flowers	182
Tender fragrant shrubs	184

Evergreen foliage	186
Colorful fall foliage	188
Coarse bold leaves	190
Blue-gray or silver leaves	191
Golden or yellow leaves	192
Red or bronze leaves	193
Variegated leaves	194
Thorny shrubs	195
Ornamental berries and fruits	196
The fruit garden	198
Herbs for mixed borders	199
Specimens	200
Hedges and screenings	202
Container-grown	204
Groundcovers	206
Resistant to deer-browsing	208
Resistant to rabbit-feeding	210
Attractive to butterflies	212
Attractive to hummingbirds	214
Notable and reliable roses	216

CONIFERS

Dry soils and sunny sites	220
Clay Soils	222
Large stature	224
Medium stature	226
Small stature	228
Miniature stature	230
Spreading or weeping	232
Columnar	233
Deciduous	234
Blue-gray or silver leaves	235
Golden or yellow leaves	236
Low-maintenance	238
Hedges and screening	240
Groundcover	241

CLIMBERS

Sunny sites	244
Shady to deeply shady sites	246
Hot and humid sites	248
Fragrant flowers	250
Evergreen foliage	251

HERBACEOUS

Moist soils and sunny sites	254
Moist to wet soils in shade	258
Dry soils in sunny sites	260
Dry soils in shady sites	264
Drought-tolerant	266
Acidic soils	270
Alkaline soils	274
Clay soils	278
Warm sheltered sites	282
Coastal exposure	284
Exposed windy sites	286
Air-polluted sites	288
Yellow flowers	292
Orange or yellow flowers	294
Red or pink flowers	296
Blue flowers	298
White or creamy flowers	300
Purple, violet, or lilac flowers	302
Winter and early spring flowers	304
Late spring or early summer flowers	306
Mid- to late summer flowers	308
Fall flowers	310
Extended bloom season	312
Fragrant	314
Evergreen leaves	316
Blue-green or gray leaves	318
Golden or yellow leaves	320
Purple, red, or bronze leaves	321
Variegated leaves	322
Herbs for borders	324
Herbs and vegetables for mixed borders	326
Rock gardens and screes	328
Groundcovers for sunny sites	330
Groundcovers for shady sites	332
Tender, container-grown	334
Resistant to deer-browsing	336
Resistant to rabbit-feeding	338
Slug-proof	340
Attractive to hummingbirds	342
Attractive to butterflies	344
For use as cut foliage	346
For use as cut flowers	348
Notable and reliable daylilies	350
Notable and reliable ferns	352

ANNUALS AND BIENNIALS

For full sun	354
For shade	356
For use as cut flowers	358
Fragrant	360

BULBS, CORMS, AND TUBERS

Focal points	362
Formal beds	364
Mixed borders	366
For naturalizing	368
For woodlands	370
Bulbs for naturalizing in woodlands	372
Shallow aquatic marginals	374
Deep aquatic marginals	378
Waterlilies	380

TREES

WHEN ONE THINKS OF TREES in the Northwest, the giant western hemlocks and Douglas firs of the wild forests may spring to mind, or perhaps the lush rainforests of the Olympic Peninsula in Washington or the redwoods of the southern coast of Oregon. However, there are many smaller trees that can provide a cornerstone or accent for your yard and provide year-round interest, offering their showy or fragrant blossoms, colorful fruit, brilliant autumn foliage, attractive shape, patterned bark, or other characteristics.

Amelanchier arborea (Downy serviceberry)
This small tree produces clusters of star-shaped white flowers in midspring. In summer, small red fruits attract tanagers, grosbeaks, and other birds.

Acer triflorum (Threeflower maple)
Like most maples, this tree is noted for its stunning fall foliage. Once the leaves have dropped, the peeling, gray-brown bark is revealed.

Depending on the size of your garden, you may opt for a small grove or maybe just a single tree. Either way, the tree is likely to be around for years and possibly generations to come, so consider all the options before you make a decision. Determine which features are most important to you, and be sure to check the maximum height and width of the tree – the plant at

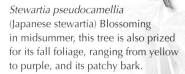

Stewartia pseudocamellia (Japanese stewartia) Blossoming in midsummer, this tree is also prized for its fall foliage, ranging from yellow to purple, and its patchy bark.

the garden center that fits initially may ultimately outgrow its spot, creating hard choices if it has become a cherished family member. Heat and cold tolerance are also important, although you may have a broader choice if you choose to grow trees in containers that are moved indoors for the winter. Finally, do a soil test before you plant: some trees prefer an acidic or alkaline soil, and trees that need a considerable amount of moisture won't do well in a fast-draining soil.

To help the tree become established, provide it with plenty of water for the first couple of years. You should also fertilize and mulch it regularly, and keep the surrounding area free of weeds or grass. Relatively little care will provide you with many years of enjoyment.

Malus 'Snowdrift'
Aptly named for the blizzard of white blossoms in spring, this dense and rounded crabapple also bears glossy, dark green foliage. Its orange red fruits attract a variety of wildlife in fall.

Trees for moist or wet soils

Waterlogged soil is a challenge for any plant, because oxygen levels are very low. Many trees have adapted to life next to streams or lakes and grow well in these situations. The trees presented here perform well in a garden area where the soil stays wet for part or most of the year.

Acer rubrum
RED MAPLE

Ⓝ ☼ ◑ ◐ 🌡 Z3–9 H9–1 ↕70ft (20m) ↔30ft (9m)
Tiny red flowers emerging before the leaves herald the arrival of spring in Eastern North America. For the best display of vivid red fall color, grow in acidic soil.

Magnolia grandiflora 'Little Gem'
LITTLE GEM SOUTHERN MAGNOLIA

Ⓝ ☼ ◑ ◐ Z7–9 H9–3 ↕20ft (6m) ↔10ft (3m)
More compact and upright than the species, with smaller, very fragrant flowers. Prefers well-drained soil. Prone to leaf spots, cankers, mildew, and scale insects.

Platanus occidentalis
BUTTONWOOD

Ⓝ ☼ ◐ Z5–8 H8–3
↕80ft (24m) ↔70ft (20m)
Wide-spreading tree with very attractive, flaking brown, gray, and cream bark. Produces green, then brown, fruit clusters that hang on in fall and winter.

Acer rubrum 'Franksred'
FRANKSRED MAPLE

Ⓝ ☼ ◐ Z3–9 H9–1 ↕100ft (30m) ↔75ft (22.5m)
Also known as 'Red Sunset', this tree, the standard to which others are compared, was developed by Frank Schmidt, Jr. Vigorous growth and lustrous green foliage.

Acer rubrum 'October Glory'
OCTOBER GLORY MAPLE

Ⓝ ☼ ◐ ◐ Z3–9 H9–1 ↕70ft (20m) ↔40ft (12m)
Forms a rounder profile and has glossier deeper green leaves than the species. One of the hardiest of the red maples, it is very fast-growing and nearly pest-free.

Nyssa sylvatica
BLACK GUM, SOUR GUM

Ⓝ ☼ ◑ ◐ Z5–9 H9–7 ↕70ft (20m) ↔30ft (9m)
Has a cone-shaped head with straight trunk and horizontal branches. Useful as a street tree or specimen. Tolerates coastal conditions, but not shade.

Populus alba
WHITE POPLAR

☼ ◐ Z4–9 H9–1 ↕70–130ft ↔50 ft (15m)
Easy to grow and very tolerant of air pollution and salt spray. However, it is weak-wooded and roots clog drain tiles and sewers, so site it carefully.

Populus trichocarpa
BLACK COTTONWOOD

Ⓝ ☼ ◊ Z4–9 H9–1
‡100ft (30m) ↔30ft (9m)
Early-leafing, very fast-growing tree with foliage that emits a balsam fragrance, especially when it first emerges. Turns yellow in autumn. Native to western North America.

Quercus bicolor
SWAMP WHITE OAK

Ⓝ ☼ ◐ ◊ Z4–8 H8–1
‡70ft (20m) ↔50ft (15m)
Found in the wild in swampy areas, it develops into a fine specimen tree with yellow to red fall color. Very drought resistant. Native to the eastern half of the United States.

Pyrus calleryana
CALLERY PEAR

☼ ◊ Z5–8 H8–2 ‡50 ft (15m) ↔50 ft (15m)
Very thorny, cone-shaped tree with foliage that turns red in late fall. Foliage is followed by small, round brown fruit. Readily sheds branches in ice storms.

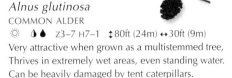

Alnus glutinosa
COMMON ALDER

☼ ◊ ◖ Z3–7 H7–1 ‡80ft (24m) ↔30ft (9m)
Very attractive when grown as a multistemmed tree, Thrives in extremely wet areas, even standing water. Can be heavily damaged by tent caterpillars.

Quercus nigra
WATER OAK

Ⓝ ☼ ◐ ◊ ꝑ Z7–9 H9–7 ‡50 ft (15m) ↔40ft (12m)
Broadly conical tree produces leaves in various shapes and sizes that drop late in fall. Smooth bark starts out brown and turns dark gray. Requires acidic soil.

Pyrus calleryana 'Bradford'
BRADFORD CALLERY PEAR

☼ ◊ Z5–8 H8–2 ‡↔40ft (12m)
Pyramidal tree that grows quickly, tolerates pollution, and is adaptable to many soil types. Tight branch crotches are weak and break easily. May be overused.

MORE CHOICES

- Acer rubrum and cultivars Z3–9 H9–1
- Alnus tenuifolia Z2–6 H6–1
- Betula fontinalis Z2–7 H7–1
- Fraxinus latifolia Z6–8 H8–6
- Magnolia grandiflora Z7–9 H9–1
- Nyssa aquatica Z5–9 H9–5
- Platanus racemosa Z3–8 H8–5
- Platanus x acerifolia Z5–8 H8–5
- Populus balsamifera Z5–9 H9–5
- Populus deltoides 'Siouxland' Z2–9 H9–1
- Populus fremontii Z1–8 H8–1
- Populus nigra 'Afghanica' Z3–9 H9–1
- Populus tremuloides Z1–8 H8–1
- Pyrus calleryana and cultivars Z5–8 H8–3
- Salix alba 'Tristis' Z3–9 H9–1
- Salix integra var. busninski Z6–9 H9–4
- Salix matsudana Z4–9 H9–4
- Sorbus aucuparia Z2–7 H7–1

TREES

Trees for dry, sunny sites

Trees, being the largest members of the plant kingdom, are generally accustomed to sunny sites, but it takes a rugged tree to survive a combination of dry soil and full sun. In locations where the soil is exceptionally well drained and/or where rainfall is sparse, a tree's roots will need to be efficient at water extraction for the tree to survive.

Koelreuteria paniculata
PANICLED GOLDEN RAIN TREE
☀ ◊ Z6–9 H9–1 ↕↔30ft (10m)
Fast-growing tree with purplish red new leaves that turn golden yellow in fall. Flowers appear in summer, followed by inflated pods.. Perfect small shade tree.

Quercus macrocarpa
BUR OAK, MOSSYCUP OAK
Ⓝ ☀ ☀ ◊ Z3–9 H9–1 ↕50ft (15m) ↔30ft (9m)
Develops a massive trunk and widely spreading habit with age. Foliage turns yellow in fall. Acorns are oval and distinctly fringed on the caps.

Pistacia chinensis
CHINESE PISTACHE
☀ ◊ Z6–9 H9–6 ↕80ft (25m) ↔30ft (10m)
Shiny, dark green leaves hold on late into fall before coloring up. Flowers (before the leaves) are followed by fruit that ripens from light blue to red. Pest-free.

Evodia danielli
KOREAN EVODIA
☀ ◊ Z5–8 H8–5 ↕↔50ft (15m)
Mid- to late summer flowers appear when few other trees are in bloom. Fruit changes from red to black in early fall to extend the show.

Fraxinus americana
WHITE ASH
Ⓝ ☀ ◊ Z6–9 H9–6 ↕80ft (24m) ↔50 ft (15m)
Pyramidal tree with yellow to dark purple to deep red fall color early in the season. Prune in fall. Ashes are susceptible to a variety of diseases and insects.

Celtis occidentalis
COMMON HACKBERRY
Ⓝ ☀ ◊ Z2–9 H9–1 ↕70ft (20m) ↔50 ft (15m)
Similar in outline at maturity to the American elm. Orange-red to deep purple, fleshy fruit ripen in early fall and hang on into winter. Good for large spaces.

Umbellularia californica
CALIFORNIA LAUREL
Ⓝ ☀ ◊ Z7–9 H9–7 ↕100ft (30m) ↔75ft (23m)
Round-headed, dense evergreen with aromatic foliage and late winter flowers. Use as a specimen or prune into a hedge or screen.

Gymnocladus dioica
KENTUCKY COFFEETREE
Ⓝ ☼ ◊ Z5–9 H9–2
↕70ft (20m) ↔50 ft (15m)
Spreading tree with pink-edged young leaves, then yellow foliage in fall. Clusters of white flowers bloom in early summer, followed by hanging pods on females.

Lagerstroemia indica
COMMON CRAPE MYRTLE
☼ ◊ Z7–9 H9–6 ↕20ft (6m) ↔20ft (6m)
Upright habit and peeling gray and brown bark. Flowers may be white, red, or purple, blooming from summer to fall. Native to China.

MORE CHOICES

- *Cladrastis kentukea* Z4–9 H9–1
- *Gleditsia triacanthos* and cultivars Z3–7 H7–1
- *Gleditsia triacanthos* f. *inermis* Z3–7 H7–1
- *Robinia pseudoacacia* and cultivars Z4–9 H9–4
- *Sophora japonica* Z5–9 H9–1

Maackia amurensis
AMUR MAACKIA
☼ ◊ Z5–7 H7–5 ↕50 ft (15m) ↔30ft (9m)
Shiny, curling bronze-colored bark and late summer flowers offer outstanding landscape appeal. Use as a street tree or grow in large containers. Pest-free.

Phellodendron amurense
AMUR CORKTREE
☼ ◊ Z3–7 H7–1 ↕45ft ↔50 ft (15m)
Broad, spreading tree with yellow fall foliage. Notable for its deeply ridged, corklike, gray-brown bark on mature trees. Requires a large space.

Robinia pseudoacacia
BLACK LOCUST
Ⓝ ☼ ◊ Z4–9 H9–4 ↕80ft (24m) ↔50 ft (15m)
Very fragrant flowers in late spring to early summer are followed by flat brown pods. Tolerant of salt. Bees are very attracted to the flowers, producing a rich honey.

Trees for acidic soils

Many of the acidic-soil loving plants available to gardeners are of woodland origin. The constant accumulation of leaf litter on the soil surface contributes to the acidity of woodland soils, so it stands to reason that many of the trees for acidic soils are a part of a woodland ecosystem in their native regions.

Magnolia x soulangiana 'Lennei'
SAUCER MAGNOLIA
☼ ◑ ♦ Z5–9 H9–6 ↕↔20ft (6m)
Flowers are much white than most saucer magnolias and appear sporadically throughout summer. Tree habit is stiff and broadly shaped with a flat top.

Betula pendula 'Youngii'
YOUNG'S EUROPEAN BIRCH
☼ ◑ ♦ Z3–7 H7–1 ↕↔30ft (10m)
Thin branches hang directly down. Often grafted on a standard and used as a specimen. Very susceptible to leaf miner and bronze birch borer.

Fagus sylvatica 'Purpurea Pendula'
PURPLE-LEAVED WEEPING BEECH
☼ ◑ ◊ ♦ Z5–7 H7–5 ↕↔10ft (3m)
Excellent mushroom-shaped weeper perfect for a large container or as a focal point. Grows slowly, and the leaves fade to purplish green in summer.

Oxydendrum arboreum
SOURWOOD
Ⓝ ☼ ♦ pH Z5–9 H9–3 ↕↔50ft (15m)
Slow-growing, pyramidal US native, rounded at the top. Flowers in summer, foliage turns yellow, red, and purple in autumn. Excellent as a specimen.

Liquidambar styraciflua 'Worplesdon'
WORPLESDON SWEET GUM
Ⓝ ☼ ♦ Z6–9 H9–6 ↕100ft (30m) ↔75ft (23m)
Symmetrical, cone-shaped tree, perfect for a large lawn, woodland, or street planting. Spiky, round fruit and good fall color are further assets.

Cornus nuttallii
PACIFIC DOGWOOD
Ⓝ ☼ ◊ Z7–8 H8–7 ↕↔50ft (15m)
Bracts surround showy purple- and green-colored true flowers. Orange to red fruit follows. May develop splitting bark from cold intolerance.

Sassafras albidum
COMMON SASSAFRAS

Ⓝ ☼ ◖ ꚛ Z4–8 H8–3 ↕100ft (30m) ↔75ft (23m)
Forms thickets of flat-topped, short, twisted branches.
Features mahogany-brown bark and fall foliage in
shades of yellow to orange to red and purple.

Styrax obassia
FRAGRANT SNOWBELL

☼ ☀ ● Z6–8 H8–6
↕40ft (12m) ↔22ft (7m)
Wonderful winter shape has many winding,
turning branches. Leaves are easily injured in
early spring, because they emerge very early.

MORE CHOICES

- *Acer palmatum* and cultivars Z5–8 H8–2
- *Acer palmatum* 'Atropurpureum' Z6–8 H8–2
- *Acer palmatum* [Dissectum selections]
  Z6–8 H8–2
- *Betula pendula* and cultivars Z2–7 H7–1
- *Fagus sylvatica* Z4–7 H9–4
- *Franklinia alatamaha* Z6–9 H9–6
- *Halesia monticola* Z6–9 H9–6
- *Liquidambar styraciflua* Z6–9 H9–6
- *Magnolia denudata* Z6–9 H9–6
- *Nyssa sylvatica* Z4–9 H9–2
- *Populus alba* Z3–9 H9–1
- *Quercus robur* Z5–8 H8–3
- *Quercus robur* 'Fastigiata' Z5–8 H8–3
- *Quercus rubra* Z5–9 H9–5
- *Sorbus intermedia* Z5–8 H8–3
- *Stewartia pseudocamellia* Z5–8 H8–1
- *Styrax japonicum* Z6–8 H8–6

Acer japonicum 'Sango Kaku'
CORALBARK MAPLE

☼ ◖ Z5–8 H8–2 ↕↔20ft (6m)
Upright tree with brightly colored stems. Best used as
a specimen or accent plant; also nice in a group or
border. Like all Japanese maples, it has few problems.

Halesia diptera var. magniflora
TWO-WINGED SILVERBELL

Ⓝ ☼ ☀ ◖ Z4–8 H8–1 ↕20ft (6m) ↔30ft (10m)
Larger flowers than the species. Winged green fruit
appear after the flowers. Foliage on this rounded tree
turns yellow in autumn. Protect from wind.

Acer japonicum 'Aconitifolium'
FULL-MOON MAPLE

☼ ◖ Z5–7 H7–5 ↕↔30ft (10m)
Small red flowers appear in early spring before the
leaves. Leaves are very divided and sharply toothed
on the edges. One of the best trees for red fall color.

Acer palmatum
JAPANESE MAPLE

☼ ◖ Z5–8 H8–2 ↕↔20ft (6m)
Leaves vary greatly in color and shape, and habot
ranges from upright to weeping. Can be grown as a
single-stemmed tree or multistemmed large shrub.

Trees for alkaline soils

On the opposite end of the scale from acidic soils are alkaline soils, also called white alkali soils. They are most often the result of the geology of the surrounding minerals and the presence of limestone or chalky deposits. Although the mineral content is higher in these soils, organic matter is often low. Here are some trees that are adaptable to high-pH conditions.

Koelreuteria paniculata
PANICLED GOLDEN RAIN TREE
☼ ◊ Z6–9 H9–1 ↕↔30ft (10m)
Showy yellow flowers give way to fruit in midsummer. New leaves are purplish red, turning to bright green and finally to yellow and orange-yellow in autumn.

Acer campestre
HEDGE MAPLE
☼ ☼ ◊ Z6–8 H8–4 ↕↔25–55ft (8–17m)
Slow-growing, very adaptable tree. Often used as a street tree in urban areas: it tolerates compaction around the roots, heavy pruning, and air pollution.

Acer negundo 'Flamingo'
FLAMINGO BOXELDER
Ⓝ ☼ ☼ ◊ Z5–8 H8–3 ↕50ft (15m) ↔30ft (10m)
Pink young leaves age to green with white edges. To encourage production of more pink leaves, prune plants in late winter. Grows very quickly.

Acer platanoides
NORWAY MAPLE
☼ ☼ ◊ Z3–7 H7–1 ↕80ft (25m) ↔50 ft (15m)
Tolerates a wide variety of adverse conditions, such as pollution and extremes in soil type and moisture, so it is widely used in parks and street-tree plantings.

Acer negundo 'Variegatum'
VARIEGATED BOXELDER
Ⓝ ☼ ◊ Z5–8 H8–3 ↕↔50ft (15m)
An excellent specimen tree for smaller gardens. The fruits are variegated like the leaves. Prune out shoots with all-green or all-white foliage to maintain plant.

Albizia julibrissin
SILK-TREE, MIMOSA

☼ ◊ Z6–9 H9–6 ‡↔30ft (10m)

Light gray-brown seedpods persist through the winter. Grows quickly and normally is not long-lived. Very susceptible to wilt and webworm. Self-sows strongly.

Fagus sylvatica
EUROPEAN BEECH

☼ ☀ ◊◑ Z5–7 H7–5 ‡80ft (24m) ↔50 ft (15m)

Very formal, pyramidal tree that branches to the ground. Produces triangular nuts inside a bristly, woody husk. Bronze-russet fall color.

Morus nigra
BLACK MULBERRY

☼ ◊ Z5–9 H9–5

‡40ft (12m) ↔50ft (15m)

Rounded tree with dense branching. Fruits are edible and relished by birds and wildlife. Fall color ranges from green to yellow-green to yellow. Native to China.

Fagus sylvatica 'Dawyck Purple'
DAWYCK PURPLE EUROPEAN BEECH

☼ ☀ ◊◑ Z5–7 H7–5 ‡70ft (20m) ↔15ft (5m)

Makes a wonderful focal point in the garden and is relatively pest-free, except for bark diseases. Plant with green-leaved plants for foliage contrast.

Malus floribunda
JAPANESE FLOWERING CRABAPPLE

☼ ◊ Z4–8 H8–1 ‡↔30ft (10m)

Fragrant flowers, produced each year, are followed by small yellow and red fruit that usually drops soon after ripening. Prone to scab, fireblight, and powdery mildew.

MORE CHOICES

- *Acer campestre* 'Evelyn' Z6–8 H8–6
- *Acer negundo* and cultivars Z5–8 H8–3
- *Acer platanoides* and cultivars Z3–7 H7–1
- *Fagus sylvatica* Z4–7 H9–4
- *Laburnum alpinum* Z5–8 H8–5
- *Populus alba* Z3–9 H9–1
- *Prunus serrulata* 'Shirotae' Z5–8 H8–5
- *Quercus macrocarpa* Z3–9 H9–1
- *Sophora japonica* Z5–9 H9–1
- *Tilia tomentosa* Z6–9 H9–6

Aesculus californica
CALIFORNIA BUCKEYE

Ⓝ ☼ ◊ Z7–8 H8–7 ‡↔30ft (10m)

Fragran flowers may also be pink. Long, pear-shaped fruit capsules follow the flowers. Rounded, symmetrical growth habit. Native to California.

Paulownia tomentosa
ROYAL PAULOWNIA, EMPRESS TREE

☼ ◊ Z5–8 H8–5 ‡40ft (12m) ↔30ft (9m)

Light brown, hairy flower buds are apparent all winter. A closeup of the vanilla-scented flowers reveals yellow stripes inside spotted, pale violet petals.

TREES

Trees for clay soils

Clay soils are a double-edged sword. Clay by nature has the ability to hold large quantities of nutrients, but its physical characteristics make it a challenge for even the most stalwart trees. In the presence of too much water, clay soils expand and will not drain well, and with too little water, they contract and crack. These trees can meet the challenge of clay soils.

Fraxinus excelsior
EUROPEAN ASH
☼ ◐ ◑ Z5–8 H8–3 ‡100ft (30m) ↔70ft (20m)
Rounded, spreading profile with upcurving lower branches. Foliage sometimes turns yellow in fall. Susceptible to borer damage.

MORE CHOICES

- *Acer pseudoplatanus* Z4–7 H7–1
- *Aesculus x carnea* 'Briotii' Z5–9 H9–5
- *Carpinus betulus* 'Fastigata' Z4–8 H8–3
- *Cercis canadensis* Z6–9 H9–3
- *Cercis mexicana* Z6–9 H9–3
- *Crataegus viridis* Z5–7 H7–1
- *Eucalyptus glaucescens* Z9–10 H10–9
- *Fraxinus excelsior* and cultivars Z5–8 H8–5
- *Magnolia x soulangiana* Z5–9 H9–5
- *Magnolia x soulangiana* var. *lennei* Z5–9 H9–5
- *Populus nigra* 'Afghanica' Z3–9 H9–1

Aesculus x carnea
RED HORSE CHESTNUT
☼ ◑ ◐ Z7–8 H8–6
‡70ft (20) ↔50ft (15)
Flowers appear late spring to early summer, followed by spiny fruit. Distinctive, rounded growth habit. Prone to canker, Japanese beetles, and scale insects.

Magnolia x soulangiana
SAUCER MAGNOLIA
☼ ◑ ◐ Z5–9 H9–5 ‡20ft (6m) ↔20ft (6m)
Often grown as a low-branched, multistemmed tree. Flowers at an early age and early in the season; they are often damaged by frost. Tolerant of pollution.

Cercis canadensis var. *alba*
EASTERN REDBUD
Ⓝ ☼ ◑ ◐ Z6–9 H9–3 ‡↔30ft (10m)
Early spring flowers often last 2 to 3 weeks. This appealing small tree looks well used in a woodland border and other naturalized situations.

Carpinus betulus
EUROPEAN HORNBEAM
☼ ◑ ◐ Z4–8 H8–1
‡80ft (25m) ↔70ft (20m)
The smooth gray bark is fluted and muscly-looking. Leaves are yellow in fall and unusually free of pests. Excellent as a screening plant, as a hedge, or in planters.

Quercus palustris
PIN OAK
Ⓝ ☼ ◑ ◐ Z5–8 H8–3 ‡70ft (20m) ↔40ft (12m)
Very striking growth form, with a clearly pyramidal outline and horizontal branching habit. Fall color can be an outstanding red. Tolerant of city conditions.

Prunus 'Okame'
OKAME CHERRY

☼ ◊ ◐ Z5–8 H8–5 ↕30ft (10m) ↔25ft (8m)

Flowers appear in early spring. Narrowly oblong leaves are sharply toothed and turn orange and red in autumn. A cross between Taiwan cherry and Fuji cherry.

Quercus robur
ENGLISH OAK

☼ ◑ ◊ Z5–8 H8–3 ↕120ft (37m) ↔80ft (24m)

Open, massive tree, valuable for parks and other large sites. Mildew can be a serious problem. Native to Europe, northern Africa, and western Asia.

Malus hupehensis
TEA CRABAPPLE

☼ ◊ Z5–8 H8–5 ↕↔50ft (15m)

Deep pink buds open to fragrant white flowers in mid- to late spring. Fast growing and vase-shaped when young, then spreads. Fireblight prone. Native to China.

Betula jacquemontii
WHITE-BARKED HIMALAYAN BIRCH

☼ ◑ ◐ Z5–7 H7–3 ↕60ft (18m) ↔30ft (9m)

Tapered dark green leaves turn yellow in autumn. Striking focal point in the garden. Appears to be resistant to borer. Native to China and the Himalayas.

Sorbus alnifolia
KOREAN MOUNTAIN ASH

☼ ◑ ◊ Z5–8 H8–5 ↕50ft (15m) ↔25ft (8m)

A specimen tree for the yard, not the street, this species of mountainash is too little known and used. Leaves turn yellow and orange in fall. Round fruit in shades of red persist into winter for a spectacular effect.

TREES

Trees for coastal exposure

As anyone a "salt spray" away from the coast can attest only the toughest trees around can survive the coast. They must endure both high winds as well as the effects of salt laden air not to mention the very porous sandy soils. These are a selection of trees that work well as a first line of defense for your coastal garden.

Populus alba
WHITE POPLAR

☀ ◊ Z4–9 H9–1 ‡70–130ft ↔50 ft (15m)

Wavy-edged leaves turn yellow in fall on this wide-spreading tree. Drought-tolerant, it grows in any kind of soil except saturated. Native to North Africa, Turkey, and the former USSR.

Ulmus parvifolia
CHINESE ELM

☀ ◊ Z5–9 H9–5 ‡↔50ft (15m)

Spreading tree with flaking orange and brown bark. Very small red flowers appear in late summer, followed by green fruit and yellow/red leaves in late fall.

Ulmus pumila
SIBERIAN ELM

☀ ◊ Z3–9 H9–1 ‡50ft (15m) ↔40ft (12m)

Although fast-growing and very tolerant, this should be planted with a caveat in mind: it has a tendency to break up in ice storms. Often better as a hedge.

Acer platanoides 'Royal Red'
NORWAY MAPLE

☀ ◐ ◊ Z3–7 H7–1 ‡80ft (25m) ↔50 ft

Fast-growing European native with clusters of small yellow flowers in spring and (often) yellow leaves in fall. Shown is a dark-leaved selection.

Ilex aquifolium
ENGLISH HOLLY

☀ ◐ ● ◊ Z7–9 H9–7 ‡70ft (20m) ↔20ft (6m)

Upright evergreen with dense foliage and gray bark. Berries are prized for winter decorations. Grows best in well-drained soil. Native to Europe, N Africa, Asia.

Acer platanoides 'Deborah'
NORWAY MAPLE

☀ ◐ ◊ Z3–7 H7–1 ‡80ft (24m) ↔50 ft (15m)

Leaves open bright red, become deep reddish green in summer, and turn orange-yellow in fall. Prefers well-drained soil. Excellent contrast to other green shades.

Acer platanoides 'Drummondii'
NORWAY MAPLE

☀ ◐ ◊ Z3–7 H7–1 ‡80ft (25m) ↔50 ft

Situate carefully: the variegated leaves are prone to burning in full sun. Use as a focal point or with red-leaved trees and shrubs to set off the showy foliage.

TREES

Ilex opaca
AMERICAN HOLLY
Ⓝ ☼ ☼ ☀ ◐ Z5–9 H9–5
↕45ft (14m) ↔4ft (1.2m)
Crimson (sometimes yellow or
orange) berries enhance this
evergreen in winter. Like most
hollies, spiny leaves are
occasionally smooth-
edged. May be pruned
hard once established.

Fraxinus excelsior
EUROPEAN ASH
☼ ◐ Z5–8 H8–3 ↕100ft (30m) ↔70ft (20m)
Fast-growing, wide-spreading European tree with
distinctive black buds in winter and yellow leaves
in fall. Makes an excellent specimen tree.

MORE CHOICES

- *Acer platanoides* 'Columnarbroad'
  Z3–7 H7–1
- *Acer platanoides* 'Columnare' Z3–7 H7–1
- *Acer platanoides* 'Crimson Sentry' Z3–7 H7–1
- *Acer platanoides* 'Emerald Queen'
  Z3–7 H7–1
- *Acer platanoides* 'Globosum' Z3–7 H7–1
- *Acer platanoides* 'Pond' Z3–7 H7–1
- *Acer platanoides* 'Princeton Gold' Z3–7 H7–1
- *Acer platanoides* 'Royal Red' Z3–7 H7–1
- *Acer platanoides* 'Summershade' Z3–7 H7–1
- *Arbutus menziesii* Z7–9 H9–7
- *Crataegus crus-gallli* Z34–7 H7–1
- *Fraxinus excelsior* 'Aureafolia' Z5–8 H8–3
- *Salix alba* 'Tristis' Z3–9 H9–1
- *Sorbus aucuparia* Z2–7 H7–1

TREES

Tilia cordata
SMALL-LEAVED LINDEN
☼ ◑ ◊ Z3–8 H8–1 ↕100ft (30m) ↔40ft (12m)
Pyramidal tree with smooth, silver-gray bark and
yellow leaves in autumn. The midsummer flowers are
fragrant. Excellent as a large hedge.

Trees for exposed, windy sites

The effects of high winds on plants are twofold. First, the sheer force of the wind structurally challenges (or even damages) the plants. Second, the wind dries the foliage and robs the plants of moisture. The following are rugged enough to withstand high wind areas, and some can also be used as windbreaks.

Ilex decidua
POSSUMHAW

Ⓝ ☼ ◐ ◌ Z5–9 H9–1 ↕↔6–20ft (2–6m)

Foliage turns yellow in fall. Fruits ripen in September, hanging onto the tree throughout winter. The light gray stems stand out against an evergreen backdrop.

Crataegus phaenopyrum
WASHINGTON HAWTHORN

Ⓝ ☼ ◌◌ Z4–8 H8–1 ↕↔30ft (9m)

Very dense, thorny US native with white flowers in early summer and red to orange fruit in fall. Good specimen plant.

Crataegus viridis 'Winter King'
GREEN HAWTHORN

Ⓝ ☼ ◌◌ Z5–7 H7–5 ↕20ft (6m) ↔15ft (5m)

Rounded and very thorny, with gray-green, waxy stems. Fruits persist into winter and are larger than the species. Less rust-susceptible than other hawthorns.

Crataegus x lavallei
LAVALLE HAWTHORN

☼ ◌◌ Z5–7 H7–4
↕22ft (7m) ↔30ft (9m)

Bright red to orange-red fruit with brown speckles complement the bronze to coppery red leaves in fall. The fruit last well into winter if not eaten by birds.

TREES

Carpinus caroliniana
AMERICAN HORNBEAM

Ⓝ ☼ ◐ ◊ Z3–9 H9–1 ↕↔30ft (9m)

Slow grower with smooth gray bark that is sinewy and fluted, much like muscles. Leaves change to yellow, orange, and red in fall. Tolerates seasonal flooding.

MORE CHOICES

- *Acer platanoides* and cultivars Z3–7 H7–1
- *Carpinus betulus* Z4–8 H8–1
- *Carpinus betulus* 'Fastigata' Z4–8 H8–3
- *Carpinus japonica* Z5–8 H8–1
- *Crataegus crus-galli* 'Inermis' Z4–7 H7–1
- *Crateagus laevigata* 'Paul's Scarlet' Z5–8 H8–3
- *Crataegus punctata* 'Ohio Pioneer' Z5–7 H7–1
- *Crataegus viridis* Z5–7 H7–1
- *Crataegus x mordensis* 'Snowbird' Z3–8 H8–1
- *Eucalyptus archeri* Z9–10 H10–9
- *Eucalyptus coccifera* Z9–11 H12–10
- *Eucalyptus crenulata* Z9–10 H10–9
- *Eucalyptus glaucescens* Z9–10 H10–9
- *Eucalyptus gregsoniana* Z9–10 H10–9
- *Eucalyptus mitchelliana* Z8–10 H10–8
- *Eucalyptus neglecta* Z8–10 H10–8
- *Eucalyptus parvula* Z8–10 H10–8
- *Eucalyptus pauciflora* ssp. *debeuzevillei* Z8–10 H10–8
- *Eucalyptus stellulata* Z8–10 H10–8
- *Eucalyptus subcrenulata* Z8–10 H10–8
- *Eucalyptus urnigera* Z8–10 H10–8
- *Ilex aquifolium* Z7–9 H9–7
- *Ilex opaca* Z5–9 H9–5
- *Ilex x attenuata* 'Fosteri' Z6–9 H9–4
- *Nyssa sylvatica* Z4–9 H9–2
- *Platanus x acerifolia* Z5–8 H8–5
- *Platanus x acerifolia* 'Bloodgood' Z5–8 H8–1
- *Populus alba* Z3–9 H9–1
- *Populus balsamifera* Z5–9 H9–5
- *Populus deltoides* 'Siouxland' Z2–9 H9–1
- *Populus fremontii* Z1–8 H8–1
- *Populus nigra* 'Afghanica' Z3–9 H9–1
- *Populus tremuloides* 'Erecta' Z1–8 H8–1
- *Ulmus parvifolia* Z5–9 H9–5

Eucalyptus pauciflora ssp. niphophila
ALPINE SNOW GUM

☼ ◊ Z8–9 H10–8 ↕↔to 20ft (6m)

Spreading and hardier than the species, this bears white flowers from late spring to summer and long, narrow leaves. Native to Australia and Tasmania.

Ilex x 'Nellie R. Stevens'
NELLIE R. STEVENS HOLLY

☼ ◐ ◊ Z7–9 H9–7 ↕22ft (6.5m) ↔12ft (4m)

Very heavy producer of red, rounded fruit. Needs a male holly (such as *Ilex cornuta*) that flowers at the same time to pollinate it effectively. Fast-growing.

Populus trichocarpa
BLACK COTTONWOOD

Ⓝ ☼ ◊◑ Z5–9 H9–1 ↕100ft (30m) ↔30 ft (9m)

Fast-growing tree with glossy, oval, balsam-scented leaves, white beneath, and turning yellow in the fall. Native to western North America.

Eucalyptus perriniana
SPINNING GUM

☼ ◊ Z8–10 H10–8 ↕↔30ft (9m)

A dense, basally branching tree with smooth, flaking, off-white, gray, or green bark. Bears white flowers in summer. Aromatic, as is typical for gums.

Eucalyptus nicholii
NARROW-LEAVED BLACK PEPPERMINT

☼ ◐ ◊◑ Z9–10 H10–9 ↕50ft (15m) ↔40ft (12m)

Peppermint-scented leaves and gray to reddish brown bark characterize this stately tree with white flowers borne in autumn. Aphids and scale can be a problem.

Trees for air-polluted sites

When contemplating planting street trees or other specimens in a highly polluted area, remember that some pollutants (including gases such as carbon monoxide and sulfur compounds) exert a strong negative impact on the health of plants. Presented here are some trees that have shown tolerance to the often damaging effects of air pollutants.

Amelanchier laevis
ALLEGHENY SERVICEBERRY
Ⓝ ☼ ◑ Z5–9 H9–3 ‡↔30ft (10m)
Purple-black, sweet fruits, relished by birds and animals, follow the spring flowers. May be grown in large containers. Leaves turn orange-red to bright red in fall.

Laburnum x waterei 'Vossii'
VOSS'S GOLDENCHAIN TREE
☼ ◑ Z5–8 H8–3 ‡↔30ft (10m)
Has a denser habit and longer flower clusters than its hybrid parent, plus olive green, fissured bark. Plant in protected spots near buildings.

Morus alba 'Chaparral'
CHAPARRAL MULBERRY
☼ ◑◐ Z3–8 H8–1 ‡6–8ft (2–2.5m) ↔8–12ft (2.5–4m)
Nonfruiting form of the common mulberry, usually grafted on a standard. Easily transplanted, withstands droughty conditions, and very salt tolerant.

Prunus 'Tai Haku'
GREAT WHITE CHERRY
☼ ◐◑ Z6–8 H8–6 ‡↔30ft (10m)
Leaves are reddish bronze as they unfold and turn yellow-orange in autumn. Habit is an inverted cone. As with other cherries, prone to many problems.

Liriodendron tulipifera
TULIPTREE
Ⓝ ☼ ☼ ▥ Z5–9 H9–1 ‡100ft (30m) ↔50 ft (15m)
Fast-growing tree with golden yellow foliage in fall. Aphids are a big problem, as are scale, powdery mildew, and leaf spot. Native to the eastern US.

Malus 'Indian Magic'
INDIAN MAGIC CRABAPPLE

☼ ☽ ◊ Z4–8 H8–1 ↕↔20ft (6m)

Small, glossy red fruits, changing to orange, follow the flowers and hang on into winter. Prune immediately after flowering. Moderately susceptible to scab.

Malus 'Royalty'
ROYALTY CRABAPPLE

☼ ☽ ◊ Z4–8 H8–1 ↕↔25ft (8m)

Bears sparse, dark red-purple fruits after the spring flowers. Upright grower, with brilliant purple foliage in fall. Severely prone to scab and fireblight.

Ginkgo biloba 'Autumn Gold'
AUTUMN GOLD MAIDENHAIR TREE

☼ ◊ Z3–9 H9–1 ↕50 ft (15m) ↔30ft (9m)

Bright green, distinctly fan-shaped leaves turn gold in fall. Used extensively in urban and suburban sites because of its tough constitution. Basically pest free..

Malus 'Donald Wyman'
DONALD WYMAN CRABAPPLE

☼ ☽ ◊ Z4–8 H8–1 ↕20ft (6m) ↔25ft (8m)

Red to pink flower buds open white. Tends to flower more heavily every other year. Eventually large and spreading, so situate where it can reach its potential.

Magnolia denudata
YULAN MAGNOLIA

☼ ☽ ◊ Z6–9 H9–6 ↕30ft (9m) ↔30ft (9m)

Very early-blooming fragrant flowers are sometimes injured by late spring freezes. Plant as a specimen in a large yard or park situation. Native to central China.

MORE CHOICES

- *Acer pseudoplatanus* Z4–7 H7–1
- *Carpinus betulus* Z4–8 H8–1
- *Carpinus betulus* 'Fastigata' Z4–8 H8–3
- *Celtis occidentalis* Z2–9 H9–1
- *Crataegus laevigata* 'Crimson Cloud' Z5–8 H8–3
- *Fagus sylvatica* Z4–7 H9–4
- *Fraxinus americana* Z6–9 H9–6
- *Fraxinus americana* 'Junginger' Z4–9 H9–1
- *Ginkgo biloba* Z5–9 H9–3
- *Koelreuteria paniculata* Z6–9 H9–1
- *Liriodendron tulipifera* 'Fastigiatum' Z5–9 H9–2
- *Magnolia grandiflora* Z7–9 H9–1
- *Malus* hybrids and cultivars Z4–8 H8–2
- *Morus nigra* Z5–9 H9–5
- *Phellodendron amurense* Z4–7 H8–5
- *Platanus occidentalis* Z5–8 H8–3
- *Populus alba* Z3–9 H9–1
- *Quercus rubra* Z5–9 H9–5
- *Robinia pseudoacacia* Z4–9 H9–4
- *Sophora japonica* Z5–9 H9–1
- *Tilia cordata* Z3–8 H8–1

TREES

Large trees

These are trees that normally reside in forest conditions, where large size rules. They need plenty of room in a garden setting, but, when given the proper setting, they can be impressive specimens. The life span of many of these trees can be measured in centuries, so these trees can easily become living legacies.

MORE CHOICES

- *Acer saccharinum* Z4–8 H8–1
- *Acer saccharum* Z4–8 H8–1
- *Carya ovata* Z4–8 H8–1
- *Catalpa speciosa* Z4–8 H8–1
- *Cercidiphyllum japonicum* Z4–8 H8–1
- *Corylus colurna* Z5–7 H7–5
- *Fraxinus americana* Z6–9 H9–6
- *Liquidambar styraciflua* Z6–9 H9–6
- *Magnolia acuminata* Z4–8 H8–2
- *Nyssa sylvatica* Z4–9 H9–2
- *Quercus frainetto* Z5–8 H8–1

TREES

Acer macrophyllum
OREGON MAPLE

Ⓝ ☼ ◊ Z5–9 H9–4 ↕100ft (30m) ↔75ft (23m)
Fragrant yellow flowers appear with the large leaves in spring. A rounded head and yellow-orange fall color are other features.

Acer platanoides
NORWAY MAPLE

☼ ◐ ◊ Z3–7 H7–1 ↕80ft (25m) ↔50 ft
Leaves drop late in the season after turning a golden yellow. Develops a symmetrical, rounded crown with age. Easy to transplant and pollution tolerant.

Magnolia acuminata
CUCUMBERTREE MAGNOLIA

Ⓝ ☼ ◐ ◊ Z4–8 H8–2 ↕70ft (20m) ↔30ft (9m)
Wide-spreading branches and freedom from pests make this tree perfect for parks, estates, and golf courses. Pinkish red, cucumber-like fruit in fall.

Fagus sylvatica 'Asplenifolia'
ASPLENIFOLIA EUROPEAN BEECH

☼ ◐ ◊◊ Z5–7 H7–5 ↕80ft (24m) ↔50 ft (15m)
Deeply cut, almost feathery foliage turns golden brown in fall. A fine specimen tree that withstands heavy pruning if needed to correct growth faults.

Betula pendula
EUROPEAN WHITE BIRCH

☼ ◐ ◊ Z2–7 H7–1 ↕80ft (24m) ↔30ft (9m)
Leafs out early and tends to hold its leaves later in fall, when they turn yellow-green. It transplants easily and grows quickly. Very susceptible to miners and borers.

Quercus alba
WHITE OAK

Ⓝ ☼ ◐ ◊ ☙ Z5–9 H8–1 ↕↔60–100ft (30m) (18–30m)

A handsome oak with majestic, wide-spreading branches at maturity. Foliage turns a rich wine red in fall. Its acorns are relished by birds and mammals.

Quercus myrsinifolia
CHINESE EVERGREEN OAK

☼ ◊ Z7–9 H9–6 ↕40ft (12m) ↔30ft (9m)

Underused, round-headed tree with emerging purple-bronze foliage. Excellent as a street tree; no pest or disease problems. Tolerant of heat and a range of soils.

Quercus macrocarpa
BUR OAK, MOSSYCUP OAK

Ⓝ ☼ ◐ ◊ Z3–9 H9–1 ↕50 ft (15m) ↔30ft (9m)

Coarse but stately tree with a huge trunk and broadly spreading crown. Foliage turns yellow in fall, and the acorns have distinctive fringing on the edges.

Gymnocladus dioica
KENTUCKY COFFEETREE

Ⓝ ☼ ◊ Z5–9 H9–2 ↕70ft (20m) ↔50 ft (15m)

Of greatest interest is the dark brown, scaly, curly bark, found even on young branches. Very late to leaf out in spring. Thick, leathery pods hang on through winter.

Liriodendron tulipifera
TULIPTREE

Ⓝ ☼ ◐ ☙ Z5–9 H9–1 ↕100ft (30m) ↔50 ft (15m)

Greenish yellow flowers in late spring are followed by conical seedheads that persist into winter. Yellow fall color brightens large spaces, where this tree does best.

TREES

Medium-sized trees

For the owner of an average-sized property, medium-sized trees fit the scale of the landscape much better than very large trees. In this smaller scale, these trees can be used as specimens, or they can be used as a part of a more integrated garden setting to provide cover for shade-loving perennials or a garden chair.

Acer campestre
HEDGE MAPLE
☼ ☀ ◊ Z6–8 H8–4 ‡↔25–55ft (8–17m)
A dense, roughly pyramidal, slowly growing tree tolerant of adverse growing conditions. Pest-free and perfect for urban plantings.

Stewartia pseudocamellia
JAPANESE STEWARTIA
☼ ◊ ⊟ Z5–8 H8–0 ‡↔50ft (15m)
A Japanese tree valued for its red to purple fall color, distinctive sinewy and peeling bark that is particularly interesting in winter, and its pyramidal shape.

Acer japonicum
FULL-MOON MAPLE
☼ ☀ ◊ Z5–7 H7–1 ‡↔30ft (9m)
After flowering, soft green leaves appear then turn golden yellow and red in fall. A lovely feature in a border or used a specimen. Native to Japan.

Koelreuteria paniculata
PANICLED GOLDEN RAIN TREE
☼ ◊ Z6–9 H9–1 ↕↔30ft (10m)
Opening leaves are purplish red, become bright green, then turn golden yellow in fall. Yellow flowers appear in midsummer and become inflated fruit.

Magnolia x loebneri 'Leonard Messel'
LEONARD MESSEL MAGNOLIA
☼ ☼ ◊ Z5–9 H9–5 ↕25ft (8m) ↔20ft (6m)
A broad-rounded tree with fragrant, early flowers. As with other magnolias, pests and diseases can attack , such as scale, thrips, mildews, and anthracnose.

Oxydendrum arboreum
SOURWOOD
Ⓝ ☼ ◊ pH Z5–9 H9–3 ↕↔50ft (15m)
Produces early fall color in a superb display of yellow, red, and purple, often all at once. Good specimen for the home landscape, but intolerant of city conditions.

Parrotia persica
PERSIAN PARROTIA
☼ ◊ Z4–7 H7–1 ↕↔50 ft (15m)
A useful accent tree with yellow, orange, and red fall color; peeling gray, green, white, and brown bark; and excellent pest and disease resistance. Native to Iran.

MORE CHOICES

- *Acer griseum* Z4–8 H10–3
- *Acer grosseri* Z6–8 H8–5
- *Cladrastis kentukea* Z4–9 H9–1
- *Cornus kousa* var. *chinensis* Z5–8 H8–4
- *Davidia involucrata* Z6–8 H8–6
- *Gleditsia triacanthos* Z3–7 H7–1
- *Pterostyrax hispida* Z5–8 H8–5
- *Robinia pseudoacacia* Z4–9 H9–3
- *Styrax japonicus* Z6–8 H8–6

Sassafras albidum
COMMON SASSAFRAS
Ⓝ ☼ ◊ pH Z4–8 H8–3 ↕100ft (30m) ↔75ft (23m)
Yellow, slightly fragrant flowers appear before the leaves in early spring, followed by dark blue fruit on bright red stems. Excellent multicolor fall display.

Styrax obassia
FRAGRANT SNOWBELL
☼ ☼ ◊ Z6–8 H8–6 ↕40ft (12m) ↔22ft (7m)
Open and rounded at maturity, this Japanese native makes a nice focal point for the home garden. Offers flowers in spring and twisting branches in winter.

TREES

Small trees

Where space is limited, small trees lend the grace and presence that their larger relatives also provide, including flowers, fruit, bark, fall foliage color, and overall form, all of which are important elements of landscape design in any garden. However, unlike their bigger cousins, small trees can be accommodated in all but the smallest of landscapes.

Prunus 'Okame'
OKAME CHERRY
☼ ◊ ◖ Z5–8 H8–5 ↕30ft (10m) ↔25ft (8m)
Fast-growing, with dark green, finely textured leaves that turn yellow-orange to orange-red in fall. Prized for its burst of spring color after a dreary winter.

Acer palmatum
JAPANESE MAPLE
☼ ◊ Z5–8 H8–2 ↕↔20ft (6m)
Slow-growing, usually multistemmed tree. New foliage is often bright red, and fall color is scarlet, orange, or yellow. Growth habit tends to be in horizontal planes.

Cercis chinensis
CHINESE REDBUD
☼ ☀ ◖ Z6–9 H9–3 ↕20ft (6m) ↔15ft (5m)
Glossy, dark green, heart-shaped leaves expand after the flowers appear in early spring. Plant where it will stay, because larger specimens resent transplanting.

Carpinus caroliniana
AMERICAN HORNBEAM
Ⓝ ☼ ☀ ◊ Z3–9 H9–1 ↕↔30ft (9m)
Because there appear to be muscles flexing beneath the undulating surface of blue-gray, smooth bark, this tree acquired the common name of Musclewood.

TREES

MORE CHOICES

- *Acer triflorum* z4–8 H8–1
- *Aesculus pavia* z5–9 H9–5
- *Aesculus pavia* 'Atrosanguinea' z5–9 H9–5
- *Aralia elata* z4–9 H9–1
- *Arbutus unedo* 'Compacta' z8–9 H9–6
- *Cercis occidentalis* z8–10 H12–9
- *Cornus alternifolia* 'Argentea' z4–8 H8–1
- *Cornus florida* z5–8 H8–5
- *Eucalyptus pauciflora* ssp. *niphophila* z9–10 H10–9
- *Eucryphia glutinosa* z8–11 H12–8
- *Ficus carica* z7–11 H12–1
- *Laburnum alpinum* z5–8 H8–5
- *Laburnum anagyroides* z6–9 H8–5
- *Magnolia* x *soulangiana* z5–9 H9–5
- *Ostrya virginiana* z5–9 H9–2
- *Rhus trichocarpa* z7–9 H9–7
- *Sorbus vilmorinii* z6–8 H8–6
- *Sorbus vilmorinii* 'Pearly King' z6–8 H8–6
- *Viburnum prunifolium* z3–9 H9–1

TREES

Aesculus californica
CALIFORNIA BUCKEYE

Ⓝ ☼ ◊ z7–8 H8–7 ↕↔30ft (10m)

A closeer look of the foliage reveals glossy, dark green leaves that, in dry climates, may drop in midsummer. If given plenty of moisture, the leaves persist into fall.

Laburnum x *watereri*
GOLDENCHAIN TREE

☼ ◊ z6–8 H8–3 ↕↔25ft (8m)

Upright oval- to round-shaped tree. Group in threes and fives for a spectacular show in spring. Twig blight is a common problem.

Labernum alpinum
SCOTCH LABURNUM

☼ ◊ z5–8 H8–5 ↕↔30ft (10m)

A round- to flat-shaped crown and a short, brawny trunk support the foliage. Use as a focal point in a small garden. Native to the southern Alps, Yugoslavia, Czechoslovakia, and northern Apennines.

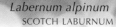

Cercis canadensis
EASTERN REDBUD

Ⓝ ☼ ◑ ◊ z6–9 H9–3 ↕↔30ft (10m)

Best when situated in a naturalized garden or border, alone or in groups. New leaves open reddish purple and change to yellow in fall.

Trees that spread or weep

Weeping trees create have an undeniably recognizable presence in a garden. They can be used as specimens or as a part of a larger garden design, perhaps to echo a waterfall or water feature. Many weeping trees are sports that must be grafted to a standard trunk; otherwise, they would simply grow horizontally and cover the ground.

Malus 'Red Jade'
RED JADE CRABAPPLE

☼ ☀ ◑ Z4–8 H6–1 ↕12ft (4m) ↔20ft (6m)

Deep pink flower buds open white and then mature to glossy red fruit relished by birdsa and animals. A perfect specimen for featuring in the front yard.

Morus alba 'Chaparral'
CHAPARRAL MULBERRY

☼ ◑◐ Z3–8 H8–1 ↕6–8ft (2–2.5m) ↔8–12ft (2.5–4m)

A nonfruiting selection with yellow-green fall color. Dense and fast-growing, so it can be used to hide unsightly objects such as wellheads and tree stumps.

Betula pendula 'Youngii'
YOUNG'S EUROPEAN BIRCH

☼ ☀ ◑ Z3–7 H7–1 ↕↔30ft (10m)

Usually grafted as a standard to give it some intitial height. Leafs out early in spring and holds leaves later in fall than other birches. Tolerates wet or dry soils.

Betula pendula 'Dalecarlica'
WEEPING BIRCH

☼ ☀ ◑ Z2–7 H7–1 ↕80ft (24m) ↔30ft (9m)

Both branches and leaves weep, making a very graceful statement. Yellow-green to yellow fall color. Transplant in spring, and prune in summer or fall.

MORE CHOICES

- *Carpinus betulus* 'Pendula' Z4–8 H8–1
- *Eucalyptus pauciflora* 'Pendula' Z9–11 H10–8
- *Fraxinus excelsior* 'Pendula' Z5–8 H8–5
- *Ginkgo biloba* var. *pendula* Z5–9 H9–3
- *Malus* 'Sinai Fire' Z4–8 H8–1
- *Malus* 'Weeping Canzam' Z4–8 H8–1
- *Salix* 'Prarie Cascade' Z3–9 H9–1
- *Sophora japonica* 'Pendula' Z5–9 H9–5
- *Ulmus glabra* 'Camperdownii' Z4–7 H7–3

Prunus subhirtella 'Pendula Plena Rosea'
WEEPING HIGAN CHERRY

☼ ◊ ◑ Z6–8 H8–6 ‡↔25 ft (8m)

Double flowers last a long time and are followed by red fruits that mature to glossy black. As with other cherries, many diseases and insects can attack.

Fagus sylvatica 'Purpurea Pendula'
WEEPING PURPLE-LEAVED BEECH

☼ ☀ ◊ ◑ Z5–7 H7–5 ‡↔10ft (3m)

Never gets very large and grows slowly, so it is well suited as a focal point for the front foundation or rock garden planting. Originated in Germany.

Fagus sylvatica 'Pendula'
WEEPING EUROPEAN BEECH

☼ ☀ ◊ ◑ Z5–7 H7–5 ‡80ft (24m) ↔50 ft (15m)

As branches touch the ground they root in place, often creating a cavernous shelter. Bronze fall color. Withstands heavy pruning and dislikes extreme heat.

Prunus subhirtella 'Pendula'
WEEPING HIGAN CHERRY

☼ ◊ Z6–8 H8–6 ‡ ↔30ft (10m)

A graceful, artistic weeper that grows quickly. The bark is particularly distinct, with gray-brown lenticels (corky pores) in stripes on the younger branches.

Cercidiphyllum japonicum 'Pendulum'
WEEPING KATSURA TREE

☼ ☀ ◊ Z3–7 H7–1 ‡20ft (6m) ↔25ft (8m)

Fast-growing tree that matures smaller than other weeping forms of Katsuratree. Bark becomes shaggy with age. Good focal point in a large rock garden.

TREES

Trees with ornamental spring flowers

A single spring-flowering tree can present one of the most wonderful of all garden displays, rivaling the impact from massed bulbs or an entire bed of early perennials. For this reason, many savvy gardeners consider the ornamental characteristics and placement of small trees long before they begin to choose and site herbaceous plants.

TREES

Chionanthus virginicus
WHITE FRINGETREE

Ⓝ ☼ ◊ Z4–9 H9–1 ↕↔20ft (6m)

A tree with a variable habit: some are open and spreading; others are denser. Lightly fragrant flowers precede dark blue, oval fruits with a white coating.

Cornus florida
FLOWERING DOGWOOD

Ⓝ ☼☽ ◊ Z5–8 H8–3 ↕20ft (6m) ↔25ft (8m)

Early flowering in pink or white, with clusters of glossy red fruit following in fall. Birds devour them. Excellent red to reddish purple fall color.

Prunus mume
JAPANESE APRICOT

☼ ◊◊ Z6–8 H8–6 ↕↔28ft (9m)

Fragrant flowers are borne singly or in pairs in late winter to early spring before the leaves. Round yellow fruits follow. A range of cultivars is available.

Aesculus californica
CALIFORNIA BUCKEYE

Ⓝ ☼ ◊ Z7–8 H8–7 ↕↔30ft (10m)

Broadly rounded tree with glossy leaves. Fragrant flowers also come in pink. Avoid planting in regions where night temperatures and humidity are high.

Prunus subhirtella
HIGAN CHERRY

☼ ◊◊ Z6–8 H8–6 ↕↔25 ft (8m)

Finely toothed leaves are shiny, dark green above and fuzzy on the veins below. These cherries are relatively long-lived and tolerant of cold, heat, and stress.

MORE CHOICES

- *Aesculus glabra* Z3–7 H7–1
- *Catalpa speciosa* Z4–8 H8–1
- *Cercis canadensis* Z4–9 H9–2
- *Cercis occidentalis* Z8–10 H12–9
- *Cornus angustata* Z6–8 H8–6
- *Cornus controversa* Z6–9 H9–6
- *Cornus kousa* Z5–8 H8–5
- *Cornus walteri* Z5–8 H8–5
- *Cornus rutgersensis* Z5–8 H8–3
- *Crataegus crus-galli inermis* Z4–7 H7–1
- *Crataegus laevigata* Z5–8 H8–3

Crataegus x lavallei
LAVALLE HAWTHORN

☼ ◊ ❋ Z5–7 H7–4 ↕22ft (7m) ↔30ft (9m)

Red to orange-red, brown-speckled fruit follow the flowers in late fall, hanging on into winter. Oval-crowned and dense. Not as plagued by rust as others.

Halesia diptera var. magniflora
TWO-WINGED SILVERBELL

Ⓝ ☼ ☼ ◊ Z4–8 H8–1 ↕20ft (6m) ↔30ft (10m)

Larger flowers than the species, appearing in early summer and preceding 2-winged green fruit. Ususally multistemmed or branched close to the ground.

Paulownia tomentosa
ROYAL PAULOWNIA, EMPRESS TREE

☼ ◊ Z5–8 H8–5 ↕40ft (12m) ↔30ft (9m)

Flowers appear in early summer and have yellow stripes inside. Dark green leaves are densely hairy beneath. Grows quickly and has few problems.

Pyrus calleryana
CALLERY PEAR

☼ ◊ Z5–8 H8–2 ↕↔50 ft (15m)

Glossy, dark green leaves turn red and purple shades in fall. Tolerates drought and pollution and is mostly free of pests and diseases. Native to Korea and China.

MORE CHOICES

- *Crataegus phaenopyrum* z4–8 H8–1
- *Crataegus punctata* 'Ohio Pioneer' z5–7 H7–1
- *Crataegus viridis* z5–7 H7–1
- *Davidia involucrata* z6–8 H8–6
- *Halesia monticola* z6–9 H9–6
- *Laburnum anagyroides* z6–8 H8–5
- *Laburnum* x *watereri* and cultivars z6–8 H8–5
- *Magnolia accuminata* z4–8 H8–2
- *Magnolia liliflora* z4–9 H9–1
- *Magnolia macrophylla* z6–9 H9–6
- *Magnolia sieboldii* z6–9 H9–6
- *Magnolia virginiana* z6–9 H9–6
- *Magnolia* x *loebneri* and cultivars z5–9 H9–5
- *Magnolia* x *soulangiana* and cultivars z6–9 H9–6
- *Prunus sargentii* and cultivars z5–9 H9–5
- *Prunus serrulata* and cultivars z6–8 H8–6

Magnolia 'Galaxy'
GALAXY MAGNOLIA

☼ ☼ ◊ Z6–9 H9–6 ↕40ft (12m) ↔25ft (8m)

Pyramidal, single-trunked tree with late-opening flowers that are rarely hurt by spring frost. Use as a specimen where the 6in flowers can be appreciated.

Magnolia denudata
YULAN MAGNOLIA

☼ ☼ ◊ Z6–9 H9–6 ↕↔30ft (9m)

Fragrant flowers on a rounded tree. Young plants are very upright but become open with age. Flowers are easily injured by late freezes. Native to central China.

TREES

Summer-blooming trees

Trees, the solid and long-lasting sentinels of the garden, are often overlooked as sources of summer interest; most are grown for spring flowers or fall color. This group of trees offers flowering interest that can be used to play off of summer-flowering perennials and shrubs, adding a new dimension to your gardening.

TREES

Lagerstroemia indica
COMMON CRAPE MYRTLE
☀ ◦ Z7–9 H9–6 ↕20ft (6m) ↔20ft (6m)
White, purple, and deep red cultivars bloom over a long season, extending into fall. Fall color ranges from yellow to orange and red. Native to China and Korea.

Stewartia pseudocamellia
JAPANESE STEWARTIA
☀ ◦ ᵖᴴ Z5–8 H8–0 ↕↔50ft (15m)
Pyramidal to oval tree with yellow or red to dark purple foliage in autumn. Exceptional sinuous, peeling bark provides year-round interest. Native to Japan.

Stewartia monadelpha
TALL STEWARTIA
☀ ◦ ᵖᴴ Z6–9 H9–6 ↕↔50ft (15m)
This pyramidal-rounded, shrubby tree displays deep red fall color on leaves that hang on into winter. Flowers appear for at least a month. Native to Japan.

MORE CHOICES

- *Albizia julibrissin* Z6–9 H9–6
- *Chionanthus retusus* Z5–9 H9–3
- *Robinia pseudoacacia* and cultivars Z4–9 H9–4
- *Sophora japonica* Z5–9 H9–1
- *Stewartia pteropetiolata* var. *koreana* Z5–8 H8–4
- *Stewartia ovata* Z3–9 H8–1
- *Stewartia sinensis* Z5–8 H8–5

Vitax agnus-castus
CHASTE TREE
☀ ◦ Z6–9 H9–6 ↕↔8ft (2.5m)
Fragrant flowers appear through much of summer. Deadhead to encourage repeat bloom. Prefers hot weather. Native to southern Europe and western Asia.

Evergreen trees

Compared to conifers (cone-bearing trees), the broadleaf (seed-bearing) evergreen tree selection is quite small, but among the choices are some of the most tresured of all garden subjects. These trees work as well for hedging and screening as they do for either specimen use or mass planting. All can add year-round interest to almost any landscape.

Ilex aquifolium
ENGLISH HOLLY

☼ ☼ ☀ ◊ Z7–9 H9–7 ↕70ft (20m) ↔20ft

A popular species that is available in a wide range of cultivars selected for their leaf and fruit color as well as for their leaf and overall plant shape.

Magnolia grandiflora
SOUTHERN MAGNOLIA

Ⓝ ☼ ☀ ◊ Z7–9 H9–1 ↕↔30ft (9m)

Wonderfully fragrant white flowers in late spring to early summer are followed by conelike fruit ripening in fall to expose red seeds. Normally pest-free.

Trachycarpus fortunei
CHUSAN PALM

☼ ◊ Z8–11 H12–8 ↕↔50ft (15m)

Long clusters of small yellow flowers hang from the leaf bases in early summer, followed by round, blue-black fruit on females. Protect from strong or cold winds.

MORE CHOICES

- *Arbutus menziesii* Z7–9 H9–7
- *Arbutus unedo* Z8–9 H9–6
- *Eucalyptus coccifera* Z9–11 H12–10
- *Eucalyptus gunnii* Z8–10 H10–8
- *Ilex aquifolium* Z7–9 H9–7
- *Trachycarpus fortunei* Z8–11 H12–8

Eucalyptus pauciflora
CABBAGE GUM

☼ ◊ Z9–11 H12–10 ↕↔50ft (15m)

A closeup look reveals narrow, hanging, shiny, blue-green leaves. Clusters of white flowers are borne from late spring to summer. Native to Australia.

Ilex opaca
AMERICAN HOLLY

Ⓝ ☼ ☼ ☀ ◊ Z5–9 H9–5 ↕45ft (14m) ↔4ft (1.2m)

In old age, the habit becomes more open and irregular. Fragrant white flowers in early summer are followed by small, persistent red fruit. Not for dry, windy areas.

Trees with colorful fall foliage

As deciduous trees prepare for winter, previously hidden colors of pigments in leaf cells are liberated from their mask of green chlorophyll, which decomposes in fall. Shades of red, yellow, and purple emerge, lighting up the landscape. The richness of the tapestry of fall color can be brought into your garden with this group of trees.

Acer rubrum 'Franksred'
FRANKSRED MAPLE
Ⓝ ☼ ◊ Z4–9 H9–1 ‡45ft (14m) ↔35ft (11m)
Glossy, thick leaves hang on late into fall. One of the best red maples for the West. Susceptible to salt damage and leaf scorch and may be damaged in storms.

Acer japonicum 'Sango Kaku'
CORALBARK MAPLE
☼ ◊ Z5–8 H8–2 ‡↔20ft (6m)
New leaves are tinged red then become light green in summer. Bright red color is best on young branches; as they mature, the color darkens. Upright habit.

Acer palmatum 'Waterfall'
WATERFALL JAPANESE MAPLE
☼ ☼ ◊ Z5–8 H8–2 ‡6ft (2m)
↔10ft (3m)
Regarded as the best green cutleaf form because of the many deep dissections and the leaf's larger size. Tolerates heat well. Good as an accent plant near a patio.

Acer japonicum 'Aconitifolium'
FULL-MOON MAPLE
☼ ◊ Z5–7 H7–5 ‡↔30ft (10m)
Leaf lobes are divided twice and sharply toothed; they change from light green to golden yellow and red in fall. Protect from wind and late spring frost.

Parrotia persica
PERSIAN PARROTIA
☼ ◊ Z4–7 H7–1 ‡↔50 ft (15m)
Leaves open reddish purple and age to shiny mid- to dark green in summer. Tiny red flowers appear before the leaves in early spring.

Zelkova serrata
JAPANESE ZELKOVA

☼ ◑ ◐ Z5–9 H9–5 ↕100ft (30m) ↔60ft (18m)

As it matures, smooth gray bark flakes off to reveal orange patches. Rough-textured, elmlike leaves have toothed edges. Native to Japan, Taiwan, and South Korea.

Quercus coccinea
SCARLET OAK

Ⓝ ☼ ◐ ◐ ❧ Z5–9 H9–4 ↕70ft (20m) ↔50 ft (15m)

Round and open at maturity, with glossy dark green foliage in summer and brilliant red fall color. Intolerant of adverse conditions, but fine to garden beneath.

MORE CHOICES

- *Acer rubrum* Z3–9 H9–1
- *Acer saccharum* Z4–8 H8–1
- *Amelanchier arborea* Z4–9 H9–4
- *Carya ovata* Z4–8 H8–1
- *Cercidiphyllum japonicum* Z4–8 H8–1
- *Franklinia alatamaha* Z6–9 H9–6
- *Fraxinus americana* Z6–9 H9–6
- *Liquidambar styraciflua* Z6–9 H9–6
- *Phellodendron amurense* Z3–7 H7–1
- *Pistacia chinensis* Z5–8 H8–5
- *Populus balsamifera* Z5–9 H9–5
- *Populus deltoides* Z3–9 H9–1
- *Populus tremuloides* Z1–8 H8–1

Liquidambar styraciflua
AMERICAN SWEET GUM

Ⓝ ☼ ◐ Z6–9 H9–6 ↕100ft (30m) ↔75ft (23m)

Narrow and upright when young, but lower limbs spread with age. Furrowed bark and corky wings on twigs add to its winter interest. Native to eastern US.

TREES

Quercus phellos
WILLOW OAK

Ⓝ ☼ ◐ ◐ Z6–9 H9–3 ↕70ft (20m) ↔50 ft (15m)

Fast-growing, with a cone-shaped growth habit. Smooth gray bark ages with shallow ridges. In warmer areas, dead leaves hang on through winter.

Ginkgo biloba 'Autumn Gold'
AUTUMN GOLD MAIDENHAIR TREE

☼ ◐ Z3–9 H9–1 ↕50 ft (15m) ↔30ft (9m)

Features attractive and unusual light green, fan-shaped leaves. Leaves linger into late fall. Excellent as backyard tree, but just as "at home" on the street. Pest-free.

Nyssa sylvatica
BLACK GUM, SOUR GUM

Ⓝ ☼ ◐ ◐ Z5–9 H9–2 ↕70ft (20m) ↔30ft (9m)

Slow-growing, pyramidal tree that spreads and becomes more irregular with maturity. Leaves emerge late in spring. Females produce black fruit that birds devour.

Trees with decorative fruit

Although fall color is usually associated with tree leaves, there are numerous species that produce very ornamental fruit, many of which color up in shades or red, orange, and yellow from late summer into fall. These berries can last into the winter, but since birds often eat them, they may not last nearly that long.

Sorbus intermedia
SWEDISH WHITEBEAM

☼ ☼ ◐ ◊ Z5–8 H8–3 ↕↔40ft (12m)

Round-headed tree with dense clusters of white flowers in late spring. As with other *Sorbus*, fireblight, powdery mildew, borers, and scale insects are common problems.

Ilex decidua
POSSUMHAW

Ⓝ ☼ ☼ ◐ ◊ Z5–9 H9–1 ↕↔6–20ft (2–6m)

Horizontal and upward-facing branches bear yellow leaves and fruit in fall. Fruit may persist until the following spring.

Ilex aquifolium
ENGLISH HOLLY

☼ ☼ ◐ ◊ Z7–9 H9–7 ↕70ft (20m) ↔20ft (6m)

Upright trees with gray bark. Long-lasting fruit is yellow or orange on some cultivars. Female trees need males pollinators nearby. Aphids may attack young branches.

Malus huphensis
TEA CRABAPPLE

☼ ◊ Z5–8 H8–5 ↕↔50ft (15m)

Deep pink buds open to fragrant white flowers in late spring. Vase-shaped (becoming spreading) and vigorous. Very susceptible to fireblight. Native to China.

Crataegus viridis 'Winter King'
GREEN HAWTHORN

Ⓝ ☀ ◊◦ Z5–7 H7–5 ↕20ft (6m) ↔15ft (5m)

Rounded to vase-shaped form. Clusters of white flowers are followed by the fruit, which lasts through winter. Fruit is larger than the species. Relatively trouble-free.

MORE CHOICES

- *Arbutus unedo* Z8–9 H9–6
- *Castanea mollissima* Z4–8 H8–1
- *Crataegus crus-galli inermis* Z4–7 H7–1
- *Crataegus laevigata* Z5–8 H8–3
- *Crataegus punctata* 'Ohio Pioneer' Z0 H7–1
- *Ilex opaca* (female) and cultivars Z5–9 H9–5
- *Phellodendron amurense* Z4–7 H8–5
- *Sorbus alnifolia* Z3–6 H8–1
- *Sorbus aucuparia* Z2–7 H7–1
- *Sorbus thuringiaca* Z5–7 H7–5

Koelreuteria paniculata
PANICLED GOLDEN RAIN TREE

☀ ◊ Z6–9 H9–1 ↕↔30ft (10m)

Spreading tree with divided, fernlike leaves that turn yellow in autumn. Large clusters of small yellow flowers bloom in mid- to late summer.

Crataegus x lavallei
LAVALLE HAWTHORN

☀ ◊◦ Z5–7 H7–4 ↕22ft (7m) ↔30ft (9m)

Upright and open branching habit. Foliage turns bronze red in autumn and hangs on into winter. White flowers give way to the fruit, which lasts all winter.

Crataegus phaenopyrum
WASHINGTON HAWTHORN

Ⓝ ☀ ◊◦ Z4–8 H8–1 ↕↔30ft (9m)

Graceful, open shape and spectacular orange, red, and purplish foliage in fall. Clusters of small white flowers become orange fruit.

Malus 'Donald Wyman'
DONALD WYMAN CRABAPPLE

☀ ☀ ◦ Z4–8 H8–1 ↕20ft (6m) ↔25ft (8m)

Wide-growing tree with pink to red buds that open into single white flowers. Flowers best in alternate years. Shows good disease resistance.

Morus nigra
BLACK MULBERRY

☀ ◊ Z5–9 H9–5 ↕40ft (12m) ↔50ft (15m)

A dense, spreading crown arises from a short trunk. Fruit has a slightly acidic flavor. Protect from cold, dry winds. Probably native to southwest Asia.

TREES

Trees with ornamental and edible fruit

If you want your tree and eat it too, then consider this selection of ornamental and tasty choices. They perform equally well in a dedicated orchard or as specimen trees, provided their cultural conditions (especially regarding pests and diseases) are met. In smaller gardens, grow cultivars that are grafted onto a dwarfing rootstock, which will control their ultimate size.

MORE CHOICES

- *Asimina triloba* Z6–8 H8–6
- *Asimina triloba* 'Pennsylvania Golden' Z6–8 H8–6
- *Diospyros kaki* 'Chocolate' Z4–9 H9–1
- *Diospyros kaki* 'Fuyu' Z4–9 H9–1
- *Diospyros kaki* 'Tamppan' Z4–9 H9–1
- *Ficus carica* Z7–11 H12–1
- *Ficus carica* 'Brown Turkey' Z7–11 H12–7
- *Ficus carica* 'Desert King' Z7–11 H12–7
- *Ficus carica* 'Hardy Chicago' Z7–11 H12–7
- *Malus* 'Empire' Z4–8 H8–1
- *Malus* 'Gravenstein' Z5–8 H8–1
- *Malus* 'Hopa' Z5–9 H9–1

Malus cultivars
APPLE, CRABAPPLE

☼ ◐ Z3–8 H8–1 ↕ ↔ 3–20ft (1–6m)

Most apples and crabapples require an extensive pest-control program to produce the sort of perfect fruit seen in markets. Organic methods are available.

Asimina triloba
PAWPAW

Ⓝ ☼ ◐ Z6–8 H8–6 ↕↔12ft (4m)

Both females and males are required to produce fruit. When fully ripe, the banana-flavored interior is yellow and custardlike. Has few pest problems.

Prunus persica var. *nectarina*
NECTARINE

☼ ◐ Z4–8 H8–1 ↕ ↔6–12 ft (2–6m)

Nectarines and their kin, peaches, thrive in areas with hot, dry summers. In cooler areas, smaller-growing grafted cultivars can be grown in a large greenhouse.

Prunus persica
PEACH

☼ ◖ Z4–8 H8–1 ↕ ↔6–12 ft (2–6m)

Like nectarines, peaches have a mimimum winter chilling requirement. Ask a fruit expert for good choices if you live in Zone 8 or warmer.

Prunus avium 'Stella'
SWEET CHERRY

☼ ◖ Z4–8 H8–1 ↕↔10–12ft (3–3.5m)

Most sweet cherries have rather complex pollination requirements, but 'Stella' is self-fertile, making it an ideal choice for a smaller garden. Birds relish the fruit.

Prunus x domestica
PLUM

☼ ◖ Z5–8 H8–3 ↕↔6–12 ft (2–6m)

This is one of several kinds of plums. All flower early in spring, so avoid growing in a frosty microclimate. Pollination requirements vary among cultivars.

MORE CHOICES

- *Malus* 'Liberty' Z4–8 H8–1
- *Malus* 'McIntosh' Z4–8 H8–1
- *Malus* 'William's Pride' Z4–8 H8–1
- *Prunus armeniaca* H8–1
- *Prunus avium* Z4–8 H8–1
- *Prunus avium* 'Plena' Z4–8 H8–4
- *Prunus cerasus* H8–1
- *Prunus x domestica* Z5–8 H8–3
- *Prunus* 'Kristin' Z5–8 H8–4
- *Prunus persica* Z4–8 H8–1
- *Prunus persica* 'Klara Meyer' Z4–8 H8–1
- *Prunus persica* var. *nucipersica* Z4–8 H8–1
- *Prunus persica* 'Prince Charming' Z6–9 H9–6
- *Prunus* 'Stella' Z5–8 H8–4
- *Punica granatum* 'Nana' Z7–10 H10–7
- *Punica granatum* 'Wonderful' Z7–10 H10–7
- *Pyrus communis* Z4–9 H9–1
- *Pyrus communis* 'Bartlett' Z5–9 H9–5
- *Pyrus communis* 'Beach Hill' Z5–9 H9–5
- *Pyrus communis* 'Bosc' Z5–9 H9–1
- *Pyrus pyrifolia* Z5–8 H9–4
- *Pyrus serotina* Z7–9 H9–4

Ficus carica
COMMON FIG

☼ ◖ Z7–11 H12–1 ↕10ft (3m) ↔12ft (4m)

Most figs bear on the previous season's growth, so protect plants in winter in the northern part of their range. Rarely bothered by pests and diseases.

Pyrus communis
PEAR

☼ ◖ Z4–9 H9–1 ↕↔9–12ft (3–4m)

Pears need more consistently warm conditions than apples to grow and bear well. The soil must be well-drained. Watch out for fireblight, a serious disease.

TREES

Trees with ornamental bark

Although all trees have interesting and identifiable bark, there are some that have special merit. Those with peeling patches or mottled or vibrant coloration in bold patterns - that often can be seen from a distance – provide visual interest to a landscape. This feature can be particularly striking during winter, when many trees are leafless.

Acer capillipes
SNAKEBARK MAPLE

☼ ◊ Z5–7 H7–5 ↕↔50ft (15m)
Spreading, drooping branches bear red young shoots, streaked with green and white at maturity. Leaves change to bright red in fall. Native to Japan.

Stewartia pseudocamellia
JAPANESE STEWARTIA

☼ ◗ ᴾᴴ Z5–8 H8–0 ↕↔50ft (15m)
Deeply grooved, muscly bark with peeling patches makes a statement in the garden. Leaves turn yellow to red and reddish purple in fall. Native to Japan.

MORE CHOICES

- *Arbutus menziesii* Z7–9 H9–7
- *Betula nigra* Z4–9 H9–1
- *Betula utilis var. jacquemontii* Z5–7 H7–3
- *Carpinus betulus* Z4–8 H8–3
- *Eucalyptus gunnii* Z8–10 H10–8
- *Lagerstroemia indica* Z7–9 H9–7
- *Platanus x acerifolia* Z5–8 H8–5
- *Prunus serrulata* Z5–8 H8–5
- *Stewartia sinensis* Z5–8 H8–5
- *Ulmus parvifolia* Z6–9 H9–3

Acer griseum
PAPERBARK MAPLE

☼ ◊ Z4–8 H8–1 ↕↔30ft (10m)
Bark character develops at a young age. Dark bluish green leaves turn bronzy red and are held well into late fall. Native to central China. Pest-free.

Betula papyrifera
PAPER BIRCH

Ⓝ ☼ ☼ ◊ Z2–7 H7–1 ↕70ft (20m) ↔30ft (9m)
Bark turns white in its third or fourth year and stays white longer than many other white-barked birches. Yellow leaves in fall. Grows quickly.

Pseudocydonia sinensis
CHINESE QUINCE

☼ ◊ Z6–8 H8–4 ↕↔20ft (6m)

Dense, upright tree with dark green foliage that turns yellow to red in fall. Light pink, early spring flowers precede egg-shaped, aromatic, yellow fruit in autumn.

Syringa reticulata
JAPANESE TREE LILAC

☼ ◊ Z3–8 H8–3 ↕30ft (10m) ↔20ft (6m)

Fragrant flowers in early summer last at least two weeks. Stiff, spreading branches become more graceful with age. Excellent specimen or street tree.

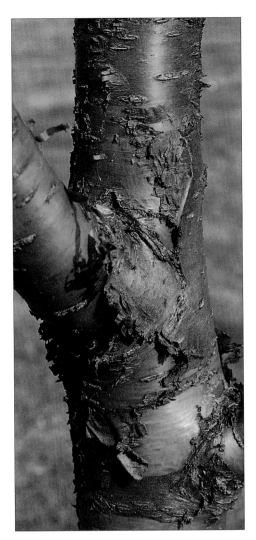

Prunus maackii
AMUR CHOKECHERRY

☼ ◊ Z3–7 H7–1 ↕↔50 ft (15m)

Pyramid-shaped when young, aging to round-headed. Profuse white flowers in midspring are followed by tiny red fruit that mature to black in late summer.

Platanus occidentalis
SYCAMORE, BUTTONWOOD

Ⓝ ☼ ◊ Z5–8 H8–3 ↕80ft (24m) ↔70ft (20m)

Brown bark flakes off irregularly, exposing whitish inner bark to produce a mottled appearance with age. Leafs out late. Used extensively as a street tree.

Lagerstroemia fauriei
CRAPE MYRTLE

☼ ◊ Z7–9 H9–7 ↕↔25ft (8m)

White flowers in summer. Fast-growing, developing bark characteristics early. Use in groups and underplant with groundcover. Mildew resistant. Japanese native.

Trees for use as specimens

Many of these trees are native to forests around the world, where they grow large in the competition for nutrients and sunshine. Given a prime location in a large garden, these trees will achieve their full majesty, grace, and form. Some are slower-growing, long-lived trees such as *Ginkgo*, or faster-growing, short-lived trees such as *Paulownia*.

Paulownia tomentosa
ROYAL PAULOWNIA, EMPRESS TREE
☀ ◊ Z5–8 H8–5 ↕40ft (12m) ↔30ft (9m)
Vanilla-scented flowers have yellow stripes inside and appear in early spring before the large, fuzzyleaves. Leaves on vigorous growth can be 2ft (60cm) wide.

Eucalyptus pauciflora subsp. *niphophila*
ALPINE SNOW GUM
☀ ◊ Z8–9 H10–8 ↕↔to 20ft (6m)
Narrow, drooping, shiny leaves. Bark peels from late summer to autumn. Yellow or red twigs. White to cream flowers appear in late spring to summer.

Ginkgo biloba
MAIDENHAIR TREE
☀ ◊ Z5–9 H9–3 ↕100ft (30m) ↔25ft (8m)
Narrow to spreading young tree becomes umbrella-shaped. Slow-growing, tolerant of pollution and heat, and free of pests. Outstanding yellow fall foliage.

Fraxinus americana
WHITE ASH

Ⓝ ☀ ◐ ♦ Z6–9 H9–6
↕80ft (24m) ↔50 ft (15m)

Develops an open, rounded head at maturity with yellow to red to dark purple foliage in early fall. Excellent for lawns and other large spaces.

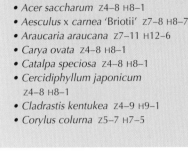

MORE CHOICES

- *Acer saccharinum* Z4–8 H8–1
- *Acer saccharum* Z4–8 H8–1
- *Aesculus* x *carnea* 'Briotii' Z7–8 H8–7
- *Araucaria araucana* Z7–11 H12–6
- *Carya ovata* Z4–8 H8–1
- *Catalpa speciosa* Z4–8 H8–1
- *Cercidiphyllum japonicum* Z4–8 H8–1
- *Cladrastis kentukea* Z4–9 H9–1
- *Corylus colurna* Z5–7 H7–5

Fagus sylvatica 'Dawyck Purple'
UPRIGHT PURPLE-LEAVED BEECH

☀ ◐ ◊ ♦ Z5–7 H7–5 ↕70ft (20m) ↔15ft (5m)

Leaves emerge late in spring and turn bronzy in fall. Slow-growing, with smooth, gray bark. Plant among green-leaved trees to serve as foils for the foliage color.

Zelkova serrata
JAPANESE ZELKOVA

☀ ◐ ♦ Z5–9 H9–5 ↕100ft (30m) ↔60ft (18m)

Vase-shaped in youth. Dark green leaves in summer and late, persistent fall color. Reddish brown bark with many horizontal markings is similar to cherries.

Liriodendron tulipifera
TULIPTREE

Ⓝ ☀ ◐ ♦ Z5–9 H9–1 ↕100ft (30m) ↔50 ft (15m)

Fast-growing, with golden yellow foliage late into fall. Greenish yellow flowers in early summer ususally flower high up in trees. Requires a large space.

Corylus colurna
TURKISH FILBERT

☀ ◐ ◊ Z5–7 H7–5 ↕70ft (20m) ↔22ft (7m)

Heavy textured, very leathery leaves turn yellow to purple in autumn. Aging bark flakes off to reveal orange-brown patches beneath. Needs room.

Magnolia acuminata
CUCUMBERTREE MAGNOLIA

Ⓝ ☀ ◐ ◊ Z4–8 H8–2 ↕70ft (20m) ↔30ft (9m)

Broadly rounded at maturity, with magnificent, wide-spreading branches. Interesting light brown fall color and pinkish red, cucumber-like fruit. Needs space.

Trees for screening and windbreaks

Planting rows of trees to break the wind that sweeps across farmers' fields is a tried-and-true practice. Likewise, homeowners may live in areas where there are high winds, usually coming from the west and north. These trees can resist the damaging effects of wind and also provide protection to anything on their leeward side as well.

Celtis occidentalis
COMMON HACKBERRY

Ⓝ ☼ ◊ Z2–9 H9–1 ‡70ft (20m) ↔50 ft (15m)
Light green leaves turn yellow in fall. White flowers mature into round, orange-red to deep purple fruit that ripens in early fall and hangs on for many weeks.

Quercus rubra
RED OAK

Ⓝ ☼ ☼ ◊ ꝏ Z5–9 H9–5 ‡80ft (24m) ↔70ft (20m)
Fast-growing, round-headed, symmetrical tree with pinkish red unfurling leaves and red fall foliage. Deep ridges add interest on old bark. Tolerates pollution.

Maclura pomifera
OSAGE-ORANGE

Ⓝ ☼ ◊ Z5–9 H9–5 ‡50 ft (15m) ↔40ft (12m)
Fast-growing tree with low, rounded, irregular head and stiff, thorny branches. Deep orange-brown bark with wavy, deep ridges. Very tough and durable.

MORE CHOICES

- *Acer saccharinum and cultivars* Z4–8 H8–1
- *Carpinus betulus* 'Fastigata' Z4–8 H8–3
- *Fagus sylvatica* Z4–7 H9–4
- *Gleditsia triacanthos* Z3–7 H7–1
- *Populus trichocarpa* Z4–9 H9–1
- *Salix* 'Prairie Cascade' Z4–9 H9–1
- *Salix alba* 'Tristis' Z3–9 H9–1
- *Tilia cordata* Z3–8 H8–1
- *Ulmus parvifolia* Z3–9 H9–1

Acer platanoides
NORWAY MAPLE

☼ ☼ ◊ Z3–7 H7–1 ‡80ft (24m) ↔50 ft (15m)
Round to broadly rounded crown with showy flower in spring. Yellow fall color late in the season. Use in large yards between properties. Tolerates pollution.

Acer campestre
HEDGE MAPLE

Ⓝ ☼ ☼ ◊ Z6–8 H8–4 ‡↔25–55ft (8–16m)
Rounded, heavy-looking, and often branched to the ground. Turns yellow in late fall and remains so for a long time Tolerates dry, compacted soil and pollution.

Fraxinus pennsylvanica
GREEN ASH

Ⓝ ☼ ◊ Z4–9 H9–4 ‡↔70ft (20m)
Upright and spreading tree with age. Shiny foliage turns yellow in autumn. Avoid seedling-grown trees; many bear nuisance fruit. Prone to borers and scale.

Juglans nigra
BLACK WALNUT

Ⓝ ☼ ◊ Z5–9 H9–5 ‡100ft (30m) ↔75ft (23m)
Oval to rounded habit. Huge taproot makes it difficult to transplant. Many plants are affected by chemicals emitted from this tree and cannot grow under it.

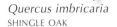

Quercus alba
WHITE OAK

Ⓝ ☼ ◐ ◊ pH Z5–9 H8–1 ↕↔60–100ft (18–30m)
Slow-growing, upright, round-headed tree with
spreading branches at maturity. Rich red wine-colored
foliage in fall. Acorns relished by birds and mammals.

Quercus macrocarpa
BUR OAK, MOSSYCUP OAK

Ⓝ ☼ ◐ ◊ Z3–9 H9–1 ↕50ft (15m) ↔30ft (9m)
Broad-spreading tree with a massive, deeply ridged
trunk with age. Produces yellow fall color and deep-
cupped acorns with distinctly fringed edges.

Quercus bicolor
SWAMP WHITE OAK

Ⓝ ☼ ◐ ◊ Z4–8 H8–1 ↕70ft (20m) ↔50ft (15m)
Broad, open, coarse-looking crown with a short trunk.
Yellow to red-purple fall color. Rugged, deep fissures
in bark at maturity. Excellent drought tolerance.

Quercus imbricaria
SHINGLE OAK

Ⓝ ☼ ◐ ◊ Z5–8 H8–4 ↕70ft (20m) ↔50ft (15m)
Reddish unfurling leaves turn russet-red in autumn and
hang on through winter. Tolerates heavy pruning and
so makes a good hedge plant.

Quercus phellos
WILLOW OAK

Ⓝ ☼ ◐ ◊ Z6–9 H9–3 ↕70ft (20m) ↔50ft (15m)
Dense, oval to rounded head at maturity. Prune early
in life to form shapely crown. Transplants more easily
than other oaks. Adaptable to poor habitats. Pest-free.

TREES

Trees that are resistant to deer browsing

The buds, leaves, and twigs of most fully grown large trees are out of the range of most deer, but younger and smaller trees are often on a deer's menu. The leaves and branches of these trees are spiny or thorny or contain unpalatable chemicals that protect them from browsing. Remember: when desperate, deer will eat almost anything, so have protective measures ready.

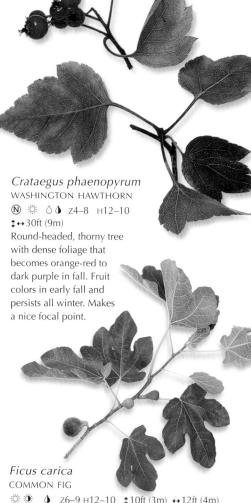

Crataegus phaenopyrum
WASHINGTON HAWTHORN

Ⓝ ☼ ◊◊ Z4–8 H12–10
↕↔30ft (9m)
Round-headed, thorny tree
with dense foliage that
becomes orange-red to
dark purple in fall. Fruit
colors in early fall and
persists all winter. Makes
a nice focal point.

Crataegus viridis 'Winter King'
GREEN HAWTHORNE

Ⓝ ☼ ◊◊ Z5–7 H7–5 ↕20ft (6m) ↔15ft (5m)
Rounded, vase-shaped habit and gray-green, waxy
stems. Fruit, larger than the species, hangs on into
winter. Less susceptible to rust than other hawthorns.

Magnolia grandiflora
SOUTHERN MAGNOLIA

Ⓝ ☼ ☼ ◊ Z7–9 H9–1 ↕↔30ft (9m)
Slow-growing, pyramidal evergreen that branches close
to the ground. Fragrant, large white flowers bloom
from late spring to early summer. Pest-free.

Magnolia macrophylla
BIGLEAF MAGNOLIA

☼ ☼ ◊ Z6–9 H12–10 ↕↔30ft (9m)
A rounded tree with huge, fragrant flowers and large,
oval, reddish, conelike fruit. Immense
leaves are sometimes over two feet
long. Needs a large setting to
remain in scale with the rest
of the landscape.

Ficus carica
COMMON FIG

☼ ☼ ◊ Z6–9 H12–10 ↕10ft (3m) ↔12ft (4m)
Young green fruit mature to darker green, purple, or
brown. Mulch annually to protect roots and conserve
moisture. Native to W Asia and E Mediterranean area.

Magnolia x loebneri
LOEBNER MAGNOLIA

☼ ☼ ◊ Z5–9 H12–10 ↕30ft (9m) ↔22ft (7m)
Very fragrant flowers in early spring. Some cultivars
have pink-flushed petals. Blooms at an early age.
A magnificent specimen tree, needing room to spread.

Magnolia acuminata
CUCUMBERTREE MAGNOLIA

Ⓝ ☼ ☼ ◊ Z4–8 H8–2 ↕70ft (20m) ↔30ft (9m)
Broad, spreading tree with leaves turning ashy brown
in fall. Slightly fragrant, late spring blooms precede
pinkish red, cucumber-like fruit in midautumn.

Quercus muehlenbergii
CHINKAPIN OAK

Ⓝ ☼ ☼ ◑ ◊ Z4–8 H8–2 ‡50 ft (15m) ↔40ft (12m)
Open, rounded head with a spread greater than its height at maturity. Yellow to orange-brown color in fall. Flaking gray bark and a massive trunk. Pest-free.

MORE CHOICES

- *Acer palmatum* and cultivars Z5–8 H8–2
- *Albizia julibrissin* Z6–9 H9–6
- *Celtis occidentalis* Z2–9 H9–1
- *Crataegus punctata* 'Ohio Pioneer' Z5–7 H7–1
- *Crataegus x lavallei* Z5–7 H7–4
- *Crataegus x lavallei* 'Carrierei' Z5–7 H7–4
- *Crataegus x mordensis* 'Snowbird' Z3–8 H8–1
- *Crateagus laevigata* 'Paul's Scarlet' Z5–8 H8–3
- *Fraxinus americana* Z6–9 H9–6
- *Fraxinus excelsior* Z5–8 H8–5
- *Fraxinus latifolia* Z6–8 H8–6
- *Fraxinus pennsylvanica* Z3–9 H9–4
- *Gingko biloba* Z5–9 H9–3
- *Magnolia denudata* Z6–9 H9–6
- *Magnolia liliflora* Z4–9 H9–1
- *Magnolia sieboldii* Z6–9 H9–6
- *Magnolia stellata* Z5–9 H9–5
- *Magnolia virginiana* Z6–9 H9–6
- *Quercus agrifolia* Z9–11 H12–9
- *Quercus alba x Quercus robur* 'Crimschmidt' Z5–9 H9–3
- *Quercus alba* Z5–9 H8–1
- *Quercus bicolor* Z4–8 H8–1
- *Quercus falcata* Z6–9 H9–5
- *Quercus frainetto* 'Schmidt' Z5–8 H8–1
- *Quercus gambelii* Z5–8 H8–1
- *Quercus garryana* Z5–9 H9–7
- *Quercus imbricaria* Z5–8 H8–4
- *Quercus lobata* Z7–9 H9–7
- *Quercus macrocarpa* Z3–9 H9–1
- *Quercus nigra* Z7–9 H9–7
- *Quercus palustris* Z5–8 H8–5
- *Quercus phellos* Z6–9 H9–3
- *Quercus robur* 'Fastigiata' Z5–8 H8–3
- *Quercus robur* 'Pyramich' Z5–8 H8–4
- *Quercus robur* Z5–8 H8–4
- *Quercus rubra* Z5–9 H9–5
- *Quercus sadleriana* Z7–9 H9–7
- *Quercus shumardii* Z5–8 H8–1

Quercus coccinea
SCARLET OAK

Ⓝ ☼ ☼ ◑ ◊ Z5–9 H9–4 ‡70ft (20m) ↔50 50ft (15m)
Rounded and open-headed, with shiny, dark green leaves blazing red in fall. Difficult to find true scarlet oak in commerce. Less susceptible to chlorosis than other oaks.

Quercus myrsinifolia
CHINESE EVERGREEN OAK

☼ ◊ Z7–9 H9–6 ‡40ft (12m) ↔30ft (9m)
Rounded crown with purple-bronze new leaves. Slow-growing, excellent subject for planters. Native to E Asia, from Japan and Formosa to China and the Himalayas.

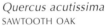

Quercus acutissima
SAWTOOTH OAK

☼ ◑ ◊ Z6–9 H8–3 ‡50 ft (15m) ↔70ft (20m)
Wide-spreading tree with foliage that emerges bright yellow in early spring and returns to yellow late in fall. Acorns have long, recurving scales. Pest-free.

Fraxinus oxycarpa 'Raywood'
CLARET ASH

☼ ◊ Z6–9 H9–6 ‡↔70ft (20m)
Crown opens up with age. A closeup of the leaves reveals sharply toothed, shiny, fernlike foliage, which turns plum-purple in fall. Developed in Australia.

TREES

SHRUBS

SHRUBS CAN SERVE A MULTITUDE of purposes in your garden, whether as a hedge or groundcover, a block of color that is the first harbinger of spring, or an enticement to attract birds and butterflies to your yard. They are the middle players between trees and perennials and can be combined with larger and smaller plants, producing a multi-tiered effect that provides color or shape throughout the year. If you have a small garden, a few well-placed shrubs may be in better scale with the space than one or more trees, and the blossoms, foliage, or shape of many shrubs make them good specimen plants.

Acer palmatum 'Bloodgood' (Japanese maple)
Clusters of small, reddish purple flowers appear in midspring on a bushy-headed shrub or small tree. The palmate leaves change to a brilliant red in fall. This cultivar grows more quickly than many other Japanes maples.

Shrubs, like trees, are woody plants, but instead of a single trunk that branches some distance up, shrubs branch freely at or near ground level. Shrubs are often used as foundation planting to serve as a transition between the rigid lines of the building and the softer lines of border plants and lawn. Alternatively, they can be planted in containers to allow more flexibility in arrangement around a patio and a greater latitude in hardiness, since the containers can be moved indoors during cold weather.

Growing a variety of shrubs in a bed or border that blends different textures, colors, and shapes together produces a graceful and natural look. Make sure that you allow enough space between them – if you continually need to prune a shrub in order to make it fit into a particular space, its resistance to disease may be weakened, and it will not be as attractive as it could be. While some shrubs are grown for their colorful fruit, others, such as rhododendrons and lilacs, will bloom more profusely the next season if faded blossoms are deadheaded promptly so that the plant does not expend energy in setting seed. Most shrubs should be fertilized annually, early in spring.

Callicarpa bodinieri var. *giraldii* 'Profusion'
The young leaves of this native of central and eastern China are bronze. Pale pink flowers are followed by an abundance of dark purple fruit.

Daphne odora 'Aureomarginata'
(Variegated winter daphne)
Some daphnes, such as this species, are evergreen, but these shrubs are more likely to be chosen for their beautifully fragrant, tubular flowers.

Hydrangea macrophylla 'Ayesha' (Bigleaf hydrangea) Here is one of the Hortensia types, commonly known as mophead hydrangeas because of their nearly spherical flowerheads.

Shrubs for dry soil and sunny sites

Shrubs that flourish in dry, sunny sites hail from regions of the world where these growing conditions are the norm. Both non-native plants from regions such as the Mediterranean or southern Africa, as well as Northwest natives, share the ability to make the most of small amounts of available soil water.

Buddleja davidii 'Fascinating'
FASCINATING BUTTERFLY BUSH
☼ ◊ Z6–9 H10–4 ↕10ft (3m) ↔15ft (5m)
Very sturdy, unusually long and wide clusters of fragrant flowers appear throughout summer and into fall if deadheaded regularly.

Buddleja davidii 'White Profusion'
WHITE BUTTERFLY BUSH
☼ ◊ Z6–9 H10–4 ↕10ft (3m) ↔15ft (5m)
Small clusters of fragrant flowers attract butterflies and bees. Best planted in groups in a border. Has no serious pests. Transplants easily and can self-sow profusely.

Buddleja davidii 'Royal Red'
RED BUTTERFLY BUSH
☼ ◊ Z6–9 H10–4 ↕10ft (3m) ↔15ft (5m)
Acclaimed as the best "red" (actually red-violet) butterfly bush. Fragrant flowers are borne in long clusters. Grows in a wide range of conditions.

Buddleja davidii 'Harlequin'
HARLEQUIN VARIEGATED BUTTERFLY BUSH
☼ ◊ Z6–9 H10–4 ↕↔20ft (6m)
Expanding leaves are yellow, old leaves almost white. Less vigorous and smaller than many butterfly bushes. Flowers can be cut, but they do not last long.

Rosa rugosa 'Alba'
WHITE RUGOSA ROSE
☼ ◊ Z2–9 H9–1 ↕↔3–6ft (1–2m)
Fast-growing, beach-loving shrub with fragrant flowers in spring, followed by bright red fruit (hips) ripening in late summer to fall. Yellow to orange to red fall foliage.

Lavatera thuringiaca 'Kew Rose'
KEW ROSE TREE MALLOW
☼ ◊ Z8–10 H9–7 ↕↔6ft (2m)
Flowers profusely in summer Rounded leaves have heart-shaped bases. Protect from cold, drying winds. Prone to scale, root rot, rust, and leaf spot.

Lavandula angustifolia
ENGLISH LAVENDER
☼ ◊ Z5–8 H8–5 ↕3ft (1m) ↔4ft (1.2m)
Slow-growing, evergreen shrub with fragrant foliage. Summer flowers are white to blue-purple. Leaves and flowers can be dried for sachets.

Nandina domestica
HEAVENLY BAMBOO
☼ ◐ Z6–9 H9–3 ↕6ft (2m) ↔5ft (1.5m)
Upright shrub blooming in late spring to early summer, Bright red, round berries follow in early fall and hang on through winter. Pest-free. Native to China.

MORE CHOICES

- *Artemisia arborescens* 'Powis Castle' Z6–9 H9–6
- *Buddleja davidii* 'Black Knight' Z6–9 H9–1
- *Buddleja davidii* 'Charming Summer' Z6–9 H9–1
- *Buddleja davidii* 'Dartmoor' Z6–9 H9–1
- *Buddleja davidii* 'DuBonnet' Z6–9 H9–1
- *Buddleja davidii* 'Lilac' Z6–9 H9–1
- *Buddleja davidii* 'Lochinch' Z6–9 H9–1
- *Buddleja davidii* 'Nanjo Blue' Z5–9 H9–2

Rhus copallina
DWARF SUMAC
Ⓝ ☼ ◊ Z5–9 H9–5 ↕↔3–5ft (1–1.5m) or more
Compact in youth, this ages to an open, irregular shrub with spreading branches and shiny, dark green foliage. Greenish yellow flowers occur in late summer.

SHRUBS

Santolina chamaecyparissus
LAVENDER COTTON

☼ ◊ Z6–9 H9–4 ‡20in (50cm) ↔3ft (1m)

Spreading, evergreen mound bears summer flowers, best removed after they fade. Use in a mass planting, in rock gardens, or as a low hedge. Salt-tolerant.

Mahonia aquifolium
OREGON GRAPE HOLLY

Ⓝ ◐ ◊ Z6–9 H9–6 ‡↔5ft (1.5m)

Slow-growing, upright, evergreen shrub turns purplish bronze in fall. Blue-black, wax-coated berries ripen in early fall and hang on through winter.

MORE CHOICES

- *Cotoneaster adpressus* 'Little Gem' Z4–7 H7–3
- *Cotoneaster dammeris* 'Coral Beauty' Z6–8 H8–4
- *Cotoneaster lacteus* Z7–9 H9–7
- *Cytisus scoparius* Z6–8 H8–6
- *Elaeagnus commutata* Z2–6 H6–1
- *Elaeagnus* x *ebbingei* 'Gift Edge' Z7–11 H12–7
- *Gaultheria shallon* Z6–8 H8–6
- *Hypericum calycinum* Z5–9 H9–4
- *Lavandula stoechas* Z8–9 H9–8
- *Lavandula* x *inter.* 'Grosso' Z5–8 H8–5
- *Lavandula* x *inter* 'Provence' Z5–8 H8–5
- *Lavatera thuringiaca* 'Kew Rose' Z7–9 H9–7
- *Leucophyllum frutescens* 'Green Cloud' Z8–10 H10–8
- *Mahonia fortunei* Z8–9 H9–4

Rosa 'Frau Dagmar Hartopp'
FRAU DAGMAR HARTOPP ROSE

☼ ◊ Z2–9 H9–1 ‡3ft (1m) ↔4ft (1.2m)

Prolific, fragrant flowers produce very large red hips, ripening as early as midsummer. Yellow to orange fall color. Resistant to blackspot and powdery mildew.

Pyracantha 'Mohave'
MOHAVE FIRETHORN

☼ ◊ Z6–9 H9–6 ‡12ft (4m) ↔15ft (5m)

Upright grower with white flowers in spring giving way to the fruit, which ripen in early fall and hang on through winter. Resistant to scab and fireblight.

Teucrium fruticans
BUSH GERMANDER

☼ ◊ Z8–9 H9–8 ‡24–40in (60–100cm) ↔12ft (4m)

Bushy, evergreen shrub with arching branches and aromatic leaves. Flowers in summer. Stays compact if grown on poor soil. Native to the western Mediterranean.

Holodiscus discolor
OCEAN SPRAY

Ⓝ ☼ ◊ Z6–9 H9–5 ‡↔20ft (6m)

Flowers bloom in midsummer, and foliage is white-hairy beneath. Plant in a mixed border or woodland setting, or as a specimen. Native to W. North America.

Rhus glabra 'Laciniata'
CUTLEAF SMOOTH SUMAC
Ⓝ ☼ ◐ Z2–8 H9–3 ↕↔8ft (2.5m)
A cutleaf form female of the smooth sumac, this produces bright red fruits that hang on through winter. Foliage turns orange, red, and purple in fall.

Cotinus coggygria 'Royal Purple'
ROYAL PURPLE SMOKEBUSH
☼ ◐ ◐◐ Z5–8 H8–3 ↕↔15ft (5m)
Upright and spreading shrub with clusters of purple-red flowers all summer and red-purple fall color. Nonfading foliage is the darkest of the cultivars.

MORE CHOICES

- *Phlomis fruticosa* Z8–9 H9–8
- *Potentilla fruticosa* 'Abbotswood' Z3–7 H7–1
- *Potentilla fruticosa* 'Tangerine' Z3–7 H7–1
- *Pyracantha coccinea* Z6–9 H9–6
- *Pyracantha* 'Gnozam' Z5–9 H9–5
- *Rhus aromatica* Z2–8 H8–1
- *Rhus trilobata* Z4–6 H6–2
- *Rhus typhina* Z3–8 H8–1
- *Ribes sanguineum* Z6–8 H8–6
- *Rosa rugosa* Z2–9 H9–1
- *Rosa* 'Blanc Double de Coubert' Z3–9 H9–1
- *Rosa rugosa* hybrids 'Jens Munk' Z2–8 H8–1
- *Rosa* (Pavement Series) Z2–9 H9–1
- *Rosa* 'Roseraie de l'Hay' Z4–9 H9–1
- *Rosa rugosa* hybrids 'Charles Albanel' Z2–9 H9–1
- *Rosa* 'Henry Hudson' Z2–9 H9–1

Rosmarinus officinalis 'Roseus'
PINK ROSEMARY
☼ ◐ Z8–11 H12–8 ↕↔5ft (1.5m)
Upright, evergreen shrub with with very narrow, leathery, aromatic, dark green leaves. Midspring to early summer flowers, reblooming in autumn. Native to the Mediterranean.

Cytisus x praecox 'Allgold'
ALLGOLD WARMINSTER BROOM
☼ ◐ Z6–9 H9–6 ↕4ft (1.2m) ↔5ft (1.5m)
Late-spring flowers, deeper yellow than the species, are produced in late spring and have an unpleasant odor. Effective in large groups to light up the landscape.

SHRUBS

Shrubs for shade

Many shrubs naturally carved themselves out a niche in the shade of larger woodland trees. In the garden, these shrubs can be used in a woodland setting as well as on the northwest and northeast sides of the house, where the plants are shaded for most of the day. They comprise the backbone of a well-designed mixed border in shade.

Hydrangea arborescens 'Grandiflora'
SMOOTH HYDRANGEA
Ⓝ ☼ ◑ ◐ Z4–9 H9–1 ‡↔8ft (2.4m)
The flowerheads of this cultivar are smaller overall than many hydrangeas, although individual sterile flowers are large. Reliable in dry soils.

Hydrangea quercifolia 'Snow Queen'
SNOW QUEEN OAKLEAF HYDRANGEA
Ⓝ ☼ ◑ ◐ Z5–9 H9–5 ‡6ft (2m) ↔8ft (2.5m)
Dense, upright flowerheads composed mostly of large sterile flowers. Dark green oaklike leaves turn crimson, orange, and purple in fall.

Hydrangea macrophylla 'Altona'
ALTONA MOPHEAD HYDRANGEA
☼ ◑ ◐◐ Z6–9 H9–2 ‡3ft (1m) ↔5ft (1.5m)
Large, nearly spherical flowerheads are composed of bright pink to deep purple-blue flowers with yellow centers. Grows into a low, rounded shrub.

Hydrangea macrophylla 'Blue Wave'
BLUE WAVE LACECAP HYDRANGEA
☼ ◑ ◐◐ Z6–9 H9–2 ‡6ft (1m) ↔8ft (2.5m)
Sterile flowers in the center of the flowerhead are surrounded by the showier fertile flowers. Color varies in intensity, depending on soil pH.

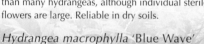

Hydrangea serrata 'Rosalba'
ROSALBA LACECAP HYDRANGEA
☼ ☀ ◊ Z6–9 H10–8 ‡↔4ft (1.2m)
Flowerheads consist of small, pink fertile flowers and white sterile flowers, which become red-marked with age. Blooms in mid- to late summer.

MORE CHOICES

- *Camellia japonica* Z7–8 H8–7
- *Camellia sasanqua* Z7–8 H8–7
- *Daphne bholua* Z7–9 H9–7
- *Daphne x burkwoodii* Z4–7 H7–1
- *Daphne odora* Z7–9 H9–7
- *Euonymus fortunei* Z5–9 H9–2
- *Gaultheria shallon* Z6–8 H8–6
- *Hamamelis mollis* Z5–8 H9–1
- *Hamamelis vernalis* Z4–8 H8–1
- *Hydrangea aspera* Z7–9 H9–7
- *Hydrangea paniculata* Z3–8 H8–1
- *Ilex crenata* 'Sky Pencil' Z5–7 H7–5
- *Kalmia latifolia* Z5–9 H9–5
- *Leucothoe fontanesiana* Z5–8 H8–5
- *Loropetalum chinensis* var. *rubrum* Z7–9 H9–3
- *Pieris floribunda* Z5–8 H8–5
- *Rhododendron macrophyllum* Z7–9 H9–7

Aucuba japonica
JAPANESE LAUREL
☼ ☀ ◊ Z6–15 H12–6 ‡10ft (3m) ↔10ft (3m)
Glossy-leaved evergreen shrub produces small, red-purple flowers in midspring. In fall, female plants produce red berries. Disliked by rabbits.

Hydrangea serrata 'Blue Bird'
BLUE BIRD LACECAP HYDRANGEA
☼ ☀ ◊ Z6–9 H10–8 ‡↔4ft (1.2m)
Flowers, which are most colorful in acidic soils, appear from summer to fall. Dark green leaves take on red shades in fall.

Kalmia polifolia
EASTERN BOG LAUREL
Ⓝ ☼ ☀ ◊ ᵖᴴ Z2–7 H7–1 ‡24in (60cm) ↔3ft (1m)
Blossoms in mid- to late spring. Glossy dark green leaves, arranged in opposite pairs or whorls of 3, have rolled-back margins and glandular hairs underneath.

Enkianthus cernuus var. *rubens*
RED ENKIANTHUS
☼ ◊ ᵖᴴ Z6–8 H8–6 ‡↔10ft (3m)
Blossoms in late spring. Bushy shrub with leaves that are tinged purple in summer and turn dark red-purple in fall. Dislikes dry soils. Native to Japan.

Enkianthus campanulatus
RED VEIN ENKIANTHUS
☼ ☀ ◊ ◊ ᵖᴴ Z5–8 H8–4 ‡↔12–15ft (4–5m)
Creamy yellow, bell-shaped flowers with pink or red veins bloom in late spring to early summer. Dull green leaves turn orange to red in fall. Native to Japan.

Rhododendron occidentale
DECIDUOUS AZALEA
Ⓝ ☼ ◐ ◊ ᴾᴴ Z7–9 H9–7 ↕↔5–8ft (1.5–2.5m)
Sweetly scented, funnel-shaped flowers are creamy
white to pale pink, with a yellow-orange blotch inside.
Glossy leaves turn yellow or orange in fall.

Rhododendron calendulaceum
FLAME AZALEA
Ⓝ ☼ ◐ ◊ ᴾᴴ Z5–8 H9–4 ↕↔6–10ft (2–3m)
Robust, sun-loving azalea has funnel-shaped flowers
of orange or scarlet, although there is also a yellow
variant. Leaves are softly hairy on top and bottom.

MORE CHOICES

- *Rhododendron prunifolium* Z6–9 H8–6
- *Rhododendron vaseyi* Z5–8 H8–4
- *Rhododendron viscosum* Z3–9 H9–1
- *Ribes sanguineum* Z6–8 H8–6
- *Sarcococca humilis* Z6–9 H9–6
- *Symphoricarpos albus* Z3–7 H7–1
- *Vaccinium parvifolium* Z5–8 H8–5
- *Vaccinium uliginosum* Z7–9 H9–7

Rhododendron austrinum
FLORIDA AZALEA
Ⓝ ☼ ◐ ◊◐ ᴾᴴ Z6–10 H10–5 ↕↔10ft (3m)
Fragrant, tubular-funnel-shaped flowers, which may
also be yellow or orange, bloom in clusters of 8 to 15.
They bloom early in the rhododendron season.

Rhododendron arborescens
SWEET AZALEA

Ⓝ ☀ ☼ ◊ ᴾᴴ Z5–9 H9–4 ↕↔8–20ft (2.5–6m)

Clove-scented flowers of this upright azalea are produced in clusters of 3 to 7. Blooms late in the season, and the leaves turn reddish green in fall.

Daphne genkwa
LILAC DAPHNE

☀ ◊ Z6–9 H9–6 ↕↔5ft (1.5m)

Faintly scented flowers bloom in clusters in mid- to late spring, before the leaves appear. Leaves are bronze when young. An upright, open shrub native to China.

Hamamelis x intermedia 'Jelena'
JELENA WITCH HAZEL

☀ ☼ ◊◊ Z5–9 H9–5 ↕↔12ft (4m)

Bright green leaves turn orange and red in fall and drop off before blossoms appear in early to midwinter. Dislikes dry soils.

Skimmia japonica
JAPANESE SKIMMIA

☀ ◊ Z7–8 H9–7 ↕↔5ft (1.5m)

Has slightly fragrant leaves as well as fragrant red- or pink-tinged white flowers. If both sexes are present, female plant bears red fruit.

Clethra alnifolia
SUMMERSWEET

Ⓝ ☀ ● ᴾᴴ Z3–9 H9–1 ↕↔8ft (2.5m)

The fragrant, bell-shaped white flowers of this shrub form elegant spires. Upright shrub often increases through suckering. Leaves turn yellow in fall.

Lindera benzoin
SPICE BUSH

Ⓝ ☀ ◊ ᴾᴴ Z4–9 H8–1 ↕↔10ft (3m)

Grown for its aromatic foliage, which turns yellow in fall. It bears tiny, yellow-green, star-shaped flowers, followed by red berries on female plants.

Shrubs for moist to wet soils

Gardeners often must deal with areas on their property that stay constantly wet or flood occasionally. These shrubs naturally grow along the banks of freshwater lakes, streams, and rivers and tolerate the oxygen-poor soils of wetland areas. They will survive and even thrive in these conditions, often providing some much- needed erosion control.

Myrica cerifera
WAX MYRTLE
Ⓝ ☼ ◐ ☀ ◊ ◊ ◊   Z6–9 H9–6   ↕↔15ft (5m)
This shrub produces small, yellow-green catkins in spring. Following these, dense clusters of waxy gray fruit appear along the shoots and last through winter.

MORE CHOICES

- *Aesculus parviflora* Z5–9 H9–4
- *Amelanchier alnifolia* Z4–9 H9–3
- *Aronia arbutifolia* Z5–9 H9–4
- *Aronia melanocarpa* 'Morton' Z3–8 H8–1
- *Calycanthus floridus* 'Athens' Z4–9 H8–4
- *Calycanthus floridus* 'Michael Lindsey' Z5–9 H9–5
- *Cephalanthus occidentalis* Z5–11 H12–3
- *Cornus stolonifera* Z2–8 H8–1
- *Gaultheria shallon* Z6–8 H8–6
- *Hammamelis vernalis* Z4–8 H8–1
- *Ilex glabra* and cultivars Z5–9 H9–3
- *Physocarpus opulifolius* and cultivars Z3–7 H7–1
- *Physocarpus opulifolius* Z3–7 H7–1
- *Rhododendron occidentale* Z7–9 H9–7
- *Rhododendron vaseyi* Z5–8 H8–4
- *Viburnum sieboldii* Z5–8 H8–5

Vaccinium corymbosum
HIGHBUSH BLUEBERRY
Ⓝ ☼ ◑ ☀ ◊ ◊ ᵖᴴ Z3–7 H7–1
↕↔5ft (1.5m)
Clusters of cylindrical white flowers appear from late spring to early summer. The blueberries that follow are blue-black with a white bloom (powdery coating).

Cornus alba 'Elegantissima'
VARIEGATED RED TWIG DOGWOOD
☼ ◊ Z2–8 H8–1 ↕↔10ft (3m)
Gray-green leaves have an irregular white margin. White flowers appear in late spring and early summer, followed by white fruit. Shoots are bright red in winter.

Itea virginica
VIRGINIA SWEETSPIRE
Ⓝ ☼ ◊ Z6–9 H10–7 ↕↔5ft (1.5m)
Fragrant white flowers bloom in dense, elongated clusters. Open shrub grows upright, then arching. Dark green leaves turn red to purple in fall.

Lindera benzoin
SPICE BUSH
Ⓝ ☼ ◑ ◊ Z4–9 H8–1 ↕↔10ft (3m)
A rounded shrub with upright branches and aromatic, bright green foliage. Yellow-green, star-shaped flowers blossom in midspring. Females bear red berries.

Ilex verticillata
WINTERBERRY

Ⓝ ☀ ◐   Z5–8 H8–5   ‡↔15ft (5m)

Deciduous shrub bears bright green, saw-toothed leaves. White flowers are followed by fruit that may be dark red to scarlet, or sometimes orange or yellow.

Rhodotypos scandens
JETBEAD

☀ ◐   Z5–8 H8–5   ‡↔5ft (1.5m)

Four-petaled white flowers bloom singly from shoot tips in late spring. Round, glossy black berries follow the flowers. Has dark green, deeply toothed leaves.

Viburnum opulus 'Aureum'
GOLDEN-LEAVED GUELDER ROSE

☀ ☀ ◐ ◐   Z3–8 H8–1   ‡↔5–10ft (1.5–3m)

White flowerheads of clustered, tubular fertile flowers, surrounded by flat sterile flowers, are of secondary interest. Foliage may scorch in strong sun and dry soil.

Clethra alnifolia
SUMMERSWEET

Ⓝ ☀ ◐ ◐ ᵖᴴ   Z3–9 H9–1   ‡↔8ft (2.5m)

An upright shrub with oval, toothed leaves. Spikes of white flowers bloom in late summer and early fall. Can be planted in a woodland garden or mixed border.

Zenobia pulverulenta
DUSTY BLUE HONEYCUPS

Ⓝ ☀ ◐   Z5–8   H8–5   ‡6ft (2m)   ↔5ft (1.5m)

Pendent, bell-shaped, fragrant white flowers bloom in early to midsummer. Blue-green to dark green leaves have a bluish white underside when young.

Physocarpus opulifolius 'Dart's Gold'
DART'S GOLDEN NINEBARK
Ⓝ ☼ ◑ ◊ ◗　Z3–7 H7–1　‡6ft (2m)　↔8ft (2.5m)
This compact shrub features attractively peeling bark
with age. Clusters of shallow, cup-shaped flowers in
white or pale pink blossom in late spring.

Arctostaphylos patula
GREEN-LEAF MANZANITA
Ⓝ ☼ ◑ ◗　Z6–9 H9–6　‡↔6ft (2m)
An evergreen shrub with red-brown bark and leathery,
bright green leaves. It produces urn-shaped white or
pink flowers, followed by flattened red-brown fruit.

Shrubs tolerant of drought

These shrubs do well in parts of the Northwest that experience either low average rainfall or long periods of drought (usually in summer). Once they are established, they can survive on natural rainfall except in extreme cases. Xeriscaping, the art and science of growing plants under drought conditions, relies on such plants for success.

Cistus salviifolius
SAGELEAF ROCKROSE
☼ ◊　Z8–11 H12–8　‡↔5ft (1.5m)
This evergreen shrub bears
a profusion of flowers in early summer.
Can be grown in a shrub border,
on sunny banks, or
next toa wall or
paved area.

Cistus x purpureus
ORCHID ROCKROSE
☼ ◊　Z9–10 H10–8　‡↔3ft (1m)
Evergreen shrub with sticky, red-flushed shoots and
dark green leaves. Does well in coastal areas because
of resistance to sea winds. Flowers are short-lived.

SHRUBS

Rosa 'Frau Dagmar Hartopp'
FRAU DAGMAR HARTOPP ROSE
☼ ◊ Z2–9 H9–1 ↕3ft (1m) ↔4ft (1.2m)
Like many of its Rugosa rose relatives, this clove-scented, shrubby and suckering, thorny beauty requires very little maintenance once it is established.

MORE CHOICES

- *Amelanchier alnifolia* Z4–9 H8–3
- *Arctostaphylos alpina* Z2–7 H7–1
- *Baccharis pilularis* Z3–7 H7–1
- *Ceanothus ovatus* Z8–10 H10–8
- *Ceanothus thyrsiflorus* and cultivars Z7–11 H10–3
- *Kerria japonica* Z4–9 H9–1
- *Parrotia persica* Z4–7 H7–1
- *Penstemon angustifolius* Z7–10 H12–3
- *Physocarpus malvaceus* Z3–7 H7–1
- *Pyracantha coccinea* Z6–9 H9–6
- *Yucca recurvifolia* Z7–9 H9–7

Cistus ladanifer
COMMON GUM CISTUS, LAUDANUM
☼ ◊ Z7–10 H10–7 ↕↔5ft (1.5m)
Flowers grow from the tips of short sideshoots. Narrow, dark green leaves are sticky and aromatic. This evergreen shrub resents being transplanted.

Rhus glabra 'Laciniata'
CUTLEAF SMOOTH SUMAC
Ⓝ ☼ ◑ Z2–8 H9–3 ↕↔8ft (2.5m)
Pinnate leaves are 20in (50cm) long, composed of 11–13 narrow, rich green leaflets. Yellow-green flowers are followed by spherical, bristly red fruit.

Rosmarinus officinalis 'Roseus'
PINK ROSEMARY
☼ ◊ Z8–11 H12–8 ↕↔5ft (1.5m)
Cultivated for its pink flowers and as a culinary herb for its leaves rich in aromatic oils. Often grown in an herb garden, it also does well in borders and beds.

Rosmarinus officinalis
ROSEMARY
☼ ◊ Z8–11 H12–8 ↕↔5ft (1.5m)
Evergreen, aromatic leaves. Rosemary is a popular culinary herb and an attractive garden plant. Flowers are produced mostly at or near shoot tips .

Shrubs for acidic soils (pH below 6)

Soil acidity increases the availability of some minerals, such as iron and magnesium. Some plants, including rhododendrons and azaleas and their relatives, are more efficient at absorbing nutrients from acidic soils than many other plants. Most of these plants evolved in woodlands, where the build up of humic acid in leaf litter decreases the soil's pH.

SHRUBS

Corylopsis pauciflora
BUTTERCUP WINTER HAZEL
☀ ◐ ◊ ◑ ◉ 🌣 Z6–9 H9–6 ‡ 5ft (1.5m) ↔ 8ft (2.5m)
Fragrant flowers are produced in pendent clusters in midspring. This dense, bushy shrub has bright green leaves with bristlelike teeth.

Hydrangea macrophylla 'Blue Wave'
BLUE WAVE LACECAP HYDRANGEA
☀ ☀ ◊ ◑ Z6–9 H9–2 ‡6ft (1m) ↔8ft (2.5m)
These shrubs make excellent border plants. The lacecap flowerheads in shades of blue and pink are long-lasting and can be dried for flower arrangements.

Itea virginica
VIRGINIA SWEETSPIRE
☀ ◑ Z6–9 H10–7 ‡5–10ft (1.5–3m) ↔5ft (1.5m)
Fragrant flowers bloom in summer. Good in a shrub or mixed border, but it may require some support while it is establishing.

Enkianthus campanulatus
RED VEIN ENKIANTHUS
☀ ◑ ◊ ◑ 🌣 Z5–8 H8–4 ‡↔12–15ft (4–5m)
Tiny red veins on the flowers produce a pinkish cast. A treelike shrub with whorled branches and toothed leaves. Grows well in an open woodland site.

Enkianthus cernuus var. *rubens*
RED ENKIANTHUS
☀ ◑ Z6–8 H8–6 ‡↔10ft (3m)
A bushy shrub with toothed leaves 2in (5cm) long. Clusters of 5–12 flowers with finely toothed mouths blossom in late spring and early summer.

MORE CHOICES

- *Amelanchier alnifolia* Z4–9 H8–3
- *Andromeda polifolia* Z2–6 H6–1
- *Arbutus unedo* 'Compacta' Z7–9 H9–3
- *Camellia japonica* Z7–8 H8–7
- *Camellia sasanqua* Z7–8 H8–7
- *Clethra alnifolia* Z3–9 H9–1
- *Fothergilla gardenii* Z4–8 H8–1
- *Gaultheria shallon* Z6–8 H8–6
- *Halesia carolina* Z5–8 H8–4
- *Kalmia latifolia* Z5–9 H9–5
- *Magnolia liliflora* Z4–9 H9–1
- *Pernettya mucronata* Z6–7 H7–6
- *Pieris japonica* Z6–8 H8–6
- *Rhododendron macrophyllum* Z7–9 H9–7
- *Skimmia japonica* Z7–9 H9–7
- *Viburnum nudum* 'Winterthur' Z5–9 H9–5

Rhododendron arborescens
SWEET AZALEA
Ⓝ ☼ ☀ ◊ ᴾᴴ Z5–9 H9–4 ↕↔8–20ft (2.5–6m)
Funnel-shaped flowers are white to light pink, often
with red stamens, and have a clove fragrance. Shiny,
dark green leaves are 1¼–3in (3–8cm) long.

Rhododendron calendulaceum
FLAME AZALEA
Ⓝ ☼ ☀ ◊ ᴾᴴ Z5–8 H9–4 ↕↔6–10ft (2–3m)
Bright yellow, orange, or scarlet flowers bloom in late
midseason of rhododendron time and at the same time
as the leaves emerge, or shortly thereafter.

Rhododendron prunifolium
PLUMLEAF AZALEA
Ⓝ ☼ ◊ Z6–9 H8–6 ↕8–10ft (2.5–3m) ↔6–8ft (2–2.5m)
A hairless, evergreen shrub with medium-sized, elliptic
leaves. Orange-red to red flowers blossom very late in
the rhododendron season.

Rhododendron austrinum
FLORIDA AZALEA
Ⓝ ☼ ☀ ◊◊ ᴾᴴ Z6–10 H10–5 ↕↔10ft (3m)
Fragrant flowers bloom in clusters of dense 8–15
blossoms. This deciduous azalea bears softly hairy,
midgreen leaves.

Zenobia pulverulenta
DUSTY BLUE HONEYCUPS
Ⓝ ☼ ◊ Z5–8 H8–5 ↕6ft (2m) ↔5ft (1.5m)
Scented flowers bloom in clusters 8in (20cm) long.
Arching shoots are bluish with a white coating. May
be deciduous or semi-evergreen.

SHRUBS

Shrubs for alkaline soils (pH above 8)

Alkaline soils often result from the geological parent material lying under the soil. Although alkaline soils can be high in minerals, they are chemically bound up in the soil, and only specialized plants can extract them with their root systems. This soil is often called white alkali soil, suggested by the white crust that forms on the surface from mineral buildup.

Buddleja davidii 'White Profusion'
WHITE BUTTERFLY BUSH
☼ ◊ Z6–9 H10–4 ↕10ft (3m) ↔15ft (5m)
A fast-growing shrub with long, arching shoots. It produces fragrant, yellow-eyed flowers in dense panicles from summer to fall.

Choisya ternata 'Aztec Pearl'
AZTEC PEARL ORANGE
Ⓝ ☼ ◊ Z8–10 H10–8 ↕↔8ft (2.5m)
Evergreen; glossy, aromatic leaves are composed of 3 stalkless leaflets. Bears clusters of 3–6 fragrant flowers in late spring and again in late summer and fall.

Chimonanthus praecox
WINTERSWEET
☼ ◊ Z7–9 H9–7 ↕8ft (2.5m) ↔10ft (3m)
In winter, this shrub produces fragrant, pendent, cup-shaped flowers. Leaves are lance shaped and glossy, arranged in opposite pairs.

MORE CHOICES

- *Deutzia scabra* 'Pink Minor' Z8–10 H10–8
- *Hibiscus syriacus* Z5–9 H10–3
- *Kolkwitzia amabilis* Z5–9 H9–5
- *Sarcococca hookeriana* var. *digyna* Z6–9 H9–6
- *Yucca filamentosa* Z4–11 H12–5

Buddleja davidii 'Harlequin'
HARLEQUIN VARIEGATED BUTTERFLY BUSH
☼ ◊ Z6–9 H10–4 ↕↔20ft (6m)
Long, pointed, dark green leaves have yellow margins when young and creamy margins when mature. Blooms from midsummer to fall. Fast-growing.

Buddleja davidii 'Fascinating'
FASCINATING BUTTERFLY BUSH
☼ ◊ Z6–9 H10–4 ↕10ft (3m) ↔15ft (5m)
This shrub attracts many insects, especially butterflies. Tubular flowers with a sweet fragrance form dense clusters 4in (10cm) or more across.

Buddleja davidii 'Royal Red'
RED BUTTERFLY BUSH
Ⓝ ☼ ◊ Z6–9 H10–4 ↕10ft (3m) ↔15ft (5m)
Clusters to 20in (50cm) long bloom in summer. Dark green leaves are white-felted underneath. The flowers are particularly attractive to butterflies.

Rosa rugosa 'Alba'
WHITE RUGOSA ROSE

☀ ◊ Z2–9 H9–1 ↕↔3–6ft (1–2m)

Pale pink buds open into fragrant, cupped flowers from summer through fall. Flowers are followed by large, tomato-shaped red to orange-red hips.

Hydrangea paniculata 'Grandiflora'
PEEGEE HYDRANGEA

☀ ☀ ◊◊ Z4–8 H8–1 ↕22ft (7m) ↔8ft (2.5m)

Clusters, composed mainly of sterile flowers, turn pink or red with age and can be used in dried arrangements. Prune back hard in spring for larger flowerheads.

Cotinus coggygria 'Royal Purple'
ROYAL PURPLE SMOKEBUSH

☀ ☀ ◊◊ Z5–8 H8–1 ↕↔15ft (5m)

Tiny, deep pink flowers blossom in summer. The masses of flower stalks give the impression of smoke. Dark purplish red leaves turn scarlet in fall.

Rhus typhina 'Dissecta'
STAGHORN SUMAC

Ⓝ ☀ ◊ Z3–8 H8–1 ↕15ft (5m) ↔20ft (6m)

Staghorn sumac is named for the texture of the velvety red shoots. Leaves turn brilliant orange-red in fall. This cutleaf form makes an especially attractive specimen.

Philadelphus x lemoinei 'Belle Etoile'
BELLE ETOILE MOCK ORANGE

☀ ☀ ◊ Z5–8 H8–1 ↕4ft (1.2m) ↔8ft (2.5m)

Small, extremely fragrant flowers are produced in clusters of 3–5 in early or midsummer. Upright or slightly arching; makes a good shrub border addition.

SHRUBS

Shrubs for clay soils

Clay soil feels "greasy" when you rub a wet bit of it between your fingers , and its surface cracks when it dries out, making penetration by rain or irrigation water difficult. However, clay soils can be among the most fertile of all garden soils, and they hold added nutrients well. Presented here are some rugged plants that can make themselves at home in clay soils.

SHRUBS

Viburnum plicatum f. *tomentosum* 'Mariesii'
MARIESII DOUBLEFILE VIBURNUM
☼ ◊ Z4–8 H8–1 ↕↔20ft (6m)
Bushy, spreading shrub with distinctively tiered branches. Blooms in late spring and early summer.

Berberis thunbergii 'Aurea'
YELLOW-LEAVED JAPANESE BARBERRY
☼ ◊ Z5–8 H8–5 ↕↔5ft (1.5m)
Foliage is bright yellow when young. Leaves turn orange and red in fall, especially if the plant is in sun. Small flowers are followed by glossy red fruit.

Viburnum x bodnantense 'Dawn'
DAWN FRAGRANT VIBURNUM
☼ ◊ Z7–8 H8–7 ↕↔10ft (3m)
Flowers during mild periods from late fall to early spring. Oval leaves are bronze when young, turning dark green as they mature.

MORE CHOICES

- *Aucuba japonica* Z6–15 H12–6
- *Berberis darwinii* Z7–9 H9–7
- *Buxus microphylla* Z6–9 H9–6
- *Cornus stolonifera* Z2–8 H8–1
- *Cotinus coggygria* Z5–9 H9–3
- *Forsythia* x *intermedia* Z6–9 H9–3
- *Hydrangea arborescens* 'Annabelle' Z4–9 H9–1
- *Kerria japonica* Z4–9 H9–1
- *Lonicera fragrantissima* Z4–8 H8–3
- *Mahonia bealei* Z7–8 H8–7
- *Philadelphus* x *virginalis* 'Minnesota Snowflake' Z4–7 H7–1
- *Pieris floribunda* Z5–8 H8–5
- *Ribes sanguineum* Z6–8 H8–6

Mahonia aquifolium
OREGON GRAPE HOLLY

Ⓝ ☼ ◑ ◊ Z6–9 H9–6 ↕↔5ft (1.5m)

Flowers are followed by round, blue-black berries
Evergreen shrub with glossy, bright green leaves.
Can be grown as a hedge or screen.

Potentilla fruticosa 'Abbotswood'
ABBOTSWOOD POTENTILLA

Ⓝ ☼ ◊ Z3–7 H7–1 ↕30in (75cm) ↔4ft (1.2m)

Dark blue-green leaves consist of five leaflets.
Relatively large, saucer-shaped flowers are borne
throughout summer and fall.

Potentilla fruticosa 'Goldfinger'
GOLDFINGER POTENTILLA

Ⓝ ☼ ◊ Z3–7 H7–1 ↕3ft (1m) ↔4ft (1.2m)

Flowers up to 2in (5cm) across blossom profusely
among the leaves, composed of 5 narrowly oblong
leaflets. Potentillas can be cut to the ground in spring.

Viburnum plicatum f. tomentosum 'Pink Beauty'
PINK BEAUTY DOUBLEFILE VIBURNUM

☼ ◊ Z4–8 H8–1 ↕↔10ft (3m)

Produces attractive lacecap flowerheads of showy sterile flowers and
unassuming fertile flowers. Sterile flowers emerge white and turn pink
with age.

Hydrangea arborescens 'Grandiflora'
SMOOTH HYDRANGEA

Ⓝ ☼ ☼ ◑ ◊ Z4–9 H9–1 ↕↔8ft (2.4m)

Although the acidity of the soil influences the color of
many pink and blue hydrangeas, the coloring of this
shrub's flowers is unaffected by soil pH.

SHRUBS

Lonicera fragrantissima
WINTER HONEYSUCKLE

☼ ☼ ◊ Z4–8 H8–3 ‡6ft (2m) ↔12ft (4m)

Very fragrant, short-tubed flowers are produced during winter and early spring and are welcomed by bees. Berries are dull red.

Spiraea x vanhouttei
VANHOUTTE SPIRAEA

☼ ◊ Z4–8 H8–1 ‡6ft (2m) ↔5ft (1.5m)

Flowers are borne in abundance in late spring and early summer and almost completely cover the dark green leaves. Very adaptable and tolerant.

MORE CHOICES

- *Rhododendron occidentale* Z7–9 H9–7
- *Spiraea japonica* and cultivars Z4–9 H9–1
- *Syringa vulgaris* and cultivars Z4–8 H8–1
- *Viburnum carlesii* 'Compactum' Z4–7 H7–1
- *Viburnum tinus* 'Spring Bouquet' Z7–11 H12–7
- *Weigela florida* Z5–9 H9–1

Spiraea japonica 'Little Princess'
LITTLE PRINCESS JAPANESE SPIREA

☼ ◊ Z4–9 H9–1 ‡↔5ft (1.5m)

Blooms profusely in mid- to late summer on a dense mound. Slower growing and less tolerant of severe pruning than many other spireas.

Rhododendron occidentale
DECIDUOUS AZALEA

Ⓝ ☼ ☼ ◊ ᵖᴴ Z7–9 H9–7 ‡↔5–8ft (1.5–2.5m)

Fragrant flowers, 2½–3½in (6–8cm) across, can be pale pink as wellas white and bloom in the midle of rhododendron season. Grows best in sun.

Syringa vulgaris 'Président Grévy'
PRESIDENT GREVY LILAC

☼ ◊◊ ◑ Z4–8 H8–1 ‡↔22ft (7m)

Very fragrant, double flowers open from red-violet buds. Clusters can reach 10in (25cm) long. Can be cut back severely to control its size.

Pyracantha 'Mohave'
MOHAVE FIRETHORN

☼ ◊ Z6–9 H9–6 ‡12ft (4m) ↔15ft (5m)

This vigorous evergreen works well as a hedge, screen, or accent. Small white flowers are followed by masses of long-lasting berries in early fall.

Skimmia japonica
JAPANESE SKIMMIA

☼ ◑ ◊ Z7–8 H9–7 ‡↔5ft (1.5m)

Fragrant white flowers, produced in mid- to late spring, are sometimes tinged pink or red. Both sexes must be grown for the females to produce bright red fruits.

Aucuba japonica
JAPANESE LAUREL
☼ ◊ Z6–15 H12–6 ↕↔10ft (3m)
Rounded, evergreen shrub with long, glossy, dark green leaves. Female plants produce round to egg-shaped red berries in fall.

Cytisus x praecox 'Allgold'
ALLGOLD WARMINSTER BROOM
☼ ◊ Z6–9 H9–6 ↕4ft (1.2m) ↔5ft (1.5m)
This compact shrub has arching shoots that, in mid- to late spring, are covered with pealike flowers ½–¾in (1–2cm) long. Tolerates nitrogen-poor soils.

Berberis thunbergii
JAPANESE BARBERRY
☼ ◊ Z5–8 H8–5 ↕↔5ft (1.5m)
Most of the many selections of Japanese barberry are widely adaptable to a range of conditions. Most produce red fruit that birds will take and disperse.

Shrubs for coastal exposure

Saltspray and wind are two of the elements that make coastal exposures difficult for most plants. Likewise, runoff along streets and roads treated with salt in winter present the same challenges. Here are some shrubs that tolerate these situations and can also be used as barriers to keep wind and saltspray out of the garden so that more sensitive plants can be grown.

Berberis thunbergii
JAPANESE BARBERRY
☼ ◐ ◊ Z5–8 H8–5 ↕↔5ft (1.5m)
Japanese barberry is available in a wide range of foliage colors and plant habits. Virtually all of the selections are very rugged and tolerant.

Berberis darwinii
DARWIN'S BARBERRY
☼ ◑ ◊◊ Z7–9 H9–4 ↕↔10ft (3m)
Arching evergreen, covered in mid- to late spring with copious hanging clusters of 10–30 flowers. Bluish black fruit are produced in fall.

Berberis thunbergii 'Aurea'
YELLOW-LEAVED JAPANESE BARBERRY
☼ ◊ Z5–8 H8–5 ↕↔5ft (1.5m)
This bushy, spiny shrub produces red-tinged, pale yellow flowers ½in (1.5cm) long in midspring and red berries in fall. May scorch in full sun in hot weather.

Rhus copallina
DWARF SUMAC
Ⓝ ☼ ◊ Z5–9 H9–5 ↕↔3–5ft (1–1.5m)
Tiny yellow-green flowers bloom in dense clusters in summer, followed by round, egg-shaped fruits in fall. Reddish green shoots are softly hairy.

Holodiscus discolor
OCEAN SPRAY
Ⓝ ☀ ☼ ◊ Z6–9 H9–5 ‡↔20ft (6m)
Hanging plumes of tiny flowers blossom in midsummmer. Good in a mixed or shrub border or in light woodland. Grows quickly.

Nerium oleander
OLEANDER
☀ ◊ Z13–15 H12–1 ‡↔20ft (6m)
Red, pink, white, apricot, or yellow flowers, often on dark red stalks, are produced in summer and followed by beanlike seed pods. Evergreen, upright shrub.

Potentilla fruticosa 'Goldfinger'
GOLDFINGER POTENTILLA
Ⓝ ☀ ◊ Z3–7 H7–1 ‡3ft (1m) ↔4ft (1.2m)
These long-flowering plants are terrific in mixed or shrub borders or as low hedges. The flowers bloom in abundance from late spring to midfall.

Arctostaphylos uva-ursi
COMMON BEARBERRY, KINNIKINICK
Ⓝ ☀ ☼ ◐ Z2–6 H6–1 ‡4in (10cm) ↔20in (50cm)
This mat-forming shrub can be grown as a groundcover or in a rock garden. Flowers are followed by round, bright scarlet fruit.

MORE CHOICES

- *Elaeagnus x ebbingei* 'Gilt Edge' Z7–11 H12–7
- *Garrya elliptica* Z8–11 H12–8
- *Laurus nobilis* Z8–11 H12–1
- *Lavandula angustifolia* and cultivars Z5–8 H8–1
- *Myrica californica* Z7–10 H10–7
- *Myrica pensylvanica* Z3–6 H6–1
- *Rhus aromatica* 'Gro-Low' Z4–9 H9–1
- *Shepherdia argentea* Z3–6 H6–1
- *Ulex europaeus* Z6–8 H8–6

Potentilla fruticosa
SHRUBBY CINQUEFOIL
Ⓝ ☀ ◊ Z3–7 H7–1 ‡3ft (1m) ↔5ft (1.5m)
These compact, deciduous shrubs have pinnate leaves composed of 5–7 dark green leaflets. Flowers from spring to midfall. Grows well in dry, sunny sites.

Cotoneaster lacteus (C. parneyi)
MILKFLOWER COTONEASTER
☀ ☼ ◊ Z7– 9 H9–7 ‡↔12ft (4m)
This evergreen shrub produces clusters of up to 100 white flowers in early to mid-summer, followed by fruit that last through winter. Makes a good hedge.

Cotoneaster adpressus 'Little Gem'
LITTLE GEM COTONEASTER
☀ ☼ ◊ Z4–7 H7–3 ‡2ft (60cm) ↔6ft (2m)
The dark green leaves of this deciduous shrub turn red in fall. Five-petaled, red-tinged white flowers blossom in summer. Berries are ¼in (6mm) long.

Lonicera nitida
BOXLEAF HONEYSUCKLE
☀ ◊ Z6–9 H9–5 ‡6ft (2m) ↔10ft (3m)
This evergreen honeysuckle produces fragrant flowers up to ½in (1.5cm) long, followed by round purple berries. Makes a good hedge.

SHRUBS

Shrubs for exposed windy sites

These tough and resilient shrubs have leathery leaves and a strong, flexible branch structure. Most are large enough to plant around the perimeter of a garden to absorb strong winds, thus protecting less resistant shrubs and perennials growing on the leeward side. They can of course be used in combination with trees suitable for windy sites for multilevel wind control.

Elaeagnus angustifolia
OLEASTER
☀ ◊ Z2–8 H8–1 ‡↔20ft (6m)
Fragrant creamy yellow flowers appear in summer, followed by edible yellow fruit. Branches are red-tinted with silvery scales. Deciduous.

Elaeagnus x ebbingei 'Gilt Edge'
GILT EDGE SILVERBERRY
☀ ◊ Z7–10 H12–7 ‡↔12ft (4m)
Leaves are silvery underneath. Produces fragrant silvery white flowers, followed by edible red fruit. Makes a good low-maintenance hedge.

Myrica californica
PACIFIC WAX MYRTLE
Ⓝ ☀ ☀ ◊ Z7–10 H10–7 ‡30ft (9m) ↔12ft (4m)
Evergreen shrub that can also become a small tree or trimmed to form a hedge.Prefers organic soil. Birds eat the waxy purple fruit.

Rhus aromatica 'Gro-Low'
GRO-LOW FRAGRANT SUMAC
Ⓝ ☀ ◊ Z4–9 H9–1 ‡18in (75cm) ↔8ft (2.5m)
Tiny yellow flowers blossom in midspring, followed by round red fruit. Glossy green leaves turn red-orange in fall. Makes a good groundcover.

Lavatera bicolor (L. maritima)
TREE MALLOW
☀ ◊ Z6–8 H8–6 ‡5ft (1.5m) ↔3ft (1m)
Flowers can be pink, lilac-pink, or white, with magenta markings. Gray-green leaves are toothed and hairy, growing to 2½in (6cm) long.

Pyracantha 'Mohave'
MOHAVE FIRETHORN
☼ ◊ Z6–9 H9–6 ↕12ft (4m) ↔15ft (5m)
Clusters of white flowers blossom in early summer, followed by long-lasting, orange-red fruit. Good resistance to fireblight and other diseases.

Berberis julianae
WINTER BARBERRY
☼ ◊ Z6–9 H9–4 ↕↔10ft (3m)
Dense, bushy shrub. Leaves are dark green and glossy above and pale green underneath. Yellow or red-tinged flowers are followed by egg-shaped black fruits.

MORE CHOICES

- *Amelanchier alnifolia* Z4–9 H8–3
- *Berberis darwinii* Z7–9 H9–7
- *Berberis thunbergii* and cultivars Z5–8 H8–5
- *Buxus microphylla* var. *japonica* Z7–9 H9–5
- *Buxus microphylla* var. *koreana* Z6–9 H9–5
- *Buxus microphylla* Z6–9 H9–6
- *Buxus sempervirens* Z6–8 H8–6
- *Cotoneaster adpressus* 'Little Gem' Z4–7 H7–3
- *Cotoneaster apiculatis* Z6–9 H9–6
- *Elaeagnus commutata* Z2–6 H6–1
- *Laurus nobilis* Z8–11 H12–1
- *Lavandula* x *intermedia* Z5–8 H8–5
- *Leucophyllum frutescens* Z8–9 H9–8
- *Rhus aromatica* Z2–8 H8–1
- *Rhus copallina* Z5–9 H9–5
- *Rhus typhina* Z3–8 H8–1
- *Viburnum dentatum* Z3–8 H8–1

Myrica pensylvanica
BAYBERRY
Ⓝ ☼ ☀ ◊ Z3–6 H6–1 ↕9ft (2.5m) ↔5–12ft (1.5–4m)
Bears yellowish green male catkins in spring before the leaves. Waxy gray fruit produced in autumn last through winter. Works well in a seashore garden.

Cotoneaster lacteus (C. parneyi)
MILKFLOWER COTONEASTER
☼ ☀ ◊ Z7–9 H9–7 ↕↔12ft (4m)
Produces clusters of up to 100 cup-shaped white flowers in early to midsummer, followed by red berries that last from fall to winter.

Ligustrum japonicum 'Texanum'
TEXANUM JAPANESE PRIVET
Ⓝ ☼ ☀ ● ⏚ Z7–12 H12–4 ↕↔6–9ft (2–3m)
Fragrant white flowers bloom in clusters 6in (15cm) long from midsummer to early fall, followed by black fruit. Cut back midspring to limit growth.

Cotoneaster 'Coral Beauty'
CORAL BEAUTY COTONEASTER
☼ ☀ ◊ Z–8 H8–7 ↕3ft (1m) ↔6ft (2m)
Mound-forming evergreen. Produces small white flowers in summer, followed by profuse clusters of orange fruit. Makes a good groundcover.

SHRUBS

Shrubs for air-polluted sites

The busier the road, the more carbon monoxide and other noxious gasses can accumulate. Most shrubs will show signs of stress under these conditions, but those presented here offer you tolerant choices, and many make useful screens from road noise as well. These shrubs are particularly useful as barrier plantings in roadside strips.

Berberis thunbergii 'Aurea'
YELLOW-LEAVED JAPANESE BARBERRY
☼ ◊ Z5–8 H8–5 ↕↔5ft (1.5m)
Dense and arching. Yellow leaves turn orange-red in fall. Produces red-tinged yellow flowers in midspring and egg-shaped red fruits. Does well in urban settings.

MORE CHOICES

- *Arbutus unedo* 'Compacta' Z7–9 H9–3
- *Berberis darwinii* Z7–9 H9–7
- *Buxus sempervirens* Z6–8 H8–6
- *Camellia japonica* Z7–8 H8–7
- *Clethra alnifolia* and cultivars Z3–9 H9–1
- *Cornus stolonifera* Z2–8 H8–1
- *Cotoneaster dammeri* Z5–8 H8–3
- *Deutzia scabra* 'Pink Minor' Z6–8 H8–6
- *Eucalyptus gunnii* var. *divaricata* Z8–10 H10–8

Hydrangea macrophylla
BIG-LEAF HYDRANGEA
☼ ☼ ◊ Z6–9 H9–6 ↕5–6ft (1.5–2m) ↔6–8ft (2–2.5m)
Flowers grown in acidic soil are blue or purple; flowers grown in neutral or alkaline soil are pink or red. Dried flowerheads are good for arrangements.

Buddleja davidii 'Royal Red'
RED BUTTERFLY BUSH
☼ ◊ Z6–9 H10–4 ↕10ft (3m) ↔15ft (5m)
From midsummer to fall produces plumes of fragrant flowers up to 20in (50cm) long. Undersides of dark green leaves are white-felted.

Buddleja davidii 'Fascinating'
FASCINATING BUTTERFLY BUSH
☼ ◊ Z6–9 H10–4 ↕10ft (3m) ↔15ft (5m)
Attractive to insects, especially butterflies. Fast growing. Dense clusters of lilac-pink flowers are produced from summer to fall.

Buddleja davidii 'Harlequin'
HARLEQUIN VARIEGATED BUTTERFLY BUSH
☼ ◊ Z6–9 H10–4 ↕↔20ft (6m)
Green leaves have a yellow border when young and a cream border when mature. Bears plumes of fragrant, dark red-purple flowers.

Syringa vulgaris 'Sensation'
SENSATION LILAC
☼ ◊ ◑ Z4–8 H8–1 ↕↔22ft (7m)
Flowers are very fragrant. Deadhead the plant for the first few years and cut out weak shoots in winter. Suitable for heavy clay soils.

Syringa vulgaris 'Charles Joly'
CHARLES JOLY LILAC
☼ ◊ ◑ Z4–8 H8–1 ↕↔22ft (7m)
Conical clusters of Sweetly scented, dark purple-red, double flowers. Requires little pruning, although it may grow to be treelike.

Syringa vulgaris 'Monge'
MONGE LILAC
☼ ◊ ◑ Z4–8 H8–1 ↕↔22ft (7m)
Produces very large, single flowers in abundance. Flowers have strong, pleasant aroma. Makes a nice addition to a shrub border.

Syringa vulgaris 'Président Grévy'
PRESIDENT GREVY LILAC
☼ ◊ ◑ Z4–8 H8–1 ↕↔22ft (7m)
Produces red-violet buds that open into lilac-blue flowers. The fragrant double flowers form very large clusters up to 10in (25cm) long.

SHRUBS

SHRUBS

Philadelphus x lemoinei 'Belle Etoile'
BELLE ETOILE MOCK ORANGE

☀ ◐ ◊ Z5–8 H8–1 ‡4ft (1.2m) ↔8ft (2.5m)

Large numbers of extremely fragrant flowers bloom in early or midsummer. Grow in a shrub border or in a woodland garden.

Aucuba japonica
JAPANESE LAUREL

☀ ◊ Z6–15 H12–6 ‡↔10ft (3m)

Females produce red berries in fall. Good for areas with rabbit problems, because foliage is unpalatable to rabbits. Grows well in heavy clay soils.

Viburnum tinus 'Spring Bouquet'
SPRING BOUQUET LAURUSTINUS

☀ ◐ ● ‡6ft (2m) ↔3ft (1m) Z8–11 H12–8

White flowers open from pink buds in late winter and spring, followed by egg-shaped. blue-black fruit. Good for attracting wildlife. Evergreen.

MORE CHOICES

- *Euonymus fortunei* Z4–9 H9–5
- *Forsythia* x *intermedia* and cultivars Z6–9 H9–6
- *Hibiscus syriacus* Z5–9 H10–3
- *Hydrangea petiolaris* Z4–9 H9–1
- *Kerria japonica* Z4–9 H9–1
- *Pernettya mucronata* Z6–7 H7–6
- *Philadelphus coronarius* Z4–9 H9–4
- *Philadelphus lewisii* Z5–8 H8–1
- *Philadelphus* x *virginalis* 'Minnesota Snowflake' Z4–7 H7–1
- *Pyracantha coccinea* Z6–9 H9–6
- *Ribes sanguineum* Z6–8 H8–6
- *Rosa* 'Albéric Barbier' Z5–9 H9–7
- *Rosa rugosa* and cultivars Z2–9 H9–1
- *Sambucus nigra* Z6–8 H8–6
- *Skimmia japonica* Z7–9 H9–7

Hypericum 'Hidcote'
HIDCOTE ST. JOHN'S WORT

☀ ◐ ◊◑ Z6–9 H9–6 ‡4ft (1.2m) ↔5ft (1.5m)

Evergreen or semi-evergreen. Produces large flowers from summer through fall. Vigorous. Grows well in a mixed or shrub border or a rock garden.

Garrya elliptica
SILK-TASSEL BUSH

Ⓝ ☀ ◊ Z8–11 H12–8 ‡↔20ft (6m)

Produces pendent catkins from midwinter to early spring. Catkins are 6–8in (15–20cm) on male plants and shorter on female plants.

Leycesteria formosa
HIMALAYAN PHEASANTBERRY
☼ ◊ Z7–9 H9–6 ↕↔6ft (2m)
Attractive first-year shoots are bamboolike and blue-green. Flowers produced in summer and early fall, followed by round, reddish purple fruit.

Rhus typhina
STAGHORN SUMAC
Ⓝ ☼ ◊ Z3–8 H8–1 ↕15ft (5m) ↔20ft (6m)
Erect conical clusters of yellow-green flowers to 8in (20cm) long appear in summer. In fall, female plants produce dense clusters of bright crimson fruit.

MORE CHOICES

- *Syringa microphylla* 'Superba' Z5–8 H8–5
- *Ulex europaeus* Z6–8 H8–6
- *Vinca minor* Z4–9 H9–1
- *Weigela florida* Z5–9 H9–1

Ligustrum japonicum
JAPANESE PRIVET
☼ ☼ ◊ Z7–10 H10–7 ↕10ft (3m) ↔8ft (2.5m)
Small white flowers forming large cones blossom in midsummer and early fall, followed by black fruit. Grows well along shady walls.

Ribes sanguineum
FLOWERING CURRANT
Ⓝ ☼ ◊ Z6–8 H8–6 ↕↔6ft (2m)
Attractive flowers blossom in spring, followed by white-coated, blue-black fruit. Works well as an informal hedge. Can be grown in heavy clay soil.

SHRUBS

Large shrubs

Although large shrubs may be as tall as small trees, their branching habit gives them a very different outline in the landscape. Since most shrubs come from forests and forest edges, they do better in partial shade than many comparably sized trees. In medium-size yards these shrubs make fine specimen plants that will complement the scale of the landscape.

Nerium oleander
OLEANDER
☼ ◊ Z13–15 H12–1 ↕↔20ft (6m)
Grown for its fragrant flowers and shiny, elongated leaves. Tip-pruning promotes branching. Can be grown in sandy soil. Adaptable a coastal setting.

Aesculus parviflora
BOTTLEBRUSH BUCKEYE
Ⓝ ☼ ☼ ◊ ◊ Z5–9 H8–4 ↕10ft (3m) ↔15ft (5m)
Young bronze leaves turn dark green in summer and yellow in fall. Sometimes slow to establish. Best grown in a large or medium-sized garden.

Magnolia cylindrica
LILY-FLOWERED MAGNOLIA
☼ ☼ ◊ Z6–9 H9–6 ↕↔15ft (5m)
Fragrant flowers produced in midspring, before or with the leaves. Young leaves turn darker green. Deciduous and slow growing.

Viburnum plicatum f. *tomentosum* 'Mariesii'
MARIESII DOUBLEFILE VIBURNUM
☀ ◐ Z4–8 H8–1 ‡↔20ft (6m)
Densely layered, tiered branches. Large clusters of white flowers are followed by ornamental red fruit. Dark green leaves turn reddish purple in fall.

Viburnum plicatum f. *tomentosum* 'Summer Snowflake'
SUMMER SNOWFLAKE DOUBLEFILE VIBURNUM
☀ ☀ ◐ Z5–8 H8–1 ‡10ft (3m) ↔12ft (4m)
Tiered branches. Lacecap flowerheads blossom in late spring and summer; red fruit ripens to black

Hydrangea macrophylla 'Pia'
PINK ELF HYDRANGEA
☀ ☀ ◐ Z6–11 H9–5 ‡24in (60cm) ↔3ft (1m)
A miniature hydrangea with profuse blossoms. Grows well in a container and makes a nice garden accent or border addition. Grows quickly. Deciduous.

MORE CHOICES

- *Chionanthus virginicus* Z4–9 H9–1
- *Exochorda racemosa* Z5–9 H9–5
- *Heptacodium miconioides* Z5–9 H9–4
- *Hibiscus syriacus* Z5–9 H10–3
- *Hydrangea macrophylla* Z6–9 H9–3
- *Kolkwitzia amabilis* Z5–9 H9–5
- *Loropetalum chinense* and cultivars Z7–9 H9–3
- *Nerium oleander* Z13–15 H12–1
- *Viburnum setigerium* Z5–7 H7–5
- *Vitex agnus-castus* Z6–9 H9–6

Hydrangea macrophylla 'Mariesii'
LACECAP HYDRANGEA
☀ ☀ ◐◐ Z6–9 H8–3 ‡↔4ft (1.2m)
From mid- to late summer produces flowerheads of pale pink to pale blue, depending on soil pH. Attractive in a shrub border.

Hydrangea macrophylla 'Blue Wave'
BLUE WAVE LACECAP HYDRANGEA
☀ ☀ ◐◐ Z6–9 H9–2 ‡6ft (1m) ↔8ft (2.5m)
Grows well in acidic soils. All parts may cause stomach upset if ingested; foliage may cause skin irritation on contact. Makes a good border plant.

SHRUBS

Medium-sized shrubs

These midsized woody plants should be considered the backbone of of well-designed landscape. They mix well with smaller shrubs as well as perennials in large mixed borders. They hold their own as specimen plants in a small lawn or other open garden area, and they can be used to face down larger shrubs or even small trees.

SHRUBS

Cornus alba 'Elegantissima'
VARIEGATED RED TWIG DOGWOOD
☼ ◊ Z2–8 H8–1 ↕↔10ft (3m)
In winter, young shoots are bright red. Creamy white flowers blossom in late spring and early summer, followed by white berries. Can grow on streambanks.

Exochorda x macrantha 'The Bride'
THE BRIDE PEARLBUSH
☼ ◐ ◊ Z5–9 H9–5 ↕6ft (2m) ↔10ft (3m)
In late spring and early summer, arching branches form a mound of abundant white flowers and dense, dark green leaves.

Philadelphus coronarius 'Variegatus'
VARIEGATED MOCK ORANGE
☼ ◐ ◊ Z5–8 H8–3 ↕8ft (2.5m) ↔6ft (2m)
This deciduous shrub is grown for its attractive foliage, as well as the very fragrant flowers produced in late spring and early summer.

Kalmia polifolia
EASTERN BOG LAUREL
Ⓝ ☼ ◐ ◊ ⌀ Z2–6 H6–1 ↕24in (60cm) ↔3ft (1m)
Sparsely branched shrub. Leathery leaves have rolled-back edges and glandular hairs underneath. Grows readily from softwood cuttings. Evergreen.

MORE CHOICES

- *Chaenomeles japonica* Z5–9 H9–1
- *Clerodendrum bungei* Z8–10 H12–8
- *Daphne aurenmarginata* Z7–9 H9–1
- *Daphne odora* Z7–9 H9–7
- *Deutzia x* 'Rosealind' Z6–8 H8–6
- *Forsythia x intermedia* 'Lynwood' Z6–9 H9–6
- *Hydrangea aspera* Z7–9 H9–7
- *Ilex crenata* 'Sky Pencil' Z5–7 H7–5
- *Paeonia suffruticosa* and cultivars Z3–8 H8–1

Viburnum dilatatum
LINDEN VIBURNUM
☼ ☼ ◊ Z5–8 H8–5 ↕10ft (3m) ↔6ft (2m)
Small, star-shaped white flowers are produced in late spring and early summer, preceding bright red berries. Dark green leaves turn bronze and red in fall.

Viburnum plicatum f. *tomentosum* 'Pink Beauty'
PINK BEAUTY DOUBLEFILE VIBURNUM
☼ ◊ Z4–8 H8–1 ↕↔10ft (3m)
Produces attractive lacecap flowerheads of showy sterile flowers and unassuming fertile flowers.

MORE CHOICES

- *Philadelphus coronarius* 'Variegatus' Z5–9 H9–5
- *Pieris japonica* and cultivars Z6–8 H8–6
- *Viburnum nudum* 'Winterthur' Z5–9 H9–5
- *Weigela florida* Z5–9 H9–5

Viburnum opulus 'Aureum'
EUROPEAN CRANBERRYBUSH VIBURNUM
☼ ☼ ● Z3–8 H8–1 ↕↔ 8–15ft (2.5–4.5m)
Grown mostly for its bright golden spring leaf coloration, which may last into summer if grown shaded from the hottest afternoon sun.

Daphne odora 'Aureomarginata'
VARIEGATED WINTER DAPHNE
☼ ◊ Z7–9 H9–7 ↕↔ 5ft (1.5m)
Very fragrant flowers blossom from midwinter through early spring, followed by fleshy, round red fruit. Grows well in a sheltered area.

Spiraea x vanhouttei
VANHOUTTE SPIRAEA
☼ ◊ Z4–8 H8–1 ↕6ft (2m) ↔5ft (1.5m)
Makes a great informal hedge. Bears profuse clusters of white flowers in late spring and early summer. Tolerates streambanks and heavy clay soils.

SHRUBS

Small shrubs

Small shrubs are versatile. They can be used with larger shrubs to create spectacular shrub borders that require far less maintenance than perennial borders, because they do not require routine division. Of course, they can be combined with perennials and other herbaceous plants to provide year-round bloom in a smallish spot.

Potentilla fruticosa 'Abbotswood'
ABBOTSWOOD POTENTILLA
Ⓝ ☀ ◊ Z3–7 H7–1 ‡3ft (1m) ↔5ft (1.5m)
Dense, bushy shrub. Long flowering season from late spring to midfall. Leaves composed of 5 leaflets. Good in a shrub border.

Choisya ternata
MEXICAN ORANGE BLOSSOM
☀ ◊ Z8–10 H10–8 ‡↔8ft (2.5m)
Fragrant flowers bloom in late spring and sometimes again in late summer or fall. Dense, aromatic, evergreen foliage. Grows well in heavy clay soil.

Potentilla fruticosa 'Goldfinger'
GOLDFINGER POTENTILLA
Ⓝ ☀ ◊ Z3–7 H7–1 ‡3ft (1m) ↔4ft (1.2m)
Produces abundant flowers from late spring to midautumn. Finely textured leaves. Good in a shrub border and tolerates coastal exposures.

Spiraea japonica 'Little Princess'
LITTLE PRINCESS JAPANESE SPIREA
☀ ◊ Z4–9 H9–1 ‡↔5ft (1.5m)
Terrific in a shrub border. Abundant rose-pink flowers produced in mid- to late summer. Young bronze leaves turn dark green as they mature. Slow-growing.

Aucuba japonica
JAPANESE LAUREL
☀ ◊ Z6–15 H12–6 ‡10ft (3m)
Small, red-purple flowers bloom in midspring. Females produce red fruit if male pollinators are nearby. Tolerant of heavy air pollution. Grows well in clay soils.

Phygelius x rectus 'Salmon Leap'
CAPE FUCHSIA
☀ ◊◑ Z8–9 H9–8 ‡4ft (1.2m) ↔5ft (1.5m)
Upright shrub. Flowers grow in open clusters up to 18in (45cm). Performs best in sheltered location. Native to wet slopes and streambanks of South Africa.

Skimmia japonica
JAPANESE SKIMMIA

☀ ◐ ◊ Z7–8 H9–7 ↕↔5ft (1.5m)

Bears white flowers in spring, followed by red berries on female plants. Evergreen. Does well in heavy clay soil. Slow-growing, and good in containers.

Cistus x purpureus
ORCHID ROCKROSE

☀ ◊ Z9–10 H10–8 ↕↔3ft (1m)

Bears flowers from early to midsummer among narrow, evergreen, gray-green leaves. Tolerant of little maintenance, sandy soils, and drought. Good in a rock garden.

Daphne x burkwoodii
BURKWOOD DAPHNE

☀ ◊ Z4–7 H7–1 ↕↔5ft (1.5m)

Densely branched, semievergreen shrub bears fragrant flowers in clusters in late spring and sometimes again in fall, especially if given some water in summer.

Sarcococca humilis
SWEET BOX

☀ ◊ Z6–9 H9–6 ↕↔5ft (1.5m)

Powerfully fragrant flowers blossom in early spring, followed by round, dark blue-black berries. Clump-forming with upright shoots. Makes a good groundcover.

Fothergilla gardenii
WITCH ALDER

Ⓝ ☀ ◑ ◊ ᵖᴴ Z4–8 H8–1 ↕↔3ft (1m)

Bears spikes of fragrant flowers in spring, before the leaves. Dark blue-green leaves turn orange, red, and purple in fall. Good for a woodland garden.

MORE CHOICES

- *Artemisia arborescens* Z5–9 H9–5
- *Berberis thunbergii* 'Aurea' Z4–8 H8–1
- *Deutzia gracilis* 'Nikko' Z4–8 H8–1
- *Hydrangea macrophylla* 'All Summer Beauty' Z5–8 H8–3
- *Pieris japonica* 'Pygmaea' Z6–8 H8–5
- *Prunus glandulosa* Z5–8 H8–3
- *Sarcococca hookeriana* var. *humilis* Z6–9 H9–6

SHRUBS

Shrubs with yellow or orange flowers

When in bloom, these cheerful shrubs provide a visual sensation of warmth to a planting. When integrating them into a border design, consider matching them up with red-flowering shrubs and perennials to increase the sense of warmth, or use them as bright accents in a predominantly blue to purple shrub or mixed border.

Michelia figo
BANANA SHRUB
☼ ◊ Z12–15 H12–10 ↕↔30ft (10m)
Bears flowers with a banana-like fragrance in spring and summer. Bushy, evergreen shrub with lightly hairy, yellow-brown stems. Slow growing.

Phlomis lanata
JERUSALEM SAGE
☼ ◊ Z4–9 H9–1 ↕20in (50cm) ↔30in (75cm)
Sage-green leaves are deeply veined and scaly. Yellow flowers covered with brown hairs blossom in summer. Terrific as part of a rock garden.

Forsythia x intermedia
BORDER FORSYTHIA
☼ ◑ ◊ Z6–9 H9–3 ↕↔5ft (1.5m)
Profuse flowers are produced in early and midspring, before the leaves. Remove oldest stems after flowering to rejuvenate the plant. Useful as a hedge or screen.

Corylopsis pauciflora
BUTTERCUP WINTER HAZEL

☼ ◐ ◐ ◐ pH Z6–9 H9–6 ↕5ft (1.5m) ↔8ft (2.5m)

Dense and bushy. Young bronze leaves turn bright green as they mature. Bears fragrant flowers in profusion from early to midspring.

Mahonia aquifolium
OREGON GRAPE HOLLY

Ⓝ ☼ ◐ Z6–9 H9–6 ↕↔5ft (1.5m)

Dense, low evergreen. Birds feed on the fleshy blue-black berries that follow the flowers. Leaves are prickly. Grows well in clay soils and containers.

Buddleja globosa
ORANGE BALL TREE

☼ ◐ Z7–9 H9–6 ↕↔15ft (5m)

In early summer, this bears fragrant flowers in tiny, dense, round clusters. Tolerates coastal exposure. Native to Chile and Argentina.

Hamamelis x intermedia 'Arnold Promise'
ARNOLD PROMISE WITCH HAZEL

Ⓝ ☼ ☼ ◐ Z5–9 H9–5 ↕↔12ft (4m)

Open, spreading shrub. Bears large, fragrant flowers in mid- and late winter. Green leaves turn yellow in fall. Resistant to cold.

Rhododendron calendulaceum
FLAME AZALEA

Ⓝ ☼ ☼ ◐ pH Z5–8 H9–4 ↕↔6–10ft (2–3m)

Produces yellow, scarlet, or orange flowers in early summer, with or just after the leaves. Midgreen leaves are softly hairy both above and underneath.

MORE CHOICES

- Berberis chinensis Z5–8 H8–5
- Clematis tangutica Z6–9 H9–6
- Corylopsis spicata Z5–8 H8–5
- Corylopsis 'Winterthur' Z5–8 H8–6
- Forsythia x intermedia Z6–9 H9–6
- Hamamelis mollis 'Goldcrest' Z5–8 H8–4
- Hamamelis mollis 'Pallida' Z5–9 H9–5
- Phlomis fruticosa Z8–9 H9–8
- Potentilla fruticosa 'Tangerine' Z3–7 H7–1
- Rhododendron bakeri Z5–7 H9–7
- Ribes aureum Z5–8 H8–3

Potentilla fruticosa 'Goldfinger'
GOLDFINGER POTENTILLA

Ⓝ ☼ ◐ Z3–7 H7–1 ↕3ft (1m) ↔4ft (1.2m)

Grows well in clay soil and tolerates coastal exposure. Bears large flowers from late spring to midfall. Grow in mixed or shrub borders or as a low hedge.

Shrubs with blue, purple, lilac flowers

These shades are considered "cool" colors. When used in a planting, cool colors give the impression that the flowers are farther away than they are, and can be used in narrow beds to make them look even smaller. Cool colors can be used together to produce an analogous color scheme or contrasted with warm, complementary colors of yellow, orange, and red.

Lavandula angustifolia
ENGLISH LAVENDER
☼ ◊ Z5–8 H8–5 ‡3ft (1m) ↔4ft (1.2m)
Aromatic leaves and fragrant flowers are borne in mid- and late summer. Excellent in a permixedennial border or low hedge. Deer avoid English lavender.

Lavandula stoechas
SPANISH LAVENDER
☼ ◊ Z8–9 H9–8 ‡↔5ft (1.5m)
Grown for its aromatic silver-gray leaves and fragrant purple flowers borne in late spring and summer. Adaptable and easy to care for.

Leucophyllum frutescens
TEXAS RANGER, SILVERLEAF TEXAS SAGE
Ⓝ ☼ ◊ Z8–9 H9–8 ‡8ft (2.5m) ↔6ft (2m)
Compact, arching shrub. Tolerance to salt makes this ideal for seaside gardens. Bears rose-purple flowers in summer. Native to Mexico and Texas.

Hydrangea macrophylla 'Blue Wave'
BLUE WAVE LACECAP HYDRANGEA
☼ ◐ ◊◊ Z6–9 H9–2 ‡6ft (1m) ↔8ft (2.5m)
Tolerates acidic soils and areas with significant air pollution. In spring, prune older shoots to the base and trim back winter-damaged shoots.

Caryopteris x clandonensis 'Worcester Gold'
WORCESTER GOLD BLUE MIST SHRUB
Ⓝ ☼ ◐ ◊ Z6–9 H9–2 ‡3ft (1m) ↔5ft (1.5m)
Blue or purple-blue flowers produced in late summer and early fall. Plant in a perennial border or shrub bed. Cut back hard in spring. Dense and bushy.

Caryopteris x clandonensis 'Dark Night'
DARK NIGHT BLUE MIST SHRUB
☼ ◐ ◊ Z6–9 H9–2 ‡3ft (1m) ↔5ft (1.5m)
Bears fragrant, small, dark purple-blue flowers Compact, mounding shrub. Grown for its silvery gray foliage. Perfect for a mixed or shrub border.

Buddleja davidii 'Black Knight'
BLACK KNIGHT BUTTERFLY BUSH

☼ ◊ Z6–9 H10–4 ↕10ft (3m) ↔15ft (5m)

Bears conical clusters of fragrant, dark purple flowers in summer. Attracts butterflies. Useful as an accent plant. Fast grower.

Ceratostigma plumbaginoides
LEADWORT, PLUMBAGO

☼ ◊ Z6–9 H9–6 ↕18in (45cm) ↔12 in (30cm)

Clusters of small, dark blue flowers bloom in late summer and fall. Bright green leaves turn brilliant red in fall. Wiry, reddish stems. Use as groundcover or in a rock garden.

Rosmarinus officinalis
ROSEMARY

☼ ◊ Z8–11 H12–8 ↕↔5ft (1.5m)

Aromatic leaves used as a culinary herb. Grow outdoors or in a container inside. Tolerant of drought, and unappealing to rabbits.

Syringa vulgaris 'Sensation'
SENSATION LILAC

☼ ◊◊ Z4–8 H8–1

↕↔22ft (7m)

Suitable for air-polluted sites. Cut out weak shoots in winter. Large clusters of unusual white-edged purple flowers bloom in late spring and early summer.

MORE CHOICES

- *Amorpha fruticosa* Z2–8 H8–1
- *Buddleja davidii* 'Nanjo Blue' Z5–9 H9–2
- *Caryopteris x clandonensis* 'Longwood Blue' Z6–9 H9–1
- *Hibiscus syriacus* 'Blue Bird' Z5–9 H9–5
- *Hydrangea serrata* 'Blue Billow' Z5–8 H8–3
- *Lavandula x intermedia* Z5–8 H8–5
- *Leucophyllum frutescens* 'Green Cloud' Z8–10 H10–8
- *Rhododendron cumberlandense* Z5–8 H8–4

Syringa vulgaris 'Charles Joly'
CHARLES JOLY LILAC

☼ ◊◊ Z4–8 H8–1 ↕↔22ft (7m)

Bears fragrant flowers in late spring and early summer. Tolerates significant amounts of air pollution. Suitable for use as a screen or in a border.

Shrubs with red/pink flowers

Red is one of the "warm" colors that command a viewer's attention. Pure red flowers will appear to pop out toward the viewer. Red is a complementary color to green, so red flowers against green foliage create a sharp contrast. As the tint shifts from red to pink the effect is more subdued, creating a more peaceful mood.

Clethra alnifolia 'Ruby Spice'
RUBY SPICE SUMMERSWEET
Ⓝ ☼ ☀ ● Z3–9 H9–1 ↕↔6–8ft (2–2.5m)
This cultivar has darker pink flowers than the species. Fragrant flowers from late summer to early fall. Tolerant of seaside conditions.

Spiraea japonica 'Neon Flash'
NEON FLASH JAPANESE SPIRAEA
☼ ☀ ● Z3–9 H9–1 ↕4ft (1.2m) ↔5 (1.5m)
Flowers appear from mid- to late summer. Leaves are reddish when they emerge and retain a purplish hue even after they mature. Prefers fertile soil.

Kalmia polifolia
EASTERN BOG LAUREL
Ⓝ ☼ ☀ ● pH Z2–6 H6–1 ↕24in (60cm) ↔3ft (1m)
Bears clusters of flowers in mid- and late spring. Mulch every spring with leaf mold or pine needles. Native to Canada and the northeastern United States.

Fuchsia x hybrida 'Magellanica'
LADY'S EARDROPS
☼ ● Z9–11 H12–9 ↕10ft (3m) ↔6ft (2m)
Bears flowers throughout summer, followed by oblong red-purple fruit. Does well in sheltered sites but also tolerates the wind and salt spray of a coastal location.

MORE CHOICES

- *Camellia japonica* 'Covina' z8–10 H8–7
- *Camellia japonica* 'Debutant' z7–11 H8–7
- *Camellia reticulata* 'Buddha' z7–9 H9–7
- *Clerodendrum bungei* z8–10 H12–8
- *Clethra alnifolia* 'Pink Spires' z3–9 H9–1
- *Daphne bholua* z7–9 H9–7
- *Daphne genkwa* z6–9 H9–6
- *Daphne odora* z7–9 H9–7
- *Hamamelis x intermedia* 'Diane' z5–9 H9–1
- *Hibiscus syriacus* 'Pink Giant' z5–9 H9–1
- *Hydrangea serrata* 'Preziosa' z5–8 H8–1
- *Kalmia latifolia* z5–91 H9–5
- *Kolkwitzia amabilis* z5–9 H9–5
- *Lonicera henryi* z3–8 H8–1
- *Lonicera involucrata* z6–8 H8–5
- *Loropetalum chinense* var. *rubrum* z7–9 H9–3
- *Rhododendron macrophyllum* z7–9 H9–7
- *Rhododendron occidentale* z7–9 H9–7
- *Spiraea x bumalda* 'Anthony Waterer' z3–9 H9–1
- *Viburnum x bodnantense* 'Dawn' z7–8 H8–7
- *Weigela florida* 'Java Red' z4–8 H8–1

Lonicera tatarica 'Rosea'
ROSEA TATARIAN HONEYSUCKLE

☼ ☼ ◊ Z3–9 H8–1 ↕12ft (4m) ↔8ft (2.5m)

In late spring bears fragrant flowers in red, white, or pink. Red fruit is produced after the flowers from late summer into the fall.

Buddleja davidii 'Royal Red'
RED BUTTERFLY BUSH

Ⓝ ☼ ◊ Z6–9 H10–4 ↕10ft (3m) ↔15ft (5m)

Richly fragrant flowers attract butterflies. Open shrub that grows quickly, tolerates air pollution, and does well in alkaline soils.

Rosa 'Frau Dagmar Hartopp'
FRAU DAGMAR HARTOPP ROSE

☼ ◊ Z2–9 H9–1 ↕3ft (1m) ↔4ft (1.2m)

This cultivar is much more compact than the species. The leaves turn purplish and yellow after frost. Like many rugosas, it bears fragrant flowers and red fruit.

Ribes sanguineum
FLOWERING CURRANT

Ⓝ ☼ ◊ Z6–8 H8–6 ↕↔6ft (2m)

Flowers precede round, blue-black fruit. Tolerates air pollution and grows in heavy clay soil. Attracts hummingbirds and flickers. Suitable for a hedge.

Syringa meyeri 'Palibin'
DWARF KOREAN LILAC

☼ ◊ Z4–7 H7–9 ↕↔5ft (1.5m)

Dense clusters of single, lilac-pink flowers bloom in late spring and early summer. Deadheadrecently planted lilacs. Older plants can be cut back hard.

Rosa rugosa 'Hedgehog'
RUGOSA ROSE

☼ ☼ ◊ pH Z2–9 H9–1 ↕↔6ft (2m)

Flowers in mid- to late summer are followed by edible red fruit (hips). Highly resistant to rose fungal diseases. Prefers a fertile, organic soil.

SHRUBS

Shrubs with white or creamy flowers

There is something very clean, crisp, and elegant about a shrub with white or creamy flowers, especially when the flowers are highlighted against a backdrop of rich green foliage. Consider using these shrubs in a thematic white garden or as bright accents in a broader design scheme. Pure white is a stronger color that many people realize, so use it with care.

Rosa rugosa 'Alba'
WHITE RUGOSA ROSE
☼ ◊ Z2–9 H9–1 ↕↔3–6ft (1–2m)
Dense and vigorous. Flowers produced from summer through fall, followed by large, round hips. Grows well in alkaline soils.

Exochorda x macrantha 'The Bride'
THE BRIDE PEARLBUSH
☼ ☼ ◊ Z5–9 H9–5 ↕ 6ft (2m) ↔10ft (3m)
Dramatic flowers in late spring and early summer. Thin old shoots after flowering to promote new growth. Susceptible to chlorosis in shallow, alkaline soil.

Leucothoe fontanesiana
DROOPING LEUCOTHOE
Ⓝ ☼ ☼ ◊ ᴾᴴ Z5–8 H8–5 ↕5ft (1.5m) ↔10ft (3m)
Evergreen shrub produces clusters of flowers from mid- to late spring. Glossy, leathery leaves have sharp teeth. Makes a nice hedge.

Potentilla fruticosa 'Abbotswood'
ABBOTSWOOD POTENTILLA
Ⓝ ☼ ◊ Z3–7 H7–1 ↕30in (75cm) ↔4ft (1.2m)
Compact shrub bears flowers continuously from spring to midfall. Succeeds in clay soils or in windy, coastal environments.

MORE CHOICES

- *Choisya ternata* Z8–10 H10–8
- *Clerodendrum trichotomum* Z7–9 H9–7
- *Exochorda giraldii var* 'Wilsonii' Z6–9 H10–4
- *Exochorda racemosa* Z5–9 H9–5
- *Exochorda serratifolia* Z6–9 H9–6
- *Fuchsia magellanica* 'Alba' Z9–11 H12–9
- *Hibiscus syriacus* 'Diana' Z5–9 H9–1
- *Jasminum officinale* Z8–11 H12–8
- *Loropetalum chinense* Z7–9 H9–3
- *Philadelphus coronarius* Z5–9 H9–5
- *Philadelphus lewisii* Z5–8 H8–1
- *Philadelphus x virginalis* 'Minnesota Snowflake' Z4–7 H7–1
- *Pieris floribunda* Z5–8 H8–5
- *Rhododendron arborescens* Z5–9 H9–4
- *Rhododendron periclymenoides* Z4–9 H9–5
- *Rhododendron viscosum* Z3–9 H9–1
- *Ribes aureum var. villosum* Z5–8 H8–3
- *Syringa reticulata* 'Ivory Silk' Z4–8 H8–1

Buddleja davidii 'White Profusion'
WHITE BUTTERFLY BUSH
Ⓝ ☼ ◊ Z6–9 H10–4 ↕10ft (3m) ↔15ft (5m)
Fragrant flowers produced from summer to fall attract insects, especially butterflies. Able to extract necessary minerals from alkaline soil. Fast growing.

Philadelphus 'Snowflake'
SNOWFLAKE MOCK ORANGE

☀ ☀ ◐ ◐ Z4–8 H8–1 ‡8ft (2.4m) ↔6ft (1.8m)

Fragrant flowers. Cut back old shoots after flowering to allow younger growth to flower the following year. Prone to aphid infestations.

Philadelphus x lemoinei 'Belle Etoile'
BELLE ETOILE MOCK ORANGE

☀ ☀ ◐ Z5–8 H8–1 ‡4ft (1.2m) ↔8ft (2.5m)

Grows well in alkaline soil and tolerates air-polluted sites. Fragrant flowers blossom in early or midsummer. Terrific in a shrub border.

Camellia japonica 'Alba Plena'
ALBA PLENA JAPANESE CAMELLIA

☀ ◐ ◐ Z7–8 H8–7 ‡30ft (9m) ↔25ft (8m)

Erect, evergreen shrub produces profuse double flowers in late fall and early winter. Very versatile, it can be grown in open ground or a container.

Spiraea x vanhouttei
VANHOUTTE SPIRAEA

☀ ◐ Z4–8 H8–1 ‡6ft (2m) ↔5ft (1.5m)

Elegant, arching branches bear clusters of white flowers in early summer. Makes an excellent hedge. Tolerates clay or wet soils and streambanks.

Hydrangea quercifolia
OAKLEAF HYDRANGEA

Ⓝ ☀ ☀ ◐ Z5–9 H9–2 ‡6ft (2m) ↔8ft (2.5m)

From midsummer through midfall bears flowers that become pink-tinged with age. Leaves turn red and purple in fall. Distinctive, peeling orange-brown bark.

Clethra alnifolia
SUMMERSWEET

Ⓝ ☀ ◐ ⚘ Z3–9 H9–1 ‡↔8ft (2.5m)

Fragrant flowers borne in late summer and early fall attract butterflies. Attractive in a woodland garden or mixed border. Thrives in acidic soils.

Winter-blooming shrubs

Few things can lift a gardener out of the winter doldrums as fast as the sight of a winter-flowering shrub. Whether viewed from a window or up close in a late winter garden, these shrubs are better than a shot of Vitamin B-12. Many of these shrubs also have the added benefit of spirit-lifting, fragrant flowers.

Erica x *darleyensis* 'Mediterranean Pink'
MEDITERRANEAN PINK HEATH
☼ ☼ ● Z7–8 H8–7 ‡24in (60cm) ↔12–24in (30–60cm)
Mounding, evergreen foliage. Flowers borne in late winter and early spring. Good as a groundcover or border. Establishes quickly.

Lonicera fragrantissima
WINTER HONEYSUCKLE
☼ ☼ ◊ Z4–8 H8–3 ‡6ft (2m) ↔12ft (4m)
Can be planted in heavy clay soils. Fragrant flowers emerge in winter and early spring. Dull dark green leaves have bristly edges when young.

Garrya elliptica
SILK-TASSEL BUSH
Ⓝ ☼ ◊ Z8–11 H12–8 ‡↔20ft (6m)
Performs well along busy roads and in other sites with heavy pollution. Catkins on male plants grow to 8in (20cm), slightly less on female plants.

MORE CHOICES

- *Camellia reticulata* Z7–8 H8–7
- *Camellia sasanqua* Z7–8 H8–7
- *Corylus avellana* Z3–9 H9–1
- *Hamamelis mollis* Z5–8 H9–1
- *Hamamelis vernalis* Z4–8 H8–1
- *Lonicera fragrantissima* Z4–8 H8–3
- *Lonicera* x *purpusii* Z7–9 H9–7
- *Loropetalum chinense* Z7–9 H9–3
- *Mahonia* x *media* Z8–9 H9–8
- *Sarcococca confusa* Z6–9 H9–6
- *Viburnum farreri* Z6–8 H8–6
- *Viburnum tinus* Z8–10 H10–8

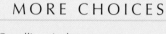

Daphne odora 'Aureomarginata'
VARIEGATED WINTER DAPHNE
☼ ◊ Z7–9 H9–7 ‡↔ 5ft (1.5m)
Very fragrant flowers precede fleshy, round fruit. Prefers a warm, sheltered corner. Performs well as a foundation plant. Evergreen.

Camellia japonica
JAPANESE CAMELLIA

☀ ◐ ◌ ◌ Z7–8 H8–7 ‡30ft (9m) ↔25ft (8m)

Grows best in a sheltered environment. Pruning is required to keep this shrub from attaining treelike dimensions. Evergreen and long-lived.

Viburnum tinus 'Spring Bouquet'
SPRING BOUQUET LAURUSTINUS

☀ ◐ ● Z8–11 H12–8 ‡6ft (2m) ↔3ft (1m)

Flowers are followed by dark blue-black, ovoid fruit. Leaves are smaller than the species. Prefers moderately fertile soil. Also known as 'Compactum'.

Viburnum x bodnantense 'Dawn'
DAWN FRAGRANT VIBURNUM

☀ ◐ ◌ Z7–8 H8–7 ‡10ft (3m) ↔6ft (2m)

Richly fragrant flowers appear before the leaves. Flowers vary in color from rose-red to pink-white. Sparse fruit is small, round, and blue-black or purple.

Camellia sasanqua
SASANQUA CAMELLIA

☀ ◐ ◌ Z7–8 H8–7 ‡10ft (3m) ↔5ft (1.5m)

Adaptable to the cool, sheltering shade of a wall or fence. Can be trimmed for a low hedge or border, or allow it to grow higher as a screen.

Sarcococca hookeriana var. *digyna*
SLENDER SWEET BOX

☀ ◐ ◌ ◌ Z6–9 H9–6 ‡5ft (1.5m) ↔6ft (2m)

Dense, clump-forming evergreen groundcover. Sweetly scented white flowers are succeeded by round black fruits. Male flowers have cream anthers.

Hamamelis x intermedia
HYBRID WITCH HAZEL

☀ ◐ ◌ Z5–9 H9–1 ‡↔12ft (4m)

Fragrant yellow, dark red, or orange flowers appear on bare branches. Bright green leaves turn yellow in fall. Grows well in acidic soil.

Chimonanthus praecox
WINTERSWEET

☀ ◌ Z7–9 H9–7 ‡ 8ft (2.5m) ↔10ft (3m)

Very fragrant flowers 1in (2.5cm) across emerge during mild periods in winter. Glossy, midgreen leaves grow to 8in (20cm). Adaptable to alkaline soils.

SHRUBS

Early spring-blooming shrubs

These beautiful flowering shrubs bloom as the lion and the lamb of spring do their annual dance. This group includes both deciduous and evergreen flowering shrubs, and in all cases the flowers make attractive additions to the landscape. Be prepared to protect the blooms from the ravages of frosts and freezes if practical to do so.

Cistus x purpurens
ORCHID ROCKROSE
☼ ◊ Z9–10 H10–8 ↕↔3ft (1m)
Bears short-lived flowers and sticky, red-flushed shoots. Tolerates drought as well as sea winds, salt spray, and sandy soils in coastal areas. Evergreen.

Magnolia cylindrica
LILY-FLOWERED MAGNOLIA
☼ ☼ ◊ Z6–9 H9–6 ↕ 30ft (6–9m) ↔ 13ft (3.9m)
Fragrant white or yellow-white flowers appear before or with the leaves and grow to 4in (10cm) long. Slow-growing. Native to eastern China.

Lindera benzoin
SPICE BUSH
Ⓝ ☼ ☼ ◊ ᵖᴴ Z4–9 H8–1 ↕↔10ft (3m)
Bears tiny, star-shaped flowers. Aromatic green foliage turns yellow in fall. Can be grown in areas with wet soil or along streambanks. Uninteresting to deer.

Viburnum plicatum f. *tomentosum* 'Pink Beauty'
PINK BEAUTY DOUBLEFILE VIBURNUM
☼ ☼ ◊ Z4–8 H8–1 ↕10ft (3m) ↔12ft (4m)
Produces flowerheads of sterile (outer) and fertile (inner) flowers. Bears red fruit that matures to black. Dark green leaves turn red-purple in fall.

SHRUBS

Abeliophyllum distichum
WHITE FORSYTHIA, KOREAN ABELIA LEAF
☼ ◐ ◊ Z5–9 H9–1 ↕↔4ft (1.2m)
Flowers bloom in late winter or early spring but may be damaged by hard frosts. Grows well when provided the shelter and warmth of a wall. Native to Korea.

Corylopsis pauciflora
BUTTERCUP WINTER HAZEL
☼ ◐ ◊◊◊ ᴾᴴ Z6–9 H9–6 ↕5ft (1.5m) ↔8ft (2.5m)
Dense, bushy shrub bears an abundance of fragrant flowers in early to midspring, but late frosts may damage them. Bronze young leaves turn bright green.

Syringa vulgaris 'Charles Joly'
CHARLES JOLY LILAC
☼ ◊ ◊ Z4–8 H8–1 ↕↔22ft (7m)
Flowers have a wonderful, classic fragrance. Open branched; requires little pruning. Tolerates air-polluted sites. Grow as a screen or border.

Pieris japonica 'Mountain Fire'
MOUNTAIN FIRE PIERIS
☼ ◐ ◊ ᴾᴴ Z5–9 H9–1 ↕↔10ft (3m)
Evergreen leaves are brilliant red when young, turning chestnut brown as they mature. Produces abundant clusters of flowers. Deer find this shrub unappealing.

Cornus mas
CORNELIAN CHERRY
☼ ◐ ◊ Z5–8 H8–4 ↕↔15ft (5m)
Star-shaped flowers on bare branches precede edible, egg-shaped, bright red fruit that entice birds into the garden. Dark green leaves turn reddish purple in fall.

Late spring-blooming shrubs

If your garden ebbs in interest between flower-laden midspring and the verdance of early summer, consider planting some of these shrubs to fill in the gap. Because peak seasons of interest may overlap, it is important to work out color schemes that are complementary with neighboring earlier- and later- performing plants.

Leucothoe fontanesiana
DROOPING LEUCOTHOE
Ⓝ ☀ ☀ ◐ ◖ ᵖᴴ Z5–8 H8–5 ↕5ft (1.5m) ↔10ft (3m)
Upright, with arching branches. Glossy, leathery, teethed leaves are lighter green underneath. Flowers ¼in (6mm) long form clusters. Makes a nice hedge.

Hydrangea arborescens
SMOOTH HYDRANGEA
Ⓝ ☀ ☀ ◐ Z4–9 H9–1 ↕↔3–5ft (1–1.7m)
Clusters of flowers up to 6in (15cm) across may be domed or flattened. Dark green leaves up to 7in (18cm) are lighter underneath.

MORE CHOICES

- *Berberis darwinii* Z7–9 H9–7
- *Berberis thunbergii* and cultivars Z4–8 H8–3
- *Ceanothus americanus* Z4–8
- *Ceanothus thyrsiflorus* Z7–11 H10–3
- *Cotinus coggygria* Z5–9 H9–3
- *Enkianthus cernuus* f. *rubens* Z6–8 H8–6
- *Gaultheria shallon* Z6–8 H8–6
- *Hypericum androsaemum* Z5–7

Kalmia polifolia
EASTERN BOG LAUREL
Ⓝ ☀ ☀ ◐ ◖ ᵖᴴ Z2–7 H7–1 ↕2ft (60cm) ↔3ft (1m)
Sparsely branched shrub. Leathery leaves have rolled-back edges and glandular hairs underneath. Grows readily from softwood cuttings. Evergreen.

Rhododendron occidentale
DECIDUOUS AZALEA
Ⓝ ☼ ◐ ◊ ♨ Z7–9 H9–7 ↕↔5–8ft (1.5–2.5m)
Leaves turn yellow or orange in fall. Fragrant flowers can sometimes be pale pink. Grows well in clay and wet soils and on streambanks.

Styrax obassia
FRAGRANT SNOWBELL
☼ ◐ ● Z6–8 H8–6 ↕40ft (12m) ↔22ft (7m)
Fragrant, bell-shaped flowers form long clusters. Dark green leaves are blue-gray underneath and turn yellow in fall. Adaptable to acidic soil.

Kerria japonica
GLOBEFLOWER, JAPANESE KERRIA
☼ ◊ Z4–9 H9–1 ↕6ft (2m) ↔8ft (2.5m)
Flowers may be single or double, depending on cultivar. Tolerates shade well, although its blooms will be reduced. Suitable for a shrub or mixed border.

MORE CHOICES

- *Illicium henryi* Z7–9 H9–7
- *Kalmia latifolia* Z5–9 H9–5
- *Magnolia liliflora* Z4–9 H9–1
- *Magnolia stellata* Z5–9 H9–5
- *Magnolia virginiana* Z6–9 H9–6
- *Mahonia aquifolium* Z6–9 H9–6
- *Paeonia suffruitcosa* Z3–8 H8–1
- *Philadelphus coronarius* Z4–9 H9–4
- *Phlomis fruitcosa* Z8–9 H9–8
- *Poncirus trioliata* and cultivars Z4–9 H9–1
- *Syringa microphylla* and cultivars Z5–8 H8–5
- *Syringa reticulata* Z3–8 H8–3
- *Trochodendron araliodies* Z6–11 H12–10
- *Ulex europaeus* Z6–8 H8–6
- *Vaccinium corymbosum* Z3–7 H7–1
- *Viburnum carlesii* Z5–8 H8–5
- *Viburnum* x *burkwoodii* Z5–8 H8–1

Exochorda x macrantha 'The Bride'
THE BRIDE PEARLBUSH
☼ ◐ ◊ Z5–9 H9–5 ↕6ft (2m) ↔10ft (3m)
Arching branches are dense and mound-forming. Copious white flowers cover dark green leaves. Prone to chlorosis if grown in shallow, alkaline soil

Spiraea japonica 'Little Princess'
LITTLE PRINCESS JAPANESE SPIREA
☼ ◊ Z4–9 H9–1 ↕↔5ft (1.5m)
Forms a dense, compact mound. Suitable for shrub borders. Tiny flowers form clusters 1½in (4cm) across. Young bronze leaves mature to dark green.

Spiraea japonica 'Gold Flame'
GOLD FLAME SPIREA
☼ ◊ Z4–9 H9–1 ↕↔30in (75cm)
Young orange-red leaves turn bright yellow and then pale green when mature. In fall they become orange, red, and yellow.

SHRUBS

Early summer-flowering shrubs

Taking the baton from spring-flowering shrubs, these summer-flowering ones will keep the excitement going as the longest and warmest days of the year set in. The freshness of these flowering shrubs will make you feel cool as you relax with family and friends in your backyard sanctuary, and many of them will lure butterflies or hummingbirds as well.

Abelia chinensis
CHINESE ABELIA

☼ ◐ ◊ Z7–9 H9–7 ‡5ft (1.5m) ↔8ft (2.5m)

Fragrant flowers ¼in (6mm) long attract butterflies. Spreading shrub; to limit growth, remove dead wood and prune older branches after flowering.

Zenobia pulverulenta
DUSTY BLUE HONEYCUPS

Ⓝ ☼ ◊ Z5–8 H8–5 ‡6ft (2m) ↔5ft (1.5m)

Leaves are glaucous blue-black to dark green. Can be grown in oxygen-poor environments such as wetlands and streambanks, as well as in acidic soils.

Viburnum sieboldii
SIEBOLD VIBURNUM

☼ ◐ ◊ Z5–8 H8–5 ‡12ft (4m) ↔20ft (6m)

Thrives in permanently moist soils found in streambanks. White flowers are followed by clusters of ovoid red fruits that turn black when fully ripe.

Potentilla fruticosa 'Abbotswood'
ABBOTSWOOD POTENTILLA

Ⓝ ☀ ◊ Z3–7 H7–1 ↕30in (75cm) ↔4ft (1.2m)

Dwarf, compact, bushy shrub. Bears abundant flowers from summer through fall. Suitable for locations with heavy clay soil.

Potentilla fruticosa 'Goldfinger'
GOLDFINGER POTENTILLA

Ⓝ ☀ ◊ Z3–7 H7–1 ↕3ft (1m) ↔4ft (1.2m)

Can be grown in clay soils. Tolerates wind and saltspray of coastal exposures. Great for a shrub border or low hedge.

Rhododendron prunifolium
PLUMLEAF AZALEA

Ⓝ ☀ ◊ Z6–9 H8–6 ↕8–10ft (2.5–3m) ↔6–8ft (2–2.5m)

Evergreen azalea. Orange-red to red flowers are 1–1¼in (2.5–3cm) across. Native to eastern Alabama and southwestern Georgia.

Weigela florida 'Variegata'
VARIEGATED WEIGELA

☀ ◊ Z5–8 H8–1 ↕↔6–8ft (2–2.5m)

Dense, bushy shrub. Prune old, straggly plants hard. Can grow near roads and in urban environments due to tolerance of air pollution. Easy to grow.

Symplocos paniculata
SAPPHIREBERRY

☀ ◊ Z5–8 H8–4 ↕↔10ft (3m)

Cultivation of several plants together results in more abundant production of their egg-shaped, metallic blue fruit. Small flowers have pleasant scent.

Hydrangea macrophylla 'Pia'
PINK ELF HYDRANGEA

☀ ☀ ◊ Z6–11 H9–5 ↕24in (60cm) ↔3ft (1m)

Fast-growing miniature hydrangea. Thrives in a container or in an open garden. Produces a profusion of red-pink flowers.

MORE CHOICES

- *Abelia chinensis* Z5–9 H9–3
- *Aesculus pavia* Z5–9 H9–5
- *Amorpha fruticosa* Z2–8 H8–1
- *Buddleja alterifolia* Z6–9 H10–1
- *Cephalanthus occidentalis* Z5–11 H12–3
- *Enkianthus campanulatus* Z4–7 H7–3
- *Exochorda serratifolia* Z6–9 H9–6
- *Fothergilla major* Z4–8 H9–2
- *Hydrangea serrata* Z6–9 H9–6
- *Kolkwitzia amabilis* Z5–9 H9–5
- *Lonicera involucrata* Z6–8 H8–5
- *Lonicera tatarica* Z3–9 H9–1
- *Paeonia lutea* Z3–8 H8–1
- *Pernettya mucronata* Z6–7 H7–6
- *Rhododendron perclymenoides* Z4–9 H9–5
- *Spiraea douglasii* Z5–8 H8–5
- *Vaccinium ovatum* Z6–8 H8–6
- *Viburnum lentago* Z2–8 H8–1

Lonicera tatarica
TATARIAN HONEYSUCKLE

☀ ◊ Z3–9 H9–1 ↕↔10ft (3m)

Fragrant white, pink, or red flowers are borne in late spring, followed by red fruit in late summer through fall. May become invasive.

SHRUBS

Mid- to late summer- blooming shrubs

As the garden moves into the dog days of summer, these shrubs will not swelter. Instead, they will thrill you with their showy blooms and will keep up with any of your perennials and annuals. These shrubs, combined with a carefully considered selection of other seasonally flowering shrubs, will give you a nearly everblooming garden.

SHRUBS

MORE CHOICES

- *Abelia x grandiflora* Z6–9 H9–1
- *Amorpha fruticosa* Z2–8 H8–1
- *Arbutus unedo* 'Compacta' Z7–9 H9–3
- *Ceanothus thyrsiflorus* Z7–11 H10–3
- *Clerodendrum trichotomum* Z7–9 H9–7
- *Clethra fargesii* Z5–8 H8–4
- *Hibiscus syriacus* Z5–9 H10–3
- *Hydrangea quercifolia* Z5–9 H9–1
- *Neviusia alabamensis* Z4–8 H10–9
- *Philadelphus x lemoinei* Z5–8 H8–5
- *Rubus odoratus* Z3–7 H7–1
- *Viburnum opulus* Z3–8 H8–1

Buddleja davidii 'White Profusion'
WHITE BUTTERFLY BUSH
Ⓝ ☼ ◐ Z6–9 H10–4 ‡10ft (3m) ↔15ft (5m)
Fragrant flowers form dense conical clusters 16in (40cm) long. Terrific plant for attracting butterflies into your yard. Grows in alkaline soil. Fast-growing.

Hydrangea paniculata 'Grandiflora'
PEEGEE HYDRANGEA
☼ ◐ ◐◑ Z4–8 H8–1 ‡10–22ft (3–7m) ↔8ft (2.5m)
White flowers turn pink or red as they age. Prune back hard in spring to promote larger but fewer clusters of flowers. Extremely tolerant and durable shrub.

Hydrangea quercifolia 'Snow Queen'
SNOW QUEEN OAKLEAF HYDRANGEA
☼ ◐ ◑ Z5–9 H9–5 ‡6ft (2m) ↔8ft (2.5m)
Bears upright flowerheads of densely clustered sterile flowers. Flowerheads can be dried for arrangements. Deeply lobed leaves resemble oak leaves.

Teucrium fruticans
BUSH GERMANDER
☼ ◊ Z8–9 H9–8 ↕24–40in (60–100cm) ↔12ft (4m)
Thrives in a sheltered border or by a warm, sunny wall. Can be used as topiary. Stems and undersides of leaves are white-woolly.

Fuchsia x hybrida 'Magellanica'
LADY'S EARDROPS
☼ ◐ ◊ Z9–11 H12–1 ↕10ft (3m) ↔6ft (2m)
Produces pendent flowers in summer, followed by red-purple berries. Suitable for warm, sheltered sites as well as coastal locations. Makes a great hedge.

Aesculus parviflora
BOTTLEBRUSH BUCKEYE
Ⓝ ☼ ◐ ◊ ◑ Z5–9 H8–4 ↕10ft (3m) ↔15ft (5m)
Mound-forming. Leaves are bronze when young and turn dark green as they mature and yellow in fall. Slow to establish but eventually spreads widely.

Clethra alnifolia
SUMMERSWEET
Ⓝ ☼ ◑ ⏚ Z3–9 H9–1 ↕ 8ft (2.5m) ↔8ft (2.5m)
Fragrant flowers attract butterflies. Suitable for a woodland garden or mixed border. Can be grown in wetland areas and along streams and riverbanks.

Philadelphus x lemoinei 'Belle Etoile'
BELLE ETOILE MOCK ORANGE
☼ ◐ ◊ Z5–8 H8–1 ↕4ft (1.2m) ↔8ft (2.5m)
Suitable for sites with high levels of air pollution, as well as spots with alkaline soil. Richly scented flowers. Grow in a shrub border or woodland garden.

Clerodendrum bungei
GLORY BOWER
☼ ◊ Z8–10 H12–8 ↕↔10 ft (3m)
Small, fragrant flowers on purple shoots are dark pink in bud and age to red-pink. Attracts butterflies, but may become invasive. Native to China.

Viburnum opulus 'Aureum'
GOLDEN-LEAVED GUELDER ROSE
☼ ◐ ◑ Z3–8 H8–1 ↕15ft (5m) ↔12ft (4m)
Grown mostly for its bright golden spring leaf coloration, which may last into summer if grown shaded from the hottest afternoon sun.

SHRUBS

Fragrant shrubs

Whether we admit it or not, our experience in the garden is not limited to our dominant sense of sight: our sense of smell also plays an important role. These shrubs have both visual and olfactory beauty, and not just in the flowers; the leaves and fruit of many plants have interesting fragrances of their own. Another sense – touch – can play a role in enjoying fragrance.

Itea virginica
VIRGINIA SWEETSPIRE

Ⓝ ☼ ◔ Z6–9 H10–7 ‡5–10ft (1.5–3m) ↔5ft (1.5m)

Dark green foliage turns red and purple in fall. Upright-arching habit. Able to grow in the oxygen-poor soil of wetland areas.

Elaeagnus angustifolia
OLEASTER

☼ ◔ Z2–8 H8–1 ‡↔20ft (6m)

Flexible shrub able to absorb strong winds and grow in exposed sites. Silvery white flowers in mid- to late autumn are followed by edible yellow fruit.

Myrica pensylvanica
BAYBERRY

Ⓝ ☼ ◑ ◔◔ Z3–6 H6–1 ‡9ft (2.5m) ↔12ft (4m)

Bears yellow-green catkins in spring before the leaves. Waxy layer on the outside of the berries is used to make candles. Interesting hedge or screen.

Rosa rugosa 'Hedgehog'
RUGOSA ROSE

☼ ◑ ◔ ᵖᴴ Z2–9 H9–x1 ‡↔6ft (2m)

Flowers borne in mid- to late summer precede large, edible red hips. Grows best in fertile, organic soil but tolerates much poorer. Resistant to fungal diseases.

Abeliophyllum distichum
WHITE FORSYTHIA, KOREAN ABELIALEAF
☼ ◊ Z5–9 H9–1 ↕↔4ft (1.2m)
Cut out older shoots after flowering to promote young, more floriferous growth. Thrives when planted next to walls or fences. Attracts early butterflies.

Buddleja davidii
BUTTERFLY BUSH
☼ ◊ Z6–9 H10–4 ↕10ft (3m) ↔15ft (5m)
Dense cones of lilac to purple flowers are 12in (30cm) in length. Attracts insects, especially bees and butterflies. Cut back hard in spring.

Lonicera fragrantissima
WINTER HONEYSUCKLE
☼ ☼ ◊ Z4–8 H8–3 ↕6ft (2m) ↔12ft (4m)
Intensely fragrant flowers bloom in late winter through midspring and can scent a large area. Remove a few of the largest branches after bloom to manage growth.

MORE CHOICES

- *Buddleja alternifolia* Z6–9 H10–1
- *Buxus microphylla* Z6–9 H9–6
- *Calycanthus floridus* Z5–9 H9–1
- *Cephalanthus occidentalis* Z5–11 H12–3
- *Clethra alnifolia* Z3–9 H9–1
- *Daphne* x *burkwoodii* Z4–7 H7–1
- *Elaeagnus angustifolia* Z2–8 H8–1
- *Elaeagus* x *ebbingei* Z7–11 H12–7
- *Fothergilla gardenii* Z4–8 H8–1
- *Fothergilla major* Z4–8 H9–2
- *Hamamelis vernalis* Z4–8 H8–1

Malus sargentii
SARGENT CRABAPPLE
☼ ◊ Z4–8 H8–1 ↕↔20ft (6m)
White flowers open from red buds in late spring. Birds feed on long-lasting, dark red fruit ⅜in (9mm) across. Native to Japan.

Rosa 'Frau Dagmar Hartopp'
FRAU DAGMAR HARTOPP ROSE
☼ ◊ Z2–9 H9–1 ↕3ft (1m) ↔4ft (1.2m)
This compact shrub bears clove-scented flowers, followed by large red to ornage-red fruit. Dark green leaves turn yellow and purple after frost in fall.

Clethra alnifolia
SUMMERSWEET
Ⓝ ☼ ● ☷ Z3–9 H9–1 ↕↔8ft (2.5m)
Midgreen leaves turn yellow in fall. Suitable for planting in oxygen-poor soil of wetlands and riverbanks, as well as in acidic soil.

SHRUBS

Tender fragrant shrubs (zone 7 and up)

Here are some shrubs that are not reliably cold hardy in most parts of the Northwest. However, they have such exquisite fragrances that you may be inclined to try to grow them in protected outdoor areas (such as at or near the base of a south-facing wall) or in containers that can be brought indoors to provide winter protection

Osmanthus heterophyllus 'Goshiki'
VARIEGATED FALSE HOLLY
☼ ◐ ◊ Z7–9 H9–7 ↕↔15ft (5m)
White flowers bloom in small clusters in late summer and fall, followed by egg-shaped, blue-black berries. Excellent as a hedge or topiary. Trim hedges in spring.

Chilopsis linearis
DESERT WILLOW
Ⓝ ☼ ◊ Z8–9 H9–8 ↕↔6–25ft (2–8m)
Yellow-mottled flowers in white, pink, lilac, lavender, or purple are produced sporadically in summer. Seedlings are susceptible to root rot.

Michelia figo
BANANA SHRUB
☼ ◊ Z12–15 H12–10 ↕↔30ft (10m)
Freely branching evergreen. In spring and summer bears flowers with a banana-like scent. Yellow-brown stems are lightly hairy. Native to China.

Chimonanthus praecox
WINTERSWEET
☼ ◊ Z7–9 H9–7
↕ 8ft (2.5m) ↔10ft (3m)
Flowers blossom during mild periods in winter on bare branches, before leaves emerge. Waxy yellow flowers with purple markings. Grows well in alkaline soil.

MORE CHOICES

- *Buddleja globosa* Z7–9 H9–7
- *Choisya ternata* Z8–10 H10–8
- *Citrus mitis* Z0 H12–1
- *Clerodendrum bungei* Z8–10 H12–8
- *Clerodendrum trichotomum* Z7–9 H9–7
- *Corylopsis* hybrids Z3–9 H9–1
- *Corylopsis pauciflora* Z3–9 H9–1
- *Corylopsis spicata* Z5–8 H8–5
- *Daphne bhoula* Z7–9 H9–7
- *Eucalyptus gunnii* var. *divaricata* Z8–10 H10–8
- *Eucalyptus perriniana* Z8–10 H10–8
- *Illicium anisatum* Z7–9 H9–7
- *Illicium floridanum* Z7–9 H9–4
- *Ilicium parviflorum* Z7–9 H9–7
- *Osmanthus* x *fortunei* Z8–9 H9–8
- *Rhododendron arborescens* Z5–9 H9–4
- *Rhododendron* x *loderi* Z7–9 H9–7
- *Sarcococca orientalis* Z7–8 H8–7

Daphne odora 'Aureomarginata'
VAREIGATED WINTER DAPHNE

☼ ◊ Z7–9 H9–7 ↕↔5ft (1.5m)

Rounded, evergreen shrub bears flowers from midwinter to early spring, followed by spherical, fleshy red fruit. Species is native to China and Japan.

Lavandula stoechas
SPANISH LAVENDER

☼ ◊ Z8–9 H9–8 ↕↔5ft (1.5m)

Thrives when grown in a warm, sheltered site, or in a container that can be moved indoors during bad weather. Bears flowers in late spring and summer.

Skimmia japonica
JAPANESE SKIMMIA

☼ ◐ ◊ Z7–8 H9–7 ↕↔5ft (1.5m)

Makes a good hedge and grows well in a container. White flowers blossom in spring. Female bears red fruit if a male pollinator is present.

Buddleja globosa
ORANGE BALL TREE

☼ ◊ Z7–9 H9–6 ↕↔15ft (5m)

Densely clustered flowers bloom in early summer. Deciduous to semi-evergreen. Thrives in the shelter of a wall or fence. Native to Chile and Argentina.

Eucalyptus perriniana
SPINNING GUM

☼ ◊ Z8–10 H10–8 ↕↔30ft (10m)

Young silvery blue leaves turn blue-green as they mature. Smooth, flaking bark is off-white, gray, or green. Grows quickly.

Evergreen shrubs

Here are some shrubs that will pull double and triple duty in your landscape: they bear leaves throughout the year, they produce often very attractive flowers, and some have ornamental fruit that attract birds and other wildlife. All of these traits make them highly desirable options for any landscape design.

SHRUBS

Berberis julianae
WINTER BARBERRY
☀ ◊ Z6–9 H9–4 ↕↔10ft (3m)
A durable shrub that survives in exposed, windy sites. Flowers borne in late spring and early summer are followed ovoid black berries.

Arctostaphylos uva-ursi
COMMON BEARBERRY, KINNIKINICK
Ⓝ ☀ ☀ Z2–6 H6–1 ↕4in (10cm) ↔20in (50cm)
Mat-forming shrub. Flowers precede bright scarlet berries. Suitable for use as a groundcover or in a rock garden. Withstands sea winds and salt spray.

Camellia japonica
JAPANESE CAMELLIA
☀ ◊ ◊ Z7–8 H8–7 ↕30ft (9m) ↔25ft (8m)
Bears flowers in winter and early spring. Numerous cultivars flower over a longer period. Native to China, Korea, and Japan.

Skimmia japonica
JAPANESE SKIMMIA
☀ ◊ Z7–8 H9–7 ↕↔5ft (1.5m)
Fragrant white flowers borne in spring; females later bear red berries. Best if grown in a sheltered area or container, but it can survive in heavy, clay soil.

MORE CHOICES

- *Ardisia japonica* Z6–9 H9–1
- *Buxus sempervirens* Z6–8 H8–6
- *Ceanothus* 'Dark Star' Z9–11 H12–9
- *Ceanothus thyrsiflorus* Z7–11 H10–3
- *Choisya ternata* and cultivars Z8–10 H10–8
- *Eucalyptus gunnii* var. *divaricata* Z8–10 H10–8
- *Euonymus fortunei* Z4–9 H9–5
- *Gaultheria shallon* Z6–8 H8–6
- *Ilex crenata* and cultivars Z5–7 H7–5
- *Leucothoe fontanesiana* Z5–8 H8–5
- *Mahonia aquifolium* Z6–9 H9–6
- *Mahonia nervosa* Z5–7
- *Pieris japonica* Z6–8 H8–6
- *Santolina chamaecyparissus* Z6–9 H9–4
- *Santolina rosmarinifolia* Z6–9 H9–6
- *Viburnum japonicum* Z8–9 H9–8

Camellia sasanqua
SASANQUA CAMELLIA
☀ ◊ Z7–8 H8–7 ↕10ft (3m) ↔5ft (1.5m)
Bears fragrant flowers in fall. In colder areas, grow in a container and move indoors to flower. Outside, plants prefer the shelter of a wall or fence. Fast-growing.

Viburnum tinus 'Spring Bouquet'
SPRING BOUQUET LAURUSTINUS
☼ ◑ ◖ ● z8–11 H12–8 ↕6ft (2m) ↔3ft (1m)
Flowers are followed by dark blue-black, ovoid fruit.
Has smaller leaves than the species. Prefers
moderately fertile soil. Also known as 'Compactum'.

Daphne odora 'Aureomarginata'
VAREIGATED WINTER DAPHNE
☼ ◖ z7–9 H9–7 ↕↔5ft (1.5m)
Very fragrant flowers blossom from midwinter to early
spring and followed by fleshy red fruit. Grows best in a
sheltered site.

Sarcococca humilis
SWEET BOX
◑ ◖ z6–9 H9–6 ↕↔5ft (1.5m)
Bears fragrant, pink-tinged white flowers in spring,
followed by blue-black berries. Dwarf, clump-forming
shrub makes a good groundcover. Native to China.

Kalmia polifolia
EASTERN BOG LAUREL
Ⓝ ☼ ◑ ◖ z5–9
H9–5 ↕24in (60cm) ↔36in (90cm)
Sparsely branched, open shrub
produces clusters of bowl-
shaped, purple-pink flowers in
mid-and late spring. Native to the
eastern United States and Canada.

Shrubs with fall foliage color

You might believe that fall color comes exclusively from trees, but think again: these shrubs will give many trees a run for their money. Use them as specimens or focal points, or group them in threes or larger masses for even bigger impact. No well-rounded garden should be without one of these fall foliage monarchs.

Berberis thunbergii 'Atropurpurea Nana'
CRIMSON PYGMY BARBERRY

☼ ◊ Z5–8 H8–5 ↕↔24in (60cm)

This densely branched, dwarf shrub can be grown in a container or rock garden or as a small hedge. Attractive reddish purple leaves turn red-orange in fall.

Berberis thunbergii 'Dart's Red Lady'
DART'S RED LADY JAPANESE BARBERRY

☼ ◊ Z4–8 H8–3 ↕2–3ft (60–90cm) ↔2ft (60cm)

Produces small yellow flowers, followed by shiny red fruit favored by birds. Very dark reddish purple leaves turn bright red in fall. Dense, round shrub.

Hamamelis virginiana
COMMON WITCH HAZEL

Ⓝ ☼ ◊ ⌘ Z3–8 H8–1 ↕↔20ft (6m)

Bears small spidery yellow flowers in fall, unlike the rest of its spring-blooming relatves. Grows well in the shade of a wall or fence. Native to E North America.

Euonymus alatus
BURNING BUSH

☼ ☼ ◊ Z4–9 H9–1 ↕6ft (2m) ↔10ft (3m)

Corky wings decorate green shoots. Leaves are dark green in spring and summer. Bears yellowish fruit that split open to reveal orange seeds. Rabbits avoid it.

Rhus copallina
DWARF SUMAC

Ⓝ ☼ ◊ Z5–9 H9–5 ↕3–5ft (1–1.5m) or more

Reddish green twigs have a hairy covering. Yellow-green flowers appear in dense, erect clusters, followed by red fruit on female plants.

MORE CHOICES

- *Acer palmatum* Z6–8 H8–2
- *Amelanchier alnifolia* Z4–9 H8–3
- *Aronia melanocarpa* Z3–8 H8–1
- *Berberis thunbergii* Z5–8 H8–5
- *Callicarpa americana* Z7–9 H9–6
- *Calycanthus floridus* Z5–9 H9–1
- *Chimonanthus praecox* Z7–9 H9–7
- *Clethra alnifolia* Z3–9 H9–1
- *Cotinus coggygria* Z5–9 H9–3
- *Fothergilla gardenii* Z4–9 H9–1
- *Fothergilla major* Z4–8 H9–2
- *Hamamelis mollis* Z5–8 H9–1
- *Hamamelis x intermedia* Z5–9 H9–1
- *Hamamelis virginiana* Z3–8 H8–1
- *Hydrangea quercifolia* Z5–9 H9–5
- *Itea virginica* Z5–9 H10–7
- *Kerria japonica* Z4–9 H9–1
- *Lagerstroemia indica* Z7–9 H9–7
- *Lindera benzoin* Z4–9 H8–1
- *Nandina domestica* Z6–9 H9–3
- *Philadelphus coronarius* Z4–9 H9–4
- *Philadelphus lewisii* Z5–8 H8–1
- *Philadelphus x lemonei* Z5–8 H8–3
- *Rhus glabra* Z2–8 H8–1
- *Rhus aromatica* Z2–8 H8–1

Acer palmatum 'Bloodgood'
JAPANESE MAPLE
☼ ◐ ◊ z5–8 H8–2 ‡↔15ft (5m)
Reddish purple flowers blossom in midspring,
followed by winged red fruit. Foliage often turns bright
red in fall. Grow as a shrub or small tree.

Acer japonicum 'Sango Kaku'
CORALBARK MAPLE
☼ ◐ ◊ z5–8 H8–2 ‡20ft (6m) ↔15ft (5m)
Young orange-yellow leaves mature to green before
turning pink and yellow in fall. Twigs are coral-pink
in winter then darken as the season warms up.

Acer palmatum (Dissectum Group)
THREADLEAF JAPANESE MAPLE
☼ ◐ ◊ z6–8 H8–6 ‡6ft (2m) ↔10ft (3m)
Mound-forming shrub with arching shoots bears finely
cut red-purple leaves that turn gold in fall. Produces
tiny purple-red flowers in late summer.

Shrubs with coarse, bold leaves

Combining flower and foliage colors is just one way to achieve visual effects in a garden. Leaf texture (not the surface qualities but the visual delicacy or massiveness of the foliage) can also be exploited to create different pictures and feelings. However, be judicious in your use of coarse, bold leaves: too many in a design can create a heavy, dense, ponderous mood.

Viburnum sieboldii
SIEBOLD VIBURNUM
☀ ☼ ◐ Z5–8 H8–5 ↕12ft (4m) ↔20ft (6m)
Flowers in late spring. Ovoid red berries on red stalks ripen to black. Able to grow in the wet soil found along streams and on riverbanks.

Hydrangea macrophylla 'Pia'
PINK ELF HYDRANGEA
☀ ☼ ◐ Z6–11 H9–5 ↕24in (60cm) ↔3ft (1m)
Fast-growing, miniature hydrangea for a container or small spot in a bed. Flowers in early summer. Dry flowerheads for long-lasting floral arrangements.

MORE CHOICES

- *Aralia elata* 'Variegata' Z4–9 H9–1
- *Aralia spinosa* Z4–9 H9–1
- *Hibiscus syriacus* Z5–9 H10–3
- *Hydrangea aspera* Z7–9 H9–7
- *Nandina domestica* Z6–9 H9–3

Hydrangea quercifolia
OAKLEAF HYDRANGEA
Ⓝ ☀ ☼ ◐ Z5–9 H9–2 ↕6ft (2m) ↔8ft (2.5m)
White flowers borne from midsummer to midfall become pink-tinged as they age. Deeply lobed leaves turn red, purple, and bronze in fall.

Eriobotrya japonica
LOQUAT
☀ ◐ Z8–11 H12–8 ↕↔25ft (8m)
Bears clusters of fragrant white flowers in early fall. Pear-shaped, orange-yellow fruit are edible. Native to China and Japan.

Aucuba japonica
JAPANESE LAUREL
☀ ◐ Z6–15 H12–6 ↕↔10ft (3m)
Can be grown in heavy clay soil. If both male and female plants are grown, female plant bears red fruit in fall. Rabbits do not disturb this evergreen shrub.

Rhus glabra 'Laciniata'
CUTLEAF SMOOTH SUMAC
Ⓝ ☀ ◐ Z2–8 H9–3 ↕↔8ft (2.5m)
Bears tightly clustered yellow-green flowers in erect panicles 8in (20cm) long in summer, followed by hairy red fruit. Leaves turn orange to reddish purple in fall.

Shrubs with blue-gray/silvery leaves

These shrubs add lightness and openness to a garden, breaking up the sometimes monotonous greens of other plants. Because many of these shrubs have contrasting leaf undersides, they can bring animation into a garden when a breeze catches them. They can also be used together in a Mediterranean theme garden in a dry, sunny spot.

MORE CHOICES

- *Artemisia californica* z0–0
- *Artemisia filifolia* z0–0
- *Elaeagnus commutata* z2–6 H6–1
- *Eucalyptus gunnii var divaricata* z8–10 H10–8
- *Shepherdia argentea* z3–6 H6–1

Buddleja davidii 'White Profusion'
WHITE BUTTERFLY BUSH
☼ ◊ z6–9 H9–6 ↕8ft (2.5m) ↔10ft (3m)
Vigorous, spreading shrub with arching shoots. Flowers are borne from late summer through fall on clusters up to 16in (40cm). Attracts butterflies and other insects.

Cistus salviifolius
SAGELEAF ROCKROSE
☼ ◊ z8–11 H12–8 ↕↔5ft (1.5m)
Dense, bushy, evergreen shrub flowers copiously in summer. Leaves are slightly wrinkled. Native to southern Europe.

Teucrium fruticans
BUSH GERMANDER
☼ ◊ z8–9 H9–8 ↕24–40in (60–100cm) ↔12ft (4m)
Bears pale blue flowers in summer among aromatic leaves. Thrives when grown in the shelter of a border or a wall or fence. Can be trained into topiary.

Helianthemum nummularium
SUNROSE
☼ ◊ z6–8 H8–6 ↕6–8in (15–20cm) ↔3ft (1m)
Many members of this mostly evergreen genus bear linear, silvery to gray-green leaves. Flowers in a wide color range bloom from late spring to midsummer.

Andromeda polifolia
COMMON BOG ROSEMARY, MARSH ANDROMEDA
☼ ☼ ◊ z2–6 H6–1 ↕16in (40cm) ↔24in (60cm)
White or pale pink flowers bloom in spring and early summer among leathery, dark green leaves. Native to northern Europe.

Artemisia 'Powis Castle'
POWIS CASTLE WORMWOOD
☼ ◊ z7– 9 H12–8 ↕2ft (60cm) ↔3ft (1m)
Low, mound-forming, evergreen shrub with aromatic foliage. Bears sparse clusters of yellow-tinged silver flowers in summer.

Shrubs with golden or yellow foliage

A visual vibrancy and warmth emanates from golden- and yellow-leaved plants. They can be used to great effect in shady or partially shady locations to give the illusion that more light is present than there actually is. They can also be used to provide a contrast to deep green or bronze foliage, and they coordinate beautifully with purple-pink or darker blue flowers

Caryopteris x clandonensis 'Worcester Gold'
WORCESTER GOLD BLUE MIST SHRUB
☼ ☼ ◊ Z6–9 H9–2 ‡3ft (1m)
↔5ft (1.5m)
Dense, mound-forming shrub. Bears clusters of lavender-blue flowers in late summer. Good in perennial borders.

Sambucus racemosa 'Aurea'
YELLOW-LEAVED EUROPEAN RED ELDERBERRY
☼ ☼ ◊◊ Z3–7 H7–1
‡↔8–10ft (2.5–3m)
Bushy shrub with arching shoots. Bears clusters of star-shaped yellow flowers in midspring, followed by round red berries in summer.

MORE CHOICES

- *Berberis thunbergii* 'Aurea' Z4–8 H8–1
- *Ilex crenata* 'Golden Gem' Z5–7 H7–5
- *Rubus cockburnianus* 'Aureus' Z6–8 H8–6
- *Spiraea japonica* 'Gold Flame' Z4–9 H9–1

Viburnum opulus 'Aureum'
GOLDEN-LEAVED GUELDER ROSE
☼ ☼ ◊ Z3–8 H8–1 ‡↔5–10ft
(1.5–3m)
Young leaves are reddish bronze. Flowers in summer, followed by fleshy red berries in fall.

Elaeagnus x ebbingei 'Gilt Edge'
GILT EDGE SILVERBERRY
☼ ◊ Z7–10 H12–7 ‡↔12ft (4m)
Resistant to heat and wind; requires little maintenance. Bears tiny, fragrant silver flowers, followed by red berries.

Osmanthus heterophyllus 'Goshiki'
VARIEGATED FALSE HOLLY
☼ ◊ Z7–9 H9–7 ‡↔15ft (5m)
Bears fragrant white flowers in fall, followed by egg-shaped blue-black fruit. Makes a good hedge or topiary.

Spiraea japonica 'Gold Flame'
GOLD FLAME SPIRAEA
☼ ◊ Z4–9 H9–1 ‡↔30in (75cm)
Flowers on current year's growth, so plant can be cut back hard in early spring. Young reddish bronze leaves mature to yellow-green.

Shrubs with purple, red, or bronze leaves

When used judiciously, these shrubs make a perfect contrast to other plants' brightly colored foliage or flowers. In very sunny locations, these plants will make the light in an area appear more subdued than it actually is, creating a feeling of calm and stability. These can also be used as focal points to draw the eye and hold it.

Cotinus coggygria 'Royal Purple'
ROYAL PURPLE SMOKEBUSH
☼ ☀ ◊ ◊ Z5–8 H8–1
↕↔15ft (5m)
Dense, mound-forming shrub. Bears tiny pink flowers in airy clusters that have the appearance of smoky clouds. Leaves turn scarlet in fall. Grows well in heavy clay soils.

Acer palmatum var. atropurpureum
RED JAPANESE MAPLE
☼ ☀ ◊ Z5–8 H8–2 ↕15–25ft (5–8m) ↔20ft (6m)
Bushy-headed shrub to open-branched small tree. Reddish purple leaves turn bright red in fall. Bears small red-purple flowers in midspring.

Itea virginica 'Henry's Garnet'
HENRY'S GARNET SWEETSPIRE
Ⓝ ☼ ◊ Z6–9 H10–7 ↕3–4ft (1–1.5m) ↔6ft (2m)
Bears fragrant, creamy white flowers in dense clusters in summer. Leaves turn red-purple and orange in fall. Native to the eastern United States.

Pieris japonica 'Mountain Fire'
MOUNTAIN FIRE PIERIS
☀ ◊ ◊ ᵖᴴ Z5–9 H9–1 ↕↔10ft (3m)
Brilliant red leaves turn glossy dark green as they mature. Produces abundant drooping clusters of white flowers. Evergreen and slow-growing.

Acer palmatum 'Bloodgood'
JAPANESE MAPLE
☼ ☀ ◊ Z5–8 H8–2 ↕↔15ft (5m)
Bushy-headed shrub or small tree bears clusters of purple-red flowers in midspring, followedy by winged red fruit. Leaves turn bright red in fall.

MORE CHOICES

- *Nandina domestica* 'Nana Purpurea' Z6–11 H12–4
- *Sambucus nigra* 'Guinocho Purple' Z6–8 H8–6
- *Weigela florida* 'Java Red' Z4–8 H8–1

SHRUBS

Shrubs with variegated leaves

Variegation usually arises as a mutation within a plant's actively growing cells, manifesting itself as growth with areas colored differently than the normal green. Vegetative propagation (done mainly by cuttings and grafting) preserves the coloration and gives rise to entirely variegated plants. Variegated shrubs provide striking visual interest in a landscape.

Weigela florida 'Variegata'
OLD-FASHIONED WEIGELA
☼ ◐ ◊ z5–8 H8–1 ↕↔8ft (2.5m)
In addition to its variegation, this is also more compact than the species. Flowers appear from late spring to early summer. Best if grown in fertile soil.

Elaeagnus x *ebbingei* 'Gilt Edge'
GILT EDGE SILVERBERRY
☼ ◊ z7–10 H12–7 ↕↔12ft (4m)
An evergreen shrub with leathery leaves. The flowers are silver-scaly, creamy white, and borne in fall. Best grown in fertile soil. Tolerates coastal wind.

Daphne odora 'Aureomarginata'
VARIEGATED WINTER DAPHNE
☼ ◊ z7–9 H9–7 ↕↔ 5ft (1.5m)
Beautifully fragrant flowers appear from midwinter to early spring, followed by fleshy red fruit. Best in moderately fertile, organic, well-drained soil.

Osmanthus heterophyllus 'Goshiki'
VARIEGATED FALSE HOLLY
☼ ☼ ◊ z7–9 H9–7 ↕↔15ft (5m)
Tubular, fragrant white flowers are borne in clusters from late summer through fall. Slower growing than the species.

Philadelphus coronarius 'Variegatus'
VARIEGATED MOCK ORANGE
☼ ☼ ◊ z5–8 H8–3
↕8ft (2.5m) ↔6ft (2m)
Produces more of a show from its foliage than from the flowers, which are less profusely borne than on the species.

MORE CHOICES

- *Berberis thunbergii* 'Rose Glow' z5–8 H8–5
- *Buxus sempervirens* 'Elegantissima' z5–9 H10–4
- *Cottoneaster horizontalis* 'Variegatus' z4–7 H7–3
- *Viburnum tinus* 'Variegatum' z8–11 H12–8

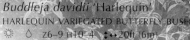

Buddleja davidii 'Harlequin'
HARLEQUIN VARIEGATED BUTTERFLY BUSH
☼ ◊ z6–9 H10–4 ↕↔20ft (6m)
Yellow-margined young leaves mature to cream-margined. Fragrant flowers borne from summer to fall are attractive to pollinating insects.

Cornus alba 'Elegantissima'
VARIEGATED RED TWIG DOGWOOD
☼ ◊ z2–8 H8–1 ↕↔10ft (3m)
White flowers in flat clusters are borne in late spring and early summer, followed by bluish fruit. Winter shoots are red.

Thorny shrubs

Although usually not of major aesthetic value, when large or borne in quantity, thorns make useful deterrents. Thorny plants are often sited in strategic locations to deter uninvited or unwanted guests, whether two- or four-legged. While their thorns may be unfriendly to encounter, these shrubs are still beautiful plants to admire from a safe distance.

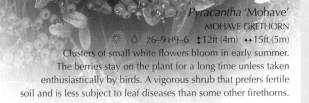

Berberis julianae
WINTER BARBERRY
☀ ◊ Z6–9 H9–4 ‡↔10ft (3m)
Red-tinged flowers appear in clusters in late spring, followed by dark black fruit with a whitish coat in fall. Evergreen and dense, making it a good choice for a hedge or nesting site for birds.

MORE CHOICES

- *Aralia spinosa* Z4–9 H9–1
- *Berberis thunbergii* and cultivars Z4–8 H8–3
- *Poncirus trifoliata* Z5–9 H9–5
- *Rosa rugosa* Z2–9 H9–1

Pyracantha 'Mohave'
MOHAVE FIRETHORN
☀ ◊ Z6–9 H9–6 ‡12ft (4m) ↔15ft (5m)
Clusters of small white flowers bloom in early summer. The berries stay on the plant for a long time unless taken enthusiastically by birds. A vigorous shrub that prefers fertile soil and is less subject to leaf diseases than some other firethorns.

Berberis darwinii
DARWIN'S BARBERRY
☀ ☀ ◊ ◊ Z7–9 H9–4 ‡↔10ft (3m)
Profuse flowers in mid-and late spring ripen into spherical, white-coated, blue-black fruit. May bloom again in fall. A choice, upright evergreen.

Ribes silvestre
WHITE CURRANT
☀ ◊ Z6–8 H8–1 ‡6ft (2m) ↔5ft (1.5m)
Though not as notoriously thorny as their gooseberry (*R. uva-crispa*) relatives, currants occasionally produce a few thorns. Fruit attracts many birds.

Ulex europaeus
GORSE
☀ ◊ Z6–8 H8–6 ‡8ft (2.5m) ↔6ft (2m)
An upright to rounded, densely bushy shrub. Coconut-scented, pealike flowers are produced mainly in spring and intermittently throughout the year.

Shrubs with ornamental fruit

Color in the garden doesn't necessarily need to be provided by flowers or foliage color; fruit can also liven up the landscape from summer to well into winter. Also, fruit-bearing plants provide food for wildlife, adding the animated colors of birds, insects, mammals, and other wildlife to the overall garden picture.

SHRUBS

Lindera benzoin
SPICE BUSH
Ⓝ ☼ ◊ pH Z4–9 H8–1 ↕↔10ft (3m)
This aromatic, spreading, deciduous shrub flowers in midspring, followed by ovoid red berries on female plants. Best in fertile soil. Needs minimal pruning.

Callicarpa bodinieri var. *giraldii*
BEAUTYBERRY
☼ ◊ Z4–7 H7–1 ↕10ft (3m) ↔8ft (2.5m)
An upright, deciduous shrub. Produces lavender-pink flowers from late spring to early summer on current year's growth. Prune in spring. Prefers fertile soil.

Cornus mas
CORNELIAN CHERRY
☼ ☼ ◊ Z5–8 H8–4 ↕ 15ft (5m) ↔15ft (5m)
This vigorous, deciduous shrub can be trained into a small tree. Slightly fragrant flowers appear in late winter, followed by oblong, bright red fruit in summer.

MORE CHOICES

- *Amelanchier* x *grandiflora* 'Autumn Brilliance' Z3–7 H7–1
- *Amelanchier* x *grandiflora* 'Cole's Secret' Z0–0 H8–1
- *Aronia arbutifolia* 'Brilliantissima' Z5–9 H9–4
- *Aronia melanocarpa* 'Morton' Z3–8 H8–1
- *Berberis thunbergii* Z5–8 H8–5
- *Callicarpa americana* Z7–9 H9–6
- *Callicarpa bodinieri* var. *giraldi* 'Profusion' Z5–8 H8–3
- *Cornus racemosa* Z4–8 H8–3
- *Corylus cornuta* Z0–0 H
- *Cotoneaster horizontalis* Z5–7 H7–5
- *Gaultheria shallon* Z6–8 H8–6
- *Kolkwitzia amabilis* Z5–9 H9–5
- *Leycesteria formosa* Z7–9 H9–6
- *Mahonia aquifolium* Z6–9 H9–6
- *Mahonia fortunei* Z8–9 H9–4
- *Mahonia nervosa* Z5–7 H
- *Mahonia repens* Z5–8 H8–3
- *Nandina domestica* Z6–9 H9–3
- *Rhus typhina* Z3–8 H8–1
- *Ribes aureum* Z5–8 H8–3
- *Ribes aureum* var. *villosum* Z5–8 H8–3
- *Ribes laxiflorum* Z0–0 H
- *Ribes sanguineum* Z6–8 H8–6

Vaccinium corymbosum
HIGHBUSH BLUEBERRY
Ⓝ ☼ ☼ ◊ ◊ pH Z3–7 H7–1 ↕↔5ft (1.5m)
An upright, twiggy, deciduous shrub. This is the species most commonly grown for edible blueberries. Many cultivars are available. Birds relish the fruit.

Rosa rugosa 'Hedgehog'
RUGOSA ROSE
☀ ☀ ◐ ○ pH Z2–9 H9–1
↕↔6ft (2m)
Flowers from mid- to late summer, followed by edible red hips. Like most of the rugosas, this is highly resistant to rose fungal diseases. Prefers fertile, organic soil.

Cotoneaster apiculatus
CRANBERRY COTONEASTER
☀ ○ Z5–7 H7–5 ↕3ft (1m) ↔8ft (2.5m)
This species has vigorous, prostrate growth. Solitary, red- tinged white flowers are borne in summer, followed by abundant fruit in fall. Prefers moderately fertile soil.

Ribes silvestre
WHITE CURRANT
☀ ○ Z6–8 H8–1 ↕6ft (2m) ↔5ft (1.5m)
Both red and white currants bear abundant crops of fruit in summer that may be stripped by birds as soon as they ripen. Prefers moderately fertile soil.

Amelanchier x *grandiflora*
APPLE SERVICEBERRY
☀ ☀ ○ Z5–8 H7–1 ↕25ft (8m) ↔30ft (10m)
A spreading shrub that can be trained into a tree. White flowers in spring are soon followed by tasty, blue-black fruit. Leaves turn orange and red in fall.

Mahonia japonica 'Bealei'
LEATHERLEAF MAHONIA
☀ ○ Z7–8 H8–7 ↕↔10ft (3m)
Mildly fragrant, pale yellow flowers appear in early spring. Fruits ripen to blue-purple. Prefers moderately fertile, organic soil. Oldest leaves turn orange in fall.

SHRUBS

Shrubs with edible fruit

These fruiting shrubs are often grown in dedicated fruit gardens to provide mouthwatering fruit to eat fresh or to preserve. The shrubs presented here are beautiful in their own right, so there is no need to relegate them exclusively to the fruit garden. Try including them in your ornamental garden beds, where they will provide a tasty treat to a wandering visitor.

Rubus idaeus
RASPBERRY

(N) ☼ ◊ Z7–9 H9–1 ‡6ft (2m) ↔5ft (1.5m)

Everbearing selections produce flowers and fruit all summer. The red and yellow cultivars are hardier than the black and purple types.

Vaccinium corymbosum
HIGHBUSH BLUEBERRY

(N) ☼ ☼ ◊ ◊ pH Z3–7 H7–1 ‡↔5ft (1.5m)

An upright, twiggy, deciduous shrub with elliptical green leaves. The urn-shaped flowers appear in late spring and early summer. Prefers highly organic soil.

Ribes silvestre
WHITE CURRANT

☼ ◊ Z6–8 H8–1 ‡6ft (2m) ↔5ft (1.5m)

Easily grown fruit have a pleasant sweet/tart flavor and are rich in vitamin C. Flowers in spring. Grows best in loam but will tolerate heavy or sandy soil.

MORE CHOICES

- *Ribes uva-crispa* z5–9 H9–2
- *Rubus ssp.* z4–9 H9–1
- *Vaccinium vitis-idaea* z2–6 H6–1

Vaccinium macrocarpon
CRANBERRY

(N) ☼ ◊ ◊ pH Z2–7 H7–1 ‡6in (15cm)

↔indefinite

A spreading, mat-forming evergreen shrub that turns bronze in winter. It forms bell shaped white flowers in summer, followed by fruit in fall. Best in a bog.

Ribes sativum
RED CURRANT

☼ ◊ Z6–8 H9–2 ‡6ft (2m) ↔4½ft (1.5m)

Light green spring flowers are followed by fruit in summer. Fruit can be eaten fresh or used to make jams and syrups or dried like raisins. Grows best in loam.

Herbs for mixed borders

These subshrubs are as equally at home in a dedicated herb garden as they are in a bed filled with perennials and shrubs. Each has a great deal to offer in shape, texture, and flower. They also offer their fragrance as well as culinary attributes to the kitchen and are attractive to pollinators and other beneficial insects.

Thymus vulgaris
COMMON THYME
☼ ◊ Z4–9 H9–1 ↕6–12in (15–30cm) ↔16in (40cm)
This bushy, cushion-forming subshrub produces purple or white flowers in spring and early summer. The most commonly grown thyme for culinary use.

Thymus pseudolanuginosus
WOOLLY THYME
☼ ◊ Z4–9 H9–1 ↕1–2in (2.5–5cm) ↔8in (20cm)
This low-maintenance subshrub is a creeper, making it an ideal groundcover. Tiny, tubular pink flowers appear in summer. Foliage is not highly fragrant.

MORE CHOICES

- Lavandula angustifolia and cultivars Z5–8 H8–1
- Laurus nobilis 'Aureus' Z8–11 H12–1
- Salvia officinalis and cultivars Z5–8 H8–5

Rosemarinus officinalis
ROSEMARY
☼ ◊ Z8–11 H12–8 ↕↔5ft (1.5m)
An upright to rounded, dense, strongly aromatic shrub. Blue flowers appear from midspring to early summer. Prefers marginally to moderately fertile soil.

Thymus x citriodorus
LEMON-SCENTED THYME
☼ ◊ Z6–9 H9–6 ↕12in (30cm) ↔10in (25cm)
A bushy rounded subshrub with strongly lemon-scented foliage. Pale lavender-pink flowers appear in summer. A cross between T. pulegiodes and T. vulgaris.

Thymus herba-barona
CARAWAY THYME
☼ ◊ Z6–9 H9–6 ↕2–4in (5–10cm) ↔8in (20cm)
This loosely matting subshrub bears pale pink flowers in midsummer that are attractive to bees. The foliage of this culinary thyme smells like caraway seeds.

Lavendula stoechas 'Otto Quast'
OTTO QUAST SPANISH LAVENDER
☼ ◊ Z7–9 H9–7 ↕28in (70cm) ↔3ft (1m)
A compact Mediterranean plant. Flowers appear from late spring to summer. This cultivar's flower bracts are larger than the species. Prefers moderately fertile soil.

SHRUBS

Shrubs for use as specimens

Specimen plants are used as focal points in a garden design to stop and hold the eyes as the viewer surveys the landscape. The shrubs presented here are all worthy of "specimen" status because they are impressive, interesting flowering shrubs that have character. They can be used as the "stars" in a mixed border or on their own in a lawn or courtyard.

Eriobotrya japonica
LOQUAT
☼ ◊ Z8–11 H12–8 ↕↔25ft (8m)
Bears large panicles of fragrant white flowers from fall to winter that ripen to spherical, edible, orange-yellow fruit in spring. Spreading, evergreen shrub or small tree.

Exochorda x *macrantha* 'The Bride'
THE BRIDE PEARLBUSH
☼ ☼ ◊ Z5–9 H9–5 ↕ 6ft (2m) ↔10ft (3m)
Abundant flowers appear from late spring to early summer and can weigh down the branches. An arching, mound-forming plant that prefers fertile soil.

Choisya ternata 'Aztec Pearl'
AZTEC PEARL ORANGE
☼ ◊ Z8–10 H10–8 ↕↔8ft (2.5m)
 Fragrant flowers, sometimes pink-tinged, bloom in late spring and again in late summer through fall. A compact shrub with slender branches.

Vitex agnus-castus var. *latifolia*
CHASTE TREE
☼ ◊ Z6–9 H9–6 ↕↔6–25ft (2–7.5)
An open, spreading, deciduous shrub with aromatic leaves and flowers that bloom from late summer to midfall. Grows more vigorously than the species.

Hydrangea macrophylla 'Monred'
RED 'N' PRETTY HYDRANGEA
☼ ◊◐ Z7–9 H9–7 ↕6ft (2m) ↔4ft (1.2m)
Flowers from mid to late summer. Best when grown in
moderately fertile, organic soil. Prune back to large,
healthy-looking buds from early to midspring.

Viburnum plicatum f. tomentosum 'Pink Beauty'
PINK BEAUTY DOUBLEFILE VIBURNUM
☼ ☼ ◊ Z4–8 H8–1 ↕10ft (3m) ↔12ft (4m)
Sterile outer florets turn pink as they mature. Fertile
flowers are followed by red fruits that ripen to black.

MORE CHOICES

- *Aesculus parviflora* Z5–9 H9–4
- *Buddleja alternifolia* Z6–9 H10–1
- *Ceanothus* cultivars Z7–11 H10–3
- *Clerodendrum trochotomum* Z7–9 H9–7
- *Exochorda racemosa* Z5–9 H9–5
- *Heptacodium miconioides* Z5–9 H9–4
- *Kolkwitzia amabilis* Z5–9 H9–5
- *Loropetalum chinense* Z7–9 H9–3
- *Pernettya mucronata* Z6–7 H7–6
- *Phormium tenax* Z9–11 H12–6

Cornus alba 'Elegantissima'
VARIEGATED RED TWIG DOGWOOD
☼ ◊ Z2–8 H8–1 ↕↔10ft (3m)
White flowers in flat clusters are borne in late spring
and early summer. Cut back to the ground or remove
oldest stems in spring to promote red bark coloration.

Nerium oleander
OLEANDER
☼ ◊ Z13–15 H12–1 ↕↔20ft (6m)
Pink, red, white, yellow, or salmon flowers appear in
summer. An erect to spreading, shrub suitable for
specimen use in containers. Prefers fertile soil mix.

Hydrangea macrophylla 'Blue Wave'
BLUE WAVE LACECAP HYDRANGEA
☼ ☼ ◊◐ Z6–9 H9–2 ↕6ft (1m) ↔8ft (2.5m)
Sterile outer flowers can also be mauve or pink.
Makes a splendid specimen, or grow as a group in a
large shrub border. Also known as 'Mariesii Perfecta'.

SHRUBS

Shrubs for hedges and screening

It is a long-standing gardening tradition to use shrubs as screens and barriers. With good reason: there are many choices that will address various situations. Presented here are tall, vigorous growers that help screen out the views and sounds of major roadways, as well as smaller shrubs to delineate areas and prevent foot traffic but allow a view of distant areas.

MORE CHOICES

- *Amelanchier alnifolia* Z4–9 H8–3
- *Berberis darwinii* Z7–9 H9–7
- *Berberis thunbergii* and cultivars Z5–8 H8–5
- *Buxus microphylla* var. *japonica* Z7–9 H9–5
- *Buxus microphylla* var. *koreana* Z6–9 H9–5
- *Buxus microphylla* Z6–9 H9–6
- *Buxus sempervirens* Z6–8 H8–6
- *Cotoneaster adpressus* 'Little Gem' Z4–7 H7–3
- *Cotoneaster apiculatis* Z5–7 H7–5
- *Elaeagnus commutata* Z4–7 H7–3
- *Laurus nobilis* Z8–11 H12–1
- *Lavandula stoechas* Z8–9 H9–8
- *Lavandula* x *intermedia* Z5–8 H8–5
- *Lavatera thuringiaca* 'Barnsley' Z6–8 H8–6
- *Leucophyllum frutescens* Z8–9 H9–8
- *Nandina domestica* Z6–9 H9–3
- *Pyracantha coccinea* Z6–9 H9–6
- *Rhus copallina* Z5–9 H9–5
- *Rhus trilobata* Z4–6 H6–2
- *Rosmarinus officinalis* Z8–11 H12–8

Viburnum prunifolium
BLACKHAW VIBURNUM

Ⓝ ☼ ☼ ◒ ◐ Z3–9 H9–1 ‡15ft (5m) ↔12ft (4m)

Shrub or small tree. Fruits persist through winter and attract cedar waxwings and other birds. Creamy white flowers in late spring. Best in moderately fertile soil.

Spiraea japonica 'Little Princess'
LITTLE PRINCESS JAPANESE SPIREA

☼ ◌ Z4–9 H9–1 ‡↔5ft (1.5m)

Flowers from mid- to late summer. Grows well in a mixed shrub border with fertile soil. Many attractive cultivars of the species are available.

Nerium oleander
OLEANDER

☼ ◌ Z13–15 H12–1 ‡↔20ft (6m)

Erect to spreading shrubs bear flowers in pink, red, white, yellow, or salmon in summer. Prefer fertile soil. Excellent in a large container.

Viburnum tinus 'Spring Bouquet'
SPRING BOUQUET LAURUSTINUS

☼ ☼ ● Z8–11 H12–8 ‡6ft (2m) ↔3ft (1m)

Flowers appear from late winter to spring, followed by dark blue-black, ovoid fruit. Prefers moderately fertile soil. Also known as 'Compactum'.

Syringa vulgaris 'Monge'
MONGE LILAC

☼ ◌ ◐ Z4–8 H8–1 ‡↔22ft (7m)

Profuse, very large, single, fragrant flowers bloom from late spring to early summer. Best in fertile, organic soil. Deadhead flowers soon after they fade.

Osmanthus heterophyllus 'Goshiki'
VARIEGATED FALSE HOLLY

☼ ☼ ◌ Z7–9 H9–7 ‡↔15ft (5m)

A compact, mound forming variety with pink-tinged young foliage. Tubular white flowers from late summer to autumn are followed by ovoid, blue-black fruit.

Camellia sasanqua
SASANQUA CAMELLIA

☀ ◐ ○ z7–8 H8–7 ‡10ft (3m) ↔5ft (1.5m)

Fragrant flowers are borne in fall and early winter. An upright to spreading shrub with eliptical leaves. There are many nice named cultivars. Prefers organic soil.

Euonymus alatus
BURNING BUSH

☀ ◐ ○ z4–9 H9–1 ‡6ft (2m) ↔10ft (3m)

A deciduous shrub with dark green leaves that turn red in fall. Also produces orange fruit. Tolerant of many soil types. 'Compacta' is more compact, with pinker fall color.

Camellia japonica
JAPANESE CAMELLIA

☀ ◐ ○ z7–8 H8–7 ‡30ft (9m) ↔25ft (8m)

An upright to spreading shrub with many cultivars. Flowers appear from winter to early spring and some-times into late spring. Superb evergreen foliage.

Myrica cerifera
WAX MYRTLE

Ⓝ ☀ ◐ ○ z6–9 H9–6 ‡↔15ft (5m)

A rounded, deciduous or evergreen shrub with upright branches. Inconspicuous flowers are borne in spring. Spherical, waxy, gray-white fruit ripen in fall.

Rosa rugosa 'Alba'
WHITE RUGOSA ROSE

☀ ○ z2–9 H9–1 ‡↔3–6ft (1–2m)

Fragrant flowers are followed by large red fruit called hips. Tolerant of many soil types, including nearly pure sand. Makes a good sheared or unsheared hedge.

Ligustrum japonicum 'Texanum'
TEXANUM JAPANESE PRIVET

☀ ◐ ○ z7–12 H12–4 ‡6–9ft (2–3m) ↔3ft (1m)

More compact, denser growth than the species. White flowers from midsummer to early fall are followed by small, round black fruit. Also known as L. texanum.

Shrubs for containers

There are few things that can make as striking an impact in a garden setting as a large urn or tub containing a bold shrub. Here are some shrubs whose root systems remain healthy in close quarters. Be sure to grow shrubs that are at least two USDA hardiness zones colder than yours, or you will need to protect their rootballs (if not the entire plant) during winter.

Aloysia triphylla
LEMON VERBENA

☼ ◊ Z8–11 H12–8 ‡6ft (2m) ↔6ft (2m)

Deciduous shrub with lemon-scented leaves. Tiny. pale lilac to white flowers in slender clusters appear in late summer. Also known as A. *citriodora*.

Choisya ternata 'Aztec Pearl'
AZTEC PEARL ORANGE

☼ ◊ Z8–10 H10–8 ‡↔8ft (2.5m)

Compact shrub with slender branches. Flowers, sometimes pink tinged, bloom in late spring and again in late summer through fall. Use a soil-based potting mix.

Skimmia japonica
JAPANESE SKIMMIA

☼ ◊ Z7–8 H9–7 ‡↔5ft (1.5m)

Fragrant white flowers are sometimes tinged pink or red and bloom in mid- to late spring. The flower buds can also be red. Fruit may cause mild stomach upset.

Berberis thunbergii
JAPANESE BARBERRY

☼ ◊ Z5–8 H8–5 ‡↔5ft (1.5m)

Japanese barberries, in their wide range of plant habit and foliage coloration, adapt very well to containers. However, be careful where you site the thorny plants.

Rosmarinus officinalis
ROSEMARY
☼ ◊ Z8–11 H12–8 ↕↔5ft (1.5m)
An upright to rounded, dense shrub.
Flowers appear from midspring to early
summer. The foliage is strongly aromatic.
Prefers marginally to moderately fertile soil.

Spiraea japonica 'Shibori'
SHIBORI SPIREA
☼ ◊ Z4–9 H9–1 ↕↔24in (60cm)
Produces both pink and white flowers on the same
plant from mid- to late summer.
Prefers fertile soil. Also known
as 'Shirobana'.

Mahonia aquifolium
OREGON GRAPE HOLLY
Ⓝ ☼ ◊ Z6–9 H9–6 ↕↔5ft (1.5m)
Fragrant flowers are borne in spring and are
attractive to pollinating insects. Foliage turns bronzy
in fall. Open habit; combine with other plants in a pot.

Lantana camara 'Miss Huff'
MISS HUFF BUSH LANTANA
☼ ◊ Z7–11 H12–1 ↕5ft (1.5m) ↔10ft (3m)
Flowers from late spring to early fall. It is almost
sterile, so there is no need to deadhead flowers
except to improve appearance.

Acer palmatum dissectum 'Inabe Shidare'
INABE SHIDARE JAPANESE MAPLE
☼ ◑ ◊ Z5–8 H8–2 ↕6ft (2m) ↔10ft (3m)
This upright then cascading cultivar retains its purple-
red foliage color into summer. Tiny purple-red flowers
appear in spring.

MORE CHOICES

- *Acer palmatum* (Dissectum group)
  Z6–8 H8–2
- *Berberis thunbergii* and cultivars
  Z5–8 H8–5
- *Berberis thunbergii* var. *atropurpurea*
  Z5–8 H8–5
- *Deutzia scabra* 'Pink Minor' Z6–8 H8–6
- *Eucalyptus gunnii* var. *divaricata*
  Z8–10 H10–8
- *Hibiscus syriacus* Z5–9 H10–3
- *Hypericum* 'Hidcote' Z6–9 H9–6
- *Laurus nobilis* Z8–11 H12–1
- *Lavandula stoechas* Z8–9 H9–8
- *Lavandula* x *intermedia* Z5–8 H8–5
- *Punica granatum* Z7–10 H12–1
- *Spiraea douglasii* Z5–8 H8–5
- *Spiraea japonica* cultivars Z4–9 H9–1
- *Yucca filamentosa* Z4–11 H12–5

Lavandula angustifolia
ENGLISH LAVENDER
☼ ◊ Z5–8 H8–5
↕3ft (1m) ↔4ft (1.2m)
Compact and bushy evergreen shrub with sweetly
aromatic foliage. Flowers from mid- to late summer.
Prefers moderately fertile soil. Prune in early spring.

Syringa meyeri 'Palibin'
DWARF KOREAN LILAC
☼ ◊ Z4–7 H7–9 ↕↔5ft (1.5m)
Grows much more slowly than the species. Fragrant
flowers appear late spring/early summer. Use a fertile,
organic, soil-based mix. Also called *S. palibiniana*.

Cistus x purpureus
ORCHID ROCKROSE
☼ ◊ Z9–10 H10–8 ↕ 3ft (1m) ↔3ft (1m)
Rounded shrub with sticky, red-flushed shoots. Flowers
in summer. Does well in marginally to moderately
fertile soil. Hybrid of *C. creticus* and *C. ladanifer*.

Shrubs for groundcover

Many smaller, lower-growing shrubs straddle the line between what are considered perennials and shrubs. Often referred to as subshrubs, many have a spreading habit, which makes them ideal for growing on slopes or other locations where a groundcover is needed. The larger species are good for stabilizing banks and controlling erosion.

Mahonia repens
CREEPING BARBERRY

Ⓝ ☼ ◐ ◑ ❍ Z5–8 H8–3 ↕1ft (30cm) ↔6ft (2m)

An upright, suckering plant. Dark yellow flowers form from mid to late spring. Blue-black berries follow. Best if grown in moderately fertile, organic soil.

Rhus aromatica 'Gro-Low'
GRO-LOW FRAGRANT SUMAC

Ⓝ ☼ ❍ Z4–9 H9–1 ↕2–2½ft (60–75cm) ↔6–8ft (2–2.5m)

Very vigorous, spreading, and much more compact than the species. Foliage turns red-orange in fall. Small yellow flowers appear in midspring, followed by red fruit.

Cornus canadensis
CREEPING DOGWOOD

Ⓝ ☼ ❍ Z2–7 H7–1 ↕6in (15cm) ↔indefinite

Flowers in late spring to early summer are followed by red fruit. Prefers moist, organic soil where summers are cool. Can be difficult to get established.

Vinca minor 'Atropurpurea'
WINE PERIWINKLE

☼ ◐ ❍ ❍ Z4–9 H9–1 ↕4–8in (10–20cm) ↔indefinite

Flowers from midspring to fall. Tolerant of many soil conditions. Also known as 'Purpurea' and 'Rubra'.

Vinca minor 'Green Carpet'
GREEN CARPET COMMON PERIWINKLE

☼ ◐ ❍ Z4–9 H9–1 ↕4–8in (10–20cm) ↔indefinite

A mat-forming, evergreen subshrub. Flowers from mid- spring to autumn. Grows well in most soils. Cut back in spring to control growth. Good in a woodland garden.

Vinca major 'Maculata'
MACULATA GREATER PERIWINKLE

☼ ◐ ❍ ❍ Z7–9 H9–6 ↕18in (45cm) ↔indefinite

This cultivar's evergreen leaves sport yellow-green centers. Flowers from midspring to autumn. Can also be grown in containers.

Leucothoe fontanesiana
DROOPING LEUCOTHOE

Ⓝ ☀ ☀ ◐ ♔ z5–8 H8–5 ↕5ft (1.5m) ↔10ft (3m)

Cylindrical, creamy white, mildly fragrant flowers appear in spring. Gracefully arching branches become more pronounced as the plant matures.

Arctostaphylos uva-ursi
COMMON BEARBERRY, KINNIKINICK

Ⓝ ☀ ☀ ◐ z2–6 H6–1 ↕4in (10cm) ↔20in (50cm)

Flowers appear in summer and are followed by spherical, bright scarlet fruit in fall. Multibranching, mat-forming habit. Best in moderately fertile soil.

Rosa rugosa 'Roseraie de l'Hay'
ROSERAIE DE L'HAY RUGOSA ROSE

☀ ◐ z4–9 H9–1 ↕7ft (2.2m) ↔6ft (2m)

A vigorous rugosa hybrid with strongly scented blooms from summer to fall. Canes are thick and heavily bristled with thin thorns. Has typical rugosa disease resistance.

MORE CHOICES

- *Aronia melanocarpa* 'Morton' z3–8 H8–1
- *Calluna vulgaris* z5–7 H7–5
- *Ceanothus thyrsiflorus* var. *repens* z8–11 H12–8
- *Cornus canadensis* z2–7 H7–1
- *Cotoneaster dammeri* 'Lowfast' z6–8 H8–6
- *Erica cinerea* 'Atropurpurea' z6–8 H8–6
- *Euonymus fortunei* z4–9 H9–5
- *Gaultheria shallon* z6–8 H8–6
- *Helianthemum nummularium* z6–8 H8–6
- *Hypericum calycinum* z5–9 H9–4
- *Mahonia nervosa* z5–7
- *Rubus pentalobus* z6–9 H9–2
- *Sacococca hookeriana* var. *humilis* z6–9 H9–6
- *Spiraea bumalda* z4–9 H10–2
- *Vaccinium vitis-idae* var. *minus* z2–6 H6–1
- *Vinca major* 'Maculata' z7–11 H12–7
- *Vinca minor* z4–9 H9–1

Skimmia japonica
JAPANESE SKIMMIA

☀ ◐ z7–8 H9–7 ↕↔5ft (1.5m)

Male plants bear showier buds and flowers than the females, which bear red fruit in fall if males are present. Flowers are slightly fragrant on both.

Ceratostigma plumbaginoides
LEADWORT, PLUMBAGO

☀ ◐ z6–9 H9–6 ↕18in (45cm) ↔12 in (30cm)

Flowers in late summer. A rhizomatous, spreading, woody-based perennial. Prefers moderately fertile soil. Prune in early to midspring.

Rosmarinus officinalis 'Huntington Carpet'
HUNTINGTON CARPET ROSEMARY

☀ ◐ z8–10 H10–12 ↕1–2ft (30–60cm) ↔8ft (2.5m)

Flowers appear from midspring to early summer. The foliage is strongly aromatic and prozed for its culinary value. Prefers marginally to moderately fertile soil.

SHRUBS

Shrubs resistant to deer browsing

Shrubs are usually the perfect height for deer browsing; in the wild, native shrubs make up an integral part of a deer's diet. When dislocated from its wild environs, a deer will feast on your shrubs, focusing on the tender new growth and flower buds. Here are some shrubs that have been found to be less palatable to deer than most.

Erica vagans 'Mrs. D. F. Maxwell'
MAXWELL'S CORNISH HEATH
☼ ◊ Z7–9 H5–8 ‡12in (30cm) ↔18in (45cm)
This cultivar was selected for the deep color of its flowers that are borne from midsummer to midfall. Prune the evergreen foliage back after bloom.

Daphne genkwa
LILAC DAPHNE
☼ ◊ Z6–9 H9–6 ‡ 5ft (1.5m) ↔5ft (1.5m)
An upright, open, deciduous shrub. Fragrant flowers are borne from mid- to late spring before the leaves emerge. Produces gray-white, oval, dry fruit.

Lavatera thuringiaca 'Barnsley'
TREE MALLOW
☼ ◊ Z6–8 H8–6 ‡↔6ft (2m)
This cultivar has a more extended bloom season than the species. Blooms from summer until frost. Best when grown in moderately fertile soil.

Hypericum frondosum
GOLDEN ST. JOHN'S WORT
Ⓝ ☼ ◐ ◊ ◗ Z6–8 H8–4 ‡↔2–4ft (60–120cm)
An erect, deciduous shrub with thick, flaking stems. Flowers from mid- to late summer on the current season's growth. Prefers moderately fertile soil.

Rhus glabra 'Laciniata'
CUTLEAF SMOOTH SUMAC
Ⓝ ☼ ◗ Z2–8 H9–3 ‡↔8ft (2.5m)
A spreading and suckering, deciduous shrub that turns orange to red-purple in fall. In summer, yellow-green flowers appear and are followed by bristly red fruit.

Sarcococca hookeriana var. digyna
SLENDER SWEET BOX
☼ ◊◗ Z6–9 H9–6 ‡5ft (1.5m) ↔6ft (2m)
This variety has more slender, tapered leaves than the species. Fragrant flowers emerge in early spring. Grow in moderately fertile, organic soil.

Mahonia repens
CREEPING BARBERRY

☼ ◐ ◊　Z5–8 H8–3　↕1ft (30cm)　↔6ft (2m)

An upright, suckering plant. Dark yellow flowers bloom from mid to late spring. Blue-black berries follow. Best if grown in moderately fertile, organic soil.

Syringa reticulata
JAPANESE TREE LILAC

☼ ◊　Z3–8 H8–3　↕30ft (10m)　↔20ft (6m)

Fragrant flowers are borne from early to midsummer. Bark is shiny reddish brown when young. A very upright shrub that can be trained as a small tree.

Viburnum plicatum f. tomentosum 'Summer Snowflake'
SUMMER SNOWFLAKE DOUBLEFILE VIBURNUM

☼ ◐ ◊　Z5–8 H8–1　↕10ft (3m)　↔12ft (4m)

Blooms in spring and again throughout summer and into early fall. Birds and other wildlife eat the fruit.

Kerria japonica
GLOBEFLOWER, JAPANESE KERRIA

☼ ◊　Z4–9 H9–1　↕6ft (2m)　↔8ft (2.5m)

A suckering shrub with arching green shoots. Flowers appear form mid- to late spring. Grow in fertile soil in a shrub border or open position in a woodland garden.

MORE CHOICES

- *Abelia* x *grandiflora* and cultivars Z6–9 H9–1
- *Aesculus californica* Z7–8 H8–7
- *Berberis darwinii* Z7–9 H9–7
- *Berberis thunbergii* and cultivars Z5–8 H8–5
- *Buddleja alternifolia* Z6–9 H10–1
- *Buxus microphylla* var. *japonica* Z7–9 H9–5
- *Buxus microphylla* var. *koreana* Z6–9 H9–5
- *Buxus sempervirens* Z6–8 H8–6
- *Cotoneaster* spp. Z7–9 H8–3
- *Daphne bholua* Z7–9 H9–7
- *Daphne* x *burkwoodii* Z4–7 H7–1
- *Elaeagnus commutata* Z2–6 H6–1
- *Erica cinerea* 'Atropurpurea' Z6–8 H8–6
- *Erica* x *darleyensis* Z7–8 H8–7
- *Gaultheria shallon* Z6–8 H8–6
- *Ilex* spp. Z4–10 H9–3
- *Nandina domestica* Z6–9 H9–3
- *Nerium oleander* Z13–15 H12–1
- *Penstemon angustifolius* Z7–10 H12–3
- *Potentilla fruticosa* Z3–7 H7–1
- *Quercus sadleriana* Z7–9 H9–7
- *Rhododendron macrophyllum* Z7–9 H9–7
- *Santolina chamaecyparissus* Z6–9 H9–4
- *Santolina rosmarinifolia* Z6–9 H9–6
- *Sarcococca orientalis* Z7–8 H8–7
- *Syringa vulgaris* Z4–8 H8–1
- *Vaccinium ovatum* Z6–8 H8–6
- *Zauschneria californica* Z8–11 H12–8

SHRUBS

Cotoneaster apiculatus
CRANBERRY COTONEASTER

☼ ◊　Z5–7 H7–5　↕ 3ft (1m)　↔8ft (2.5m)

Solitary, red-tinged white flowers are borne in summer. Foliage turns purple-red in fall. Prefers moderately fertile, well-drained soil. Can be pruned hard.

Shrubs resistant to rabbit feeding

Most shrubs will outgrow a rabbit's reach if given the chance, but persistent rabbit grazing on newly planted shrubs can stunt or even kill some shrubs. Here is a variety of beautiful shrubs that rabbits are unlikely to bother. It is safe to assume that other cultivars of the species represented here are also rabbit resistant.

Pieris japonica 'Mountain Fire'
MOUNTAIN FIRE PIERIS
☀ ◐ ◯ pH   Z5–9 H9–1   ↕↔10ft (3m)
Red young leaves turn glossy chestnut brown before maturing to dark green. Flowers from late winter to spring. Best in moderately fertile, organic soil.

MORE CHOICES

- *Arbutus unedo* 'Compacta' z7–9 H9–3
- *Berberis julianae* z6–9 H9–4
- *Ceanothus americanus* z4–8
- *Ceanothus thyrsiflorus* z7–11 H10–3
- *Cornus alba* 'Elegantissima' z2–8 H8–1
- *Cornus sericea* z2–8 H8–1
- *Cotoneaster horizontalis* z4–7 H7–3
- *Daphne* x *burkwoodii* z4–7 H7–1
- *Elaeagnus* x *ebbingei* 'Gilt Edge' z7–11 H12–7
- *Euonymus alatus* z4–9 H9–1
- *Gaultheria shallon* z6–8 H8–6
- *Hydrangea aspera* and cultivars z7–9 H9–7
- *Ilex crenata* 'Sky Pencil' z5–7 H7–5
- *Ilex vomitoria* z7–11 H12–7
- *Lindera benzoin* z4–9 H8–1
- *Pernettya mucronata* z6–7 H7–6
- *Rhus aromatica* 'Gro-Low' z4–9 H9–1
- *Rhus glabra* 'Laciniata' z2–8 H9–3
- *Ribes aureum* var. *villosum* z5–8 H8–3
- *Ribes sanguineum* z6–8 H8–6
- *Sambucus racemosa* and cultivars z3–8 H8–1
- *Skimmia japonica* z7–9 H9–7
- *Symphoricarpos albus* z3–7 H7–1
- *Syringa meyeri* and cultivars z4–8 H8–1
- *Ulex europaeus* z6–8 H8–6
- *Viburnum tinus* 'Spring Bouquet' z8–11 H12–8
- *Weigela florida* z5–9 H9–1

Hydrangea quercifolia
OAKLEAF HYDRANGEA
Ⓝ ☀ ◐ ◯   Z5–9 H9–2   ↕6ft (2m)   ↔8ft (2.5m)
A deciduous, mound-forming shrub. Flowers midsummer to autumn and become pink-tinged with age. The peeling bark is an attractive orange-brown.

Aucuba japonica
JAPANESE LAUREL
☀ ◯   Z6–15 H12–6   ↕↔10ft (3m)
Bears small red-purple flowers in midspring. Female plants produce bright red berries if a male plant is growing nearby. Tolerant of most soil types.

Spiraea japonica cultivars
JAPANESE SPIREA
☀ ◯   Z5–8 H9–1   ↕6ft (2m)   ↔5ft (1.5m)
Flowers from mid- to late summer. Grows well in a shrub or mixed border in fertile soil. Many attractive cultivars are available.

Hydrangea macrophylla cultivars
BIG-LEAF HYDRANGEA
☼ ☼ ◊ Z6–9 H9–6 ↕5–6ft (1.5–2m) ↔6–8ft (2–2.5m)
Rounded, deciduous shrubs with many good cultivars.
that fall into two groups: lacecaps, with flattened
flowerheads, and hortensias, with nearly spherical ones.

Ilex verticillata 'Jim Dandy'
MALE WINTERBERRY
Ⓝ ☼ ◊ Z4–8 H8–1 ↕6ft (2m) ↔4ft (1.2m)
A dwarf, upright, rounded, and slow-growing male
cultivar. The fruit (shown) are borne only on female
shrubs within a quarter mile of a male pollinator.

Buddleja davidii 'Black Knight'
BLACK KNIGHT BUTTERFLY BUSH
☼ ◊ Z6–9 H10–4 ↕10ft (3m) ↔15ft (5m)
Fragrant flowers, darker purple than the species, appear
in summer. A deciduous shrub with long, arching shoots.
Suitable for a mixed or shrub border.

Kalmia polifolia
EASTERN BOG LAUREL
Ⓝ ☼ ☼ ◊ ♨ Z2–7 H7–1 ↕24in (60cm) ↔36in (90cm)
Flowers are produced from mid to late spring on a
sparsely branched shrub. Best when grown in organic
soil. Good for borders or woodland gardens.

Cotoneaster apiculatus
CRANBERRY COTONEASTER
☼ ◊ Z5–7 H7–5 ↕ 3ft (1m) ↔8ft (2.5m)
Solitary, red-tinged white flowers are borne in summer.
They are followed by fruit that mature to red. Vigorous
prostrate growth. Prefers moderately fertile soil.

Philadelphus 'Snowflake'
SNOWFLAKE MOCK ORANGE
☼ ☼ ◊ ◊ Z4–8 H8–1 ↕8ft (2.4m) ↔6ft (1.8m)
An upright and heavily branched, deciduous shrub.
The fragrant flowers appear in midsummer. Best if
grown in moderately fertile soil.

Daphne odora 'Aureomarginata'
VAREIGATED WINTER DAPHNE
☼ ◊ Z7–9 H9–7 ↕↔5ft (1.5m)
A variegated, rounded, evergreen shrub. Bears fragrant
flowers from midwinter to early spring, followed by fleshy
red, spherical fruit. Also known as 'Aureomarginata'.

Shrubs that attract butterflies

Among the nectar-feeding insects, none is more regal and elegant as the butterfly as it floats from flower to flower and from plant to plant sipping nectar. Although these shrubs also attract other beneficial insects, they are especially attractive to butterflies. Grow them in a dedicated butterfly garden (with food plants for caterpillars), as specimens, or in borders.

Rosmarinus officinalis
ROSEMARY

☼ ◊ Z8–11 H12–8 ↕↔5ft (1.5m)

Flowers appear from midspring to early summer among strongly aromatic foliage. An upright to rounded, dense shrub that prefers marginally to moderately fertile soil.

Potentilla fruticosa subsp. scouleri f. albus
SHRUBBY CINQUEFOIL

Ⓝ ☼ ◊ Z4–9 H9–1 ↕↔6–12in (15–30cm)

An evergreen, spreading, upright subshrub. The species normally has purplish blue flowers that appear from late spring to early summer. Grows best in marginally to moderately fertile soil.

Spiraea japonica 'Little Princess'
LITTLE PRINCESS JAPANESE SPIREA

☼ ◊ Z4–9 H9–1 ↕↔5ft (1.5m)

Flowers from mid- to late summer. Denser and more mounded than the species, with smaller leaves. Prefers fertile soil and can be used as a groundcover.

Syringa vulgaris 'Sensation'
SENSATION LILAC

☼ ◊ ◊ Z4–8 H8–1 ↕↔22ft (7m)

Distinctively edged, fragrant flowers appear from late spring to early summer. Prefers organic rich, fertile soil. Nongrafted shrubs can be cut nearly to the ground in early spring to rejuvenate them.

Rhus trilobata
SKUNKBUSH

 ☀ ◊ Z4–6 H6–2 ↕3–6ft (1–2m) ↔6–8ft (2–2.5m)

Produces panicles of greenish yellow flowers in spring, followed by spherical red fruit. Foliage, fetid when crushed, turns yellow-red in fall.

Buddleja 'Pink Delight'
PINK DELIGHT BUTTERFLY BUSH

☀ ☀ ◊ Z6–9 H9–1 ↕8ft (2.5m) ↔6ft (2m)

Produces larger flower spikes and deeper green leaves than the species. Orange-eyed flowers bloom from summer to fall. Prefers fertile soil.

MORE CHOICES

- *Abelia* x *grandiflora* and cultivars Z6–9 H9–1
- *Ceanothus griseus* and cultivars Z9–11 H12–9
- *Clethra alnifolia* and cultivars Z3–9 H9–1
- *Lavandula* x *intermedia* Z5–8 H8–5
- *Mahonia bealei* Z7–8 H8–7
- *Philadelphus coronarius* and cultivars Z5–8 H8–4
- *Potentilla fruticosa* and cultivars Z3–7 H7–1
- *Sambucus nigra* ssp. *canadensis* Z0–0 H
- *Spiraea densiflora* var. *splendens* Z6–9 H9–1

Syringa meyeri 'Palibin'
DWARF KOREAN LILAC

☀ ◊ Z4–7 H7–1 ↕5–6ft (1.5–2m) ↔5ft (1.2m)

Compact, rounded shrub bears fragrant flowers in small clusters from late spring to early summer. Also known as *S. palibiana*, *S. patula*, and *S. velutina*.

Mahonia aquifolium
OREGON GRAPE HOLLY

 ☀ ◊ Z6–9 H9–6 ↕↔5ft (1.5m)

Fragrant flowers are borne in spring and are attractive to pollinating insects. Foliage becomes bronze in fall. An open, suckering shrub.

Spiraea nipponica 'Snowmound'
SNOWMOUND SPIREA

☀ ◊ Z4–8 H8–1 ↕↔4ft (1.2m)

Flowers appear in midsummer. Fast-growing and spreading, deciduous shrub that Prefers fertile soil. Also known as *S. nipponica* var. *tosaensis*.

Ribes sanguineum
FLOWERING CURRANT

 ☀ ◊ Z6–8 H8–6 ↕↔6ft (2m)

Spring flowers are followed by spherical, white-coated, blue-black fruit. The deciduous leaves are aromatic. Can be used as an informal hedge.

SHRUBS

Shrubs to attract butterflies and hummingbirds

Watching a butterfly or hummingbird moving from flower to flower sipping nectar is one of the great pleasures of gardening. The butterfly, using its uncurling proboscis, and the hummingbird, extending its tongue, can reach deeply into flowers to sip their nectar reward. These shrubs will attract both kinds of creature, not only for their benefit but also for your enjoyment.

Syringa vulgaris 'Monge'
MONGE LILAC
☀ ◐ ◑   Z4–8 H8–1   ↕↔22ft (7m)
Bears a profusion of very large, single, fragrant flowers from late spring to early summer. Best if grown in fertile, organic soil. Deadhead flowers after blooming.

Syringa meyeri
MEYER LILAC
☀ ◐   Z4–7 H7–1   ↕5–6ft (1.5–2m) ↔4ft (1.2m)
Fragrant flowers appear in late spring and early summer on the previous season's growth. A compact, rounded shrub. Best when grown in fertile, organic soil.

Fuchsia x hybrida 'Magellanica'
LADY'S EARDROPS
☀ ◐   Z9–11 H12–9   ↕10ft (3m) ↔6ft (2m)
More than 8,000 species and cultivars have been developed in a wide range of plant habit and flower color and form. All prefer fertile soil.

MORE CHOICES

- *Abelia chinensis* Z5–9 H12–6
- *Arctostaphylos uva-ursi* Z2–6 H6–1
- *Buddleja davidii* Z6–9 H9–1
- *Buddleja davidii* 'Royal Red' Z6–9 H9–6
- *Eucalyptus gunnii* var. *divaricata* Z8–10 H10–8
- *Eucalyptus perriniana* Z8–10 H10–8
- *Fuchsia magellanica* Z9–11 H12–9
- *Hibiscus syriacus* Z5–9 H10–3

Lavandula stoechas 'Otto Quast'
OTTO QUAST SPANISH LAVENDER
☀ ◐   Z7–9 H9–7   ↕28in (70cm) ↔3ft (1m)
A compact Mediterranean herb. Flowers appear from late spring to summer. This cultivar's flower bracts are larger than the species. Prefers moderately fertile soil.

Lantana camara 'Miss Huff'
MISS HUFF BUSH LANTANA
☼ ◊ z7–11 H12–1 ‡5ft (1.5m) ↔10ft (3m)
Lantanas are woody shrubs frequently grown as annuals for their nonstop flower displays from late spring until fall frost. They tolerate poor soil.

Leucophyllum frutescens
TEXAS RANGER, SILVERLEAF TEXAS SAGE
Ⓝ ☼ ◊ z8–9 H9–8 ‡8ft (2.5m) ↔6ft (2m)
Flowers appear during summer on compact, arching plants. The wooly foliage is evergreen. Best if grown in marginally fertile, sandy soil.

MORE CHOICES

- *Kolkwitzia amabilis* z5–9 H9–5
- *Lavandula angustifolia* z6–9 H12–7
- *Lavandula stoechas* z8–9 H9–8
- *Rosmarinus officinalis* z8–11 H12–8
- *Sambucus nigra* z6–8 H8–6
- *Sambucus racemosa* z3–7 H7–1
- *Syringa microphylla* z5–8 H8–5
- *Syringa* x *prestoniae* z2–7 H7–1
- *Weigela florida* 'Java Red' z4–8 H8–1
- *Weigela florida* 'Red Prince'

Weigela florida 'Variegata'
VARIEGATED WEIGELA
☼ ◊ z5–8 H8–1 ‡↔6–8ft (2–2.5m)
In addition to being variegated, this cultivar is also more compact than the species. The flowers appear in late spring to early summer. Best if grown in fertile soil.

Ribes sanguineum
FLOWERING CURRANT
Ⓝ ☼ ◊ z6–8 H8–6 ‡↔6ft (2m)
Spherical, powdery blue-black fruit provide an additional attraction for wildlife. The deciduous leaves are aromatic. Can be grown as an informal hedge.

Abelia x grandiflora
GLOSSY ABELIA
☼ ◊ z6–9 H9–1 ‡10ft (3m) ↔12ft (4m)
Evergreen or semi-evergreen shrub. Fragrant flowers are borne from midsummer to fall. Irresistible to many butterflies. Also known as *A. rupestris.*

SHRUBS

Notable and reliable roses

Roses are often thought of as the divas of the plant world. Most people readily acknowledge their unsurpassed beauty but also begrudge their need for high maintenance. Here are some down-to-earth beauties that are resistant to the major diseases affecting roses, minimizing the need for spraying and other coddling.

Rosa rugosa 'Alba'
WHITE RUGOSA ROSE
☼ ◊ Z2–9 H9–1 ↕↔3–6ft (1–2m)
Except for the white flowers, this cultivar is nearly identical to the species. Tolerant of many soils, including nearly pure sand. Makes a good hedge.

Rosa 'Kiftsgate'
KIFTSGATE CLIMBER ROSE
☼ ◊ Z6–9 H9–6 ↕↔30ft (10m) or more
Rampant growth can reach extraordinary lengths, easily covering gazebos or large gates. Flowers in early summer. Prefers moderately fertile, organic soil.

Rosa rugosa 'Roseraie de l'Hay'
ROSERAIE DE L'HAY RUGOSA ROSE
☼ ◊ Z4–9 H9–1 ↕7ft (2.2m) ↔6ft (2m)
A vigorous, disease-resistant rugosa hybrid with strongly scented blooms that appear from summer to fall. Canes are thick and heavily bristled.

Rosa wichurana 'Albéric Barbier'
WICHURANA RAMBLER ROSE
☀ ◊ Z5–9 H9–7 ↕6ft (2m) ↔20ft (6m)
Flower produced in spring emerge creamy yellow then
mature to pure white. Foliage is semi-evergreen.
Prefers moderately fertile, organic soil.

Rosa 'Tuscany'
TUSCANY GALLICA ROSE
☀ ◊ Z3–9 H9–1 ↕18–24in (45–60cm) ↔3ft (1m)
Scented flowers bloom in early summer. Typical of a
Gallica rose, it bears dark green leaves and spreads by
suckering from the roots. Resistant to blackspot.

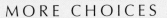

MORE CHOICES

- *Rosa* 'Blush Noisette' z6–9
- *Rosa* 'Mutabilis' z5–9 H9–5
- *Rosa pimpinellifolia* 'Petite Pink' z0 H8–1
- *Rosa* 'Blanc Double de Coubert'
  z3–9 H9–1
- *Rosa* 'Conrad Ferdinand Meyer'
  z4–9 H9–1
- *Rosa* (Pavement Series) z2–9 H9–1
- *Rosa* 'Charles Albanel' z2–9 H9–1
- *Rosa* 'Henry Hudson' z2–9 H9–1

Rosa x odorata 'Mutabilis'
CHINA ROSE
☀ ◊ Z7–9 H9–7 ↕↔3ft (1m)
Flowers from summer to fall, changing from light
yellow to copper-pink then to deep pink. Will climb if
given support. Also known as *R. chinensis* 'Mutabilis'.

Rosa rugosa
RUGOSA ROSE
☀ ◊ Z2–9 H9–1 ↕↔3–6ft (1–2m)
Produces fragrant flowers from spring to fall, followed
by bright red hips. One of the easiest roses to growand
is resistant to most fungal diseases.

Rosa rugosa 'Therese Bugnet'
THERESE BUGNET RUGOSA ROSE
☀ ◊ Z3–9 H9–1 ↕↔6ft (2m)
Another very fragrant rugosa hybrid that repeat blooms
from summer to fall. A low-maintenance rose for use
in a rose garden or a mixed border.

Rosa 'Frau Dagmar Hartopp'
FRAU DAGMAR HARTOPP ROSE
☀ ◊ Z2–9 H9–1 ↕3ft (1m) ↔4ft (1.2m)
Clove-scented flowers bloom on a shrub more
compact than the species.The leaves turn purplish
and yellow after frost.

SHRUBS

CONIFERS

UNLIKE FLOWERING PLANTS, BOTH WOODY and herbaceous, the pollen and seeds of most conifers develop within cones. Thus, the predominant color display of conifers comes from the varying shades of their foliage – gradations of yellow, green, blue, and gray. Most are evergreen, although some are deciduous; the foliage of ginkgos and larches turns brilliant yellow in fall before dropping to the ground. Conifers come in a wide variety of sizes and shapes, ranging from the enormous cypresses and redwoods to miniature false cypress cultivars. A variety of conifers can be massed in one bed for a dramatic display of color, texture, size, and shape.

Thuja occidentalis 'Rheingold' (American arborvitae) This cultivar grows as a conical bush with golden yellow leaves that are tinted with pink when young. Unlike its much larger parent species, it will fit in almost any garden.

Pseudolarix amabilis (Golden larch) Here is one of the few deciduous conifers, its long needles turning golden orange before dropping off in fall. Although it will take many years to reach its maximum height of 50–70ft (15–20m), it is not a tree for a small garden.

Conifers are woody plants that grow either as trees or shrubs but, since they have more in common with each other than with flowering trees or shrubs, they are commonly considered separately from other woody plants. The usually full, dense, and often evergreen foliage contributes color and texture to the garden throughout the year.

Many grow branches almost down to the ground even as they increase in height, a habit that makes them an excellent choice for use as hedging or a windscreen for the rest of the garden. Evergreen hedges need regular trimming to keep them under control. This will not hurt the individual plants, but if you don't have the time to keep your hedge cut back on a regular basis, some of the slower-growing conifers would make a better choice and, ultimately, will fill the space just as well.

Most conifers grow best in moist but well-drained soils, although they are among the most adaptable plants.

Picea pungens (Colorado spruce)
Like other spruces, the needlelike leaves are arranged spirally around the shoots. The pendent, cylindrical, light brown cones have papery scales.

Taxodium ascendens (Pond cypress)
Upright shoots become pendent with age, creating a soft, flowing overall appearance. Cypresses grow very well in waterlogged sites but are adaptable.

Cryptomeria japonica (Japanese cedar)
Narrowly wedge-shaped needles point forward in five-ranked spirals around the shoots. Cones can be abundant. Many cultivars are available.

Conifers for dry soils and full sun

These conifers (or the species from which they were selected) hail from regions of the world where dry soils and sunny summers are a rule and so are adaptable to dry, sunny sites. Ranging from low-growing shrubs to stately trees, these make ideal choices for specimen plants, screens and hedges, and groundcovers.

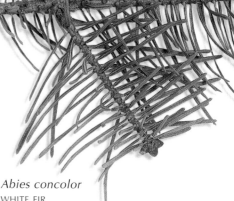

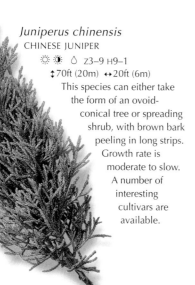

Juniperus chinensis
CHINESE JUNIPER

☼ ☼ ◊ Z3–9 H9–1

↕70ft (20m) ↔20ft (6m)

This species can either take the form of an ovoid-conical tree or spreading shrub, with brown bark peeling in long strips. Growth rate is moderate to slow. A number of interesting cultivars are available.

Juniperus chinensis 'Tortulosa'
HOLLYWOOD JUNIPER

☼ ☼ ◊ Z6–9 H9–1 ↕70ft (20m) ↔20ft (6m)

This cultivar has an upright, shrubby to treelike habit with intriguing, twisting stems. Foliage is pungently scented. Moderate growth rate.

Abies concolor
WHITE FIR

Ⓝ ☼ ◊ Z3–7 H7–1 ↕100ft (30m) ↔25ft (8m)

Columnar tree that maintains its foliage to the ground. Slow to moderate growth. Cylindrical cones measure up to 5in (25cm) and disintegrate before falling.

MORE CHOICES

- *Cedrus libani ssp. atlantica* 'Glauca Pendula' Z6–9 H9–3
- *Cupressus arizonica* Z6–9 H9–2
- *Juniperus communis* 'Berkshire'
- *Juniperus conferta* Z6–9 H9–1
- *Juniperus horizontalis* Z3–9 H9–1
- *Juniperus squamata* 'Meyeri' Z4–9 H9–1
- *Juniperus virginiana* 'Burkii' Z3–9 H9–1
- *Juniperus virginiana* 'Canaertii' Z3–9 H9–1
- *Picea pungens* 'Bakerii' Z2–8 H8–1
- *Pinus contorta* Z6–8 H8–6
- *Pinus virginiana* Z3–7 H7–1
- *Tsuga heterophylla* 'Western Hemlock' Z6–8 H8–6

Juniperus scopulorum 'Skyrocket'
SKYROCKET JUNIPER

Ⓝ ☼ ☼ ◊ Z4–7 H7–1 ↕20ft (6m) ↔24in (60cm)

This cultivar is much more upright than the species. Growth rate is moderate, and it tolerates poor soil. May also be offered as *J. virginiana* 'Skyrocket'.

Taxus cuspidata
JAPANESE YEW

Ⓝ ☼ ☼ ☼ ◊ Z5–7 H7–1 ↕50ft (15m) ↔25ft (8m)

Soft-textured conifer that can be grown as a shrub or a small tree. Fleshy fruit are scarlet, and dark green needles turn red-green in winter. Slow-growing.

Picea pungens 'Glauca Globosa'
GLOBE BLUE SPRUCE

Ⓝ ☼ ◊ Z2–8 H8–1 ↕↔3ft (1m)

This is a truly dwarf cultivar of the blue gray form of *P. pungens*. It can be found grafted onto a standard trunk. Growth rate is slow.

Picea pungens 'Hoopsii'
HOOPSII BLUE SPRUCE

Ⓝ ☼ ◊ Z3–8 H8–1

↕50ft (15m) ↔15ft (5m)

This cultivar is more blue-white than others. Growth open and uneven when young, becoming more even with age.

Picea pungens
COLORADO SPRUCE

Ⓝ ☼ ◊ Z3–8 H8–1

↕50ft (15m) ↔15ft (5m)

Gray-green needles are less prominent in the landscape than those of bluer cultivars. Very tough and adaptable.

Cedrus atlantica f. glauca
BLUE ATLAS CEDAR

☼ ◊ Z6–9 H9–3

↕100ft (30m) ↔75ft (22m)

Scrawny and awkward when young, it fills out as it matures, with horizontally spreading branches. Growth rate is moderate. Also known as *C. libani* subsp. *atlantica* f. *glauca*.

Pinus bungeana
LACEBARK PINE

☼ ◊ Z4–7 H7–1 ↕↔30ft (9m)

Bark of this tree is smooth when young, becoming colorfully flaky with age. Often has multiple trunks. Young shoots are olive green. Growth rate is slow.

Picea glauca
WHITE SPRUCE

Ⓝ ☼ ◊ Z3–6 H6–1

↕30–50ft (9–15m) ↔12–15ft (3.5–5m)

A narrowly or broadly conical tree. Bark is ash-gray becoming scaly with age. Growth rate is moderate. 'Densata' grows more slowly.

Cedrus deodara
DEODAR CEDAR

☼ ◊ Z6–9 H9–6 ↕50–80ft (15–24m)

↔15–30ft (5–9m)

Starts out conical and becomes wide-spreading with age. Bark is dark brown to black. Moderate growth rate.

Pinus sylvestris
SCOTS PINE

☼ ◊ Z3–7 H7–1 ↕80ft (24m)

↔30ft (9m)

Bluish needles twisted and long. Irregularly pyramidal in youth, it matures to a columnar-conical tree.

Conifers for clay soils

High levels of clay in soil results in reduced air space in the root zone. Clay soils also take longer to dry out in spring and are more difficult to moisten when they get very dry. This group of conifers can handle the challenging conditions presented by clay soils.

Taxodium ascendens
POND CYPRESS
Ⓝ ☼ ◊◊◊ Z5–11 H12–5
↕50–60ft (15–18m) ↔10–15ft (3–5m)
Narrowly conical, deciduous conifer producing erect young shoots that become pendent with age. Moderate growth rate.

Ginkgo biloba
MAIDENHAIR TREE
☼ ◊ Z5–9 H9–3 ↕100ft (30m) ↔75ft (22m)
An upright, deciduous, columnar tree when young, spreading with age. Female trees produce plumlike, malodorous yellow-green fruit in fall. Tolerant of most conditions.

Ginkgo biloba 'Autumn Gold'
AUTUMN GOLD MAIDENHAIR TREE
☼ ◊ Z3–9 H9–1 ↕50ft (15m) ↔30ft (10m)
This is a male cultivar, so it does not produce fruit. It has a conical habit and produces brilliant color in fall before all the foliage drops, often overnight.

MORE CHOICES

- *Chamaecyparis obtusa* 'Crippsii' Z4–8 H8–1
- *Chamaecyparis obtusa* Z4–8 H8–1
- *Chamaecyparis pisifera* 'Boulevard' Z4–8 H8–1
- *Chamaecyparis pisfera* 'Snow' Z4–8 H8–1
- *Crytomeria japonica* Z6–9 H9–4
- *Ginkgo biloba* 'Princeton Sentry' Z5–9 H9–2
- *Ginkgo biloba* 'Saratoga' Z5–9 H9–3
- *Ginkgo biloba* 'Shangri-la' Z3–9 H9–1
- *Larix decidua* Z3–6 H6–1
- *Metasequoia glypostroboides* Z4–11 H12–1
- *Picea glauca* Z2–6 H6–1
- *Pinus strobus* 'Nana' Z3–9 H9–1
- *Pinus thunbergiana* Z5–8 H8–5
- *Thuja plicata* Z6–8 H8–6
- *Tsuga heterophylla* 'Western Hemlock' Z6–8 H8–6

Taxodium distichum
BALD CYPRESS
Ⓝ ☼ ☼ ◊◊ Z5–11 H12–5 ↕80ft (24m) ↔25ft (8m)
The needles turn rust-brown in fall before dropping. Pale brown, shallowly fissured bark. Distinctive aerial roots ("knees") form around the base of the tree in wet sites. Moderate growth rate.

Pinus strobus
EASTERN WHITE PINE

Ⓝ ☼ ◑ Z4–9 H9–1 ‡100ft (30m)
↔75ft (22m)

A conical tree that becomes irregular
and flat-topped with age. Smooth gray
bark becomes black and cracked.

Pinus mugo
MUGO PINE

☼ ◌ Z3–7 H7–1 ‡10–15ft (3–5m)
↔15–25 ft (5–8m)

Resinous green stems age to brown.
Bark is scaly and gray. Some of the
shorter cultivars can be used as shrubs.

Pinus thunbergii
JAPANESE BLACK PINE

☼ ◑ Z5–8 H8–5 ‡↔50ft (15m)

Conical younger trees become more rounded and picturesquely irreglar with age.
Bark is dark purplish gray, and the shoots and buds are covered with downy white
scales. Moderate growth rate.

Pinus strobus 'Pendula'
WEEPING WHITE PINE

Ⓝ ☼ ◑◕ Z4–9 H9–1 ‡6–12ft
(1.8–3.6m) ↔25–35ft (7.5–10.5m)

Twisted, hanging branches give this
cultivar a very distinctive outline.
Makes a striking specimen tree.

Chamaecyparis obtusa 'Filicoides'
FERNSPRAY FALSE CYPRESS

☼ ◐ ◑ Z4–8 H8–1 ‡8ft (2.4m) ↔10ft (3m)

An open, irregular shrub to small tree good as a specimen or hedge.
Female cones start green and turn brown as they ripen in fall. Tolerates
alkaline soil. Growth rate is moderate.

Chamaecyparis nootkatensis
WEEPING ALASKAN CEDAR

Ⓝ ☼ ◐ ◑ Z4–7 H7–1 ‡50ft (15m)
↔20ft (6m)

Brown-gray bark peels in large plates.
Small green female cones ripen in spring.

Larix kaempferi
JAPANESE LARCH

☼ ◌ Z3–6 H6–1
‡80ft (24m) ↔30ft (9m)

A conical tree with scaly, fissured,
rust-brown to gray bark. Needles are
shed in fall, revealing purplish red
winter shoots covered in a waxy bloom.
Also known as L. leptolepis.

CONIFERS

Large conifers (more than 50ft/15m)

Because the majority of conifers are evergreen, these large species provide a sense of stability and constancy to any garden setting that can accommodate their size. Even the deciduous species such as *Ginkgo* have been revered for centuries for the sense of permanence they provide.

CONIFERS

Picea pungens
COLORADO SPRUCE
Ⓝ ☀ ◊ Z3–8 H8–1 ‡50ft (15m) ↔15ft (5m)
A conical to columnar tree with scaly, purplish gray bark. Pale brown female cones hang down. Growth rate is morderate to slow. Tolerant of winter salt spray.

Cedrus atlantica f. *glauca*
BLUE ATLAS CEDAR
☀ ◊ Z6–9 H9–3 ‡100ft (30m) ↔75ft (22m)
Scrawny when young but fills out as it matures with horizontally spreading branches. Moderate growth rate. Also known as *C. libani* subsp. *atlantica* f. *glauca*.

Picea omorika
SERBIAN SPRUCE
☀ ◊ Z4–8 H8–1 ‡100ft (30m) ↔75ft (22m)
Brown bark cracks into square patches. Bears oblong red-brown cones that turn brown. Growth rate is slow. Tolerates alkaline soil.

Tsuga heterophylla
WESTERN HEMLOCK
Ⓝ ☀ ◊ Z6–8 H8–6 ‡70–100ft (21–30m) ↔30ft (9m)
A tightly conical tree with cracked, purple-brown bark. Branches droop horizontally. Needles have two white bands on the underside. Prefers organic soil. Growth rate is fast.

Ginkgo biloba 'Autumn Gold'
AUTUMN GOLD MAIDENHAIR TREE
☀ ◊ Z3–9 H9–1 ‡50ft (15m) ↔30ft (9m)
Although slow-growing, ginkgos can attain a massive size, so site accordingly when planting one. This male cultivar does not produce malodorous fruit.

Pseudotsuga menziesii
DOUGLAS FIR
Ⓝ ☼ ◊ Z5–7 H7–5 ‡80ft (24m) ↔25–40ft (8–12m)
Trees start out conical and become columnar, with spreading branches. Growth rate is moderate. Variety *glauca* does well in the eastern sections of the NW.

Metasequoia glyptostroboides
DAWN REDWOOD
☼ ● Z4–11 H12–1 ‡100ft (30m) ↔75ft (22m)
Foliage turns orange-brown before it sheds in late fall. Bark is orange-brown year round, and the trunk becomes inversely fluted with age. Growth rate is fast.

Sequoiadendron giganteum
GIANT REDWOOD
Ⓝ ☼ ◊ Z6–9 H9–4 ‡100ft (30m) ↔75ft (22m)
A conical tree that becomes increasingly flat-topped with age. Vary attractive reddish brown bark. Prefers moderately fertile soil Growth rate is moderate.

Pinus sylvestris
SCOTS PINE
☼ ◊ Z3–7 H7–1 ‡50–80ft (15–24m) ↔30ft (9m)
Bluish needles are twisted and 2–3in (5–8cm) long. Irregularly pyramidal in youth, maturing columnar-conical. Small cones. Moderate growth rate.

MORE CHOICES

- *Abies firma* Z6–9 H9–6
- *Abies grandis* Z5–6 H6–5
- *Abies nordmanniana* Z4–6 H6–4
- *Araucaria araucana* Z7–11 H12–6
- *Calocedrus decurrens*
- *Cedrus atlantica* 'Fastigiata' Z6–9 H9–3
- *Cedrus libani* Z6–9 H9–3
- *Chamaecyparis lawsoniana* 'Wisselii' Z5–9 H9–5
- *Cryptomeria japonica* Z6–9 H9–6
- x *Cupressocyparis leylandii* Z6–9 H9–3
- *Cupressus sempervirens*
- *Juniperus virginiana* 'Canaertii' Z3–9 H9–1
- *Larix decidua* Z3–6 H6–9
- *Larix kaempferi* Z5–7 H7–4
- *Picea abies* Z3–8 H8–1
- *Picea englemannii* Z3–8 H8–1
- *Picea orientalis* Z7–8 H8–5
- *Pinus cembra* Z3–7 H7–1
- *Pinus jeffrei* Z6–8 H8–6
- *Pinus nigra* Z5–8 H8–4
- *Pinus resinosa* Z3–7 H7–1
- *Pinus strobus* Z4–9 H9–1
- *Pinus strobus* 'Fastigiata' Z4–9 H9–3
- *Taiwania cryptomerioides* Z0–10 H9–7
- *Taxodium distichum* 'Shawnee Brave' Z5–11 H12–5
- *Tsuga canadensis* Z4–8 H8–1

Abies concolor
WHITE FIR
Ⓝ ☼ ◊ Z3–7 H7–1 ‡100ft (30m) ↔25ft (8m)
Columnar tree that maintains its foliage to the ground. Needles curve up from twigs. Cylindrical cones are up to 5in (13cm) long. Slow to moderate growth rate.

Medium-sized conifers

These trees and large shrubs, ranging from 20 to 50 feet tall (6–15m), make excellent additions to all but the smallest gardens. They are superb specimen plants and contribute to the "backbone" of the garden, having a presence all year. These conifers can be added to large borders to serve as a backdrop for more colorful plants.

Pinus bungeana
LACEBARK PINE

☀ ◊ Z4–7 H7–1 ↕↔30ft (9m)

Bark of this tree is smooth and olive green when young, becoming patchy and flaky with age. Often forms multiple trunks. Growth rate is slow.

Cephalotaxus harringtonia
COW'S-TAIL PINE

☀ ◊ Z6–9 H9–3 ↕15ft (5m) ↔10ft (3m)

Can be a large shrub or small tree as it ages. Female plants produce small, egg-shaped, olive green fruit in fall. Prefers fertile soil. Tolerates severe cutting back.

Chamaecyparis obtusa
HINOKI CYPRESS

☀ ☼ ◊ ◑ Z4–8 H8–1 ↕70ft (20m) ↔15ft (5m)

An open, irregular shrub to small tree, depending on the cultivar. Small cones start green and turn brown as they ripen in fall. Growth rate is moderate.

Juniperus chinensis 'Keteleeri'
CHINESE JUNIPER

☀ ◊ Z3–9 H9–1 ↕↔50ft (15m)

This cultivar is much more conical (and foliage is grayer) than the species. Brown bark peels in long strips. Needs very little pruning. Growth is moderate to slow.

Juniperus virginiana 'Burkii'
BURK'S BLUE CEDAR

Ⓝ ☀ ☼ ◊ Z4–8 H8–1 ↕to 20ft (6m) ↔3ft (1m)

Dense, upright small tree that produces attractive blue-gray foliage that takes on purple tints in winter. Like the species, it is susceptible to cedar rust.

Pseudolarix amabilis
GOLDEN LARCH

☼ ◑ z5–9 H9–4 ↕↔50ft 915m)

This broadly conical tree becomes quite open as it ages. Needles turn a golden yellow before they drop in fall. Growth rate is slow. Also known as *P. kaempferi*.

Cunninghamia lanceolata
CHINESE FIR

☼ ◑ z7–9 H9–7 ↕↔50ft (15m)

A conical tree that becomes more rounded or dome-topped as it ages. Growth rate is slow to moderate. Also known as *C. lanceolata* var. *sinensis*.

MORE CHOICES

- *Abies balsamea phanerolepis* z3–6 H6–1
- *Abies koreana* z5–6 H6–5
- *Chamaecyparis obtusa* 'Crippsii' z4–8 H8–1
- *Chamaecyparis pisifera* 'Squarrosa' z4–8 H8–1
- *Cupressus arizonica* 'Pyramidalis' z7–9 H9–7
- *Juniperus scopulorum* z3–7 H7–1
- *Juniperus virginiana* 'Canaertii' z3–9 H9–1
- *Larix laricina* z5–7 H6–1
- *Picea glauca* 'Densata' z2–6 H6–1
- *Picea mariana* z3–6 H6–1
- *Pinus aristata* z2–10 H9–1
- *Pinus contorta* var. *contorta* z6–8 H8–6
- *Pinus eldarica* z6–8 H8–4
- *Pinus virginiana* z3–7 H7–1
- *Sciadopitys verticillata* z5–9 H9–4
- *Taxodium distichum* var. *imbricatum* 'Nutans' z5–11 H12–5
- *Thuja koraiensis* z5–7 H7–5
- *Thuja occidentalis* 'Sprialis' z2–7 H7–1
- *Tsuga mertensiana* z6–8 H8–6

Taxodium distichum
BALD CYPRESS

Ⓝ ☼ ◑ z5–11 H12–5 ↕100ft (30m) ↔75ft (22.5m)

A deciduous, columnar tree with erect shoots that become pendent when mature. Bark is pale brown and shallowly fissured. Growth rate is moderate.

Picea glauca 'Coerulea'
WHITE SPRUCE

Ⓝ ☼ ◑ z3–6 H6–1 ↕↔50ft (15m)

Short, dense, bright blue-green needles and a narrowly conical mature habit are the attributes of this sport of *P. glauca* var. *densata*. Growth rate slow.

Small conifers

Here are some excellent choices for gardeners wanting to include the grace, elegance, and texture of much larger-scale conifers in an average-size yard. These conifers, which range from 3 to 20 feet (1–6m), fit well into dedicated beds and mixed borders and are in scale with most homes and properties. Being evergreen, they make the ideal backbone for year-round interest.

Pinus mugo cultivars
DWARF MOUNTAIN PINE, SWISS MOUNTAIN PINE
☼ ◊ Z3–7 H7–1 ↕10–15ft (3–5m) ↔15–25 ft (5–8m)
This species is variable, so it is best to research and buy known cultivars before including them in your landscape. Growth rate is slow.

Juniperus sabina var. *tamariscifolia*
TAMARISK JUNIPER
☼ ◊ Z4–7 H7–1 ↕to 12ft (4m) ↔10–15ft (3–5m)
The horizontal tiers of spreading branches create a mounding form. Growth rate is slow. The flattened, spherical fruit turns bluish black with a white coating.

Juniperus squamata 'Chinese Silver'
CHINESE SILVER JUNIPER
☼ ☀ ◊ Z4–9 H9–1 ↕↔10–12ft (3–5m)
Prominent white stomata (pores) give the leaves of this cultivar a more silvery appearance than the species. Growth rate is slow. Tolerant of many soil types.

Juniperus sabina 'Cupressifolia'
SAVIN JUNIPER
☼ ◊ Z4–7 H7–1 ↕6ft (2m) ↔12ft (4m)
This low, compact female cultivar bears abundant cones that contrast with the blue-green adult foliage. Growth rate is moderate to fast.

Juniperus squamata 'Holger'
HOLGER'S SINGLESEED JUNIPER
☼ ☀ ◊ Z4–9 H9–1 ↕↔6ft (2m)
This cultivar has a spreading habit. The young leaves are a striking sulfur yellow that contrasts with the steely blue older foliage. Bears ovoid, glossy black fruit.

Picea glauca 'Conica'
DWARF ALBERTA SPRUCE
Ⓝ ☀ ◊ z3–6 H6–1 ‡6–15ft (2–5m) ↔3–6ft (1–2m)
A dwarf variety that maintains a neat, conical shape.
Growth is slow, and be watchful of reverted growth.
Also known as *P. glauca* var. *albertiana* 'Conica'

Pinus sylvestris 'Gold Coin'
GOLD COIN SCOTS PINE
☀ ◊ z3–7 H7–1 ‡↔6ft (2m)
Slower-growing than the species, with a golden cast
replacing the typical blue-green leaves. Bark peels off
in thin flakes. Works well in a mixed border.

MORE CHOICES

- *Chamaecyparis lawsoniana* 'Ellwood's Gold' z4–8 H8–3
- *Chamaecyparis obtusa* 'Nana' z4–8 H8–1
- *Chamaecyparis obtusa* 'Nana Aurea' z3–7 H7–1
- *Chamaecyparis obtusa* 'Rigid Dwarf' z3–7 H7–1
- *Chamaecyparis obtusa* 'Tempelhof' z4–8 H8–1
- *Cryptomeria japonica* 'Black Dragon' z6–8 H8–6
- *Cryptomeria japonica* 'Spiralis' z6–9 H9–6
- *Juniperus chinensis* 'Aurea' z3–9 H9–1
- *Juniperus chinensis* 'Kaizuka Variegated' z3–9 H9–1
- *Juniperus communis* 'Gold Cone' z2–6 H6–1
- *Juniperus communis* 'Hibernica' z2–6 H6–1
- *Juniperus scopulorum* 'Gray Gleam' z3–7 H7–1
- *Picea pungens* 'Kosteri' z3–8 H8–1
- *Thuja occidentalis* 'Pendula' z3–7 H7–1
- *Thuja occidentalis* 'Smaragd' z2–7 H7–1
- *Thuja occidentalis* 'Sunkist' z3–8 H8–1
- *Thuja plicata* 'Stoneham Gold' z6–8 H8–6
- X *Cupressocyparis leylandii* 'Hyde Hall' z6–9 H9–6

Thuja orientalis 'Semperaurea'
ORIENTAL ARBORVITAE
☀ ◊ z6–9 H9–6 ‡10ft (3m) ↔6ft (2m)
The new growth of this cultivar is golden yellow.
Foliage may turn bronze in winter. Slower-growing
and more compact than the species.

Juniperus chinensis 'Stricta'
CHINESE JUNIPER
☀ ◊ z3–9 H9–1 ‡to 15ft (5m) ↔to 3ft (1m)
A distinctly upright, blue-gray leaved selection of an
amazingly variable species. Makes a striking contrast
of form and color in a border. Growth rate moderate.

CONIFERS

Dwarf conifers less than 3ft (1m) tall

These selections are all slow-growing sports (naturally occurring variants) of much larger conifers. Their size makes them ideal for very small suburban lots and for container gardening. They are also ideal for rock gardens and screes, where their forms and silhouettes can be used to evoke the sculpting effects of strong mountaintop winds .

Chamaecyparis lawsoniana 'Minima'
DWARF LAWSON FALSE CYPRESS
Ⓝ ☼ ◊ Z5–9 H9–5 ↕↔3ft (1m)
A very compact form of this very large species. Maintains a rounded to conical habit. Needs little to no pruning to maintain form.Will tolerate alkaline soils.

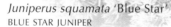

Juniperus squamata 'Blue Star'
BLUE STAR JUNIPER
☼ ☼ ◊ Z4–9 H9–1 ↕20in (50cm) ↔24in (60cm)
This very dense bush has more bluish gray leaves than the species. Good for a rock garden or groundcover. Needs little to no pruning.

Thuja orientalis 'Aurea Nana'
DWARF GOLDEN ARBORVITAE
☼ ◊ Z6–9 H9–6 ↕↔24in (60cm)
Yellow green leaves in distinct planes turn bronze in the winter. Forms upright, flask-shaped, gray-coated female cones. Prefers deep soils.

Thuja plicata 'Hillieri'
WESTERN ARBORVITAE
Ⓝ ☼ ◊ Z6–8 H8–6 ↕↔3ft (1m)
Foliage is more blue-green than the species, and growth is much slower. Prefers deep, well drained soil. Nice alpine garden plant.

Thuja occidentalis 'Caespitosa'
AMERICAN WHITE CEDAR
Ⓝ ☼ ◊ Z2–7 H7–1 ↕30–60ft (9–18m) ↔10–15ft (3–5m)
There are many other dwarf cutivars of this large tree, including 'Golden Globe', 'Hetz Midget', 'Little Gem', 'Emerald' and 'Wansdyke Silver'.

MORE CHOICES

- *Abies balsamea* 'Nana' Z3–6 H6–1
- *Abies concolor* 'Compacta' Z3–7 H7–2
- *Cedrus libani* 'Sargentii' Z7–9 H9–7
- *Chamaecyparis lawsoniana* 'Gnome' Z5–9 H9–5
- *Chamaecyparis obtusa* 'Hage' Z4–8 H8–1
- *Chamaecyparis obtusa* 'Juniperoides' Z4–8 H8–1
- *Cryptomeria japonica* 'Vilmoriniana' Z6–9 H9–6
- *Juniperus communis* 'Compressa' Z2–8 H6–1
- *Juniperus squamata* 'Blue Star' Z4–8 H8–1
- *Picea abies* 'Little Gem' Z3–8 H8–2
- *Picea glauca* var. *albertina* 'Echiniformis' Z3–6 H6–1
- *Pinus mugo* Z3–7 H7–1
- *Pinus strobus* 'Minima' Z3–9 H9–1
- *Pinus sylvestris* 'Beuvronensis' Z3–7 H7–1
- *Thuja plicata* 'Rogersii' Z6–8 H8–6
- *Tsuga canadensis* 'Jeddeloh' Z4–8 H8–1

Picea abies 'Reflexa'
NORWAY SPRUCE

☼ ◊ Z3–8 H8–1 ↕12in (30cm) ↔15ft (5m)

A prostrate sport, often grafted to a tall stock to produce a weeping plant. Ungrafted, it will gracefully cascade over the side of a retaining wall.

Picea pungens 'Montgomery'
BLUE SPRUCE

Ⓝ ☼ ◊ Z3–8 H8–1 ↕↔3ft (1m)

A very slow-growing cultivar that maintains its broad conical habit as it ages. Leaves are much more silver than the species. A good focal point for a border.

Juniperus communis 'Compressa'
COMMON JUNIPER

Ⓝ ☼ ◐ ◊ Z2–6 H6–1 ↕30in (75cm) ↔6in (15cm)

Growth rate is very slow. Works well in a trough or in a rock garden, where it makes a nice specimen plant.. Very tolerant of poor soils.

Pinus sylvestris 'Doone Valley'
SCOTS PINE

☼ ◊ Z3–7 H7–1 ↕↔3ft (1m)

A dwarf cultivar of the much larger species. Forms ovoid, conical, green female cones that ripen to gray or red-brown. Tolerant of any well-drained soil.

CONIFERS

Conifers that spread or weep

Spreading conifers produce distinctly horizontal growth. Weeping plants can be tall specimens with graceful, pendulous branches, or spreading cultivars grafted to a standard (upright) trunk. Weepers make very strong accent plants, providing visual interest to the landscape. Spreaders can be used as specimens or massed for a bolder effect.

Taxodium distichum
BALD CYPRESS
Ⓝ ☼ ☼ ◐ ● Z5–11 H12–5 ‡80ft (24m) ↔25ft (8m)
Side branches on main stems weep slightly. The needles turn rust-brown in fall before dropping. Growth rate is moderate.

Juniperus cultivars
JUNIPER
☼ ◊ Z3–9 H9–1 ‡2ft (60cm) ↔10ft (3m)
Many juniper species spread naturally or have had cultivars selected from them that do so. All make excellent groundcovers for large areas and slopes.

Larix decidua 'Pendula'
WEEPING EUROPEAN LARCH
☼ ◊ Z3–6 H6–1 ‡100ft (30m) or more ↔20ft (6m)
Branches are more pendulous than the species. Scaly, gray bark becomes ridged with age. Deciduous.

MORE CHOICES

- *Abies concolor* 'Pendula' Z3–7 H7–1
- *Cedrus deodara* 'Pendula' Z7–9 H9–6
- *Juniperus scopulorum* 'Tolleson's Weeping' Z3–7 H7–1
- *Tsuga canadensis* 'Ashfield Weeper' Z4–8 H8–3
- *Taxus baccata* 'Dovastonii Aurea' Z7–8 H8–7

Juniperus cultivars
JUNIPER
☼ ◊ Z3–9 H9–1 ‡2ft (60cm) ↔10ft (3m)
Spreading junipers are available in a wide range of colors, from green to blue-green, silvery green, and yellow-green. Colors fade if not grown in full sun.

Pinus strobus 'Pendula'
WEEPING WHITE PINE
Ⓝ ☼ ◊ Z4–9 H9–1 ‡to 120ft (35m) ↔20–25ft (6–8m)
A horizontally growing sport of *P. strobus* that is usually grown as a standard. Smooth gray bark turns black and cracked with age. Moderate growth rate.

Columnar conifers

On the other extreme from spreaders and weepers (see left), these conifers produce strongly vertical growth, giving them a distinctive, spirelike outline. Their strong vertical lines make them "exclamation points" in a landscape design. These selections maintain their vertical habit with little or no pruning, but be sure to remove heavy snow loads as soon as possible.

Juniperus chinensis 'Keteleeri'
CHINESE JUNIPER
☼ ◊ Z3–9 H9–1 ↕↔50ft (15m)
This cultivar is much more narrowly conical than the species, and its foliage is darker gray and much more dense. Growth rate is moderate to slow.

Cryptomeria japonica 'Sekkan-sugi'
JAPANESE CEDAR
◐ ◊ Z6–9 H9–6 ↕30ft (10m) ↔10–12ft (3–4m)
A wonderful cultivar that produces creamy yellow leaves that turn almost white in winter. Sometimes is more conical than columnar. Moderately fast grower.

Juniperus scopulorum 'Skyrocket'
SKYROCKET JUNIPER
Ⓝ ☼ ◐ ◊ Z4–7 H7–1 ↕20ft (6m) ↔24in (60cm)
This cultivar is valued for its upright habit and blue foliage, which becomes bronze-tinted in cold winter areas. Growth rate is moderate. Tolerates poor soil.

CONIFERS

Cryptomeria japonica 'Pyramidata'
JAPANESE CEDAR
☼ ◊ Z6–9 H9–6 ↕30ft (10m)
Much more narrowly columnar than the species. Prefers deep, fertile, organic soil. Deep green leaves turn bronze in winter. Growth rate is moderate.

MORE CHOICES

- *Abies alba* 'Columnaris' Z5–8 H8–5
- *Abies balsamea* 'Columnaris' Z3–6 H6–1
- *Abies concolor* 'Fastigiate' Z3–7 H7–1
- *Chamaecyparis lawsoniana* 'Columnaris' Z2–7 H7–1
- *Cupressus sempervirens* 'Swane's Gold' Z7–9 H9–6
- *Pinus sylvestris* 'Fastigiata' Z2–7 H7–1
- *Thuja occidentalis* 'Holmstrup' Z2–7 H7–1
- *Thuja occidentalis* 'Spiralis' Z2–7 H7–1
- x *Cupressocyparis leylandii* 'Hyde Hall' Z6–9 H9–6

Thuja occidentalis
AMERICAN WHITE CEDAR
Ⓝ ☼ ◊ Z2–7 H7–1 ↕30–60ft (9–18m) ↔15ft (5m)
Remains very full to the ground as it matures. Growth rate is slow to moderate. Some especially columnar cultivars are 'Pyramidalis' and 'Hetz Wintergreen'.

Deciduous conifers

Conifers by definition are cone-bearing plants (as opposed to flowering plants, such as maples and lilies). The vast majority of conifers are evergreen, but there are a few noteworthy conifers that drop their foliage every fall, providing attractive color and then revealing very interesting bark coloration and branch structure.

Ginkgo biloba
MAIDENHAIR TREE

☼ ◊ Z5–9 H9–3 ‡100ft (30m) ↔75ft (22m)
An upright, columnar tree when young that spreads with age. Female trees produce plumlike, silvery yellow, ill-scented fruit in fall. Good golden fall color.

Larix occidentalis
WESTERN LARCH

Ⓝ ☼ ◊ Z4–8 H8–1 ‡80ft (25m) ↔15ft (5m)
Blue-green to gray-green leaves emerge from orange-brown twigs. Young bark is orange-brown and hairy becoming furrowed. Moderate growth rate.

Ginkgo biloba 'Autumn Gold'
AUTUMN GOLD MAIDENHAIR TREE

☼ ◊ Z3–9 H9–1 ‡50ft (15m) ↔30ft (9m)
This male cultivar has a rather regular, conical form and produces brilliant fall color. Being male, it does not produce malodorous fruit like the females

MORE CHOICES

- *Ginkgo biloba* 'Saratoga' Z5–9 H9–3
- *Larix decidua* Z3–6 H6–1
- *Larix decidua* 'Fastigiana' Z3–6 H6–1
- *Larix decidua* 'Pendula' Z3–6 H6–1
- *Larix kaempferi* Z5–7 H7–5
- *Larix kaempferi* 'Pendula' Z5–7 H7–5
- *Metasequoia glypostroboides* Z4–7 H12–1
- *Metasequoia glypostroboides* 'National' Z4–7 H12–1
- *Taxodium ascendens* Z5–11 H12–5
- *Taxodium ascendens* 'Prairie Sentinel' Z5–11 H12–5
- *Taxodium distichum* 'Shawny Brave' Z5–11 H12–5

Pseudolarix amabilis
GOLDEN LARCH

☼ ◊ Z5–9 H9–4 ‡↔50ft (915m)
Grow this plant if you want an interesting contrast to most conifers: it is open and gracefully tiered with age and produces very delicate-looking foliage.

Taxodium distichum
BALD CYPRESS

Ⓝ ☼ ☼ ◊ ◊ Z5–11 H12–5 ‡80ft (24m) ↔25ft (8m)
Very fine needles turn rusty brown in fall before shedding and making the tree "bald." Pale brown bark becomes shallowly fissured. Growth rate is moderate.

Conifers with blue-gray or silvery foliage

Although many conifers have blue-green foliage, there are many cultivars that exhibit a grayer or even silvery cast. These specimens are particularly handsome when contrasted with darker-foliaged plants. The contrast is especially pronounced and visually exciting when the darker plant has large, coarse leaves (especially those of broadleaf evergreens).

Juniperus squamata 'Meyeri'
FISHBACK JUNIPER
☼ ☀ ◊ Z4–9 H9–1 ↕↔15ft (5m)
Has spreading, arching shoot tips and a more rounded habit than the species. Grows slowly. Trim dead foliage out of this shrub to keep it looking its best.

Juniperus scopulorum 'Skyrocket'
SKYROCKET JUNIPER
☼ ☀ ◊ Z4–7 H7–1 ↕20ft (6m) ↔20–24in (50–60cm)
This cultivar is known for being much more upright than the species. Moderate growth rate. Tolerates poor soil. It may also be listed as *J. virginiana* 'Skyrocket'.

Picea glauca 'Coerulea'
WHITE SPRUCE
Ⓝ ☼ ◊ Z3–6 H6–1 ↕↔50ft (15m)
An attractive selection of an already blue-foliaged species, it becomes denser and regularly conical with age. Watch for competing leaders when young, removing the weaker of the two if they appear.

MORE CHOICES

- *Abies concolor* 'Candicans' Z3–7 H7–1
- *Chamaecyparis lawsoniana* 'Pelt's Blue' Z5–9 H9–5
- *Cupressus arizonica* 'Pyramidalis' Z7–9 H9–7
- *Juniperus communis* 'Compressa' Z2–6 H6–1
- *Juniperus communis* 'Hibernica' Z2–6 H6–1
- *Juniperus horizontalis* 'Douglasii' Z3–9 H9–1
- *Juniperus horizontalis* 'Glauca' Z3–9 H9–1
- *Juniperus sabina* 'Blue Danube' Z3–7 H7–1
- *Juniperus virginiana* 'Glauca' Z3–9 H9–1
- *Pseudotsuga menziesii* 'Glauca' Z5–7 H7–5

Cedrus atlantica f. *glauca*
BLUE ATLAS CEDAR
☼ ◊ Z6–9 H9–3 ↕100ft (30m) ↔75ft (22m)
Scrawny-looking when young, but like most cedars, it fills out attractively as it matures, with horizontally spreading branches. Growth rate is moderate.

Picea pungens 'Koster'
BLUE SPRUCE
Ⓝ ☼ ◊ Z3–8 H8–1 ↕↔50ft (15m)
Foliage is much more silvery blue than the species. A conical to columnar tree with scaly, purplish gray bark. Growth rate is slow. Pale brown cones persist.

Conifers with golden or yellow leaves

There is a multitude of conifers, both large and small, that can give the illusion of capturing the warmth of the sun. There are many variations on the coloration: some exhibit a golden cast evenly across the plant, others have swirls of yellow mixed with the standard green, and sometimes the color is limited to the new growth.

Pinus sylvestris 'Aurea'
SCOTS PINE

☼ ◐ Z3–7 H7–1 ↕80ft (24m) ↔30ft (9m)
The foliage becomes increasingly golden as weather cools, then it retuns to normal blue green for the growing season. Growth rate is slow to moderate.

Thuja occidentalis 'Rheingold'
AMERICAN ARBORVITAE

Ⓝ ☼ ◐ Z2–7 H7–1 ↕10–12ft (3–4m) ↔6–12ft (2–4m)
This cultivar is smaller and shrubbier than the species. Foliage is pink tinted when young, and the growth rate is slow. Also called *T. o.* 'Ellwangeriana Aurea'.

Thuja plicata 'Collyer's Gold'
WESTERN RED CEDAR

Ⓝ ☼ ◐ Z6–8 H8–6 ↕6ft (2m) ↔3ft (1m)
A dense, upright shrub form of the species. Young shoots are gold, so prune older plants to encourage more new growth. Growth rate is slow

Picea orientalis 'Aurea'
ORIENTAL SPRUCE

☼ ◐ Z5–8 H8–5 ↕70ft (21m)
↔15ft (5m)
The bright coloration persists for only the first six weeks on new growth. A broadly columnar tree, it is conical when young. Growth rate is slow.

Chamaecyparis obtusa 'Tetragona Aurea'
HINOKI CYPRESS

☼ ◐ Z4–8 H8–1 ↕30ft (m) ↔10ft (3m)
Must be grown in full sun to maintain its bright yellow-bronze leaves. Grows as an open irregular shrub and then eventually as a small tree. Growth rate is moderate.

Juniperus chinensis 'Aurea'
CHINESE JUNIPER

☼ ☼ ◊ Z3–9 H9–1
↕70ft (20m) ↔20ft (6m)
This columnar tree produces abundant cones in midspring. Growth rate is moderate to slow. Other golden cultivars include 'Kuriwao Gold' and 'Old Gold'.

Ginkgo biloba 'Autumn Gold'
AUTUMN GOLD MAIDENHAIR TREE

☼ ◊ Z5–9 H9–3 ↕50ft (15m) ↔30ft (10m)
A male cultivar, so it does not produce smelly fruit. It has a rather regular (for a ginkgo), conical form. The foliage turns a brilliant gold in fall before it drops.

Cryptomeria japonica 'Sekkan-sugi'
JAPANESE CEDAR

☼ ◊ Z6–9 H9–6 ↕30ft (10m) ↔12ft (4m)
A wonderful cultivar that produces creamy yellow leaves turning almost white in winter. A conical or columnar tree, it is a moderately fast grower.

CONIFERS

Juniperus cultivars
JUNIPER

☼ ◊ Z3–9 H9–1 ↕1–70ft (0.3–21m)
This genus of 50–60 shrubs and trees includes many golden cultivars. Leaves are scalelike. Females produce berrylike fruits. Growth rate is slow to moderate.

MORE CHOICES

- *Abies concolor* 'Aurea' Z3–7 H7–1
- *Abies concolor* 'Wintergold' Z3–7 H7–1
- *Abies nordmanniana* 'Golden Spreads' Z4–6 H6–4
- *Chamaecyparis lawsoniana* 'Killiney Gold' Z5–9 H9–5
- *Chamaecyparis lawsoniana* 'Robusta Aurea' Z5–9 H9–5
- *Chamaecyparis obtusa* 'Fernspray Gold' Z4–8 H8–1
- *Chamaecyparis pisifera* 'Filifera Aurea' Z5–8 H8–1
- *Cupressus macrocarpus* 'Goldcrest' Z7–11 H12–7
- *Cupressus sempervirens* 'Swane's Golden' Z7–9 H9–6
- x *Cupressocyparis leylandii* 'Robinson's Gold' Z6–9 H9–6
- *Juniperus chinensus* 'Blue and Gold' Z3–9 H9–1
- *Juniperus communis* 'Gold Cone' Z2–6 H6–1
- *Picea abies* 'Aurea' Z3–8 H8–1
- *Picea orientalis* 'Skylands' Z5–8 H8–5
- *Pinus sylvestris* 'Gold Coin' Z3–7 H7–1
- *Taxus baccata* Z7–8 H8–7
- *Taxus baccata* 'Adpressa Aurea' Z7–8 H8–7
- *Thuja occidentalis* 'Holmstrup' Z2–7 H7–1
- *Thuja occidentalis* 'Rheingold' Z2–7 H7–1
- *Thuja plicata* 'Aurea' Z6–8 H8–6
- *Tsuga canadensis* 'Aurea Compacta' Z4–8 H8–1

Chamaecyparis lawsoniana 'Hillieri'
LAWSON FALSE CYPRESS

Ⓝ ☼ ◊ Z5–9 H9–5 ↕130ft (40m) ↔15ft (5m)
The foliage is borne in large, flattened sprays on a columnar tree. Moderate growth rate. 'Lane', 'Lutea', and 'Winston Churchill' are other golden cultivars.

Low-maintenance conifers

Low-maintenance plants are almost every gardener's wish. Conifers as a group are very adaptable, but this group is particularly well behaved, requiring minimal care. These conifers also have relatively few insect or disease problems. Once established they should provide years of carefree service and beauty.

Taxus species and cultivars
YEW

☼ ◐ ◊ Z4–8 H8–1 ‡3–60ft (1–18m)

A genus of 5–10 species of broadly rounded to upright shrubs or small trees. Female plants form a fleshy red, single-seeded fruit. Growth rate is slow to moderate.

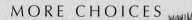

MORE CHOICES

- *Abies fraseri* Z4–7 H7–2
- *Cephalotaxus harringtonia* 'McCorkle Form' H9–6
- *Chamaecyparis obtusa* Z4–8 H8–3
- *Chamaecyparis obtusa* 'Crippsii' Z4–8 H8–1

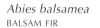

Abies balsamea
BALSAM FIR

Ⓝ ☼ ◊ Z3–6 H6–1

‡50ft (15m) ↔15ft (5m)

A conical tree with smooth gray bark when mature. Produces a fragrant resin reminiscent of balsam and orange peels. Prefers fertile soil.

Abies concolor
WHITE FIR

Ⓝ ☼ ◊ Z3–7 H7–1 ‡100ft (30m) ↔25ft (8m)

Columnar tree that maintains its foliage to the ground. Slow to moderate growth rate. Cylindrical cones are 3-5in long and shatter before falling from the tree.

Cupressus arizonica var. glabra
SMOOTH CYPRESS

Ⓝ ☼ ◊ Z7–9 H9–7 ‡50ft (15m) ↔30 (9m)

Bark is smooth and reddish purple. Bears soft needles and spherical brown, prickly, 1in cones. Moderate to fast growth. The cultivar 'Glauca' has very blue leaves.

Juniperus cultivars
JUNIPER

☼ ◊ Z3–9 H9–1 ‡1–50ft (.3–15m) ↔10–15ft (3–5m)

Genus of 50–60 shrubs and trees. Leaves are scalelike. Females produce fleshy, berrylike fruits. Growth rate slow to moderate. Tolerant of many types of soil.

Chamaecyparis obtusa 'Filicoides'
FERNSPRAY FALSE CYPRESS

☼ ◐ ● Z4–8 H8–1 ‡8ft (2.4m) ↔10ft (3m)

An open, irregular shrub to small tree. Cones start green and turn brown as they ripen in fall. Tolerates alkaline soil. Growth rate is moderate.

Cedrus deodara
DEODAR CEDAR

☀ ◐ Z6–9 H9–6 ‡80ft (24m) ↔30ft (9m)
Starts out conical and becomes wide-spreading with age. Needles are sharply pointed. Moderate growth rate. Tolerant of many soil types.

Taxodium distichum
BALD CYPRESS

Ⓝ ☀ ◐ ◐◐ Z5–11 H12–5 ‡80ft (24m) ↔25ft (8m)
Needles become rust-brown in fall before dropping. Growth rate is moderate. Distinctive "knees" form around the base of the tree in wet sites.

Picea omorika
SERBIAN SPRUCE

☀ ◐ Z4–8 H8–1 ‡100ft (30m) ↔75ft (22m)
Unusually narrow growth habit and semi-pendulous branches set this spruce apart from the rest. Growth rate is slow and tolerates alkaline soil.

MORE CHOICES

- *Cupressus sempervirens* Z7–9 H9–3
- *Larix decidua* Z3–6 H6–1
- *Larix kaempferi* Z5–7 H7–4
- *Picea glauca* Z2–7 H7–2
- *Picea orientalis* Z5–8 H8–5
- *Pinus mugo* Z3–7 H7–1
- *Pinus strobiformis* Z3–9 H9–1
- *Pinus strobus* Z3–9 H9–1
- *Pinus thunbergii* Z5–8 H8–5
- *Taxodium ascendens* Z5–11 H12–5
- *Thuja plicata* Z6–8 H8–6

Thuja occidentalis
ARBORVITAE

Ⓝ ☀ ◐ Z2–7 H7–1 ‡60ft (18m) ↔15ft (5m)
There are many cultivars available; most stay very full to the ground, even as they mature. Growth rate is slow to moderate. The bark shreds away with age.

Calocedrus decurrens
INCENSE CEDAR

Ⓝ ☀ ◐ ◐ Z5–8 H8–5 ‡130ft (40m) ↔28ft (9m)
Matures into a narrow-crowned, columnar tree with cinnamon-red bark. Growth rate is moderate. Very attractive when grown as a specimen or in a group.

Metasequoia glyptostroboides
DAWN REDWOOD

◐ ◐ Z4–11 H12–1 ‡100ft (30m) ↔75ft (22m)
Foliage becomes orange-brown before it drops in late fall. The bark is also orange-brown, and the trunk becomes inversely fluted with age. Growth rate is fast.

Conifers for hedges/screening

No matter which size of hedge you may desire, there is a conifer that will meet your needs. It is best to pick a plant whose mature size is close to the ultimate size of your hedge to minimize the necessary pruning and other maintenance. These evergreen choices make ideal year-round visual screens that will also provide shelter from wind.

Pinus sylvestris
SCOTS PINE

☼ ◊ Z3–7 H7–1 ‡80ft (24m) ↔30ft (9m)

Normally bluish green needles are twisted and 2–3in (5–8cm) long. Irregularly pyramidal in youth, it matures to a columnar-conical tree. Growth rate is moderate.

Cryptomeria japonica
JAPANESE CEDAR

◐ ◊ Z6–9 H9–4 ‡70ft (20m) ↔25ft (8m)

Cryptomeria is one of the few conifers that can be successfully coppiced (cut back severely). Normally a conical or columnar tree, it is a moderately fast grower.

Thuja plicata 'Collyer's Gold'
WESTERN RED CEDAR

Ⓝ ☼ ◐ Z6–8 H8–6 ‡6ft (2m) ↔3ft (1m)

A dense, upright shrub form of the species. Growth rate is slow. Young shoots are gold, so repeated cutting back will keep the foliage bright.

Thuja occidentalis 'Caespitosa'
AMERICAN ARBORVITAE

Ⓝ ☼ ◐ ◊ Z2–7 H7–1 ‡50ft (15m) ↔10–15ft (3–5m)

This cultivar grows slowly into a cushion- or bun-shaped shrub. Good for a low-growing hedge between formal garden areas or in restricted areas.

Abies concolor
WHITE FIR

Ⓝ ☼ ◊ Z3–7 H7–1 ‡100ft (30m) ↔25ft (8m)

Columnar tree that maintains its foliage to the ground. Slow to moderate growth rate. When planted closely it makes a tall, dense, sound-absorbing barrier.

MORE CHOICES

- *Calocedrus decurvens* Z5–8 H8–5
- *Chamaecyparis lawsonia* Z5–9 H9–5
- x *Cupressocyparis leylandii* 'Harlequin' Z6–9 H9–6
- *Juniperus conferta* 'Blue Pacific' Z5–9 H9–1
- *Juniperus horizontalis* 'Blue Chip' Z3–9 H9–1
- *Juniperus horizontalis* 'Douglasii' Z3–9 H9–1
- *Juniperus horizontalis* 'Glauca' Z3–9 H9–1
- *Juniperus horizontalis* 'Plumosa' Z3–9 H9–1
- *Juniperus horizontalis* 'Wiltonii' Z3–9 H9–1
- *Juniperus procumbens* 'Nana' Z3–9 H9–1
- *Juniperus squamata* 'Blue Carpet' Z4–9 H9–1
- *Microbiota decussata* Z3–7 H7–1
- *Picea abies* 'Reflexa' Z3–8 H8–1
- *Picea pungens* 'Procumbens' Z2–8 H8–1
- *Podocarpus alpinus* Z7–10 H10–7
- *Taxus cuspidata* Z5–7 H7–3
- *Tsuga caroliniana* Z3–8 H8–1

Groundcover conifers

These low-growing, spreading conifers are very effective in crowding out weeds and stabilizing slopes. Their carpetlike, evergreen foliage also softens the impact of hard rains or excessive watering. Many cultivars not shown provide a variety of foliage colors, from bright green and golden yellow to blue-green and gray-green.

Cephalotaxus harringtonia cultivars
COW'S-TAIL PINE
☼ ◊ Z6–9 H9–3 ‡15ft (5m) ↔10ft (3m)
The cultivar 'Prostrata', while not a carpetlike spreader, does produce attractive, arching branches that make an attractive higher groundcover. 'Duke Gardens' is similar.

Juniperus sabina var. *tamariscifolia*
TAMARISK JUNIPER
☼ ◊ Z4–7 H7–1 ‡3ft (1m) ↔6ft (2m)
Horizontal tiers of spreading branches create a mounded form. Flattened spherical fruit turns bluish black with a white bloom. Growth rate is slow.

MORE CHOICES

- *Cryptomeria japonica* Z6–9 H9–6
- *Juniperus communis* 'Berkshire' Z2–6 H6–1
- *Picea abies* Z3–8 H8–1
- *Pseudotsuga menziesii* Z5–7 H7–5
- *Thuja plicata* Z6–8 H8–6
- *Tsuga heterophylla* Z6–8 H8–6

Juniperus procumbens 'Nana'
JAPANESE GARDEN JUNIPER
☼ ◊ Z3–9 H9–1 ‡6–8in (15–20cm) ↔30in (75cm)
A dwarf, compact form of an already procumbent shrub results in a low, mat-forming plant. Foliage turns slightly purple in winter. Growth rate is slow.

Picea pungens cultivars
COLORADO SPRUCE
Ⓝ ☼ ◊ Z3–8 H8–1 ‡50ft (15m) ↔15ft (5m)
'Montgomery' is a slow-growing plant with silvery gray-blue leaves. 'Mrs. Cesarini' has blue green foliage. 'Globosa' makes a tight mound.

Juniperus conferta 'Blue Pacific'
SHORE JUNIPER
☼ ◑ ◊ Z5–9 H9–1 ‡12in (30cm)
This cultivar is more trailing than the species and has a deeper blue cast to the foliage. Produces black fruit with a silvery white coating. Growth rate is moderate.

CLIMBERS

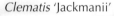

A NUMBER OF USEFUL FLOWERING plants grow as climbers (often also called vines), including both woody and herbaceous species and their selections. As a group, climbers are extremely versatile: they can hide an unattractive wall, decorate a lamppost, obscure an unsightly chain-link fence, clamber into a shrub or tree, adorn a garden arbor, decorate a utilitarian or ornate support in a container planting, or run along horizontally as a groundcover. Some need to be tied to a support, while others attach themselves to a surface without any assistance by their aerial roots, adhesive pads, tendrils, or twining stems.

Lonicera x *tellmanniana* (Honeysuckle)
The tubular, fragrant blossoms, borne from late spring through midsummer, attract a wide variety of hummingbirds and insects.

Clematis 'Jackmanii'
A favorite climber, this clematis holds on to a trellis and other supports with its twining leaf stalks. It is one of the later-flowering cultivars.

When climbers are grown against a warm wall, they benefit from the reflected heat, which initiates the formation of flower buds. However, the roots of climbers such as wisteria and clematis need shade, which can be provided by a large stone or tile. If you are growing a climber through another plant for variety and seasonal interest, remember that the climber and the host plant will compete for food and moisture; to limit the competition, plant the roots of the climber as far away as possible, rather than right up against the other plant. Walls and other solid supports create a rain shadow, so climbers grown in these locations should be placed 18in (45cm) away from the support in order to receive sufficient moisture without requiring additional watering once they are adapted to the site.

Parthenocissus tricuspidata (Boston ivy)
Boston ivy, a vigorous, woody climber that clings to walls with disk-tipped tendrils, is grown primarily for its spectacular fall color.

Allamanda cathartica 'Hendersoni'
One of the genera commonly known as trumpet vine, *Allamanda* consists of evergreen, woody climbers native to tropical North, Central, and South America.

Climbers for sunny sites

Here are some perennial climbers that cover fences, walls, pillars, pergolas, or any other structures you may provide for them. Many also can be used as vigorous groundcovers. All provide attractive foliage, flowers, or both, and some release a sweet fragrance into your garden or bear fruit for the birds and your enjoyment.

Parthenocissus tricuspidata
BOSTON IVY, JAPANESE IVY
☼ ◊ Z4–8 H8–1 ↕to 70ft (20m)
Red to purple color appears in fall. In warmer regions, Boston Ivy may hold its leaves through winter. Makes a good substitute for English Ivy in colder regions.

Clematis 'Jackmanii'
CLEMATIS
☼ ☼ ◊ Z4–9 H9–1
↕10ft (3m)
This large-flowering, fast-growing variety flowers on the current season's shoots, so it should be pruned in spring. Blooms in late summer and continues lightly into fall.

MORE CHOICES

- *Bignonia capreolata* Z6–9 H9–6
- *Bignonia capreolata* 'Atrosanguinea' Z6–9 H9–3
- *Campsis radicans* Z5–9 H9–3
- *Euonymus fortunei* Z4–9 H9–5
- *Lonicera nitida* 'Baggesen's Gold' Z6–9 H9–6
- *Lonicera nitida* 'Ernest Wilson' Z6–9 H9–7
- *Lonicera periclymenum* Z5–9 H9–5
- *Lonicera periclymenum* 'Belgica' Z5–9 H9–5
- *Lonicera periclymenum* 'Graham Thomas' Z5–9 H9–5
- *Lonicera periclymenum* 'Le Gasnerie' Z4–8 H8–1

Parthenocissus quinquefolia
FIVE-LEAVED IVY, VIRGINIA CREEPER
Ⓝ ☼ ☼ ◊ Z7–9 H9–1 ↕50ft (15m) or more
Grows very vigorously and climbs over and onto anything in its path. Brilliant red fall foliage and dark blue fruits are additional virtues.

Lonicera x *tellmanniana*
CLIMBING HONEYSUCKLE
☼ ◊ Z7–9 H9–7 ↕to 15ft (5m)
This deciduous climber of moderate growth flowers from late spring to midsummer. Red berries provide interest in fall as well.

Lonicera periclymemnum 'Serotina'
LATE DUTCH HONEYSUCKLE
☼ ☼ ● ◊ Z5–9 H9–5 ↕to 22ft (7m)
This cultivar was chosen for its uniquely dark red-streaked, fragrant white flowers that bloom from mid-to late summer. Bears red fruit in fall.

Jasminum officinale 'Aureovariegatum'
COMMON JASMINE
☼ ◊ Z8–11 H12–8 ↕to 40ft (12m)
This vigorous climber is prized for its wonderful fragrance. Normally deciduous, it holds its leaves in the southernmost areas of the Northwest.

Rosa 'Kiftsgate'
KIFTSGATE CLIMBER ROSE
☼ ◊ Z6–9 H9–6 ↕↔30ft (10m) or more
Early-summer sprays of creamy white flowers are
exquisitely fragrant and cover the plant. Rampant
growth can reach extraordinary lengths if not pruned.

Clematis armandii
EVERGREEN CLEMATIS
☼ ☼ ◊ Z7–9 H9–7 ↕15ft (5m) ↔10ft (3m)
The wonderfully scented flowers are produced in early
spring on last season's growth, so prune immediately
after flowering. Slow to establish. Better in warmer areas.

Gelsemium rankinii
SWAMP JESSAMINE
Ⓝ ☼ ☼ ◊ ◖ Z7–9 H9–7 ↕10–20ft (3–6m)
Very similar to *G. sempervirens*, but its flowers are not
sweetly scented, and it will tolerate much wetter soils.
Best grown in the southern extremes of the Northwest.

MORE CHOICES

- *Lonicera* x *heckrottii* Z6–9 H9–6
- *Lonicera* x *heckrottii* 'Goldflame' Z6–9 H9–6
- *Parthenocissus tricuspidata* 'Fenway Park'
  Z4–8 H8–1
- *Parthenocissus tricuspidata* 'Lowii' Z4–8 H8–1
- *Parthenocissus tricuspidata* 'Veitchii
  Boskoop' Z3–8 H8–1
- *Passiflora lutea* Z6–10 H12–1
- *Vitis vinifera* Z5–9 H9–1
- *Wisteria floribunda* Z5–9 H9–3
- *Wisteria floribunda* 'Pink Ice' Z5–8 H8–3
- *Wisteria floribunda* 'Snow Showers' Z5–8 H8–1
- *Wisteria sinensis* 'Prolific' Z6–8 H8–6

Gelsemium sempevirens 'Pride of Augusta'
CAROLINA JASMINE
Ⓝ ☼ ◊ Z7–9 H9–7 ↕to 20ft (6m)
Like *G. rankinii*, this native of SE United States is best
grown in the southernmost regions of the Northwest.
Elsewhere, it must be overwintered indoors.

Wisteria sinensis 'Purpurea'
PURPLE CHINESE WISTERIA
☼ ◊ Z5–8 H8–1 ↕28ft (9m)
This cultivar was selected for the purity of its purplish
violet flowers. The pealike, fragrant blooms hang from
dense, pendent, foot-long racemes in early spring.

Wisteria floribunda 'Macrobotrys'
JAPANESE WISTERIA
☼ ◊ Z5–8 H8–3 ↕to 28ft (9m)
Japanese wisteria is nearly as vigorous as its Chinese
cousin. This cultivar's unusually long flowers clusters
open from the stem end then down to the tips.

Wisteria sinensis 'Alba'
WHITE CHINESE WISTERIA
☼ ◊ Z5–8 H8–5 ↕to 28ft (9m)
This cultivar makes a wonderful color contrast when
grown with *Wisteria sinensis* 'Purpurea' (see left). The
flower clusters of this species open up all at once.

Climbers for shade

Most of these climbers grow naturally in woodlands where their climbing ability is used to scale other plants and position themselves to get as much as possible. They also prefer the cooler temperatures that are found in the shade of woodlands. They can be used to cover trellises, fences, or walls, or to spread over the ground.

CLIMBERS

Hedera helix 'Manda's Crested'
ENGLISH IVY
☀ ☀ ☀ ◐ ◊ Z5–11 H12–6 ↕↔6ft (2m)
This cultivar's foliage takes on coppery tints in cold weather. Good for growing on a wall or fence or as a groundcover. Evergreen.

MORE CHOICES

- *Campsis radicans* 'Flava' Z5–9 H9–5
- *Hedera helix* 'California Gold' Z5–11 H12–6
- *Hedera helix* 'Gold Heart' Z5–11 H12–6
- *Hydrangea anomala* Z4–9 H9–1
- *Kadsura japonica* 'Alba' Z7–9 H9–1
- *Parthenocissus tricuspidata* 'Fenway Park' Z4–8 H8–1
- *Parthenocissus tricuspidata* 'Lowii' Z4–8 H8–1
- *Parthenocissus tricuspidata* 'Veitchii Boskoop' Z3–8 H8–1
- *Trachelospermum jasminoides* 'Madison' Z7–9 H9–7

Parthenocissus tricuspidata
BOSTON IVY, JAPANESE IVY
☀ ◐ ◊ Z4–8 H8–1 ↕to 70ft (20m)
Bright green leaves turn red to purple in autumn. Can hold its leaves through winter in warmer regions. Prefers fertile soil but is tolerant. Prune in late winter.

Humulus lupulus 'Aureus'
GOLDEN HOPS
Ⓝ ☀ ◊ Z4–8 H8–1 ↕to 20ft (6m)
Foliage becomes more golden in partial shade. In summer, female plants bears fragrant green flower spikes that turn straw colored and are used to flavor beer.

Parthenocissus quinquefolia
FIVE-LEAVED IVY, VIRGINIA CREEPER
Ⓝ ☀ ◐ ◊ Z7–9 H9–1 ↕50ft (15m) or more
Dull green leaves are followed by brilliant red fall color. Will run along the ground and can be used as a groundcover for slopes.

Clematis 'Nelly Moser'
NELLY MOSER CLEMATIS

☼ ◐ ◊ Z4–9 H9–1 ‡3ft (1m)

A compact, deciduous climber that flowers in early summer on the previous year's growth, and in late summer on the current season's growth.

Akebia quinata
CHOCOLATE VINE

☼ ◊ Z5–9 H9–5 ‡30ft (10m) or more

Spicily scented flowers appear in early spring, followed by sausage-shaped, purple-fleshed fruits. Prefers fertile soil. Prune after flowering to restrict growth.

Clematis 'Ernst Markham'
ERNST MARKHAM CLEMATIS

☼ ◊ Z4–9 H9–1 ‡10–12ft (3–4m)

Flowers in summer on the current year's growth. Best if grown in a fertile, organic soil. A vigorous, deciduous choice for covering a pergola or trellis.

Clematis 'Comtesse de Bouchaud'
COMTESSE DE BOUCHAUD CLEMATIS

☼ ◐ ◊ Z4–9 H9–1 ‡6–10ft (2–m)

A very strong-growing, deciduous climber with midgreen leaves. Flowers bloom on current season's shoots from summer to late autumn.

Clematis 'Jackmanii'
CLEMATIS

☼ ◐ ◊ Z4–9 H9–1 ‡10ft (3m)

Flowers appear in mid- to late summer on previous season's growth and are followed by decorative, silver-gray seedpods. Prefers fertile, organic soil.

Climbers for heat and humidity

If you've ever said the phrase " It's not the heat, it's the humidity," then you have a sense of what plants go through in the same situation. Whereas we perspire, plants transpire, releasing water from their leaves, thereby cooling them . High humidity reduces a plant's ability to cool itself in warm weather. These vines hold up well despite these challenging conditions.

Passiflora incarnata
PASSION FLOWER

Ⓝ ☀ ☼ ◐ Z6–8 H10–7 ↕6ft (2m)

This tender climber flowers in summer, followed by sweet, edible, oval-shaped, yellow fruits. Slender stems bear grasping tendrils and lobed, dark green leaves.

MORE CHOICES

- *Actinidia deliciosa* Z7–9 H9–7
- *Campsis radicans* 'Flava' Z5–9 H9–5
- *Euonymus fortunei* Z4–9 H9–5
- *Parthenocissus tricuspidata* and cultivars Z4–8 H8–2
- *Trachelospermum jasminoides* 'Madison' Z7–9 H9–7
- *Wisteria brachbotrys* Z0 H8–5
- *Wisteria floribunda* and cultivars Z5–9 H9–4

Wisteria floribunda 'Macrobotrys'
JAPANESE WISTERIA

☀ ◐ Z5–8 H8–3 ↕to 28ft (9m)

Early spring flowers clusters open from the base down to the tips. This cultivar has flowers that are four times as long as the species, which is only 1ft (30cm) long.

Wisteria sinensis 'Purpurea'
PURPLE CHINESE WISTERIA

☀ ◐ Z5–8 H8–5 ↕to 100ft (30m)

Dense, pendent clusters bear fragrant blooms in early spring. In the wild, wisterias climb trees, but in gardens we can train them up walls and on pergolas.

Lonicera fragrantissima
WINTER HONEYSUCKLE

☀ ☼ ◐ Z4–8 H8–3 ↕6ft (2m) ↔12 ft (4m)

This long-stemmed shrub can be grown as a climber by removing all but a few of its main branches that arise from the ground, then training the survivors.

Lonicera x *purpusii*
HYBRID WINTER HONEYSUCKLE

☀ ◐ Z7–9 H9–7 ↕ ↔5ft (1.5m)

Like *L. fragrantissima* (left), this shrub can be maintained as a climber through selective and diligent pruning to encourage trainable shoots.

Parthenocissus tricuspidata
BOSTON IVY, JAPANESE IVY
☀ ◊ Z4–8 H8–1 ↕to 70ft (20m)
Bright green leaves turn red to purple in fall. Holds its leaves through winter in warmer regions of the Northwest. Prefers fertile soil. Prune in early winter.

Actinidia kolomikta 'Arctic Beauty'
KIWI VINE
☀ ◊ Z5–8 H8–5 ↕12ft (4m)
Male plants of this dioecious species are more colorful. Leaves become variegated as they mature. Fragrant, inconspicuous flowers bloom in early summer.

Parthenocissus quinquefolia
FIVE-LEAVED IVY, VIRGINIA CREEPER
Ⓝ ☀ ☀ ◊ Z7–9 H9–1 ↕50ft (15m) or more
If not supported, it will run along the ground and so can be used as a groundcover for slopes. Dull green leaves are followed by brilliant red fall color.

Lonicera periclymenum 'Serotina'
LATE DUTCH HONEYSUCKLE
☀ ☀ ☀ ◊ Z5–9 H9–5
↕to22ft (7m)
This cultivar was chosen for its attractively dark red-streaked, fragrant white flowers produced in mid to late summer. Fall berries are an added benefit

Akebia quinata
CHOCOLATE VINE
☀ ◊ Z5–9 H9–5 ↕30ft (10m) or more
Spicily scented flowers appear in early spring, followed by sausage-shaped, purple-fleshed fruits. Prefers fertile soil. Prune after flowering to contain rampant growth.

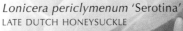

Climbers with fragrant flowers

Nothing provides a welcome like the fragrance of flowers. Many of these climbers grow big enough to cover an arbor entrance, inviting guests inside. Breezes can waft their fragrance throughout the garden, or they can be grown over a gazebo, where you can relax as the floral aromas surround you.

Gelsemium rankinii
SWAMP JESSAMINE
Ⓝ ☼☀ ◐◆ ᵖᴴ Z7–9
H9–7 ↕15in ↔10in
Flowers appear from late winter to early spring. Needs winter protection in all but the southern extremes of the Northwest.

Lonicera fragrantissima
WINTER HONEYSUCKLE
☼ ☀ ◊ Z4–8 H8–3 ↕6ft (2m) ↔12 ft (4m)
Actually a shrub, this winter bloomer can be trained to send its long branches over a trellis or gazebo like its more trailing relatives. Very adaptable and tolerant.

Jasminum officinale 'Aureovariegatum'
COMMON JASMINE
☼ ◊ Z8–11 H12–8 ↕to 40ft (12m)
Flowers from summer to early autumn. Deciduous, but it will hold its leaves through winter in the southern-most parts of the Northwest. Prefers fertile soil.

MORE CHOICES

- *Actinidia deliciosa* Z7–9 H9–7
- *Actinidia kolomikta* Z3–11 H12–1
- *Actinidia kolomikta* 'Arctic Beauty' Z5–8 H8–5
- *Decumaria barbara* Z6–9 H9–6
- *Jasminum officinale* 'Aureovariegatum' Z9–11 H12–9
- *Lonicera periclymenum* Z5–9 H9–5
- *Trachelospermum jasminoides* Z11–11 H12–6

Rosa 'Kiftsgate'
KIFTSGATE CLIMBER ROSE
☼ ◊ Z6–9 H9–6 ↕↔30ft (10m) or more
Flowers appear in early summer. Very strong, rampant growth can reach extraordinary lengths; provide a very strong support. Prefers moderately fertile, organic soil.

Rosa wichuraiana 'Albéric Barbier'
WICHURANA RAMBLER ROSE
☼ ◊ Z5–9 H9–7 ↕15ft (5m) ↔10ft (3m)
Flowers produced in spring are creamy yellow at first and then mature to pure white. Foliage is semi-evergreen. Prefers moderately fertile, organic soil.

Evergreen climbers

The majority of evergreen climbers are from tropical regions and are therefore unsuitable for growing outside all year, but there are a few from temperate regions that do well in Northwestern gardens. Whether you are interested in upgrading a chain-link fence for privacy or hiding unsightly structures, these evergreen climbers are ideal for providing year-round cover. Their flowers and fruits are added bonuses.

CLIMBERS

Gelsemium sempervirens 'Pride of Augusta'
CAROLINA JASMINE

Ⓝ ☼ ◊ z7–9 H9–7 ↕to 20ft (6m)
This is a twining perennial often confused with true jasmine because of its fragrant yellow, tubular flowers. Prefers moderately fertile soil.

Clematis armandii
EVERGREEN CLEMATIS

☼ ☼ ◊ z7–9 H9–7 ↕10–15ft (3–5m) ↔6–10ft (2–3m)
Slow to start, but once it is established it will grow rather rapidly. Its wonderfully scented flowers are produced in early spring. Prune after flowers fade.

MORE CHOICES

- *Bignonia capreolata* 'Atrosanguinea' z6–9 H9–3
- *Euonymus fortunei* z4–9 H9–5
- *Hedera helix* 'California Gold' z5–11 H12–6
- *Hedera helix* 'Gold Heart' z5–11 H12–6
- *Lonicera sempervirens* 'Alabama Crimson' z4–9 H9–1
- *Lonicera sempervirens* 'Blanche Sandman' z5–8 H8–1
- *Lonicera sempervirens* 'John Clayton' z5–8 H8–1
- *Lonicera sempervirens* 'Major Wheeler' z4–8
- *Trachelospermum jasminoides* 'Madison' z7–9 H9–7

Jasminum grandiflorum
COMMON JASMINE

☼ ◊ z9–11 H12–9 ↕to 40ft (12m)
Also known as *J. officinale* f. *affine*. Pink-tinged flowers bloom from summer to early autumn and are larger than *J. officinale*. Grows vigorously.

Hedera helix
ENGLISH IVY

☼ ☼ ☼ ◊ z5–11 H12–6 ↕30ft (10m) ↔15ft (5m)
A self-clinging climber best grown in fertile, organic soil. Good for growing on a wall or as a groundcover, but avoid planting near trees or allowing it to grow up trees.

HERBACEOUS PLANTS

HERBACEOUS PLANTS – BY DEFINITION, those that die down to ground level each year – are the multifaceted components of almost every gardener's palette. Whatever the size of your garden, you can use them to produce infinite combinations of colors, textures, scents, and shapes and to provide interest throughout most of the year (all year, in the case of evergreen herbaceous plants). They often require more time investment than woody plants but repay rich dividends.

Rudbeckia species and cultivars
The black-eyed Susan and its relatives bloom from late summer through midfall. Many can be grown as biennials or short-lived perennials.

The backbone of the herbaceous garden is often the bulbs – the crocuses and snowdrops, narcissus and tulips. Among the first and most dependable harbingers of spring, some bloom well into summer. Many bulbous plants last for years, often naturalizing and, in many cases, spreading well beyond the area where they were originally planted.

At the other end of the spectrum are the decorative grasses, whose leaves and seedheads remain until they are pruned back in spring. Some of these grasses can be used on the edge of a pond or if you have a particularly damp area.

Another group of perennials well suited to difficult growing conditions are the alpine plants, those that are native to regions of high altitude. They do well in dry, windy sites and are often used in rock gardens because of their small size and creeping habit.

Regardless of any limitations of your garden, you will be able to find many herbaceous plants to provide a kaleidoscope of color and texture.

Hemerocallis 'Red Rum'
Most daylilies are summer bloomers, providing color for a few to several weeks, mostly in summer. As their name suggests, each flower lives only a single day.

Tulipa 'Pink Beauty'
Available in nearly every color and many differnt forms beyond the simple goblet shape shown above, tulips are excellent in a bed or border.

Aquilegia McKana hybrids
The characteristic spurred blossoms of this white example could be the centerpiece of a perennial bed or grown for use as a cut flower.

Viola x wittrockiana, Ultima Series (Pansies)
A bed of these colorful small perennials remains in bloom from winter throughout spring.

Perennials for moist soil in sun

Here are some suitable garden plants that in the wild live along the sunny borders of lakes and streams or in moist glades and glens and sunny wetland areas. If you have a similar site in your garden, the following plants will serve you well through their strong constitution as well as their beauty of flower and foliage.

Geranium sanguineum 'Album'
WHITE CRANESBILL
☼ ◊ Z4–8 H8–1 ‡12in (30cm) ↔16in (40cm)
Blooms freely throughout summer. Prefers moderately fertile, organic, well-drained soil. Prone to the same problems as the species (see right).

Geranium sanguineum
BLOODY CRANESBILL
☼ ◊ Z3–8 H8–1 ‡10in (25cm) ↔12in (30cm)
Blooms during summer. Prefers moderately fertile, organic, well-drained soil. Prone to bacterial blight, downy and powdery mildew, gray mold, leaf spot, leaf miner, and slugs.

Geranium sanguineum 'Max Frei'
MAX FREI CRANESBILL
☼ ◊ Z4–8 H8–1 ‡6in (15cm) ↔9in (23cm)
A more mounded selection, it prefers the same conditions and suffers from the same maladies as the species (see above).

Geranium sanguineum 'Striatum'
STRIPED BLOODY CRANESBILL
☼ ◊ Z3–8 H8–1 ‡4–6in (10–15cm) ↔12in (30cm)
This more compact form of the species prefers the same conditions and is prone to the same problems as the species (see above).

Cortaderia selloana
PAMPAS GRASS
☀ ◊ Z7–11 H12–7 ‡8ft (2.5m) ↔4ft (1.2m)
Blooms in late summer; the plumes persist into winter.
Tolerant of most watering regimes. Prefers fertile, well-
drained soil. Susceptible to *Helminthosporium* leaf spot.

Cortaderia selloana 'Aureolineata'
GOLD-EDGE PAMPAS GRASS
☀ ◊ Z7–11 H12–7 ‡7ft (2.2m) ↔4ft (1.2m)
The rich yellow-margined leaves of this cultivar age to
a dark golden yellow. It is tolerant of most watering
regimes. Prefers fertile, well-drained soil.

Geranium macrorrhizum 'Spessart'
SPESSART SCENTED CRANESBILL
☀ ◊ Z4–8 H8–1 ‡20in (50cm) 24in (60cm)
Blooms appear in early summer, followed by
distinctive seedheads. Prefers moderately fertile,
organic, well-drained soil.

Cortederia selloana 'Pumila'
DWARF PAMPAS GRASS
☀ ◊ Z7–10 H12–7 ‡5ft (1.5m) ↔4ft (1.2m)
Valued for its size, which is about half that of the
species and which makes it suitable for large
containers. Needs the same conditions as the species.

Geranium x 'Johnson's Blue'
JOHNSON'S BLUE CRANESBILL
☀ ◊ Z4–8 H8–1 ‡12in (30cm) ↔24in (60cm)
This interspecific hybrid blooms in summer. Prefers
moderately fertile, organic, well-drained soil. Prone to
problems that affect others in the genus (see opposite).

HERBACEOUS PLANTS

Monarda didyma 'Jacob Cline'
JACOB CLINE BEE BALM

☼ ◐ ◊ ◑ Z4–11 H12–1 ‡18in (45cm) ↔2ft (60cm)
Blooms from mid- to late summer. Grow in moderately fertile, organic, well-drained soil. More resistant to powdery mildew and rust than the species.

Heliopsis helianthoides 'Ballerina'
BALLERINA SMOOTH OXEYE

Ⓝ ☼ ◑ Z4–9 H9–4 ‡3ft (1m) ↔24in (60cm)
This semidouble form blooms from midsummer to early autumn. Prefers moderately fertile, organic, well drained soil. Prone to powdery mildew and rust.

Monarda didyma 'Marshall's Delight'
MARSHALL'S DELIGHT BEE BALM

Ⓝ ☼ ◐ ◑ Z4–8 H8–1 ‡3ft (1m) ↔24in (60cm)
Blooms from mid- to late summer. Prefers moderately fertile, organic, well-drained soil. Highly resistant to powdery mildew. Susceptible to leaf spots and rust.

Carex siderosticha 'Variegata'
VARIEGATED CREEPING BROADLEAF SEDGE

☼ ◐ ◑◐ Z6–9 H9–3 ‡12in (30cm) ↔16cm (40cm)
Slowly spreading, this tough and adaptable perennial has pale brown flower spikes in late spring. Prone to rust, smuts, leaf spots, and aphids.

Monarda didyma
BEE BALM, SWEET BERGAMOT

Ⓝ ☼ ◐ ◑◐ Z4–10 H10–1 ‡3ft (1m) ↔24in (60cm)
A bushy clump-former that blooms from mid- to late summer. Prefers moderately fertile, organic, well drained soil. Prone to powdery mildew and rust.

Phlox paniculata 'David'
DAVID GARDEN PHLOX

Ⓝ ☼ ☀ ◐ 〇 Z4–8 H8–1 ‡↔42in (1.2m)

This robust variety blooms from midsummer to early autumn and is mildew resistant, which is unusual for this species. Grows best in fertile soil.

Phlox paniculata 'Starfire'
STARFIRE GARDEN PHLOX

Ⓝ ☼ ☀ ◐ 〇 Z4–8 H8–1 ‡3ft (1m) ↔42in (1.2m)

Prized for its intense flower color on display from summer well into fall above deep green leaves. Grows best in fertile soil. Susceptible to powdery mildew.

MORE CHOICES

- *Cortaderia selloana* 'Monvin P.P.' Z7–11 H12–7
- *Geranium sanguineum* 'Striatum (Lancastriense)' Z4–8 H12–2
- *Hemerocallis fulva* 'Kwansa' Z3–10 H12–1
- *Hemerocallis hybrids* Z3–10 H12–1
- *Phlox paniculata* 'Blue Boy' Z4–8 H8–1
- *Phlox paniculata* 'Bright Eyes' Z4–8 H8–1

- *Phlox paniculata* 'Darwin's Joyce' Z4–8 H8–1
- *Phlox paniculata* 'Laura' Z4–8 H8–1
- *Phlox paniculata* 'Orange Perfection' Z4–8 H8–1
- *Phlox paniculata* 'Pink Gown' Z4–8 H8–1
- *Silphium perfoliatum* Z5–9 H9–5

Sarracenia x 'Dixie Lace'
DIXIE LACE PITCHER PLANT

Ⓝ ☼ ◑ 〇 ⚘ Z6–9 H9–4 ‡12in (30cm) ↔18in (45cm)

Flowers appear in mid to late spring. Best grown in acidic, organic soil or wet sphagnum moss. This insectivorous plant is a hybrid of four different species.

Nerine bowdenii
GUERNSEY LILY

☼ ◐ 〇 Z8–10 H10–8 ‡18in (45cm) ↔3in (8cm)

This bulbous perennial blooms in autumn. The cultivar 'Alba' bears white flowers. Best if grown in well-drained soil. Susceptible to slug damage.

Hibiscus moscheutos
ROSE MALLOW, SWAMP HIBISCUS

Ⓝ ☼ ◑ Z5–10 H12–1 ‡8ft (2.5m) ↔3ft (1m)

Blooms during summer. Prefers well-drained, organic soil, in which it will grow rapidly to shrub size. Watch out for Japanese beetle infestations in summer.

HERBACEOUS PLANTS

Perennials for moist to wet soils in shade

Plants that grow in wet soils and shade must be both efficient at absorbing sunlight and tolerant of wet and often oxygen-poor soils. Many of the plants presented here evolved in wet woodlands, where these traits served them well. These adaptable plants can liven up similar areas of your garden.

Lysichiton americanus
YELLOW SKUNK CABBAGE
Ⓝ ☼ ● Z7–9 H9–7
↕3ft (1m) ↔30in (75cm)
The flowers appear in early spring before the large, strappy leaves. The flowers have a musky aroma, and the leaves are quite pungent when bruised.

Trillium chloropetalum
GIANT WAKE ROBIN
Ⓝ ☼ ◑ ● Z6–9 H9–6 ↕16in (40cm) ↔8in (20cm)
The spring-blooming fragrant flowers also occur in yellow and brownish purple. Prefers acidic to neutral soil rich in organic matter. Mulch in fall with leaf mold.

Menyanthes trifoliata
BOG BEAN, BUCKBEAN
Ⓝ ☼ ● Z4–8 H8–1 ↕9in (23cm) ↔12in (30cm)
Flowers briefly in summer. Suitable for muddy pond margins and peaty bogs, it can also grow partially submerged. Susceptible to leaf gall.

Vancouveria hexandra
AMERICAN BARRENWORT

Ⓝ ☼ ◊ Z5–8 H8–5 ↕8in (20cn) ↔indefinite
Flowers emerge in late spring on leafless stems. This rhizomatous perennial prefers moderately fertile, organic soil. Can be attacked by vine weevil.

Cimicifuga racemosa
BLACK BUGBANE, BLACK COHOSH

Ⓝ ☼ ◊ Z3–8 H12–1 ↕4–7ft (1.2–2.2m) ↔24in (60cm)
A clump-forming perennial that blooms in mid-summer. Flowers are scented, but many people find them disagreeable. Prefers moist, fertile, organic soil.

MORE CHOICES

- *Aconitum columbianum* Z3–8 H8–3
- *Actaea rubra* Z4–8 H8–1
- *Ageratina altissima* var. *altissma* Z0
- *Anemone quinquefolia* Z4–8 H8–1
- *Campanula scouleri* Z0 H7–3
- *Cardamine concatenata* Z0
- *Caulophyllum thalictroides* Z4–7 H
- *Clintonia andrewsiana* Z8–9 H8–1
- *Sanguinaria canadensis* Z3–9 H8–1
- *Tiarella trifoliata* Z4–7 H
- *Tricyrtis hirta* Z4–9 H9–1

Convallaria majalis
LILY-OF-THE-VALLEY

☼ ◊ Z2–7 H7–1 ↕6in (15cm) ↔indefinite
Bears sweetly scented spring flowers. A handful of cultivars show varying flower color and leaf variegation. Prefers moist, organic soil and leaf mold mulch.

Hydrophyllum virginianum
VIRGINIA WATERLEAF

Ⓝ ☼ ☼ ◊◗ Z4–9 H9–1 ↕30in (75cm)
This solid performer blooms in late spring and prefers fertile, organic soils. Native to the eastern side of the Northwest in upland woods and shady floodplains.

Polemonium foliosissimum
LEAFY JACOB'S LADDER

Ⓝ ☼ ☼ ◊ Z4–8 H8–1 ↕30in (75cm) ↔24in (60cm)
This clump forming, midsummer-blooming perennial can also be found in shades of cream and white. Prefers fertile, well-drained soils. Can be affected by powdery mildew.

Uvularia grandiflora
BELLWORT, MERRY BELLS

Ⓝ ☼ ◊◗ Z3–7 H7–1 ↕24in (60cm) ↔12in (30cm)
Upright stems bear hanging flowers from mid- to late spring. Slowly spreads from creeping rhizomes. Prefers fertile, organic soil.

Corydalis flexuosa 'China Blue'
CHINA BLUE FUMEWORT

☼ ◊ Z6–8 H8–3 ↕6–8in (16–20cm) ↔8in (20cm)
Blooms appear from late spring to summer and may repeat if deadheaded. It prefers moderately fertile, organic, well-drained soils.

HERBACEOUS PLANTS

Perennials for dry soil in sun

Bright sunlight shining on a perennial increases the amount of water it needs to transpire. Dry soil minimizes the amount of water a plant has to utilize in this process. These plants have developed mechanisms to minimize transpiration (such as hairs on the leaves) and to maximize their root systems' ability to wring out as much water from the soil as possible.

Guara lindheimeri
WHIRLING BUTTERFLIES

☼ ◊ Z6–8 H9–6 ‡4ft (1.2m) ↔3ft (1m)

Blooms appear from midsummer to early fall. Prefers rich soil. Forms a large taproot, so it is best transplanted when young. Upright habit.

Baptisia australis
FALSE INDIGO

Ⓝ ☼ ◊ Z3–9 H9–1 ‡30in (75cm) ↔24in (60cm)

Blooms in early summer. Seedpods are ornamental. Best used in the back of a border or as a specimen plant. This member of the pea family attracts birds.

Echinops ritro
SMALL GLOBE THISTLE

☼ ◊◑ Z3–9 H12–1 ‡to 24in (60cm) ↔18in (45cm)

Flowers in late summer. Prefers marginally fertile soil. and self-sows freely. Good for large borders. Attracts insects and birds but is unpalatable to deer.

Guara lindheimeri 'Siskiyou Pink'
SISKIYOU PINK WHIRLING BUTTERFLIES

Ⓝ ☼ ◊ Z6–9 H9–6 ‡3–4ft (1–1.3m) ↔3ft (1m)

Blooms midsummer to early fall. The tall flower spikes are attractive in the back of a border. To ensure long blooming period, deadhead spent flower spikes.

Catananche caerulea
CUPID'S DART

☼ ◊ Z3–8 H8–1 ‡2–36in (50–90cm) ↔12in (30cm)

Blooms from midsummer to autumn. A relatively short-lived clump-forming perennial that requires only moderate fertilization. Sensitive to wet winter soil.

Echinacea purpurea
PURPLE CONEFLOWER

Ⓝ ☼ ◊ Z3–9 H9–3 ‡to 5ft (1.5m) ↔18in (45cm)

Flowers from midsummer to early autumn and prefers deep, organic soil. The cultivars bred from this native plant are often more suitable for the garden border.

Papaver orientale 'Turkenlouis'
TURKENLOUIS ORIENTAL POPPY
☼ ◊ Z3–8 H8–1 ‡↔3ft (1m)
Blooms from late spring to midsummer. Large flowers may require staking. Reasonably long-lived, but best if divided every four years or so.

Papaver orientale 'Picotee'
PICOTEE ORIENTAL POPPY
☼ ◊ Z3–8 H8–1 ‡↔3ft (1m)
Blooms from late spring to midsummer. A good plant to combine with spring flowering bulbs, because it will fill in over the dying foliage. Relatively long-lived.

MORE CHOICES

- *Guara lindheimeri* 'Corries Gold' Z6–9 H9–6
- *Guara lindheimeri* 'Variegata' Z6–9 H9–6
- *Liatris punctata* Z3–9
- *Opuntia basilaris* Z11–12 H12–9

Achillea millefolium 'Paprika'
PAPRIKA YARROW
Ⓝ ☼ ◊ Z3–9 H8–2 ‡↔24in (60cm)
Blooms from early to late summer. Seedheads persist through the winter if not cut back, but yarrows tend to self sow, producing possibly unwanted "volunteers."

Achillea millefolium 'Summer Pastels'
SUMMER PASTELS YARROW
Ⓝ ☼ ◊ Z3–9 H9–2 ‡↔24in (60cm)
Blooms from early to late summer. This is a mat forming, rhizomatous perennial with fragrant foliage. Tolerates a wide range of soil conditions.

MORE CHOICES

- *Achillea millefolium* 'Cassis' Z3–9 H9–1
- *Achillea* 'Coronation Gold' Z3–9 H9–1
- *Achillea millefolium* 'Heidi' Z3–9 H9–1
- *Achillea millefolium* 'Hoffnung' Z3–9 H9–1
- *Achillea* x *kellererii* Z5–7 H7–5

Achillea taygetea 'Moonshine'
MOONSHINE YARROW
☼ ◊ Z3–9 H9–1 ‡24in (60cm) ↔20in (50cm)
Produces flowerheads (excellent for cutting) from mid- to late summer. The species and its cultivars are more clump-forming than *A. millefolium*.

Achillea ptarmica 'The Pearl Superior'
THE PEARL SUPERIOR SNEEZEWORT
☼ ◊ Z3–8 H8–1 ‡↔30in (75cm)
Blooming from early to late summer. The fresh flowers make nice additions to a flower arrangement. The flowers can also be used for dried arrangements.

HERBACEOUS PLANTS

Asclepias tuberosa
BUTTERFLY WEED

Ⓝ ☼ ◊ Z4–9 H9–2 ‡30in (75cm) ↔18in (45cm)
Blooms in midsummer. Prefers fertile, well-drained, loamy soil. Susceptible to aphids and mealybugs when in bloom.

Rudbeckia maxima
GREAT CONEFLOWER

Ⓝ ☼ ☼ ◊ Z4–8 H8–1 ‡5–6ft (1.5–2m) ↔24in (60cm)
Blooms in late summer. Flowers rise above large bluish leaves. Prefers moderately fertile, well-drained soil.

Sedum acre
GOLDEN CARPET STONECROP

Ⓝ ☼ ◊ Z3–8 H8–1
‡2in (5cm) ↔indefinite
Blooms in late spring to early summer. Prefers moderately fertile, well drained, soil and moderate to little water. Susceptible to mealybugs, scale insects, slugs and snails.

Hylotelephium erythrostichium 'Mediovariegatum'
STRIPED STONECROP

☼ ◊ Z3–8 H8–1 ‡12in (30cm) ↔18in (45cm)
Prized for its showy variegation that fades as the season progresses. Cut out any all-green growth. Greenish white flowers in late summer.

Sedum aizoon
AIZOON STONECROP

Ⓝ ☼ ◊ Z3–8 H8–1 ‡↔18in (45cm)
Flowers in summer. The cultivar 'Aurantiacum' produces dark red stems followed by showy red fruit. Prefers well-drained soil, as do all sedums.

Sedum 'Autumn Joy'
AUTUMN JOY STONECROP

Ⓝ ☼ ◊ Z3–8 H8–1 ‡↔to 24in (60cm)
This hybrid is a very upright, clumping perennial tha blooms early autumn. Very popular plant with gardeners and butterflies. Also offered as 'Herbstfreude'.

MORE CHOICES

- *Papaver orientale* 'Helen Elizabeth' Z4–9 H9–1
- *Papaver orientale* 'Perry's White' Z4–9 H9–1
- *Sedum emarginatum* 'Eco-Mt Emei' Z6–8 H8–3
- *Sedum oreganum* Z0–0 H–
- *Sedum rubrechtii* Z0–0 H8–1
- *Sedum spurium* 'Dragons Blood' Z3–8 H8–1
- *Sedum spurium* 'Red Carpet' Z3–9 H9–1
- *Sedum spurium* 'Tricolor' Z4–9 H9–1
- *Sedum* 'Frosty Morn' Z4–9 H9–1
- *Silphium laciniatum* Z5–9 H9–5
- *Yucca baccata* Z5–9 H12–9
- *Yucca brevifolia* Z0–0 H
- *Yucca filamentosa* Z4–11 H12–5

Sedum kamtschaticum 'Floriferum'
ORANGE STONECROP

Ⓝ ☼ ◊ Z5–8 H8–1 ‡2–3in (5–7.5cm) ↔12in (30)
This very floriferous cultivar flowers in early summer. and makes an attractive contrast with its relative 'Variegatum' especially when out of bloom.

Sedum kamtschaticum 'Variegatum'
VARIEGATED ORANGE STONECROP

☼ ◊ Z4–8 H9–1 ‡2–3in (5–8cm) ↔8in (20cm)
This cultivar has pink-tinted, midgreen leaves with cream margins. Early summer flowers take on red tints as they age, extending the floral interest.

Hylotelephium sieboldii
OCTOBER STONECROP

☼ ◊ Z3–8 H8–1 ‡4in (10cm) ↔8in (20cm)

Star-shaped pink flowers appear in fall. Its cultivar 'Mediovariegatum' has red-edged leaves splashed with cream. Both are excellent for featuring in containers.

Sedum 'Vera Jameson'
VERA JAMESON STONECROP

☼ ◊ Z4–9 H9–1 ‡12in (30cm) ↔18in (45cm)

This hybrid blooms on purple stems from late summer to early autumn. Like most sedums, it prefers moderately fertile soil but is tolerant of poorer ones.

Sedum telephium
ORPINE

☼ ◊ Z4–9 H9–1 ‡↔2ft (60cm)

Blooms late summer to early autumn. Its variant, subsp. *maximum* 'Atropurpureum', produces strikingly dark purple stems and flowers with orange-red centers.

Sedum spectabile 'Brilliant'
BRILLIANT STONECROP

☼ ◊ Z4–9 H9–1 ‡↔12–18in (30–45cm)

The late-summer flowers are deeper pink than the species'. Like most sedums, it is susceptible to mealybugs, scale insects, slugs, and snails.

Gaillardia aristata
BLANKET FLOWER

Ⓝ ☼ ◊ Z3–8 H8–1 ‡24in (60cm) ↔20in (50cm)

Blooms freely from summer to autumn. Prefers fertile, well-drained soil but will tolerate poor soil conditions except for very heavy clay, in which it will die out.

Yucca filamentosa 'Golden Sword'
GOLDEN SWORD YUCCA

Ⓝ ☼ ◊ Z4–11 H12–5 ‡6ft (2m) ↔5ft (1.5m)

Yellow-centered leaves distinguish this cultivar. It flowers from late spring into summer. Prefers well-drained soil, and it tolerates drought.

Yucca filamentosa 'Ivory Tower'
IVORY TOWER YUCCA

Ⓝ ☼ ◊ Z5–9 H12–1 ‡22in (55cm) ↔5ft (1.5m)

This cultivar's flower face outward, unlike the species', which droop. Prefers well-drained soil and tolerates drought. Makes a bold statement

Sedum spurium 'Bronze Carpet'
BRONZE CARPET STONECROP

☼ ◊ Z3–9 H9–1 ‡4in (10cm) ↔24in (60cm)

The pink flowers of this improved cultivar bloom from early to late summer. Excellent in rock gardens and in the cracks between ornamental garden stones.

Zauschneria californica (Epilobium canum)
CALIFORNIA FUCHSIA

Ⓝ ☼ ◊ Z8–11 H12–8 ‡↔18in (45cm)

Flowers from late summer to early fall. Prefers moderately fertile, well-drained soil. Young growth is susceptible to slug and snail damage.

HERBACEOUS PLANTS

Perennials for dry soil in shade

Dry soil frequently occurs underneath trees or large shrubs, which cast shade onto the soil below and also remove most of the soil moisture with their large root systems. Avoid planting perennials where tree or shrub roots are at or just below the surface. Instead, find soil pockets in which to plant these drought- and shade-tolerant plants.

Epimedium grandiflorum 'Rose Queen'
ROSE QUEEN BISHOP'S HAT

☼ ◊ Z4–8 H8–2 ↕↔12in (30cm)

The young leaves are dark bronze-purple. Other cultivars have flowers in shades of white, yellow, and pink. All prefer fertile, organic, well-drained soil.

Anemone multifida
CUT-LEAF ANEMONE, PACIFIC ANEMONE

Ⓝ ☼ ☀ ◊ Z3–6 H6–1 ↕12in (30cm) ↔6in (15cm)

This robust rhizomatous perennial flowers in summer. It tolerates dry conditions (especially during summer) and does best well-drained, organic soil.

Iris foetidissima
GLADWIN, STINKING IRIS

☼ ☀ ◊ Z4–9 H9–2 ↕3ft (1m) ↔indefinite

This summer-blooming beardless iris gets its name from the foliage, which smells rank when bruised. Prefers moderately fertile, well-drained soil.

Epimedium x youngianum
YOUNG'S BARRENWORT

☼ ◊ Z5–9 H8–5 ↕12in (30cm) ↔12in (30cm)

Flowers can also occur in shades of rose-pink and purple. Prefers fertile, organic, well-drained soil. Interspecific cross of E. grandiflorum and E. diphyllum.

Epimedium x versicolor 'Sulphureum'
BARRENWORT

☼ ◊◊ Z5–8 H8–5 ↕12in (30cm) ↔3ft (1m)

Other cultivars of this hybrid cross have pink to copper-red flowers. Prefers fertile, organic, well-drained soil. Susceptible to vine weevil and mosaic virus.

MORE CHOICES

- *Epimedium* x *cantabrigiense* Z5–8 H8–5
- *Epimedium* x *perralchicum* 'Frohnleiten' Z5–8 H8–5
- *Epimedium younganium* 'Roseum' Z5–9 H8–5
- *Hellebrous* x *hybridus* (Royal Heritage strain) Z6–9 H9–1
- *Tolmiea menziesii* Z6–9 H9–6

Liriope muscari
LILYTURF
☼ ◊ Z6–10 H10–6 ↕12in (30cm) ↔18in (45cm)
Flowers of this evergreen perennial's cultivars range from white to violet. Prefers a light moderately fertile, well-drained soil. Moisture is welcome.

Pachysandra terminalis 'Green Shade'
GREEN SHADE JAPANESE SPURGE
◑ ◐ ◊ Z4–8 H8–1 ↕8in (20cm) ↔12in (30cm)
This groundcover, grown for its lush foliage, is a very vigorous spreader and so should be used judiciously; it is much more manageable in dry areas.

Euphorbia amygdaloides
WOOD SPURGE
☼ ◊ Z6–9 H10–2 ↕32in (80cm) ↔12in (30cm)
Bears terminal yellow-green flower clusters from midspring to early summer. Best in organic soil and will tolerate drought, but it prefers moderate water levels.

Epimedium x *rubrum*
RED BARRENWORT
◑ ◊ Z4–8 H8–1 ↕12in (30cm) ↔8in (20cm)
Evergreen leaves are red when young and also turn red with the arrival of cool fall weather. Prefers fertile, organic, well-drained soil.

Vinca major 'Maculata'
MACULATA GREATER PERIWINKLE
☼ ◑ ◊◊ Z7–11 H9–6 ↕18in (45cm) ↔indefinite
Prefers average soil. To control rampant growth, cut back hard in early spring. May be attacked by leaf spot, leafhoppers, scale insects, aphids, and dieback.

HERBACEOUS PLANTS

Perennials tolerant of drought

The southern regions of the Northwest are notoriously dry, as are the areas in what are called the "rain shadows" (eastern sides) of the mountains that bisect the region. Even the wetter Pacific Northwest areas can have very dry summers, where months can go by without rainfall. These perennials are adaptable to conditions with minimal irrigation.

Liatris microcephala
SMALLHEAD GAYFEATHER
Ⓝ ☼ ☀ ◊ Z6–8 H8–5
↕12–24in (30–60cm)
Summer blooms open from the top of the spike to the bottom. Prefers light, moderately fertile, well-drained, organic soil. In cooler regions, mulch plants during winter.

Euphorbia pulcherrima
POINSETTIA
☼ ◊ Z13–15 H12–10 ↕↔10ft (3m)
Usually grown indoors but can grow outdoors in warmer areas. Prefers light soil. Susceptible to nematodes, spider mites, aphids, and mealybugs.

Liatris 'Kobold'
KOBOLD GAYFEATHER
☼ ◑ Z4–9 H8–1 ↕↔16–20in (40–50cm)
Long-lasting flowers bloom in midsummer. Prefers light, moderately fertile, well-drained, organic soil. In cooler regions, mulch plants during winter.

Euphorbia polychroma
CUSHION SPURGE
☼ ◑ Z5–9 H9–5 ↕↔20in (50cm)
Long-lasting flowers bloom from midspring to summer. Prefers light to organic soil. Susceptible to nematodes, spider mites, aphids, and mealybugs.

Artemisia 'Powis Castle'
POWIS CASTLE WORMWOOD
☼ ◊ Z6–9 H9–6 ↕24in (60cm) ↔36in (90cm)
The silver, almost lacy leaves provide a beautiful contrast to bold foliage and pastel-colored flowers. Provide good drainage and less-than-fertile soil.

Festuca ovina 'Glauca'
BLUE FESCUE
☼ ◊ Z4–8 H8–1 ↕↔4in (10cm)
Flowers appear in early to midsummer and persist. Can grow in moderately to marginally fertile soil. Prone to a number of fungal diseases.

Liatris spicata
DENSE GAYFEATHER
Ⓝ ☼ ◊ Z4–9 H9–5 ↕24in (60cm) ↔12in (30cm)
Long-lasting flowers bloom from late summer to early fall. Prefers light, moderately fertile, well-drained, organic soil. In cooler areas, mulch during winter.

MORE CHOICES

- *Achillea millefolium* Z3–9 H9–1
- *Achillea millefolium* 'Cerise Queen' Z3–9 H9–1
- *Achillea ptarmica* 'The Pearl Superior' Z3–8 H8–1
- *Achillea* 'Coronation Gold' Z3–9 H9–1
- *Achillea* 'Moonshine' Z3–8 H8–1
- *Achillea x kellerii* Z5–7 H7–5
- *Artemisia lactiflora* Z5–8 H8–5
- *Artemisia ludoviciana* Z7–9 H12–8
- *Artemisia schmidtiana* 'Silver Mound' Z5–8 H8–3
- *Baptisia alba* Z3–9 H9–2
- *Baptisia australis* Z3–9 H9–1
- *Centranthus ruber* Z5–8 H8–5
- *Coreopsis grandiflora* Z4–9 H12–1

Kniphofia uvaria
RED-HOT POKER

☼ ☀ ◐ Z6–9 H9–1 ↕4ft (1.2m) ↔24in (60cm)

Blooms appear from late summer to early fall. Flowers are red in bud, open orange, and turn yellow. Best if grown in fertile, organic, rich, sandy soil.

Romneya coulteri
TREE POPPY

Ⓝ ☼ ◐ Z8–10 H9–2 ↕↔6ft (2m)

Blooms for a long time in summer. Prefers fertile soil and a dry winter mulch. Shelter plants from cold winds. Susceptible to *Verticillium* wilt and caterpillars.

Penstemon barbatus
BEARDLIP PENSTEMON

Ⓝ ☼ ☀ ◐ Z4–9 H9–2 ↕3ft (1m) ↔1ft (30cm)

Blooms from early summer to early autumn. Grow in moderately to marginally fertile soil. Prone to powdery mildew, rust, leaf spots, and slugs and snails.

Penstemon digitalis 'Husker Red'
HUSKER RED PENSTEMON

Ⓝ ☼ ☀ ◐ Z3–8 H8–1 ↕30in (75cm) ↔12in (30cm)

Flowers appear from early to late summer. Tolerant of high humidity. Grow in moderately fertile to marginally fertile soil. Prone to foliage diseases and slugs and snails.

Penstemon serrulatus
CASCADE PENSTEMON

Ⓝ ☼ ◐ Z3–9 H9–1 ↕24in (60cm) ↔12in (30cm)

Grow in moderately to marginally fertile soil. Prone to powdery mildew, rust, and leaf spots as well as slugs and snails (especially young plants).

HERBACEOUS PLANTS

HERBACEOUS PLANTS

Yucca glauca
SPANISH DAGGER

Ⓝ ☼ ◊ Z5–10 H10–5 ↕↔4ft (1.2m)

This clump-forming evergreen flowers in summer. Grows well in most soil types. Susceptible to cane borers, scale insects, and fungal leaf spot.

Yucca filamentosa 'Variegata'
VARIEGATED YUCCA

Ⓝ ☼ ◊ Z5–10 H12–1 ↕30in (75cm) ↔5ft (1.5m)

Flowers appear from late spring into summer. Grows well in most soil types. Clump forming. Susceptible to cane borers, scale insects, and fungal leaf spot.

MORE CHOICES

- *Coreopsis lanceolata* 'Baby Gold' Z4–9 H12–1
- *Coreopsis tripteris* Z4–9 H9–1
- *Coreopsis verticillata* 'Moonbeam' Z3–8 H9–1
- *Coreopsis verticillata* 'Zagreb' Z4–9 H9–1
- *Gaillardia aristata* Z3–8 H8–1
- *Gaura lindheimeri* Z6–9 H9–6
- *Liatris pycnostachya* Z3–9 H9–2
- *Melampodium leucanthum* Z4–9 H12–3
- *Oenothera fruticosa* Z4–8 H8–1
- *Oenothera fruticosa* 'Summer Solstice' Z4–8 H8–1

Phormium tenax
NEW ZEALAND FLAX

☼ ◊ Z9–11 H12–6 ↕10ft (3m) ↔3–6ft (1–2m)

This bold plant blooms in summer. Prefers fertile soil. Cultivars are available with purple to bronze leaves. Leaf edges can be sharp. Susceptible to leaf spot.

Hesperaloe parviflora
RED YUCCA

Ⓝ ☼ ◊ Z6–11 H12–6 ↕3ft (1m) ↔6ft (2m)

It looks like a *Yucca* and is sometimes labeled as such: they are closely related. Blooms in summer. Prone to scale insects and aphids when blooming.

Sedum spectabile 'Frosty Morn'
FROSTY MORN STONECROP

☼ ◐ ◊ Z3–8 H8–1 ↕↔18in (45cm)

Offers star-shaped, pale pink flowers in late summer. Prefers moderately fertile soil. Susceptible to mealybugs, scale insects, slugs, and snails.

Santolina chamaecyparissus
LAVENDER COTTON

☼ ◊ Z6–9 H9–4 ↕20in (50cm) ↔3ft (1m)
Flowers appear from mid- to late summer. Grow in marginally to moderately fertile soil. In colder areas it may die back to the ground during winter.

Verbena canadensis 'Summer Blaze'
SUMMER BLAZE ROSE VERVAIN

Ⓝ ☼ ◊ Z4–7 H7–1 ↕5–10in (13–25cm) ↔spreading
Blooms in summer. Prefers moderately fertile soil. Prone to insects, slugs, snails, powdery mildew, leaf spot, and rust. Fragrant flowers attract butterflies.

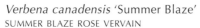

MORE CHOICES

- *Penstemon angustifolius* Z7–10 H12–3
- *Penstemon cobaea* Z7–10 H12–7
- *Perovskia atriplicifolia* Z6–9 H9–6
- *Perovskia atriplicifolia* 'Longin' Z6–9 H9–6
- *Phormium tenax* Z9–11 H12–6
- *Santolina rosmarinifolia* Z6–9 H9–6
- *Sedum acre* Z3–8 H8–1
- *Sedum emarginatum* 'Eco-Mt. Emei' Z6–8 H8–3
- *Sedum spectabile* (*Hylotelephium spectabile*) Z4–9 H9–1
- *Sedum spectabile* 'Brilliant' Z4–9 H9–1
- *Verbascum thapsus* Z3–9 H9–1
- *Verbena canadensis* 'Alba' Z4–7 H7–1
- *Yucca baccata* Z5–9 H12–9
- *Yucca filamentosa* 'Golden Sword' Z4–11 H12–5
- *Zinnia grandiflora* Z0 H12–1

Verbena hastata
BLUE VERVAIN

Ⓝ ☼ ◐ Z3–9 H9–1 ↕5ft (1.5m) ↔24in (60cm)
Flowers apear from early summer to early autumn. Prefers moderately fertile soil. Prone to a variety of diseases and insects but normally tolerates them.

Salvia azurea
BLUE SAGE

Ⓝ ☼ ◑ ◊ Z4–7 H12–1 ↕to 5ft (1.5m) ↔3ft (1m)
Flowers from late summer to autumn. Grows best in light, moderately fertile, organic soil. A variety of maladies may attack, but the plant grows back.

Oenothera macrocarpa
OZARK SUNDROPS

Ⓝ ☼ ◊ Z5–8 H8–3 ↕↔6in (15cm)
Flowers from late spring to early fall. Grow in marginally to moderately fertile soil. Tolerant of rocky soil. Prone to leaf gall, mildews, rust, and leaf spot.

Linum lewisii
COMMON FLAX

Ⓝ ☼ ◊ Z0 H8–1 ↕30in (75cm) ↔24in (60cm)
Blooms from late spring to early fall. Grow in light, moderately fertile, organic soil. Susceptible to stem rot, rust, wilt, anthracnose, slugs, snails, and aphids.

HERBACEOUS PLANTS

Perennials for acidic soils

The following plants prefer soil acidity that is below the average garden level of between 6.5 and 7 (neutral). These plants are often found growing in woodlands and moist areas, especially those rich in organic matter. They are also well adjusted to the high availability of some minerals that is associated with low pH levels.

Iris ensata 'Variegata'
VARIEGATED JAPANESE WATER IRIS

☼ ☼ ◊ Z5–8 H8–4 ↕3ft (1m) ↔indefinite

Blooms in early summer. Leaves and stems are attractively white-striped. Prefers well-drained, fertile soil and dislikes high levels of nitrogen. Plant from midsummer to early fall.

Asclepias tuberosa
BUTTERFLY WEED

Ⓝ ☼ ◊ Z4–9 H9–2 ↕30in (75cm) ↔18in (45cm)

Blooms in midsummer. Prefers fertile, well-drained, loamy soil. Susceptible to aphids, mealybugs, rust, and bacterial and fungal leaf spots.

MORE CHOICES

- *Aruncus dioicus* Z3–7 H7–1
- *Chelone lyonii* 'Hot Lips' Z3–8 H8–1
- *Dodecatheon meadia* Z4–8 H8–1
- *Iris ensata* and cultivars Z3–9 H9–1

Cornus canadensis
CREEPING DOGWOOD

Ⓝ ☼ ◊ ☙ Z2–7 H7–1 ↕6in (15cm) ↔12in (30cm)

Flowers in late spring to early summer, followed by ornamental red fruit. Prefers organic soil and is best grown where summers are cool.

Iris versicolor
BLUE FLAG, WILD IRIS

Ⓝ ☼ ◊◊ Z3–9 H9–1 ↕2ft (60cm) ↔indefinite

Blooms in early to midsummer. Prefers fertile, well-drained, loamy soil. Susceptible to aphids and mealybugs, especially when in bloom.

Iris laevigata 'Snowdrift'
SNOWDRIFT JAPANESE WATER IRIS

☼ ☼ ◊ Z5–9 H9–1 ↕2ft (0.6m) ↔indefinite

Blooms from late spring to early summer. Has broad leaves and spreads by rhizomes to form open clumps. Prefers fertile, well-drained, loamy soil.

Iris innominata
WOODLAND IRIS

Ⓝ ☼ ☼ ◊ Z7–9 H9–7 ↕6–20in (6–25cm) ↔indefinite

Flowers can also be cream to pale lavender and purple. Prefers fertile, well-drained, loamy soil. Susceptible to aphids and mealybugs, especially when in bloom. Also predisposed to infections from rust and bacterial and fungal leaf spots.

Erythronium grandiflorum
AVALANCHE LILY

Ⓝ ☼ ◊ Z4–9 H9–1 ↕12in (30cm) ↔3cm (8cm)
The delicate blooms appear in spring. Grow in fertile, organic, well drained soil. Prone to rust, smuts, fungal spots, and slugs. Native to the western US.

Erythronium americanum
YELLOW TROUT LILY

Ⓝ ☼ ◊ Z3–9 H9–1 ↕2–10in (5–25cm) ↔2–3in (5–8cm)
Blooms in spring. Prefers organic, well-drained soil that is not too rich. Prone to rust, smuts, fungal spots, and slugs. Native to the eastern US.

Digitalis purpurea
COMMON FOXGLOVE

☼ ◊ Z4–8 H9–1 ↕3–5ft (1–1.5m) ↔2ft (60cm)
Blooms appear in early summer. These variable plants can be biennial or perennial. Prefers well-drained soil and tolerates poor, dry soils. Prone to crown and root rot as well as rust.

Erythronium oregonum
GIANT WHITE FAWNLILY

Ⓝ ☼ ◊ Z3–9 H9–1 ↕14in (35cm) ↔5in (12cm)
Blooms appear in spring. Grow in fertile, organic well-drained soil. Prone to rust, smuts, fungal spots, and slugs. Native from Vancouver, BC, to Oregon.

Erythronium albidum
WHITE DOG'S-TOOTH VIOLET

Ⓝ ☼ ☼ ◊ Z3–9 H9–1 ↕12in (30cm) ↔6in (15cm)
Blooms appear in late spring. Grow in fertile, organic well-drained soil. Prone to rust, smuts, fungal spots and slugs. Native to the central US.

Cimicifuga racemosa
BLACK BUGBANE, BLACK COHOSH

Ⓝ ☼ ◊ Z3–8 H12–1 ↕4–7ft (1.2–2.2m) ↔24in (60cm)
A clump-forming perennial that blooms in midsummer. Flowers are scented, but many people find them disagreeable. Prefers fertile, organic soil.

Asclepias incarnata
SWAMP MILKWEED

Ⓝ ☼ ◊ Z3–8 H8–1 ↕4ft (1.2m) ↔24in (60cm)
Blooms midsummer to early autumn. Prefers fertile, well-drained, loamy soil. Susceptible to aphids and mealybugs, especially when in bloom.

Kirengeshoma palmata
YELLOW WAX-BELLS

☼ ◊ pH Z5–8 H8–5 ↕3ft (1m) ↔2ft (60cm)
This clump-forming perennial flowers from late summer to early fall. Prefers highly organic soil. Young plants are susceptible to slugs and snails.

HERBACEOUS PLANTS

MORE CHOICES

- *Lewisia cotyledon* Z5–8 H8–1
- *Phlox stolonifera* 'Pink Ridge' Z4–8 H8–1
- *Phlox stolonifera* 'Sherwood Purple' Z3–8 H8–1
- *Trillium catesbaei* Z7–9 H8–1
- *Trillium* 'Nodding Red' Z4–8 H8–1
- *Trillium sessile* Z4–8 H8–1
- *Trillium* 'Snowy White' Z4–8 H8–1

Viola pedata
BIRD'S-FOOT VIOLET

Ⓝ ☀ ◌ Z4–8 H8–1 ↕2in (5cm) ↔3in (8cm)
Flowers in late spring to early summer. Prefers well-drained, peaty, sandy soil. Susceptible to a variety of problems, but seedlings perpetuate the planting.

Uvularia grandiflora
BELLWORT, MERRY BELLS

Ⓝ ☀ ◌◌ Z3–7 H7–1 ↕24in (60cm) ↔12in (30cm)
Flowers are borne from mid- to late spring on upright stems. This is a slowly spreading plant with creeping rhizomes. Prefers fertile, organic soil.

Mertensia virginica
VIRGINIA BLUEBELLS

Ⓝ ☀ ◌ Z3–7 H7–1 ↕24in (60cm) ↔18in (45cm)
Flowers open from pink-tinted buds in mid- to late spring. Grow in well-drained, organic soil. Prone to problems but usually outgrows them

Osmunda regalis
ROYAL FERN

Ⓝ ☀ ● Z2–10 H9–1 ↕6ft (2m) ↔3ft (1m)
A deciduous fern that produces its ornamental fertile fronds in summer. Grow in fertile, organic soil. It is prone to rust. Rootstock is source of osmunda fiber.

Lilium pardalinum
LEOPARD LILY, PANTHER LILY

Ⓝ ☀ ◌ Z5–8 H8–5 ↕↔6–10ft (2–3m)
Blooms from late spring into summer. Prefers organic, well-drained soil. Prone to gray mold, red lily beetles, slugs, and snails. Also attractive to foraging animals.

Lewisia rediviva
BITTERROOT

Ⓝ ☀ ◌ 🌱 Z4–9 H9–1 ↕1½in (4cm) ↔2in (5cm)
Flowers from early spring to summer, after which the leaves die back. Grow in moderately fertile, very well-drained, organic soil.

Vancouveria hexandra
AMERICAN BARRENWORT

Ⓝ ☀ ◐ Z5–8 H8–5 ‡8in (20cm) ↔indefinite

Flowers in late spring on leafless stems. Rhizomatous; prefers moderately fertile, organic soil. Susceptible to vine weevil.

Tricyrtis formosana
TOAD LILY

☀ ☀ ◐ Z6–9 H9–6 ‡3ft (1m) ↔18in (45cm)

Blooms in early fall. Leaves dark green with purple-green spots. Slugs and snails attack soft young growth.

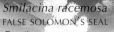

Smilacina racemosa
FALSE SOLOMON'S SEAL

Ⓝ ☀ ◐ Z4–9 H9–1 ‡3ft (1m) ↔18in (45cm)

Flowers are produced from mid- to late spring, followed by ornamental red berries. Prefers moderately fertile, well-drained, organic soil.

Trillium erectum
PURPLE TRILLIUM

Ⓝ ☀ ◐ Z4–9 H7–3 ‡20in (50cm) ↔12in (30cm)

Outward-facing flowers appear in spring. Prefers acidic to neutral soil rich in organic matter. Mulch in fall with leaf mold.

Trillium grandiflorum
WAKE ROBIN

Ⓝ ☀ ☀ ◐◐ Z4–7 H7–3 ‡18in (45cm) ↔12in (30cm)

Flowers bloom in midspring and often turn pink as they age. Prefers acidic to neutral soil rich in organic matter. Mulch in fall with leaf mold.

Trillium chloropetalum
GIANT WAKE ROBIN

Ⓝ ☀ ☀ ◐ Z6–9 H9–6 ‡16in (40cm) ↔8in (20cm)

The fragrant flowers appear in spring. Prefers acidic to neutral, organic soil. Mulch in fall with leaf mold. Susceptible to rust, smut, fungal spot, slugs, and snails.

Trillium luteum
YELLOW TRILLIUM

Ⓝ ☀ ☀ ◐◐ Z5–7 H7–4 ‡16in (40cm) ↔12in (30cm)

Sweetly fragrant flowers appear in spring. Prefers acidic to neutral, organic soil. Mulch in fall with leaf mold. Susceptible to rust, smut, fungal spot, slugs, and snails.

Trillium ovatum
COAST TRILLIUM

Ⓝ ☀ ◐◐ Z5–8 H8–5 ‡15in (38cm) ↔8in (20cm)

Spring-blooming flowers often turn pink or red. Prefers acidic to neutral, organic soil. Mulch in fall with leaf mold. Prone to rust, smut, spots, slugs, and snails.

Perennials for alkaline soil

Alkaline soils are usually rich in minerals necessary for plant growth, but because of their high pH (reading 8 or more), the minerals in them are not easily absorbed by most plants. The selections on these four pages represent plants that either thrive in or are amenable to soils with high pH. Some alkaline soils are referred to as "white alkali" or "caliche."

Dianthus chinensis
INDIAN PINK

☼ ◊ z9–11 H12–1 ↕↔6–12in (15–30cm)
Scentless flowers appear in summer. Cultivars offer flowers in shades of pink, red, and white with variable patterns and fringing. Normally short-lived perennials.

Echinops ritro
SMALL GLOBE THISTLE

☼ ◊ ◊ z3–9 H12–1 ↕to 24in (60cm) ↔18in (45cm)
Flowers in late summer. Prefers marginally fertile soil. Self sows freely. Good for large borders. Attractive to insects and birds, but unpalatable to deer.

Aurinia saxatilis
BASKET OF GOLD

☼ ◊ z4–8 H8–1 ↕8in (20cm) ↔12in (30cm)
Flowers are produced from late spring to early summer. Evergreen and mound-forming. Prune plants back after flowering to keep plant from becoming leggy.

Acanthus mollis
BEAR'S BREECHES

☼ ☼ ◊ z7–11 H12–7 ↕4ft (1.2m) ↔18in (45cm)
Produces flowers in late summer. The flower bracts are purple, as the flower stalk may also be. Performs best when grown in deep, fertile, loamy soil.

Anchusa azurea
BLUE BUGLOSS,
ITALIAN ALKANET

☼ ◊ z3–8 H8–1 ↕5ft (1.5m) ↔2ft (60cm)
Flowers appear in early summer on clumping, upright plants. Flowers turn from gentian blue to blue-purple with age. Prefers moderately fertile soil.

Platycodon grandiflorus 'Mariesii'
MARIESII BALLOON FLOWER

☼ ☼ ◊ z4–9 H9–3 ↕18in (45cm) ↔12in (30cm)
In late summer, large, balloonlike buds precede the flowers, which reach 2 in. wide. This semi dwarf subspecies prefers deep, fertile, loamy soil.

MORE CHOICES

- *Achillea millefolium* z3–9 H9–1
- *Achillea millefolium* 'Paprika' z3–9 H8–2
- *Anemone blanda* z4–8 H8–1
- *Atemisia lactiflora* z5–8 H8–5
- *Campanula glomerata* z3–8 H8–1
- *Campanula lactiflora* 'Pouffe' z3–9 H9–1
- *Campanula punctata* 'Elizabeth' z3–9 H9–1
- *Coreopsis grandiflora* z4–9 H12–1

Centaurea dealbata
WHITEWASH CORNFLOWER, PERSIAN CORNFLOWER

☼ ◊ z3–9 H9–1 ↕3ft (1m) ↔2ft (60cm)

A clump-forming plant with midsummer flowers good for cutting. Performs well in most garden soils. Self-seeding, so cut flowers off after they finish blooming.

Coreopsis grandiflora 'Early Sunrise'
EARLY SUNRISE TICKSEED

Ⓝ ☼ ☼ ◊ z3–9 H9–1 ↕↔18in (45cm)

Flowers appear from late spring to late summer and make good cut flowers. This cultivar blooms the first year from seed and is sometimes treated as an annual.

Coreopsis verticillata 'Moonbeam'
MOONBEAM TICKSEED

Ⓝ ☼ ☼ ◊ z3–8 H9–1 ↕18in (45cm)

Flowers freely from early summer to autumn. Deaheading helps extend the bloom period. This cultivar has an upright habit and is drought resistant.

Perovskia atriplicifolia 'Blue Spire'
BLUE SPIRE RUSSIAN SAGE

Ⓝ ☼ ◊ z6–8 H9–6 ↕↔5ft (1.5m)

This cultivar is much more floriferous than the species. The flower spikes create a purple haze of color above the foliage. Flowers in late summer and early autumn.

Centranthus ruber
RED VALERIAN

☼ ◊ z5–8 H8–5 ↕3ft (1m) ↔2ft (60cm)

Fragrant flowers appear spring to late summer. Also available with white and rose-pink flowers. Self-sows freely. Prefers minimally to moderately fertile soil.

Perovskia atriplicifolia
RUSSIAN SAGE

☼ ◊ z6–9 H9–6 ↕4ft (1.2m) ↔3ft (1m)

Flowers from summer to early autumn. Bloom period can be extended by deadheading older flowers. Grows well in minimally to moderately fertile soil.

HERBACEOUS PLANTS

Campanula lactiflora 'Lodden Anna'
LODDEN ANNA BELLFLOWER
☼ ◊ Z4–8 H8–1
↕4ft (1.2m) ↔2ft (60cm)
This cultivar is identical to 'Pritchard's Variety', with the exception of the flower color. The unbranched stems arise from a basal clump. Prefers fertile soil.

Campanula lactiflora 'Prichard's Variety'
PRICHARD'S BELLFLOWER
☼ ☼ ◊ Z5–7 H7–5 ↕to 30in (75cm) ↔24in (60cm)
A vigorous, upright perennial that flowers freely from early summer to early autumn. Works well in both a herbaceous border and a naturalistic garden.

Geranium cinereum 'Ballerina'
BALLERINA CRANESBILL
☼ ◊ Z4–9 H9–3 ↕4in (10cm) ↔12in (30cm)
Flowers from late spring to early summer. This cultivar has grayer leaves than the species. Excellent in a rock or alpine garden it also grows well in a container.

Geranium sanguineum
BLOODY CRANESBILL
☼ ◊ Z3–8 H8–1 ↕10in (25cm) ↔12in (30cm)
Blooms during summer. Prefers moderately fertile soil, so do not over fertilize. Divide in spring every few years to keep plants vigorous and healthy.

Geranium 'Brookside'
BROOKSIDE CRANESBILL
☼ ☼ ◔ Z5–8 H8–1 ↕↔2ft (60cm)
A cultivar that blooms in midsummer and produces coiled pods that scatter seeds far and wide when they burst. Bees visit the flowers, and birds eat the seeds.

Kniphofia 'Royal Standard'
ROYAL STANDARD RED-HOT POKER
☼ ◊ Z5–8 H9–4 ↕3–4ft (1–1.2m) ↔2ft (60cm)
Flowers are borne on thick stems from mid- to late summer. Good hummingbird plant. Prefers sandy soil that is deep, fertile, and high in organic content.

Thalictrum flavum subsp. glaucum
DUSTY MEADOW RUE

☼ ◑ ◊◑ Z6–8 H8–4 ↕3ft (1m) ↔2ft (60cm)

Fragrant flowers appear in summer and may need staking. Flowers are paler (and stems are more blue-green) than the species. Prefers organic soil.

Sedum 'Autumn Joy'
AUTUMN JOY STONECROP

☼ ◊ Z3–8 H8–1 ↕↔to 2ft (60cm)

This hybrid is a very upright, clumping perennial that blooms early autumn. Prefers moderately fertile soil. Also sold under the name 'Herbsfreude'.

Hypericum 'Hidcote'
HIDCOTE ST. JOHN'S WORT

◑ ◊ Z6–9 H9–6 ↕↔5ft (1.5m)

Flowers from midsummer to early autumn This dense and bushy hybrid bears evergreen to semi-evergreen foliage and prefers moderately fertile soil.

MORE CHOICES

- *Eryngium alpinum* 'Blue Star' Z6–9 H9–6
- *Geranium cinereum* 'Splenders' Z3–9 H9–3
- *Geranium cinereum* var. *subcaulescens* Z5–9 H9–3
- *Gypsophila paniculata* Z5–9 H9–1
- *Kniphofia* 'Uvaria Early' Z5–9 H9–1
- *Kniphofia* 'Malibu Yellow' Z5–9 H9–1
- *Kniphofia* 'Springtime' Z5–9 H9–1
- *Papaver orientale* Z4–9 H9–1
- *Papaver orientale* 'Helen Elizabeth' Z4–9 H9–1
- *Papaver orientale* 'Perry's White' Z4–9 H9–1
- *Papaver orientale* 'Picotee' Z3–8 H8–1
- *Papaver orientale* 'Turenlouis' Z3–8 H8–1
- *Perovskia atriplicifolia* 'Longin' Z6–9 H9–6
- *Platycodon grandiflorus* 'Alba' Z3–8 H8–1
- *Platycodon grandiflorus* 'Shell Pink' Z4–9 H9–3
- *Salvia superba* Z5–9 H9–5
- *Veronicastrum virginicum* Z4–8 H8–3

Sidalcea malviflora
CHECKERBLOOM

☼ ◑ Z5–7 H8–2 ↕4ft (1.2m) ↔18in (45cm)

This erect perennial blooms in early to midsummer. Grows best in moderately fertile, organic, sandy soil. Will often rebloom if cut back hard after flowering.

Aubrieta deltoidea
LILACBUSH

☼ ◑ ◑ Z5–7 H7–5 ↕6ft (1.8m) ↔18in (50cm)

Cut back hard after sping bloom to keep the plant dense. This mat-former is excellent in rock gardens and screes. Prefers moderately fertile soil.

Verbascum thapsus
DENSEFLOWER MULLEIN

☼ ◊ Z3–9 H9–1 ↕4–6ft (1.2–2m) ↔18in (45cm)

The flowering spike towers above the wooly, rosette-forming foliage in summer. A short-lived perennial that is sometime treated as a biennial.

HERBACEOUS PLANTS

Perennials for clay soil

Soils rich in clay present a challenge to perennials growing in them, particularly when the soils are low in organic matter. In this situation, pore spaces in these soils are small, so oxygen levels at the roots can be low. In addition, the soil can fluctuate from sticky and wet to bricklike and dry. These perennials are adaptable to clay soils.

HERBACEOUS PLANTS

Aster x frikartii
MICHAELMAS DAISY, FRIKART'S ASTER

☀ ◐ Z4–8 H8–1 ↕28in (70cm) ↔18in (45cm)
Flowers from late summer to early fall. This hybrid of *A. amellus* and *A. thomsonii* prefers moderately fertile soil. Susceptible to *Verticillium* wilt and other diseases.

Aster novi belgii 'Alma Potschke'
ALMA POTSCHKE NEW ENGLAND ASTER

Ⓝ ☀ ◑ ◐ Z4–8 H9–1 ↕4ft (1.2m) ↔24in (60cm)
Flowers in late summer to midautumn. The original species has blue-violet flowers. Prefers fertile soil. Susceptible to *Verticillium* wilt and other diseases.

Aster novi belgii 'Persian Rose'
PERSIAN ROSE DWARF ASTER

Ⓝ ☀ ◑ ◐ ◔ Z4–8 H8–1 ↕↔12–15in (30–38cm)
Like other *Aster novi-belgii*, this one is the result of a native American species going to "finishing school" in Europe and then returning home as a cultivar.

Brunnera macrophylla 'Dawson's White'
SIBERIAN BUGLOSS

☀ ◔ Z3–7 H7–1 ↕18in (45cm) ↔24in (60cm)
Flowers from mid- to late spring. Prefers moderately fertile, organic soil. Equally at home in a woodland setting as in a border. Species has deep green leaves.

Paeonia lactiflora cultivars
GARDEN PEONY

☀ ◑ ◔ Z3–8 H8–1 ↕↔20–28in (50–70cm)
Fragrant flowers, ranging from red to white, bloom from late spring to early summer. Grow in deep, fertile, organic soil. Peonies are long-lived.

Aquilegia 'Nora Barlow'
NORA BARLOW COLUMBINE

☀ ◑ ◔ Z4–7 H7–1 ↕3ft (1m) ↔18in (45cm)
This double-flowered selection flowers in late spring. Prefers fertile soil. Susceptible to a range of diseases and insects but often outgrows them.

Polemonium caeruleum
JACOB'S LADDER

☼ ◊ Z4–9 H9–1 ↕↔18–24in (40–60cm)

Blooms in early summer. Although not as common, this can also be found with white flowers. Grow in fertile soil. Prone to powdery mildew.

Rheum palmatum 'Atrosanguineum'
CHINESE PURPLE RHUBARB

☼ ◑ ◊ Z5–9 H9–1 ↕↔6ft (2m)

Flowers in early summer. Has a massive rhizomatous rootstock. Leaves are vivid crimson when young. Grow in deep, organic soil. Susceptible to rots and rust.

Hosta 'June'
JUNE HOSTA

☼ ◑ ◊ Z3–8 H9–2 ↕16in (45cm) ↔28in (70cm)

A variegated sport of H. 'Halcyon', this bears gray-lavender flowers on a gray-green flower stalk in summer. Prefers fertile soil. Prone to slugs and snails.

Rudbeckia fulgida 'Deamii'
DEAMII CONEFLOWER

Ⓝ ☼ ◑ ◊ ◐ Z4–9 H9–1 ↕3ft (1m) ↔2ft (60cm)

A free-flowering form that is more drought tolerant than the species. Blooms from late summer to midautumn. Prefers moderately fertile soil.

Hemerocallis 'Stella D'Oro'
STELLA D'ORO DAYLILY

☼ ◊ Z3–9 H12–1 ↕12in (30cm) ↔18in (45cm)

Vigorous and free flowering, blooming early and repeating throughout the season. Prefers fertile soil. Arguably the finest of all daylilies.

Rodgersia aesculifolia
FINGERLEAF RODGERSIA

Ⓝ ☼ ◑ ◑ Z5–8 H8–1 ↕to 6ft (2m) ↔3ft (1m)

Blooms in midsummer above horsechestnut-like foliage. A pink-flowered form is available. Grow in soil rich in organic matter. Can be subject to slug damage.

Solidago rugosa 'Fireworks'
GOLDENROD

Ⓝ ☼ ◑ ◊ Z4–9 H9–1 ↕4ft (1.2m) ↔3–4ft (1–1.2m)

Late-summer blooming. Flowers are attractive to bees and butterflies. Grow in marginal to moderately fertile soil. Prone to powdery mildew, leaf spots, and rust.

HERBACEOUS PLANTS

Aconitum x cammarum 'Bicolor'
BICOLOR MONKSHOOD

☼ ◊ Z3–8 H8–3 ‡4ft (1.2m) ↔20in (50cm)

Blooms from mid- to late summer. Prefers fertile soil but is fairly tolerant of other soil types. All parts of monkshoods are highly poisonous.

Helenium autumnale
SNEEZEWEED

Ⓝ ☼ ◊ Z4–8 H8–1 ‡5ft (1.5m) ↔18in (45cm)

Flowers appear from late summer to midautumn. Prefers fertile soil. Susceptible to powdery mildew, rust, leaf smut, and fungal spot diseases.

Aconitum napellus
HELMET FLOWER

◊ Z3–8 H8–3 ‡5ft (1.5m) ↔1ft (30cm)

Blooms from mid- to late summer. Prefers fertile soil; fairly tolerant of other soil types. Prone to aphids, stem rots, mildews, crown rot rust, and *Verticillium* wilt.

Ajuga reptans 'Caitlin's Giant'
CATLIN'S GIANT CARPET BUGLE

☼ ☼ ◑ ● Z3–9 H9–1 ‡6in (15cm) ↔3ft (1m)

This large-leafed and large-flowered form blooms from late spring to early summer. Grows well in most soil types. Prone to fungal leaf spot and crown rot.

Eupatorium purpureum
PURPLE JOE PYE WEED

Ⓝ ☼ ☼ ● Z3–9 H9–1 ‡7ft (2.2m) ↔3ft (1m)

Blooms from midsummer to early autumn. Leaves smell like vanilla when bruised. Prone to rust, powdery mildew, white smut, and leaf spots.

Aster novi belgii 'Purple Dome'
PURPLE DOME NEW ENGLAND ASTER

Ⓝ ☼ ☼ ● Z4–8 H9–1 ‡18in (45cm) ↔30in (75cm)

Flowers in late summer to midautumn. Flower color is similar to the species. Prefers fertile soil. Susceptible to *Verticillium* wilt and other fungal diseases.

Astilbe simplicifolia 'Inshriach Pink'
INSHRIACH PINK ASTILBE

☀ ◐ ◊ z5–8 H8–2 ↕↔12in (30cm)
Flowers in late summer. Grow in fertile, organic soil. Forms clumps like other Astilbes. Prone to tarnished plant bug, powdery mildew, and leaf spots.

Astilbe simplicifolia 'Sprite'
SPRITE ASTILBE

◊ z4–8 H8–1 ↕20in (50cm) ↔3ft (1m)
Flowers in summer. Divide clumps every 3-4 years and replant into fertile, organic soil to keep them in top shape and flowering well.

Astilbe chinensis 'Pumila'
DWARF FALSE GOATSBEARD

☀ ◊ z4–8 H8–1 ↕12in (30cm) ↔8in (20cm)
Flowers in late summer. Grow in fertile, organic soil. They are easy to propagate by division, which should be done in spring just as the new growth emerges.

MORE CHOICES

- *Aruncus dioicus* z3–7 H7–1
- *Aster novi belgii* z4–8 H8–1
- *Astilbe chinensis* z3–8 H8–2
- *Astilbe japonica* and cultivars z3–8 H8–2
- *Astilbe slimplicifolia* z4–8 H8–2
- *Astilbe* x *arendsii* 'Fanal' z3–9 H9–1
- *Astilbe* x *arendsii* 'Rheinland' z3–9 H9–1
- *Astrantia major* 'Lars' z4–7 H7–1
- *Brunnera macrophylla* 'Variegata' z3–7 H7–1
- *Helianthus microcephalis* z4–9 H9–1
- *Helianthus salicifolius* z6–9 H9–6
- *Heliopsis helianthoides* 'Ballerina' z4–9 H9–4
- *Monarda didyma* z4–10 H10–1
- *Monarda didyma* 'Jacob Cline' z4–11 H12–1
- *Monarda didyma* 'Marshall's Delight' z4–8 H8–1
- *Rudbeckia fulgida* var. *speciosa* 'Newmanii' z4–9 H9–2

Astilbe japonica 'Deutschland'
DEUTSCHLAND ASTILBE

☀ ◐ ◊ ◖ z4–9 H8–2 ↕20in (50cm) ↔12in (30cm)
Flowers in late spring. Requires fertile, organic soil and good drainage, especially in the Pacific NW and other areas with wet winters.

Astilbe japonica 'Irrlicht'
IRRLICHT ASTILBE

☀ ◐ ◊ ◖ z4–9 H8–2 ↕↔18in (45cm)
Late spring- and early summer-blooming flowers appear over attractive clumps of dark green foliage. Divide regularly.

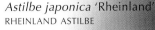

Astilbe japonica 'Rheinland'
RHEINLAND ASTILBE

☀ ◐ ◊ ◖ z4–8 H8–2 ↕20in (50cm) ↔18in (45cm)
Flowers in summer. The leaves, suggestive of ferns, form bushy mounds that are especially lush when clumps are grown in fertile, organic soil.

HERBACEOUS PLANTS

Perennials for warm, sheltered sites

The adventurous gardener likes to push the envelope occasionally when selecting garden plants. One way to expand your choices is to identify microclimates in your garden than can support plants that normally grow in areas that are one USDA hardiness zone warmer than your area. South-facing alcoves, especially against walls, are ideal.

Nerine bowdenii
GUERNSEY LILY

☼ ◊ Z8–10 H10–8 ↕18in (45cm) ↔3in (8cm)
This bulbous perennial blooms in autumn. The cultivar 'Alba' has white flowers. Best if grown in well-drained soil. Susceptible to slug damage.

Lobelia erinus
STRING PEARLS

☼ ◊ Z9–10 H7–1 ↕8in (20cm) ↔6in (15cm)
Flowering from summer through autumn, these trailing perennials (often grown as annuals) occur in shades of blue, purple, red, and white.

Bletilla striata
HARDY ORCHID

☼ ◊ Z5–8 H8–5 ↕↔to 24in (60cm)
These beautiful terrestrial orchids flower from spring to early summer. Cultivars are available with white to pale yellow flowers. Prefer organic soil.

Clivia miniata
CLIVIA

☼ ◊ Z12–15 H12–10 ↕16in (40cm) ↔24in (60cm)
Clivias, evergreen bulbous perennial from South Africa, flower from spring to summer. Flowers are mostly orange or yellow. They prefer fertile, organic soil.

MORE CHOICES

- *Acidanthera 'Abyssinian Glad'* z0 H12–4
- *Bletilla striata* z5–8 H8–5
- *Clivia miniata* z12–15 H12–10
- *Coleus blumei* z11–12 H12–1
- *Consolida orientalis* z0 H12–1
- *Cortaderia selloana* z7–11 H12–7
- *Erodium corsicum* z4–7 H7–1
- *Gloxinia sylvatica* z9–11 H12–9
- *Oxalis brazilensis* z8–10 H10–8
- *Pennisetum alopecuroides 'Rubrum'*
  z6–9 H9–6

Agapanthus campanulatus
AFRICAN BLUE LILY

☼ ◐ z7–11 H12–7 ↕4ft (1.2m) ↔20in (50cm)
Flowers, ranging from deep violet to pale blue, appear during summer. Prefers fertile soil. Benefits from winter mulching where marginally hardy.

Oxalis tetraphylla 'Iron Cross'
WOODSORREL

☼ ◐ z8–10 H10–6 ↕↔to 6in (15cm)
Flat-topped clusters of funnel-shaped, reddish purple flowers with greenish yellow throats appear in summer. Prefers fertile, organic soil.Clump-forming bulb.

Eucomis 'Bicolor'
PINEAPPLE FLOWER

☼ ◐ z8–10 H10–8 ↕↔12–24in (30–60cm)
This bulbous perennial should be planted just below the soil surface in very well-drained, moderately fertile soil. Restrict water during winter dormancy.

Salvia uliginosa
BOG SAGE

☼ ◑ ◐ z8–11 H12–7 ↕to 6ft (2m) ↔36in (90cm)
A clump-forming, rhizomatous perennial with deeply toothed, very aromatic leaves. Flowers from late summer to midautumn. Flowers can also be white.

Delosperma cooperi
ICE PLANT

☼ ◐ z8–10 H10–8 ↕2in (5cm) ↔indefinite
Creeping succulent with cylindrical, light green,. evergreen to semi-evergreen foliage. Flowers from mid- to late summer. Prefers sharply drained soil.

HERBACEOUS PLANTS

Perennials for coastal exposure

Where gardens are within wind distance of salt water, the plants growing in them must be tolerant of salt, both in the air and in the soil. Salt desiccates (dries out) delicate leaves, causing "burn," and draws moisture from the roots, both of which can lead to their death. The following perennials show high levels of tolerance for coastal conditions.

MORE CHOICES

- *Allium giganteum* z3–9 H9–5
- *Armeria maritima* 'Cotton Tail' z3–9 H9–1
- *Asclepias tuberosa* z4–9 H9–2
- *Aurinia saxatilis* 'Sunnyborder Apricot' z4–8 H8–3
- *Baptisia australis* z3–9 H9–1
- *Centranthus ruber* z5–8 H8–5
- *Eryngium planum* z4–9 H9–1
- *Festuca ovina* 'Glauca' z4–8 H8–1
- *Geranium sanguineum* and cultivars z3–8 H8–1
- *Helianthemum nummularium* z6–8 H8–6
- *Hibiscus moscheutos* z5–10 H12–1
- *Kniphofia uvaria* z6–9 H9–1
- *Liriope minor* z6–9 H9–4
- *Ophiopogon japonicus* 'Variegatus' z7–10 H10–1

Heuchera sanguinea 'Splendens'
SPLENDENS CORAL BELLS
Ⓝ ☼ ◐ ◊ z3–8 H8–1 ‡28in (70cm)
Clump-forming perennial with flowers carried in summer well above the kidney-shaped leaves. Prefers fertile, organic soil. Can be grown as a groundcover.

Gypsophila paniculata
BABY'S BREATH
☼ ◊ z5–9 H9–1 ‡8–12in (20–30cm) ↔6in (15cm)
Flowers in mid- to late summer. Forms a long taproot, so it should be transplanted when young or sown where it will grow. A common "filler" used by florists.

Ophiopogon japonicus
MONDO GRASS
☼ ◐ ◊ z7–10 H12–1 ‡↔12in (30cm)
Tuberous-rooted, clump-forming perennial bears short racemes of bell-shaped white flowers in summer. Produces blue-black berries in fall. Good groundcover.

Crambe cordifolia
COLEWORT
☼ ◊ z6–9 H9–6 ‡to 6ft (2m) ↔4ft (1.2m)
This plant makes a bold statement with spectacular blooms rising above the foliage from late spring to midsummer. Best if sited toward the back of a border.

Iberis sempervirens
CANDYTUFT
☼ ◊ z5–9 H9–3 ‡12in (30cm) ↔24in (60cm)
Flowers appear from late spring to early summer on this spreading evergreen perennial. Prefers marginally to moderately fertile soil; does well in a rock garden.

Platycodon grandiflorus 'Mariesii'
MARIESII BALLOON FLOWER
☼ ◐ ◊ z4–9 H9–3 ‡18in (45cm) ↔12in (30cm)
In late summer, large balloonlike buds precede the flowers, which often reach 2in wide. Prefers deep, fertile, loamy soil. This is a semidwarf subspecies.

Liriope muscari
LILYTURF

☼ ◊ Z6–10 H10–6 ‡12in (30cm) ↔18in (45cm)
The flowers emerge from the evergreen leaves of this tuberous perennial from early to late autumn. Prefers light, moderately fertile soil.

Liriope muscari 'White'
WHITE LILYTURF

☼ ◊ Z6–11 H12–1 ‡12in (30cm) ↔18in (45cm)
This white form of the species makes a good border and path edging. It does well in rock gardens and *en masse* as an evergreen groundcover.

Liriope gigantea
GIANT LILYTURF

☼ ◊◊ ᵖᴴ Z6–11 H12–6 ‡3ft (1m) ↔2ft (60cm)
True to its species name, this is the largest of all the *Liriope* species. The violet flower spikes appear in midsummer. Makes a useful accent plant.

Armeria maritima 'Bloodstone'
COMMON THRIFT

Ⓝ ☼ ◊ z3–9 H9–1
‡4in (10cm) ↔6in (15cm)
Flowers bloom from late spring to summer above clump-forming plants. Prefers marginally to moderately fertile soil and tolerates almost pure sand. Divide every 4–5 years, before the center dies out.

MORE CHOICES

- *Ophiopogon planiscapus* and cultivars Z6–11 H12–1
- *Pennisetum alopecuroides* and cultivars Z6–9 H9–6
- *Platycodon grandiflorum* and cultivars Z3–7 H9–3
- *Santolina chamaecyparissus* Z6–9 H9–4
- *Sedum acre* Z3–8 H8–1
- *Sedum kamtschaticum* and cultivars Z4–9 H9–1
- *Sedum oreganum* Z0–0 H
- *Sedum rubrechtii* Z0–0 H8–1
- *Sedum spectabile (Hylotelephium spectabile)* Z4–9 H9–1
- *Sedum spurium* and cultivars Z4–9 H9–4
- *Yucca filamentosa* Z4–11 H12–5

Liriope spicata 'Silver Dragon'
SILVER DRAGON LILYTURF

☼ ◐ ◊ Z6–11 H12–1 ‡↔12–15in (30–38cm)
The light purple flowers appear in late summer. It is similar to the species, except the foliage is striped silver, and it is slower growing.

Perennials for exposed, windy sites

Plants tolerant of wind must be both physically sturdy to withstand the physical force as well as be fortified against the desiccating effect of constant high winds. These perennials do an admirable job of holding up against these challenging sites with their sturdy stems, thick leaves, and hairy or waxy leaf surfaces.

Santolina chamaecyparissus
LAVENDER COTTON
☀ ◊ Z6–9 H9–4 ↕20in (50cm) ↔3ft (1m)
Flowers appear from mid- to late summer. Grow in marginally to moderately fertile soil. May die back to the ground in colder areas of the Northwest.

Brunnera macrophylla 'Dawson's White'
SIBERIAN BUGLOSS
◐ ◊ Z3–7 H7–1 ↕18in (45cm) ↔24in (60cm)
Flowers from mid- to late spring. Prefers moderately fertile, organic soil. Equally at home in a woodland setting or in a border. Species has deep green leaves.

Cortaderia selloana 'Pumila'
DWARF PAMPAS GRASS
☀ ◊ Z7–10 H12–7 ↕5ft (1.5m) ↔4ft (1.2m)
Blooms in late summer, the plumes persisting into winter. When cutting back, wear gloves and long sleeves to protect against the sharp-edged foliage.

Anaphalis margaritacea
PEARLY EVERLASTING
Ⓝ ☀ ◊ Z4–8 H8–1 ↕30in (75cm) ↔24in (60cm)
Flowers appear from midsummer to early autumn on erect, leafy stems. Good for screes and rock gardens. Prefers moderately fertile soil.

Agapanthus campanulatus
'Headbourne Hybrids'
HEADBOURNE HYBRID AFRICAN BLUE LILY
☀ ◑ ◊ Z8–11 H12–3 ↕30in (75cm) ↔12in (30cm)
Flowers appear during summer and range from deep violet to pale blue. Prefers fertile soil. Benefits from a winter mulch where marginally hardy.

Yucca filamentosa 'Variegata'
VARIEGATED YUCCA

Ⓝ ☼ ◊ Z5–10 H12–1 ‡30in (75cm) ↔5ft (1.5m)
The nodding, bell-shaped white flowers appear on an upright stalk from late spring into summer. Yellow leaf margins may be infused with pink during winter.

MORE CHOICES

- *Achillea ptarmica 'The Pearl Superior'*
  Z3–8 H8–1
- *Anaphalis margaritacea* Z4–8 H8–1
- *Asclepias tuberosa* Z4–9 H9–2
- *Brunnera macrophylla* Z3–7 H7–1
- *Carex buchananii 'Fox Red'* Z6–9 H9–5
- *Carex comans* Z7–9 H9–7
- *Carex conica 'Hime Kansugi'* Z5–9 H9–5
- *Carex glauca* Z5–9 H9–3
- *Carex morrowii* Z5–9 H12–1
- *Carex plantaginea* Z5–7 H7–4
- *Carex siderosticha 'Variegata'* Z6–9 H9–3
- *Cortaderia selloana* Z7–11 H12–7
- *Echinops bannaticus* Z5–9 H9–5
- *Euphorbia marginata* Z13–15 H12–1
- *Euphorbia polychroma* Z5–9 H9–5
- *Santolina rosmarinifolia*
- *Yucca filamentosa*
  Z4–11 H12–5
- *Yucca glauca*
  Z5–10 H10–5

Anchusa azurea
BLUE BUGLOSS, ITALIAN ALKANET

☼ ◊ Z3–8 H8–1 ‡3–5ft
(1–1.5m) ↔2ft (60cm)
Flowering panicles appear in early summer. Plants are clump forming and upright in habit. Prefers moderately fertile soil.

Phlomis frutiocosa
JERUSALEM SAGE

☼ ◊ Z8–9 H9–8 ‡↔5ft (1.5m)
Flowering from early and midsummer, this mound-forming plant resembles sage, its close relative. The undersides of the leaves are woolly. Prefers fertile soil.

Astilbe chinensis
FALSE GOATSBEARD, CHINESE SPIRAEA

☼☼ ◊◊ Z4–8 H8–2 ‡↔24in (60cm)
Flowers in late summer. Grow in fertile, organic soil. Easy to propagate by division, which should be done in spring, just as the new growth emerges.

Phormium tenax
NEW ZEALAND FLAX

☼ ◊ Z9–11 H12–6 ‡10ft (3m) ↔3–6ft (1–2m)
This bold plant blooms in summer and prefers fertile soil. Cultivars are available with variegated as well as purple to bronze leaf color. Leaf edges can be sharp.

Carex hachijoensis 'Evergold'
VARIEGATED JAPANESE SEDGE

☼ ◊ Z6–9 H9–6 ‡8in (20cm) ↔6–8in (15–20cm)
Bears small brown flower spikes in mid to late spring. Best when grow in fertile soil. Can be used as an accent plant in borders or *en masse* as a groundcover.

Perennials for air-polluted sites

Air pollution is not only hazardous to people and animals but also to plants. The gases produced from the internal combustion engine and other sources can also wreak havoc with plants' respiratory and photosynthetic processes. The seletions presented here grow reliably in areas high in pollution, such as roadsides and industrial belts.

Achillea millefolium
YARROW

☼ ◗ Z3–9 H10–1 ↕↔24in (60cm)

Blooms from early to late summer. Tolerates a wide range of soil conditions. Self-sows, so deadhead after blooming if you don't want volunteers popping up.

Chrysanthemum x superbum
SHASTA DAISY

☼ ☼ ◗ Z5–8 H8–5 ↕3ft (1m) ↔24in (60cm)

Flowers from early summer to early autumn. Good border plant and great source of cut flowers. Easy to grow and long lived. Prefers moderately fertile soil.

Achillea ptarmica 'The Pearl Superior'
THE PEARL SUPERIOR SNEEZEWORT

☼ ◗ Z3–8 H8–1 ↕↔30in (75cm)

Blooms from early to late summer. The fresh flowers make nice additions to an arrangement and can also be used for dried arrangements.

Sedum kamtschaticum 'Variegatum'
ORANGE STONECROP

☼ ◗ Z3–8 H8–1 ↕2–3in (5–8cm) ↔8in (20cm)

Late summer flowers slowly fade to crimson as they age. Clump-forming, thick rhizomes should be divided every 4 to 5 years. Prefers moderately fertile soil.

Geranium macrorrhizum
SCENTED CRANESBILL

☼ ☼ ◗ Z4–8 H8–1 ↕20in (50cm) ↔24in (60cm)

Early summer blooms mature into distinctive seedheads. Prefers moderately fertile, organic soil. Self sows freely and is attractive to beneficial insects and birds.

Veronica spicata
SPIKE SPEEDWELL

☼ ◊ Z3–8 H8–1 ↕24in (60cm) ↔18in (45cm)

Early to late summer blooms can be used in fresh arrangements.. Prefers moderately fertile soil. Resistant to deer browsing. Many good cultivars are available.

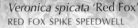

MORE CHOICES

- *Achillea millefolium* Z3–9 H10–1
- *Artemisia ludoviciana* 'Silver Queen' Z5–8 H8–5
- *Aster novae angliae* and cultivars Z4–8 H8–1
- *Coreopsis grandiflora* Z4–9 H12–1
- *Geranium pratense* Z4–8 H8–1
- *Hemerocallis spp.* Z3–8 H12–1
- *Miscanthus giganteus* Z5–9 H8–1
- *Miscanthus sinensis* (various cultivars) Z6–9 H9–1
- *Monarda didyma* Z4–10 H10–1
- *Origanum vulgare* 'Hirtum' Z4–9 H10–2
- *Pennisetum alopecuroides* (various cultivars) Z6–9 H9–6

Veronica spicata 'Red Fox'
RED FOX SPIKE SPEEDWELL

☼ ◊ Z3–8 H8–3 ↕↔12in (30cm)

Flowers from late spring to early summer. Attracts bees and butterflies. It makes a good midground perennial and can also be used as a focal point in a bed.

Pennisetum alopecuroides 'Little Bunny'
LITTLE BUNNY DWARF MOUNTAIN GRASS

☼ ◊ Z5–9 H9–1 ↕10in (25cm) ↔12in (30cm)

Bears flower spikes from summer to fall. Use to soften the foreground of a bed or in a mass planting. Prefers poor to moderately fertile soil.

Monarda fistulosa
WILD BEE BALM

Ⓝ ☼ ◊ Z3–9 H9–1 ↕4ft (1.2m) ↔18in (45cm)

Flowers from midsummer through early fall in light pink to lilac-purple. Spicily aromatic leaves are reminiscent of thyme and oregano. Clump-forming.

Pennisetum alopecuroides 'Moudry'
BLACK FLOWERING MOUNTAIN GRASS

☼ ◊ Z5–9 H9–1 ↕↔3ft (1m)

Bears flower spikes from summer to fall. Seeds of this cultivar are black, giving the spikes a dark cast. Prefers moderately fertile soil.

Pennisetum alopecuroides
CHINESE FOUNTAIN GRASS

☼ ◊ Z6–9 H9–6 ↕3ft (1m) ↔18in (45cm)

Bears flower spikes from summer to autumn which persist into winter. May be freely self-sowing in some locations if flowers not cut back in late summer.

HERBACEOUS PLANTS

Miscanthus sinensis
EULALIA, MAIDENGRASS

☼ ◑ Z4–9 H9–1 ‡to 12ft (4m) ↔4ft (1.2m)

Flower clusters appear in fall; seedheads persist throughout winter. Prefers moderately fertile soil. Cut to the ground in early spring before new growth begins.

Miscanthus sinensis 'Gracillimus'
EULALIA, MAIDENGRASS

☼ ◑ Z5–9 H9–1 ‡4ft (1.2m) ↔30in (45cm)

Leaves of this cultivar are more narrow and curved than the species and have white midribs. Flowers appear in fall; seedheads persist throughout winter.

Miscanthus sinensis 'Kirk Alexander'
KIRK ALEXANDER MAIDENGRASS

☼ ◑ Z4–9 H9–1 ‡6ft (2m) ↔3ft (1m)

This cultivar has tan flowers in fall and yellow banding on the leaves. It is also more compact than the species, making it a good candidate for smaller borders.

Miscanthus sinensis 'Morning Light'
VARIEGATED MAIDENGRASS

☼ ◑ Z5–9 H9–1 ‡↔4ft (1.2m)

Resembles *M. sinensis* 'Gracillimus' except for its narrow white leaf edges. Like other slender-leaved grasses, it looks beautiful when backlit by the sun.

Miscanthus sinensis 'Purpurascens'
EULALIA, FLAME GRASS

☼ ◑ Z5–9 H9–1 ‡↔4ft (1.2m)

Leaves are purplish green with pink midribs in summer, turning reddish orange and purple-red in late fall. Flowers are silvery when they emerge in early fall.

Miscanthus transmorrisonensis
EVERGREEN MAIDENGRASS

☼ ◑ Z7–10 H10–7 ‡7ft (2.1m) ↔4ft (1.2m)

Blooms late summer into fall. Panicles (flower clusters) open in sequence as they form. Originally collected from Taiwan by the Morris Arboretum, PA in 1979.

Phlox paniculata 'Starfire'
STARFIRE GARDEN PHLOX
☼ ◑ ◊ Z4–8 H8–1 ↕3ft (1m) ↔24–40in (60cm–1m)
Bronzy green foliage shows off vivid flowers that
bloom from summer to early fall. Grows best in fertile
soil. Attracts hummingbirds and butterflies.

Phlox subulata 'Candy Stripe'
CANDY STRIPE CREEPING PHLOX
 Ⓝ ☼ ◑ ◊ Z3–8 H8–1 ↕6in (15cm) ↔20in (50cm)
Flowers from late spring to early summer and some-
times again in fall. Evergreen. Prefers fertile soil.
Creeping stems good for groundcover or rock gardens.

Ajuga reptans 'Catlin's Giant'
CATLIN'S GIANT CARPET BUGLE
☼ ◑ ● ◊ Z3–9 H9–1 ↕6in (15cm) ↔3ft (1m)
Has unusually large leaves and flowers from late
spring to early summer. Grows well in most soil types.
Dense and spreading groundcover.

Mentha spicata
SPEARMINT
☼ ◊ Z3–7 H7–1 ↕to 3ft (1m)
↔indefinite
Grow this vigorously spreading
perennial where it can be
contained. Flowers in pink
or white appear during
summer. Valued for
its sweet-smelling
(sometimes pungent)
leaves.

MORE CHOICES

- *Phlox paniculata* (various cultivars)
- *Phlox subulata* (various cultivars)
- *Potentilla fruticosa* 'Tangerine'
- *Sedum acre*
- *Sedum aizoon*
- *Sedum alboroseum mediovariegata*
- *Sedum* 'Autumn Joy'
- *Sedum emarginatum* 'Eco-Mt. Emei'
- *Sedum kamtschaticum* '(various cultivars)
- *Sedum oreganum*
- *Sedum rubrechtii*
- *Sedum sieboldii (Hylotelephium sieboldii)*
- *Sedum spectabile* ((various cultivars)
- *Sedum spurium* (various cultivars)
- *Sedum telephium*
- *Sedum x* (various cultivars)
- *Verbena canadensis* (various cultivars)
- *Yucca baccata*
- *Yucca filamentosa* (various cultivars)

Nepeta cataria
CATNIP
☼ ◑ ◊ Z3–7 H7–1 ↕to 36in (90cm) ↔18in (45cm)
Purple-spotted white flowers appear in summer and
fall above woolly, aromatic foliage.. Grows well in
most soils. Neighborhood cats may flatten your plants.

HERBACEOUS PLANTS

Perennials with yellow flowers

Yellow-flowering perennials bring visual warmth to a garden, especially if they are combined with other warm colors (orange and red). They can also be contrasted with purple flowers: in a predominantly yellow border, purple flowers serve as focal points, and in a predominantly purple border, yellow flowers will be the focal points.

Aquilegia chrysantha
YELLOW COLUMBINE

Ⓝ ☀ ◊ Z3–8 H8–1 ↕4ft (1.2m) ↔2ft (60cm)

Flowers from late spring to late summer. Sepals can sometimes be tinged pink. Vigorous and erect, with midgreen leaves divided into leaflets. Prefers fertile soil.

Corydalis lutea
YELLOW CORYDALIS

☀ ◊ Z5–8 H8–4 ↕↔8–12in (20–30cm)

A beautiful evergreen plant. Flowers from late spring to early fall. Will self-sow readily but can be controlled. Best if grown in fertile to moderately fertile soil.

Heliopsis scabra
SMOOTH OXEYE

Ⓝ ☀ ◊ Z4–9 H9–1 ↕3ft (1m) ↔2ft (60cm)

Bears 1 to 4 flower heads per stalk from midsummer to early fall. Grow in moderately fertile, organic soil. Also known as H. helianthoides subsp. scabra.

Rudbeckia laciniata 'Goldquelle'
GOLDQUELLE CONEFLOWER

Ⓝ ☼ ◊ Z4–8 H8–1 ↕6ft (2m) ↔30in (75cm)

Blooms from midsummer to midfall. Basal leaves are pinnate and lobed, becoming less so as they move up the stem. Also called 'Golden Fountain'.

Rudbeckia nitida 'Herbstonne'
HERBSTONNE CONEFLOWER

Ⓝ ☼ ◊ Z4–8 H8–1 ↕7ft (2.3m) ↔30in (75cm)

The long summer bloom period can be extended into early fall by deadheading. Best grown in fertile soil. Drought-tolerant once established.

MORE CHOICES

- *Bletilla striata* 'Yellow' z5–9 H8–2
- *Coreopsis grandiflora* z4–9 H9–1
- *Coreopsis lanceolata* 'Baby Gold' z4–9 H12–1
- *Coreopsis tripteris* z4–9 H9–1
- *Coreopsis verticillata* 'Zagreb' z4–9 H9–1
- *Digitalis ambigua* z3–8 H8–1
- *Helianthus microcephalus* z4–9 H9–1
- *Helianthus salicifolius* z6–9 H9–6
- *Hemerocallis* 'Stella d'Oro' z3–10 H12–2
- *Iris pumila* 'Salem Yellow' z4–9 H9–1
- *Kniphofia uvaria* 'Malibu Yellow' z5–9
- *Lamiastrum galeobdolon* z4–8 H8–1
- *Ligularia przewalskii* z5–8 H8–1
- *Oenothera biennis* z4–8 H8–1
- *Oenothera missourensis* z5–8 H8–3
- *Oenothera fruticosa* 'Summer Solstice' z4–8 H8–1

Sternbergia lutea
AUTUMN DAFFODIL

☼ ◊◊◊ Z7–9 H9–6 ↕6in (15cm) ↔3in (8cm)

Flowers appear in fall. Plant bulbs in late summer. Best when grown in moderately fertile soil. Prefers dry soil while it is dormant. Excellent rock garden plant.

Mimulus luteus
YELLOW MONKEY FLOWER

☼ ◊ Z7–9 H9–7 ↕↔12in (30cm)

Vigorous, spreading plant blooms spring into summer. Will self-sow. Prefers fertile, organic soil. Can tolerate standing water levels up to 3in (8cm) deep.

Helianthus giganteus 'Sheila's Sunshine'
SHEILA'S SUNSHINE GIANT SUNFLOWER

Ⓝ ☼ ◊◊ Z6–8 H8–3 ↕10ft (3m)

Large flowers up to 1ft (30cm) in diameter appear in late summer. May need staking and protection from wind. Grow in moderately fertile to fertile soil.

Helianthus pauciflorus
STIFF SUNFLOWER

Ⓝ ☼ ◊ Z5–9 H9–5 ↕6ft (2m) ↔24in (60cm)

Flowers are borne in late summer on a clump-forming perennial with lance-shaped leaves. Prefers moderately fertile, organic soil. Also known as *H.rigidus*.

HERBACEOUS PLANTS

Perennials with orange-yellow flowers

Orange-yellow flowers contrast attractively with violet and blue flowers. Interestingly, a border with predominantly orange-yellow flowers will appear to be closer to the viewer, making the bed appear smaller than it actually is. Orange-yellow flowers also work harmoniously with the blue-green foliage that is found in plants such as hostas.

Coreopsis auriculata 'Nana'
DWARF LOBED TICKSEED
Ⓝ ☼ ☼ ◊ Z4–9 H9–1 ‡8in (20cm) ↔24in (60cm)
This compact cultivar has full-size blooms appearing from late spring into summer. Deadheading promotes flowering into fall. Best when grown in fertile soil.

Rudbeckia fulgida 'Deamii'
DEAMII CONEFLOWER
Ⓝ ☼ ☼ ◊ Z4–9 H9–1 ‡3ft (1m) ↔2ft (60cm)
Blooms freely from late summer to midautumn. Prefers moderately fertile, heavy soil. More drought-tolerant than some in the genus.

Rudbeckia hirta
BLACK-EYED SUSAN
Ⓝ ☼ ☼ ◊ Z3–7 H7–1 ‡3ft (1m) ↔18in (45cm)
Flowers freely throughout much of summer. Strains are available in a variety of heights and doubleness. Easy from seed; often short lived. Tolerates heavy clay.

Canna x *generalis*
CANNA LILY
☼ ◊ Z7–11 H12–1 ‡4ft (1.2m) ↔20in (50cm)
Flowers in red, pink, orange and yellow from summer to fall. Deadheading spent flowers will promote continued flowering. They prefer fertile soil.

Kniphofia uvaria 'Royal Standard'
RED-HOT POKER
☼ ◊ Z5–8 H9–4 ‡3–4ft (1–1.2m) ↔2ft (60cm)
Bloom from late summer to early fall. Flowers are red in bud, open orange, and fade to yellow. Best if grown in fertile, organic, sandy soil.

MORE CHOICES

- *Achillea* 'Coronation Gold' z3–9 H9–1
- *Crocosmia* 'Challa' z6–9 H9–2
- *Crocosmia* x *crocosmiflora* 'Constance' z6–9 H9–2
- *Crocosmia masoniorum* z6–9 H9–2
- *Crocosmia* 'Venus' z6–9 H9–2
- *Helenium autumnale* z4–8 H8–1
- *Helenium hoopesii* z3–7 H7–1
- *Helianthus* x *multiflorus* z5–9 H9–5
- *Hemerocallis* 'Midnight Orange' z3–9 H12–1
- *Ligularia dentata* 'Desdemona' z4–8 H8–1
- *Ligularia dentata* 'Othello' z4–8 H8–1
- *Lysimachia punctata* z4–8 H8–1
- *Phlox paniculata* 'Orange Perfection' z4–8 H8–1
- *Rheum palmatum* z4–9 H9–1
- *Rudbeckia fulgida* var. *speciosa* 'Newmanii' z4–9 H9–2
- *Rudbeckia fulgida* var. *sullivanti* z3–9 H9–1
- *Rudbeckia fulgida* var. *sullivantii* 'Goldsturm' z5–9 H9–5
- *Solidago* 'Goldenmosa' z5–9 H9–5

Lilium pardalinum
LEOPARD LILY, PANTHER LILY

Ⓝ ☀ ◊ z5–8 H8–5 ‡↔6–10ft (2–3m)
Blooms May to July in Oregon, where it is native. One of the easiest of the West Coast lilies to grow. Prefers deep, loose, organic soil. Very disease resistant.

Lilium columbianum
AMERICAN LILY,
COLUMBIA TIGER LILY

Ⓝ ☀ ◊ z6–8 H8–6 ‡5–6ft (1.5–1.8m) ↔12–24in (30–60cm)
Stems often bear dozens of blooms during summer. Prefers well drained soil. There is a dwarf variety available for smaller gardens.

Asclepias tuberosa
BUTTERFLY WEED

Ⓝ ☀ ◊ z4–9 H9–2 ‡30in (75cm) ↔18in (45cm)
Blooms in midsummer. Prefers fertile, well-drained loamy soil. Forms a large taproot and is long-lived, so transplant when young. Easy from seed.

Crocosmia 'Emily McKenzie'
EMILY MCKENZIE MONTBRETIA

☀ ◊ z6–9 H9–2 ‡24in (60cm) ↔6–8in (15–20cm)
Flowers in late summer. Prefers moderately fertile, organic soil. Mixes well with shrubs in a border and provides excellent cut flowers.

Perennials with red or pink flowers

Red flowers blend well with flowers in the other two primary colors (blue and yellow) and also work in tandem with equally warm yellow and orange shades. More muted than red, pink works well with others pastels, creating a gentler mood than do pure, more saturated colors. Both pink and red combine very well with complementary green.

Dicentra formosa 'Bacchanal'
BACCHANAL BLEEDING HEART

Ⓝ ☼ ◊ Z4–8 H10–1 ‡18in (45cm) ↔12in (30cm)
Flowers from late spring to early summer. Sometimes reblooms in fall. A wide-spreading perennial good as a woodland groundcover. Prefers fertile, organic soil.

Potentilla astrosanguinea 'Gibson's Scarlet'
GIBSON'S SCARLET HIMALAYAN CINQUEFOIL

☼ ◊ Z4–7 H7–1 ‡3ft (1m) ↔24in (60cm)
Very free-flowering from summer to fall on a clump-forming, semi evergreen plant. Grows in marginally to moderately fertile, gritty soil. Good rock garden plant.

Sidalcea hybrida 'Elsie Heugh'
ELSIE HEUGH PRAIRIE MALLOW

☼ ◊ Z5–8 H8–3 ‡3ft (1m) ↔18in (45cm)
Flowers from early to midsummer. Grow in moderately fertile, organic soil. Cut flower stems back hard after bloom to encourage repeat bloom.

Hemerocallis 'Pardon Me'
PARDON ME DAYLILY

Ⓝ ☼ ◊ Z5–11 H12–1 ‡↔18in (45cm)
A free-flowering repeat bloomer bearing fragrant 3in (7cm) flowers in summer. Attractive arching foliage is deciduous.

Epimedium grandiflorum 'Rose Queen'
ROSE QUEEN BISHOP'S HAT

☼ ◊ Z4–8 H8–2 ‡↔12in (30cm)
Young leaves are dark bronze-purple. Other cultivars bear flowers in shades of white, yellow, and pink. Prefers fertile, organic, well-drained soil. Susceptible to vine weevil and mosaic virus.

Monarda didyma 'Jacob Cline'
JACOB CLINE BEE BALM

☀ ☀ ◌ ◌ Z4–11 H12–1 ↕4ft (1.2m) ↔2ft (60cm)
Blooms mid- to late summer. Grow in moderately fertile, organic, well-drained soil. More resistant to powdery mildew and rust than the species.

MORE CHOICES

- *Achillea millefolium* 'Red' z3–9 H9–1
- *Armeria maritima* 'Bloodstone' z3–9 H9–1
- *Astilbe* 'Straussenfeder' z3–8 H8–2
- *Astilbe* 'Venus' z3–8 H8–2
- *Bergenia* 'Morning Red' z4–8 H8–1
- *Boltonia asteroides* 'Pink Beauty' z4–8 H9–2
- *Canna* x *generalis* 'Cherry Red' z7–11 H12–1
- *Delphinium nudicaule* z5–7 H7–5
- *Delphinium* 'Red Rocket' z3–8 H6–1
- *Dictamnus albus* var. *purpureus* z3–8 H8–1
- *Eremurus robustus* z5–8 H8–5
- *Filipendula rubra* z3–9 H9–1
- *Gaillardia aristata* z3–8 H8–1
- *Geum rivale* z3–7 H7–1
- *Geum triflorum* z1–7
- *Heuchera sanguinea* 'Splendens' z3–8 H8–1
- *Lavatera cachemiiriana* z4–9 H9–1
- *Lobelia cardinalis* z2–8 H8–1
- *Lupinus* x *hybrida* 'My Castle' z4–7 H7–1
- *Lychnis chalcedonica* z4–8 H8–1
- *Malva moschata* z4–8 H8–1
- *Monarda didyma* z4–10 H10–1
- *Monarda didyma* 'Gardenview Scarlet' z4–8 H8–1
- *Paeonia lactiflora* 'Double Red' z3–8 H8–1
- *Paeonia lactiflora* 'Sarah Bernhardt' z3–8 H8–1
- *Penstemon barbatus* 'Prairie Dusk' z4–8 H8–1
- *Penstemon barbatus* 'Prairie Fire' z4–8 H8–1
- *Penstemon digitalis* 'Husker Red' z3–8 H8–1
- *Sidalcea* 'Sheron' z5–7 H8–5
- *Verbena bonariensis* z7–11 H12–7
- *Veronica spicata* 'Red Fox' z3–8 H8–3

Dianthus chinensis
INDIAN PINK

☀ ◌ Z4–8 H8–1 ↕8in (20cm) ↔9in (25cm)
Scentless flowers appear in summer. Other cultivars produce flowers in shades of red and white with variable patterns and fringing. Short-lived perennial.

Kniphofia uvaria
RED-HOT POKER

☀ ☀ ◌ Z6–9 H9–1 ↕4ft (1.2m) ↔24in (60cm)
Blooms from late summer to early fall. Flowers are red in bud, open orange, then fade to yellow. Best if grown in fertile, organic, sandy soil.

Aquilegia formosa
RED COLUMBINE, SCARLET COLUMBINE

Ⓝ ☀ ☀ ◌ Z4–7 H7–1 ↕3ft (1m) ↔18in (45cm)
Flowers appear from late spring to early summer. A very open, airy plant with blue-green foliage. A Northwest native for rocky soil. Self-sows.

Crocosmia x 'Lucifer'
LUCIFER MONTBRETIA

☀ ◌ Z6–9 H9–6 ↕to 3ft (1m) ↔10in (25cm)
This robust hybrid that in blooms midsummer prefers moderately fertile, organic soil. Can be dug up and stored like gladiolus where not hardy.

Perennials with blue flowers

Pure blue is a relatively rare flower color. Much more common are blue-violet flowers, which have a degree of red in them. Like pure blue flowers, they have a calming and cooling effect in a garden bed. Blue and blue-violet flowers contrast well with yellow and orange flowers, as do pure blues with oranges and yellows.

Aquilegia caerulea
ROCKY MOUNTAIN COLUMBINE

Ⓝ ☼ ◐ ◊ Z4–7 H7–1 ↕24in (60cm) ↔12in (30cm)

This upright plant blooms from late spring to midsummer. Flowers are 2in (5cm) across and spurred. A very attractive and popular Northwest native plant.

Verbena hastata
BLUE VERVAIN

Ⓝ ☼ ◐ Z3–9 H9–1 ↕5ft (1.5m) ↔24in (60cm)

Flowers from early summer to early fall on an upright plant. Also available in white. Valuable later-season nectar source for bees and butterflies.

Perovskia atriplicifolia
RUSSIAN SAGE

☼ ◊ Z6–9 H9–6 ↕4ft (1.2m) ↔3ft (1m)

Flowers from summer to early autumn. Bloom period can be extended by deadheading older flowers. Grows well in minimally to moderately fertile soil.

Anchusa azurea
BLUE BUGLOSS, ITALIAN ALKANET

☼ ◊ Z3–8 H8–1 ↕3–5ft (1–1.5m) ↔2ft (60cm)

Flowers appear in early summer on clump-forming, upright plants. Flowers turn from gentian to blue purple with age. Prefers moderately fertile soil.

Sisyrinchium angustifolium
NARROWLEAF BLUE-EYED GRASS

☼ ◊ Z5–8 H8–5 ↕12in (30cm) ↔3in (8cm)

Short-lived individual flowers are borne in succession during summer on a self-seeding, semievergreen, delicate-looking perennial.

Scabiosa columbaria 'Butterfly Blue'
BUTTERFLY BLUE PINCUSHION FLOWER

☼ ◊ Z5–9 H9–3 ↕to 16in (40cm) ↔to 3ft (1m)

Flowers from mid- to late summer. More compact than the species. Prefers moderately fertile soil. Deadhead to extend bloom. Nectar source for bees and butterflies.

Corydalis flexuosa 'China Blue'
CHINA BLUE FUMEWORT

☼ ◊ Z6–8 H8–3 ‡6–8in (16–20cm)
↔8in (20cm)
This deceptively delicate-looking perennial blooms from late spring to summer and may repeat bloom if deadheaded. It prefers moderately fertile, organic soil.

Amsonia tabernaemontana
WILLOW BLUESTAR

Ⓝ ☼ ◊ Z3–9 H9–1 ‡18-24in (45-60cm) ↔12in (30cm)
An erect, clump-forming perennial. Will grow in most soil types but prefers sandy soil. Cut plant back by one-third after it finishes flowering in spring.

MORE CHOICES

- *Anagallis monelii* 'Pacific Blue' Z7–8
- *Aster dumosus* 'Lady in Blue' Z4–8 H8–1
- *Baptisia australis* Z3–9 H9–1
- *Campanula portenschlagiana* (*C. muralis*) Z4–7 H7–1
- *Campanula rotundifolia* Z5–7 H7–3
- *Centaurea montana* 'Blue' Z3–9 H9–1
- *Clematis integrifolia* 'Caerulea' Z3–7 H7–1
- *Delphinium glareosum* Z0–0 H
- *Delphinium tricorne* Z3–8 H7–3
- *Penstemon azureus* Z7–10 H10–7
- *Phlox paniculata* 'Blue Boy' Z4–8 H8–1
- *Rosmarinus officinalis* 'Tuscan Blue' Z9–10 H10–8
- *Salvia azurea* var. *grandiflora* Z9–11 H12–9
- *Veronica spicata* 'Sunny Border Blue' Z3–8 H8–1

Amsonia hubrichtii
NARROW-LEAF BLUESTAR

Ⓝ ☼ ☼ ◊ Z6–8 H8–5 ‡3ft (1m) ↔4ft (1.2m)
Flowers in late spring. Willowlike midgreen leaves turn bright yellow in fall. Tolerant of most soil types. Equally at home in a wildflower garden or border.

Brunnera macrophylla 'Dawson's White'
SIBERIAN BUGLOSS

☼ ◊ Z3–7 H7–1 ‡18in (45cm)
↔24in (60cm)
Flowers from mid- to late spring. Prefers moderately fertile, organic soil. Equally suitable for a woodland or border. Species has deep green leaves.

Campanula isophylla 'Mayi'
MAY'S ITALIAN BELLFLOWER

☼ ◊ Z0 H12–1 ‡4in (10cm) ↔12in (30cm)
Flowers in midsummer over a 2–3 month period. Soft, trailing stems become woody at the base. Best grown in fertile soil. Grown as an annual in areas with frost.

Catananche caerulea
CUPID'S DART

☼ ◊ Z3–8 H8–1 ‡2–36in (50–90cm) ↔12in (30cm)
Blooms from midsummer to autumn. A relatively short-lived, clump-forming perennial, it requires only moderately fertile soil. Intolerant of wet winter soil.

HERBACEOUS PLANTS

Perennials with white or cream flowers

White flowers can be used in borders with great impact, seemingly popping out of or floating above a green background of foliage. They can be used either to rest the eyes when used in quantity or to arrest the eyes when used judiciously in a design. White gardens are hauntingly beautiful on a moonlit night and attract nocturnal moths and other creatures.

Aruncus dioicus
GOATSBEARD

Ⓝ ☼ ◊ Z3–7 H7–1 ‡6ft (2m) ↔4ft (1.2m)
Flowers appear from early to midsummer and make good cut flowers. Fernlike, alternately pinnate, midgreen leaves can grow 3ft long. Best grown in fertile soil.

Dicentra spectabilis 'Alba'
WHITE BLEEDING HEART

☼ ◊ Z3–9 H9–1 ‡4ft (1.2m) ↔18in (45cm)
Flowers appear from late spring to early summer. Plants normally die back to the thick, fleshy roots in midsummer. Prefers fertile, organic soil.

Caltha palustris 'Alba'
WHITE MARSH MARIGOLD

Ⓝ ☼ ◊ Z3–7 H7–1
‡9in (22cm) ↔12in (30cm)
This cultivar is more compact than the yellow-flowered species. Prefers rich soil and open sites. Can grow in standing water to 2in (5cm) deep.

Crambe cordifolia
COLEWORT

☼ ◊ Z6–9 H9–6 ‡to 6ft (2m) ↔4ft (1.2m)
Spectacular blooms rise in a white cloud above the foliage from late spring to midsummer. Most effective when placed toward the back of a border.

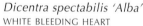

Aruncus aethusifolius
GOATSBEARD

☼ ☼ ◊ Z3–9 H10–1 ‡16in (40cm) ↔12in (30cm)
Flowers appear from early to midsummer, and leaves turn yellow in fall. Can be used as a compact groundcover. Best if grown in fertile soil.

Anemone x hybrida
HYBRID ANEMONE

☼ ◐ ◒ Z4–8 H8–5 ↕5ft (1.5m) ↔2ft (60cm)
Flowers appear from late summer to midautumn in shades of white, pink, and purple. This garden hybrid is also called *A*. x *elegans* and *A. japonica*.

Stokesia laevis 'Alba'
STOKES' ASTER

Ⓝ ☼ ◐ Z5–9 H9–4 ↕↔12–18in (30–45cm)
Flowers appear from midsummer to early autumn above this rosettes of oval-shaped to lance-shaped, evergreen leaves. Prefers light, fertile soil.

Achillea ptarmica 'The Pearl Superior'
THE PEARL SUPERIOR SNEEZEWORT

☼ ◐ Z3–8 H8–1 ↕↔2ft (60cm)
Blooms from early to late summer; the fresh flowers make nice additions to a flower arrangement. The flowers can also be used for dried arrangements.

MORE CHOICES

- *Aruncus dioicus* 'Kneiffii' Z3–7 H7–1
- *Astrantia maxima* 'Alba' Z4–7 H7–1
- *Baptisia alba* Z3–9 H9–2
- *Bletilla striata* 'Alba' Z5–9 H8–2
- *Chelone obliqua* 'Alba'
- *Fuchsia magellanica* 'Alba'
- *Hepatica acutiloba* 'Alba' Z4–9 H9–3
- *Iris cristata* 'Alba' Z4–10 H10–1
- *Lespedeza thunbergii* 'Alba' Z5–11 H12–3
- *Paeonia officinalis* 'Alba Plena' Z3–8 H8–1
- *Salvia verticillata* 'Alba' Z6–8 H8–6
- *Verbena canadensis* 'Alba' Z4–7 H7–1

Liriope muscari 'White'
WHITE LILYTURF

☼ ◐◐ Z6–11 H12–1 ↕18in (45cm) ↔24in (60cm)
This white form of the species makes a good border and path edging. It does well in rock gardens and *en masse* as an evergreen groundcover.

HERBACEOUS PLANTS

Perennials with purple/violet/lilac flowers

All three of the colors in this group harmonize with each other attractively. An entire garden bed could be dedicated to these colors to create a very soothing, serene effect. They contrast nicely when used with plants that have yellow- or white-variegated or yellow-green foliage or those with yellow-green flowers.

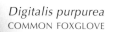

Polemonium caeruleum
JACOB'S LADDER

☼ ◊ Z4–9 H9–1 ↕↔18–24in (40–60cm)

Blooms in early summer. Although not as common, it can also be found with white flowers. Grow in fertile soil. Good border or woodland garden plant.

Digitalis purpurea
COMMON FOXGLOVE

☼ ◊ Z4–8 H9–1 ↕3–5ft (1–1.5m) ↔2ft (60cm)

Rosette-forming plant with a large flower spike that blooms in early summer. These variable plants can be biennial or perennial. Tolerates poor and arid soils.

Aster cordifolius
BLUE WOOD ASTER

Ⓝ ☼ ◆ Z5–8 H8–1 ↕↔2–5ft (60cm–1.5m)

Flowers from late summer to midautumn. Clump-forming plant with long-stalked, oval to heart shaped leaves. Best if grown in moderately fertile soil.

Echinacea purpurea
PURPLE CONEFLOWER

Ⓝ ☼ ◊ Z3–9 H9–3 ↕to 5ft (1.5m) ↔18in (45cm)

Flowers from midsummer to early autumn. Prefers deep, organic soil. Cultivars of this native plant are often more suitable for the border than the species.

Platycodon grandiflorus 'Mariesii'
MARIESII BALLOON FLOWER

☼ ◑ ◊ Z4–9 H9–3 ‡18in (45cm) ↔12in (30cm)

This is a semidwarf subspecies. In late summer, large balloonlike buds precede the 2in flowers. Prefers deep, fertile, loamy soil. Emerges late in spring.

Liriope muscari 'Lilac Beauty'
BIG BLUE LILYTURF

☼ ◑ ◊ Z6–10 H12–1 ‡↔2ft (60cm)

Flowers in fall and are held higher above the foliage than the species. Foliage is evergreen. Prefers a light, moderately fertile soil. Good for garden borders.

Viola labradorica
ALPINE VIOLET

Ⓝ ☼ ◑ ◊ Z2–8 H8–1 ‡3in (8cm) ↔indefinite

Short-spurred flowers appear in spring and summer. above spreading, semievergreen foliage. Prefers fertile, organic soil. Can become invasive.

MORE CHOICES

- *Campanula glomerata* Z3–8 H8–1
- *Campanula medium* Z5–8 H8–5
- *Erica cinerea* 'Atropurpurea' Z6–8 H8–6
- *Nepeta* x *faassenii* 'Six Hills Giant' Z4–8 H8–1
- *Thalictrum dasycarpum* Z3–6 H9–1
- *Trillium erectum* Z4–9 H9–1
- *Viola odorata* Z6–8 H8–6

Liriope muscari
LILYTURF

☼ ◊ Z6–10 H12–1 ‡12in (30cm) ↔18in (45cm)

This evergreen perennial blooms in fall. Flowers of cultivars range from white to violet. Prefers a light, moderately fertile soil. Excellent groundcover.

Geranium viscosissimum
STICKY PURPLE CRANESBILL

Ⓝ ☼ ◊◑ Z4–9 H9–1 ‡↔12–24in (30–60cm)

Blooms from late spring through summer. Clump-forming perennial covered with sticky hairs. A nice addition to a meadow or woodland-edge garden.

Sisyrinchium bellum
BLUE-EYED GRASS

Ⓝ ☼ ◊ Z7–8 H8–7 ‡5in (12cm) ↔4in (10cm)

Flowers during the summer among narrow, linear, semievergreen foliage. Self-sows freely. This Northwest native prefers marginally to moderately fertile soil.

Winter- and early spring-flowering perennials

One of the most anxious times of the horticultural year for avid northern gardeners is right after the holidays, as they wait for some evidence of spring to lift them out of winter gardening purgatory. Here are some spirit-lifting plants that perform just when winter-weary gardeners need a boost to get them ready for the season ahead.

Helleborus argutifolius
CORSICAN HELLEBORE
☀ ◯ Z6–9 H9–6 ↕24in (60cm) ↔18in (45cm)
This species works well naturalized or in a woodland garden. Best if grown in highly organic soils. Also called *H. corsicus* (it is native to Corsica).

Trillium erectum
PURPLE TRILLIUM
Ⓝ ☀ ☀ ◐ ◑ Z4–9 H7–3 ↕t20in (50cm) ↔12in (30cm)
Prefers soil rich in organic matter. Mulch in fall with leaf mold. The flowers are rather malodorous. Excellent in a woodland garden.

MORE CHOICES

- *Aurinia saxitilis* Z4–8 H8–1
- *Bergenia cordifolia* Z3–8 H8–1
- *Brunnera macrophylla* Z3–7 H7–1
- *Cardamine diphylla* Z4–8 H8–3
- *Chionodoxa lucilae* Z3–9 H9–1
- *Cyclamen coum* Z5–9 H9–5
- *Dicentra formosa* Z4–8 H10–1
- *Eranthis hyemalis* Z4–9 H9–1
- *Helleborus* (Royal Heritage Strain) Z4–9 H9–1

Galanthus nivalis
COMMON SNOWDROP
☀ ◐ ◯ Z3–8 H8–1 ↕4–6in (10–15cm) ↔2–3in (5–8cm)
A bulbous perennial native from the Pyrenees to Ukraine. Suitable for naturalizing in grass or in a woodland but also at home in borders and rock gardens.

Euphorbia polychroma
CUSHION SPURGE
☀ ◐ Z5–9 H9–5 ↕↔20in (50cm)
Bright yellow-green flowerheads are showy for a long time. Foliage turns red, orange, and purple in fall. Prefers light, organic soil, in which it will self-sow.

Trillium ovatum
COAST TRILLIUM
Ⓝ ☀ ☀ ◐ ◑ Z5–8 H8–5 ↕10–15in (25–38cm)
The spring flowers often turn pink or red. Prefers acidic to neutral soil rich in organic matter. Mulch in fall with leaf mold.

Trillium chloropetalum
GIANT WAKE ROBIN
Ⓝ ☀ ☀ ◐ Z6–9 H9–6 ↕to 16in (40cm) ↔to 8in (20cm)
Fragrant flowers appear in spring. Mulch in fall with leaf mold. Like most trilliums, it prefers organic soil. Lovely under the cover of trees.

Iberis sempervirens
CANDYTUFT
☼ ◊ Z5–9 H9–3 ‡12in (30cm) ↔24in (60cm)
A spreading, evergreen, long-blooming perennial, it is best grown in marginally to moderately fertile soil. Excellent in a rock garden.

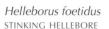

Helleborus foetidus
STINKING HELLEBORE
☼ ◊ Z6–9 H9–6
‡↔18in (45cm)
Although the foliage is rank when bruised, the flowers can have a pleasant aroma. A nice complement to spring-flowering bulbs. Often self-sows.

Phlox subulata 'Candy Stripe'
CANDY STRIPE CREEPING PHLOX
Ⓝ ☼·☼ ◊ Z3–8 H8–1 ‡2–6in (5–15cm)
↔20in (50cm) or more
A dense evergreen or semi-evergreen that prefers fertile soil. Makes a nice addition to the rock garden.

MORE CHOICES

- *Helleborus orientalis* Z4–8 H8–3
- *Iberis sempervirens* Z5–9 H9–3
- *Iris germanica* Z3–9 H9–1
- *Lamiastrum galeobdolon* Z4–8 H8–1
- *Mertensia virginica* Z3–7 H7–1
- *Phlox divaricata* Z4–8 H8–1
- *Phlox pilosa* Z4–9 H9–3
- *Phlox speciosa ssp. occidentalis* Z5–8 H8–5
- *Phlox stansburyi* Z5–8 H8–5
- *Phlox stolonifera* Z4–8 H8–1
- *Pulmonaria angustifolia* Z2–7 H8–1
- *Trillium catesbaei* Z7–9 H8–1
- *Trillium erectum* Z4–9 H9–1
- *Trillium grandiflorum* Z4–7 H7–3
- *Trillium luteum* Z5–7 H7–4
- *Trillium species* Z2–9 H8–1
- *Trillium sessile* Z4–8 H8–1

Pulmonaria saccharata 'Mrs. Moon'
MRS. MOON LUNGWORT
☼·☼ ◊ Z3–8 H8–1 ‡12in (30cm) ↔24in (60cm)
Flowers of this clump-forming, rhizomatous cultivar start as pink buds. Grow in organic fertile, organic soil. Remove old leaves after flowering.

Cyclamen coum
HARDY CYCLAMEN
☼ ◊ Z5–9 H9–5 ‡to 4in (10cm) ↔2–4in (5–10cm)
Prefers moderately fertile, organic soil. Grows well under trees and large shrubs and benefits from a mulch of leaf mold after the leaves die back.

Helleborus niger
CHRISTMAS ROSE
☼ ◊ Z3–8 H8–1 ‡↔12in (30cm)
A clump-forming plant with overwintering dark green, leathery leaves. Flowers can also be flushed with pink. Prefers fertile organic soil. Very early blooming.

Late spring/early summer-blooming perennials

Spring (and sometimes even early summer) is the time when many gardens often look worse for the wear after a long winter. What better way to be welcomed back out into the garden than by these floriferous harbingers of spring and summer? They breathe life into your garden as the rising temperatures and finer weather bring you back outdoors.

Geranium sanguineum
BLOODY CRANESBILL
☼ ◊ Z3–8 H8–1 ↕10in (25cm) ↔12in (30cm)
Dense, clump-forming plant with spreading rhizomes. Prefers moderately fertile soil. Divide every few years in spring to keep plants vigorous and healthy.

Dicentra cucullaria
DUTCHMAN'S BREECHES
Ⓝ ☼ ◊ Z4–8 H8–1 ↕8in (20cm) ↔10in (25cm)
Flowers are sometimes pink-flushed on this clumping, tuberous perennial that dies back to the ground after flowering. Best grown in fertile, organic soil.

MORE CHOICES

- *Acanthus mollis* Z7–11 H12–7
- *Aquilegia caerulea* Z4–7 H7–1
- *Aquilegia flavescens* Z4–7 H7–1
- *Aquilegia formosa* Z4–7 H7–1
- *Caltha palustris* Z3–7 H7–1
- *Dianthus plumarius* Z4–9 H9–1
- *Geum rivale* Z3–7 H7–1
- *Geum triflorum* Z1–7 H7–1
- *Paeonia lactiflora* Z3–8 H8–1
- *Paeonia officinalis* Z3–8 H8–1
- *Phlox diffusa* Z4–8 H8–1
- *Phlox subulata* Z3–8 H8–1
- *Thalictrum aquilegifolium* Z5–9 H9–5
- *Thalictrum dasycarpum* Z4–8 H8–1
- *Veronica peduncularis* Z6–8 H8–6

Veronica peduncularis
VERONICA
☼ ◊ Z6–8 H8–6 ↕4in (10cm) ↔24in (60cm)
Branching rhizomes bear freely branched stems. Regular deadheading promotes a longer bloom period. Grows best in light, moderately fertile soil.

Baptisia australis
FALSE INDIGO
Ⓝ ☼ ◊ Z3–9 H9–1 ↕30in (75cm) ↔24in (60cm)
Seed pods are ornamental. Best used in the middle or back of a border or as a specimen plant. This member of the pea family attracts native birds.

Trollius laxus
AMERICAN GLOBEFLOWER
Ⓝ ☼ ☼ ◊ ◔ Z3–7 H8–5 ↕20in (50cm) ↔2ft (60cm)
Often found growing naturally in subalpine meadow communities, it adapts well to growing in rock gardens. Sometimes called *T. americanus*.

Thalictrum delavayi 'Hewitt's Double'
CHINESE MEADOW-RUE
☼ ◊ Z6–8 H8–4 ↕4ft (1.2m) ↔24in (60cm)
The flowers lack stamens, which are replaced with mauve sepals. An erect, clump-forming, rhizomatous plant.. Divide every 2 to 3 years to keep it vigorous.

Armeria maritima 'Bloodstone'
COMMON THRIFT

Ⓝ ☼ ◊ Z3–9 H9–1 ‡4in (10cm) ↔6in (15cm)

Clump-forming, evergreen plants bear an abundance of flowers. Prefers marginally to moderately fertile soil. Divide every 4 to 5 years as the center dies out.

Amsonia tabernaemontana
WILLOW BLUESTAR

Ⓝ ☼ ◊ Z3–9 H9–1 ‡24in (60cm) ↔12in (30cm)

An erect, bushy, clump-forming perennial that grows in most soil types but does best in sandy soil. Cut back by one-third after it finishes flowering.

Phlox maculata 'Natascha'
MEADOW PHLOX

Ⓝ ☼ ☼ ◊ Z4–8 H8–1

‡2ft (60cm) ↔18in (45cm)

An upright, clumping plant best grown in fertile soil. Try to keep foliage dry when watering to decrease mildew. Deadheading promotes repeat bloom.

Aquilegia chrysantha
YELLOW COLUMBINE

Ⓝ ☼ ◊ Z3–8 H8–1 ‡4ft (1.2m) ↔2ft (60cm)

A vigorous, erect plant with midgreen leaves divided into three leaflets. Sepals can sometimes be tinged pink. Prefers fertile soil but tolerates less fertility.

Aquilegia caerulea
ROCKY MOUNTAIN COLUMBINE

Ⓝ ☼ ☼ ◊ Z4–7 H7–1 ‡24in (60cm) ↔12in (30cm)

Upright plants live at most for 4 to 5 years, but their self-sowing nature guarantees plenty of replacements. Used in the breeding of many hybrid columbines.

Aquilegia canadensis
CANADIAN COLUMBINE

Ⓝ ☼ ☼ ◊ Z3–8 H8–1 ‡3ft (1m) ↔12in (30cm)

A delicate-looking perennial with dark green leaves divided into leaflets. Prefers fertile soil, but too much fertility causes lanky growth. Often self-sows.

HERBACEOUS PLANTS

Midsummer/late summer-blooming perennials

These perennials carry the baton from earlier- flowering plants deep into the heart of the growing season. They are particularly rugged perennials, thriving in the warm and long dog days of summer. Their colors range across the floral spectrum, giving you ample material to achieve beautiful effects in your garden.

HERBACEOUS PLANTS

Rudbeckia maxima
GREAT CONEFLOWER

Ⓝ ☀ ◐ ◊ Z4–8 H8–1 ‡5–6ft (1.5–2m) ↔2ft (60cm)

Flowers appear in late summer. An erect and stiff plant with oval, gray-green leaves. Prefers moderately fertile soil. Good for the back of a border.

Filipendula rubra
QUEEN OF THE PRAIRIE

Ⓝ ☀ ● Z3–9 H9–1 ‡6–8ft (2–2.5m) ↔4ft (1.2m)

Fragrant flowers in midsummer. A spreading plant, it forms large clumps of irregularly cut, pinnate leaves. Prefers moderately fertile, leafy soil.

MORE CHOICES

- *Campanula rotundifolia* Z5–7 H7–3
- *Cimicifuga racemosa* Z3–8 H12–1
- *Coreopsis grandiflora* Z4–9 H9–1
- *Coreopsis lanceolata* Z4–9 H9–1
- *Coreopsis rosea* Z4–8 H8–1
- *Delphinium nudicaule* Z5–7 H7–5
- *Deschampsia caespitosa viviparia* Z0 H9–2
- *Dianthus deltoides* Z3–10 H10–1
- *Digitalis purpurea* Z4–8 H9–1

Salvia uliginosa
BOG SAGE

☀ ◐ ● Z8–11 H12–7 ‡to 6ft (2m) ↔36in (90cm)

A clump-forming, rhizomatous perennial with deeply toothed, midgreen, aromatic leaves. Flowers from late summer to midfall. Flowers can also be white.

Catananche caerulea
CUPID'S DART

Ⓝ ☀ ◊ Z3–8 H8–1 ‡3ft (1m) ↔12in (30cm)

A relatively short-lived, clump-forming perennial that Requires only moderate fertilization. Sensitive to wet winter soil. Blooms from midsummer to fall.

Asclepias syriaca
BUTTERFLY WEED

Ⓝ ☀ ◊ Z3–9 H9–2 ‡3ft (1m)

A vigorous, spreading plant with upright stems. Flowers are scented and appear in summer. Ornamental fruit are pendulous and softly spiny. Prefers loamy soil.

Oenothera fruticosa
SUNDROPS

Ⓝ ☀ ● Z4–8 H8–1 ‡3ft (1m) ↔12in (30cm)

Flowers from late spring to late summer on erect, branching plants. Foliage turns dull red after fall frosts. Prefers moderately fertile to fertile soil.

Tradescantia virginiana
HYBRID SPIDERWORT

Ⓝ ☼ ◐ ◗ Z5–9 H9–5 ↕24in (60cm) ↔24in (60cm)
Tufted, branching plants. Flowers from early summer to early fall in shades of blue, purple,and rose-pink as well as white. Deadheading encourages repeat bloom.

Heliopsis scabra
HELIOPSIS

Ⓝ ☼ ◗ Z4–9 H9–1 ↕3ft (1m) ↔2ft (60cm)
Bears 1–4 flowerheads per flower stalk from midsummer to early fall. Grow in moderatley fertile, organic soil. Also known as *H. helianthoides* subsp. *scabra*.

MORE CHOICES

- *Euphorbia marginata* Z13–15 H12–1
- *Gypsophila repens* Z4–7 H7–1
- *Hemerocallis* ssp. Z3–8 H12–1
- *Heuchera americana* Z4–8 H8–1
- *Heuchera micrantha* Z4–7 H8–2
- *Heuchera sanguinea* Z3–8 H8–1
- *Kniphofia uvaria* Z5–9 H9–1
- *Liatris spicata* Z4–9 H9–1
- *Salvia guaranitica* Z5–8 H8–5
- *Salvia officinalis* Z5–8 H8–5
- *Salvia splendens* Z9–11 H12–1
- *Stokesia laevis* Z5–9 H9–5
- *Thalictrum delavayi* Z4–7 H7–1
- *Thalictrum rochebrunianum* 'Lavender Mist' Z4–11 H12–3
- *Veronica spicata* Z3–8 H8–1

Alchemilla mollis
LADY'S MANTLE

Ⓝ ☼ ◊ Z4–7 H7–1 ↕↔20in (50cm)
Tiny flowers produced from early summer to early fall can be used in fresh and dreid arrangements. This sturdy, drought-tolerant groundcover prefers organic soil.

Liatris pychnostachya
CAT-TAIL GAYFEATHER

Ⓝ ☼ ◊ Z3–9 H9–2 ↕5ft (1.5m) ↔18in (45cm)
Flowers from midsummer to early fall above densely clustered, basal leaves. 'Alexander' is less likely to need staking. Prefers moderately fertile soil.

Boltonia asteroides
CHRISTMAS ROSE

Ⓝ ☼ ◐ ◊ Z4–8 H9–1 ↕6ft (2m) ↔3ft (1m)
A strong-stemmed plant with blue-green leaves and flowers from late summer into early fall in white, lilac, or pinkish purple. Divide every few years.

Astilbe x arendsii
FALSE GOATSBEARD

☼ ◐ ◊ ◗ Z4–9 H9–1
↕3ft (1m) ↔2ft (60cm)
Flowers appear in midsummer. Prefers organic soil. Divide every four years to maintain bloom quality. Many cultivars have arisen from this hybrid.

HERBACEOUS PLANTS

Fall-blooming perennials

After the glut of spring and summer flowers has passed, many gardens contain little or no floral interest. If you add these gems to your borders, you will keep garden interest going into some of the nicest weather of the year. Those returning from summer vacations will believe you didn't miss a thing while being away from home.

Colchicum 'Waterlily'
AUTUMN CROCUS

☼ ◊ Z4–9 H9–1 ↕6in (15cm) ↔8in (20cm)
This is just one of many *Colchicum* selections to choose from. It prefers deep, fertile, well-drained soil that is not too dry. Plant in early summer.

Aster dumosus
PACIFIC HYBRID ASTER

Ⓝ ☼ ◊◊ Z4–8 H8–1 ↕↔12–36in (30–90cm)
Leaves are linear, and flowers can be white, pink, to the pictured lavender-blue. Often hybridized with *A. novi-belgii* but labeled as *A.* x *dumosus*.

Cyclamen hederifolium (C. neapolitanum)
HARDY CYCLAMEN

☼ ◊ Z5 7 H9–7 ↕4in (10cm) ↔4–6in (10–15cm)
Scented flowers bloom in shades of pink or white. Leaf shape ranges from triangular to heart shaped. Prefers moderately fertile, organic soil.

Molina caerulea
PURPLE MOOR GRASS

☼ ◊ Z4–8 H8–1 ↕8ft (2.2m) ↔2ft (60cm)
Slow-growing grass bears dense purple, tufted flower clusters that age to tan. Grows well in most soils. Works well in a mixed border or woodland garden.

MORE CHOICES

- Aconitum carmichaelii Z3–8 H8–3
- Aster laevis Z4–8 H8–4
- Aster novae-angliae Z4–8 H8–1
- Cortaderia selloana Z4–11 H9–7
- Eupatorium maculatum Z5–11 H9–1
- Eupatorium purpureum Z3–9 H9–1
- Gentiana andrewsii Z3–7 H8–1
- Ligularia dentata Z4–8 H8–1

Pennisetum alopecuroides 'Little Bunny'
LITTLE BUNNY DWARF MOUNTAIN GRASS

☼ ◊ Z5–9 H9–1 ↕10in (25cm) ↔12in (30cm)
A very nice compact form of the species, this can be used to soften the foreground of a bed. Prefers poor to moderately fertile soil.

Solidago rugosa 'Fireworks'
GOLDENROD

Ⓝ ☼◑ ◊ Z4–9 H9–1 ↕4ft (1.2m) ↔3–4ft (1–1.2m)
More compact than the species. Flowers appear in late summer and are attractive to bees and butterflies. Prefers marginal to moderately fertile soil.

Nerine bowdenii
GUERNSEY LILY

☼ ◊ Z8–10 H10–8 ↕18in (45cm) ↔3in (8cm)
Lightly scented flowers, also in white, red, and orange, appear in autumn. Do not divide unless very crowded. Benefits from the heat radiated off of a sunny wall.

Ceratostigma plumbaginoides
LEADWORT, PLUMBAGO
☼ ◊ Z6–9 H9–6 ↕18in (45cm) ↔12 in (30cm)
A spreading, woody-based perennial with contrasting
red-tinted foliage in autumn. Prefers light, moderately
fertile soil. Good rock garden plant.

Anemone x hybrida
JAPANESE WINDFLOWER
☼ ◊ ⌖ Z4–8 H8–5 ↕5ft (1.5m) ↔2ft (60cm)
Flower color occurs in shades of white, pink, and
purple. Prefers fertile organic soil. This garden hybrid
is also named *A.* x *elegans* and *A. japonica*.

Hosta 'Gold Standard'
PLANTAIN LILY
☼ ☼ ◊ Z3–8 H9–2 ↕30in (75cm) ↔3ft (1m)
Funnel-shaped, lavender-blue flowers bloom high
above the foliage. Can be used as an accent plant or
groundcover under deciduous trees. Best in fertile soil.

MORE CHOICES

- *Miscanthus* spp. Z5–9 H8–1
- *Schizachyrium scoparium* Z4–8 H9–1
- *Schizostylis coccinea* Z7–9 H9–7
- *Sedum* x 'Frosty Morn' Z4–9 H9–1
- x *Solidaster luteus* Z5–8 H8–5
- *Tricyrtis hirta* Z4–9 H9–1
- *Vernonia noveboracensis* Z4–8 H8–3

Aster divaricatus
WHITE WOOD ASTER
Ⓝ ☼ ◊ Z4–8 H9–1 ↕↔24in (60cm)
Clump-forming plant with arching and wiry, blackish
purple stems and midgreen leaves. Best when grown
in moderately fertile soil. Also known as *A. corymbosus*.

Cimicifuga simplex 'White Pearl'
KAMCHATKA BUGBANE
☼ ◊◊ Z4–8 H12–1 ↕3ft (1m) ↔24in (60cm)
Clump-forming perennial with light green to purplish
green, irregularly lobed leaves. Grow in fertile, organic
soil. Excellent plant for a woodland garden.

Hylotelephium sieboldii
OCTOBER STONECROP
☼ ◊ Z3–8 H8–1 ↕4in (10cm) ↔8in (20cm)
Pink, star-shaped flowers bloom in flat-topped clusters.
A good rock garden or mixed border plant,and it grows
nicely in containers. Prefers moderately fertile soil.

Eupatorium perfoliatum
BONESET
Ⓝ ☼ ◊ Z3–9 H8–1 ↕to 5ft (1.5m) ↔3ft (1m)
White flower heads are often purple tinged and
provide nectar to bees and butterflies. This clump-
forming perennial prefers moderately fertile soil.

Perennials with extended bloom season

These perennials provide the most bang for your buck, often without the deadheading needed to extend bloom on other perennials. The plants featured here normally bloom for up to a quarter of the year, while the average perennial blooms for 2 to 4 weeks at the most. They straddle growing seasons, either from spring to summer or summer into fall.

Geranium pratense
MEADOW CRANESBILL

☼ ◑ ◊ ◗ Z4–8 H8–1 ‡30in (75cm) ↔24in (60cm)
Flower colors range from blue or violet to white. Blooms appear early to midsummer. Best when grown in moderately fertile organic soil. Self-sows freely.

Dianthus deltoides
MAIDEN PINK

☼ ◊ Z3–10 H10–1 ‡6in (15cm) ↔12in (30cm)
Scentless flowers borne in summer. Flower colors can range from white, to deep pink and red. A mat-forming plant that makes a good groundcover. Self-sows.

Astrantia major 'Lars'
LARS GREAT MASTERWORT

☼ ◑ ◊ Z4–7 H7–1 ‡3ft (1m) ↔18in (45cm)
Flowers fromearly to midsummer on a clump-forming perennial with deeply lobed leaves. Prefers fertile, organic soil. Flowers can be dried for arrangements.

Boltonia asteroides
WHITE DOLL'S DAISY

Ⓝ ☼ ◑ ◊ Z4–8 H9–1 ‡6ft (2m) ↔3ft (1m)
Flowers in white or pinkish purple bloom from late summer into early fall. A strong-stemmed plant with lance-shaped, blue-green leaves. Divide every few years.

Aster x frikartii 'Mönch'
MÖNCH MICHAELMAS DAISY

☼ ◑ ◊ Z4–8 H8–1 ‡30in (75cm) ↔18in (45cm)
Flowers appear from late summer to early fall. Upright plant with dark green oval-shaped leaves. Best if grown in moderately fertile soil. Tolerates clay.

Phlomis fruticosa
JERUSALEM SAGE

☼ ◊ Z8–9 H9–8 ‡↔5ft (1.5m)
This mound-forming plant resembles culinary sage, its close relative. Flowers appear early to midsummer. Leaf undersides are woolly. Prefers fertile soil.

Campanula lactiflora
BELLFLOWER, MILKY BELLFLOWER

☼ ◑ ◐ ◊ Z5–7 H7–5 ‡4ft (1.2m) ↔2ft (60cm)
A vigorous, upright perennial that flowers freely from early summer to early fall. Works well in both a herbaceous border or in a naturalistic garden.

Coreopsis auriculata
LOBED TICKSEED

Ⓝ ☼ ◐ ◊ z4–9 H9–1 ↕32in (80cm) ↔24in (60cm)
Flowers appear from late spring into summer. Erect
stems bear oval as well as palmately lobed, midgreen
leaves. Best when grown in fertile soil.

Mimulus luteus
YELLOW MONKEY FLOWER

☼ ● z7–9 H9–7 ↕↔12in (30cm)
Vigorous, spreading plant blooms from spring into
summer. Will self-sow. Prefers fertile, organic soil.
Tolerates standing water levels up to 3in (8cm).

Mimulus lewisii
PINK MONKEY FLOWER

Ⓝ ☼ ◊ z5–8 H8–5 ↕24in (60cm) ↔18in (45cm)
Vigorous, spreading plant blooms spring into summer.
Will self sow. Prefers fertile, organic soil. Can tolerate
standing water levels up to 3in (8cm).

Corydalis lutea
YELLOW CORYDALIS

☼ ◊ z5–8 H8–4 ↕↔8–12 (20–30cm)
Flowers from late spring to early autumn. Will self-sow
readily. Best if grown in moderately fertile to fertile
soil. A beautiful evergreen plant.

Tradescantia virginiana
HYBRID SPIDERWORT

☼ ☀ ● z5–9 H9–5 ↕16–24in (40–60cm)
↔18–24in (45–60cm)
Flowers from early summer to
early fall bloom in shades of
blue, purple, and rose-pink
as well as white. These are
tuftedplants with erect,
branching stems.

MORE CHOICES

- *Achillea filipendula* 'Parker's Variety'
  z3–9 H9–1
- *Achillea millefolium* and cultivars
  z3–9 H9–1
- *Achillea millefolium* 'Cerise Queen'
  z3–9 H9–1
- *Achillea ptarmica* 'The Pearl Superior'
  z3–8 H8–1
- *Chrysogonum virginianum* z5–9 H9–2
- *Coreopsis grandiflora* z4–9 H9–1
- *Coreopsis integrifolia* z7–9 H9–5
- *Coreopsis lanceolata* z4–9 H9–1
- *Coreopsis rosea* z4–8 H8–1
- *Coreopsis verticillata* and cultivars
  z4–9 H9–1
- *Dianthus caryophyllus* z7–10 H10–7
- *Dicentra eximia* and cultivars z4–8 H8–4
- *Gaura lindheimeri* z6–9 H9–6
- *Geranium endressii* z5–8 H8–5
- *Geranium macrorrhizum* z4–8 H8–1
- *Geranium sanguineum* and cultivars
  z3–8 H8–1
- *Geum triflorum* z1–7
- *Hemerocallis sp.* z3–8 H12–1
- *Kniphofia uvaria* z5–9 H9–1
- *Mimulus ringens* z4–9 H9–4
- *Oenothera missourensis* z5–8 H8–3
- *Phygelius* x *rectus* and cultivars z8–9 H9–8

HERBACEOUS PLANTS

Fragrant perennials

Nothing rounds out a garden better than plants that engage the sense of smell. Some plants have delightful fragrance during the day when the sun is warm and the air is still, while others emit often powerful fragrances as evening approaches or at night. These flowers attract not only the human nose but also pollinating insects, including butterflies and moths.

Amsonia hubrictii
NARROW-LEAF BLUE-STAR

Ⓝ ☼ ◐ ◊ Z6–8 H8–5 ‡3ft (1m) ↔4ft (1.2m)

Sky blue flowers emit a very delicate scent in spring. Shrubby mounds of willowy leaves turn bright yellow in fall. Tolerates dry, clay soils.

Monarda fistulosa
WILD BEE BALM

Ⓝ ☼ ◊ Z3–9 H9–1 ‡4ft (1.2m) ↔18in (45cm)

Flowers from midsummer through early fall vary from light pink to lilac purple. Spicily aromatic leaves are reminiscent of thyme and oregano. Clump-forming.

Dodecatheon meadia
SHOOTING STARS

Ⓝ ☼ ◐ ◊ Z4–8 H8–1 ‡8in (20cm) ↔6in (15cm)

Lightly fragrant flowers appear to explode over low rosettes of midgreen foliage in mid- and late spring. Provide well-drained, organic soil.

Crambe cordifolia
COLEWORT

☼ ◊ Z6–9 H9–6 ‡to 6ft (2m) ↔4ft (1.2m)

A mass of spectacular, honey-scented blooms rises above the foliage from late spring to midsummer. Best placed toward the back of a border.

MORE CHOICES

- Agrimonia odorata Z0 H8–1
- Amaryllis belledonna 'Hathor' Z7–11 H12–7
- Amsonia tabernaemontana Z3–9 H9–1
- Aquilegia caerulea Z4–7 H7–1
- Aquilegia canadensis Z3–8 H8–1
- Aquilegia chrysantha Z3–8 H8–1
- Aquilegia cultivars Z4–7 H7–1
- Centaurea montana Z3–9 H9–1
- Cheiranthus cheiri Z3–7 H7–1
- Clematis integrifolia 'Caerulea' Z3–7 H7–1
- Convallaria majalis Z2–7 H7–1
- Coreopsis lanceolata Z4–9 H9–1
- Coreopsis tripteris Z4–9 H9–1
- Cosmos atrosanguineus Z8–11 H12–8
- Dianthus barbatus Z3–8 H9–1
- Dianthus caryophyllus Z7–10 H10–7
- Dianthus chinensis Z9–11 H12–1
- Dianthus plumarius and cultivars Z4–9 H9–1
- Filipendula ulmaria Z3–9 H9–1
- Hedychium coronarium Z7–11 H12–6
- Hesperis matronalis Z4–9 H9–1
- Hosta 'Honeybells' Z3–9 H9–1
- Hosta plantaginea 'Aphrodite' Z3–9 H9–1
- Hosta plantaginea Z3–9 H9–1
- Iberis sempervirens Z5–9 H9–3

Achillea ptarmica 'The Pearl Superior'
THE PEARL SUPERIOR SNEEZEWORT

☼ ◊ Z3–8 H8–1 ‡↔30in (75cm)

Blooms from early to late summer. The flowers make nice additions to a fresh flower arrangement and can also be used for dried arrangements.

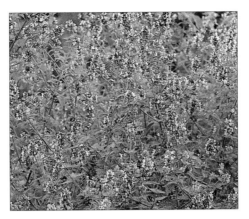

Nepeta cataria
CATNIP
☼ ☼ ◊ Z3–7 H7–1 ‡to 36in (90cm) ↔18in (45cm)
Purple-spotted white flowers bloom in summer and
fall. Woolly foliage is aromatic. Grows well in most
soils. Neighborhood cats may flatten your plants.

Nepeta x *faassenii*
CATMINT
☼ ◊ Z4–8 H8–1 ‡↔18in (45cm)
Flowers from early summer to early autumn. Cut back
scented foliage after flowering to keep plants tight and
encourage repeat flowering. Also known as *N. mussinii*.

Convallaria majalis var. *rosea*
PINK LILY-OF-THE-VALLEY
☼ ◊ Z2–7 H7–1 ‡6in (15cm) ↔indefinite
Spreading rhizomes give rise to scented flowers in
spring. Prefers organic soil (but tolerates clay) and an
application of leaf mold in fall.

MORE CHOICES

- *Lilium candidum* Z6–9 H9–6
- *Lilium* 'Cinnabar' Z3–8 H8–1
- *Lilium pumilum* Z3–8 H8–1
- *Nicotiana alata* Z0 H12–1
- *Oenothera missourensis* Z5–8 H8–3
- *Oenothera speciosa* Z5–8 H8–1
- *Paeonia lactiflora* 'Sarah Bernhardt'
  Z3–8 H8–1
- *Palianthes tuterosa* Z7–11 H11–7
- *Phlox divaricata* Z4–8 H8–1
- *Phlox maculata* 'Alpha' Z5–8 H8–1
- *Primula alpicola* Z4–8 H8–1
- *Primula vulgaris* Z4–8 H8–1
- *Thermopsis caroliniana* Z6–9 H9–3
- *Viola odorata* Z6–8 H8–6
- *Yucca filamentosa* Z4–11 H12–5
- *Yucca glauca* Z5–10 H10–5

Asclepias incarnata
SWAMP MILKWEED
Ⓝ ☼ ◊ Z3–8 H8–1 ‡4ft (1.2m) ↔24in (60cm)
Fragrant blooms appear from midsummer to early
autumn. Prefers fertile soil. Susceptible to aphids and
mealybugs, especially when in bloom.

Thalictrum flavum subsp. *glaucum*
DUSTY MEADOW RUE
☼ ☼ ◊◊ Z6–8 H8–4 ‡3ft (1m) ↔24in (60cm)
Stems are more blue-green and flowers are paler than
the species. Fragrant flowers appear in summer and
may need staking. Prefers soil rich in organic matter.

Dianthus gratianopolitanus
MAIDEN PINK
☼ ◊ Z3–10 H10–1 ‡6in (15cm) ↔12in (30cm)
Very fragrant, single flowers are produced during
summer. Good for the edge of a border or for a rock
garden. Also known as *D. caesius*.

HERBACEOUS PLANTS

Evergreen perennials

Evergreen plants are an important component of a well-designed landscape, giving it year-long structure. However, evergreen perennials are definitely in the minority in the world of herbaceous plants, but within this minority are plants that have four-season interest. Almost all of these perennials have the added bonus of showy flowers.

Arum italicum
LORDS AND LADIES
☼ ◐ ◊ Z7–9 H9–3 ↕12in (30cm) ↔6in (15cm)
Pale greenish white spathes surround early summer blooms. Fruit (shown) appear in fall. Arrow-shaped leaves have white veins. Prefers organic soil.

Hemerocallis x 'Mini Pearl'
MINI PEARL DAYLILY
Ⓝ ☼ ◊ Z5–11 H12–1 ↕18in (45cm) ↔24in (60cm)
Repeat bloomer that starts in midsummer and continues periodically until fall. Semi-evergreen in colder climates. Best transplanted in spring.

Carex morrowii 'Ice Dance'
ICE DANCE JAPANESE SEDGE
☼ ◐ ◊ Z5–9 H12–1 ↕20in (30cm) ↔12in (30cm)
Bears panicles of green and brown flower spikes in late spring. Clump-forming perennial with short rhizomes. Best grown in fertile soil.

Dianthus deltoides
MAIDEN PINK
Ⓝ ☼ ◊ Z3–10 H10–1 ↕6in (15cm) ↔12in (30cm)
Scentless flowers are borne in summer on a mat-forming plant that makes a good groundcover. Flower colors range from white to deep pink and red. Self-sows..

Hemerocallis x 'Summerwine'
SUMMERWINE DAYLILY
☼ ◊ Z5–11 H12–1 ↕30in (75cm)
Flowers in midsummer. A great accent plant for the middle of a mixed border, or grow it in large sweeps. Prefers fertile soil and is best transplanted in spring.

HERBACEOUS PLANTS

MORE CHOICES

- *Acanthus mollis* z7–11 H12–7
- *Ajuga reptans* z3–9 H9–1
- *Arabis x arendsii* 'Coccinea' z5–8 H8–5
- *Cheiranthus cheiri* z7–8 H9–2
- *Clematis armandii* z7–9 H9–7
- *Dianthus caryophyllus* z7–10 H10–7
- *Helleborus argutifolius* z6–9 H9–6
- *Helleborus orientalis* z4–9 H8–3
- *Hylotelephium sieboldii* z3–8 H8–1
- *Iberis sempervirens* z5–9 H9–3
- *Iris foetidissima* z3–9 H9–2
- *Liriope muscari* and cultivars z6–10 H12–1
- *Miscanthus transmorrisonenesis* z4–9 H9–4
- *Phlox subulata* 'Candy Stripe' z2–8 H9–4
- *Polystichum munitum* z3–8 H8–1
- *Santolina chamaecyparissus* z6–9 H9–4
- *Santolina rosmarinifolia* z6–9 H9–6
- *Sedum acre* z3–8 H8–1
- *Sedum spurium* and cultivars z3–8 H8–1
- *Yucca filamentosa* z4–11 H12–5

Tellima grandiflora
FRINGECUP
Ⓝ ☀ ◊ z4–8 H8–1 ↕↔24in (30cm)
Rosette-forming, hairy plant flowers from late spring to midsummer. Grows best in organic soil and self-sows freely. 'Purpurteppich' has purple-tinged leaves.

Pulmonaria saccharata 'Mrs. Moon'
MRS. MOON LUNGWORT
☀ ☀ ◊ z3–8 H8–1 ↕12in (30cm) ↔24in (60cm)
Pink buds open from late winter to late spring. A clump-forming rhizomatous perennial best grown in fertile, organic soil. Remove old leaves after flowering.

Arabis ferdinandi-colburgi 'Variegata'
ROCK CRESS
☀ ☀ ◊◖ z5–8 H8–3 ↕↔3–4in (7.5–19cm)
Flowers are borne from spring to early summer. This mat-forming perennial is good in rock gardens and as a groundcover. Also called *A. procurrens* 'Variegata'.

Armeria maritima 'Bloodstone'
COMMON THRIFT
Ⓝ ☀ ◊ z3–9 H9–1 ↕4in (10cm) ↔6in (15cm)
Flowers bloom from late spring to summer. Prefers marginally to moderately fertile soil and will tolerate almost pure sand. Divide every 4 to 5 years..

Helictotrichon sempervirens
BLUE OAT GRASS
☀ ◊ z4–9 H9–1 ↕3ft (1m) ↔2ft (60cm)
Straw-colored spikelets bloom on stiff, upright stems from early to midsummer. Grow in marginally to moderately fertile soil. Clean up plants in spring.

Armeria alliacea 'Sea Pink'
SEA PINK
☀ ◊ z7–8 H8–5 ↕↔20in (50cm)
White to deep red-purple flowers appear in summer above tight tufts of leaves. Best if grown in marginally to moderately fertile soil. Also listed as *A. arenaria*.

Polystichum acrostichoides
CHRISTMAS FERN
Ⓝ ☀ ◊ z3–8 H8–1 ↕24in (60cm) ↔18in (45cm)
Shuttlecock-like, evergreen foliage emerges from clumping rhizomes as silvery fiddleheads . Clumps enlarge over time but do not spread aggressively.

Perennials with blue-green/gray leaves

These plants have the subtle and useful ability to lighten a bed or border without being overpowering the way plants with white- or yellow-variegated foliage can sometimes be. They also work well with flowers in shades of red as well as white. Adventuresome gardeners combine these with yellow-green flowers and foliage.

HERBACEOUS PLANTS

Hosta 'Blue Moon'
BLUE MOON HOSTA

☼ ◐ ◊ Z3–8 H9–2 ↕5in (12cm) ↔12in (30cm)
Bears dense racemes of bell-shaped, pale mauve-gray flowers in midsummer. This slow-growing hosta does best in fertile, organic soil. Watch for slug damage.

Dicentra formosa 'Bacchanal'
LANGTREES BLEEDING HEART

Ⓝ ☼ ◊ Z3–8 H10–1 ↕12in (30cm) ↔18in (45cm)
Flowers from midspring to midsummer. A vigorous rhizomatous perennial, it prefers fertile, organic soil. Also called D. 'Bacchanal'.

Helictotrichon sempervirens
BLUE OAT GRASS

☼ ◊ Z4–9 H9–1 ↕3ft (1m) ↔24in (60cm)
In early to midsummer, straw-colored spikelets bloom on stiff, upright stems. Clean up old growth in spring. Grow in marginally to moderately fertile soil.

Anaphalis margaritacea
PEARLY EVERLASTING

Ⓝ ☼ ◊ Z4–8 H8–1 ↕30in (75cm) ↔24in (60cm)
Flowers are borne from midsummer to early fall on erect, leafy stems. Prefers moderately fertile soil. Good for screes and rock gardens.

MORE CHOICES

- *Achillea* x *kellererii* Z5–7 H7–5
- *Achillea* 'Moonshine' Z3–8 H8–1
- *Artemisia absinthium* Z3–9 H10–4
- *Artemisia arborescens* 'Powis Castle' Z6–9 H9–6
- *Artemisia lactiflora* and cultivars Z5–8 H8–5
- *Artemisia schmidtiana* 'Silver Mound' Z5–8 H8–3
- *Artemisia* 'Silver Brocade' Z3–7 H7–1
- *Cerastium tomentosum* Z3–7 H7–1
- *Festuca ovina* var. *glauca* Z4–8 H8–1
- *Heuchera americana* 'Pewter Veil' Z4–8 H8–1
- *Hosta* 'Hadspen Blue' Z3–9 H9–1
- *Hylotelephium* 'Autumn Joy' Z4–9 H9–1
- *Nepeta cataria* Z3–7 H7–1
- *Nepeta cataria* ssp. *citriodora* Z3–7 H7–1
- *Nepeta grandiflora* Z3–8 H8–1
- *Origanum majorana* Z7–9 H8–1
- *Perovskia atriplicifolia* and cultivars Z6–9 H9–6
- *Phlomis fruticosa* Z8–9 H9–8
- *Rudbeckia maxima* Z4–8 H8–1
- *Salvia argentea* Z5–8 H8–5
- *Teucrium fruticans* Z8–9 H9–8
- *Thalictrum aquilegifolium* Z5–9 H9–5
- *Thymus pseudolanuginosus* Z4–9 H9–1

Veronica incana
SILVER SPEEDWELL

☼ ◊ Z3–8 H8–1 ↕↔12in (30cm)
Flowers in from early to late summer on a mat-forming perennial with stems that root as they creep along the ground. Also called V. spicata subsp. incana.

Festuca glauca 'Elijah Blue'
ELIJAH BLUE FESCUE

☼ ◊ Z4–8 H8–1 ↕8in (20cm) ↔10in (25cm)
Produces spikelets of violet-flushed, blue-green
flowers in early to midsummer. Prefers marginally to
moderately fertile soil. Divide every 3 to 4 years.

Ruta graveolens
RUE

☼ ☼ ◊ Z5–9 H9–5 ↕3ft (1m) ↔30in (75cm)
Flowers borne in summer. Prefers moderately fertile
soil. Seedpods can be used in dried designs and wreaths.
Contact with leaf oils can cause severe dermatitis.

Androsace lanuginosa
ROCK JASMINE

☼ ◊ Z5–7 H7–3 ↕1½in (4cm) ↔7in (18cm)
An evergreen mat-former with reddish green stems.
Flowers from mid- to late summer. Best if grown in
gritty, moderately fertile soil. Ideal for a rock garden.

Nepeta x faassenii
CATMINT

☼ ◊ Z4–8 H8–1 ↕↔18in (45cm)
Flowers from early summer to early fall. Cut back after
flowering to keep plants tight and
to encourage repeat flowering.

Cynara cardunculus
CARDOON

☼ ◊ Z7–9 H9–7 ↕6ft (2m) ↔3ft (1m)
Flowers from early summer to early fall with purple
flower heads. A clump forming perennial that is also
an old vegetable related to the artichoke .

Romneya coulteri
TREE POPPY

Ⓝ ☼ ◊ Z8–10 H9–2 ↕↔6ft (2m)
The blooms last throughout the summer. Best when
grown in fertile soil. Shelter plants from cold winds
against a sunny wall. Appreciates dry winter mulch.

Artemisia ludoviciana 'Silver King'
CUDWEED, WHITE SAGE

Ⓝ ☼ ◊ Z5–9 H12–8 ↕4ft (1.2m) ↔24in (60m)
A clump-forming perennial with foliage that turns red
in fall. Flower heads are borne from midsummer to
autumn. Best in well-drained, low-fertility soil.

HERBACEOUS PLANTS

Perennials with golden or yellow leaves

Most perennials that feature light green or yellow foliage are "sports" that have been selected from greener-leafed species or other selections. They add visual interest when contrasted with dark green or purple, bronze or red leaves, such as those presented on the oppostie page. Those that are adapted to shade can also brighten up the darker corners of your garden.

Hosta 'Birchwood Parky's Gold'
BIRCHWOOD PARKY'S GOLD HOSTA

☼ ◐ ◌ z3–8 H9–2 ‡16in (40cm) ↔30in (75cm)
Pale lavender-blue, bell-shaped flowers appear atop slender stems in midsummer. Leaves become yellower as the season progresses. Prefers rich soil.

Hosta 'Sum and Substance'
SUM AND SUBSTANCE HOSTA

☼ ☼ ◌ z3–8 H9–2 ‡↔3ft (1m)
Dense racemes of bell-shaped pale lilac flowers appear in mid- to late summer. Puckering of leaves increases as the season progresses. Prefers fertile soil.

Lysimachia nummularia 'Aurea'
GOLDEN CREEPING JENNY

☼ ◌ z4–8 H8–1 ‡2in (5cm) ↔indefinite
A very vigorous, stem-rooting evergreen that can cover a fairly large area in just one season. Bright yellow, cup-shaped flowers in summer add interest.

Hosta 'Zounds'
ZOUNDS HOSTA

☼ ◌ z3–8 H9–2 ‡↔3ft (1m)
Thick leaves have an almost metallic luster. Leafy flower stems bear funnel-shaped, pale lavender-blue flowers in early summer. Prefers rich soil.

MORE CHOICES

- *Carex elata* 'Aurea' z5–9 H9–3
- *Lamium maculatum* 'Cannon's Gold' z4–8 H8–1
- *Selaginella kraussiana* 'Aurea' z6–9 H5
- *Tanacetum vulgare* 'Isla Gold' z4–8 H8–1

Hosta 'Gold Standard'
GOLD STANDARD HOSTA

☼ ◐ ◌ z3–8 H9–2 ‡30in (75cm) ↔3ft (1m)
Funnel-shaped, lavender-blue flowers are borne in mid-summer. Can be used as an accent plant or groundcover under deciduous trees. Best if grown in fertile soil.

Perennials with purple, red, or bronze leaves

As for lighter-colored foliage (see the opposite page) plant breeders have also selected for darker foliage colors. Some plants exhibit the colors in new foliage, while others show it in their mature growth. Dark-foliaged plants provide richness to very sunny garden areas, where the subtlety of the green hues may be washed away, and bring an air of mystery to shady spots.

Sedum 'Matrona'
MATRONA STONECROP
☼ ◐ Z4–9 H9–4 ↕24in (60cm) ↔24in (60cm)
This mounded, upright selection was created by crossing *S.* 'Atropurpureum' and *S.* 'Autumn Joy'. Flowers appear in late summer.

Epimedium x *youngianum* 'Roseum'
PINK YOUNG'S BARRENWORT
☼ ◐ Z5–9 H8–5 ↕12in (30cm) ↔12in (30cm)
Flowers of dusky pink to purple bloom from mid- to late spring. Foliage is variable. Prefers fertile, organic soil. Also goes by the cultivar name 'Lilacinum'.

Imperata cylindrica 'Rubra'
JAPANESE BLOOD GRASS
☼ ◐ Z5–9 H9–3 ↕20in (50cm) ↔indefinite
Leaves start green but quickly transform to deep blood red. This perennial grass is a slow spreader. Also known as *I. cylindrica* 'Red Baron'.

Euphorbia amygdaloides 'Purpurea'
PURPLE WOOD SPURGE
☼ ◑ ◐ Z6–10 H10–2 ↕↔1ft (30cm)
Bears terminal yellow-green flower clusters from midspring to early summer. Prefers organic soil and tolerates dry conditions.

MORE CHOICES

- *Artemesia lactiflora* 'Guizhou' Z5–8 H8–5
- *Epimedium* x *youngianum* 'Niveum' Z5–9 H9–5
- *Imperata cylindrica* 'Rubra' Z5–9 H9–3
- *Ligularia dentata* 'Desdemona' Z4–8 H8–1

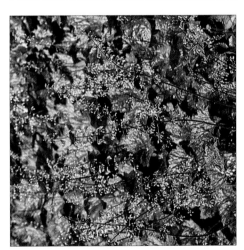

Heuchera micrantha
CREVICE ALUM ROOT
Ⓝ ☼ ◑ ◐ ◐ Z4–7 H8–2 ↕36in (90cm) ↔18in (45cm)
Flowers are produced in early summer. This mound-forming Northwest native makes a good groundcover and grows best in fertile soil.

Epimedium grandiflorum 'Rose Queen'
BISHOP'S HAT
☼ ◐ Z4–8 H8–2 ↕↔12in (30cm)
The young leaves of this cultivar are dark bronze purple. Other cultivars have flowers in shades of white, yellow, and pink. Prefers fertile, organic soil.

Perennials with variegated leaves

There are many plants that have natural variegation, and others are chance sports of more common, all-green perennials. The variegation can range from yellow to white to cream and can take on various patterns. In all cases, variegated plants can be used to brighten a shady location in the garden or to add visual interest in a perennial border.

Hosta 'Gold Standard'
GOLD STANDARD HOSTA

☼ ☼ ◑ ◊ Z3–8 H9–2 ‡30in (75cm) ↔3ft (1m)
Funnel-shaped, lavender-blue flowers are borne in mid summer. Can be used as an accent plant or ground-cover under deciduous trees. Best grown in fertile soil.

Fritillaria imperialis 'Variegata'
VARIEGATED CROWN IMPERIAL

☼ ◊ Z5–9 H9–4 ‡3ft (1m) ↔9–12in (23–30cm)
Flowers appear in late spring. This bulbous plant is excellent for massing in formal beds. Best when grown in fertile soil. Also called *F. imperialis* 'Aureomarginata'.

Carex siderosticha 'Variegata'
VARIEGATED CREEPING BROADLEAF SEDGE

☼ ☼ ◊ ◊◊ Z6–9 H9–3 ‡12in (30cm) ↔16cm (40cm)
This slowly spreading perennial produces pale brown flower spikes in late spring. Best when grown in fertile soil, but it tolerates other types.

Brunnera macrophylla 'Dawson's White'
DAWSON'S WHITE SIBERIAN BUGLOSS

☼ ◊ Z3–7 H7–1 ‡18in (45cm) ↔24in (60cm)
Flowers from mid- to late spring. Prefers moderately fertile, organic soil. Equally suitable in a woodland or a border. Plant with green-leaved plants for contrast.

Arundo donax 'Versicolor'
GIANT REED

☼ ◊ Z7–15 H12–1 ‡8–10ft (2.5–3m) ↔2ft (60cm)
Terminal clusters of light green to purple spikelets are produced from mid- to late fall. The plant habit is very suggestive of corn. Also called *A. donax* 'Variegata'.

Iris pseudacorus 'Variegata'
VARIEGATED YELLOW FLAG

☼ ● Z5–8 H8–3 ‡6ft (2m) ↔indefinite

A vigorous iris that blooms from mid- to late summer. Will grow well at the margins of garden ponds or lakes. Variegation normally fades in summer.

MORE CHOICES

- *Acorus calamus* 'Variegatus' Z10–11 H12–2
- *Arabis ferdinandi-coburgi* 'Variegata' Z3–7 H8–1
- *Arum italicum* 'Pictum' Z7–9 H9–6
- *Bletilla striata* 'Alba Variegata' Z5–9 H8–2
- *Cortaderia selloana* 'Monvin' PP5136 Z7–11 H12–7
- *Euphorbia marginata* Z13–15 H12–1
- *Filipendula ulmaria* 'Variegata' Z4–7 H8–1
- *Gaura lindheimeri* 'Variegata' Z6–9 H9–6
- *Hakonechloa macra* 'Aureola' Z5–9 H9–5
- *Kalimeris incisa* 'Variegata' Z4–8 H8–1
- *Ophiopogon japonicus* 'Variegatus' Z7–10 H10–1
- *Pentas* 'Stars and Stripes' Z10–11 H12–3
- *Pulmonaria saccharata* 'Mrs. Moon' Z3–8 H8–1
- *Sedum kamtschaticum* 'Variegatum' Z4–8 H9–1

Miscanthus sinensis 'Zebrinus'
ZEBRA GRASS

☼ ◊ Z4–9 H9–1 ‡4ft (1.2m) ↔3ft (1m)

Fall-blooming flowers are initially copper then fade to creamy white. Makes a very interesting living screen. Flowers can be cut for fresh or dry arrangements.

Miscanthus sinensis 'Variegatus'
VARIEGATED MAIDENGRASS

☼ ◊ Z5–9 H9–1 ‡6ft (2m) ↔4ft (1.2m)

Autumn-flowering panicles persist throughout winter. Cut back in early spring before new growth starts. Prefers moderately fertile soil. Great accent plant.

Iris pallida 'Aureo Variegata'
ORRIS

☼ ◊ Z4–9 H9–2 ‡3ft (1m) ↔indefinite

Scented flowers bloom from late spring to early summer. In warmer locations, the foliage can be evergreen. Also known as *I. pallida* var. *dalmatica*.

Vinca minor 'Variegata'
VARIEGATED PERIWINKLE

☼ ☼ ◊ ● ● Z4–x9 H9–1 ‡8in (20cm) ↔indefinite

Flowers from midspring to autumn. A mat-forming plant that makes a good groundcover and grows well in most soils. Cut back in spring to control growth.

HERBACEOUS PLANTS

Centranthus ruber
RED VALERIAN
☼ ◊ Z5–8 H8–5 ‡3ft (1m) ↔24in (60cm)
Fragrant flowers appear in spring to late summer.
Cultivars available in white and red shades. Self-sows
freely. Prefers minimally to moderately fertile soil.

Petroselinum crispum var. **neapolitanum**
ITALIAN PARSLEY
☼ ☼ ◊ Z5–9 H9–1 ‡32in (80cm) ↔24in (60cm)
This is the less commonly grown flat-leaf parsley. It is
more pungent than the curly cultivars and is better for
use in cooking. Prefers moderate fertility. Biennial.

Angelica archangelica
ANGELICA
☼ ◊ Z4–9 H9–1 ‡6ft (2m) ↔3ft (1m)
Graceful pinnate leaves arise from long stalks, making
it an elegant bedding plant suggestive of the tropics.
The sap can cause a rash in the presence of sunlight.

Perennial herbs for borders

Many gardeners segregate their ornamental plants from their vegetable and
herb gardens. This method works well for the utilitarian gardener, but there
are many culinary and medicinal herbs that merit consideration for dual
usage: their foliage texture as well as their floral displays make them very
attractive ornamental plants.

Monarda fistulosa
WILD BEE BALM
Ⓝ ☼ ◊ Z3–9 H9–1 ‡4ft (1.2m) ↔18in (45cm)
Flowers from midsummer through early fall. Flowers
vary from light pink lilac purple. Spicy aromatic leaves
reminiscent of thyme and oregano. Clump forming.

Althaea officinalis
MARSH MALLOW

☼ ◊ Z3–9 H9–1 ‡6ft (2m) ↔5ft (1.5m)
Flowers from midsummer to early autumn. Upright grower with soft, hairy leaves. A paste of the roots was once used to make marshmallows. Prefers fertile soil.

Monarda didyma
BEE BALM, SWEET BERGAMOT

Ⓝ ☼ ☼ ◊◊ Z4–10 H10–1 ‡3ft (1m) ↔24in (60cm)
This bushy, clump-forming perennial blooms mid- to late summer. Used by Native Americans and early colonists as a tea. Prone to powdery mildew.

Monarda didyma 'Marshall's Delight'
MARSHALL'S DELIGHT BEE BALM

☼ ☼ ◊ Z4–8 H8–1 ‡3ft (1m) ↔24in (60cm)
Blooms mid to late summer. Prefers moderately fertile, organic soil, and it spreads slowly by runners. Good hummingbird plant. Highly resistant to powdery mildew.

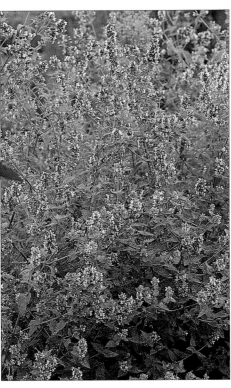

Nepeta cataria
CATNIP

☼ ☼ ◊ Z3–7 H7–1 ‡to 36in (90cm) ↔18in (45cm)
White flowers have purple spots and bloom in summer and fall. Woolly foliage is aromatic. Grows well in most soils. Neighborhood cats may flatten your plants.

MORE CHOICES

- *Allium schoenoprasum* Z5–11 H12–1
- *Artemisia absinthium* Z4–8 H9–1
- *Artemisia lactiflora* Z5–8 H8–5
- *Eupatorium purpureum* Z3–9 H9–1
- *Leonurus cardiaca* Z0 H8–1
- *Levisticum officinale* Z4–8 H8–1
- *Scutellaria lateriflora* Z3–9 H8–1
- *Thymus praecox* spp *arcticus* Z5–9 H9–4
- *Verbascum olympicum* Z5–9 H9–5

Eupatorium perfoliatum
BONESET

Ⓝ ☼ ☼ ◊ Z3–9 H8–1 ‡to 5ft (1.5m) ↔3ft (1m)
The white flowerheads that appear in late summer to autumn are often purple tinged. Prefers moderately fertile soil. This is a useful clump-forming perennial.

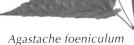

Agastache foeniculum
ANISE HYSSOP

Ⓝ ☼ ◊ Z6–10 H9–5 ‡5ft (1.5m) ↔12in (30cm)
Blooms from midsummer to early autumn. Flowers can also be white. Good at the back of borders. Leaves have the scent and flavor of licorice.

Ruta graveolens
RUE

☼ ☼ ◊ Z5–9 H9–5 ‡3ft (1m) ↔30in (75cm)
Flowers appear in summer. Blue-green foliage is a good contrast to gray-leaved plants. Prefers moderately fertile soil. Leaf oils can cause a severe rash.

Achillea ptarmica 'The Pearl Superior'
THE PEARL SUPERIOR SNEEZEWORT

☼ ◊ Z3–8 H8–1 ‡↔30in (75cm)
Blooms from early to late summer. The fresh flowers make nice additions to a flower arrangement. The flowers can also be used for dried arrangements.

Herbs and vegetables for mixed borders

It is probably out of habit or convenience that most gardeners still relegate vegetables to their own section of the garden, away from more ornamental areas. But increasingly more gardeners realize that many herbs and vegetables can add visual excitement to other areas, so they are moving ornamental edibles out of the back quarter and into the flower garden.

Levisticum officinale
LOVAGE

☼ ◐ ◑ Z4–8 H8–4 ↕3–6ft (1–2m) ↔3ft (1m)
Flowers appear high above the celery-like leaves in early to midsummer. The seeds, leaves, and hollow stems all smell and taste of celery. Perennial.

Eupatorium purpureum
PURPLE JOE PYE WEED

Ⓝ ☼ ◑ ◑ Z3–9 H9–1 ↕7ft (2.2m) ↔3ft (1m)
Blooms from midsummer to early autumn. Leaves smell like vanilla when bruised. A native that has been used for its purported medicinal properties. Perennial.

Borago offinalis
BORAGE

☼ ◐ H12–1 ↕3ft (1m) ↔1ft (30cm)
Flowers appear from late spring to late summer and are attractive to bees. Used for its cucumber-like taste and its medicinal properties. Annual or biennial.

Brassica oleracea Capitata group
CABBAGE

Ⓝ ☼ ◐ ◑ Z7–8 H9–1 ↕↔1–2ft (30–60cm)
Many gardeners use flowering cabbage in their flower beds, but this even more edible relative makes a nice addition, too. Cultivars come in shades of green and with red hues. Biennial grown as an annual.

Solanum melongena
EGGPLANT

☼ ◐ ◑ Z11 H12–1 ↕↔2–3ft (60–90cm)
Highly attractive vegetables with large lilac flowers that resemble tomato blooms. Fruits come in white, purple, white speckled purple, and green. Annual.

Capsicum annuum
SWEET PEPPER

☼ ◊ Z9–11 H12–1 ‡5ft (1.5m) ↔20in (50cm)
Sweet peppers come in a variety of sizes and shapes.
White flowers are followed by green fruit than turn
shades of red, yellow, orange, purple, and ivory. Annual.

Beta vulgaris (Cicla group)
SWISS CHARD

☼ ☀ ◊ Z7–12 H12–1 ‡9in (23cm) ↔to 18in (45cm)
This beet variety does not produce swollen roots but is
instead grown for its highly ornamental, edible leaves.
'Bright Lights' is the most ornamental variety. Biennial.

Verbena officinalis
HERB OF THE CROSS

☼ ◊ Z4–8 H8–1 ‡4–5ft (1.3–1.6m) ↔2ft (60cm)
This medicinal herb blooms from late spring to early
summer. A wonderful plant for the back of the border.
Prefers light, moderately fertile soil. Perennial.

MORE CHOICES

- *Alchemilla vulgaris* Z4–7 H7–1
- *Allium schoenoprasum* Z5–11 H12–1
- *Allium tuberosum* Z4–8 H8–1
- *Foeniculum vulgare* 'Rubrum' Z4–10 H10–2
- *Levisticum officinale* Z4–8 H8–1
- *Ocimum basilicum* 'African Blue' Z9–11
- *Ocimum basilicum* 'Dark Opal'
  Z9–11 H12–1
- *Ocimum basilicum* 'Purple Ruffles'
  Z9–11 H12–1
- *Rheum rhabarbarum* Z5–9 H9–1
- *Stachys officinalis* Z5–8 H8–4
- *Tanacetum parthenium* Z4–9 H9–1
- *Zea mays* 'Indian Summer' Z0 H12–1

Tagetes lucida
MEXICAN TARRAGON

☼ ◊ Z8–13 H12–1 ‡30in (75cm) ↔18in (45cm)
Flowers appear from late summer to early autumn.
This is a tender perennial relative of the marigold. The
leaves are sometimes used as a tarragon substitute.

Monarda didyma 'Jacob Cline'
JACOB CLINE BEE BALM

☼ ☀ ◊◊ Z4–11 H12–1 ‡4ft (1.5m) ↔2ft (60cm)–spreading
Blooms mid- to late summer. Grow in moderately
fertile, organic, well-drained soil. More resistant to
powdery mildew and rust than the species. Perennial.

Capsicum annuum
HOT PEPPER

☼ ◊ Z9–11 H12–1 ‡5ft (1.5m) ↔20in (50cm)
Hot pepper fruit tend to be smaller than the sweet
peppers, but they are no less ornamental and can be
found all the same colors (see above). Annual.

Perennials for rock gardens and screes

Although the sharp drainage and low moisture levels of rock gardens and screes present a survival challenge to some perennials, others will thrive. The plants presented here grow naturally in alpine areas, coastal regions, or well-drained hillsides. Sloping, open sites – not necessarily rock gardens or screes, and not always in full sun – are excellent places for displaying these selections.

Armeria maritima 'Bloodstone'
COMMON THRIFT

(N) ☼ ◊ Z3–9 H9–1 ↕4in (10cm) ↔6in (15cm)
Flowers from late spring to summer. Prefers marginally to moderately fertile soil and tolerates almost pure sand. Divide every 4–5 years as the center dies out.

Sedum spurium 'Bronze Carpet'
BRONZE CARPET STONECROP

☼ ◊ Z3–9 H9–1 ↕4in (10cm) ↔24in (60cm)
The pink flowers of this improved cultivar bloom from early to late summer. Trailing stems make a good groundcover. Prefers moderately fertile soil.

Aster alpinus
ALPINE ASTER

(N) ☼ ◊ Z5–7 H7–1 ↕10in (25cm) ↔18in (45cm)
Flowers from early to midsummer on mound-forming plants. Cultivars sre available in shades of pink and white. Prefers moderately fertile soil.

Sedum kamtschaticum 'Variegatum'
VARIEGATED ORANGE STONECROP

☼ ◊ Z4–8 H9–1 ‡2–3in (5–8cm) ↔8in (20cm)

Blooms in late summer, the flowers slowly fading to crimson as they age. Prefers moderately fertile soil and should be divided every 4 to 5 years.

Dryas octopetala
MOUNTAIN AVENS

Ⓝ ☼ ◊ Z3–6 H6–1 ‡2½in (6cm) ↔indefinite

Late spring to early summer flowers, followed by ornamental seedpods, decorate evergreen to nearly evergreen mats. Best if grown in gritty, organic soil.

Penstemon hirsutus
HAIRY PENSTEMON

Ⓝ ☼ ◊ Z3–9 H9–1 ‡3ft (1m) ↔2ft (60cm)

Summer-flowering, spreading to upright evergreen, this may also be useful in a border. Best grown in marginally to moderately fertile soil.

Armeria alliacea
SEA PINK

☼ ◊ Z7–8 H8–5 ‡↔20in (50cm)

Blooms in summer. Flowers also occur in white or deep red-purple. Best if grown in marginally to moderately fertile soil. Also listed as *A. arenaria*.

Dodecatheon hendersonii
SAILOR CAPS

Ⓝ ☼ ◊ Z5–7 H7–5 ‡12in (30cm) ↔3in (8cm)

Flowers appear in early summer, after which the oblong, fleshy, dark green leaf rosettes go dormant. Prefers organic soil and does well in a woodland.

Iberis sempervirens
CANDYTUFT

☼ ◊ Z5–9 H9–3 ‡12in (30cm) ↔24in (60cm)

Flowers appear from late spring to early summer above evergreen foliage. Deadhead after bloom. Prefers marginally to moderately fertile soil.

Silene acaulis
MOSS CAMPION

Ⓝ ☼ ◊ Z3–5 H5–1 ‡1in (2.5cm) ↔6in (15cm)

Spring flowers also occur in white. Attractive mosslike foliage is evergreen. Grow in moderately fertile soil. Unusually, it is also native to mountains in Eurasia.

MORE CHOICES

- *Achillea* x *kellererii* Z5–7 H7–5
- *Aubrieta deltoidea* Z5–7 H7–5
- *Aurinia saxitillis* Z4–8 H8–1
- *Delosperma cooperi* Z8–10 H10–8
- *Dodecatheon meadia* Z4–8 H8–1
- *Dryas drummondii* Z2–6 H6–1
- *Gentiana andrewsii* Z3–7 H8–1
- *Geranium cinereum* Z5–9 H9–5
- *Gysophila repens* Z4–7 H7–1
- *Hepatica acutiloba* Z4–9 H9–3
- *Hepatica americana* Z4–8 H8–1
- *Heuchera rubescens* Z3–7 H
- *Lewisia cotyledon* Z5–8 H8–1
- *Lewisia rediviva* Z4–9 H9–1
- *Saxifraga oppositifolia* Z1–7 H7–1
- *Sedum acre* Z3–8 H8–1

Groundcover perennials for sun

These plants can be used as a grass alternative where there is no foot traffic, or in sunny areas where grass is hard to maintain, such as on slopes. They are also useful between larger perennials, where they will suppress weeds as well as keep the soil cool and moist. Most of these groundcovers will also bloom, so make sure they fit in with your garden's color scheme.

Sedum kamtschaticum 'Variegatum'
VARIEGATED ORANGE STONECROP

☼ ◊ Z4–8 H9–1 ↕2–3in (5–8cm) ↔8in (20cm)
Late summer flowers slowly age to crimson. Thick, clump-forming rhizomes should be divided every 4 to 5 years. Prefers moderately fertile soil.

Sedum kamtschaticum
ORANGE STONECROP

☼ ◊ Z3–8 H8–1 ↕3in (8cm) ↔8in (20cm)
Late summer-blooming clump-former, good at the front of a bed or in a rock garden. Cut back after flowering to keep compact. Prefers moderately fertile soil.

Aubrieta deltoidea
LILACBUSH

☼ ☼ ◐ ● Z5–7 H7–5 ↕6in (15cm) ↔18in (50cm)
Flowers appear in spring. Cut back hard after bloom. This mat-forming plant, suited to rock gardens and screes, prefers moderately fertile soil.

Armeria maritima
SEA PINK

Ⓝ ☼ ◊ Z3–9 H9–1 ↕4in (10cm) ↔6in (15cm)
Flowers from late spring to summer. Prefers marginally to moderately fertile soil and will tolerate almost pure sand. Divide every 4 to 5 years as center dies out.

Alyssum saxatile
BASKET OF GOLD

☼ ◊ Z4–8 H8–1 ↕8in (20cm) ↔12in (30cm)
Flowers are produced from late spring to early summer on this evergreen mound. Prune plants back after flowering to keep them from becoming leggy.

MORE CHOICES

- *Arabis caucasica* z4–8 H8–1
- *Erigeron x hybrida* 'Wayne Roderick' z5–8 H8–1
- *Festuca glauca* 'Elijah Blue' z4–8 H8–1
- *Geranium sanguineum* 'Striatum' z3–8 H8–1
- *Iberis sempervirens* z5–9 H9–3
- *Oenothera tetragona* z4–8 H8–1
- *Phlox subulata* 'Candy Stripe' z2–8 H9–4
- *Phlox subulata* 'Red Wings' z3–8 H8–1
- *Sedum kamtschaticum* 'Floriferum' z4–9 H9–1
- *Sedum spurium* z4–9 H9–1

Geranium 'Anne Folkard'
ANNE FOLKARD CRANESBILL

☀ ◊ ◑ z5–9 H9–3 ‡20in (50cm) ↔3ft (1m)
Spreading perennial. Leaves emerge yellow-green and become greener with age. Flowers appear from midsummer to midautumn. Prefers moderately fertile soil.

Festuca glauca 'Wayne Roderick'
WAYNE RODERICK FESCUE

☀ ◊ z4–9 H9–1 ‡↔4in (10cm)
Produces spikelets of violet-flushed, blue-green flowers in summer. Prefers poor to moderately fertile soil. Divide every 3 years to maintain vigor and leaf color.

Lirope muscari
LILYTURF

☀ ◊ z6–10 H10–6 ‡12in (30cm) ↔18in (45cm)
Flowers emerge from the evergreen leaves from early to late autumn. Prefers light, moderately fertile soil bit is tolerant of a range of conditions. Tuberous perennial.

Erigeron glaucus 'Sea Breeze'
SEA BREEZE SEASIDE DAISY

☀◑ ◊ z5–8 H8–5 ‡12in (30cm) ↔18in (45cm)
Flowers appear from late spring to early summer. Stems bear succulent-looking leaves. Suitable for a garden bed or rock garden. Prefers fertile soil.

Silene acaulis
MOSS CAMPION

☀ ◊ z3–5 H5–1 ‡1in (2.5cm) ↔6in (15cm)
Blooms in spring; flowers can also be white. Attractive mosslike foliage is evergreen. A good addition to a rock garden or scree. Grow in moderately fertile soil.

Phlox subulata 'Candy Stripe'
CANDY STRIPE CREEPING PHLOX

Ⓝ ☀◑ ◊ z3–8 H8–1 ‡6in (15cm) ↔20in (50cm)
Flowers from late spring to early summer, and it sometimes blooms again in fall. Dense evergreen or semievergreen perennial. Prefers fertile soil.

Ceratostigma plumbaginoides
LEADWORT, PLUMBAGO

☀ ◊ z6–9 H9–6 ‡18in (45cm) ↔12 in (30cm) A spreading, woody-based perennial. Blooms appear in late summer. The foliage becomes red-tinted in autumn. Prefers light, moderately fertile soil.

HERBACEOUS PLANTS

Groundcover perennials for shade

These plants are at home both in a woodland bed between larger plants as well as under trees and other locations too shady for grass. They do need ample water, so grow them where they receive little or no competition from shallow-rooted trees. Some of these are also evergreen, providing year-round cover and interest.

Epimedium x cantabrigiense
BARRENWORT

☀ ◑ Z5–8 H8–5 ‡24in (60cm) ↔24in (60cm)
Flowers appear from midspring to late spring. Flowers can also be yellow. Clump-forming plant with evergreen foliage. Prefers organic, fertile soil.

Hosta 'Blue Angel'
BLUE ANGEL HOSTA

☀ ☀ ◑ Z3–8 H9–2 ‡36in (90cm) ↔4ft (1.2m)
A slow-growing, clump-forming cultivar. Bears bell-shaped, grayish white flowers on leafy, grayish green flower stalks in early summer.

Asarum caudatum
WILD GINGER

Ⓝ ☀ ◑ Z4–8 H8–1 ‡3in (8cm) ↔10in (25cm)
Unusual reddish brown flowers appear below the leaves in late spring/early summer. Prefers moderately fertile, organic soil. Evergreen in warmer areas.

Convallaria majalis var. *rosea*
PINK LILY-OF-THE-VALLEY

☀ ☀ ☀ ◑◑ Z4–9 H9–1 ‡9in (23cm) ↔indefinite
Spreading rhizomes give rise to strongly scented flowers in spring. Species' flowers are white. Prefers moist, organic soil and leaf-mold mulch in fall.

Cyclamen hederifolium
BABY CYCLAMEN

☀ ◑ Z5–7 H9–7 ‡4in (10cm) ↔4–6in (10–15cm)
Scented flowers in shades of pink to white are produced from mid- to late autumn. Leaves vary from triangular to heart-shaped. Also called *C. neapolitanum*.

Gymnocarpium dryopteris
OAK FERN
Ⓝ ☼ ◗ Z4–8 H8–1 ‡8in (20cm) ↔indefinite
Deciduous foliage is yellow green when young and darkens with age. Fiddleheads (new shoots) appear in sets of three throughout the growing season.

Mitchella repens
PARTRIDGE BERRY
Ⓝ ☼ ◗ Z4–9 H9–1 ‡2in (5cm) ↔indefinite
Mat-forming, prostrate stems root at the nodes (joints). White or pink-flushed flowers appear in early summer, followed in fall by colorful berries. Best in organic soil.

Lirope gigantea
GIANT LILYTURF
☼ ☀ ◗◗ Z6–11 H12–6 ‡3ft (1m) ↔2ft (60cm)
True to its botanical name, this is the largest of all the *Liriope* species. Violet flower spikes appear in mid summer. Makes a great accent plant.

Lirope muscari 'Lilac Beauty'
BIG BLUE LILYTURF
☼ ◗ Z6–10 H10–6 ‡12in (30cm) ↔18in (45cm)
This cultivar makes a good border and path edging. It does well in rock gardens and *en masse* as an evergreen groundcover.

Pachysandra terminalis 'Green Sheen'
GREEN SHEEN JAPANESE SPURGE
☼ ☀ ◗ ◗ Z6–9 H9–6 ‡12in (30cm) ↔indefinite
This cultivar's leaves are a glossier and darker green than the species'. Tiny white flowers are produced on short spikes in early summer. Grows well on most soils.

Galium triflorum
FRAGRANT BEDSTRAW
Ⓝ ☼ ◗◗ Z5–8 H8–5 ‡12in (30cm) ↔4ft (1.2m)
Blooms from late spring into late summer. Best if grown in soil rich in organic matter. Can spread quickly. Leaves can be used for tea and flavoring wine.

MORE CHOICES

- *Ajuga reptans* 'Catlin's Giant' Z3–9 H9–1
- *Asarum canadense* Z2–8 H8–1
- *Epimedium perralchicum* 'Frohleiten' Z5–9 H9–4
- *Epimedium* x *youngianum* 'Niveum' Z5–9 H9–5
- *Euphorbia amygdaloides* Z6–10 H10–2
- *Galium odoratum* Z5–8 H8–5
- *Geranium macrorrhizum* Z4–8 H8–1
- *Heuchera americana* Z4–8 H8–1
- *Lamium maculatum* 'Beedham's White' Z4–8 H8–1
- *Maianthemum canadense* Z4–7 H7–1
- *Pulmonaria angustifolia* 'Smokey Blue' Z3–8 H8–1
- *Tiarella cordifolia* Z3–8 H7–1
- *Vancouveria hexandra* Z5–8 H8–1

HERBACEOUS PLANTS

Tender perennials for containers

These perennials, often grown as annuals in colder regions of the Northwest, are adaptable to being grown in containers. Once planted up, set the containers out on patios or sink them into the ground during the frost-free months, then bring them indoors into a frost-free sunroom or garage (or greenhouse) until warm weather returns.

Agapanthus campanulatus
AFRICAN BLUE LILY

☼ ◊ Z7–11 H12–7 ‡4ft (1.2m) ↔20in (50cm)

Best if grown in a soil-based potting mix. Fertilize from spring until it flowers in late summer. Overwinter in a cool, bright location, and water sparingly.

Zephyranthes candida
RAIN LILY

☼ ◊ Z7–9 H9–6 ‡10in (25cm) ↔3in (8cm)

Blooms late summer to early fall. Plant this bulbous perennial 4in deep in a soil-based potting mix. Keep soil evenly moist during the overwintering period.

Erysimum cheiri
WALLFLOWER

☼ ◊ Z7–8 H9–2 ‡10–32in (25–80cm) ↔12–16in (30–40cm)

Particularly adapted to restricted soil conditions; it grows well in the cracks of walls where it is hardy. Spring flowers are fragrant.

Kniphofia uvaria
RED-HOT POKER

☼ ◐ ◊ Z6–9 H9–1 ‡4ft (1.2m) ↔24in (60cm)

Where winter lows drop below 0 degrees F, this South African native is best grown in a container. A soil mix formulated for cacti and succulents works best.

Helianthemum nummularium
SUNROSE

☼ ◊ Z7–9 H9–4 ‡8in (20cm) ↔3ft (1m)

Where winters fall below 0°F (-18°C), grow this in a container, where its prostrate growth will spill over the sides. Best in a soil mix designed for cacti and succulents.

Eucomis 'Bicolor'
PINEAPPLE LILY

☼ ◊ Z8–10 H10–8 ‡↔12–24in (30–60cm)

Plant this bulbous perennial just below the soil surface in soil-based potting mix, with pumice or grit added for increased drainage.

MORE CHOICES

- *Cortaderia selloana* 'Aureolineata'
  Z7–11 H12–7
- *Cortaderia selloana* 'Monvin' PP5136
  Z7–11 H12–7
- *Fuchsia* 'Double Otto' Z7–11 H12–9
- *Laurentia fluviatilis* Z7–9 H9–6
- *Lavandula stoechas* Z8–9 H9–8
- *Lavatera trimestris* cultivars Z11–12 H12–1
- *Salvia farinacea* Z8–11 H12–1

Nassella tenuissima
FINE-STEM TUSSOCK GRASS

☼ ◐ ◊ Z7–9 H9–6 ↕↔24in (60cm)

This grass makes a great container plant, adding movement and a backdrop to a mixed container. Flowers from summer to fall, followed by downy, oat-colored seedheads.

Origanum majorana
KNOTTED MARJORAM,
SWEET MARJORAM

☼ ◊ Z7–9 H8–1

↕32in (80cm) ↔18in (45cm)

Although often grown as an annual, this culinary herb can be kept as a perennial if maintained over winter on a windowsill or cool greenhouse.

Mirabilis jalapa
FOUR O'CLOCK, MARVEL OF PERU

☼ ◊ Z11–15 H12–9 ↕24in (60cm)

Although grown as an annual, this lovely, bushy plant will form swollen storage roots reminiscent of dahlias. Keep soil on the dry side during winter.

Tagetes lucida
MEXICAN TARRAGON

☼ ◊ Z8–13 H12–1 ↕30in (75cm) ↔18in (45cm)

Flowers appear from late summer to early autumn. This perennial relative of the common annual marigold bears leaves with the taste and aroma of anise.

Pennisetum alopecuroides 'Rubrum'
PURPLE FOUNTAIN GRASS

☼ ◊ Z8–11 H12–8 ↕4ft (1.2m) ↔3ft (1m)

Flower spikes arise from this distinguished grass from summer to autumn. Use a soil-based potting mix. Overwinter in a frost-free garage, and water sparingly.

Perennials resistant to deer browsing

Gardeners are increasingly facing the unenviable position of sharing their gardens with deer. The potential devastation hungry deer can inflict on an unprotected garden is enormous. Short of erecting tall barriers around a garden, one way gardeners can cope is by selecting plants that are uninteresting or unpalatable to deer. However, remember that if hungry enough, deer may consume virtually any plant.

HERBACEOUS PLANTS

Digitalis purpurea
COMMON FOXGLOVE

☼ ◐ Z4–8 H9–1
↕3–5ft (1–1.5m) ↔2ft (60cm)
Rosette-forming biennial or short-lived perennial with a towering flower spike that blooms in early summer. White, pink, and apricot forms also occur. Tolerates poor soils.

Achillea millefolium
YARROW

Ⓝ ☼ ◐ Z3–9 H10–1 ↕↔24in (60cm)
Blooms from early to late summer. Tolerates a wide range of soil conditions. Will self-sow, so cut back flowers after blooming if you don't want volunteers.

Acanthus mollis
BEAR'S BREECHES

☼ ◐ ◊ Z7–11 H12–7 ↕4ft (1.2m) ↔18in (45cm)
Produces flowers in late summer. The flower bracts are purple, as the flower stalks may also be. Performs best when grown in deep, fertile, loamy soil.

Aquilegia canadensis
CANADIAN COLUMBINE

Ⓝ ☼ ◐ ◊ Z3–8 H8–1 ↕3ft (1m) ↔12in (30cm)
A delicate-looking perennial with dark green leaves divided into leaflets. Nodding flowers appear from midspring to midsummer. Prefers fertile soil.

Echinacea purpurea
PURPLE CONEFLOWER

Ⓝ ☼ ◊ Z3–9 H9–3 ↕to 5ft (1.5m) ↔18in (45cm)
Flowers from midsummer to early autumn and prefers deep, organic soil. The cultivars bred from this native plant are often more suitable for the garden border.

Iberis sempervirens
CANDYTUFT

☼ ◊ Z5–9 H9–3 ↕12in (30cm) ↔24in (60cm)
Flowers appear from late spring to early summer above evergreen foliage. Prefers marginally to moderately fertile soil. Good in a rock garden.

Centranthus ruber
RED VALERIAN

☼ ◊ Z5–8 H8–5 ↕3ft (1m) ↔24in (60cm)

Fragrant flowers in white, carmine-red, and rose pink appear from spring to late summer. Self sows freely. Prefers minimally to moderately fertile soil.

Monarda fistulosa
WILD BEE BALM

Ⓝ ☼ ◊ Z3–9 H9–1 ↕4ft (1.2m) ↔18in (45cm)

Flowers ranging from light pink to lilac-purple bloom from midsummer through early fall. Spicily aromatic leaves are reminiscent of thyme and oregano.

Miscanthus sinensis 'Morning Light'
VARIEGATED MAIDENGRASS

☼ ◊ Z5–9 H9–1 ↕↔4ft (1.2m)

Resembles *M. sinensis* 'Gracillimus' except for its narrow white leaf margins. Flowering panicles appear in autumn and persist throughout winter.

Amsonia tabernaemontana
WILLOW BLUESTAR

☼ ◊ Z3–9 H9–1 ↕18-24in (45-60cm) ↔12in (30cm)

Flowers appear from late spring to mid summer. A clump-forming perennial, it and other *Amsonia* are usually very long lived and require little maintenance.

MORE CHOICES

- *Actaea rubra* Z4–8 H8–1
- *Anemone japonica* Z4–8 H8–5
- *Armeria maritima* 'Cottontail' Z3–9 H9–1
- *Bergenia cordifolia* Z3–8 H8–1
- *Coreopsis lanceolata* 'Baby Gold' Z4–9 H12–1
- *Epimedium grandiflorum* 'Rose Queen' Z5–8 H8–5
- *Euphorbia marginata* Z13–15 H12–1
- *Helleborus argutifolius* Z6–9 H9–6
- *Kniphofia uvaria* Z5–9 H9–1
- *Lamium maculatum* 'Beedham's White' Z4–8 H8–1
- *Lysimachia clethroides* Z4–9 H9–1
- *Nepeta cataria* Z3–7 H7–1
- *Nepeta x faassenii* Z4–8 H8–1
- *Paeonia* 'Bowlof Beauty' Z3–8 H8–1
- *Papaver orientalis* Z5–7 H9–2
- *Penstemon barbatus* Z4–9 H9–1
- *Phlox subulata* Z3–9 H9–1
- *Rudebeckia hirta* Z3–7 H7–1
- *Veronica noveboracensis* Z4–8 H8–3

Hemerocallis 'Eenie Weenie'
EENIE WEENIE DAYLILY

☼ ◊ Z3–9 H12–1 ↕↔10in (25cm)

This is a compact cultivar with neat, mounded foliage. Very free-flowering, it usually blooms more than once during the season. Best when grown in fertile soil.

HERBACEOUS PLANTS

Perennials resistant to rabbit feeding

Although rabbits are much easier to exclude from a garden than deer, there are many situations where it is not feasible to attempt to keep rabbits out of an area. As natural habitats decrease, rabbits increasingly move into residential areas, chewing many plants to the ground. Here are some perennials that rabbits normally avoid.

Anemone x *hybrida*
JAPANESE WINDFLOWER

☼ ◐ ⚘ Z4–5 H8–5 ↕5ft (1.5m) ↔2ft (60cm)
Flowers in shades of white, pink, and purple appear from late summer to midautumn. This garden hybrid is also called *A.* x *elegans* and *A. japonica*.

Anemone narcissiflora
NARCISSUS ANEMONE

Ⓝ ☼ ◊ Z5–8 H8–5 ↕24in (60cm) ↔20in (50cm)
The daffodil-like flowers bloom from late spring to early summer. Plants are clump-forming, with a slightly woody rootstock. Prefers organic soil.

Aqulegia canadensis
CANADIAN COLUMBINE

Ⓝ ☼ ☀ ◊ Z3–8 H8–1 ↕3ft (1m) ↔12in (30cm)
Racemes of nodding flowers appear from midspring to midsummer. This delicate-looking perennial with dark green leaves divided into leaflets prefers fertile soil.

MORE CHOICES

- *Acanthus mollis* Z7–11 H12–7
- *Aconitum columbianum* Z3–8 H8–3
- *Anemone multifida* Z3–6 H6–1
- *Convallaria majalis* Z2–7 H7–1
- *Epimedium sulphureum* Z0 H8–5
- *Eryngium planum* Z4–9 H9–1
- *Euphorbia dulcis* 'Chameleon' Z4–9 H9–1
- *Euphorbia marginata* Z13–15 H12–1
- *Geranium* spp. and cultivars Z4–8 H12–2
- *Helleborus foetidus* Z6–9 H9–6
- *Helleborus niger* Z3–8 H8–1
- *Helleborus* x *hybridus* (Royal Heritage Strain) Z6–9 H9–1
- *Lamium maculatum* 'Beedham's White' Z4–8 H8–1
- *Nepeta* x *faassenii* Z4–8 H8–1
- *Paeonia officinalis* and cultivars Z3–8 H8–1
- *Pulmonaria saccarata* 'Mrs. Moon' Z3–8 H8–1
- *Sedum* spp. and cultivars Z6–9 H9–6
- *Tradescantia virginiana* Z5–9 H9–5
- *Trollius laxus* Z3–7 H

Bergenia 'Morgenröte'
MORNING RED HEARTLEAF SAXIFRAGE, PIGSQUEAK

☼ ☀ ☀ ◊ Z4–8 H8–1 ↕18in (45cm) ↔12in (30cm)
Flowers from mid- to late spring and will rebloom where summers are cool. Prefers organic soil but will tolerate poor soil. Also known as *B.* 'Morning Red'.

Agapanthus campanulatus
AFRICAN BLUE LILY

☼ ◊ Z7–11 H12–7 ↕4ft (1.2m) ↔20in (50cm)
Flowers appear during summer and range from deep violet to pale blue. Best grown in fertile soil. Benefits from winter mulching where marginally hardy.

Crocosmia x *crocosmiflora*
MONTBRETIA

☼ ☀ ◊ Z6–9 H9–3 ↕24in (60cm) ↔3in (8cm)
Summer flowers vary from yellow to orange to red. Prefers moderately fertile, organic soil. Hybrid cross between *C. aurea* and *C. pottsii*.

Aquilegia chrysantha
YELLOW COLUMBINE

Ⓝ ☼ ◑ ◊ Z3–8 H8–1 ‡4ft (1.2m) ↔2ft (60cm)
Flowers from late spring to late summer. Sepals can sometimes be tinged pink. A vigorous, erect plant with midgreen, divided leaves. Prefers fertile soil.

Aquilegia x hybrida
COLUMBINE HYBRIDS

☼ ◑ ◊ Z4–7 H7–1 ‡3ft (1m) ↔2ft (60cm)
A variable group. Mrs. Scott-Elliot hybrids are the tallest, followed closely by the McKana group. The Biedermeier Group has much shorter stems.

Aquilegia caerulea
ROCKY MOUNTAIN COLUMBINE

Ⓝ ☼ ◑ ◊ Z4–7 H7–1 ‡24in (60cm) ↔12in (30cm)
Spurred, 2in flowers bloom on upright plants from late spring to midsummer. The state flower of Colorado. Best in moderately fertile soil.

Astilbe chinensis var. taquetti 'Superba'
SUPERBA FALSE GOATSBEARD

☼ ◑ ◊ ● Z4–8 H8–2 ‡4ft (1.2m) ↔24in (60cm)
Flowers appear in late summer above dense, crinkled, bronze-green leaves. Prefers fertile, organic soil and is tolerant of occasional droughty conditions.

Astilbe x arendsii 'Amethyst'
AMETHYST ASTILBE

☼ ◑ ◊ ● Z4–8 H8–2 ‡60in (90cm) ↔3ft (1m)
Flowers appear in early summer above clumps of midgreen foliage divided into three leaflets. Prefers rich, organic soil. Divide every 3 to 5 years.

Aconitum 'Ivorine'
IVORINE MONKSHOOD

☼ ◊ Z3–8 H8–3 ‡5ft (1.5m) ↔20in (50cm)
Flowers are borne from late spring to early summer on upright, bushy plants. Best grown in fertile soil. May require staking. Also called A. septentrionale 'Ivorine'.

Slug-proof perennials

Slugs and snails rasp through leaves as they feed, leaving them jagged and tattered, and in some cases decimating the leaves. The thinner, smoother, and more tender the leaf, the more likely a slug will eat it. Here are some choices that are unappetizing to slugs. They either contain chemicals toxic to slugs or are notably tough-skinned or hairy.

HERBACEOUS PLANTS

Campanula rotundifolia
BLUEBELL, BLUEBELL BELLFLOWER

Ⓝ ☼ ☼ ◊ Z5–7 H7–3
↕↔5–12in (12–30cm)
This plant grows from underground runners. Blooms in summer. Flowers can also vary from lavender to purple or white. Good for rock gardens and naturalized under trees.

Corydalis lutea
YELLOW CORYDALIS

☼ ◊ Z5–8 H8–4 ↕↔8–12 (20–30cm)
Flowers from late spring to early autumn. A beautiful evergreen plant, it self-sows readily. Best if grown in moderately fertile to fertile soil.

Helleborus foetidus
STINKING HELLEBORE

☼ ◊ Z6–9 H9–6 ↕↔18in (45cm)
Flowers from midwinter to midspring. Although the foliage smells rank when bruised, the flower can have a pleasant aroma. Readily self-sows.

Artemisia absinthium
ABSINTHE, WORMWOOD

☼ ◊ Z4–8 H9–1 ↕36in (90cm) ↔24in (60cm)
A woody-based clumper with aromatic foliage. Grayish yellow flowers are borne in late summer. Cut back hard in fall to maintain a compact shape.

Epimedium x youngianum 'Roseum'
PINK YOUNG'S BARRENWORT

☼ ◊ Z5–9 H8–5 ↕12in (30cm) ↔12in (30cm)
Flowers from mid- to late spring. Flowers can be dusky pink to purple; foliage also varies. Prefers fertile, organic soil. Also goes by the cultivar name 'Lilacinum'.

Epimedium x perralchicum
BARRENWORT

☼ ◊ Z5–8 H8–5 ↕18in (45cm) ↔12in (30cm)
Pendent, bright yellow flowers bloom from mid- to late spring. The evergreen foliage of this garden hybrid is bronze when young, later turning deep green.

Heuchera micranthra
CREVICE ALUM ROOT

Ⓝ ☼ ☀ ◑ Z4–7 H8–2 ↕3ft (1m) ↔18in (45cm)

Flowers are produced in early summer. Grows best in fertile soil. Although mound-forming, it makes a good groundcover. Native to the Northwest.

Dicentra eximia 'Boothman's Variety'
BOOTHMAN'S BLEEDING HEART

Ⓝ ☀ ○ Z3–8 H10–1 ↕12in (30cm) ↔16in (40cm)

Flowers are produced from midspring to midsummer. A spreading, rhizomatous perennial, it prefers fertile, organic soil. Also goes by D. 'Stuart Boothman'.

Heuchera x brizoides
CORAL BELLS

☼ ☀ ◑ Z4–8 H8–1 ↕30in (75cm) ↔18in (45cm)

Flowers, varying from red to pink and white, bloom from late spring to early summer on mound-forming, plants. Highly attractive to hummingbirds.

MORE CHOICES

- *Achillea millefolium* Z3–9 H10–1
- *Achillea ptarmica 'The Pearl Superior'* Z3–8 H8–1
- *Achillea roseum 'Cerise Queen'* Z3–9 H9–1
- *Achillea taygetea 'Moonshine'* Z3–9 H9–1
- *Achillea x kellererii* Z5–7 H7–5
- *Artemesia lactiflora 'Guizhou'* Z5–8 H8–5
- *Artemesia ludovidiana 'Silver King'* Z5–9 H12–8
- *Artemisia 'Powis Castle'* Z6–9 H9–6
- *Artemesia 'Silver Brocade'* Z3–7 H7–1
- *Artemisia 'Silver Mound'* Z5–8 H8–3
- *Campanula persicifolia* Z3–8 H8–1
- *Epimedium x cantabrigiense* Z5–8 H8–5
- *Epimedium grandiflorum 'Rose Queen'* Z4–8 H8–2
- *Epimedium x rubrum* Z4–8 H8–1
- *Epimedium x youngianum* 'Niveum' Z5–9 H9–5
- *Euphorbia amygdaloides 'Purpurea'* Z6–10 H10–2
- *Euphorbia marginata* Z13–15 H12–1
- *Euphorbia polychroma* Z5–9 H9–5
- *Galanthus 'Atkinsii'* Z3–9 H9–1
- *Helleborus argutifolius* Z6–9 H9–6
- *Helleborus niger* Z3–8 H8–1
- *Heuchera sanguinea 'Splendens'* Z3–8 H8–1
- *Rudbeckia hirta* Z3–7 H7–1
- *Sedum spectabile* Z4–9 H9–1
- *Pulmonaria angustifolia 'Smokey Blue'* Z3–8 H8–1

Helleborus orientalis
LENTEN ROSE

☼ ◑ Z4–9 H8–3 ↕↔to 18in (45cm)

An elegant plant withleathery, deep green overwintering leaves. Flowers, most often white or greenish cream aging to pink, bloom from midwinter to midspring.

Euphorbia dulcis 'Chameleon'
CHAMELEON SPURGE

☼ ○◑ Z3–8 H10–1 ↕↔12in (30cm)

Greenish yellow flowers with purple-tinged bracts appear in early summer. Foliage changes from purple in spring to burgundy, then finally red. Self-sows.

Hosta 'Halcyon'
HALCYON HOSTA

☼ ● ◑ Z3–8 H9–2 ↕1ft (30cm) ↔3ft (1m)

Flower spikes appear during summer above smooth, thick leaves. An easy-to-grow, low-maintenance plant that can be massed or used as a specimen in borders.

Perennials to attract hummingbirds

Hummingbirds' fast metabolism requires them to take in plenty of sugars. Although many gardeners put out sugar-water feeders, nectar from plants is a superior natural alternative. Make sure to choose plants that bloom from early spring, when the first males arrive, to late summer, when all of the hummingbirds migrate southward.

HERBACEOUS PLANTS

Digitalis x mertonensis
MERTON FOXGLOVE, STRAWBERRY FOXGLOVE
☼ ◑ ◊ Z3–8 H8–1 ↕30in (75cm) ↔12in (30cm)
Flowers appear on tall flower spikes from late spring to early summer. This vigorous hybrid of *D. grandiflora* and *D. purpurea* comes true from seed.

Aquilegia chrysantha
YELLOW COLUMBINE
Ⓝ ☼ ◊ Z3–8 H8–1 ↕4ft (1.2m) ↔2ft (60cm)
A vigorous, erect plant with midgreen leaves divided into leaflets. Flowers from late spring to late summer. Sepals are sometimes tinged pink. Prefers fertile soil.

Aguilegia formosa
RED COLUMBINE, SCARLET COLUMBINE
Ⓝ ☼ ◑ ◊ Z4–7 H7–1 ↕3ft (1m) ↔18in (45cm)
Flowers appear from late spring to early summer. Very open airy plant with blue-green foliage. This Northwest native can grow in rocky soil and self-sows.

MORE CHOICES

- *Alcea rosea* Z3–9 H9–1
- *Aquilegia caerulea* Z4–7 H7–1
- *Aquilegia caerulea* 'Crimson Star' Z4–7 H7–1
- *Crocosmia* x 'Lucifer' Z6–9 H9–6
- *Delphinium nudicaule* Z5–7 H7–5
- *Delphinium* 'Red Rocket' Z3–8 H6–1
- *Epilobium canum* ssp. *latifolium* Z8–11 H12–8
- *Kniphofia uvaria* Z6–9 H9–1

Kniphofia 'Royal Standard'
ROYAL STANDARD RED-HOT POKER
☼ ◊ Z5–8 H9–4 ↕3–4ft (1–1.2m) ↔2ft (60cm)
Flowers are borne on thick stems from mid- to late summer. Prefers deep, fertile, sandy soil high in organic content. Spreads by sending out sideshoots.

Lobelia cardinalis
CARDINAL FLOWER
Ⓝ ☼ ◊ Z2–8 H8–1 ↕3ft (1m) ↔9in (23cm)
Flowers from summer to early autumn. Foliage is lance-shaped, bright green, and tinged with bronze. Best if grown in fertile, organic soil. Short-lived.

Crocosmia 'Emily McKenzie'
EMILY MCKENZIE MONTBRETIA
☼ ◊ Z6–9 H9–2 ↕24in (60cm) ↔6–8in (15–20cm)
Flowers in late summer. Prefers moderately fertile, organic soil. Mixes well with shrubs in a border and provides excellent, long-lasting cut flowers.

Heuchera sanguinea 'Splendens'
SPLENDENS CORAL BELLS
Ⓝ ☼ ◑ ◊ Z3–8 H8–1 ↕↔1–2ft (0.3–0.6m)
Flowers in summer high above kidney-shaped leaves. Prefers fertile soil high in organic matter. A clump former, but it can be grown as a groundcover.

Lupinus x hybrida 'My Castle'
MY CASTLE LUPINE

☼ ◊ Z4–7 H7–1 ↕3ft (1m) ↔30in (75cm)
Flowers bloom above clumps of palmate leaves from early to midsummer. Best grown in moderately fertile, light, sandy soil. Good in borders or naturalized areas.

Penstemon digitalis 'Husker Red'
HUSKER RED PENSTEMON

Ⓝ ☼ ☽ ◊ Z3–8 H8–1 ↕30in (75cm) ↔12in (30cm)
Flowers early to late summer. Tolerant of high humidity. Grow in moderately fertile to marginally fertile soil. Foliage/flower contrast provides a nice accent.

Asclepias tuberosa
BUTTERFLY WEED

Ⓝ ☼ ◊ Z4–9 H9–2 ↕30in (75cm) ↔18in (45cm)
Blooms in midsummer. Prefers fertile, well-drained, loamy soil. Forms a large, rather long taproot, so transplant when young. Long-lived.

MORE CHOICES

- *Lupinus hybrida* Z4–7 H7–1
- *Mimulus cardinalis* Z6–9 H9–6
- *Monarda citridora* Z4–8 H8–1
- *Monarda clinopodia* Z4–8 H8–1
- *Monarda fistulosa* 'Claire Grace' Z3–9 H9–1
- *Nicotiana alata* Z10–11 H12–1
- *Penstemon barbatus* Z4–9 H9–2

Veronica spicata 'Red Fox'
RED FOX SPIKE SPEEDWELL

☼ ◊ Z3–8 H8–3 ↕↔12in (30cm)
Blooms late spring to early summer. It makes a good midground perennial and can also be used as a focal point in the bed. Attracts bees and butterflies.

Aquilegia 'Music Medley'
HYBRID COLUMBINE

☼ ☽ ◊ Z3–7 H7–1 ↕23ft (1m) ↔18in (45cm)
This cultivar offers longer-lasting, larger blooms. Also includes solid white and yellow flowers as well as white bicolors with blue, pink, and red.

Monarda didyma 'Marshall's Delight'
MARSHALL'S DELIGHT BEE BALM

☼ ☽ ◊ Z4–8 H8–1 ↕3ft (1m) ↔24in (60cm)
Blooms mid- to late summer. Spreads slowly by runners. Prefers moderately fertile, organic soil. Attracts bees and butterflies. Resists powdery mildew.

Monarda didyma 'Jacob Cline'
JACOB CLINE BEE BALM

☼ ☽ ◊ Z4–11 H12–1 ↕3–4ft (1–1.3m) ↔2ft (0.6m)
Blooms mid- to late summer Grow in moderately fertile, organic, moist, well-drained soil. More resistant to powdery mildew and rust than the species.

HERBACEOUS PLANTS

Perennials to attract butterflies

Adult butterflies depend on nectar from flowers as their main food source. They use their retractable proboscis, which is highly specialized for siphoning up nectar, to feed from shallow disk flowers (found in the daisy family) as easily as from deep tubular flowers. Some butterflies migrate to your garden from more southerly areas, while others may overwinter.

Sedum kamtschaticum 'Variegatum'
ORANGE STONECROP

☼ ◊ Z3–8 H8–1 ‡2–3in (5–8cm) ↔8in (20cm)
Late summer flowers slowly fade to crimson as they age. Clump-forming rhizomes should be divided every 4–5 years. Prefers moderately fertile soil.

Lilium candidum
MADONNA LILY

☼ ◊ Z6–9 H9–6 ‡↔3–6ft (1–2m)
A shiny, bright green basal leaf rosette gives rise to a tall flower stalk in summer. The flowers are sweetly fragrant. Susceptible to *Botrytis* (gray mold).

MORE CHOICES

- *Achillea millefolium* 'Cerise Queen' Z3–9 H9–1
- *Aquilegia canadensis* Z4–7 H7–1
- *Aster dumosus* Z4–8 H8–1
- *Aster novi belgii* Z4–8 H8–1
- *Aubrieta deltoidea* Z5–7 H7–5
- *Centranthus ruber* Z5–8 H8–5
- *Ceratostigma plumbaginoides* Z5–9 H9–4

Liatris spicata
DENSE GAYFEATHER

Ⓝ ☼ ◊ Z4–9 H9–5 ‡24in (60cm) ↔12in (30cm)
Long-lasting flowers appear from late summer to early fall. Prefers light, moderately fertile, organic soil. In cooler regions, mulch plants during winter.

Aster cordifolius
BLUE WOOD ASTER

Ⓝ ☼ ◑ Z5–8 H8–1 ‡↔2–5ft (60cm–1.5m)
Flowers from late summer to midfall. Clump forming plant with long-stalked, oval to heart-shaped leaves. Best if grown in moderately fertile soil.

Eupatorium fistulosum
JOE PYE WEED

Ⓝ ☼ ◑ ◊ Z3–8 H8–2 ‡5ft (1.5m) ↔3ft (1m)
A compact, upright plant with wine-colored stems and whorls of lance-shaped leaves. Flowers from summer to fall. An excellent source of nectar for butterflies.

Chelone obliqua 'Alba'
TURTLEHEAD

☼ ◑ ◑ Z3–9 H9–3 ‡2–3ft (0.6–1m) ↔2ft (60cm)
Stiff, upright plants bear flowers in white, pink, or purple from late summer to midfall. They grow best in deep, fertile soil and will tolerate heavy clay soils.

Salvia chamaedryoides
GERMANDER SAGE

☼ ☼ ◐ Z7–11 H12–7 ‡12in (30cm) ↔24in (60cm)

Flowers appear in late summer on a branching, woody-based, tender perennial. Good container plant. Best if grown in light, moderately fertile, organic soil.

Allium cernuum
NODDING ONION

Ⓝ ☼ ◊ Z3–9 H9–5 ‡28in (70cm) ↔5in (12cm)

A vigorous, bulbous plant with strap-shaped, dark green basal leaves. Flowers are borne in summer. Plant the bulbs in fertile soil in fall.

MORE CHOICES

- Coreopsis tripteris Z4–9 H9–1
- Dianthus chinensis Z9–11 H12–1
- Echinacea purpurea Z3–9 H9–1
- Helianthus angustifolius Z6–9 H9–4
- Hemerocallis species and cultivars Z3–8 H12–1
- Liatris punctata Z3–9 H
- Lilium pardalinum Z5–8 H8–5
- Lobelia cardinalis Z2–8 H8–1
- Nepeta faassenii and cultivars Z4–8 H8–1
- Origanum laevigatum and cultivars Z7–11 H12–1
- Penstemon cobaea Z7–10 H12–7
- Rudbeckia hirta Z3–7 H7–1
- X Solidaster luteus Z5–8 H8–5

Penstemon serrulatus
CASCADE PENSTEMON

Ⓝ ☼ ◊ Z3–9 H9–1 ‡24in (60cm) ↔12in (30cm)

Flowers in late summer above spreading, semi-evergreen foliage. Grow in moderately to marginally fertile soil. NW native. Also known as P. difussus.

Astilbe chinensis
FALSE GOATSBEARD, CHINESE SPIRAEA

☼ ☼ ◊◐ Z3–8 H8–2 ‡4ft (1.3m) ↔2ft (60cm)

Flowers in late summer. Grow in fertile, organic soil. They are easy to propagate by division, which should be done in spring just as new growth emerges.

Verbena peruviana
PERUVIAN MOCK VERVAIN

☼ ◊ Z9–11 H12–9 ‡3in (8cm) ↔3ft (1m)

Flowers appear from summer to fall. A fast-growing, semievergreen, tender perennial also known as V. chamaedrifolia and V. chamaedriodes.

Phlox maculata
WILD SWEET WILLIAM

Ⓝ ☼ ◊ Z5–8 H8–1 ‡3ft (1m) ↔18in (45cm)

An upright, clumping plant best grown in fertile soil. Try to keep foliage dry when watering to decrease mildew. Deadhead to promote repeat bloom.

Perennials for cut foliage

A well-balanced flower arrangement does not rely exclusively on flowers. Foliage, which acts both as filler and as textural contrast, is also a integral part of any arrangement. The following are perennials that have interesting foliage that holds up well in a wet arrangement. Most of these perennials will also provide flowers as well.

HERBACEOUS PLANTS

Bergenia 'Morgenröte'
MORNING RED HEARTLEAF SAXIFRAGE, PIGSQUEAK
☼ ◑ ● ◊ Z4–8 H8–1 ‡18in (45cm) ↔12in (30cm)
Flowers from mid- to late spring and will rebloom where summers are cool. Prefers organic soil but will tolerate poor soil. Also known as 'Morning Red'.

Astilbe x *arendsii* 'Granat'
GRANAT ASTILBE
☼ ◑ ◊ Z3–8 H8–2 ‡2ft (60cm) ↔3ft (1m)
Flowers appear in midsummer above very dark green, pinnate foliage. Prefers organic, rich soil. Divide every 4 years to maintain bloom quality.

MORE CHOICES

- *Artemesia ludoviciana* 'Silver King'
  Z5–9 H12–8
- *Astilbe japonica* Z3–8 H8–2
- *Astilbe simplicifolia* Z4–8 H8–2
- *Bergenia cordifolia* 'Morning Red' Z4–8 H8–1
- *Heuchera americana* 'Pewter Veil' Z4–8 H8–1
- *Heuchera americana* 'Plum Puddin'
  Z4–8 H8–1

Astilbe 'Bronze Elegance'
BRONZE ELEGANCE ASTILBE
☼ ◑ ●● Z3–8 H8–2 ‡12in (30cm) ↔10in (25cm)
Blooms in late summer on reddish green stems. Dark green, pinnate leaves are flushed bronze. Also listed and sold as 'Bronce Elegans'.

Arum italicum
LORDS AND LADIES
☼ ◑ ◊ Z7–9 H9–3 ‡↔12–18in (30–45cm)
Blooms in early summer bear pale greenish white spathes. Fruit (shown) appear in the fall. Arrow-shaped leaves have white veins. Prefers organic soil.

Hakonechloa macra 'Aureola'
GOLDEN JAPANESE FOREST GRASS
☼ ◑ ◊ Z5–9 H9–4 ‡14in (35cm) ↔16in (40cm)
Forms mounds of arching leaves that are bright yellow with narrow green stripes until they turn red in fall. Pale green spikelets open late summer to midautumn.

Polystichum acrostichoides
CHRISTMAS FERN

Ⓝ ☀ ◗ Z3–8 H8–1 ‡24in (60cm) ↔18in (45cm)

Evergreen foliage emerges from the rhizomes looking like a shuttlecock. The fiddleheads (new shoots) have a silver cast. Clumps enlarge but do not spread widely.

Polystichum munitum
SWORD FERN

Ⓝ ☀ ◗ Z3–8 H8–1 ‡4ft (1.2m) ↔12in (30cm)

Similar in appearance but much larger than the related *P. acrostichoides* and with more leathery leaves. The large, evergreen fronds may live for several years.

Rodgersia pinnata
RODGERSIA, RODGER'S FLOWER

☀ ☀ ◗ Z3–7 H7–1 ‡to 4ft (1.2m) ↔30in (75cm)

Blooms in mid- to late summer. Flowers can also be found in white and pink. Leaf and flower stalks are reddish green. Grow in soil rich in organic matter.

Hosta 'Gold Edger'
GOLD EDGER HOSTA

☀ ◗ Z3–8 H9–2 ‡↔3ft (1m)

This beautiful, compact hosta grows to full size quickly. The white to lavender flowers appear in early summer. Prefers fertile soil and a summer mulch.

Hosta 'Halcyon'
HALCYON HOSTA

☀ ☀ ◗ Z3–8 H9–2 ‡1ft (30cm) ↔3ft (1m)

Flower spikes appear during the summer. Leaves are smooth and thick. An easy-to-grow, low-maintenance plant. Grow as a specimen or massed in mixed borders.

HERBACEOUS PLANTS

Perennials for cut flowers

One of the most pleasant ways to enjoy your garden is through cutting flowers and making flower arrangements, both fresh and dried. This brings the pleasant colors and textures into your home, where you can enjoy them when your activities require you to be inside. You can also share the beauty of your garden with someone you care about.

Tulipa 'Garden Party'
GARDEN PARTY TULIP
☼ ◊ Z3–8 H8–1 ‡12–14in (30–35cm)
This Triumph-type tulip is a midseason bloomer. A wonderful bedding plant, it can also be forced indoors for early flowering. Best when grown in fertile soil.

Achillea millefolium 'Paprika'
PAPRIKA YARROW
☼ ◊ Z3–9 H8–2 ‡↔24in (60cm)
Blooms from early to late summer. Seedheads will persist through the winter if not cut back. Self-sows, so deadhead if you don't want seedlings showing up.

Astilbe chinensis
FALSE GOATSBEARD, CHINESE SPIREA
☼☼ ◊◊ Z4–8 H8–2 ‡↔24in (60cm)
Flowers in late summer. Grow in fertile, organic soil. They are easy to propagate by division, which should be done in spring just as the new growth emerges.

MORE CHOICES

- *Achillea* 'Moonshine' Z3–8 H8–1
- *Achillea filipendula* 'Parker's Variety' Z3–9 H9–1
- *Achillea culivars* Z4–9 H9–2
- *Aster* x *frikartii* Z4–8 H8–1
- *Astilbe* x *arendsii* and cultivars Z4–8 H8–2
- *Astilbe japonica* and cultivars Z3–8 H8–2
- *Astilbe simplicifolia* and cultivars Z3–8 H8–2
- *Campanula persicifolia* Z3–8 H8–1
- *Delphinium carolinianum* Z5–8 H8–3
- *Delphinium elatum* Z3–8 H7–3
- *Delphinium nudicaule* Z5–7 H7–5
- *Delphinium* 'Red Rocket' Z3–8 H6–1
- *Echinacea purpurea* 'Magnus' Z3–9 H9–1
- *Galtonia candicans* Z7–10 H10–7
- *Gypsophila paniculata* Z5–9 H9–1

Coreopsis grandiflora
LARGEFLOWER TICKSEED
Ⓝ ☼☼ ◊ Z4–9 H12–1 ‡3ft (1m) ↔18in (45cm)
Flowers from late spring to late summer the first year from seed so is sometimes treated as an annual. Good in a natural or wild flower garden.

Convallaria majalis
LILY-OF-THE-VALLEY

☀ ◊ Z2–7 H7–1 ‡6in (15cm) ↔indefinite
Colonizing plants produce strongly sweet-scented flowers in spring. Prefers organic soil and an application of leaf mold mulch in fall.

Catananche caerulea
CUPID'S DART

☀ ◊ Z3–8 H8–1 ‡3ft (1m) ↔12in (30cm)
Blooms from midsummer to fall. A relatively short-lived, clump-forming perennial. Requires only moderate fertilization. Sensitive to wet winter soil.

Baptisia australis
FALSE INDIGO

Ⓝ ☀ ◊ Z3–9 H9–1 ‡30in (75cm) ↔24in (60cm)
Blooms in early summer and attracts native birds. Almost black seedpods are ornamental. Best used in the back of a border or as a specimen plant.

Phlox paniculata 'Starfire'
STARFIRE GARDEN PHLOX

Ⓝ ☀ ☀ ◊ Z4–8 H8–1 ‡4ft (1.2m) ↔24in (60cm)
Bronzy green foliage shows off the vivid flowers that bloom from summer to early fall. Grows best in fertile soil. Attracts hummingbirds and butterflies.

Echinacea purpurea
PURPLE CONEFLOWER

Ⓝ ☀ ◊ Z3–9 H9–3 ‡to 5ft (1.5m) ↔18in (45cm)
Flowers from midsummer to early fall. Prefers deep, organic soil. The cultivars bred from this native plant are often more suitable for the garden border.

MORE CHOICES

- *Gypsophila paniculata* 'Bristol Fairy' Z5–9 H9–1
- *Iris siberica* Z3–9 H9–1
- *Leucanthemum* x *superbum* Z5–8 H8–1
- *Leucojum aestivum* 'Gravetye Giant' Z4–9 H8–1
- *Paeonia officinalis* and cultivars Z3–8 H8–1
- *Phlox paniculata* and cultivars Z4–8 H8–1
- *Platycodon grandiflorus* and cultivars Z3–7 H9–3
- *Schizostylis coccinea* Z7–9 H9–7
- *Solidago rugosa* 'Fireworks' Z4–9 H9–1
- *Thermopsis caroliniana* Z6–9 H9–3
- *Viola odorata* Z6–8 H8–6

Paeonia 'Bowl of Beauty'
BOWL OF BEAUTY PEONY

☀ ☀ ◊ Z3–8 H8–1 ‡↔3ft (1m)
This and many similar cultivars bloom from late spring to early summer. Grow in deep, fertile, organic soil. Peonies dislike transplanting once established.

Liatris spicata
DENSE GAYFEATHER

Ⓝ ☀ ◊ Z4–9 H9–5 ‡24in (60cm) ↔12in (30cm)
Long-lasting flowers bloom from late summer to early fall. Prefers light, moderately fertile, organic soil. In cooler regions, mulch plants during the winter.

HERBACEOUS PLANTS

Notable and reliable daylilies

Daylilies are the workhorses of the perennial stable. As a group, they bloom from late spring to early fall (occasionally later), and many cultivars bloom for a month to six weeks continuously. Some cultivars, and a few of the species, are fragrant as well. They tolerate many soil types, with the exception of extremely heavy, wet clay.

Hemerocallis 'Catherine Woodbury'
CATHERINE WOODBURY DAYLILY
☼ ◑ z3–10 H12–2 ↕28in (70cm) ↔30in (75cm)
Fragrant, abundant flowers appear from early to midseason. Introduced in 1967 and still widely grown. Foliage is deciduous.

MORE CHOICES

- *Hemerocallis* 'Autumn Red' z3–9 H12–1
- *Hemerocallis* 'Bitsy' z3–11 H12–1
- *Hemerocallis* 'Black Eyed Stella' z5–11 H12–1
- *Hemerocallis* 'Chicago Royal Robe' z3–9 H12–1
- *Hemerocallis* 'Custard Candy' z3–11 H12–1
- *Hemerocallis* 'Frankly Scarlet' z5–10 H10–1
- *Hemerocallis* 'Janice Brown' z3–11 H12–1
- *Hemerocallis* 'Judith' z3–11 H12–1
- *Hemerocallis* 'LeeBea Orange Crush' z3–11 H12–1
- *Hemerocallis* 'Plum Perfect' z5–10 H10–1
- *Hemerocallis* 'Red Volunteer' z3–11 H12–1

Hemerocallis 'Stella D'Oro'
STELLA D'ORO DAYLILY
☼ ◑ z3–9 H12–1
↕12in (30cm) ↔18in (45cm)
Probably the most popular of all daylilies, 'Stella' is vigorous and free-flowering, starting early and repeating throughout the season. Fragrant. Deciduous. Introduced in 1975.

Hemerocallis 'Frans Hals'
FRANS HALS DAYLILY
☼ ◑ z3–10 H12–2 ↕↔2ft (0.6m)
A long-blooming, mid- to late-season cultivar in a seldom-seen color pattern. Deciduous. Introduced in 1955. Selected offspring of *H.* 'Baggette' x 'Corell'.

Hemerocallis 'Cherry Cheeks'
CHERRY CHEEKS DAYLILY
☼ ◑ z3–10 H12–2 ↕↔24–30in (60–75cm)
Blooms appear from early to midseason. Introduced in 1968 and is still a garden favorite. This vigorous tetraploid is deciduous.

Hemerocallis 'Joan Senior'
JOAN SENIOR DAYLILY

☀ ◊ Z3–9 H12–1 ↕↔24in (60cm)

Flowers from early to midseason and then repeats. Introduced in 1977. Semievergreen foliage. Selected offspring of *H.* 'Loving Memory' and 'Little Infant'.

Hemerocallis 'Pardon Me'
PARDON ME DAYLILY

☀ ◊ Z5–11 H12–1 ↕↔18in (45cm)

Free-flowering, bearing fragrant flowers in midseason and repeating reliably. Foliage is deciduous. Introduced in 1982. Selected descendant of *H.* 'Little Grapette'.

Hemerocallis 'Hyperion'
HYPERION DAYLILY

☀ ☀ ◊ Z3–10 H12–2
↕↔3ft (90cm)

Fragrant flowers appear from early to midseason. The narrow leaves are deciduous. Introduced in 1925 and still grown widely.

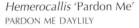

Hemerocallis 'Siloam Fairy Tale'
SILOAM FAIRY TALE DAYLILY

☀ ◊ Z3–9 H12–1 ↕20in (50cm) ↔18in (45cm)

Bears wonderfully fragrant flowers from early to midseason. Foliage is deciduous. One of many excellent members of the 'Siloam' series.

Hemerocallis 'Pink Damask'
PINK DAMASK DAYLILY

☀ ◊ Z3–9 H9–1 ↕↔3ft (1m)

A repeat-blooming plant with flowers in midseason. Foliage is deciduous. Introduced in 1951 and still treasured for its sherbetlike coloration.

HERBACEOUS PLANTS

Notable and reliable ferns

Many ferns are surprisingly tough plants that are generally easy to grow in moist, shady locations. They need some attention paid to watering when they are first planted, but once they are established they require only a minimum of routine care. They provide rich textures and a subtle, arguably primitive ambience to a garden setting.

Athyrium filix-femina
LADY FERN

Ⓝ ☀ ◐ Z4–9 H9–1 ↕4ft (1.2m) ↔3ft (1m)
The deciduous foliage radiates out from the center of the rhizome. Adaptable to many soil conditions, but it prefers fertile, highly organic soil.

Athyrium nipponicum 'Pictum'
JAPANESE PAINTED FERN

☀ ◐ Z5–8 H8–1 ↕12in (30cm) ↔indefinite
Showy, arching fronds increase slowly from spreading clumps on this deciduous fern. They color up best when the plants are grown in light shade.

Blechnum spicant
DEER FERN

Ⓝ ☀ ◐ Z10–11 H12–10 ↕30in (75cm) ↔18in (45cm)
The older, sterile fronds lay out horizontally on this tufted, evergreen fern that grows from short, creeping rhizomes. Contrasts attractively with finer foliage.

MORE CHOICES

- *Adiantum aleuticum* Z3–8 H8–1
- *Asplenium ebenoides* Z3–9 H9–1
- *Asplenium platyneuron* Z3–9 H9–1
- *Asplenium trichomanes* Z5–8 H8–3
- *Athyrium otophorum* Z5–8 H8–2
- *Athyrium pycnocarpon* Z5–8 H8–2
- *Dennstaedtia punctilobula* Z3–8 H8–1
- *Dryopteris carthusiana* Z6–8 H8–6
- *Dryopteris dilatata* Z5–8 H8–5
- *Osmunda claytoniana* Z2–10 H9–1
- *Pteridium auilinum* Z5–9 H9–1
- *Thelypteris palustris* Z5–8 H8–3
- *Woodsia obtusa* Z4–7 H7–1

Polystichum acrostichoides
CHRISTMAS FERN

Ⓝ ☀ ◐ Z3–8 H8–1 ↕24in (60cm) ↔18in (45cm)
Evergreen foliage emerges from the rhizomes looking like a shuttlecock. Fiddleheads (emerging fronds) have a silver cast. Clumps enlarge over time but do not spread.

Onoclea sensibilis
SENSITIVE FERN

Ⓝ ☀ ◐ Z4–9 H9–1 ↕↔18in (45cm)
This graceful fern produces both upright and arching , deciduous fronds. Fronds emerging in early spring can be tinted pink to bronze.

Polystichum munitum
SWORD FERN

Ⓝ ☀ ◐ Z3–8 H8–1 ↕4ft (1.2m) ↔12in (30cm)
Similar in appearance but much larger than *P. acrostichoides*, with more leathery leaves. Each large frond may live for several years. Evergreen.

Gymnocarpium dryopteris
OAK FERN

Ⓝ ☀ ◆ z4–8 H8–1 ‡8in (20cm) ↔indefinite
Deciduous foliage, pale to yellow-green when young, darkens with age. Fiddleheads, appearing in sets of three, emerge throughout the growing season.

Dryopteris filix-mas
MALE FERN

Ⓝ ☀ ◑ z4–8 H8–1 ‡4ft (1.2m) ↔3ft (1m)
Deciduous fronds emerge from the crown of a large rhizome. They open pale green and become darker and more leathery with age. Tolerant of many soil types.

Osmunda cinnamomea
CINNAMON FERN

Ⓝ ☀ ◑ z3–9 H9–1 ‡3ft (1m) ↔18in (45cm)
This upright fern's erect, fertile fronds bear cinnamon-colored sporangia in early spring. The deciduous sterile fronds turn yellow in fall.

Osmunda regalis
ROYAL FERN

Ⓝ ☀ ◆ z2–10 H9–1 ‡6ft (2m) ↔3ft (1m)
The brown, fertile fronds are produced in summer. The sterile, deciduous fronds turn yellow in autumn. Rhizomes are the source of osmunda fiber used in orchid culture.

HERBACEOUS PLANTS

Annuals and biennials for full sun

Fast-growing annuals and biennials give you the ability to realize gardening expectations very quickly. Because they are short lived, they also allow you to change the look of a garden area from one year (or even one season) to the next. They are extremely useful for filling gaps in your sunny beds as you wait for perennials and shrubs to grow.

MORE CHOICES

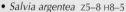

- *Antirrhinum majus* z7–9 H9–1
- *Centaurea cyanus* z0 H7–1
- *Consolida orientalis* z0 H12–1
- *Cosmos bipinnatus* z11–12 H12–1
- *Dianthus barbatus* z3–8 H9–1
- *Gypsophila elegans* z5–9 H9–1
- *Helianthus annuus* z0 H12–1
- *Helichrysum bracteatum* z10–11 H12–1
- *Lathyrus odoratus* z9–10 H8–1
- *Limonium sinuatum* z0 H9–3
- *Oenothera biennis* z4–8 H8–1
- *Salvia argentea* z5–8 H8–5

Tithonia rotundifolia
TITHONIA, MEXICAN SUNFLOWER

☼ ◊ z11 H12–1 ‡6ft (2m) ↔12in (30cm)

A vigorous annual with velvety green leaves that are hairy below. Flowers are produced from late summer to autumn. Deadheading promotes rebloom.

Alcea rosea
HOLLYHOCK

☼ ◊ z3–9 H9–1 ‡5–6ft (1.5–2m) ↔2ft (60cm)

Upright, short-lived, summer-blooming perennial usually grown as a biennial. Many colorful single and double cultivars are available. Grow in moderately fertile soil.

Scabiosa atropupurea
PINCUSHION FLOWER

☼ ◊ z10–11 H9–4 ‡3ft (1m) ↔to 9in (23cm)

Solitary, fragrant flowers are borne in summer on wiry-stemmed plants with midgreen leaves. Grow this plant in moderately fertile soil. Attractive to bees

Cleome spinosa
SPIDER FLOWER

☼ ◊ z11 H12–1 ‡4ft (1.2m) ↔18in (45cm)

Scented flowers appear in summer. Grows best in light, fertile, sandy soil. Palmate leaves clothe the strong stems. Annual.

Cosmos bipinnatus
CANDYSTRIPE COSMOS

☼ ◊ H12–1 ‡6ft (2m) ↔18in (45cm)

Flowers range from orange to yellow and single to semidouble, depending on the cultivar. Deadheading old blooms extends the bloom period. Self-sowing.

Rudbeckia triloba
BROWN-EYED SUSAN

Ⓝ ☼ ☀ ◊ z3–11 H12–1 ‡to 5ft (1.5m) ↔3ft (1m)

This branching, clump-forming biennial produces an abundance of flowers in summer and autumn the second year from sowing. Grows best in moderately fertile soil.

Dimorphotheca aurantiaca
AFRICAN DAISY

☼ ◊ Z9–11 H12–6 ‡↔12in (30cm)
Upright annual with oval to lance-shaped, aromatic leaves. Flowers in summer. Grows best in light fertile soils. Deadheading promotes rebloom.

Ageratum houstonianum
AGERATUM, FLOSS FLOWER

☼ ◊ Z10–13 H12–1 ‡↔8in (20cm)
Fast-growing, mounding annual. Flowers appear in summer and autumn and vary from bright or gray-blue to pink or white. Good butterfly plant.

Petunia x hybrida
PETUNIA

☼ ◊ Z9–11 H12–1 ‡↔12in (30cm)
Petunias bloom virtually all season in a huge range of colors except orange, including bicolors and picotees. All grow best in light, fertile soil. Annual.

Iberis umbellata
CANDYTUFT

☼ ◐ Z10–11 H10–1 ‡6–12in (15–30cm) ↔to 9in (23cm)
Bushy, mound-forming annual with scented flowers from spring to summer. Prefers moderately fertile soil.

Portulaca grandiflora
MOSS ROSE

☼ ◊ Z9–11 H12–1 ‡8in (20cm)
Flowers prolifically all summer. Available in single and double forms and in many colors. Grows well in poor, sandy soils. Annual.

Celosia cultivars
COCKSCOMB

☼ ◊ Z11 H9–2 ‡8–20in (20–50cm)
Annualcockcombs are stalwarts for summer beds. The Plumosa group has upright plumes of flowers; the Cristata group cultivars bear tight clusters.

Tagetes cultivars
MARIGOLD

☼ ◑ ◊ H12–1 ‡1–3ft (30cm–1m) ↔12–18in (30–45cm)
Flowers from late spring until frost and responds well to deadheading. Most are crosses between T. erecta and T. patula.

Brassica oleracea
FLOWERING KALE

☼ ◊ Z8–9 H9–1 ‡↔18in (45cm)
This ornamental relative of cabbage and kale is grown for its colorful fall foliage. Biennials, they flower the following year if allowed to stand.

Annuals and biennials for shade

Almost every garden has at least one small pocket that the sun barely reaches. Other gardens with structures, such as solid fences, or a large number of trees, can accommodate an entire bed of shade-loving plants. Here are some short-lived plants to fill in the gaps between shade-loving shrubs and perennials or to make up an entire bed.

Solenostemon scutellarioides cultivars
COLEUS
☼ ◊ Z11–12 H12–1 ‡18 (45cm) ↔12in (30cm)
These tender perennials are grown as annuals in most locations more for their attractive foliage than the tiny blue or white flowers. Huge range of cultivars.

MORE CHOICES

- *Begonia semperflorens* Z13–15 H12–10
- *Begonia x tuberhybrida* 'Tuberous begonia' Z13–15 H12–10
- *Caladium bicolor* 'Fancy Caladium' Z13–15 H12–10
- *Exacuum affine* Z0 H7–1
- *Fuchsia* 'Double Otto' Z7–11 H12–9
- *Impatiens* hybrids 'New Guinea Impatiens' Z13–15 H12–10
- *Mathhiola bicornis* Z7–9 H9–1
- *Mimulus hybrids* Z6–9 H9–6
- *Myosotis sylvatica* Z5–9 H9–5
- *Nemophila menziesii* Z0 H12–2
- *Viola tricolor* Z3–9 H12–1

Viola x *wittrockiana*
PANSY
☼ ◊ Z6–9 H9–1 ‡8in (20cm) ↔8in (20cm)
Bred for cool-weather flowering. Additional colors include blue, white, orange, pink, red, and purple, often in "face" patterns. Prefers fertile, organic soil.

Digitalis purpurea
COMMON FOXGLOVE
☼ ◊ Z4–8 H9–1 ‡3–5ft (1–1.5m) ↔2ft (60cm)
Rosette-forming plant with large flower spikes that bloom in early summer. Can be biennial or perennial. Tolerates poor and arid soils.

Lobelia erinus
STRING PEARLS
☼ ◊ Z9–10 H7–1 ‡↔6in (15cm)
These are bushy, trailing perennials grown as annuals for their flowers from summer through autumn in shades of blue, purple, pink, red and white.

Fuchsia 'Gartenmeister Bonstedt'
GARTENMEISTERS FUCHSIA
☼ ◊ Z9–11 H12–9 ‡↔24–36in (60–90cm)
A free-flowering, upright, tender shrub often grown as an annual. The leaves are dark bronze-red with purple undersides. Prefers fertile soil.

Fuchsia 'Autumnale'
AUTUMNALE FUCHSIA

☼ ◊ z9–11 H12–9 ↕6ft (2m) ↔20in (50cm)
This trailing, tender shrub is often grown as an annual.
Summer flowering. Foliage progresses from green-
yellow to dark red and salmon with splashes of yellow.

Fuchsia x hybrida 'Magellanica'
LADY'S EARDROPS

☼ ◊ z9–11 H12–9 ↕10ft (3m) ↔6ft (2m)
Flowers freely during summer. Flowers also occur in
deeper red or white. This erect shrub is susceptible to
frost damage and so is often grown as an annual.

Myosotis alpestris
FORGET-ME-NOT

☼ ◊ z4–8 H8–1 ↕↔4–6in (10–15cm)
Flowers from spring to early summer appear on short-
lived, clump-forming perennials grown as annuals.
Also known as *M. rupicola*.

Impatiens balsamina
ROSE BALSAM

☼ ◊◊◊ H12–1 ↕30in (75cm) ↔18in (45cm)
Flowers range from white, pink, and red to lilac as
well as bicolors and doubled forms, which have only
a light scent. Prefers organic soil.

Impatiens walleriana
BUSY LIZZIE

☼☼ ◊ z10–15 H12–1 ↕↔2ft (60cm)
A tender perennial that flowers freely the first year.
Plants start blooming in late spring and continue to
frost. Many cultivars are available.

Annuals and biennials for cut flowers

One way to enjoy your gardening more is to bring home-grown cut flowers inside for use in both fresh and long-lasting dried arrangements. Cutting annual flowers actually encourages many of them to produce more blooms, especially if done regularly. Some of these offer the added bonus of an appealing scent.

HERBACEOUS PLANTS

Centaurea cyanus
BACHELOR'S BUTTONS

☼ ◊ H7–1 ‡1–3ft (30cm–1m) ↔1ft (30cm)
Flower colors also include purple, red, pink, and white. Easy to grow from seed. The flowers last well when cut and may be dried.

Calendula officinalis
POT MARIGOLD

☼ ☼ ◊ z0 H6–1 ‡30in (75cm) ↔18in (45cm)
Also available in cream and orange shades. Normally blooms from spring to summer; can be enjoyed during winter in southernmost areas of Nevada and Utah.

Dianthus caryophyllus
CARNATION

☼ ◊ Z7–10 H10–7 ‡32in (80cm) ↔12–24in
The border forms of this species make suitable additions to the garden, and many varieties are fragrant. These are perennials grown as annuals.

MORE CHOICES

- *Antirrhinum majus* Z7–9 H9–1
- *Briza maxima* z0 H12–1
- *Consolida orientalis* z0 H12–1
- *Dianthus barbatus* Z3–8 H9–1
- *Helianthus annuus* z0 H12–1
- *Lathyrus odoratus* Z9–10 H8–1
- *Salvia horminium* Z11–15 H12–10

Erysimum cheiri
WALLFLOWER

☼ ◊ Z7–8 H9–2 ‡32in (80cm) ↔16in (40cm)
Exquisitely fragrant flowers come in shades of yellow, orange, and red. This is a perennial grown as an annual in most areas except for the Pacific Northwest.

Nigella damascena
LOVE-IN-A-MIST

☼ ◊ H10–1 ‡24in (60cm) ↔8in (20cm)
Flowers range from blue, white, to rose and then produce ornamental pods as shown. This self-sowing annual blooms freely in areas with cool summers.

Amaranthus caudatus
AMARANTHUS, LOVE-LIES-BLEEDING

☼ ◊ Z10–15 H12–1 ‡5ft (1.5m) ↔30in (75cm)
Flowers range from crimson to purple or blood red (hence the common name) or green, as in 'Viridis'. Tolerates poor soil; best in moderately fertile soil.

Cosmos bipannatus
CANDYSTRIPE COSMOS

☼ ◊ Z11 H12–1 ‡6ft (2m) ↔18in (45cm)
Colors range from clear yellow to orange and near red. Has the potential to self-sow. Bloom period can be extended greatly by removing the faded blooms.

Gypsophila elegans
BABY'S BREATH

☼ ◊ Z5–9 H9–1 ‡8–12in (20–30cm) ↔6in (15cm)

This summer-flowering annual also comes in pink. Stagger sowing to extend the bloom period. Grows best in deep, sharply drained, alkaline soil.

Gomphrena globosa
GLOBE AMARANTH

☼ ◊ Z11–12 H12–1 ‡12in (30cm) ↔8in (20cm)

Flowerheads in shades of red, pink, lavender, purple, orange, or white appear from summer to early autumn. Grows best in well-drained soils.

Molucella laevis
BELLS OF IRELAND

☼ ◊ Z9–11 H11–1 ‡3ft (1m) ↔9in (23cm)

Interesting green calyces surround the small white to pale purplish pink, fragrant flowers The flower stalks appear in late summer and can be dried.

Celosia argentea Cristata Group
COCKSCOMB

☼ ◊ Z11 H9–2 ‡6–36in (15–90cm) ↔24in (60cm)

Fan-shaped flowers bloom in shades of red, orange, yellow, and purple. Cultivars include Olympia Series and Jewel Box Mix. Best in moist, fertile soil.

Zinnia cultivars
ZINNIA

☼ ◊ H12–1 ‡↔8–36in (20–90cm)

Colors include white, yellow, orange, red, and purple. Many can be so double that they resemble dahlias. Prefer well-drained soil with plenty of organic matter.

Limonium sinuatum
STATICE

☼ ◊ H9–3 ‡8in (45cm) ↔12in (30cm)

A perennial grown as an annual except in USDA Zones 8 and 9, this flowers from summer to fall in shades of pink, white, yellow, and blue. Prefers sandy soil.

HERBACEOUS PLANTS

Annuals and biennals for fragrance

These beautiful annuals and biennials offer a feast for the eyes and for the nose as well, and together they offer fragrant flowers as well as fragrant leaves. Use these for adding "spice" to your dedicated annual and biennial beds, as filler plants in perennial and shrub borders, or in containers to bring their fragrance to many parts of your garden.

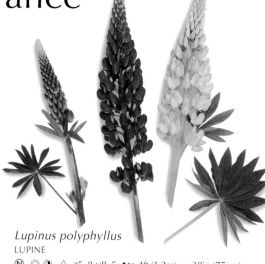

Lupinus polyphyllus
LUPINE
Ⓝ ☼ ☼ ◊ Z5–8 H8–5 ‡to 4ft (1.2m) ↔30in (75cm)
This summer-blooming annual is perennial in the southern and coastal regions of the Northwest. It prefers moderately fertile soil. Also comes in white.

Mirabilis jalapa
FOUR O'CLOCK, MARVEL OF PERU
☼ ◊ Z11–15 H12–9 ‡24in (60cm) ↔30in (75cm)
The fragrant flowers come in magenta, yellow, red, pink, and white and are often striped or mottled. Prefers a moderately fertile, well-drained soil.

Matricaria recutita
GERMAN CHAMOMILE
☼ ◊ Z0 H7–1 ‡24in (60cm) ↔15in (38cm)
This is the plant used for chamomile tea; the entire smells of pineapple. Grows well in average soil. Self-sows and naturalizes readily.

Nigella damascena
LOVE-IN-A-MIST
☼ ◊ Z0 H10–1 ‡24in (60cm) ↔8in (20cm)
The flowers range from blue, white, to rose and develop into ornamental pods, as shown. Better in areas with cool summers, where they will bloom freely.

MORE CHOICES

- *Antirrhinum majus* 'Rocket' Z7–9 H9–1
- *Cleome hassleriana* 'Cherry Queen' Z0 H12–1
- *Cleome hassleriana* 'Pink Queen' Z0 H12–1
- *Cleome hassleriana* 'Violet Queen' Z0 H12–1
- *Cosmos bipinnatus* 'Sea Shells' Z11–12 H12–1
- *Helianthus annuus* 'Autumn Beauty' Z0 H12–1
- *Helianthus annuus* 'Evening Sun' Z0 H12–1
- *Helianthus annuus* 'Teddy Bear' Z0 H12–1

Hesperis matronalis
DAME'S ROCKET
☼ ☼ ◊ Z3–8 H9–3 ‡to 36in (1m) ↔18in (45cm)
Biennial or sometimes short-lived perennial. Colors include white and purple shades. It prefers fertile, well-drained soil. Attracts beneficial insects.

Petunia x *hybrida* 'Blue Vein'
BLUE VEIN PETUNIA
☼ ◊ Z9–11 H12–1 ‡6in (15cm) ↔4ft (1.2m)
Petunias bloom in all colors except orange, with endless combinations including bicolors and picotees. The plants prefer well-drained soil.

Oenothera biennis
EVENING PRIMROSE
Ⓝ ☼ ◊ Z4–8 H8–1 ‡3–5ft (1–1.5m) ↔24in (60cm)
Flowers open at night and fold up during the day. Blooms from summer to autumn. Prefers well-drained moderately fertile soil but tolerates poor, rocky soil.

Phlox drummondii 'Sternenzauber'
DRUMMOND PHLOX
Ⓝ ☼ ◊ Z10–11 H12–1 ‡18in (45cm) ↔10in (25cm)
Flowers come in shades and combinations of purple, pink, red, lavender-blue, and white. Prefers fertile, well-drained soil. Suceptible to powdery mildew.

Viola x wittrockiana
PANSY

☼ ◐ Z6–9 H9–1 ‡6–8in (15–20cm) ↔8in (20cm)

Pansies occur in a very wide color range, many with "faces," in early spring as well as autumn to winter in milder areas. Prefer fertile, organic, well-drained soil.

Dianthus chinensis
INDIAN PINK

☼ ◐ Z7–10 H10–7 ‡32in (80cm) ↔24in (60cm)

Perennials often as annuals; in warmer areas they can be treated as perennials. Flowers of many varieties are fragrant. Both garden and florist forms are available.

Nicotiana x sanderae 'Daylight Sensation'
JASMINE TOBACCO

☼ ◑ ◐ Z10–13 H12–1 ‡24in (60cm) ↔16in (40cm)

Blooms in shades of red and green as well as white; many are night fragrant. This cultivar stays open and fragrant during the day. Prefers fertile, well-drained soil.

MORE CHOICES

- *Lathyrus odoratus* Z9–10 H8–1
- *Lobularia maritima* Z10–11 H12–1
- *Monarda cirtiodora* Z4–8 H8–1
- *Ocimum basilicum* Z9–11 H10–1
- *Ocimum basilicum* 'Dark Opal' Z9–11 H12–1
- *Scabiosa atropurpurea* Z4–11 H8–3
- *Tagetes tenuifolia* H12–1
- *Verbena bonariensis* Z7–11 H12–7

Ocimum basilicum 'Cinnamon'
CINNAMON BASIL

☼ ◐ Z9–10 H12–1

‡30in (75cm) ↔12in (30cm)

The entire plant is cinnamon-scented. Other basils offer lemon to clove or camphor scents. Prefers light, fertile, well-drained soil.

Reseda odorata
MIGNONETTE

☼ ◐ Z10–11 H6–1 ‡24in (60cm) ↔12in (30cm)

The aromatic flowers appear from summer to early autumn. The species tends to be more fragrant than the cultivars. Give well-drained, moderately fertile soil.

Impatiens balsamina
GARDEN BALSAM

☼ ◐◑ Z0 H12–1 ‡30in (75cm) ↔18in (45cm)

Colors range from white, pink, red, and lilac as well as bicolors and doubled forms with only a light scent. Prefers organic, well-drained soils.

Molucella laevis
BELLS OF IRELAND

☼ ◐ Z9–11 H11–1 ‡3ft (1m) ↔9in (23cm)

Yellow-green calyces (the bells) surround the tiny white to pale purplish pink, fragrant flowers in summer. Prefers well-drained soil.

Erysimum cheiri
WALLFLOWER

☼ ◐ Z7–8 H9–2 ‡32in (80cm) ↔16in (40cm)

Exquisitely fragrant flowers come in shades of yellow, orange, brown, and red. At home in a rock garden and will do well in poor soils. Prefers cool summers.

HERBACEOUS PLANTS

Bulbs, corms, and tubers for use as focal points

In any good garden design, focal points arrest the eye and hold it there. More often than not, they are plants that appear distinctively different from their neighbors or surroundings. If they are to remain effective as focal points, plants cannot be overused in a design.

Corydalis lutea
YELLOW CORYDALIS
☼ ◊ Z5–8 H8–4 ↕↔8–12in (20–30cm)
Flowers from late spring to early fall. Will self-sow readily. Best if grown in fertile to moderately fertile soil. Evergreen. Also known as *Pseudofumaria lutea*.

MORE CHOICES

- *Anemone* ssp. Z5–9 H9–3
- *Anemone blanda* Z4–8 H8–1
- *Anemone japonica* Z4–8 H8–1
- *Corydalis lutea* Z5–8 H8–4
- *Crocosmia* x *crocosmiiflora* Z6–9 H9–2
- *Fritillaria imperialis* Z4–9 H8–2

Allium giganteum
GIANT ORNAMENTAL ONION
☼ ◊ Z3–9 H9–5 ↕6ft (2m) ↔12–14in (30–35cm)
Amazingly dense flowerheads bloom in summer. Strap-shaped leaves wither before the plant blooms. Grows best in fertile soil. Excellent cut flower.

Lycoris radiata
RED SPIDER LILY
☼ ◊ Z7–10 H10–7 ↕16in (40cm) ↔6in (15cm)
Flowers in late summer and early autumn, held above strap-shaped, dark green leaves. Plant bulbs in fall in fertile soil, with the neck of the bulb at the surface.

HERBACEOUS PLANTS

Anemone hupehensis
CHINESE ANEMONE

☼ ☼ ◐ ● Z4–8 H9–3 ↕3ft (1m) ↔16in (40cm)
Flowers from late summer through fall. An erect plant with a rather woody base, best when grown in fertile, organic soil. Also nice when massed.

Anemone x *hybrida* 'Whirlwind'
WHIRLWIND WINDFLOWER

☼ ☼ ◐ ● Z4–8 H9–3 ↕4–5ft (1.2–1.5m) ↔indefinite
Flowers from late summer to early fall, sometimes with twisted, greenish white tepals in the center.

Crocosmia x *crocosmiiflora*
MONTBRETIA

☼ ☼ ◐ ● Z6–9 H9–3 ↕24in (60cm) ↔3in (8cm)
Summer flowers vary from yellow to orange to red. Prefers moderately fertile, organic soil, in which it may become invasive. Excellent cut flower.

Fritillaria imperialis 'Variegata'
VARIEGATED CROWN IMPERIAL

☼ ◊ Z5–9 H9–4 ↕3ft (1m) ↔9–12in (23–30cm)
Flowers appear in late spring. Excellent as a single specimen or in groups. Best when grown in fertile soil. Bulbs and foliage have a distinctly skunky odor.

Lilium candidum
MADONNA LILY

☼ ◊ Z6–9 H9–6 ↕↔3–6ft (1–2m)
Fragrant flowers bloom in summer above a rosette of lance-shaped, shiny, bright green leaves. Susceptible to *Botrytis* (gray mold) and viruses. Plant shallowly.

Fritillaria imperialis
CROWN IMPERIAL

☼ ◊ Z4–9 H8–2 ↕3ft (1m) ↔9–12in (23–30cm)
Late spring-blooming flowers are available in orange, yellow, and red. A very tolerant species that prefers fertile soil. Interesting. although malodorus, cut flower.

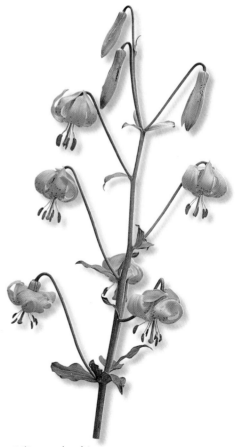

Lilium columbianum
AMERICAN LILY, COLUMBIA TIGER LILY

Ⓝ ☼ ◊ Z6–8 H8–6 ↕6ft (2m) ↔24in (60cm)
Established plants bear dozens of blooms during summer. A dwarf variety is well suited to smaller gardens. Provide fertile, well-drained soil.

HERBACEOUS PLANTS

Bulbs, corms, and tubers for formal beds

Formal gardens are usually made up of simple, geometric beds with a very finished, tidy, balanced, and symmetrical appearance. They include straight paths, clipped hedges, and formal beds such as parterres and knot gardens. These bulbous plants and their allies are suitable for use in formal settings, especially when used *en masse*.

Agapanthus spp.
BLUE AFRICAN LILY
☼ ◐ ◊ Z8–11 H12–3 ‡30in (75cm) ↔12in (30cm)
Flowers appear during summer, ranging from deep violet to pale blue and white. Prefers fertile soil. Provide winter mulch where marginally hardy.

Galtonia canadicans
SUMMER HYACINTH
☼ ◊ Z7–10 H10–7 ‡3–4ft (1–1.2m) ↔4in (10cm)
Fragrant flowers appear in late summer. Grow in fertile soil from fall-planted bulbs. Provide heavy winter mulch in colder areas, and protection from slugs.

Agapanthus 'Headbourne Hybrids'
HEADBOURNE HYBRID BLUE AFRICAN LILY
☼ ◐ ◊ Z8–11 H12–3 ‡30in (75cm) ↔12in (30cm)
These are among the hardiest members of the genus. Flowers in shades of deep violet to pale blue appear above clumps of strappy leaves in summer.

Narcissus trumpet cultivars
DAFFODIL

☼ ◌ Z3–9 H9–1 ↕5–20in (13–50cm)

Virtually all flower in spring. Excellent for massing in beds. They can also be naturalized in grass, woodland edge, or border. Not palatable to squirrels or deer.

Narcissus 'Sundisc'
SUN DISC JONQUILLA DAFFODIL

☼ ◌ Z3–9 H9–1 ↕7in (18cm)

A dwarf Jonquilla cultivar with late spring blooms on stiff stems. The outer petals fade to cream with age. Best when grown in moderately fertile soil.

Fritillaria meleagris
SNAKE'S-HEAD FRITILLARY

☼ ◌ Z4–9 H8–2 ↕12in (30cm) ↔2–3in (5–8cm)

Spring-blooming flowers vary from purple to pinkish purple and white. Can also be naturalized in grass or a rock garden in moderately fertile to fertile, organic soil.

Tulipa 'Fringed Beauty'
FRINGED BEAUTY TULIP

☼ ◌ Z3–8 H8–1 ↕12in (30cm)

Blooms late in the tulip season and makes an elegant cut flower. Deadhead and fertilize after flowering and allow foliage to yellow to encourage future blooms. .

Narcissus 'Toto'
TOTO DAFFODIL

☼ ☼ ◌ Z3–9 H9–1 ↕8in (15cm)

A compact daffodil that is at home in a rock garden as it is in a formal or woodland bed. Flowers from early to midspring. Best grown in moderately fertile soil.

Lilium candidum
MADONNA LILY

☼ ◌ Z6–9 H9–6 ↕↔3–6ft (1–2m)

A mass planting of this intensely fragrant lily makes a bold, fragrant statement in a formal bed or as part of a large mixed border. Blooms in summer on stiff stems.

MORE CHOICES

- *Allium 'Gladiator'* Z4–8 H8–1
- *Allium 'Globemaster'* Z4–8 H8–1
- *Allium 'Mars'* Z4–8 H8–1
- *Allium 'Mount Everest'* Z4–8 H8–1
- *Fritillaria imperialis* and cultivars Z5–9 H9–4
- *Fritillaria imperials 'Variegata'* Z5–9 H9–4
- *Gladiolus daleni* Z0 H12–7
- *Hyacinthus orientalis* Z5–9 H9–5

HERBACEOUS PLANTS

Bulbs, corms, and tubers for mixed borders

Bulbs and their allies are members in good standing of the herbaceous plant clan and mix well with perennials as well as shrubs. They make quick and easy additions to empty spaces in a border. These selections have easy-going, free-flowing forms that make them especially useful in less formal designs, such as naturalized plantings and cottage gardens.

HERBACEOUS PLANTS

Tigridia pavonia
PEACOCK FLOWER, TIGER FLOWER

☼ ◊ Z8–10 H12–3 ↕18in (45cm) ↔6in (15cm)

In summer, strappy foliage sets off a succession of orange, pink, red, yellow, or white flowers with contrasting centers. Plant bulbs in spring.

Lilium paradalinum
LEOPARD LILY, PANTHER LILY

Ⓝ ☼ ◊ Z5–8 H8–5 ↕↔6–10ft (2–3m)

Blooms May to July in Oregon, where it is native. One of the easiest of the West Coast native lilies to grow. Prefers deep loose organic soil. Very disease resistant.

Lilium candidum
MADONNA LILY

☼ ◊ Z6–9 H9–6 ↕↔3–6ft (1–2m)

A rosette of lance-shaped, shiny, bright green basal leaves gives rise to fragrant flowers in summer. Susceptible to *Botrytis* (gray mold) and viruses. Plant shallowly in fall.

Lycoris radiata
RED SPIDER LILY

☼ ◊ Z7–10 H10–7 ↕16in (40cm) ↔6in (15cm)

Flowers from late summer to early fall above semi-erect, strap-shaped, dark green leaves. Plant in fertile soil in fall with the neck of the bulb at the soil line.

Lilium superbum
TURK'S-CAP LILY

Ⓝ ☼ ◊ Z4–8 H8–1 ↕↔5–10ft (1.5–3m)

Flowers in mid-to late summer. Purple-mottled stems bear lance shaped leaves that spiral around the stem. Prefers organic soil.

Camassia quamash
QUAMASH

Ⓝ ☼ ☀ ◊ Z4–11 H12–1 ↕32in (80cm) ↔12in (30cm)

Flowers appear in late spring. Quickly forms large clumps. Prefers fertile, organic soil and can be naturalized in grass. NW native. Also called *C. esculenta*.

Galanthus elwesii
GIANT SNOWDROP

☀ ◊ Z3–8 H8–1 ↕12in (30cm) ↔3in (8cm)

Honey-scented flowers appear in late winter on surprisingly robust plants. Foliage is sometimes twisted. Best when grown in soil with high organic content.

Tulipa 'Fringed Beauty'
FRINGED BEAUTY TULIP

☼ ◊ Z3–8 H8–1 ↕12in (30cm)

Blooms mid- to late spring. Deadhead and fertilize plants after flowering and allow foliage to yellow to encourage future blooms. Elegant cut flowers.

Anemone x hybrida
JAPANESE ANEMONE, WINDFLOWER

☼ ◊ ᵖᴴ Z4–8 H8–5 ↕5ft (1.5m) ↔2ft (60cm)

Flower color varies among shades of white, pink, and purple. Prefers fertile, organic soil. This garden hybrid is also called *A.* x *elegans* and *A. japonica*.

MORE CHOICES

- *Allium aflatunense* Z4–8 H8–1
- *Allium cernuum* Z3–9 H9–5
- *Allium cowanii* Z6–10 H10–6
- *Allium flavum* Z4–10 H9–1
- *Allium karativiense* Z3–9 H9–5
- *Allium moly* 'Jeannine' Z3–9 H9–1
- *Anemone blanda* Z4–8 H8–1
- *Chionodoxa luciliae* Z3–9 H9–1
- *Crocus vernus* Z3–8 H8–1
- *Dahlia* hybrids Z9–11 H12–1
- *Eranthis hyemalis* Z4–9 H9–1
- *Fritillaria persica* 'Adiyaman' Z6–8 H8–6
- *Gladiolus* (Grandiflorus group) Z8–10 H9–1
- *Iris reticulata* Z5–8 H8–5
- *Narcissus* hybrids Z3–9 H9–1
- *Ranunculus asiaticus* Z7–11 H12–7

Zephyranthes candida
RAIN LILY

☼ ◊ Z7–9 H9–6 ↕6–10in (15–25cm) ↔2–3in (5–8cm)

Blooms late summer to early fall. Petals can sometimes be red-tinted on the back. Upright plants bear linear foliage. Protect against excess moisture during winter.

HERBACEOUS PLANTS

Bulbs, corms, and tubers for naturalizing

Including bulbs and similar plants is a visually exciting way to maximize the use of your lawn areas. These early spring bloomers look best when planted in sweeps (large, irregular masses). For easier planting, use a commercial bulb planter that pops out a plug of soil that is then replaced over the planted bulb. Remember: don't mow the grass until the bulbs' foliage withers.

Crocus species and cultivars
CROCUS

☼ ☀ ◊ Z3–8 H8–1 ↕2–6in (5–15cm)

Crocuses are available in many colors and patterns and bloom in spring (mostly) or fall. They vary from tolerating poor soil to preferring richer, organic soil.

Muscari species and cultivars
GRAPE HYACINTH

☼ ☀ ◊ Z2–9 H9–1 ↕4–18in (10–45cm)

These bulbs flower mostly in spring. Of the 30 species known, about a dozen are cultivated. They prefer fertile soil and will naturalize if not disturbed.

Puschkinia scilloides
STRIPED SQUILL

☼ ☀ ◊ Z3–9 H9–1 ↕8in (20cm) ↔2in (5cm)

Plant bulbs in fall for their striking late winter to early spring flowers. The variety *libanotica* is pure white. Adaptable to most soil types and will naturalize.

Scilla siberica
SIBERIAN SQUILL

☼ ☀ ◊ Z3–8 H8–1 ↕4–8in (10–20cm) ↔2in (5cm)

Flowers appear in spring. Plant bulbs in fall in moderately fertile, organic soil. Naturalizes well under trees and shrubs.

Fritillaria meleagris
SNAKE'S-HEAD FRITILLARY

☼ ◊ Z4–9 H8–2 ↕12in (30cm) ↔2–3in (5–8cm)

Blooms in spring. Flowers available in purple to pinkish purple and white. Will naturalize in grass or a rock garden. Prefers moderately fertile to fertile organic soil.

Leucojum aestivum 'Gravetye Giant'
GRAVETYE GIANT SNOWFLAKE

☼ ◊ Z4–9 H8–1 ↕3ft (1m) ↔3in (8cm)

This cultivar is much more robust than the species. Faintly chocolate-scented flowers appear in spring. Prefers organic soil. Susceptible to bulb fly.

Narcissus
DAFFODIL

☼ ☼ ◗ Z3–9 H9–1 ↕5–20in (12.5–50cm)

Most flower in spring and are good for planting between shrubs or mixed in a border. They can also be naturalized in grass or along a woodland edge.

Narcissus cyclamineus 'Mite'
MITE CYCLAMINEUS DAFFODIL

☼ ◗ Z3–9 H9–1 ↕6in (15cm)

This cultivar of a charming wild species flowers early in the daffodil season. Leaves are narrow and bright green. Plant bulbs in fall in moderately fertile soil.

MORE CHOICES

• *Crocus chrysanthus* Z3–8 H10–1
• *Crocus tomasinianus* Z3–8 H8–1
• *Crocus vernus* Z3–8 H8–1
• *Scilla campanulata* Z4–9 H9–1

Galanthus nivalis
COMMON SNOWDROP

☼ ◗ Z3–8 H8–1 ↕4–6in (10–15cm) ↔2–3in (5–8cm)

Suitable for naturalizing in either grass or woodland. It is also at home in borders and rock gardens. A bulbous perennial native to the Pyrenees and Ukraine.

Chionodoxa forbesii
GLORY OF THE SNOW

☼ ◗ Z3–9 H9–1 ↕10in (25cm) ↔2in (5cm)

Blooms in early spring. This species also has cultivars with white and pink flowers. Plant bulbs in fall. Adapts to most well-drained soils. Self-sows.

HERBACEOUS PLANTS

Bulbs, corms, and tubers for woodlands

Although not all bulbs and their relatives grow natively in deciduous woodlands, such a setting is an excellent location for many of them. Most bloom and die back to the ground before the tree and shrub canopy leafs out and completely shades the woodland floor. Plant in drifts with a few individuals scattered around them, and they will look completely natural.

Camassia quamash
QUAMASH

Ⓝ ☼ ☀ ◊ Z4–11 H12–1 ‡32in (80cm) ↔12in (0cm)

Flowers appear in late spring. Fast-growing plant that forms large clumps. Can be naturalized in rough grass. Prefers fertile organic soil. Also called *C. esculenta*.

Corydalis lutea
YELLOW CORYDALIS

☼ ◊ Z5–8 H8–4 ‡↔8–12 (20–30cm)

A beautiful evergreen plant that flowers from late spring to early fall. Self-sows readily. Best if grown in fertile to moderately fertile soil.

Leucojum aestivum 'Gravetye Giant'
GRAVETYE GIANT SNOWFLAKE

☼ ◊ Z4–9 H8–1 ‡36in (90cm) ↔3in (8cm)

This cultivar is much more robust than the species. Faintly chocolate-scented flowers appear in spring. Prefers organic soil. Susceptible to bulb fly.

Convallaria majalis var. rosea
PINK LILY-OF-THE-VALLEY

☀ ◊ Z2–7 H7–1 ‡6in (15cm) ↔indefinite

Spreading rhizomes give rise to strongly scented flower in spring. Species flowers are white. Cultivars also available with leaf variegation.

Scilla siberica
SIBERIAN SQUILL

☼ ☀ ◊ Z3–8 H8–1 ‡4–8in (10–20cm) ↔2in (5cm)

Flowers borne in spring. Plant bulbs in fall in moderately fertile, organic soil. Can naturalize to form large masses under trees and shrubs.

Cyclamen hederifolium
BABY CYCLAMEN

☀ ◊ Z5–7 H9–7 ‡4in (10cm) ↔4–6in (10–15cm)

Scented flowers in shades of pink or white. Leaf shape varies from triangular to heart-shaped. Prefers moderately fertile, organic soil. Also called *C. neapolitanum*.

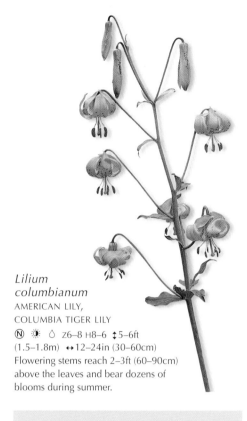

Lilium columbianum
AMERICAN LILY,
COLUMBIA TIGER LILY

Ⓝ ☼ ◊ Z6–8 H8–6 ↕5–6ft
(1.5–1.8m) ↔12–24in (30–60cm)
Flowering stems reach 2–3ft (60–90cm)
above the leaves and bear dozens of
blooms during summer.

MORE CHOICES

- *Convallaria majalis* Z2–7 H7–1
- *Convallaria majalis* cultivars Z4–9 H9–1
- *Crocus sativus* Z5–8 H8–1
- *Cyclamen coum* Z5–9 H9–5
- *Eranthis hyemalis* Z4–9 H9–1
- *Galanthus nivalis* Z3–8 H8–1
- *Leucojum aestivum and cultivars*
  Z3–9 H9–1

Lilium pardalinum
LEOPARD LILY, PANTHER LILY

Ⓝ ☼ ◊ Z5–8 H8–5 ↕↔6–10ft (2–3m)
Blooms May to July in Oregon, where it is native. One
of the easiest of the West Coast native lilies to grow.
Prefers deep, loose, organic soil. Very disease resistant.

Fritillaria pudica
YELLOW FRITILLARY

Ⓝ ☼ ◊ Z2–9 H9–1 ↕2–8in (5–20cm) ↔2in (5cm)
Early spring flowers are sometimes orange-yellow
or tinted red. Best if grown in fertile soil and where
winter rainfall is minimal.

Chionodoxa luciliae
GLORY OF THE SNOW

☼ ◊ Z3–9 H9–1 ↕10in (25cm) ↔2in (5cm)
Blooms in early spring. This species also has cultivars
with white and pink flowers. Adapts to most well-
drained soils, where it self-sows. Also called *C. forbesii*.

Fritillaria meleagris
SNAKE'S-HEAD FRITILLARY

☼ ◊ Z4–9 H8–2 ↕12in (30cm) ↔2–3in (5–8cm)
Spring. flowers vary from purple to pinkish purple and
white. Can be naturalized in grass or in a rock garden.
Prefers moderately fertile to fertile organic soil.

Bulbs for naturalizing in woodlands

Woodland bulbs take advantage of sunshine in late winter and early spring that makes its way through the overstory trees' leafless canopy. You can quickly liven up woodland borders with these early bloomers that blend well with woodland perennials such as hellebores and primroses. Sweeps of bulbs (instead of soldier rows) look more natural and make a better impact.

Chionodoxa forbesii
GLORY OF THE SNOW

☼ ◊ Z3–9 H9–1 ↕4–10in (12–25cm) ↔1–2in (2.5–5cm)
This native of western Turkey blooms in early spring. and has cultivars with white and pink flowers. Prefers well-drained soil and self-seeds voluntarily.

Colchicum 'Waterlily'
WATERLILY AUTUMN CROCUS

☼ ◊ Z4–9 H9–1 ↕4–6in (10–15cm) ↔6–8in (15–20cm)
Blooms in fall, but the leaves emerge in spring. Prefers deep, fertile, well-drained soil that is not too dry. Plant corms in in early summer. Prone to gray mold and slugs.

Crocus
E.A. BOWLES CROCUS

☼ ◊ Z3–8 H8–1 ↕4in (10cm) ↔1–3in (2.5–8cm)
More than 80 species of crocus and a few dozen cultivars are available. Their flowers come in many colors and patterns and can bloom in spring or fall.

Cyclamen coum Pewter Group
PEWTER GROUP CYCLAMEN
☼ ◊ Z5–9 H9–5 ↕4in (10cm) ↔2–4in (5–10cm)
The flowers of this species come in pink, white, and carmine red as well as bicolors. Prefers moderately fertile, well-drained, organic soil.

Tulipa 'Kees Nelis' (Triumph Group)
KEES NELIS TULIP
☼ ◊ Z3–8 H8–1 ↕10–14in (25–35cm)
Triumph Group tulips have single, cup-shaped flowers ranging from white through dark purple, many with contrasting borders, and bloom in mid- to late spring.

Tulipa kaufmanniana
WATERLILY TULIP
☼ ◊ Z3–8 H8–1 ↕4–14in (10–35cm)
Flowers can also be cream or flushed with pink, orange, or red. Blooms early to midseason. Prefers well-drained soil kept moist during the growing season.

MORE CHOICES

- *Brodiaea elegans* Z5–11 H12–6
- *Calochortus macrocarpus* Z7–10
- *Calochortus uniflorus* Z6–10
- *Camassia leichthinii* Z4–11 H10–1
- *Dichelostemma capitatum* Z6–10
- *Erythronium hendersonii* Z3–9 H9–1
- *Fritillaria affinis* var. *affinis* Z7–9
- *Fritillaria recurva* Z6–9 H9–6
- *Leucojum aestivum* Z3–9 H9–1
- *Sternbergia candida* Z8–10 H10–8
- *Tulipa biflora* Z4–8 H8–1
- *Tulipa greigii* Z3–8 H8–1
- *Tulipa tarda* Z3–8 H8–1

Puschkinia scilloides
STRIPED SQUILL
☼ ☼ ◊ Z3–9 H9–1 ↕8in (20cm) ↔2in (5cm)
Plant in fall for their striking late winter to early spring flowers. The variety *libanotica* is pure white. Prefers moist, well-drained soil in the growing season.

Sternbergia lutea
AUTUMN DAFFODIL
☼ ◊◗ Z7–9 H9–6 ↕6–9in (15–23cm) ↔3in (8cm)
Flowers appear in fall. Plant bulbs in late summer. Best when grown in moderately fertile soil. Prefers dry soil while it is dormant. Excellent rock garden plant.

HERBACEOUS PLANTS

Shallow aquatic marginals

Water features add a wonderful dimension to any garden setting. Shallow areas (up to 6in/15cm deep) can provide water for drinking and bathing to birds and other beneficial animals. Plants that grow well in shallow water not only give these animals cover but also make striking displays in your garden's water feature.

Lysichiton camtschatcensis
JAPANESE SKUNK CABBAGE

☼ ◗ Z5–9 H9–1 ↕30in (75cm) ↔24in (60cm)
Early spring flowers have a more pleasant aroma than *L. americanus*, and the plant is smaller. Prefers rich, organic soil. From bogs and wet woodlands of NE Asia.

Lysichiton americanus
YELLOW SKUNK CABBAGE

Ⓝ ☼ ◗ Z9–7 H7–9 ↕3ft (1m) ↔30in (75cm)
Yellow flowers in early spring precede large, strongly veined, bold leaves. Prefers to be in rich. organic soil. From bogs and wet woodlands of W North America.

Iris laevigata
JAPANESE WATER IRIS

☼ ☼ ◗◗ Z4–9 H9–1 ↕2–3ft (60–90cm) or more ↔indefinite
Blooms late spring to early summer in shades of blue, red, purple, and white. Forms sizeable clumps. From wet areas of Japan, N. China, Korea, C. Russia

Caltha palustris 'Alba'
WHITE MARSH MARIGOLD

Ⓝ ☼ ◗ Z3–7 H7–1 ↕9in (22cm) ↔12in (30cm)
More compact than the yellow-flowered species. Prefers rich soil and open sites. Does best if water level is less than 2in. Widespread in the N Hemisphere.

Eriophorum angustifolium
TALL COTTON GRASS

Ⓝ ☼ ◗ ᵖᴴ Z5–9 H9–5 ↕to 30in(75cm) ↔indefinite
The grasslike foliage (*Eriophorum* is not a true grass) arises from long, creeping rhizomes. The downy flowers appear above the foliage in summer.

Houttuynia cordata
CHAMELEON

☼ ◗ Z4–7 H12–1 ↕4in (10cm) ↔indefinite
Spreads rapidly in damp shade, and flowers in summer. The leaves have an orange scent when crushed. Prefers moderately fertile, organic soil.

HERBACEOUS PLANTS

Mimulus luteus
YELLOW MONKEY FLOWER

☼ ◐ Z3–9 H9–1 ↕↔12in (30cm)

Vigorous, spreading plant blooms spring to summer. Will self-sow. Prefers fertile, organic soil in a water level of less than 3 inches. Native to Chile.

Cyperus haspan
DWARF PAPYRUS

☼ ◐ ◐ Z7–11 H12–7 ↕24–36in (60–90cm) ↔18–24in (45–60cm)

Tiny summer flowers are borne in umbels and can be used in dried arrangements. Prefers loamy soil with a shallow layer of gravel on the surface. Native to C Asia.

Typha minima
DWARF CATTAIL

☼ ◐ Z3–11 H12–1 ↕18–24in (45–60cm) ↔12in (30cm)

Flowers are distinctive, cylindrical spikes that appear from mid- to late summer and can be used in dried arrangements. Can become invasive in unlined ponds.

Sagittaria sagittifolia
JAPANESE ARROWHEAD

☼ ◖ z5–11 H12–3 ‡18in (45cm) ↔12in (30cm)

Racemes of 1in white flowers with a basal spot appear during summer. Prefers gravelly soil and will spread and self-sow. From shallow to deep waters in Eurasia.

Colocasia esculenta
GREEN TARO

☼ ◖ z10–11 H12–4 ‡3ft (1m) ↔2ft (60cm)

Where these plants get enough heat, they produce large flowers resembling callas. Overwinter tubers in a dry, frost-free location. Native to tropical E Asia.

Colocasia esculenta var. *fontanesii*
VIOLET-STEM TARO

☼ ◖ z9–11 H12–8 ‡3ft (1m) ↔2ft (60cm)

Has all the attributes of the species plus highly ornamental, purple stalks and veins. Makes a bold tropical statement. Overwinter in a dry, frost-free spot.

MORE CHOICES

- *Caltha palustris* z3–7 H7–1
- *Caltha palustris* 'Multiplex' z5–9 H9–1
- *Juncus effusus* and cultivars z6–9
- *Juncus glaucus* z4–9 H9–1
- *Juncus macrophyllus* z4–9 H9–1

Sagittaria latifolia
WAPATO, DUCK POTATO

Ⓝ ☼ ◖ z5–11 H12–5 ‡5ft (1.2m) ↔2ft (60cm)

Similar in appearance and growth habits to the Japanese Arrowhead (above). Susceptible to leaf spots, leaf smut, spider mites, and aphids.

Acorus gramineus 'Ogon'
JAPANESE SWEET FLAG

☼ ◖ z10–11 H12–2 ‡to 10in (25cm) ↔6in (15cm)

Gives the impression of tall, semi-evergreen *Iris* leaves. Flowers are inconspicuous. Susceptible to wet and dry root rots, rust, and various fungal leaf spots.

Myosotis palustris
WATER FORGET-ME-NOT

☼ ☼ ◖ z3–9 H9–1 ‡6–12in (15–30cm) ↔12in (30cm)

Bears flowers in early summer and continues into fall. Grows from creeping rhizomes. Tolerates water up to 4in deep. Found in Europe, Asia, and N America.

HERBACEOUS PLANTS

Calla palustris
BOG ARUM

Ⓝ ☼ ◉ Z4–8 H8–1 ↕10in (25cm) ↔12in (30cm)
Flowers bloom in midsummer. Upright leaves emerge from creeping rhizomes. Use to soften the edges of a bog garden. From N and C Europe, Asia, and N America.

Mentha citrata (Syn. *Mentha* x *piperita* f. *citrata*)
CITRUS MINT

☼ ◐◉ Z6–11 H12–6 ↕3ft (1m) ↔spreading
Purple flowers bloom in late summer, and leaves have citrus overtones. Rhizomes can become invasive if not contained. Does best if water level is less than 2in.

Mentha aquatica
WATER MINT

☼ ◐◉ Z6–11 H12–6 ↕6–36in (15–90cm) ↔3ft (1m) or more
The essential oils in the intensely aromatic leaves are used in perfumery. It flowers in summer. Grows much like citrus mint. From Eurasia.

Scirpus lacustris (syn. *Schoenoplectus lacustris*)
BULRUSH

☼ ☼ ◉ Z4–8 H8–1 ↕3–12ft (1–4m) ↔spreading
Dark green, leafless, hollow stems emerge from a creeping rhizome. Reddish brown spikelets appear in early to late summer. Native to Europe and NW China.

Scirpus tabern 'Zebrinus'
CLUB RUSH

Ⓝ ☼ ◉ Z5–11 H12–1 ↕5ft (1.2m) ↔indefinite
Graceful, horizontally striped, leafless, hollow stems arise from rhizomes. Clusters of brown spikelets appear from early to late summer. Prefers fertile soil.

Cyperus longus
UMBRELLA GRASS

☼ ☼ ◐◉ Z3–11 H12–1 ↕5ft (1.2m) ↔indefinite
Grows in loose tufts from long, knotted rhizomes. Yellow flowers are borne in clusters in summer and turn brown with age. From N Africa and SW and C Asia.

Schoenoplectus lacustris 'Albescens'
BULRUSH

☼ ☼ ◉ Z5–11 H12–1 ↕12ft (4m) ↔spreading
The leaves of this cultivar are vertically striped and grow from creeping rhizomes. Reddish brown spikelets appear from early to late summer.

Deep aquatic marginals

These plants flourish in water from 1-3ft (30-90cm) deep, as found along the edges of a pond or water garden. Their handsome foliage and flowers complement the entire composition of water and plants. They also provide food and shelter for fish and other aquatic creatures that you may maintain or that choose to take up residence in your water garden.

Pontederia cordata 'Alba'
WHITE PICKEREL WEED

Ⓝ ☼ ◖ Z3–9 H9–1 ↕30in (75cm) ↔18in (45cm)
Flower spikes need warm, dry weather to open from late spring to fall above erect, lance shaped, glossy leaves. White cultivar of the species (see below).

Pontederia cordata
PICKEREL WEED

Ⓝ ☼ ◖ Z3–11 H12–1 ↕30in (75cm) ↔18in (45cm)
Flowers are borne from late spring to fall. When grown in an aquatic container, the soil should be a loamy and fertile. Can also be grown in water-filled barrels.

Iris pseudacorus 'Variegata'
VARIEGATED YELLOW FLAG

☼ ◖ Z5–8 H8–3 ↕6ft (2m) ↔indefinite
Four to 12 flowers per stem are borne from mid to late summer. Prefers moderately fertile soil and can be grown in a moist border. Variegation will fade in time.

Iris pseudacorus
YELLOW FLAG

☼ ◖ Z5–8 H8–3 ↕6ft (2m) ↔indefinite
A vigorous iris that blooms from mid- to late summer. Ripe seeds fall from the capsule and then float away and spread to new locations.

Saururus cernuus
LIZARD'S TAIL
Ⓝ ☼ ● z5–11 H12–5 ↕9in (23cm) ↔12in (30cm)
Flowers appear in early summer. The group of nutlets that forms along the stem resembles a lizard's tail. Spreads by runners.

Acorus calamus 'Variegatus'
VARIEGATED SWEET FLAG
Ⓝ ☼ ● z10–11 H12–2 ↕30in (75cm) ↔24in
Insignificant flowers appear from late spring to early summer. Does not produce fertile seeds, but it can spread widely by rhizomes.

Acorus calamus
SWEET-SCENTED RUSH
Ⓝ ☼ ● z4–11 H12–1 ↕3ft (1m) ↔2ft (60cm)
The leaves have a lemony scent, and the rhizomes can be used to flavor candy. Unassuming flowers appear from late spring to late summer.

Butomus umbellatus
FLOWERING RUSH
☼ ● z3–11 H8–5 ↕3ft (1m) ↔18in (45cm)
Fragrant flowers appear in late summer. Long, twisted leaves emerge bronze-purple then turn dark green. Can become invasive, so keep away from waterways.

MORE CHOICES

- *Nelumbo lutea* z4–11 H12–1
- *Nelumbo nucifera* z4–11 H12–3
- *Sparganium erectum* z5–9 H9–5
- *Thalia dealbata* z6–11 H12–6

Nuphar lutea
YELLOW POND LILY
Ⓝ ☼ ● z3–9 H9–1 ↔5ft (1.5m)
Produces peculiar-smelling flowers in summer among mid- to deep green leaves with wavy edges. Divide plants regularly to promote flowering.

Typha angustifolia
NARROW-LEAVED CATTAIL
☼ ● z2–11 H12–1 ↕5ft (1.5m) ↔indefinite
Brown flower spikes are borne in midsummer. Can spread quickly by rhizomes and become invasive if not contained.

HERBACEOUS PLANTS

Waterlilies

Few plants can rival the beautiful (and sometimes fragrant) waterlilies. As if their dark green or mottled floating lilypads were not attractive enough, their flowers peek their colorful heads just above the water surface. Hardy varieties can be overwintered outdoors. Tropicals cannot tolerate frost and must be protected or treated as aquatic annuals.

Nymphaea 'Moorei'
MOOREI WATERLILY
☼ ◑ z3–11 H12–1 ‡5in (13cm) ↔3–4ft (1–1.2m)
The 4–5in (10–13cm) flowers are barely fragrant and bloom during the day. This hardy waterlily has large green leaves with purple specks.

Nymphaea 'Albida'
ALBIDA WATERLILY
☼ ◑ z3–11 H12–1
‡4in (10cm) ↔3–4ft (1–1.2m)
The 5-6 in. flowers are fragrant and day blooming. This hardy waterlily has 9 in (23cm) dark green leaves with purple specks.

Nymphaea 'Escarboucle'
ESCARBOUCLE WATERLILY
☼ ◑ z3–11 H12–1 ↔to 10ft (3m)
Day-blooming flowers measure 7in (18cm). Hardy waterlily with 10in (25cm), midgreen leaves that are brown-tinged when young.

Nuphar lutea
YELLOW POND LILY
Ⓝ ☼ ◑ z3–9 H9–1 ↔5ft (1.5m)
This hardy waterlily relative produces peculiar-smelling flowers in summer. Mid- to deep green, wavy-edged leaves reach 16in (40cm) wide.

Nymphaea 'Rosennymphe'
ROSENNYMPHE WATERLILY
☼ ◑ z3–11 H12–1 ↔to 5ft (1.5m)
Slightly fragrant, day-blooming flowers measure up to 7in (18cm) across. Hardy waterlily with 10in (25cm) dark green leaves that are bronzy red when young.

Nymphaea 'Firecrest'
FIRECREST WATERLILY
☼ ◑ z3–11 H12–1 ↔to 4ft (1.2m)
Day-blooming flowers measure 6in in diameter. Hardy waterlily with 9in (15cm) mid-green leaves that are dark purple when young.

Nymphaea odorata
AMERICAN WHITE WATERLILY
Ⓝ ☼ ◑ z3–11 H12–1 ↔4–6ft (1.2–2m)
Day-blooming, fragrant flowers measure 4–9in (10–23cm) wide. Hardy waterlily with glossy, leathery mid-green leaves up to 12in (30cm) long.

Nymphaea 'Laydekeri Fulgens'
LAYDEKERI WATERLILY
☼ ◑ z3–11 H12–1 ↔18–30in (45–75cm)
Flowers measure 6in (15cm) across and are day-blooming. Hardy waterlily with 8in (20cm) dark green leaves that are purple or purple-marked when young.

Nymphaea 'Rose Arey'
ROSE AREY WATERLILY

☼ ● Z3–11 H12–1 ↔to 5ft (1.5m)
Day-blooming flowers measure 8in (20cm) in diameter. Hardy waterlily with 9in (23cm) bronze-green leaves that are purple when young.

Nymphaea 'James Brydon'
JAMES BRYDON WATERLILY

☼ ● Z3–11 H12–1 ↔to 8ft (2.5m)
Day-blooming flowers measure 5in (13cm) wide. Tropical waterlily with bronze-green leaves that are purple-brown with dark purple markings when young.

Nymphaea tetragona (pygmaea) 'Helvola'
HARDY DWARF WATERLILY

Ⓝ ☼ ● Z3–11 H12–1 ↔to 18in (45cm)
Slightly fragrant day-blooming flowers 3in (8cm) across. Hardy waterlily with dark green leaves mottled with purple. From Europe, Asia, and North America.

Nymphaea 'Gladstoneana''
GLADSTONEANA WATERLILY

☼ ● Z3–11 H12–1 ↔to 10ft (3m)
Day-blooming flowers measure to 7in (18cm). Tropical waterlily with 12 in (30cm), light bronze leaves with overlapping lobes, one of which is raised.

Nymphaea 'Marliacea Rosea'
MARLIACEA ROSEA WATERLILY

☼ ● Z3–11 H12–1 ↔6ft (2m)
Day-blooming flowers measure 7in (18cm) across. Hardy waterlily with deep green leaves that are purple-flushed when young.

MORE CHOICES
- *Nelumbo nucifera* 'Pekinensis Rubra' z4–11 H12–3
- *Nymphaea* 'Colonel A.J. Welsh' z3–11 H12–1
- *Nymphaea* 'Postlingberg' z3–11 H12–1
- *Nymphaea sulphurea* z3–11 H12–1
- *Nymphaea* 'Wilfron Gonnere' z3–11 H12–1
- *Nymphoides peltata* z6–11 H12–6
- *Victoria amazonica* z0 H12–2
- *Victoria cruziana* z0 H12–2

Nymphaea 'Attraction'
ATTRACTION WATERLILY

☼ ● Z3–11 H12–1 ↔6ft (2m)
Day-blooming flowers 5in (13cm) wide This hardy waterlily has bronze-green leaves that are purple-brown with dark purple markings when young.

Nymphaea 'Tetragona'
PYGMY WATERLILY

☼ ● Z3–11 H12–1 ↔to 12in (30cm)
The slightly fragrant, day-blooming flowers up to 2in (5cm) across. Hardy waterlily with 3in (8cm), dark green leaves with purple blotches.

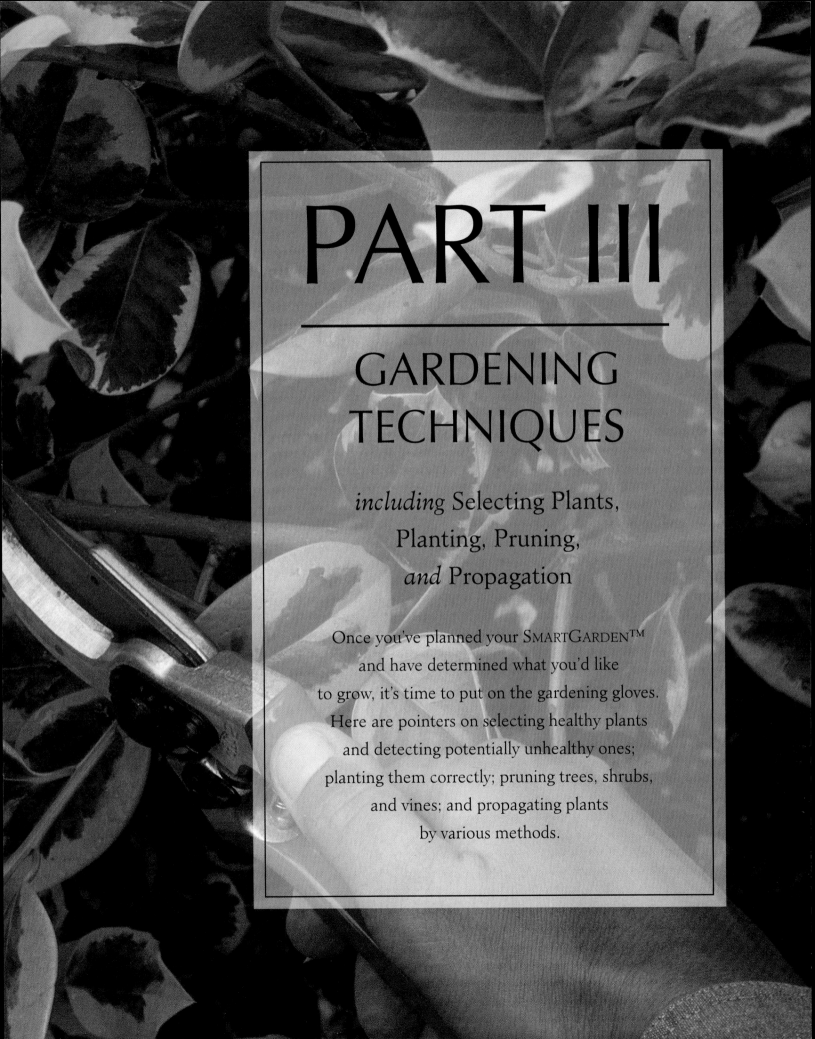

PART III

GARDENING TECHNIQUES

including Selecting Plants,
Planting, Pruning,
and Propagation

Once you've planned your SMARTGARDEN™
and have determined what you'd like
to grow, it's time to put on the gardening gloves.
Here are pointers on selecting healthy plants
and detecting potentially unhealthy ones;
planting them correctly; pruning trees, shrubs,
and vines; and propagating plants
by various methods.

SELECTING PLANTS

Choosing plants at the nursery or garden center does not need to be a long, complicated process: basically, look for plants that appear healthy and that avoid extremes, such as too much top-growth compared to the root ball, or too little foliage on stems that barely support the leaves. Spend more time on choosing longer-lived and more expensive trees and shrubs than on herbaceous plants.

CHOOSING A TREE

Container-grown tree

Before buying one of these, remove it from its container to examine the roots. Do not buy a potbound tree (with a mass of congested roots) or one with thick roots protruding from the holes.

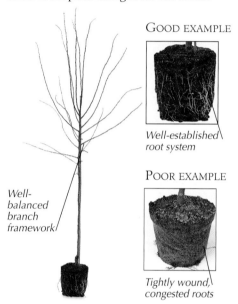

Well-balanced branch framework

GOOD EXAMPLE

Well-established root system

POOR EXAMPLE

Tightly wound, congested roots

Bare-root tree

These have virtually no soil around the roots. Examine the roots to check that they are not damaged or diseased and that there is no sign of dryness that may have been caused by exposure to air or sunlight.

GOOD EXAMPLE

Evenly distributed, spreading root system

Fibrous feeder roots

POOR EXAMPLES

Uneven, "hockey stick" roots

Tightly coiled roots

Balled-and-burlapped tree

Buy and plant a balled-and-burlapped tree when dormant in fall or early spring, following the same basic examination criteria as for both container-grown and bare-root trees.

GOOD EXAMPLE

x CUPRESSOCYPARIS LEYLANDII

Firm root ball with the covering intact

SELECTING A CONTAINER-GROWN SHRUB

Look through the drainage holes (or carefully slide the shrub out of its container) to check for a well-developed root system. If present, the shrub is probably container-grown and is not containerized (meaning it was recently removed from the open ground and put into a container). The roots should have healthy, white tips. Reject plants with poorly developed root systems, with coiled roots or root balls, or with roots protruding from the container, since these rarely establish or grow well.

GOOD EXAMPLE

Vigorous, well-balanced top-growth

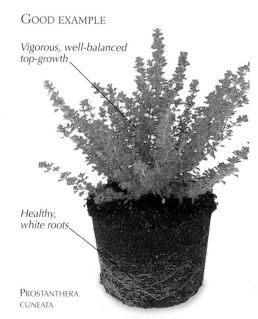

Healthy, white roots

PROSTANTHERA CUNEATA

POOR EXAMPLE

Twiggy, sparse stems showing little new growth

Potbound roots

Pruning congested roots

Tease out potbound roots, and cut back any that are very long and damaged.

SELECTING CLIMBERS

Climbing plants are usually sold container-grown, although a few may be sold bare-root. Choose a healthy-looking plant with a well-balanced framework of strong shoots, and reject any that show signs of pest infestation or disease. For potgrown plants, turn the pot over and check that the tips of the young roots are just showing. If so, the plant is well-rooted. Reject potbound plants – those that have tightly coiled roots or a mass of roots protruding through the drainage holes. Bare-root plants should have plenty of healthy, well-developed fibrous roots that are in proportion to the amount of top-growth.

GOOD EXAMPLE

Vigorous, sturdy stems

Healthy buds

LONICERA

POOR EXAMPLES

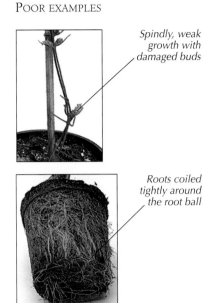

Spindly, weak growth with damaged buds

Roots coiled tightly around the root ball

SELECTING HEALTHY ROSES

Bare-root bush rose

Examine the plant carefully: if the stems appear dried out (the bark will be shriveled), or buds have started growing prematurely (producing blanched, thin shoots), do not buy it.

GOOD EXAMPLE

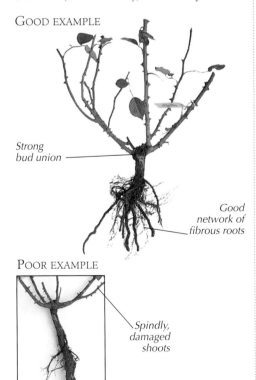

Strong bud union

Good network of fibrous roots

POOR EXAMPLE

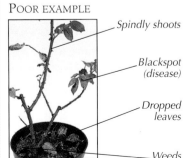

Spindly, damaged shoots

Stunted root sytem

Container-grown rose

Check that the plant has not been recently potted up: hold the plant by its main shoot and gently shake it. If it does not move around in the soil mix, it is well-established and a good buy.

GOOD EXAMPLE

Vigorous foliage of a good color

Sturdy, well-balanced top growth

Healthy root system

Moist soil mix

POOR EXAMPLE

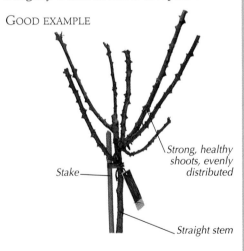

Spindly shoots

Blackspot (disease)

Dropped leaves

Weeds

Standard rose

Choose a standard rose with a balanced head of shoots, since it is likely to be viewed from all sides. A straight main stem is best, although a slightly crooked stem is acceptable.

GOOD EXAMPLE

Strong, healthy shoots, evenly distributed

Stake

Straight stem

POOR EXAMPLE

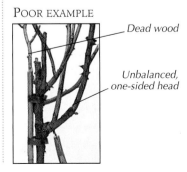

Dead wood

Unbalanced, one-sided head

CHOOSING HERBACEOUS PLANTS

Most herbaceous plants are sold container-grown, but bare-root plants are also sometimes available from fall to early spring, when they are dormant. If buying herbaceous plants at the beginning of the growing season, check that there are strong, emerging shoots. Plants that have a few fat, healthy-looking buds are better than those that have a large number of weaker ones.

GOOD EXAMPLE

IMPATIENS CULTIVAR

Bushy, sturdy growth

Healthy buds developing

Moist soil mix

GOOD EXAMPLE

Strong, healthy top growth

Moist soil mix

Established, vigorous roots

LUPINE

POOR EXAMPLES

Weak and woody top-growth

Dry soil mix

Underdeveloped root system

Leggy, bare stems

Dead leaves

Moss and weeds growing on soil mix

Potbound roots

Yellowing, discolored leaves

SELECTING BULBS, CORMS, TUBERS, AND SIMILAR PLANTS

Most bulbs are sold in a dry state during their dormant period. Buy these as early as possible before they start into growth; most daffodils, for example, normally start producing roots in late summer, and most other spring-flowering bulbs will begin to grow by early fall. Fall-flowering crocuses and *Colchicum* species and hybrids especially benefit from early planting: specialized nurseries sell them in midsummer. All fall-flowering bulbs are best bought and planted by late summer. Summer-flowering bulbs (such as *Gladiolus*, *Dahlia*, and *Canna*) are available for purchase in spring.

Bulbs tend to deteriorate if kept dry too long; they will have a shorter growing period and take some time to recover and flower satisfactorily, so buy and plant them as soon as they are available. Do not buy or plant any bulbs that are mushy or slimy, or any that feel much lighter than a bulb of similar size of the same kind (they are probably dried up and dead).

GOOD EXAMPLES

DAFFODIL (SINGLE-NOSED)   DAFFODIL (TWIN-NOSED)

Fresh, plump tubers

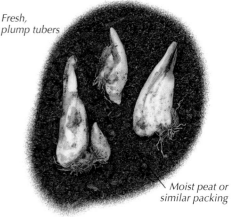

Moist peat or similar packing

ERYTHRONIUM OREGONUM

POOR EXAMPLES

Diseased tissue

Damaged outer scales

No tunic (covering)

Deterioration of bulb tissue

Small nose

Offset too small to flower

CORYDALIS SOLIDA

Distinct growing point on corm

SELECTING PLANTS FOR THE WATER GARDEN

When selecting aquatic plants at the nursery or garden center, look for clean, fresh-looking, and vigorous specimens, growing in tanks that are free from algae and duckweed (*Wolffia*). Check that the undersides of the leaves are free from jellylike deposits of snail eggs and that there are no strands of blanketweed in the foliage. Mail-order plants should appear plump and green; if they look weak and limp, they are unlikely to grow well. If buying plants by mail order, use a specialized supplier.

Marginal plant

GOOD EXAMPLE

Strong flowering stem

Healthy leaves

CALTHA PALUSTRIS

POOR EXAMPLE

Weak growth

Weed-infested soil mix

Surface floater

GOOD EXAMPLE

Young, fresh growth

STRATIOTES ALOIDES

POOR EXAMPLE

Damaged growth

Old, rotting foliage

SELECTING CACTI AND OTHER SUCCULENTS

When buying cacti and other succulents, choose healthy, pest- and disease-free, unblemished plants that show strong new growth (unless you are buying the plants when they are dormant) or have flower buds forming. Do not buy damaged or even slightly shriveled specimens, or any with dull, dry, or limp segments. Also reject plants that have outgrown their pots.

GOOD EXAMPLE

Healthy-looking body

New buds forming

REBUTIA SPECIES

POOR EXAMPLE

Damaged growth

GOOD EXAMPLE

Plump, fleshy leaves

Sturdy stem

CRASSULA OVATA

POOR EXAMPLE

Shriveled and cut leaves

PLANTING

When selecting and planting trees, shrubs, and woody climbers, it is vital to take account of the general weather pattern of your area as well as your garden's individual microclimate, because these factors will determine whether a given plant is hardy and has a reasonable chance of surviving in your garden. Proper planting and aftercare will increase the likelihood of survival.

PLANTING A CONTAINER-GROWN TREE

First, thoroughly moisten the soil mix in the container – if it is very dry, stand the container in water for half an hour or until the soil mix is moist throughout (the bubbles will stop rising). Then remove the container, cutting it away if necessary, taking care not to damage the roots excessively. Gently tease out the roots with your fingers or a hand fork (or with pruners, if the roots are thickly congested) to encourage them to grow into the surrounding soil; this is essential with a potbound plant. If there are any broken or damaged roots, trim them back with pruners. It is important to check that the planting depth is correct. If a tree is planted too deeply, its roots may not receive enough oxygen and the tree may grow more slowly or even die; if planted too shallowly, the roots may dry out.

Mark out the area of the hole to be dug – about 3 or 4 times the diameter of the tree's root ball. Remove any grass or weeds, then dig out the hole to about 1½ times the depth of the root ball.

2 Scarify the sides and bottom of the hole with a fork. There is no need to improve the soil unless the quality is very poor, such as dense, heavy clay or very infertile sand.

3 Drive a stake into the hole, just off center and on the windward side. Lay the tree on its side and slide it out of the pot. Gently tease out the roots without breaking up the root ball.

4 Hold the tree next to the stake and spread out roots. Lay a stake across the hole to check the planting depth. Adjust by adding or removing soil. Plant tree at same depth it was in its container.

5 Backfill around the tree with more topsoil, working it down the root ball, and then gently firm the soil. Build up soil around the hole to form a watering ring.

6 Cut back damaged stems, long sideshoots, and weaker, lower branches (see inset). Apply a mulch 2–3in (5–7cm) deep around the area.

PLANTING A CONTAINER-GROWN SHRUB

Fall and spring are the optimum times for planting container-grown and containerized shrubs. Planting in fall allows the roots to establish while the ground is still warm, so the shrub should be growing vigorously before hot, dry weather the next summer. In some areas, planting can be carried out during mild weather in winter, but not when the ground is very cold or frozen. Roots will not begin growth in very cold soil, and there is a risk that they may freeze. A possible disadvantage to spring planting is that top-growth is likely to develop before the roots establish adequately and, if there is a long spell of hot, dry weather, watering may be required to help the plants survive.

Using a watering ring

To help retain water, create a shallow depression and a low wall of soil around the shrub. Cover the area with mulch, then allow the ring to settle on its own.

Placing one hand on top of the soil mix and around the shrub to support it, carefully ease the plant out of its container. Place the shrub in the prepared hole.

Lay a stake alongside to check that the soil level is the same as before. If necessary, adjust the planting depth by adding or removing topsoil beneath the shrub.

Backfill around the shrub with the removed soil, firming in stages to prevent air pockets from forming. Once the hole has been filled with soil, carefully firm around the shrub with your heel or hands.

Prune any diseased, damaged, or weak wood, and cut back any inward-growing or crossing stems to an outward-growing shoot or bud.

TRANSPLANTING A SHRUB

Careful selection and siting of a shrub should make transplanting unnecessary, although sometimes it may be desirable or unavoidable. In general, the younger the shrub, the more likely it is to reestablish after being moved. Most young shrubs may be lifted bare-root when dormant. Established shrubs that have large root systems should be lifted with a ball of soil around the roots before being moved. Spring (before bud break) and mid- to late fall are the best times to do this.

Using a spade, mark out a circle around the extent of the shrub's branches (here *Ilex aquifolium* 'Golden Milkboy'). Tie in (or prune off) any trailing stems, or wrap the shrub in burlap, to prevent the stems from being damaged. Dig a circular trench around the plant.

Use a fork to loosen the soil around the root ball. Continue to carefully fork away soil from around the shrub's root ball to reduce its size and weight.

Undercut the root ball with a spade, cutting through woody roots if necessary to separate them from the surrounding soil.

Pull some burlap up around the root ball and tie it securely. Remove the shrub from its hole, then transport it to its new position.

Remove or untie the burlap when replanting. Plant with the soil mark at the same level as before. Firm, water well, and mulch.

PLANTING A CLIMBER AGAINST A WALL

Before removing the plant from its pot, make sure that the soil mix is moist. Water the plant well, so that the root ball is thoroughly wet, and then allow it to drain for at least an hour. Remove the surface layer of soil mix to eliminate weeds, and then invert the pot, taking care to support the plant as it slides out. If the roots have begun to curl around inside the pot, gently tease them out. Any dead, damaged, or protruding roots should be cut back to the perimeter of the root ball. Position the plant so that the top of the root ball is just level with the surrounding soil. It is advisable to plant clematis more deeply, however. Climbers that have been grafted (as is the case with most wisterias) should be planted with the graft union 2½in (6cm) below soil level to encourage rooting of the cultivar.

Attach a support 12in (30cm) above the soil and 2in (5cm) from the wall. Dig a hole 18in (45cm) from the wall. Loosen the soil at the base and add compost.

Soak the climbers root ball well. Position it in the hole at a 45° angle, placing a stake across to check the planting level. Spread the roots away from the wall.

Fill in around the plant and firm and level the soil, ensuring that no air pockets remain between the roots and that the plant is fully supported.

Untie the stems from the central stake and select 4 or 5 strong shoots. Insert a stake for each shoot and attach it to the lowest wire. Tie in the shoots.

Using pruners, trim back any weak, damaged, or wayward shoots to the central stem. This establishes the initial framework for the climber.

Water the plant thoroughly (here *Jasminum mesnyi*). Cover the surrounding soil with a deep mulch to retain moisture and discourage weeds.

PLANTING A BARE-ROOT ROSE

Bare-root roses are best planted just before or at the beginning of their dormant period (in fall or early winter) to lessen the shock of transplanting. Early spring is better in areas that have bad winters. Plant roses as soon as possible after purchase. If there is any delay, perhaps because of unsuitable weather, it is best to heel them into a spare piece of ground, with the roots buried in a shallow trench. Alternatively, store the roses in a cool and frost-free place, and keep the roots moist. If the roots of a bare-root rose look dry before planting, soak the roots in a bucket of water for an hour or two until they are thoroughly moist.

Remove diseased, damaged , or crossing shoots and straggly stems; trim thick roots by one-third. Dig a hole and fork in compost mixed with bone meal or fertilizer.

Center the rose in the hole and spread out the roots evenly. Lay a stake across the hole to check that the bud union will be at the correct depth for the type of rose and your climate zone.

In 2 or 3 stages, water the hole and backfill with soil after the water has drained out. Do not walk on the backfilled soil to avoid compacting the soil and breaking the roots.

PLANTING A CLIMBING ROSE

Train climbers grown against a wall or fence along horizontal wires that are about 18in (45cm) apart and held in place by vine eyes or strong nails. If the brickwork or masonry is very hard, drill holes for the vine eyes with a ³⁄₁₆in (4.7mm) bit. Keep the wires 3in (7cm) away from the wall to allow air circulation and discourage diseases. The ground next to a wall is likely to be dry, since it is in a rain shadow and the masonry absorbs moisture from the soil. Plant about 18in (45cm) from the wall where the soil is less dry and water from eaves will not drip on the

rose.Prepare the soil and planting hole, and trim the rose, as for bush roses. Fan out its roots. Train the shoots along stakes, but keep each stake far enough from the roots to avoid damaging them.

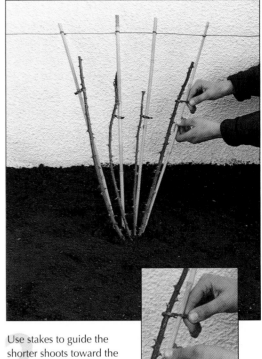

1 Place the rose in the planting hole, leaning it toward the wall at an angle of about 45° so that the shoots reach the lowest support wire. Place a stake across the hole to check the planting depth.

2 Use stakes to guide the shorter shoots toward the wires. Tie all the shoots to the stakes or wires with plastic straps (see insert).

PLANTING A STANDARD ROSE

A standard rose needs a stake, placed on the side of the prevailing wind, to support it. Paint the entire stake with a preservative that is not toxic to plants, then allow it to dry. Insert the stake very firmly near the center of the planting hole before positioning the rose to avoid damaging the roots and, as a result, encouraging suckers from below the graft union. Position the rose next to the stake, and check that it just reaches the base of the lowest branches; if necessary, adjust the height of the stake. Use a stake or rake handle to make sure that the bud union is at the correct level (above ground in warmer areas, below in colder).

1 Position the stake in the hole so that the rose stem will be in the center. Drive the stake into the ground and check that the top is just below the head of the rose.

2 Place a stake across the hole to check the planting depth. Use the old soil mark on the stem as a guide and plant at the correct depth. Fill in the hole, then water.

3 Use a tie just below the head of the rose, and another halfway up the stem, to attach the rose to the stake. Cut out weak or crossing shoots.

PLANTING A CONTAINER-GROWN PERENNIAL

Perennials grown in containers may be planted out at any time of year when the soil is workable, but the best seasons are spring and fall. Planting in fall helps the plants establish quickly before the onset of winter, because the soil is still warm enough to promote root growth, yet it is unlikely to dry out. In cold areas, however, spring planting is better for perennials that are not entirely hardy or that dislike wet conditions.

In a prepared bed, dig a hole 1½ times wider and deeper than the plant's root ball.

Gently scrape off the top 1¼in (3cm) of soil to remove weeds and weed seeds. Carefully tease out the roots around the sides and base of the root ball.

Check that the plant crown is at the correct depth when planted and fill in around the root ball. Firm gently around the plant, then water it in thoroughly.

PLANTING ANNUALS INTO OPEN GROUND

Before you plant out annuals, first prepare the bed, water the young plants thoroughly, and then allow them to drain for an hour or so. To remove a plant from its pot, invert it, supporting the stem with a finger on either side. Then tap the rim against a hard surface. If plants are in trays without divisions, hold the tray firmly with both hands, then tap one side sharply on the ground to loosen the medium.

Break the pack apart and carefully remove each seedling (here *Tagetes*) with its root ball intact.

Place each plant in a hole large enough to take its root ball, making sure the plant is slightly lower in the soil than it was in its container.

Gently firm the soil in the well around the plant so that there are no air pockets. Water the area.

PLANTING DEPTHS

ASTER

SISYRINCHIUM STRIATUM 'AUNT MAY'

GROUND-LEVEL PLANTING
The majority of perennials should be planted so that the crown of the plant is level with the surrounding soil.

RAISED PLANTING
Set plants that are prone to rot at the base, and variegated plants that tend to revert, with their crowns slightly above the ground.

While most perennials are best planted out at the same soil level as they were in their pots, a number grow better if planted higher or deeper, depending on their individual requirements. Some prefer a raised, well-drained site, while others thrive in deeper, moist conditions.

HOSTA

POLYGONATUM

SHALLOW PLANTING
Plant perennials that require a moist environment with their crowns about 1in (2.5cm) below ground level.

DEEP PLANTING
Plant perennials with tuberous root systems so that their crowns are about 4in (10cm) below the soil surface.

PLANTING LARGE BULBS IN GRASS

When planting bulbs that are to be naturalized in grass, first cut the grass as short as possible. Random rather than regimented planting achieves a more natural effect; scatter the bulbs gently by hand over the area and plant them where they have fallen, making sure that they are at least one bulb's width apart. Dig holes with a trowel or use a bulb planter, which cuts out plugs of sod and soil to a depth of about 4–6in (10–15cm); dig deeper if necessary for larger bulbs. Check that all the holes are at the correct depth and that the bulbs are the right way up before inserting them and replacing the sod, then give them a good watering.

Clean the bulbs (here daffodils), removing any loose outer coatings and old roots. Scatter the bulbs randomly over the planting area, then make sure that they are at least their own width apart.

Make an individual hole for each bulb, using a bulb planter to remove a circle of sod and a core of soil to a depth of about 4–6in (10–15cm).

Place a pinch of bone meal, mixed with a little of the soil from the core, into each hole and put in a bulb with the growing point uppermost.

Break up the underside of the core over the bulb so that it is completely covered with loose soil. Then replace the remains of the core on top of it.

Replace the lid of sod and firm it in gently, taking care not to damage the growing point of the bulb. Fill in any gaps in the grass with more soil.

PLANTING BULBS IN THE OPEN

Dry, loose bulbs should be planted as soon as possible after purchase, usually in late summer or early fall (plant summer-flowering bulbs in early to midspring); otherwise, keep them cool and dry until you can plant them. Bulbs are usually best planted several to a large hole dug out with a spade, but they may also be planted singly. Do not make the outline of the planting area or the spacing of the bulbs symmetrical: this looks unnatural, and if one or two bulbs fail, they will leave unsightly gaps.

Dig out a large hole in well-prepared ground. Plant the bulbs (here tulips), at least 3 times their own depth, and 2–3 widths apart.

For a natural effect, space the bulbs randomly. Once they are in position, gently draw the soil over them with your hand to avoid displacing or damaging them.

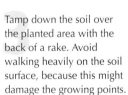

Tamp down the soil over the planted area with the back of a rake. Avoid walking heavily on the soil surface, because this might damage the growing points.

Planting bulbs

SINGLY
Plant each bulb in a separate hole at the appropriate depth. Draw back the prepared soil with a trowel, and firm it down gently afterward.

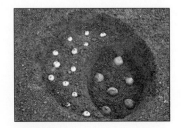

IN LAYERS
Two or more kinds of bulb may be planted in the same space. Plant each kind at its correct depth, carefully covering each layer before planting the next type of bulb.

PLANTING DEEP-WATER AND MARGINAL PLANTS

Whether planting in beds or free-standing containers, settle the plants firmly in the soil, because they are very buoyant and may become dislodged. Always plant in moist soil, and soak containers well before immersing them in the pond. A top-dressing of grit, coarse sand, or pea gravel to a depth of 1in (2.5cm) prevents soil from floating out and clouding the water and discourages hungry or curious fish from disturbing the plants. When submerging the containers in deep water, thread string through the sides to form handles; this makes it much easier to position the basket, which can then be gradually lowered onto the bottom.

1 Choose a planting basket to accommodate the plant roots, and line it with burlap or closely woven polypropylene.

2 Fill the basket with heavy, moist soil to a depth of at least 2in (5cm). Center the plant (here *Aponogeton distachyos*).

3 Fill with more soil to within ½in (1cm) of the rim of the basket, firming the plant in well to give it good anchorage.

4 Top-dress the container with washed grit or pea gravel to a depth of 1in (2.5cm).

5 Trim away any surplus liner with scissors. Tie string handles to the rim of the basket on opposite sides.

6 Hold the basket by the string handles, then gently lower it onto blocks or the marginal shelf. Release the handles.

Surface floaters

With a new planting, include some surface-floating plants to discourage the growth of algae. When the ornamental plants become more established, some of the floaters should be removed. In a large pond, a line may be drawn across the pond from both ends to bring plants within reach. Duckweed in particular is very persistent, so choose less vigorous species.

Surface-floating plants have no anchorage because their roots obtain nutrients directly from the water. Their initial positioning is unimportant, since the groups are moved around on the surface by wind.

Surface-floating plants (here *Stratiotes aloides*) may be placed on the water's surface; in warm weather they multiply rapidly, giving valuable surface shade.

PLANTING IN A HANGING BASKET

A wide range of plants can be grown in a hanging basket, including annuals, tender perennials, succulents (as shown here) and even weak-stemmed shrubs, such as fuchsias. Make sure that the basket is completely clean. Wire baskets should be lined with a commercial liner or a layer of sphagnum moss. Do not line the basket with plastic, since this restricts drainage. If using a plastic basket that has an attached drainage tray, be sure to place a piece of screening over the drainage hole(s) to prevent the soil mix from washing out.

Line a wire hanging basket with a layer of moist sphagnum moss. The layer should be 1¼in (3cm) thick when compressed.

Fill the basket almost to the brim with a mix of 1 part sharp sand to 3 parts soil-based potting mix. Prepare a hole for the plant in the center of the basket.

Insert the plant (here a *Schlumbergera*), spreading out the roots. Fill in gently but firmly with soil mix so that there are no air pockets around the roots.

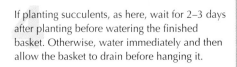

If planting succulents, as here, wait for 2–3 days after planting before watering the finished basket. Otherwise, water immediately and then allow the basket to drain before hanging it.

REPOTTING AN INDOOR PLANT

Indoor plants need repotting to accommodate their growth and to replenish the soil mix. A potbound plant has retarded growth, and water runs straight through the soil mix. Repot before this happens, so that the plant develops well. A few plants, such as amaryllis (*Hippeastrum*), enjoy confined roots, so repot them less often, and top-dress occasionally. The best time to repot is at the start of the growing season, although fast-growing plants may need repotting a few times in one season. The process may delay flowering, because the plant initially concentrates its energy on new root growth. Avoid repotting a dormant plant; it will not respond to the moisture and fertility, and it may rot.

Before potting on a plant (here *Dracaena deremensis* 'Souvenir de Schriever'), make sure that its root ball is moist by watering it thoroughly about an hour beforehand. Select a pot that is one or two sizes larger than the old one. Make sure the pot is clean (whether washed, disinfected, or new) to avoid spreading diseases. The fresh potting mix should be of the same type as that in the old pot.

Remove the plant by inverting the pot and sharply tapping the rim on a hard surface to loosen the root ball. Support the plant as it slides out of the pot.

Gently tease out the root ball with a small fork or your fingers. Put some moist potting mix in the base of the new pot.

Insert the plant so that its soil mark is level with the rim base. Fill in with soil mix to within ½in (1.5cm) of the rim, firm, water, and place in position (right).

PRUNING

Pruning and training both aim to make sure that plants are as vigorous and healthy as possible, are at the least risk of infection from disease, and are free of structural weakness at maturity. They can also create striking features by enhancing ornamental qualities, such as bark, flowers, foliage, and fruit. However, pruning always causes some stress, so learn when and how to prune.

PRUNING AND TRAINING YOUNG TREES

Young trees benefit from formative pruning to make sure that they develop a strong, well-balanced framework of evenly spaced branches. This involves the removal of dead, damaged, and diseased wood, as well as any weak or crossing branches. Formative pruning may also be used to determine the tree's shape as it grows: for example, a young feathered tree may be pruned over several years to form a standard, or perhaps trained against a wall as an espalier.

Feathered tree
Remove congested and crossing shoots, then cut out any laterals that are small, spindly, or badly positioned, to achieve a well-balanced framework of branches.

Feathered tree

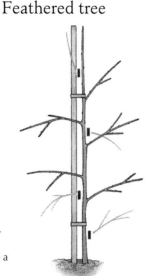

Central-leader standard

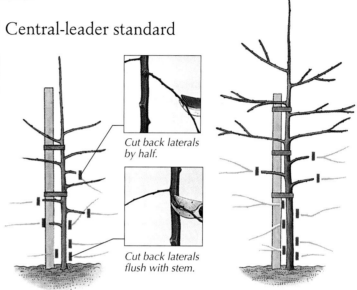

Cut back laterals by half.

Cut back laterals flush with stem.

Year 1
On the lowest third of the tree, cut back laterals to the main stem; on the middle third, cut back laterals by half. Remove any weak or competing leaders.

Years 2 and 3
Continue the process, removing the lowest laterals completely and cutting back by about half those laterals that are on the middle third of the tree.

Branched-head standard

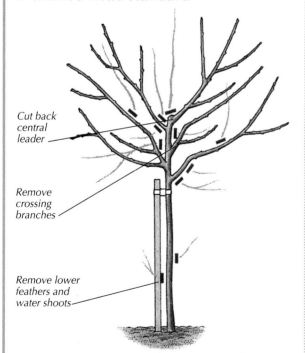

Cut back central leader

Remove crossing branches

Remove lower feathers and water shoots

Remove crossing laterals and any growths on the lower third of the tree. Cut back the leader to a healthy bud or shoot.

Weeping tree

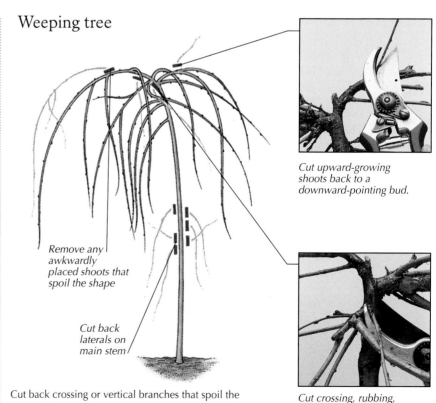

Remove any awkwardly placed shoots that spoil the shape

Cut back laterals on main stem

Cut upward-growing shoots back to a downward-pointing bud.

Cut crossing, rubbing, or congested growth.

Cut back crossing or vertical branches that spoil the symmetry of the tree. Remove any growths on the main stem.

FORMATIVE PRUNING AND TRAINING

The aim of formative pruning is to make sure that a shrub has a framework of well-spaced branches. The amount of formative pruning required depends very much on the type of shrub and on the quality of the plants available. (It is usually best to start with a quality plant from a good source.) Evergreen shrubs generally need little formative pruning. Excessive growth resulting in an unbalanced shape should be lightly pruned in midspring, after the shrub has been planted. Deciduous shrubs are much more likely to require formative pruning than evergreen shrubs. This should be carried out in the dormant season, between midfall and midspring, at or after planting.

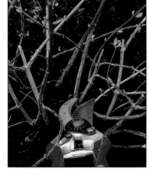

Coppicing a shrub for winter stem color

Coppicing stimulates the growth of colorful, vigorous stems. Cut back all stems to about 2–3in (5–8cm) from the base before growth begins in spring, and then fertilize and mulch well.

Prune back crossing or congested shoots to an outward-facing bud or cut right back to the base.

Prune out any very weak and spindly, or long and straggly, stems, cutting them right back to the base.

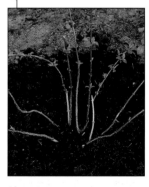

Also remove any very awkward stems that spoil the shape of the shrub, to leave an evenly balanced framework.

WHY, HOW, AND WHERE TO CUT

Pruning normally stimulates growth. The actively growing terminal shoot or dormant growth bud of a stem is often dominant, inhibiting by chemical means the growth of buds or shoots below it. Pruning to remove the ends of stems affects the control mechanism, resulting in more vigorous development of lower shoots or growth buds. Hard pruning promotes more vigorous growth than light pruning. This needs to be borne in mind when correcting the shape of an unbalanced shrub. Prune weak growth hard, but strong growth only lightly.

Opposite shoots
Prune stems with opposite buds to just above a strong pair of buds or shoots, using a clean, straight cut.

Alternate shoots
For plants with alternate buds, prune to just above a bud or shoot, using a clean, angled cut.

Making an angled cut
Angle the cut so that its lowest point is opposite the base of the bud and the top just clears the bud.

PRUNING ROSES

The purpose of pruning roses is to promote new, vigorous, disease-free shoots developing to replace the old, weakened ones, and so produce a reasonably attractive shape and the optimum display of blooms. Training a plant stimulates the production of flowering sideshoots and directs new growth. A pair of sharp, high-quality pruners is essential, and always wear thornproof gloves.

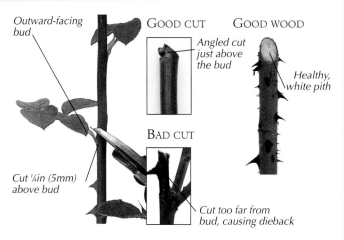

Outward-facing bud

Cut ¼in (5mm) above bud

GOOD CUT

Angled cut just above the bud

BAD CUT

Cut too far from bud, causing dieback

GOOD WOOD

Healthy, white pith

Pruning a newly planted bush rose

Prune a newly planted bush rose to about 3in (8cm) above ground level. Cut back to outward-facing buds, and remove any cold-damaged growth.

PRUNING HYBRID TEA AND GRANDIFLORA ROSES

Depending on the extent of winter kill and on the differences among cultivars, in colder areas the main shoots should be pruned back to between 8–10in (20–25cm). In milder areas, the shoots may be cut down less severely, to about 18–24in (45–60cm). For exhibition-quality blooms, cut the main shoots back hard to leave only two or three buds.

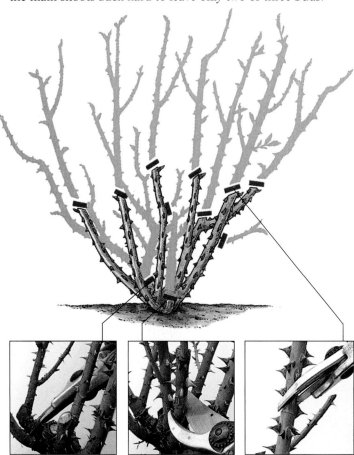

Cut out crossing, congested, and twiggy or spindly growth.

Remove dead wood and any that shows signs of damage or disease.

Prune main shoots to within about 8–10in (20–25cm) of ground level.

PRUNING FLORIBUNDA ROSES

When pruning Floribundas, cut out any unproductive wood as for Hybrid Teas. Reduce sideshoots by about one-third on smaller cultivars, and by two-thirds on taller-growing ones. Cut back the main shoots to 12–15in (30–38cm), but reduce the shoots of taller cultivars by about one-third. Do not prune them any harder, (unless growing for exhibition) because this will significantly reduce the number of blooms.

Remove crossing or congested wood and twiggy, spindly growth.

Prune out all dead, damaged or diseased wood to a healthy bud.

Prune main shoots to 12–15in (30–38cm) from ground level.

Reduce sideshoots by one- to two-thirds, cutting to a bud.

PRUNING STANDARD AND MINIATURE ROSES

Most standards are formed from Hybrid Teas or Floribundas budded onto a straight, unbranched stem. Prune as for their bush relatives, but cut back the main shoots so that they are all roughly equal in length. If the head is unbalanced, prune the shoots on the denser side less hard so that they do not produce as much new growth as those on the thinner side.

There are two methods: either give them the minimum of attention (remove dead growth, thin out tangles, and shorten overly long shoots) or treat them like small Hybrid Teas or Floribundas (remove all growth except the strongest shoots, and then cut them back by one-third or more).

Standard rose

After
All dead and damaged wood and any crossing stems have been removed to leave healthy shoots. The main shoots have been reduced to 8–10in (20–25cm), and the side-shoots by about one-third.

Before
In the spring, prune a standard rose to prevent the plant from becoming too top-heavy and to produce an evenly shaped, floriferous head.

Miniature rose

Before (Method Two)
Miniature roses often produce a mass of twiggy growth. The shape of this plant is unbalanced by overly vigorous shoots growing from the base.

After (Method Two)
Excessively twiggy and spindly growth, crossing shoots, and damaged wood have been removed, and vigorous shoots have been cut back by half.

DEALING WITH SUCKERS

Suckers usually look quite different from the rest of the plant, often with leaves of a different shape or color, and they often grow more strongly. Remove any suckers as soon as they appear. This prevents the rootstock from wasting energy on the sucker's growth. Damage to the roots, caused by severe cold or any accidental nicks from hoes, other implements, or a stake, may stimulate the production of suckers. Shoots on the stem of a standard rose are also suckers, since the stem is actually part of the understock. As with other grafted roses, any suckers will look different from the cultivar you want to grow.

REMOVING A SUCKER FROM A STANDARD ROSE
Pull away any suckers growing from the rose stem (see inset), taking care not to rip the bark.

With a trowel, carefully scrape away the soil to expose the top of the rootstock. Check that the suspect shoot arises from below the bud union.

Using gloves to protect your hands, pull the sucker down and away from the rootstock. Trim the wound, refill the hole, and gently firm the soil.

How a sucker grows

The sucker (right) grows directly from the rootstock. If cut back only at ground level it will regrow and divert further energy from the main part of the plant.

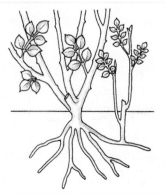

PEGGING DOWN ROSES

This technique is an effective (although time-consuming) way of increasing flower production on roses that tend to send up long, ungainly shoots with flowers only at the tips. In late summer or fall, bend the shoots over gently, taking great care not to snap them, then peg the shoots firmly into the ground. This has much the same result as horizontally training the shoots of climbing and rambler roses.

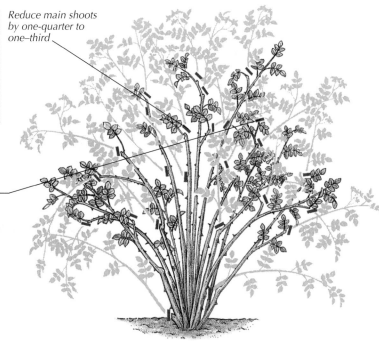

Select long, noflowering shoots, and prune the soft tips. Gently bend each shoot over, then peg it to the soil with sturdy wire pins (see insert)

PRUNING GALLICA ROSES

Many of these old-fashioned roses produce a twiggy tangle of shoots that should be regularly thinned out to improve air circulation and bloom quality and to make the plant more attractive. After flowering, shorten the sideshoots only, and remove any dead or diseased wood. Gently clip Gallica roses used for hedging to maintain a neat shape. Follow their natural outline: do not attempt to shape them into a formal hedge, since this would remove many of the sideshoots on which flowers are produced in the following year.

Thin out twiggy growth regularly, and remove spent blooms by cutting back to the main shoot.

On mature plants, cut out up to one-quarter of old main shoots at the base.

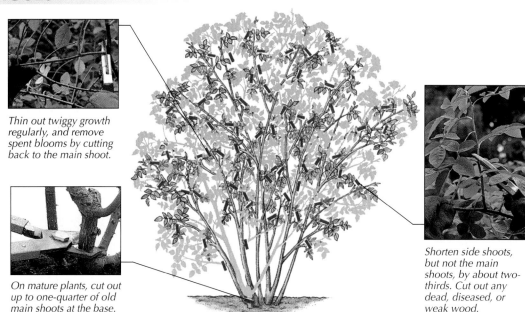

Shorten side shoots, but not the main shoots, by about two-thirds. Cut out any dead, diseased, or weak wood.

PRUNING ALBA, CENTIFOLIA, DAMASK, AND MOSS ROSES

After flowering, reduce both main shoots and sideshoots. At the end of summer, cut back any overly long shoots that might whip about in the wind and cause wind-rock damage to the roots.

A general note on pruning the old-fashioned roses: some of these roses have a very individual growth habit and do not conform neatly to a specific pruning program. For these, it is best to observe the way the plant grows for the first few years, and then adapt a specific program (such as one of those given here) to how the rose reacts to the program. Some old-fashioned roses resent pruning and will respond by turning into very unattractive plants.

Cut back any overly long, whippy shoots by about one-third.

Prune sideshoots to about two-thirds of their length.

Reduce main shoots by one-quarter to one–third

PRUNING AND TRAINING CLIMBING ROSES

These roses require minor pruning but regular annual training. In their first year (and in their second unless they have made exceptional growth), do not prune climbers, except to remove any dead, diseased, or weak growth. Never hard prune climbing sports of bush roses (roses with the word "climbing" in their name; for example 'Climbing Peace') in the first two years, since they may revert to the bush form. Begin training as soon as the new shoots are long enough to reach the supports; train them sideways along horizontal supports to encourage flowering. Where this is not possible, choose a cultivar that is halfway between a tall shrub and a climbing rose. Many of these flower well from the plant base without special training.

Reduce the sideshoots by about two-thirds or about 6in (15cm), cutting above an outward-facing bud.

Tie all new shoots into horizontal wires 6–8in (15–20cm) apart. The shoots should not cross each other.

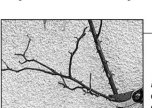

Remove any diseased, dead, or twiggy growth, cutting back to healthy wood or the main shoot.

PRUNING AND TRAINING MATURE RAMBLER ROSES

Ramblers produce much more growth from the base than most climbers and, if not carefully managed, grow into a vicious tangle of unmanageable shoots. Prune ramblers in summer, after they flower. In the first two years, restrict pruning to cutting back all the sideshoots by about 3in (7.5cm) to a vigorous shoot; also, remove dead or diseased wood. In later years, prune and train more heavily to maintain the framework: remove the oldest shoots to the ground, and train in new shoots that spring up from the base.

Cut sideshoots back to leave between 2 to 4 healthy buds or shoots.

Cut back any old, spent shoots to ground level, using loppers.

Tie all shoots to the wires as close to the horizontal as possible.

PROPAGATION

Producing new plants from existing ones is one of the most satisfying of all horticultural pursuits. From a simpler technique (sowing seeds) to the more elaborate (such as layering), growing your own allows you to raise a number of plants at minimum expense, such as for a hedge, and greatly increases your selections, especially if you grow annuals and vegetables from seed.

HARDWOOD CUTTINGS

Many deciduous trees and shrubs (as well as some ever-greens) may be rooted from hard-wood cuttings outdoors in fall and winter. If your winters are long and harsh or excessively wet, the cuttings usually die if left outside, but they can be rooted in deep boxes in a frost-free basement or root cellar instead. Select cuttings just after a hard frost. Choose strong, vigorous shoots of the current season's growth. For species that do not root easily, tie cuttings into small bundles, then plunge them into a sand bed.

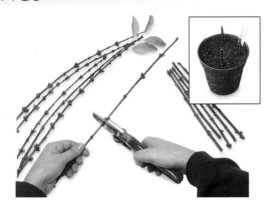

Strip leaves and sideshoots from bottom half of cutting.

For deciduous plants: trim off tips and cut stems into 8in (20cm) lengths. Make a horizontal cut just below a node, and a sloping cut to mark the top. Dip the base in hormone rooting compound. Insert them 2in (5cm) apart, 6in (5cm) deep, in soil-based rooting medium in pots, either in a cold place or outdoors.

For evergreens: cut shoots into sections 8–10in (20–25cm) long. Trim just above a leaf at the tip and below another at the base. Strip leaves from bottom half of cutting. Insert 5–8 cuttings in a 6in (15cm) pot. Place in a closed case with slight bottom heat, or in a clear plastic bag. Rooting occurs in 6–10 weeks.

SEMIRIPE CUTTINGS

Many conifers, as well as certain broadleaved evergreens such as hollies (*Ilex*) and *Magnolia grandiflora*, may be propagated readily from semiripe cuttings. After insertion, check the cuttings periodically, watering them only to keep them from drying out. Remove any fallen leaves as soon as they appear, since these may rot and spread disease to the cuttings. During cold spells, cold frames should be insulated with burlap or a similar covering.

The ideal semiripe cutting is taken from current season's growth that has begun to firm up; the base is quite firm, while the tip is soft and still actively growing. Such stems will offer some resistance when bent.

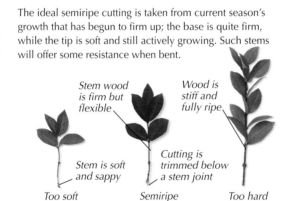

Stem wood is firm but flexible

Wood is stiff and fully ripe

Stem is soft and sappy

Cutting is trimmed below a stem joint

Too soft   Semiripe   Too hard

DISTINGUSHING SEMIRIPE WOOD

In mid- to late summer, select a healthy, semiripe shoot of the current season's growth (here, *Aucuba*), then sever the cutting jut above a stem joint with clean, sharp pruners.

Remove sideshoots from the stem with a sharp knife. Trim the stem to 4–6in (10–15cm), cutting just below a stem joint. Remove the soft tip and the lowest pair of leaves.

To stimulate rooting, cut a shallow sliver of bark, ½–1in (1–2.5cm) long, from the base of the stem; do not expose the pith. This process is known as wounding.

Dip the base of the cutting in hormone rooting compound. Make sure that the entire wound receives the thinnest possible (but uniform) coating, then shake off the excess.

Place cuttings 2–3in (5–8cm) apart in standard rooting medium in a nursery bed outdoors (or in pots in a closed case). Label with name and date. Water and cover.

SOFTWOOD AND GREENWOOD CUTTINGS

This method of propagation is suitable for some tree species, although it is more commonly used for shrubs. Softwood cuttings are taken from the fast-growing tips of new shoots and usually root very easily. They wilt rapidly, however, so it is vital to prepare and insert them as quickly as possible after removing them from the parent plant.

SOFTWOOD CUTTINGS
Take softwood cuttings in spring and early summer from the new season's growth before it has begun to firm up. Choose vigorous nonflowering shoots with 2 or 3 pairs of leaves, cutting just below a stem joint.

GREENWOOD CUTTINGS
Take greenwood cuttings in late spring to midsummer, just as new stems begin to firm up. They are less prone to wilt and easier to handle than softwood and root as readily. Treat them exactly as for softwood cuttings

Remove the soft tip, because it is vulnerable to rot and scorch

1 Remove the soft tip just above a leaf joint, as well as the lowest pair of leaves. Cut large leaves in half to reduce moisture loss. Trim the base just below a leaf joint; the stem should be 1½–2in (4–5cm) long.

2 Fill a 5in (13cm) pot with rooting medium. Make 2 or 3 holes around the edge, then insert the cuttings so that the lowest leaves lie just above the surface and are not touching each other.

Vent of closed case will be opened gradually to harden off rooted cuttings

3 After watering thoroughly with a commercial fungicidal solution, label and place pots in a closed case heated, if possible, at the base to 59°F (15°C). Keep in a shaded place, out of direct sun.

4 Once cuttings have rooted, admit more air to harden them off. Knock out of the pot, tease apart, and pot up singly into 3½in (9cm) pots of soil mix. Pinch out growing tips to encourage bushy growth.

SIMPLE LAYERING

The long, trailing shoots of climbers may often be propagated by simple layering if they do not root naturally. A shoot is wounded and pegged down into the surrounding soil. This induces it to root at a node to provide a young plant that is later separated from the parent. Layers of many climbers that have been pegged down in spring will develop strong root systems by fall, at which time they can be separated from the parent plant. Layering also works for many shrubs and a few trees.

Dig a hole, about 3in (8cm) deep in prepared soil, with a shallowly sloping side next to the parent plant and a nearly vertical slope on the far side. Mix a little sand and organic matter into the bottom of the hole if soil is heavy.

2 Trim off sideshoots and leaves. At the point where the underside of the stem touches the soil, make a slanting cut through to the middle of the stem to make a "tongue" of bark, or remove a 1in (2.5cm) sliver of bark.

3 Dust the wound with some hormone rooting compound. Peg the stem down securely into the bottom of the hole using several U-shaped, galvanized wire pins, placing them on either side of the wound.

4 Bend the stem tip up against the vertical side of the hole and secure with a stake. Backfill, firm, and water in. Keep weed-free and moist. A layer should be well rooted within a year, and can be cut from the parent.

5 Plant the layer in a 5in (13cm) pot of standard soil mix, then water and label it. You could plant it into its permanent position in the garden if it has produced enough roots. Watch its watering needs carefully.

PROPAGATING PERENNIALS BY DIVISION

This method is suitable for propagating many perennials that have a spreading rootstock and produce plenty of shoots from the base. As well as being a way of increasing stocks, in many cases division rejuvenates the plants and keeps them vigorous, since old or unproductive parts are discarded. Most plants should be divided when they are dormant (or are about to go dormant, or are just emerging from dormancy) from late fall to early spring, but not in extremely cold, wet, or dry weather, because these conditions may make it difficult for the divided plants to reestablish successfully. Try to do this on an overcast, calm day.

1 Lift the plant to be divided, taking care to insert the fork far enough away from the plant so that the roots are not damaged. Shake off surplus soil.

2 Separate plants with a woody center by chopping through the crown with a spade. Use a trowel for smaller, less dense clumps.

Alternative method

Divide densely rooted herbaceous plants (here *Hemerocallis*) using 2 forks inserted back to back in the center. Larger, tougher clumps will require the help of an assistant.

3 Divide the plant into smaller pieces by hand, retaining only healthy, vigorous sections, each with several new shoots.

4 Cut back the old top-growth, then replant the divided sections to the same depth as before. Firm in and water thoroughly.

DIVIDING HOSTAS

Large hostas with tough rootstocks should be divided using a spade or back-to-back forks. Hostas that have looser, fleshy rootstocks may be separated by hand; this technique may be necessary to avoid damaging smaller-growing cultivars. For quick reestablishment of a clump, include several buds on an individual division, but if making many plants is your goal and you can wait longer for mature clumps, separate the clump into single or double buds, as long as each division has enough roots to sustain it. Trim any damaged parts with a knife, then replant as soon as possible. If there is a delay, store the plants under cover and keep moist.

Tough, fibrous roots
Divide the crown with a spade. Each section should include several developing buds.

Loose, fleshy roots
Divide small plants and those with a loose rootstock by pulling the clump apart by hand.

DIVIDING RHIZOMATOUS PLANTS

Divide plants with thick rhizomes, such as *Bergenia* and rhizomatous irises, by splitting the clump into pieces by hand, then cutting the rhizomes into sections, each with one or more growth points. Bamboos have tough rootstocks that either form dense clumps with short rhizomes or have long, spreading rhizomes. Divide dense clumps with a spade or two back-to-back forks; cut spreading rhizomes into sections (each of which should have three nodes or joints) with pruners. In all cases, trim excessively long roots before replanting.

Lift the plant to be divided (here an iris), inserting the fork well away from the rhizomes to avoid damaging them.

Shake the clump to remove any loose soil. Using your hands or a hand fork, split the clump into manageable pieces.

Discard any old rhizomes, then detach the new, young rhizomes from the clump and neatly trim off their ends.

Dust the cut areas with fungicide. Trim long roots by one-third. For irises, cut the leaves into a "fan" about 6in (15cm) tall to prevent wind-rock.

Plant the rhizomes at least 6in (15cm) apart. The rhizomes should be half buried, with their leaves and buds upright. Firm in well, then water.

PROPAGATING PERENNIALS BY ROOT CUTTINGS

This is a useful method of propagating perennials that have fairly thick, fleshy roots, such as *Papaver orientale*; it also works very well for horseradish (*Armoracia*). Take care to minimize damage to the parent plant when cutting its roots, and replant it immediately. Root cuttings are most successful when they are taken during the plant's dormant period, usually just before winter. Note: plants with thinner roots, such as *Anemone*, are done slightly differently. Lay the cuttings flat on the medium, then cover and treat as for thicker root cuttings.

Lift the plant (here *Acanthus*) when dormant and wash the roots. Cut roots of pencil thickness close to the crown.

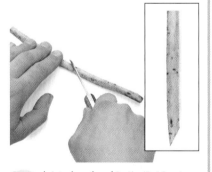

Cut each into lengths of 2–4in (5–10cm). Make a straight cut at the upper end and an angled cut at the lower (inset).

Insert the cuttings into holes made in pots of moist rooting medium, then firm. The top end of each cutting should be flush with the surface.

Top-dress the pots of cuttings with coarse grit, label them, and place them in a cold frame until the cuttings root.

When the cuttings have developed young shoots, pot them up into individual pots filled with soil-based potting mix. Water and label the pots (see inset).

SOWING IN DRILLS

Seeds sown in drills produce seedlings growing in straight rows at regular intervals, so they are readily distinguished from weed seedlings, which are randomly distributed. Using either a trowel tip or the corner of a hoe, mark out shallow drills at a width depending on the ultimate size of the plants. Sow seeds thinly and evenly by sprinkling or placing them in each drill at the appropriate depth for the plants being sown, then carefully draw back the displaced soil. Label each row, then water gently but thoroughly with a fine spray. This technique is traditionally used for sowing vegetables, but it works equally well for annuals and biennials, especially in cutting gardens.

Using a line of string as a guide, make a furrow about 1in (2.5cm) deep with a hoe.

Alternative Step

If the seeds are pelleted, place them individually in the base of the drill.

Dribble the seeds from your hand to make sure they are scattered evenly.

Carefully rake the soil back over the drill without dislodging the seeds.

BROADCAST SOWING

Before sowing, mark the outline of the area for different plants with sand to keep track the balance of colors, heights, and habits of each of the plants to be used, especially annuals. After sowing, label the area, then water the area gently but thoroughly with a fine spray. This method is particularly suitable for taprooted annuals, such as *Clarkia*, *Gypsophila*, and poppies (*Papaver*), which are best sown where they are to flower, since they do not transplant readily.

Prepare the soil by raking to produce a fine tilth. Scatter the seeds thinly over the prepared area from your hand or from the packet.

Rake over the area lightly at right angles to cover the seeds so that they are disturbed as little as possible. Water gently but thoroughly.

THINNING SEEDLINGS

To prevent overcrowding, seedlings usually need to be thinned. Do this when the soil is moist and the weather mild, taking care to retain the sturdier seedlings where possible and to achieve even spacing. To minimize disturbance to a seedling being retained, press the soil around it with your fingers as the surplus seedlings are extracted. Thinnings may be used to fill sparse areas caused by uneven sowing or irregular germination, or they may be planted elsewhere in the garden.

To thin small seedlings, nip them out at ground level so that the roots of the remaining seedlings are not disturbed.

Lift seedlings gently, keeping as much soil around them as possible. If moving them, place them in a clear plastic bag to retain moisture.

SOWING IN A TRAY

Many annuals, biennials, perennials, herbs, and vegetables are usually sown in containers so that they can germinate and develop under cover and then be planted out as young plants when conditions are favorable. Pots, seed pans (shallow pots), seed trays, and packs are all suitable containers, depending on the number of seeds to be sown and the space they require. Most seedlings will need to be pricked out before they are large enough to be planted out (see below). Peat pots are useful for seedlings that do not transplant well, since the whole pot may be planted out without disturbing the roots.

Fill the seed tray with a standard sowing medium, then level with a presser board to ½in (1cm) below the rim.

Sprinkle the seeds thinly over the surface of the medium to achieve an even distribution.

Cover the seeds with a layer of sieved, moist soil mix to about the same thickness as the seeds themselves. Water the seeds in lightly.

Place a piece of glass or clear plastic sheeting over the tray to maintain even humidity.

Shade the tray with netting if the tray is in direct sunlight. Remove both glass and netting as soon as germination starts.

PRICKING OUT OF A PACK

Seedlings raised in trays or pans need to be transplanted into larger containers before they become overcrowded, because they may quickly become weak and spindly if deprived of sufficient space or light, and damping off (a disease) may develop. This process is known as pricking out. It enables the seedlings to continue to develop properly until they are ready for planting out in the open garden. Fill the new containers with a soil-based mix, then firm gently to eliminate any air pockets. Small pots, no more than 3in (6cm) in diameter, or compartmentalized plastic packs are ideal for individual seedlings; larger pots, pans, or trays can be used for several plants.

Carefully separate the seedlings, handling them by their seed leaves, not their more delicate stems. Try to keep plenty of medium around the roots.

Transplant each seedling into a separate section of a pack. Firm the soil mix around each one with your fingers or a dibber, then water.

APPENDICES

Alaska
Cooperative Extension Service Building
PO Box 756180
Fairbanks, AK 99775-6180
(907) 474-6971 ; Fax: (907) 474-7246
http://www.uaf.edu/coop-ext

Colorado
Cooperative Extension
1 Administration Building
Colorado State University,
Fort Collins, CO 80523-4040
(970) 491-6281; Fax (970) 491-6208.
http://www.ext.colostate.edu

Idaho
University of Idaho Extension Nez Perce County
1239 Idaho Street
Lewiston, ID 83501
(208) 799-3096; Fax: (208) 799-3054
http://www.uidaho.edu/ag/extension

Kansas
Department of HFRR
Kansas State University
2021 Throckmorton Hall
Manhattan, KS. 66506-5507
(785) 532-1438; Fax: (785) 532-6949
http://www.oznet.ksu.edu

Montana
Montana State University Extension Service
Plant, Soil & Environmental Sciences Dept.
P.O. Box 173140
Bozeman, MT 59717-3120
(406) 994-6523
http://extn.msu.montana.edu

Nebraska
Nebraska Cooperative Extension
University of Nebraska- Lincoln
377 Plant Science
Lincoln, NE. 68583-0724
(402) 472-1640
http://extension.unl.edu

Nevada
Univ of NV Cooperative Extension
PO Box 11130
Reno, NV 89520-0027
(775) 784-4848; Fax: (702) 784-4881
http://www.unce.unr.edu

North Dakota
North Dakota State University Extension Service
Fargo ND 58105-5655
(701) 241-5707
http://www.ag.ndsu.nodak.edu

Oregon
Oregon State University Extension Service
4017 ALS Building
Corvallis, OR 97331-7304
(541) 737-2503; Fax: (541) 737-3479
http://extension.oregonstate.edu/index.php

South Dakota
South Dakota State University Cooperative Extension Service
Box 2140-A NPB 254-D
Brookings, SD 57007-0996
(605) 688-6253; Fax: (605) 688-4713
http://www3.sdstate.edu/CooperativeExtension

Utah
Utah State University Cooperative Extension
28 E. State Street/P.O. Box 618
Farmington, UT 84025
(801) 451-3405
http://extension.usu.edu

Washington
Washington State University Cooperative Extension
7612 Pioneer Way East
Puyallup, WA 98371-4998
(253) 445-4614
http://ext.wsu.edu

Wyoming
University of Wyoming
Cooperative Extension Service
P.O. Box 3354
Laramie, WY 82071-3354
(307) 766-5117; Fax: (307) 766-5549
http://www.uwyo.edu/ces/ceshome.htm

HORTICULTURAL WEB SITES

The Internet provides a rich source of information on every facet of the horticultural world. In addition to the web sites maintained by many botanical gardens and research facilities, many gardening centers offer their plants and horticultural products on the internet. The following sites may be particularly helpful or enlightening.

American Horticultural Society   http://www.ahs.org

Betrock's Hortworld   http:/www.hortworld.com

Elisabeth C. Miller Library: Directory of Horticulture Web Sites
http://depts.washington.edu/hortlib/resources/dir_hort_websites.shtml

GardenNet   http://gardennet.com

GardenWeb   http://www.gardenweb.com

Horticulture Guy   http://HorticultureGuy.com

Hortiplex database   http://hortiplex.gardenweb.com/plants

HortNet plant image gallery   http://www.hort.net/gallery

International Organization for Plant Information
http://plantnet.rbgsyd.gov.au

Internet Directory for Botany   http://www.botany.net/IDB

Lady Bird Johnson Wildflower Center   http://www.wildflower.org

NeoFlora   http://www.neoflora.com

Plant Facts   http://plantfacts.ohio-state.edu

RHS Horticultural Database   http://www.rhs.org.uk/databases/summary.asp

Tropicos image index   http://mobot.mobot.org/W3T/Search/vast.html

USDA Plant Database   http://plants.usda.gov

NORTHWEST REGIONAL GARDENS

Botanical gardens can be an excellent source of inspiration and information on native and exotic plants that grow particularly well in your region and microclimates.

AK

Alaska Botanical Garden
P.O. Box 202202
Anchorage, AK 99520
(907) 770-3692
http://www.alaskabg.org/

Georgeson Botanical Garden
University of Alaska Fairbanks
PO Box 757200
Fairbanks, AK 99775
(907)474-5651
http://www.uaf.edu/salrm/gbg/

CO

Betty Ford Alpine Garden
183 Gore Creek Drive
Vail, CO 81657
(970) 476-0103
http://www.bettyfordalpinegardens.org/

Denver Botanic Garden
1005 York Street
Denver, CO 80206
(720) 865-3500
http://www.botanicgardens.org/

Western Colorado Botanic Gardens
641 Struthers Avenue, Grand Junction, CO 81501
(970) 245-3288
http://www.wcbotanic.org/

ID

Idaho Botanical Gardens
2355 N. Penitentiary Rd.
(208) 343-8649
http://www.idahobotanicalgarden.org/

Sawtooth Botanical Garden
P.O. Box 928
Sun Valley, ID 83353
(208) 726-9358
http://www.sbgarden.org/

University of Idaho Arboretum & Botanical Garden
Nez Perce Drive
P.O. Box 443226
Moscow, ID 83844-3226
(208) 885-6646

KS

Botanica – The Wichita Gardens
701 Amidon, Wichita, KS 67203
(316) 264-0448
http://www.botanica.org/

Dyck Arboretum of the Plains
Hesston College
177 West Hickory Street/Box 3000
Hesston, KS 67062
(620) 327-8127
http://www.hesston.edu/arbor/

MT

Tizer Lake Gardens
38 Tizer Lake Road
Jefferson City, MT 59638
(406) 933-8789; Toll Free: (866) 933-8789
http://www.tizerlakegardens.com

Zoo Montana
2100 South Shiloh Road
Billings, MT 59106
(406) 652-8100
http://www.zoomontana.org/

NE

Nebraska Statewide Arboretum
P.O. Box 830715
University of Nebraska
Lincoln, NE 68583-0715
(402) 472-2971
http://arboretum.unl.edu/

Ohmaha's Botanical Center - Lauritzen Gardens
100 Bancroft Street
Omaha, NE 68108
(402) 346-4002
http://www.omahabotanicalgardens.org/

ND

International Peace Garden
R.R. 1, Box 116
Dunseith , ND 58329
(701)263-4390
http://www.peacegarden.com/

Dickinson Research Extension Center
1133 State Ave.
Dickinson, ND 58601
(701) 483-2348 .
http://www.ag.ndsu.nodak.edu/dickinso/

NV

University of Nevada – Las Vegas Arboretum
4505 S. Maryland Parkway/Box 451064
Las Vegas, NV 89154-1064
(702) 895-3392
http://www.unlv.edu/facilities/landscape/arboretum.html

Wilbur D. May Arboretum & Botanical Garden
Rancho San Rafael Park
1502 Washington Street Reno, NV 89503
(775) 785-4153
http://www.maycenter.com/arboretum/arbor.html

OR

Oregon Garden
879 West Main Street
PO Box 155
Silverton OR 97381
(503) 874-8100; Toll free (877) 674-2733
http://www.oregongarden.org/

Berry Botanic Garden
11505 SW Summerville Avenue
Portland, Oregon 97219
(503)-636-4112
http://www.berrybot.org/

Hoyt Arboretum
4000 SW Fairview Blvd.
Portland, Oregon 97221
(503) 228-8733
http://www.hoytarboretum.org/

Mt. Pisgah Arboretum
34901 Frank Parrish Rd
Eugene, OR 97405
(541) 741-4110
http://www.efn.org/~mtpisgah/

SD

McCrory Gardens
Horticulture, Forestry, Landscape & Parks Department
South Dakota State University
Brookings, SD 57007-0996
(605) 688-5136
http://www3.sdstate.edu/Academics/CollegeOfAgricultureAndBi
ologicalSciences/HorticultureForestryLandscapeandParks/McCr
oryGardens/Index.cfm

UT

Red Butte Garden and Arboretum - University of Utah
300 Wakara Way
Salt Lake City, Utah 84108
(801) 581-4747
http://www.redbuttegarden.org/

Utah Botanical Center - Utah State University
4055 Old Main Hill
Utah State University, Logan, UT 84322-4055
(801) 451-3204
http://www.usu.edu/ubc/

WA

Bellevue Botanical Garden
12001 Main Street
Bellevue, WA 98005
(425) 452-2750
http://www.bellevuebotanical.org/

Washington Park Arboretum
University of Washington
Box 358010
Seattle, WA 98195-8010
(206) 543-8800
http://www.wparboretum.org/

Yakima Area Arboretum
1401 Arboretum Drive
Yakima, Washington 98901
(509) 248-7337
http://www.ahtrees.org/

Manito Park
Grand Boulevard between 17th and 25th Avenue
Spokane, WA 99203
(509) 456-4331
http://www.spokaneparks.org/parks/index.htm

WY

Cheyenne Botanic Garden
710 South Lions Park Drive
Cheyenne, Wyoming 82001
(307) 637-6458
http://www.botanic.org/

INDEX

Page numbers given in italics refer to catalog pages on which the plants are illustrated. In plant entries, topics that relate to the main entries appear first; subentries for species and cultivars always follow the general subentries.

A

Abelia,
  Chinese, *178*
  glossy, *215*
Abelia
  chinensis, *178*
  x *grandiflora*, *215*
Abelia leaf, Korean, *175, 183*
Abeliophyllum distichum, *175, 183*
Abies concolor, *220, 225, 238, 240*
Abies grandis, 54
Abutilon, 38
Acanthus, 405
  mollis, *274, 336*
Acer
  campestre, *92, 104, 124*
  capillipes, *120*
  griseum, *120*
  japonicum, *104*
    'Acontifolium,' *91, 114*
    'Sango-Kaku,' *91, 114, 189*
  macrophyllum, *102*
  negundo
    'Flamingo,' *92*
    'Variegatum,' *92*
  palmatum, *91, 106*
    'Bloodgood,' *128, 189, 193*
    Dissectum Group, *189*
    'Inabe Shidare,' *205*
    var. *atropurpureum*, *193*
    'Waterfall,' *114*
  platanoides, *92, 102*
    'Deborah,' *96, 124*
    'Drummondii,' *96*
  'Royal Red,' *96*
  rubrum, *86*
    'Franksred,' *86, 114*
    'October Glory,' *86*
  triflorum, *84*
Achillea, 34
  millefolium, *288, 336*
    'Paprika,' *261, 348*
    'Summer Pastels,' *261*
  ptarmica 'The Pearl Superior,' *261, 288, 301, 314, 325*
  taygetea 'Moonshine,' *261*
Aconitum
  x *cammarum* 'Bicolor,' *280*
  'Ivorine,' *339*
  napellus, *280*
Acorus
  calamus, *379*
    'Variegatus,' *379*
  gramineus 'Ogon,' *376*
Actaea rubra, *336*
Actinidia kolomikta 'Arctic Beauty,' *249*
Aesculus
  californica, *93, 107, 110*
  x *carnea*, *94*
  parviflora, *158, 181*
Agapanthus

campanulatus, *283, 334, 338*
  'Headbourne Hybrids,' *286, 364*
Agastache foeniculum, *325*
Ageratum houstonianum, *355*
Ajuga reptans 'Caitlin's Giant,' *280, 291*
Akebia quinata, *247, 249*
Albizia julibrissin, *93*
Alcea rosea, *354*
Alchemilla mollis, *309*
Alder, common, *87*
Allamanda cathartica 'Hendersoni,' *242*
Allium
  cernuum, *345*
  giganteum, *362*
Alnus glutinosa, *87*
Aloysia triphylla, *204*
Althaea officinalis, *325*
Alyssum saxatile, *330*
Amaranth, globe, *359*
Amaranthus, 358
Amaranthus caudatus, *358*
Amelanchier
  arborea, *84*
  x *grandiflora*, *197*
  laevis, *100*
Amorpha nana, 54
Amsonia
  hubrictii, *299, 314*
  tabernaemontana, *299, 307, 337*
Anaphalis margaritacea, *286, 318*
Anchusa azurea, *274, 287, 298*
Andromeda, marsh, *191*
Andromeda polifolia, *191*
Androsace lanuginosa, *319*
Anemone, 405
  x *hybrida*, *301, 311, 338, 367*
    'Whirlwind,' *363*
  huphensis 'September Charm,' *363*
  multifida, *264*
  narcissiflora, *338*
  occidentalis, *58*
Anemone, Western, *58*
Angelica, *324*
Angelica archangelica, *324*
Annuals, definition, *34*
Antirrhinum, *39*
Apricot, Japanese, *110*
Aquilegia
  caerulea, *54, 298, 307, 339*
  canadensis, *307, 336, 338*
  chrysantha, *292, 307, 339, 342*
  flavescens, 54
  formosa, *54, 297, 342*
  x *hybrida*, *339*
  McKana hybrids, *252*
  'Music Medley,' *343*
  'Nora Barlow,' *278*
Arabis ferdinandi-colburgi 'Variegata,' *317*
Arborvitae, *239*
  American, *236, 240*
  dwarf golden, *230*
  Oriental, *229*
  Western, *230*
Arctostaphylos
  patula, *140*
  uva-ursi, *151, 186, 207*
Armeria
  alliacea, *329*
    'Sea Pink,' *317*
  maritima, *330*
    'Bloodstone,' *285, 307, 317, 328*
Armoracia, 405

Arrowhead, Japanese, *376*
Artemisia, 42
  absinthium, *340*
  frigida, 54
  'Silver King,' *319*
  'Powis Castle,' *191, 266*
Aruncus
  aethusifolius, *300*
  dioicus, *300*
Arum, bog, *377*
Arum italicum, *316, 346*
Arundo donax 'Versicolor,' *322*
Asarum caudatum, *332*
Asclepias
  incarnata, *271, 315*
  syriaca, *308*
  tuberosa, *262, 270, 295, 343*
Ash
  claret, *127*
  European, *94, 97*
  green, *124*
  Korean mountain, *95*
  white, *88, 123*
Asimina triloba, *118*
Aster
  Frikart's, *278*
  New England, *278, 280*
  Pacific hybrid, *310*
  Persian Rose, dwarf, *278*
  Stokes', *301*
  white wood, *311*
Aster, 392
  alpinus, *328*
  cordifolius, *302, 344*
  divaricatus, *311*
  dumosus, *310*
  x *frikartii*, *278*
    'Monch,' *312*
  novi belgii
    'Alma Potschke,' *278*
    'Persian Rose,' *278*
    'Purple Dome,' *280*
Astilbe
  x *arendsii*, *309*
    'Amethyst,' *339*
    'Granat,' *346*
    'Bronze Elegance,' *346*
  chinensis, *287, 345, 348*
    'Pumila,' *281*
    var. *taquetti* 'Superba,' *339*
  japonica
    'Deutschland,' *281*
    'Irrlicht,' *281*
    'Rheinland,' *281*
  simplicifolia
    'Inshriach Pink,' *281*
    'Sprite,' *281*
Astrantia major 'Lars,' *312*
Athyrium
  filix-femina, *352*
  Nipponicum 'Pictum,' *352*
Atriplex canescens, *58*
Aubrieta, 47
  deltoidea, *277, 330*
Aucuba, 402
  japonica, *135, 149, 156, 162, 190, 210*
Aurinia saxatilis, *274*
Azalea
  deciduous, *136, 148, 177*
  flame, *136, 143, 165*
  Florida, *136, 143*
  plumleaf, *143, 179*

sweet, *137, 143*
  Western, 54

B

Baby's breath, *284, 359*
Bachelor's button, *358*
Balsam, garden, *361*
Balsam, rose, *357*
Bamboo, 405
  heavenly, *131*
Banana, 42
Baptisia australis, *260, 306, 349*
Barberry
  crimson pygmy, *188*
  creeping, *206, 209*
  Darwin's, *150, 195*
  Japanese, *149, 150, 188, 204*
  winter, *153, 186, 195*
  yellow-leaved Japanese, *146, 150, 154*
Barrenwort, *264, 340*
Basil, cinnamon, *361*
Bayberry, *153, 182*
Bean, bog, *258*
Bearberry, common, *151, 186, 207*
Beardtongue, pink plains, *58*
Beautyberry, *196*
Bee balm, *256, 325*
  wild, *289, 314, 324, 337*
Beech
  European, *93*
  purple-leaved weeping, *90, 109*
  upright purple-leaved, *123*
Bells of Ireland, *359, 361*
Bellwort, *259, 272*
Beneficial organisms, *68–69*
Berberis
  darwinii, *150, 195*
  julianae, *153, 186, 195*
  thunbergii, *149, 150, 204*
    'Atropurpurea Nana,' *188*
    'Aurea,' *146, 150, 154*
    'Dart's Red Lady,' *188*
Bergamot, sweet, *256, 325*
Bergenia, 405
  'Morgenröte,' *338, 346*
Bermudagrass, 14
Beta vulgaris, *327*
Betula
  jacquemontii, *95*
  papyrifera, *120*
  pendula, *102*
    'Dalecarlica,' *108*
    'Youngii,' *90, 108*
Birch
  canoe, *120*
  European white, *102*
  white-barked Himalayan, *95*
  paper, *120*
  weeping, *108*
  Young's European, *90, 108*
Bishop's hat, *264, 296, 321*
Bitterroot, *54, 272*
Black-eyed Susan vine, *24*
Blechnum spicant, *54, 352*
Bletilla striata, *282*
Bluebell, *340*
Blueberry, highbush, *138, 196, 198*
Bluegrass, Kentucky, *14*
Blue mist shrub,
  Dark Night, *166*
  Worcester Gold, *166, 192*
Bluestar,

narrow-leaf, *299*
   willow, *299, 307, 337*
Boltonia asteroides, 309, 312
Boneset, *311, 325*
Borago offinalis, 326
Bougainvillea, 24, 38
Bouteloua gracilis, 58
Boxelder,
   Flamingo, *92*
   Variegated, *92*
Brassica, oleracea, 326, 355
Broom, Allgold Warminster, *133, 149*
Brown-eyed Susan, *354*
Brunnera macrophylla,
   'Dawson's White,' *278, 286, 299, 322*
Buchloe dactyloides, 58
Buckbean, *258*
Buckeye
   bottlebrush, *158, 181*
   California, *93, 107, 110*
Buddleja
   davidii, 183
     'Black Night,' *167, 211*
     'Fascinating,' *130, 144, 154*
     'Harlequin,' *130, 144, 154, 194*
     'Royal Red,' *130, 144, 154, 169*
     'White Profusion,' *130, 144, 170, 180, 191*
    globosa, 165, 185
    'Pink Delight,' *213*
Buffalograss, 14
Bugbane, black, *259, 271*
Bulrush, *377*
Bunchberry, 21
Burning bush, *188, 203*
Butomus umbellatus, 379
Butterfly bush. See *Buddleja*
Butterfly weed, *262, 270, 295, 308, 343*
Buttonwood, *86, 121*

C

Calendula officinalis, 34, 358
Calla palustris, 377
Callicarpa, 35
   bodinieri var. *giraldii, 128, 196*
Callirhoe involucrata, 54
Calocedrus decurrens, 239
Calochortus nuttallii, 54
Caltha
   palustris, 387
   palustris 'Alba,' *300, 374*
Camassia quamash, 54, 367, 370
Camellia
   Japanese, *173, 186, 203*
   sasanqua, *173, 186, 203*
Camellia
   japonica, 173, 186, 203
     'Alba Plena,' *171*
   sasanqua, 173, 186, 203
Campanula
   isophylla 'Mayi,' *299*
   lactiflora, 312
     'Lodden Anna,' *276*
     'Prichard's Variety,' *276*
   rotundifolia, 340
Candytuft, *284, 305, 329, 336, 355*
Canna, 38
   x *generalis, 294*
Capsicum annuum, 327
Cardinal flower, *342*
Carex
   hachijoensis 'Evergold,' *287*
   morrowii 'Ice Dance,' *316*

siderosticha 'Variegata,' *256, 322*
Carnation, *358, 361*
Carpinus
   betulus, 94
   caroliniana, 99, 106
Caryopteris x *clandonensis*
   'Dark Night,' *166*
   'Worcester Gold,' *166, 192*
Castilleja
   linariifolia, 54
   rhexiifolia, 54
Catananche caerulea, 260, 299, 308, 349
Cattail, dwarf, *375*
Cedar
   American white, *230, 233*
   blue atlas, *221, 224, 235*
   Burk's blue, *226*
   deodar, *221, 239*
   incense, *239*
   Japanese, *218, 233, 237, 240*
   weeping Alaskan, *223*
   western red, *240*
Cedrus
   atlantica f. *glauca, 221, 224, 235*
   deodara, 221, 239
Celosia, 355
   argentea Cristata Group, *359*
Celtis occidentalis, 88, 124
Centaurea
   cyanus, 358
   dealbata, 275
Centranthus ruber, 275, 324, 337
Cephalotaxus harringtonia, 226, 241
Ceratostigma plumbaginoides, 167, 207, 311, 331
Cercidiphyllum japonicum 'Pendulum,' *109*
Cercis
   canadensis, 107
     var. *alba, 94*
   chinensis, 106
Chamaecyparis
   lawsoniana,
     'Hilliari,' *237*
     'Minima,' *230*
   nootkatensis, 223
   obtusa, 226
     'Filicoides,' *223, 238*
Chameleon, *374*
Chaste tree, *112, 200*
Chelone, 34,
   obliqua 'Alba,' *344*
Chemical herbicides and pesticides, 65–67
Cherry
   Cornelian, *175, 196*
   great white, *100*
   higan, *109, 110*
   Okame, *95, 106*
   sweet, *119*
Chestnut, red horse, *94*
Chilopsis linearis, 184
Chimonanthus praecox, 144, 173
Chionanthus virginicus, 110
Chionodoxa,
   forbesii, 369, 372
   luciliae, 371
Choisya ternata, 162
   'Aztec Pearl,' *144, 200, 204*
Chokecherry, Amur, *121*
Chrysanthemum
   x *superbum, 288*

Cimicifuga
   racemosa, 259, 271
   simplex 'White Pearl,' *311*
Cinquefoil, shrubby, *151, 212*
Cistus
   ladanifer, 141
   x *purpureus, 140, 163, 174, 205*
   salviifolius, 140, 191
Cistus, common gum, *141*
Citrus, 38
Clematis, 48, *242, 244, 247*
   evergreen, *245, 251*
Clematis
   armandii, 245, 251
     'Comtesse de Bouchaud,' *247*
     'Ernst Markham,' *247*
     'Jackmanii,' *242, 244, 247*
     'Nelly Moser,' *247*
Cleome spinosa, 354
Clerodendrum, 38
   bungei, 181
Clethra alnifolia, 137, 139, 171, 181, 183
   'Ruby Spice,' *168*
Clivia miniata, 282
Cockscomb, *355, 359*
Coffeetree, Kentucky, *89, 103*
Cohosh, black, *259, 271*
Colchicum, 386
   'Waterlily,' *310, 372*
Coleus, *356*
Colewort, *284, 300, 314*
Colocasia
   esculenta, 376
   fontanesii, 376
Columbine, 54
   Canadian, *307, 336, 338*
   hybrids, *339*
   Nora Barlow, *278*
   red, *297, 342*
   Rocky Mountain, *298, 307, 339*
   scarlet, *297, 342*
   yellow, *292, 307, 339, 342*
Compost and composting, 31, 40, 56–58
Coneflower
   Deamii, *279*
   Great, *262*
   Purple, *260, 302, 349*
Convallaria majalis, 259, 349
   var. *rosea, 315, 332, 370*
Coppicing a shrub, *397*
Coral bells, *341, 342*
Coreopsis
   auriculata, 313
     'Nana,' *294*
   grandiflora, 348
     'Early Sunrise,' *275*
   tinctoria, 54
   verticillata 'Moonbeam,' *275*
Corktree, amur, *89*
Cornus
   alba 'Elegantissima,' *138, 160, 194, 201*
   canadensis, 21, *206, 270*
   florida, 110
   mas, 175, 196
   nuttalii, 90
Cortaderia
   selloana, 255
     'Aureolinata,' *255*
     'Pumila,' *255, 286*
Corydalis
   flexuosa 'China Blue,' *259, 299*

   lutea, 292, 313, 340, 362, 370
   solida, 386
Corylopsis pauciflora, 142, 165, 175
Corylus
   avellana 'Contorta,' *41*
   colurna, 123
Cosmos, candystripe, *354, 358*
Cosmos bipinnatus, 354, 358
Cotinus coggygria 'Royal Purple,' *133, 145, 193*
Cotoneaster,
   coral beauty, *153*
   cranberry, *197, 209, 211*
   little gem, *151*
   milkflower, *151, 153*
Cotoneaster
   adpressus 'Little Gem,' *151*
   apiculatas, 197, 209, 211
     'Coral Beauty,' *153*
   lacteus (*C. parneyi*), *151, 153*
Cottonwood, black, *87, 99*
Cover crops, 31
Crabapple
   Donald Wyman, *101, 117*
   Indian Magic, *101*
   Japanese flowering, *93*
   Red Jade, *108*
   Royalty, *101*
   Sargent, *183*
   tea, *95, 116*
Crambe cordifolia, 284, 300, 314
Cranesbill
   Ballerina, *276*
   bloody, *254, 276, 306*
   Brookside, *276*
   Johnson's Blue, *255*
   Max Frei, *254*
   Spessart scented, *255*
   striped bloody, *254*
   white, *254*
Crape myrtle, *89, 112*
Crassula ovata, 387
Crataegus
   x *lavallei, 98, 111, 117*
   phaenopyrum, 98, 117, 126
   viridis 'Winter King,' *98, 117, 126*
Creeper, Virginia, *244, 246, 249*
Crocosmia
   x *crocosmiiflora, 338, 363*
     'Emily McKenzie,' *295, 342*
   x 'Lucifer,' *297*
Crocus, 368, 372
Crop rotation, 63
Cryptomeria, japonica, 218, 240
   'Pyramidata,' *233*
   'Sekkan,' *233, 237*
Cunninghamia lanceolata, 227
Cupid's Dart, *260, 299, 308, 349*
x *Cupressocyparis leylandii, 384*
Cupressus arizonica var. *glabra, 238*
Currant
   flowering, *157, 169, 213, 215*
   red, *198*
   white, *195, 197, 198*
Cyclamen
   coum, 305
     Pewter Group, *373*
   hederifolium (*C. neapolitanum*), *310, 332, 370*
Cyclamen, *305, 310, 332, 370, 373*
Cynara cardunculus, 319
Cyperus
   haspan, 375

longus, 377
Cypress
  bald, *222, 227, 232, 234, 239*
  Hinoki, *226*
  pond, *218, 222*
  smooth, *238*
Cytisus x *praecox* 'Allgold,' *133, 149*

D

Daffodil, *386*
  winter, *293, 373*
Dahlia, 386
Daisy, African, *355*
Darmera peltata, 55
Dame's rocket, *360*
Daphne
  Burkwood, *163*
  lilac, *137, 208*
  October, *263*
  variegated winter, *161, 172, 185, 194*
  winter, *128, 187, 211*
Daphne
  x *burkwoodii, 163*
  genkwa, 137, 208
  odora, 128, 187, 211
  'Aureomarginata,' *161, 172, 185, 194*
Daucus carota, 50
Delosperma cooperi, 283
Delphinium carolinianum, 51
Dianthus
  caryophyllus, 358
  chinensis, 274, 297, 361
  deltoides, 312, 316
  gratianopolitanus, 315
Dicentra
  cucullaria, 306
  exima 'Boothman's Variety,' *341*
  formosa 'Bacchanal,' *296, 318*
  spectabilis 'Alba,' *300*
Digitalis, 56
  x *mertonensis, 342*
  purpurea, 271, 302, 336, 356
Dimorphotheca aurantiaca, 355
Disease-resistant plants, *62*
Diseases, common, *64*
Dodecatheon
  hendersonii, 329
  meadia, 314
Dogwood
  creeping, *206, 270*
  flowering, *110*
  Pacific, *90*
  variegated red twig, *138, 160, 194, 201*
Dracaena, 38
  deremensis 'Souvenir de Schriever,' *395*
Drainage, soil, *18–19, 26, 30, 32, 37*
Drought-tolerant plants, *26, 42*
  adaptations of, *36*
  lawn and turf grasses, *14*
Dryas octopetala, 329
Dryopteris filix-mas, 353
Dutchman's breeches, *306*

E

Echinacea purpurea, 260, 302, 349
Echinops ritro, 260, 274
Elaeagnus
  angustifolia, 152, 182
  x *ebbingei* 'Gilt Edge,' *152, 192, 194*
Elder, box, *92*
Elderberry, *192*

Elephant heads, *54*
Elm
  Chinese, *96*
  Siberian, *96*
Empress tree, *93, 111, 122*
Enkianthus
  red, *135, 142*
  red vein, *135, 142*
Enkianthus
  campanulatus, 135, 142
  cernuus var. rubens, 135, 142
Ensete, *38*
Epimedium
  x *cantabrigiense, 332*
  grandiflorum 'Rose Queen,' *264, 296, 321*
  x *perralchicum, 340*
  x *rubrum, 265*
  x *versicolor* 'Sulphureum,' *264*
  x *youngianum, 264*
  'Roseum,' *321, 340*
Erica
  x *darleyensis* 'Mediterranean Pink,' *172*
  vagans 'Mrs. D. F. Maxwell,' *208*
Erigeron glaucus 'Sea Breeze,' *331*
Eriobotrya japonica, 21, 190, 200
Eriophorum angustifolium, 374
Erysimum cheiri, 334, 358, 361
Erythronium
  albidum, 271
  americanum, 271
  grandiflorum, 271
  oregonum, 271, 386
Eucalyptus
  nicholii, 99
  pauciflora, 113
    niphophila, 99, 122
  perriniana, 99, 185
Eucomis 'Bicolor,' *283, 334*
Euonymus alatus, 188, 203
Eupatorium
  fistulosum, 344
  perfoliatum, 311, 325
  purpureum, 280, 326
Euphorbia
  amygdaloides, 265
  'Purpurea,' *321*
  dulcis 'Chameleon,' *341*
  polychroma, 266, 304
  pulcherrima, 38, 266
Evapotranspiration map, *44*
Evodia danielli, 88
Evodia, Korean, *88*
Exochorda x *macrantha* 'The Bride,' *160, 170, 177, 200*

F

Fagus
  sylvatica, 93
  'Asplenifolia,' *102*
  'Dawyck Purple,' *93, 123*
  'Pendula,' *109*
  'Purpurea Pendula,' *90, 109*
False cypress
  dwarf, *237*
  fernspray, *223, 238*
  Lawson, *230*
Fern
  Christmas, *317, 347, 352*
  cinnamon, *353*
  deer, *54, 352*
  Japanese painted, *352*

lady, *352*
  male, *353*
  oak, *333, 353*
  royal, *272, 353*
  sensitive, *352*
  sword, *347, 352*
Fertilizer, *19–20*
Fescue, *14, 266, 319, 331*
Festuca
  glauca
    'Elijah Blue,' *319*
    'Wayne Roderick,' *331*
  ovina 'Glauca,' *266*
Ficus, 38
  carica, 119, 126
Fig, common, *119, 126*
Filbert, Turkish, *123*
Filipendula rubra, 308
Fir
  Balsam, *238*
  Chinese, *227*
  Douglas, *54*
  white, *220, 225, 238, 240*
Firethorn, 'Mohave,' *132, 148, 153, 195*
Flag
  Japanese sweet, *376*
  variegated yellow, *323*
Flame thrower, *53*
Flax
  common, *269*
  New Zealand, *268, 287*
Floss flower, *355*
Forget-me-not, *56, 357*
  water, *376*
Forsythia, white, *175, 183*
Forsythia x *intermedia, 164*
Fothergilla gardenii, 163
Four o'clock, *35, 335, 360*
Foxglove, *56, 271, 302, 336, 356*
  strawberry, *342*
Fragaria, 46
Fraxinus
  americana, 88, 123
  excelsior, 94, 97
  oxycarpa 'Raywood,' *127*
  pennsylvanica, 124
Fringecup, *317*
Fringe tree, white, *110*
Fritillaria
  imperialis, 363
    'Variegata,' *322, 363*
  meleagris, 365, 368, 371
  pudica, 371
Fuchsia
  'Autumnale,' *357*
  'Gartenmeisters Bonstedt,' *356*
  x *hybrida* 'Magellanica,' *168, 181, 214, 357*
Fumewort, China blue, *259, 299*

G

Gaillardia aristata, 263
Galanthus
  elwesii, 367
  nivalis, 304, 369
Galium triflorum, 333
Galtonia candicans, 364
Garden cleanup, *59, 62*
Gardenia, *38*
Gardening
  challenges and rewards, *78*
  environmentally responsible, *40–51*
Garden journal, *70–73*

Garden plan
  adapting to existing conditions, *26–31*
  creation, *10–15, 78*
Garrya elliptica, 156, 172
Gayfeather, *266, 309, 344, 349*
Gelsemium
  rankinii, 245, 250
  sempervirens 'Pride of Augusta,' *245, 251*
Geranium
  'Anne Folkard,' *331*
  'Brookside,' *276*
  cinereum 'Ballerina,' *276*
    x 'Johnson's Blue,' *255*
  macrorrhizum, 288
  'Spessart,' *255*
  pratense, 312
  sanguineum, 254, 276, 306
  'Album,' *254*
  'Max Frei,' *254*
  'Striatum,' *254*
  viscosissimum, 303
Germander
  bush, *132, 181, 191*
Ginger, *38*
Ginkgo biloba, 122, 222, 234
  'Autumn Gold,' *101, 115, 222, 224, 234, 237*
Gladiolus, 386
Globeflower, *177, 209*
  American, *54, 306*
Glory bower, *181*
Golden chain tree, *107*
  Voss's, *100*
Golden rain tree, panicled, *88, 92, 105, 117*
Goldenrod, *279, 310*
Gomphrena globosa, 359
Gorse, *195*
Gramagrass, *14*
Grass
  black flowering mountain, *289*
  blue-eyed, *303*
  blue grama, *54*
  buffalo, *54*
  Chinese fountain, *289*
  desert, *36*
  dwarf pampas, *255, 286*
  gold-edged pampas, *255*
  lawn, *14*
  Little Bunny dwarf mountain, *289, 310*
  mondo, *284*
  pampas, *255*
  purple moor, *310*
  tall cotton, *374*
  umbrella, *377*
Growth habits, *38–39*
Guara lindheimeri, 260
  'Siskiyou Pink,' *260*
Gum
  Alpine snow, *99, 122*
  American sweet, *115*
  black, *86, 115*
  cabbage, *113*
  sour, *86, 115*
  spinning, *99, 185*
  Worplesdon sweet, *90, 115*
Gymnocarpium dryopteris, 333, 353
Gymnocladus dioica, 89, 103
Gypsophila
  elegans, 359
  paniculata, 284

H

Hackberry, common, *88, 124*
Hakonechloa macra 'Aureola,' *346*
Halesia diptera var. *magniflora, 91, 111*
Hamamelis
  x *intermedia, 173*
    'Arnold's Promise,' *165*
    'Jelena,' *137*
  virginiana, 188
Hanging baskets, 395
Hardiness Zones, 22
Hawthorn
  green, *98, 117, 126*
  lavalle, *98, 111, 117*
  Washington, *98, 117, 126*
Hazel
  buttercup winter, *142, 165, 175*
Heath
  Maxwell's Cornish, *208*
  Mediterranean pink, *172*
Heat Zones, 22
Hedera helix, 251
  'Manda's Crested,' *246*
Helenium autumnale, 280
Helianthemum nummularium, 191, 334
Helianthus
  giganteus 'Sheila's Sunshine,' *293*
  pauciflorus, 293
Heliconia, 38
Helictotrichon sempervirens, 317, 318
Heliopsis
  helianthoides 'Ballerina,' *256*
  scabra, 292, 309
Hellebore
  Corsican, *304*
  stinking, *305, 340*
Helleborus
  argutifolius, 304
  foetidus, 305, 340
  niger, 305
  orientalis, 341
Hemerocallis, 404
  'Catherine Woodbury,' *350*
  'Cherry Cheeks,' *350*
  'Eenie Weenie,' *337*
  'Frans Halls,' *350*
  'Hyperion,' *351*
  'Joan Senior,' *351*
  x 'Mini Pearl,' *316*
  'Pardon Me,' *296, 351*
  'Pink Damask,' *351*
  'Red Rum,' *252*
  'Siloam Fairy Tale,' *351*
  'Stella D' Oro,' *279, 350*
  x 'Summerwine,' *316*
Hemlock, western, *224*
Hesperaloe parviflora, 268
Hesperis matronalis, 360
Heuchera
  x *brizoides, 341*
  micrantha, 321, 341
  sanguinea 'Splendens,' *284, 342*
Hibiscus, 38
  moscheutos, 257
Holly
  American, *97, 113*
  English, *96, 113, 116*
  Nellie R. Stevens, *99*
  Oregon grape, *132, 147, 165, 205, 213*
  variegated false, *184, 192, 194, 202*
Hollyhock, 354
Holodiscus discolor, 132, 151

Honesty, 34
Honeycups, dusty blue, *139, 143, 178*
Honeysuckle
  boxleaf, *151*
  climbing, *244*
  hybrid winter, *248*
  late Dutch, *244, 249*
  rosea, *179*
  tatarian, *169*
  winter, *148, 172, 183, 248, 250*
Hops, golden, 246
Hornbeam
  American, *99, 106*
  European, *94*
Hosta, 62, 392, 404
  'Birchwood Parky's Gold,' *320*
  'Blue Angel,' *332*
  'Blue Moon,' *318*
  'Gold Edger,' *347*
  'Gold Standard,' *311, 320, 322*
  'Halcyon,' *341, 347*
  'June,' *279*
  'Sum and Substance,' *320*
  'Zounds,' *320*
Houseplants, 395
Houttynia cordata, 374
Humulus lupulus 'Aureus,' *246*
Humus, 31
Hydrangea
  Altona mophead, *134*
  bigleaf, *129, 154, 211*
  Blue Bird lacecap, *135*
  Blue Wave lacecap, *134, 142, 159, 166, 201*
  lacecap, *159*
  oakleaf, *171, 190, 210*
  peegee, *145, 180*
  pink elf, *159, 179, 190*
  'Red 'n' Pretty,' *201*
  Rosalba lacecap, *135*
  smooth, *134, 147, 176*
  'Snow Queen' oakleaf, *134, 180*
Hydrangea, 35
  arborescens, 176
    'Grandiflora,' *134, 147*
  macrophylla, 154
    'Altona,' *134*
    'Ayesha,' *129*
    'Blue Wave,' *134, 142, 159, 166, 201*
    cultivars, *211*
    'Mariesii,' *159*
    'Monred,' *201*
    'Pia,' *159, 179, 190*
  paniculata
    'Grandiflora,' *145, 180*
  quercifolia, 171, 190, 210
    'Snow Queen,' *134, 180*
  serrata
    'Blue Bird,' *135*
    'Rosalba,' *135*
Hydrophyllum virginianum, 259
Hylotelephium
  erythrostichium 'Mediovariegatum,' *262*
  sieboldii, 263, 311
Hypericum
  frondosum, 208
  'Hidcote,' *156, 277*

I

Iberis
  sempervirens, 284, 305, 329,

    336
  umbellata, 355
Ilex, 402
  aquifolium, 96, 113, 116
  decidua, 98, 116
  x 'Nellie R. Stevens,' *99*
  opaca, 97, 113
  verticillata, 139
    'Jim Dandy,' *211*
Impatiens, 35, 386
  balsamina, 357, 361
  walleriana, 357
Imperata cylindrica 'Rubra,' *321*
Indian-paintbrush
  Wyoming, 54
Indian pink, 274
Indigo, false, *260, 306, 349*
Integrated pest management (IPM), 60–69
Invasive plants, 56
Iris
  Japanese water, *270, 374*
  stinking, *264*
  wild, *270*
  woodland, *270*
Iris, 405
  ensata 'Variegata,' *270*
  foetidissima, 264
  innominata, 55, 270
  laevigata, 374
    'Snowdrift,' *270*
  pallida 'Aureo Variegata,' *323*
  pseudacorus, 378
    'Variegata,' *323, 378*
  versicolor, 270
Irrigation, 14, 42–45
Itea virginica, 138, 142, 182
  'Henry's Garnet,' *193*
Ivy
  Boston, *244, 246, 249*
  English, *246, 251*
  five-leaved, *244, 246, 249*
  Japanese, *244, 246, 249*

J

Jacob's ladder, *279, 302*
  leafy, *259*
Jasmine, 38
  Carolina, *245, 251*
  common, *244, 250, 251*
Jasminum, 38
  grandiflorum, 251
  officinale, 'Argenteo-variegatum,' *244, 250*
Jessamine, swamp, 245, 250
Jetbead, 139
Joe Pye weed, purple, 280, 326
Juglans nigra, 124
Juniper, 42, *232, 237, 238*
  Blue Star, *230*
  Chinese, *220, 226, 229, 233, 237*
  Chinese silver, *228*
  common, *231*
  fishback, *235*
  Holger's singleseed, *228*
  Hollywood, *220*
  Japanese garden, *241*
  savin, *228*
  shore, *241*
  skyrocket, *220, 233, 235*
  tamarisk, *228, 241*
Juniperus, 220
  chinensis, 220

    'Aurea,' *237*
    'Keteleeri,' *226, 233*
    'Stricta,' *229*
    'Tortulosa,' *220*
  communis 'Compressa,' *231*
  conferta 'Blue Pacific,' *241*
  cultivars, *232, 237, 238*
  procumbens 'Nana,' *241*
  sabina
    'Cupressifolia,' *228*
    var. *tamariscifolia, 228, 241*
  scopulorum 'Skyrocket,' *220, 233, 235*
  squamata
    'Blue Star,' *230*
    'Chinese Silver,' *228*
    'Holger,' *228*
    'Meyeri,' *235*
  virginiana 'Burkii,' *226*

K

Kale, flowering, 355
Kalmia polifolia, 135, 160, 168, 176, 187, 211
Katsura tree, weeping, 109
Kerria japonica, 177, 209
Kinnikinick, *151, 186, 207*
Kirengshoma palmata, 271
Kniphofia
  'Royal Standard,' *276, 342*
  uvaria, 267, 294, 297, 334
Koelreuteria paniculata, 88, 92, 105, 117

L

Laburnum
  Scotch, *107*
Laburnum
  alpinum, 107
  x *watereri, 107*
    'Vossii,' *100*
Lady's eardrops, *168, 181, 214, 357*
Lagerstroemia
  fauriei, 121
  indica, 89, 112
Landscape use checklist, 13
Lantana, 38
  camara 'Miss Huff,' *205, 215*
Larch
  golden, *227, 234*
  Japanese, *223*
  weeping European, *232*
  Western, *234*
Larix
  decidua 'Pendula,' *232*
  kaempferi, 223
  occidentalis, 234
Larkspur, prairie, 54
Laudanum, 141
Laurel
  California, *88*
  Eastern bog, *160, 168, 176, 187, 211*
  Japanese, *135, 149, 156, 162, 190, 210*
Laurustinus, Spring Bouquet, *156, 173, 187, 202*
Lavandula
  angustifolia, 131, 166, 205
  stoechas, 166, 185
    'Otto Quast,' *199, 214*
Lavatera
  bicolor (L. *maritima*), *152*
  thuringiaca
    'Barnsley,' *208*
    'Kew Rose,' *131*

Lavender
English, *131, 166, 205*
Spanish, *166, 185*
'Otto Quast,' *199, 214*
Lavender cotton, *42, 132, 269, 286*
Lawn and turf
alternatives, 14–15
irrigation, 44–45
weed control, 49
Leadplant, fragrant, 54
Leadwort, *167, 207, 311, 331*
Leucojum aestivum 'Gravetye Giant,'
368, 370
Leucophyllum frutescens, 166, 215
Leucothoe, drooping, *170, 176, 207*
Leucothoe fontanesiana, 170, 176, 207
Levisticum officinale, 326
Lewisia rediviva, 54, 272
Leycesteria formosa, 157
Liatris
'Kobold,' *266*
pychnostachya, 309
spicata, 266, 344, 349
Ligustrum japonicum, 157
'Texanum,' *153, 203*
Lilac
Charles Joly, *155, 167, 175*
dwarf Korean, *169, 205, 213*
Japanese tree, *121, 209*
Meyer, *214*
Monge, *155, 202, 214*
President Grevy, *148, 155*
Sensation, *155, 167, 212*
Lilium
candidum, 344, 363, 365, 366
columbianum, 295, 363, 371
pardalinum, 272, 295, 366, 371
superbum, 366
Lily
African blue, *283, 286, 334, 338*
American, *295, 363, 371*
avalanche, *271*
Columbia tiger, *295, 363, 371*
Guernsey, *257, 283, 310*
great white fawn-, *271*
leopard, *272, 295, 366, 371*
madonna, *344, 363, 365, 366*
panther, *272, 295, 366, 371*
plantain, *311*
rain, *334*
sego, *58*
toad, *273*
turk's-cap, *366*
yellow pond, *379, 380*
yellow trout, *271*
Lily-of-the-valley, *259, 349*
pink, *315, 332, 370*
Lilyturf, *265, 285, 303, 331*
Limonium sinuatum, 359
Linden, small-leaved, *97*
Lindera benzoin, 137, 138, 174, 196
Linum lewisii, 269
Liquidambar styraciflua, 115
'Worplesdon,' *90*
Liriodendron tulipifera, 100, 103, 123
Liriope
gigantea, 285, 333
muscari, 265, 285, 303, 331
'Lilac Beauty,' *303, 333*
'White,' *285, 301*
spicata 'Silver Dragon,' *285*
Lobelia
cardinalis, 342

erinus, 282, 356
Locust, black, 89
Lonicera, 385
fragrantissima, 148, 172, 248, 250
nitida, 151
periclymenum 'Serotina,' *244, 249*
x *purpusii, 248*
tatarica, 179
'Rosea,' *169*
x *tellmanniana, 242, 244*
Loquat, *21, 190, 200*
Love-in-a-mist, *358, 360*
Low-maintenance aspects, 13–15
Lunaria annua, 34, 56
Lupine, *343, 360, 386*
Lupinus
x *hybrida* 'My Castle,' *343*
polyphyllus, 360
Lycoris radiata, 362, 366
Lysichiton
americanus, 258, 374
camtschatcensis, 374
Lysimachia nummularia 'Aurea,' *320*

M
Maackia, amur, 89
Maackia amurensis, 89
Maclura pomifera, 124
Magnolia
bigleaf, *126*
cucumber tree, *102, 123, 126*
Galaxy, *111*
Leonard Messel, *105*
lily-flowered, *158, 174*
Little Gem Southern, *86*
Loebner, *126*
saucer, *90, 94*
Southern, *113, 126*
yulan, *101, 111*
Magnolia
acuminata, 102, 123, 126
cylindrica, 158, 174
denudata, 101, 111
'Galaxy,' *111*
grandiflora, 113, 126, 402
'Little Gem,' *86*
x *loebneri, 126*
'Leonard Messel,' *105*
macrophylla, 126
x *soulangiana, 90, 94*
Mahonia
aquifolium, 132, 147, 165, 205, 213
japonica 'Bealei,' *197*
repens, 206, 209
Mahonia, leatherleaf, *197*
Maidenhair tree, *122, 222, 234*
Autumn Gold, *101, 115, 222, 224, 234, 237*
Mallow
purple poppy, *54*
rose, *257*
scarlet globe, *54*
tree, *131, 152, 208*
Malus
'Donald Wyman,' *101, 117*
floribunda, 93
hupehensis, 95, 116
'Indian Magic,' *101*
'Red Jade,' *108*
'Royalty,' *101*
sargentii, 183
'Snowdrift,' *85*
Manzanita, green-leaf, *140*

Maple
coralbark, *91, 114, 189*
flowering, 38
Franksred, *86, 114*
full-moon, *91, 104, 114*
hedge, *92, 104, 124*
Inabe Shidare Japanese, *205*
Japanese, *91, 104, 189, 193*
Japanese threadleaf, *189*
Norway, *92, 96, 102, 124*
October Glory, *86*
Oregon, *102*
paperbark, *120*
red, *86*
red Japanese, *193*
snakebark, *120*
waterfall, Japanese, *114*
Marigold, *355*
pot, *34, 358*
Marvel of Peru, *39, 335, 360*
Mastic, Chinese, 88
Matricaria recutita, 360
Maypops, 248
Mentha
aquatica, 377
citrata (M. x *piperita* f. *citrata*), *377*
spicata, 291
Menyanthes trifoliata, 258
Mertensia virginica, 272
Metasequoia glyptostroboides, 225, 239
Michelia figo, 164, 184
Mignonette, *361*
Milkweed, swamp, *271, 315*
Mimulus
lewisii, 313
luteus, 293, 313, 375
Mint
citrus, *377*
water, *377*
Mirabilis jalapa, 35, 335, 360
Miscanthus
sinensis, 290
'Gracimillus,' *290*
'Kirk Alexander,' *290*
'Morning Light,' *290, 337*
'Purpurascens,' *290*
'Variegatus,' *323*
'Zebrinus,' *323*
transmorrisonensis, 290
Mitchella repens, 333
Molina caerulea, 310
Molucella laevis, 359, 361
Monarda
didyma, 256, 325
'Jacob Cline,' *256, 297, 327, 343*
'Marshall's Delight,' *256, 325, 343*
fistulosa, 289, 314, 324, 337
Monkey flower, *293, 313, 375*
Monkshood, bicolor, *280*
Morus
alba 'Chaparral,' *100, 108*
nigra, 93, 117
Mountain ash, Korean, *95*
Mulberry
black, *93, 117*
Chaparral, *100, 108*
Mulching, 40, 46–47
Mullein, denseflower, *277*
Musa, 38
Muscari, 368
Myosotis

alpestris, 357
palustris, 376
sylvatica, 56
Myrica
californica, 152
cerifera, 138, 203
pensylvanica, 153, 182
Myrtle
crape, *121*
Pacific wax, *152*
wax, *138, 203*

N
Nandina domestica, 131
Narcissus, 365, 369
'Mite,' *369*
'Sundisc,' *365*
'Toto,' *365*
trumpet cultivars, *365*
Nassella tenuissima, 335
Native plants, 54, 55
Natural garden, 54
Nature, working with, 52–59
Nectarine, *118*
Nepeta
cataria, 291, 315, 325
faassenii, 315, 319
Nerine bowdenii, 257, 282, 310
Nerium oleander, 151, 158, 201, 202
Nicotiana x *sanderae* 'Daylight Sensation,' *361*
Nigella damascena, 358, 360
Ninebark, Dart's golden, *140*
Northwest regional habitats, 54
Nuphar lutea, 379, 380
Nutrients, 19–20, 31
Nymphaea
'Albida,' *380*
'Attraction,' *381*
'Escarboucle,' *380*
'Firecrest,' *380*
'Gladstoneana,' *381*
'James Brydon,' *381*
'Laydekeri Fulgens,' *380*
'Marliacea Rosea,' *381*
'Moorei,' *380*
odorata, 380
'Rose Arey,' *381*
'Rosennymphe,' *380*
'Tetragona,' *381*
tetragona pygmaea 'Helvola,' *381*
Nyssa sylvatica, 86, 115

O
Oak
bur, *88, 103, 125*
Chinese evergreen, *103, 127*
chinkapin, *127*
English, *95*
mossycup, *88, 103, 125*
pin, *94*
red, *124*
sawtooth, *127*
scarlet, *115, 127*
shingle, *125*
swamp white, *87, 125*
water, *87*
white, *103, 125*
willow, *115, 125*
Ocean spray, *132, 151*
Ocimum basilicum 'Cinnamon,' *361*
Oenothera
biennis, 360

fruticosa, 308
macrocarpa, 269
Oleander, 151, 158, 201, 202
Oleaster, 152, 182
Onoclea sensibilis, 352
Ophiopogon japonicus, 284
Orange
Aztec pearl, 144, 200, 204
Belle Etoile mock, 145, 156, 171, 181
osage-, 124
Snowflake mock, 171, 211
variegated mock, 160, 194
Organic matter, 31
Origanum majorana, 335
Orpine, 263
Osmanthus heterophyllus 'Goshiki,' 184, 192, 194, 202
Osmunda
cinnamomea, 353
regalis, 272, 353
Oxalis tetraphylla 'Iron Cross,' 283
Oxeye, ballerina smooth, 256
Oxydendrum arboreum, 90, 105

P
Pachysandra terminalis
'Green Shade,' 265
'Green Sheen,' 333
Paeonia
'Bowl of Beauty,' 349
lactiflora, 278
Palm, 38
chusan, 113
Pansy, 252, 356, 361
Papaver orientale, 405
'Picotee,' 261
'Turkenlouis,' 261
Papyrus, dwarf, 375
Parasites and predators, common, 68
Parrotia persica, 105, 114
Parthenocissus
quinquefolia, 244, 246, 249
tricuspidata, 242, 244, 246, 249
Passiflora incarnata, 248
Passion flower, 248
Paulownia, royal, 93, 111, 122
Paulownia tomentosa, 93, 111, 122
Pawpaw, 118
Peach, 119
Pear, 119
Bradford callery, 87
callery, 87, 111
Pearlbush, The Bride, 160, 170, 177, 200
Pearly everlasting, 286, 318
Pedicularis groenlandica, 54
Pelargonium, 38
Pennisetum alopecuroides, 289
'Little Bunny,' 289, 310
'Moudry,' 289
'Rubrum,' 335
Penstemon
ambiguus, 54
barbatus, 54, 267
digitalis 'Husker Red,' 267, 343
hirsutus, 329
serrulatus, 267, 345
Peony
Bowl of Beauty, 349
garden, 278
Pepper
hot, 327
sweet, 327
Peppermint, narrow-leaved black, 99

Perennials
definition, 38
grown as annuals, 39
maintenance, 63
Periwinkle
common, 206
greater, 206, 265
wine, 206
Perovskia atriplicifolia, 275
'Blue Spire,' 275, 298
Pesticides
alternatives to chemical, 71–73
chemical, 53, 69–70
Pest management, 54, 63, 64–73
Pest-resistant plants, 66
Pests, common, 68
Petroselinum crispum var. *neapolitanum, 324*
Petunia
x *hybrida, 355*
'Blue Vein,' 360
pH, soil, 23, 34, 35
Pheasantberry, Himalayan, 157
Phellodendron amurense, 89
Philadelphus
coronarius 'Variegatus,' 160, 194
x *lemoinei* 'Belle Etoile,' 145, 156, 171, 181
'Snowflake,' 171, 211
Phlomis
fruticosa, 287, 312
lanata, 164
Phlox
Candy Stripe creeping, 291, 305, 331
David garden, 257
drummond, 360
meadow, 307
mountain, 58
starfire garden, 257, 291
Phlox
diffusa, 58
drummondii 'Sternenzauber,' 360
maculata, 345
'Natascha,' 307
paniculata, 349
'David,' 257
'Starfire,' 257, 291
subulata 'Candy Stripe,' 291, 305, 331
Phormium tenax, 287
'Variegatum,' 268
Phygelius x *rectus* 'Salmon Leap,' 162
Physically challenged gardeners, 17–18
Physocarpus opulifolius 'Dart's Gold,' 140
Picea
abies 'Reflexa,' 231
glauca, 221
'Coerulea,' 227, 235
'Conica,' 229
omorika, 224, 239
orientalis, 236
pungens, 218, 221, 224, 241
'Glauca Globosa,' 221
'Hoopsii,' 221
'Koster,' 235
'Montgomery,' 231
Pieris japonica 'Mountain Fire,' 175, 193, 210
Pincushion flower, 354
Pine
Aurea Scots, 236
cow's-tail, 226, 241
dwarf mountain, 228

Eastern white, 223
weeping, 223, 232
Japanese black, 223
lacebark, 221, 226
mugo, 223
pinyon, 58
Scots, 221, 225, 229, 231, 236, 240
Swiss mountain, 228
Pinus
bungeana, 221, 226
edulis, 58
mugo, 223
strobus, 223
'Pendula,' 218, 223, 232
sylvestris, 221, 225, 240
'Aurea,' 236
'Doone Valley,' 231
'Gold Coin,' 229
thunbergii, 223
Pistache, Chinese, 88
Pistacia chinensis, 88
Pitcher plant, Dixie Lace, 257
Planning your garden, 14–19, 82
Planting techniques, 390–395
Plant selection, 36–43, 56, 59, 384–387
Plant stress, 48, 63
Plant varieties and hybrids, 42, 60, 66
Platanus occidentalis, 86, 121
Platycodon grandiflorus 'Mariesii,' 274, 284, 303
Plum, 119
Plumbago, 167, 207, 311, 331
Plumeria, 42
Poinsettia, 42, 266
Polemonium
caeruleum, 279, 302
foliosissimum, 259
Polygonatum, 392
Polystichum
acrostichoides, 317, 347, 352
munitum, 347, 352
Pontederia cordata, 378
'Alba', 378
Poplar
western balsam, 87, 99
white, 86, 96
Populus
alba, 86, 96
trichocarpa, 87, 99
Portulaca grandiflora, 355
Possumhaw, 98, 116
Potato, duck, 376
Potentilla
Abbotswood, 147, 170, 179
Goldfinger, 147, 151, 162, 165, 179
Potentilla
astrosanguinea 'Gibson's Scarlet,' 296
fruticosa, 151, 162
'Abbotswood,' 147, 170, 179
'Goldfinger,' 147, 151, 162, 165, 179
subsp. *scouteri* f. *albus, 212*
Predators, common, 72
Pride of India, 88, 92, 105, 117
Primrose, evening, 360
Princess tree, 93, 111, 122
Privet
Japanese, 157
Texanum Japanese, 153, 203
Propagation techniques, 402–405
Prostanthera cuneata, 384
Pruning, 29, 39, 59, 396–401
Prunus

avium 'Stella,' 119
communis, 119
x *domestica, 119*
maackii, 121
mume, 110
'Okame,' 95, 106
persica, 119
var. *sucipersica, 118*
subhirtella, 110
'Pendula,' 109
'Pendula Plena Rosea,' 109
'Tai Haku,' 100
Pseudocydonia sinensis, 121
Pseudolarix amabilis, 218, 227, 234
Pseudotsuga menziesii, 54, 225
Pulmonaria saccharata 'Mrs. Moon,' 305, 317
Puschkinia scilloides, 368, 373
Pyracantha 'Mohave,' 132, 148, 153, 195
Pyrus
calleryana, 87, 111
'Bradford,' 87
communis, 119

Q
Quackgrass, 49
Quamash, 54, 367, 370
Queen Anne's lace, 50
Quercus
acutissima, 127
alba, 103, 125
bicolor, 87, 125
coccinea, 115, 127
imbricaria, 125
macrocarpa, 88, 103, 125
muehlenbergii, 127
myrsinifolia, 103, 127
nigra, 87
palustris, 94
phellos, 115, 125
robur, 95
rubra, 124
Quince, Chinese, 121

R
Raised beds, 13, 26-28
Raspberry, 198
Rebutia, 387
Redbud
Chinese, 106
Eastern, 94, 107
Red-hot poker, 267, 294, 297, 334
Redwood
dawn, 225, 239
giant, 225
Reseda odorata, 361
Rheum palmatum 'Atrosanguineum,' 279
Rhododendron
arborescens, 137, 143
austrinum, 136, 143
calendulaceum, 136, 143, 165
occidentale, 58, 136, 148, 177
prunifolium, 143, 179
Rhodotypos scandens, 139
Rhus
aromatica 'Gro-Low,' 152, 206
copallina, 131, 150, 188
glabra 'Laciniata,' 133, 141, 190, 208
trilobata, 213
typhina, 157
'Dissecta,' 145
Ribes

sanguineum, 157, 169, 213, 215
sativum, 198
silvestre, 195, 197, 198
Robinia pseudoacacia, 89
Rockrose
    orchid, 140, 163, 174, 205
    sageleaf, 140, 191
Rodgersia
    aesculifolia, 279
    pinnata, 347
Romneya coulteri, 267, 319
Rosa, 385
    'Albéric Barbier,' 217, 250
    'Frau Dagmar Hartopp,' 132, 141,
        169, 183, 217
    'Kiftsgate,' 216, 245, 250
    x *odorata* 'Mutabilis,' 217
    rugosa, 217
        'Alba,' 131, 145, 170, 203, 216
        'Hedgehog,' 169, 182, 197
        'Roseraie de l'Hay,' 207, 216
        'Therese Bugnet,' 217
        var. *alba,* 36
    wichurana 'Tuscany,' 217
Rose
    China, 217
    Christmas, 305
    Frau Dagmar Hartopp, 132, 141,
        169, 183, 217
    golden-leaved guelder, 139, 181, 192
    hedgehog. See *Rosa rugosa*
    Japanese. See *Rosa rugosa*
    Kiftsgate climber, 216, 245, 250
    moss, 355
    pruning techniques, 398–401
    Roseraie de l'Hay rugosa, 207, 216
    rugosa, 169, 182, 197, 217
    Therese Bugnet rugosa, 217
    Tuscany gallica, 217
    white rugosa, 131, 145, 170, 203, 216
    wichurana rambler, 217, 250
Rosemary, 141, 167, 199, 205, 212
    common bog, 191
    pink, 133, 141
Rosmarinus officinalis, 141, 167, 199,
    205, 212
    'Huntington Carpet,' 207
    'Roseus,' 133, 141
Rubus idaeus, 198
Rudbeckia, 252
    fulgida 'Deamii,' 279, 294
    hirta, 293
    laciniata 'Goldquelle,' 293
    maxima, 262, 308
    nitida 'Herbstonne,' 293
    triloba, 354
Rush, club, 377
Ruta graveolens, 319, 325
Ryegrass, perennial, 14

S
Sage
    blue, 269
    bog, 283, 308
    fringed, 54
    germander, 345
    Jerusalem, 164, 287, 312
    prairie, 58
    Russian, 275, 298
    silverleaf Texas, 166, 215
    white, 319
Sagittaria
    latifolia, 376

sagittifolia, 376
St. John's wort
    golden, 208
    Hidcote, 156, 277
Saltbush, four winged, 54
Salvia
    azurea, 269
    chamaedryoides, 345
    uliginosa, 283, 308
Sambucus racemosa 'Aurea,' 192
Santolina chamaecyparissus, 132, 269,
    286
Sapphireberry, 179
Sarcococca
    var. *digyna,* 173, 208
    humilis, 163, 187
Sarracenia x 'Dixie Lace,' 257
Sassafras, common, 91, 105
Sassafras albidum, 91, 105
Saururus cernuus, 379
Saxifrage, 43
Scabiosa
    atropurpurea, 354
    columbaria 'Butterfly Blue,' 298
Schlumbergera, 395
Schoenoplectus lacustris 'Albescens,' 377
Scilla siberica, 368, 370
Scirpus
    lacustris, 377
    tabern 'Zebrinus,' 377
Sedum
    acre, 262
    aizoon, 262
    'Autumn Joy,' 262, 277
    kamtschaticum, 330
    'Floriferum,' 262
    'Variegatum,' 262, 288, 329, 330, 344
    'Matrona,' 321
    spectabile
        'Brilliant,' 263
    'Frosty Morn,' 268
    spurium 'Bronze Carpet,' 263, 328
    telephium, 263
    'Vera Jameson,' 263
Seed sowing techniques, 406–407
Sequoiadendron giganteum, 225
Serviceberry
    Alleghany, 100
    apple, 197
Shade and light
    from limbing up a tree, 29
    plant selection, 36
    site assessment, 23, 37
Sidalcea
    hybrida 'Elsie Heugh,' 296
    malviflora, 277
Silene acaulis, 329, 331
Silk-tassel bush, 156, 172
Silk-tree, 93
Silverbell, two-winged, 91, 111
Silverberry, Gilt Edge, 152, 192, 194
Sisyrinchium
    bellum, 303
    striatum
        'Aunt May,' 392
    angustifolium, 298
Site assessment, 16–23, 37
Skimmia japonica, 137, 148, 163, 185,
    186, 204, 207
Skunkbush, 213
Skunk cabbage
    yellow, 258, 374
    Japanese, 374

Smilacina racemosa, 273
Smoke tree, royal purple, 133, 145, 193
Snapdragon, 35
Sneezeweed, 280
Sneezewort, 261, 288, 301, 314, 325
Snowbell, fragrant, 91, 105, 177
Snowdrop, common, 304, 369
Soil
    adapting to existing conditions, 30,
        39
    assessment, 16, 18–19
    improvement, 30–31
    surface, and temperature, 25
    test report for, 18
    urban, 21
Solanum melongena, 326
Solenostemon scutellarioides cultivars,
    356
Solidago rugosa 'Fireworks,' 279, 310
Sorbus
    alnifolia, 95
    intermedia, 116
Sourwood, 90, 105
Speedwell, 289, 343
Sphaeralcea coccinea, 54
Spice bush, 137, 138, 174, 196
Spider flower, 354
Spiderwort, hybrid, 309, 313
Spiraea
    japonica, 210
        'Gold Flame,' 177, 192
        'Little Princess,' 148, 162, 177, 202,
            212
    Neon Flash Japanese, 168
        'Shibori,' 205
    nipponica 'Snowmound,' 213
    x *vanhouttei,* 148, 161, 171
Spirea
    Chinese, 287, 345, 348
    Japanese, 210
    Little Princess Japanese, 148, 162,
        177, 202, 212
    Shibori, 205
    Snowmound, 213
    Vanhoutte, 148, 161, 171
Spruce
    blue, 231, 235
    Colorado, 218, 221, 224, 241
    globe blue, 221
    Hoopsii blue, 221
    Norway, 231
    Oriental, 236
    Serbian, 224, 239
    white, 221, 227, 235
Spurge, 284, 304
    chameleon, 341
    cushion, 266, 304
    Japanese, 265
    purple wood, 321
    wood, 265
Squill, 360, 370, 373
Stachys, 42
Statice, 359
Sternbergia lutea, 293, 373
Stewardship in your garden, 40–52
Stewartia
    Japanese, 84, 104, 112, 120
    tall, 112
Stewartia
    monadelpha, 112
    pseudocamellia, 84, 104, 112, 120
Stokesia laevis 'Alba,' 301
Stonecrop, 262, 263, 268, 277, 288, 311,

321, 328, 330, 344
Stratiotes aloides, 387, 394
Strawberry, 48
String pearls, 282, 356
Structures, 24–25
Styrax obassia, 91, 105, 177
Sumac,
    cutleaf smooth, 133, 141, 190, 208
    dwarf, 131, 150, 188
    Gro-Low fragrant, 152, 206
    staghorn, 145, 157
Summersweet, 137, 139, 168, 171, 181,
    183
Sunrose, 191, 334
Sweet box, 163, 187
    slender, 173, 208
Sweetgum,
    American, 115
    Worplesdon, 90
Sweetspire
    Henry's Garnet, 193
    Virginia, 138, 142, 182
Symplocos paniculata, 179
Syringa
    meyeri, 214
        'Palibin,' 169, 205, 213
    reticulata, 121, 209
    vulgaris
        'Charles Joly,' 155, 167, 175
        'Monge,' 155, 202, 214
        'President Grevy,' 148, 155
        'Sensation,' 155, 167, 212

T
Tagetes, 355
    lucida, 327, 335
Taro
    green, 376
    violet-stem, 376
Taxodium
    ascendens, 218, 222
    distichum, 222, 227, 232, 234, 239
Taxus, 238
    cuspidata, 220
Tellima grandiflora, 317
Temperature range and climate, 21,
    35–36, 63
Teucrium fruticans, 132, 181, 191
Texas ranger, 166, 215
Thalictrum
    delvayi 'Hewitt's Double,' 306
    flavum subsp. *glaucum,* 277, 315
Thistle,
    Canada, 53
    small globe, 260, 274
Thrift
    common, 285, 307, 317, 328
Thuja
    occidentalis, 233, 239
        'Caespitosa,' 230, 240
        'Rheingold,' 218, 236
    orientalis
        'Aurea Nana,' 230
        'Semperaurea,' 229
    plicata, 54
        'Collyer's Gold,' 236, 240
        'Hilleri,' 230
Thunbergia alata, 24
Thyme
    caraway, 199
    common, 199
    lemon-scented, 199
    woolly, 199

Thymus
    x citriodorus, 199
    herba-barona, 199
    pseudolanuginosus, 199
    vulgaris, 199
Tickseed, 54, 275, 348
Tigridia pavonia, 366
Tilia cordata, 97
Time
    commitment to garden and yard, 10,
        14
    as element in garden plan, 13, 28–29,
        39
Tithonia rotundifolia, 354
Tobacco, jasmine, 361
Topography, 25
Trachycarpus fortunei, 113
Tradescantia virginiana, 309, 313
Transplanting techniques, 389
Trees
    espalier, 39
    forms, 39
    planting technique, 388
    thinning, limbing up, and pruning, 29,
        39, 59, 396–397
    when to call the arborist, 29
Tricyrtis formosana, 273
Trillium
    coast, 273, 304
    purple, 273, 304
    yellow, 273
Trillium
    chloropetalum, 258, 273, 304
    erectum, 273, 304
    grandiflorum, 273
    luteum, 273
    ovatum, 273, 304
Trollius laxus, 54, 306
Tropaeolum polyphyllum, 48
Tropical plants, 38
Tsuga heterophylla, 54, 224
Tulipa, 373
    'Fringed Beauty,' 365, 367
    'Garden Party,' 348
    kaufmanniana, 373
    'Kees Nelis,' 373
    'Pink Beauty,' 252
Tuliptree, 100, 103, 123
Turtlehead, 34, 344
Typha
    angustifolia, 379
    minima, 375

U
Ulex europaeus, 195
Ulmus

    parvifolia, 96
    pumila, 96
Umbellularia californica, 88
Uvularia grandiflora, 259, 272

V
Vaccinium
    corymbosum, 138, 196, 198
    macrocarpon, 198
Valerian, red, 275, 324, 337
Vancouveria hexandra, 259, 273
Verbascum thapsus, 277
Verbena,
    canadensis 'Summer Blaze,' 269
    hastata, 269, 298
    peruviana, 345
Verbena, lemon, 204
Veronica
    incana, 318
    peduncularis, 306
    spicata, 289
    'Red Fox,' 289, 343
Vervain, 269, 298, 345
Viburnum
    blackhaw, 202
    Dawn fragrant, 146
    doublefile, 174, 201
    linden, 161
    Mariesii doublefile, 146, 159
    Pink Beauty doublefile, 161, 174,
        201
    siebold, 178, 190
    Summer Snowflake doublefile, 54,
        159, 209
Viburnum, 161
    x bodnantense, 173
    'Dawn,' 146, 173
    dilatatum, 161
    opulus 'Aureum,' 139, 161, 181, 192
    plicatum, 174, 201
    tinus 'Spring Bouquet,' 156, 173, 187,
        202
    f. tomentosum
        'Mariesii,' 146, 159
        'Summer Snowflake,' 146, 159, 209
        'Pink Beauty,' 161, 174, 201
    prunifulium, 202
    sieboldii, 178, 190
Vinca
    major 'Maculata,' 206, 265
    minor
        'Atropurpurea,' 206
        'Green Carpet,' 206
        'Variegata,' 323
Vine
    chocolate, 247, 249

    kiwi, 249
Viola
    labradorica, 303
    pedata, 272
    x wittrockiana, 252, 356, 361
Violet, bird's-foot, 272
Vitex agnus-castus, 112
    var. latifolia, 200

W
Wake robin, giant, 258, 273, 304
Walking stick, Harry Lauder's, 39
Wallflower, 334, 358, 361
Walnut, black, 124
Wapato, 376
Water
    conservation techniques, 42–45
    evapotranspiration map, 44
    quality issues, 43
    stress, 44, 59
Waterleaf, Virginia, 259
Water garden, 387, 394
Waterlilies, 380–381
Weed barriers, 47–48
Weeds and weeding, 48–49, 61, 69
Weigela florida 'Variegata,' 179, 215
Wheatgrass, fairway, 14
Whitebeam, Swedish, 116
Wildlife, 40, 50–51
Wind, 25, 36, 59
Windflower, Japanese, 311, 338
Winterberry, 139
    male, 211
Wintersweet, 144, 173
Wisteria
    Chinese, 245, 248
    Japanese, 245, 248
Wisteria
    floribunda 'Macrobotrys,' 245, 248
    sinensis,
        'Alba,' 245
        'Purpurea,' 245, 248
Witch hazel, 137, 173, 188
Wolffia, 387
Woody plant, definition, 35
Woodsorrel, 283
Wormwood, 46, 191, 266, 319, 340

Y
Yarrow. See Achillea
Yew, 238
    Japanese, 220
Yucca
    filamentosa
        'Golden Sword,' 263
        'Ivory Tower,' 263

    'Variegata,' 268, 287
    glauca, 54, 268
Yulan magnolia, 101, 111

Z
Zauschneria californica, 263
Zelkova, Japanese, 115, 123
Zelkova serrata, 115, 123
Zenobia pulverulenta, 139, 143, 178
Zephyranthes candida, 334, 367
Zinnia, 359

ACKNOWLEDGMENTS

DK Publishing Inc. and the American Horticultural Society would like to express special thanks to Dr. H. Marc Cathey for his vision of a SMARTGARDEN™ and for promoting these important principles to the American gardener; to Katy Moss Warner for her keen eye and superb leadership; to Arabella Dane for the use of her Showtime database and her countless hours of support; to Mary Ann Patterson for believing in and coordinating this project from its conception; to Mark Miller for hours of research; to David Ellis for his editor's savvy. Rita Pelczar, author of the core text for the SMARTGARDEN™ Regional Guides, has written for several American gardening magazines and has contributed to several books. As an associate editor for *The American Gardener,* she wrote a four-year series of articles highlighting principles of the SMARTGARDEN™ plan.

The Northwest regional author, Peter Punzi, is the host of the "Horticulture Guy" Radio Show as well as garden segments on cable television. Punzi holds a B.S. in Plant Science and an M.S. in Public Horticulture. He is a garden lecturer as well as a professional Garden Coach. He gardens at the "Punzi Grange" in Lakewood, Washington. For more information, visit his web site: www.HorticultureGuy.com.

PHOTO CREDITS

Abbreviations Key:
B = Bottom T = Top L = Left
R = Right C = Center

American Gardener Magazine: Mary Yee 18 L, 19 CR
Tony Avent/Plant Delights Nursery: 257 TL, 257 TR, 268 BR, 269 TL, 269 BL, 276 BL 279 BR, 281 TR, 283 TR, 299 TC, 306 RC, 307 BR, 310 BC, 314 TL,316 TC, 332 TC, 337 BL, 344 BC, 345 TL, 352 TL, 353 BL

Ball Horticultural Company: 77 R

Bromfield Aquatics, www.bromfieldaquatics.com: 270 BR, 298 BR, 300 BR, 323 L, 348 TR, 350 BR, 351 BR, 376 BL, 376 BR, 378 TL, 378 BL

Courtesy of W. Atlee Burpee: 294 TR

Dixi Carrillo/Edaw, Inc.: 76 BL

Corbis: Arthur Morris 42 TL, David Muench 54 TL, Scott T. Smith 54 BC

Emerald Coast Growers: 183 TC, 283 BR, 331 BC, 335 TL, 335 BR

Garden & Wildlife Matters Photo Library: Sheila Apps: 46B; M. Collins 60R; John Feltwell: 263 C, 281 BL, 310 BL, 359 LC, 374 BC, 376 C, 377 BR; Garden & Wildlife Matters Photo Library: 7 CL, 7 C, 7 BL, 13 TR, 26 TR, 26 BL, 32 BR, 36 CL, 37 TR, 38 BC, 39 TL, 42 BR, 45 T, 50 BL, 51 CR, 60 L, 62 B, 65 TR, 67 TR, 69 B, 69 TL, 72 TL, 72 TR, 73 B, 164 TC, 198 CR, 198 BL, 198 BR, 245 TR, 251 TL, 252 TR, 255 LC, 257 BR, 261 TR, 261 TL, 261 BC,265 TR, 266 BL, 268 TR, 274 BC, 278 TL, 279 BL, 282 L, 283 TL, 284 TR, 295 BR, 299 BR, 301 TR, 303 LC, 310 BR, 314 TR, 316 TR, 321BL, 330 BL, 331 TC, 334 TL, 338 BL, 339 TL,342 BC, 342 BR, 346 TR, 346 BL, 359 TC, 375 BL, 376 TC, 380 LC; Martin P. Land: 292 TL, 303 BL, 339 TR, 342 TL; Colin Milkins: 51 TL; John & Irene Palmer: 360 BR, 380 RC; Steffie Shields: 275 TL 288 TL 289 TL, 303 BR, 380 BR: Debi Wager: 47 TL

Garden Picture Library: David Askham: 301 TL; Mark Bolton: 277 BL, 279 C, 294 TC 311 CR, 312 TC, 340 BL, 363 BL, 364 L; Chris Burrows: 272 BL, 350 TR; Brian Carter: 122 L, 222 TL, 262 LC, 277 BC, 282 TR, 309 BL, 310 RC, 323 BR, 330 TR, 356 BC, 357 BR, 360 BL; Bob Challinor: 380 BL; Eric Crichton : 333 TL, 353 TL; Elizabeth Crowe: 380 TL, 381 LC; David England: 330 TC, 367 TL: Christopher Fairweather: 271 TL; Bjorn Forsberg: 292 BL; John Glover: 25 TL Garden Design Alan Titchmarsh, 79 Page, 177 TR, 206 BR, 245 BL, 262 BL, 265 BR, 298 TL, 307 LC,339 CR, 342 BL, 344 BL, 346 TC, 346 C, 352 BL, 363 LC, 373 TR, 380 BC, 381 BL; Sunniva Harte: 24 B Garden Design Beth Chatto, 59 TR, 269 BC, 276 TL, 306 TL, 338 TL, 374 BL; Neil Holmes: 306 BC, 306 BR, 317 LC, 339 BC, 350 BL; Jacqui Hurst: 302 RC; Lamontagne: 376 BC; Jane Legate: 29 TR, 259 BR; A.I. Lord: 324 LC; Mayer/LeScanff: 269 TR, 298 LC; Marie O'Hara: 70 BL, 82-83; Howard Rice: 19 BR, 30 BL, 255 TR, 286 TR, 292 R, 293 BR, 305 BR, 322 TL, 338 BR, 339 BR, 359 BL, 361 BC, 363 TC, 370 TL, 373 BR; Gary Rogers: 309 TR; Ellen Rooney: 23 TR; John Ferro Sims: 308 BC; JS Sira : 259 CC, 271 BL, 285 TR, 286 BL, 307 TL, 311 TC, 330 BR, 356 BR, 359 BR, 364 TR, 367 BR; Friedrich Strauss : 310 TL; Ron Sutherland: 75 Garden Design

Anthony Paul; Brigitte Thomas; 234 TR; Juliette Wade: 321 TC, 340 BR, 343 TL; Didier Willery: 332 TL

Jim Havey Productions: 76 BR

Frank Lane Picture Agency (FLPA): S. Maslowski 61

Andrew Lawson: 3-4, 161 TR, 163 TC, 163 BR, 365 TR, 365 C, 369 TR

Monrovia: Monrovia: 12 BL, 86 LC, 109 BR, 113 TR, 152 TL, 152 BR, 153 BL, 157 TR, 161 BR, 166 TL, 166 BR, 167 TL, 168 TL, 171 C, 173 TL, 173 CL, 177 BL, 184 TR, 185 TL, 186 BL, 186 BR, 192 BCL, 192 BR, 194 TL, 197 TC, 197 BR,199 BL, 201 TL, 203 TL, 203 CL, 203 BR, 206 TL, 207 BR, 209 TL, 209 CR, 209 B, 210 BL, 211 TC, 211 LC, 211 BL, 213 TR, 215 TL, 215 BR, 220 TC, 220 BR, 223 BL, 225 TC, 238 TL, 238 BR, 239 BR, 245 TC, 250 TL, 284 BR, 294 TL, 303 TL, 313 TL, 315 TR, 317 C, 319 CR, 328 TR, 343 BR, 348 BL, 352 LC; Monrovia /Hort Printing: 206 TR, 254 BR, 256 TR, 265 TC, 268 TL, 281 TL, 281 TC, 287 TL, 290 TL, 291 CR, 297 TL 343 CR, 327 BL, 316 BL, 305 TL, 305 BL; Monrovia/Peter Hogg Photography: 12 TR, 13 BR, 86 TC, 87 BL, 88 BC, 89 TL, 89 BR, 90 TR, 100 TR, 100 BR, 101 TL, 101 TR, 107 TC, 108 BL, 109 TL, 111 TR, 111 BC, 112 TR, 114 TL, 114 BL, 115 BC, 127 BR, 132 BL, 151 TR, 151 RC,152 BC, 153 C, 153 BR, 156 BL, 157 BR 159 TR, 159 BL, 159 CR, 161 BL, 164 BL, 166 RC, 168 BL, 169 TC, 170 TR, 171 TL, 172 TL, 173 TC, 175 BR, 176 TR, 178 TL, 179 BL, 181 TC, 184 TL, 185 BL, 187 TL, 190 TC, 192 BCR, 193 BR, 194 CR, 202 BL, 202 BR, 205 TC, 205 LC, 206 CL, 206 TC, 207 TL, 208 TL, 209 TR, 210 TL, 211 TL, 211 TR, 211 BR, 213 BR, 214 B, 215 TR, 215 BL, 217 CR, 221 TL, 221 TC, 222 BL, 224 BR, 232 BR, 232 TR, 234 TC, 237 TC, 237 BL, 238 BC, 247 BL, 254 TL, 256 BR, 260 C, 263 TR, 263 BR, 270 TL, 274 BR, 275 TC, 278 TR, 279 TR, 285 CR, 285 BL, 285 BR, 289 TR, 289 C, 289 BC, 291 TR, 291 CL, 291 C, 291 BL, 351 TL, 351 TR, 260 BL, 296 BL, 301 BR, 303 TC, 308 BR, 316 TL, 317 CR, 317 BC, 323 C, 323 BC, 325 BL, 328 BR, 329 LC, 329 BL,331 C, 333 BC, 333 BL, 336 BR, 338 TR, 341 TR, 343 TR, 343 BC, 345 BL

Thompson and Morgan: 307TR

Courtesy of the Online Virginia Tech Weed ID Guide, http://www.ppws.vt.edu/weedindex.htm: 73 TR

The publisher would also like to thank the following DK Photographers:

Peter Anderson, Sue Atkinson, Clive Boursnell, Deni Brown, Jonathan Buckley, Andrew Butler, Cambridge Botanic Garden, Beth Chatto, Eric Crichton, Geoff Dann, Andrew de Lory, Christine M. Douglas, Alistair Duncan, John Fielding, Neil Fletcher, Roger Foley, John Glover, Derek Hall,David W. Hardon, Jerry Harpur, Stephan Hayward, Dr. Alan Hemsley, C. Andrew Henley, Ian Howes, Jacqui Hurst, Anne Hyde, International Coffee Organization, Dave King, Howard Rice, Tim Ridley, Royal Botanical Garden, Edinburgh, Bob Rundle, Les Saucier, Savill Garden, Windsor, Mike Severns, Steven Still, Joseph Strach, Richard Surman, R. Tidman, Juliette Wade, Colin Walton, Matthew Ward, Steven Wooster, Francesca York